Still Seeing Red

Still Seeing Red

How the Cold War Shapes
the New American Politics

John Kenneth White

 WestviewPress
A Division of HarperCollins*Publishers*

Transforming American Politics

Copyright © 1997 by Westview Press, A Division of HarperCollins Publishers, Inc.

Published in 1997 in the United States of America by Westview Press, 5500 Central Avenue, Boulder, Colorado 80301-2877, and in the United Kingdom by Westview Press, 12 Hid's Copse Road, Cumnor Hill, Oxford OX2 9JJ

Library of Congress Cataloging-in-Publication Data
White, John Kenneth, 1952–
  Still seeing red : how the Cold War shapes the new American
politics / John Kenneth White.
    p.   cm.—(Transforming American politics)
  Includes bibliographical references and index.
  ISBN 0-8133-1888-2
  1. United States—Politics and government—1993– 2. Cold War—
Influence. I. Title. II. Series.
E885.W48   1997
320.973´09´049—dc21   97-9749
                                                                          CIP

The paper used in this publication meets the requirements of the American National Standard for Permanence of Paper for Printed Library Materials Z39.48-1984.

10   9   8   7   6   5   4   3   2   1

For Yvonne, aujourd'hui plus qu'hier

Gosh, I miss the Cold War.

—Bill Clinton, October 1993

Contents

Tables

Acknowledgments

Willa Cather once wrote, "A book is made with one's own flesh and blood of years. It is cremated youth." So it is with *Still Seeing Red*. From its inception in the summer of 1992 to its completion more than four years later, this book has preoccupied my late youth. A large portion of each day was spent researching, writing, or shaping the manuscript. As I delved into the Cold War, its influences on partisan politics proved greater than I first imagined. My inquiry recalled an incident involving U.S. Communist Party chairman Gus Hall. When asked in December 1994 how big the Communist Party had become, Hall succinctly replied, "I don't know." So it was when I started this book: The Cold War looms large in the forming and fragmenting of contemporary politics—a realization that seems readily apparent ever since the Soviet Union cried uncle in 1991.

In telling this story, I am indebted to several individuals whose encouragement and inspiration sustained me. A. James Reichley of Georgetown University listened to my idea for this book and closely followed its progress. Ralph Goldman, president of the Center for Party Development, provided incisive commentary as did Jerome Mileur of the University of Massachusetts, William Crotty of Northeastern University, Phillip Klinkner of Hamilton College, and Gary Rose of Sacred Heart University. Sidney Milkis of Brandeis University was an early and enthusiastic supporter of this project, as was Morton J. Tenzer, emeritus of the University of Connecticut, who closely read the manuscript and understood from the beginning exactly what I was trying to accomplish.

Research grants from the Catholic University of America and the Ford Library helped bring this book to fruition. The Research Foundation of the Catholic University provided financial assistance that allowed me to travel to the Roper Center and obtain the results of hundreds of polls from its vast collection of survey data. Everett Carll Ladd, executive director of the Roper Center, has been a longtime mentor and encouraged my return to the University of Connecticut—where I spent a portion of my youth—with ease. Lois Timms-Ferrara helped me access the polls during my two-week stay. To them and the rest of the staff at the Roper Center, I am especially grateful. At the Gerald R. Ford Library, I am indebted to William McNitt, grants coordinator, and his outstanding staff for facilitating my research there. The Ford Library is a treasure trove for those interested in studying politics from the late 1940s to the 1970s. I am also indebted to the staff at the John F. Kennedy Library in Boston for providing access to Kennedy's congressional and presidential papers.

I would also like to acknowledge the assistance I obtained as a result of research grants awarded by Catholic University. I owe a debt of deep gratitude to William Smith, a senior graduate student at Catholic University, who served as my research assistant during much of this project. Smith carefully read each chapter and completed the various tasks I gave him with care and dispatch. Elaine Jorgensen and William Carr also lent a hand when it was needed.

I spent a most pleasant sabbatical during the spring and summer of 1996 at Providence College, where the Department of Political Science graciously supplied an office, a phone, and an indispensable computer. I am grateful to the department's chair, Jim Carlson, for facilitating my stay and to Bill Hudson for encouraging me to come. The faculty and students there are outstanding. I also express my appreciation to Darrell West of Brown University for allowing me to be a visiting scholar there during the spring semester.

At Westview Press, I am especially appreciative of the encouragement given by Jennifer Knerr, acquisitions editor, and Larry Dodd, series coordinator. Both followed the progress of this book and offered encouragement at times when it was needed and appreciated. I am also indebted to Leo Wiegman, who stepped in as Westview's senior editor and made many major contributions to this project.

Finally, a personal note: In each of my previous books I have thanked my family—my mother, Margaret, and my sister, Janet—for their love and support. I do so again. But this time my family has an important addition: While working on this book I met Yvonne Prevost. We became engaged and were married on July 1, 1995. I could not have written this book without Yvonne, and so it is with great affection that I dedicate it to her.

John Kenneth White
Washington, D.C.

Introduction: Who Are We?

Life is lived forward, but understood backward.

—Soren Kierkegaard

September 1968

The presidential race had begun in earnest. The major party nominees, Hubert H. Humphrey for the Democrats and Richard M. Nixon for the Republicans, were energetically making their appeals for public support. But behind closed doors another "campaign" was taking place. The powerbrokers in the Kremlin were taking their measure of the candidates, trying to determine which would best manage the superpower relationship. It was a difficult decision. Only one month earlier the Soviet Union had invaded Czechoslovakia, ending Alexander Dubcek's brief experiment with "socialism with a human face."[1] After Dubcek's ouster, Communist party chief Leonid Brezhnev enunciated the "Brezhnev Doctrine," the fig leaf under which the Union of Soviet Socialist Republics could correct its fraternal neighbors by military invasion whenever they deviated from Moscow's hard line. The Czech invasion and the Brezhnev Doctrine met with widespread condemnation, and Oleg Kalugin, the KGB station chief in Washington, D.C., found that his informants were keeping mum. Instead of recruiting spies through ideological solidarity, the Soviets needed large sums of cold, hard cash to lure greedy Americans into snooping for Moscow—as was later disclosed in the subsequent spy cases involving John Walker and Aldrich Ames. Kalugin reported to his superiors that after the Czech fiasco publisher I. F. Stone would no longer let him pay for lunches, quoting Stone as saying: "I will never take money from your bloody government."[2] With that, the two men never saw one another again. In Kalugin's view, U.S.-Soviet relations were at an impasse and something "drastic" was required to break the deadlock.[3]

That drastic step was electing Richard Nixon president. Although Kalugin thought Nixon "unpredictable," he also believed that Nixon's longtime anticommunism might serve as a catalyst "to improve relations between our countries, for no one would ever dare accuse Nixon of being soft on communism."[4] Cloaked with a veil of secrecy, Kalugin and his KGB colleagues spun a web of intrigue. They established a back channel to the Nixon campaign, using Harvard University professor Henry Kissinger as an intermediary. Through a series of letters addressed to Kissinger, Nixon was informed that Brezhnev and the KGB would welcome his election.

But Kalugin did not speak for a unified Soviet leadership. The Soviet ambassador to the United States, Anatoly Dobrynin, already had done some politicking on his own. Believing that Hubert Humphrey would never initiate World War III and fearing that Nixon was too staunch an anticommunist (and a scoundrel besides), Dobrynin told Humphrey that the decisionmakers in the Politburo looked favorably upon him, and he offered to help the cash-starved Democratic campaign. Humphrey refused, saying it was "more than enough for him to have Moscow's good wishes."[5] After the ballots were counted and Nixon finished a hair's breadth ahead of Humphrey, the Kremlin sent a secret missive via Kissinger congratulating Nixon. Remembering the pro-Humphrey views of the Soviet ambassador, the KGB never told him about the letter. Days later an "official" communiqué from the Soviet embassy offered Moscow's best wishes to the president-elect.[6]

The point of this story is not to argue that these behind-the-scene actions affected the outcome of the 1968 contest—the Vietnam War and public disillusionment with Lyndon Johnson took care of that. Rather, it is to assert that with the end of the Cold War the blindfolds have been removed from our eyes. Since the fall of the Soviet Union in 1991, we have been learning much about what transpired behind the high walls of the Kremlin. For example, a recent search of the Soviet archives produced a 1987 plea from U.S. Communist Party chief Gus Hall to Soviet president Mikhail Gorbachev: "I don't like to raise the question of finances, but when the 'wolf' is at the door, one is forced to cry out."[7] Gorbachev ordered KGB couriers to stuff their suitcases with $2 million in cash. Further archival digging finds that Moscow gave the U.S. Communist Party substantial sums of money from its inception in 1920 until 1989. Often the cash was stashed in diplomatic pouches sent to KGB agents stationed in the United States who would, in turn, dispense it to eagerly outstretched hands.[8]

Such revelations have not been limited to the Soviet side of the Iron Curtain. In 1994, it was disclosed that thousands of Americans had been treated as human guinea pigs during the Cold War by their own government. Milton Stadt, the son of one of these unwitting subjects, described how his mother had been hospitalized for a duodenal ulcer and found herself in a U.S. government–sponsored lab where, he claimed, "these monsters were." He remembered: "My mother, Jan Stadt, had a number HP-8. She was injected with plutonium on March 9, 1946. She was forty-one years old, and I was eleven years old at the time. My mother and father were never told or asked for any kind of consent to have this done to them."[9] Jan Stadt subsequently died from the "nontherapeutic" radiation experiments performed upon her. Unfortunately, she was just one of many victims. An Advisory Committee on Human Radiation Experiments created by President Bill Clinton found numerous instances of other unsuspecting "atomic veterans," including:

- Hundreds of mentally retarded male teens who were fed a special concoction of Quaker Oats breakfast cereal containing radioactive iron and calcium at the Walter E. Fernald School in Massachusetts from the 1940s until the 1960s.
- One-hundred twenty people, most of them Eskimos and Native Americans, who were exposed to radioactive iodine in tests administered by the U.S. Air Force in 1956 and 1957.
- Thousands of uranium miners working for the U.S. government who were exposed to extraordinarily high levels of radiation. The committee found that the responsible officials knew of the hazards but never informed the miners. Hundreds subsequently died from lung cancer.[10]

Other once-secret documents show the extraordinary preparations the U.S. government undertook in preparing for a possible nuclear war. Top presidential advisers were handed a secret telephone number that granted immediate access to one another by their simply saying "Flash"—a code indicating that the call was essential to the national survival. The 2857th Test Squadron, an elite unit of helicopter pilots, staged landings on the White House lawn. In the event of a Soviet nuclear strike, they were to take the commander in chief to one of several hollowed-out mountain sites or to the heavily reinforced USS *Hampton* off the Atlantic coast. Mount Weather (code-named "High Point"), a retreat in Berryville, Virginia, would accommodate the government-in-hiding. Plans called for several thousand officials to be housed there, including the president, Cabinet members, and U.S. Supreme Court justices as well as the president's family. Photographs show that Dwight Eisenhower kept pictures of his wife and children on his desk there; John Kennedy installed a therapeutic mattress for his bad back. A crematorium and a cache of automatic weapons completed the macabre scene.[11]

Yet in the midst of such awful preparations government officials eagerly sought to reassure citizens that everything was under control. Dwight Eisenhower, however, knew better. In a top-secret 1955 memo, he wrote that if the Cold War turned hot his advisers should not be consumed by mundane questions, such as: "Who is going to bury the dead? Where would one find the tools? The organization to do it? We must not assume that we are going to handle these problems with calmness."[12] Instead of order, Eisenhower foresaw widespread panic:

> We would have to run this country as one big camp—severely regimented. In a real situation, these will not be normal people—they will be scared, will be hysterical, will be absolutely nuts. We are going to have to be prepared to operate with people who are nuts. . . . We will be running soup kitchens—we are going to be taking care of a completely bewildered population. Government which goes on with some kind of continuity will be like a one-eyed man in the land of the blind.[13]

Reflecting on the Cold War years later, schoolteacher John Driscoll, a child of the 1950s, recalled: "It seems surreal now. Every summer, when I [saw] heat lightning over the city and the sky would light up, I was convinced that it was all over. My whole childhood was built on the notion the Soviets were the real threat."[14] A 1954 poll gives credence to Driscoll's recollections: 72 percent believed that they would have to "fight it out" with the Russians; just 16 percent thought the Cold War would be resolved peacefully.[15] Driscoll and other children in elementary schools were required to practice "duck-and-cover" drills, crawling under desks and placing their arms over their heads to ward off nuclear fallout. Federal authorities distributed *55 million* palm cards advising what to do should the Soviets strike first.[16] Moreover, in one of the first PR campaigns of its kind, the U.S. government touted "Grandma's Pantry," which was nothing more than a state-of-the-art bomb shelter: "With a well-stocked pantry you can be just as self-sufficient as Grandma was. Add a first-aid kit, flashlight, and portable radio to this supply, and you will have taken the first important step in family preparedness."[17]

For the John Driscolls of America, the Cold War was a political and cultural touchstone. It provided a convenient yardstick for separating countries into those "like us" (anticommunist) and those who were "one of them" (communist). It also resulted in the invention of the "Third World" and in competition for its domination. The Cold War also shaped the culture—inspiring the spy novel as a literary genre and prompting cinematographers to preach American values to worldwide audiences. Hollywood film director Sidney Pollack recalled that the Cold War "was very good fodder for drama, because you had what was perceived as a clearly virtuous position against what was seen as clearly bad."[18] Several movies illustrate Pollack's point. In the 1963 antiwar film *Dr. Strangelove*, Slim Pickens waves his cowboy hat and yells "Yahoo, Yahoo!" as he rides a hydrogen bomb toward its Russian target. Twenty-two years later Sylvester Stallone (aka Rocky) battles a menacing Soviet boxer who threatens him by saying, "I will break you." Moments later Rocky's battered and bruised opponent collapses in the ring. In 1990, *Star Trek VI* depicts the Klingon chancellor searching for an end to decades of unremitting hostility between his empire and the Federation. Leonard Nimoy, the actor who became famous as Mr. Spock, admitted off-camera: "The Klingons have always been our stand-in for the Russians. What about a Berlin Wall coming down in space?"[19]

For decades, Cold War "victories" and "defeats" defined our national moods—reinvigorating an "American Exceptionalism" during the 1950s and 1960s and spawning an "American Pessimism" in the 1970s. It even influenced our view of the sexes: 57 percent in a 1984 Gallup survey believed a "male president would do a better job of handling our relations with the Soviet Union"; only 11 percent said a female would do better.[20] University of Minnesota professor Elaine Tyler May maintains that the 1950s-style nuclear family with its homemaker mom and working dad was a "glamorized, professionalized, and eroticized" symbol of American superiority during the Cold War.[21] Survey research supports her point. In one interview (part of a project that was conducted with 300 married couples), a man defined his family in Cold War terms: His wife and children provided him with "a sense of responsibility, a feeling of being a member of a group that in spite of many disagreements internally always will face its external enemies together."[22]

Like John Driscoll, I, too, am a baby boomer; I was born on October 10, 1952. The Cold War shaped my childhood and spanned most of my adult life, as the front-page headlines from the *New York Times* on that day illustrate: "South Korean Unit, Bayoneting Reds, Regains Key Peak"; "Work Completed on U.N. Buildings"; "Stevenson Taunts Rival for Backing McCarthy, Dirksen"; and "U.S. to Give France $525,000,000 in Aid and Hints at More."[23] Like so many of my generation, I accepted the Cold War as a fact of life. But the collapse of the Berlin Wall in November 1989 and the cascade of events that resulted in the demise of the Soviet Union two years later caught nearly everyone unawares. For example, a June 1989 poll found two-thirds disagreed with the proposition that "communism is dying out."[24] But Soviet-style communism did die—except in China, Cuba, Vietnam, and North Korea—and with it expired the political order influenced and shaped by the Cold War.

Still Seeing Red explores a heretofore little-examined aspect of the Cold War—namely, how the Cold War molded and shaped the internal politics of the United States. It argues that the Republican party was the primary beneficiary of the struggle with communism, as it succeeded in tarring liberalism with the epithet that it was "soft" on communism. Franklin Roosevelt's New Deal quickly gave way to a nationalistic, patriotic Republicanism whose leaders occupied the White House for much of the Cold War. In the ten presidential elections held from 1952 to 1988, Republicans won seven of them. Dwight Eisenhower, Richard Nixon, and Ronald Reagan are the founders of a modern Republicanism based in the Cold War era. Yet at other levels of government—particularly in Congress—New Deal Democrats reigned until they were overtaken by the race issue and the cultural liberalism of the 1970s.

The Republican party's success during the Cold War was grounded in two important yet contradictory aspects of American politics: (1) our fanatical preoccupation with communism, and (2) a robust liberalism. As to the former, the Cold War years are replete with illustrations of American anticommunism. In a revealing 1954 incident, for example, journalist Murray Kempton and former U.S. Communist Party leader Earl Browder had a chance encounter in New York City's Greenwich Village. At the time, the number of registered communists had dropped precipitously, Alger Hiss was languishing in a federal prison, the House Committee on Un-American Activities (HUAC) was grilling suspected communists, and the public was coming to grips with the specter of Senator Joseph McCarthy. Kempton tentatively suggested that the U.S. Communist Party was in danger of becoming a backwater, to which Browder responded, "It was always a political backwater."[25] Yet up to the Cold War's abrupt end Americans continued to believe that communist infiltrators were responsible for many of the country's problems. A 1989 Gallup poll found that 52 percent held communists responsible "for a lot of the unrest in the United States today."[26] Of course, the power of the U.S. Communist Party was never evidenced in massive numbers of proletarians rising in protest against capitalists. Rather, the fear of communism was mostly in our collective consciousness. As Arthur M. Schlesinger Jr. perceptively noted in the early days of the Cold War, "In its essence this crisis is internal."[27]

Fear is an animating emotion, especially in the United States. Political scientist Louis Hartz hypothesized that no other ideology, save classical liberalism, could thrive in the American polity.[28] He argued that Americans were so ideologically straitjacketed that a philosophy that did not espouse individualism, equality of opportunity, and freedom would be seen by many as alien. Alexis de Tocqueville held a similar view, writing in *Democracy in America* (1835): "I know of no country in which there is so little independence of mind and real freedom of discussion as in America."[29] Indeed, the essence of the American polity is not in the maze of structures erected by the Founders in the Constitution; rather, it is located in the shared values of its citizens. Englishman G. K. Chesterton wrote in 1920 that the United States was founded on a "creed," elaborating: "That creed is set forth with dogmatic and even theological lucidity in the Declaration of Independence; perhaps the only piece of practical politics that is also theoretical politics and also great literature."[30] This creed has little tolerance for any deviancy. Lewis Cass, the 1848 Democratic nominee for president, later told a Tammany Hall audience that he was "opposed to all the isms of the day . . . to communism and socialism, and Mormonism; to polygamy and concubinage, and to all the humbugs that are now rising among us."[31] Abraham Lincoln warned that if the Declaration of Independence was amended to read that "all men are created equal, except Negroes, and foreigners, and Catholics," then "I should prefer emigrating to some country where they make no pretense of loving liberty—to Russia, for instance, where despotism can be taken pure, and without the base alloy of hypocrisy."[32] Karl Marx acknowledged communism's failure in the United States, blaming it on "the tenacity of the Yankees" and citing their "theoretical backwardness" and their "Anglo-Saxon contempt for all theory."[33]

As the post–World War II decades passed with no end to the Cold War in sight, communism became the antithesis of the American creed. In 1964, the *World Book Encyclopedia* drew a bright line between communism and American-style democracy: "In a democratic country, the government rules by consent of the people. In a communist country, the dictator rules by force and stays in power by force. A democratic government tries to act in a way that will benefit the people. . . . Under communism, the interests of the government always come first. . . . Communism violently opposes democracy and the democratic way of life."[34] Such a robust classical liberalism that viewed communism as the antithesis of all that was good handed the Republican party an opportunity to remake itself following the twin disasters of the Great Depression and the Hoover presidency. To be sure, Republicans had long criticized Franklin D. Roosevelt for being naive when it came to Soviet intentions. But the relative success of the New Deal in transforming a generation of "have-nots" into "haves" *enhanced* the GOP's ability to make communism an issue. Repeatedly, Republicans accused Democrats of coddling communists. And just as often Democrats would howl in protest. For example, in a 1944 speech to the Foreign Policy Association, Franklin Roosevelt took note of the Republican attacks on his administration while acknowledging the prevailing antipathy toward communism. Roosevelt recounted an experience his wife, Eleanor, had with a group of elementary school students shortly after he entered the White House:

> In 1933, a certain lady who sits at a table in front of me [Eleanor Roosevelt] came back from a trip on which she had attended the opening of a schoolhouse. And she had gone to the history class, history and geography of children eight, nine, and ten, and she told me she had seen there a map of the world with a great big white space upon it; no name, no information, and the teacher told her that it was blank with no name because the school board wouldn't let her say anything about that big blank space. Oh, there were only 180,000,000 to 200,000,000 people in it, it was called Soviet Russia, and there were a lot of children and they were told that the teacher was forbidden by the school board even to put the name of that blank space on the map.[35]

Roosevelt's defense of his 1933 action permitting diplomatic recognition of the Soviet Union won him some admirers, especially as World War II neared its climax. But the subsequent slamming of the Iron Curtain on the peoples of Eastern Europe intensified the American public's anticommunism, making it an enduring political feature. In a 1983 survey, 92 percent said that in a communist country "you only hear news the government wants you to hear"; 91 percent agreed that "if you speak your mind, you risk going to jail"; 84 percent rejected the notion that life for the average communist "is pretty much the same as in the United States"; 80 percent said "you can't move or relocate without permission from the government"; 75 percent maintained that "you always have to be afraid of the police"; 75 percent agreed that "you can't pick your own job or change jobs"; 69 percent believed "there is no freedom of religion"; 65 percent disagreed that "there's less stress and tension" for the "average" communist; 61 percent said "you can't get a fair trial"; 60 percent rejected the idea that "men and women are treated equally."[36] Thus, when President Ronald Reagan dubbed the Soviet Union the "evil empire," most Americans (and many Russians) agreed with him.

This rejection of communism reinforced American nationalism, and it made the Republicans into a patriotic party. Democrats, meanwhile, became mired in debates about Soviet intentions as the New Left (led by Henry Wallace and later George McGovern) struggled not only with their feelings toward communism but with hard-line anticommunists like John F. Kennedy, Lyndon B. Johnson, and Hubert H. Humphrey who represented the old politics of the New Deal. For much of the Cold War, presidential contests were fought over the corpse of the Democratic party—especially after McGovern's rise in 1972. Republicans never wavered in their belief that Democrats were naive when it came to Soviet intentions, and they repeatedly reminded voters of the Democrats' mushy thinking. White House Chief of Staff H. R. Haldeman recalled a conversation with Richard Nixon on February 9, 1973, that illustrates this point:

> He got into Watergate strategy. He wants our people to put out that foreign or communist money came in support of the [anti–Vietnam War] demonstrations in the campaign, tie all the '72 demonstrations to McGovern and thus the Democrats as part of the peace movement. Broaden the investigation to include the peace movement and its leaders, McGovern and Teddy Kennedy. To what extent they were responsible for the demonstrations that led to violence and disruption. . . . We should itemize all the disruptions such as the Century Plaza in San Francisco, the burnings, the Statue of Liberty, etc.[37]

Despite the political charges and countercharges, most voters saw through the political smoke. A 1980 ABC News/Louis Harris poll found 50 percent agreed with this statement: "A candidate for president who says his opponent is 'soft on communism' is probably a hypocrite, because, if elected, he will soon be sitting down in Moscow and Peking to work out agreements with communist leaders."[38] Even though Americans were cynical about the Republican party's exploitation of the Cold War, when they retreated to the confines of the voting booth, they frequently chose tough-talking Republican warriors over their seemingly naive Democratic opponents. Yet once in the White House Republican executives loved to don their commander-in-chief hats, and from that moment they placed themselves above politics. In effect, the national security state smothered "traditional" politics—and this suited Americans just fine, because so many of them cared little for politics and even less about political parties. Thus, although the Cold War allowed Republicans to bask in their sunshine patriotism, the party often was headed by a patriot who disdained it as an institution.

Republican success in making liberalism a dirty word (shorthand: the "L-word") hastened its demise. By 1952, chastened Democrats were casting extensions of the New Deal not as necessary antidotes to poverty but as necessary for the nation's defense. Democratic platform writers that year pledged, "Since several million mothers must now be away from their children during the day, because they are engaged in defense work, facilities for adequate day care of these children should be provided and adequately financed."[39] Later, a Democratic Congress passed and a Republican president endorsed the National Defense Education Act and the Federal Aid Highway Act. One produced a generation of young mathematicians and scientists; the other modernized an antiquated transportation system. Both were offered as examples of anticommunist resolve, and each constituted a major rewriting of the social compact by expanding the reach of the federal government into areas once considered the province of the states. It is interesting how quickly other domestic programs became arsenals of the Cold War.

In spite of such reformulations of the Roosevelt agenda, Democrats (fairly or not) had to prove their loyalty to a skeptical electorate. Such frequent protestations left many party faithful uncomfortable with the civic rituals that accompany political campaigns. Meeting in San Francisco for the 1984 national convention, Democratic delegates waved hundreds of flags before television cameras while voters watched from their living rooms.[40] Yet there was something surreal about the scene—it looked as though the delegates were playacting, that the demonstration was staged for political purposes. It was. Reacting to Ronald Reagan's penchant for civic ritual, Democratic presidential candidate Gary Hart declared, "I don't want to be president of a country that thinks like Ronald Reagan."[41] The Democrats, too, were victims of the Cold War.

But the Cold War did more than redefine politics: It said much about who we are. The majestic words of the Declaration of Independence are worth remembering: "We hold these truths to be self-evident, that all men are created equal, that they are endowed by their Creator with certain unalienable rights, that among these are Life, Liberty, and the pursuit of Happiness." The "we" to whom Thomas Jefferson referred are Americans whose self-realization is not premised on a particular racial, ethnic, or religious bias but upon an identification with the "self-evident" truths of life, liberty, and the pursuit of happiness. In the centuries after the Declaration of Independence was written, these self-evident ideas have gone essentially unchallenged. In 1967, Lloyd Free and Hadley Cantril noted that the Mayflower Compact, the writings of John Locke, and the Declaration of Independence "reflect the basic political values that have shaped the American political system for nearly three hundred and fifty years. . . . The underlying personal political credos of the majority of Americans have remained substantially intact at the ideological level."[42] Nearly three decades later Bill Clinton observed that when one reads the Declaration of Independence and the Constitution, one discovers that "this country is an idea."[43]

During the Cold War, these creedal passions were aroused to even more intensive levels. As late as 1989 a plurality (47 percent) said they would rather fight an all-out nuclear war than live under communist rule.[44] When George Gallup asked in 1954, "Do you think a man can believe in communism and still be a loyal American, or not?" only 5 percent said yes; 87 percent answered no.[45] Those who loudly proclaimed "I'm not a communist!" included leaders of both political parties who often resorted to extreme measures to dissociate themselves from suspected communists. For example, on March 21, 1947, Harry Truman issued an executive order creating a Federal Employees Loyalty and Security Program. "Loyalty" became the touchstone for federal workers, police officers, schoolteachers, and even social workers. Ardent vocalizing of the "self-evident" truths contained in the Declaration of Independence, especially when juxtaposed against the "big lie" of communism, created a peculiar form of extremism. Political scientist Seymour Martin Lipset discovered that Joseph McCarthy's greatest source of support during the 1950s came from "nineteenth-century liberals"— those opposed to big trade unions and large corporations; in short, those who resembled Alexis de Tocqueville's America.[46]

Such extreme antipathy toward communism was not confined to the likes of Joe McCarthy. A year after the Army-McCarthy hearings a U.S. House subcommittee halted overseas distribution of a history text entitled *Profile of America* because it contained a photograph of a little red schoolhouse built in 1750. The U.S. Information Agency protested the decision, but Congress maintained that the offending picture would give the Russians the idea that one-room schools were prevalent in the United States. One member objected to the inclusion of a photograph of a Vermont schoolteacher because a friend had once seen a Russian book with a better-looking teacher. [47] At this, Emily Davie, editor of *Profile of America*, told a Senate appropriations subcommittee, "I didn't think I had to show schoolteachers looking like the Rockettes."[48]

In Florida, the "Johns Committee," chaired by State Senator Charley Johns, investigated the private lives of more than 1,000 residents from 1956 to 1964; seventy-one teachers and thirty-nine deans and college professors lost their jobs. One transcript contained the following conversation between a committee investigator and a Miami Beach housepainter suspected of being a communist:

> Investigator: Obviously, you are afraid. You have told us in so many words. You have said you would not want to be an informer, and you are afraid because of your wife and children. If we make this public, which we can do. . . .
>
> Housepainter: I know.
>
> Investigator: What about your wife and children, then what about your occupation here?[49]

A decade ago, *New York Times* columnist Anthony Lewis wondered, "Why do we have this hysterical strain in us about communism?"[50] The answer, I believe, is that communism challenged the very essence of the nation itself. Leon Samson has written that "Americanism is to the American not a tradition or a territory, not what France is to a Frenchman or England to an Englishman, but a doctrine—what socialism is to a socialist."[51] Being an American involves more than loyalty to a particular parcel of earth; rather, it means the complete acceptance of classical liberalism. To reject these political values is to risk being tarred as "un-American"—the proverbial scarlet letter in American politics. Louis Hartz argued that the danger in American society was not the Framers' fear of the "tyranny of the majority"; rather, it was "the danger of unanimity," which had manifested itself in a red scare that no other Western nation had been able to understand.[52] As historian Richard Hofstadter once observed, "It has been our fate as a nation not to have ideologies but to be one."[53]

Given this commitment to a single set of political values, the question "What does it mean to be an American?" has a special importance. Love of country has meant love of liberalism. Proving one's loyalty has meant paying homage to the values of individualism, freedom, and equality of opportunity. In a 1946 Independence Day oration, John F. Kennedy observed that the "characteristics of the American people have ever been a deep sense of religion, a deep sense of idealism, a deep sense of patriotism, and a deep sense of individualism."[54] Even when major setbacks have challenged classical liberalism, Americans have adamantly refused to abandon their ideology. A December 1939 Roper poll is illustrative. When asked, "Which one of the following most nearly represents your opinion of the American form of government? (a) Our form of government based on the Constitution is as near perfect as it can be and no important changes should be made in it; (b) the Constitution has served its purpose well, but it has not kept up with the times and should be thoroughly revised to make it fit present day needs; or (c) the systems of private capitalism and democracy are breaking down and we might as well accept the fact that sooner or later we will have to have a new form of government," 64 percent said our political system is "as near perfect as it can be" (including 58 percent who were classified as "poor")—this when so many were still in the abyss of the Great Depression.[55]

This belief that the American system was the most perfect system remained unchanged from the Great Depression through the Cold War. Americans believed the "captive peoples" in Eastern Europe and the Soviet Union wanted their system, and government leaders reflected these attitudes by creating Radio Free Europe and Radio Liberty—using funds from the Central Intelligence Agency (CIA) to do it. These radio stations beamed the American way of life in twenty-four languages each day to those behind the Iron Curtain. Dwight Eisenhower maintained that these agencies were indispensable weapons in fighting communism, and he advised that they "be guided by persons selflessly dedicated to the promotion of freedom and the propagation of truth."[56]

It was perhaps inevitable that communism, with its emphasis on group rights and its expropriation of private property, became the antithesis of everything American. Thus, the best way to defend a controversial action was to label its opponents "communists." Following the brutal slaughter of Vietnamese civilians at My Lai, for instance, First Lieutenant William L. Calley Jr. employed this strategy at his 1971 military tribunal: "Nobody in the military system ever described them [the Vietnamese] as anything other than communism. They didn't give it a race, they didn't give it a sex, they didn't give it an age. They never let me believe it was just a philosophy in a man's mind."[57] Two years earlier a passionate Al Gore (later to become vice president) wrote his father, then a U.S. senator from Tennessee, that the American antipathy toward communism had created its own form of paranoia:

> We do have inveterate antipathy for communism—or paranoia as I like to put it. My own belief is that this form of psychological ailment—in this case a national madness—leads the victim to actually create the thing which is feared the most. It strikes me that this is precisely what the U.S. has been doing. Creating—and if not creating, energetically supporting—fascist, totalitarian regimes in the name of fighting totalitarianism. Greece, South Vietnam, a good deal of Latin America. For me, the best example is the U.S. Army.[58]

Shown the letter he had written to his father while in college, Vice President Gore was horrified: "Oh, good Lord! Oh, God! Is that a private letter? Did he share that with you? Good Lord!" Gore observed that his note was "a college kid's silly language in the midst of a very intense period for the country." The vice president added that he no longer agreed with his notions of a "national madness" and "paranoia" about communism:

> I have a very strong, inveterate antipathy myself for communism. But in the context, as you will recall, the debate between North Vietnam and South Vietnam was one that was defined by one side as purely a struggle against communism, with very little appreciation for the colonial history and the nationalist dimension of the conflict. And, in that context, we certainly did have a lack of perspective on the true nature of that conflict. But communism is an evil ideology that is enslaving and doesn't work.[59]

As Gore's youthful letter illustrates, American susceptibility to anticommunist hysteria caused many to see red. In 1952, baseball's Cincinnati Reds officially changed their name to the Redlegs, not wanting their foes to believe that they might be battling the Cincinnati Communists. A local sportswriter sadly noted, "We were Reds before they were."[60] Two years later when the *Saturday Evening Post* asked "HOW RED IS INDIA?" the American response was "TOO RED!"[61] It seemed that not only the Russians were coming but also Chinese, Indians, Cubans, and nearly everyone else. Thus, during the 1980s, Congress approved annual foreign aid expenditures totaling $16 billion—much of it under the pretense that if we did not give Third World nations substantial sums of cash they would fall under the communist spell.[62]

As anticommunist hysteria grew, so did fanaticism. The world of the fanatic is a peculiar one. Eric Hoffer, the California longshoreman, describes it in *The True Believer:* "All mass movements . . . breed fanaticism, enthusiasm, fervent hope, hatred, and intolerance; all of them are capable of releasing a powerful flow of activity in certain departments of life; all of them demand blind faith and singlehearted allegiance."[63] But the American obsession with communism lasted far longer than our hatred for strange persons or other nations. The Salem witch trials; our obsession with the Germans in World Wars I and II; our desire to avenge the Japanese attack on Pearl Harbor; the transformation of the Ayatollah Khomeini into a madman after the seizure of the American hostages in 1979; and our distaste during the Persian Gulf War in 1991 for another modern-day Satan, Saddam Hussein, were relatively brief flirtations with fanaticism. But the anticommunist crusade, beginning with the Red Scare of 1920 and continuing as the Soviets expanded their reach around the globe after World War II, touched nearly every department of life. Virtually nothing was beyond its reach. Even our everyday language reflected the forty-six-year struggle with communism. Terms such as *fellow-traveler, card-carrying, containment, hawk, dove, détente, red herring, Iron Curtain, Free World, Captive Nations, McCarthyism, gulag, counterintelligence,* and *nuclear freeze* entered the popular lexicon. Cold War slogans also dominated our politics: "America: Love It or

Leave It," "Give Peace a Chance," "Peace Through Strength," "Godless Communism," "Soft on Communism," "Better Dead Than Red," "Ban the Bomb," and "Live Free or Die" are but a few examples.

Anticommunism became an integral chapter in the life stories of prominent Americans whose formative years encompassed the Cold War. For example, a youthful H. R. Haldeman became fascinated with the Alger Hiss case and soon attached himself to Richard Nixon's political fortunes. Haldeman's entry into politics was presaged by the activities of his paternal grandfather and namesake, Harry Haldeman, who organized the Better America Foundation during the Red Scare of 1920.[64] In Huntington, Indiana, young Dan Quayle was an ardent fan of Whittaker Chambers's *Witness*, arguing the merits of Chambers's prose in a college essay. In this, Quayle imitated his parents, who subscribed to John Birch Society founder Robert Welch's thesis that Dwight Eisenhower was a clandestine communist.[65] Hillary Rodham Clinton's initial foray into politics was as a "Goldwater Girl" in 1964. And on July 24, 1963, seventeen-year-old Bill Clinton had his picture taken with John F. Kennedy and heard Kennedy tell the American Legion–sponsored Boys Nation that the United States was standing guard in the battle with communism "all the way from Berlin to Saigon."[66] Listening to these words, the teenage Arkansan resolved to enter public life. He interned in the office of J. William Fulbright, chairman of the Senate Foreign Relations Committee and staunch opponent of the Vietnam War. His first taste of presidential politics was as coordinator of George McGovern's Texas effort in 1972. As Clinton himself admitted, "I am literally a child of the Cold War."[67]

The Cold War also tainted every political issue. This is especially true of civil rights. In 1983, Jesse Helms, the Republican senator from North Carolina, vehemently objected to making Martin Luther King's birthday into a national holiday. Claiming that King was a communist sympathizer, Helms implored President Reagan not to sign the bill. When asked about Helms's accusations, Reagan gave credibility to the charge, saying of King's supposed communist connections, "We'll know in about thirty-five years, won't we?"[68] During the Cold War the Soviets often exploited racial tensions in the United States for their own propaganda advantage. A 1954 *Saturday Evening Post* article penned by NAACP executive secretary Walter White contained this editor's note: "The author, a distinguished Negro spokesman, senses a changing—and heartening—attitude toward racial discrimination in our capital. But, he says, indignities are still forced on dark-skinned foreigners and Americans there—and that's the story Moscow loves to exploit."[69] From its inception, the U.S. Communist Party targeted blacks as potential recruits—often citing the 1931 Scottsboro case in which nine black men (some were barely youths, the youngest being only twelve) were accused of raping two white Alabama women. Kennedy biographer

Richard Reeves writes that James Meredith was inspired to apply to the whites-only University of Mississippi after listening to Kennedy's Inaugural Address, the most fervent of speeches ever given during the Cold War. Behind closed doors, Kennedy complained to adviser Louis Martin: "Negroes are getting ideas they didn't have before," and wondered, "Where are they getting them?" At this, Martin became irritated and shouted, "From you! You're lifting the horizons of Negroes."[70] Later, in a television address following Governor George Wallace's blocking of the schoolhouse door at the University of Alabama, Kennedy used the Cold War to justify school integration and federal involvement in the civil rights movement: "Today we are committed to a worldwide struggle to promote and protect the rights of all who wish to be free. And when Americans are sent to Vietnam or West Berlin, we do not ask for whites only. It ought to be possible, therefore, for American students of any color to attend any public institution they select without having to be backed up by troops."[71]

The federal government—that part of the American polity that is, in Lincoln's words, "of, for, and by the people"—followed public opinion by mobilizing to fight the Cold War. Nearly a dozen agencies were formed to gather intelligence or administer national security policy, including the CIA, the National Security Agency, and the Defense Intelligence Agency. At the apex of this intelligence apparatus was the "imperial presidency." When the Soviet Union collapsed in 1991, the United States had 375 military bases scattered around the globe staffed by more than a half-million personnel.[72] It was this enlarged, permanent defense establishment that prompted Bernard Baruch to warn in 1949 that Americans needed to develop "a new sense of interrelationship between war and peace, between home and abroad, between each of us and 'those bureaucrats in Washington.'"[73] But the new relationship often proved a one-way street as matters heretofore reserved to the political realm were removed from it in the name of national security. Steven Aftergood, editor of the *Secrecy and Government Bulletin*, a publication of the Federation of American Scientists, wrote in July 1991: "A whole realm of government is beyond any pretense of democratic decision-making."[74]

As if to prove the point, it was disclosed in 1995 that the National Reconnaissance Office (NRO), created in 1960 to operate spy satellites and evaluate their findings, had secretly accumulated $1.5 *billion* in unspent appropriations. The agency, whose existence was not publicly known until 1992, had ignored congressional directives to reduce its surplus. Moreover, how the NRO spent its money became a matter of controversy. In 1993, the House Appropriations Committee said the NRO had signed a multibillion-dollar contract for ocean surveillance satellites in defiance of congressional instructions. One year later the Senate Select Committee on Intelligence was surprised to learn that the NRO had spent $340 million to build a new headquarters near Dulles International Airport outside Washington, D.C. The money had been concealed in accounts that did not appear to be for construction. An NRO spokesman said the agency had been "negligent."[75]

Still Seeing Red tells the story of the politics of the Cold War. In so doing, it is my hope that a veil of misunderstanding about electoral movements and coalition-building during the Cold War will be lifted. In this, we may better understand why contemporary politics is the way it is. But this book also says much about who we are. It is a question that needs reexamination. As the famous figurative "Doomsday Clock" moved from two minutes before midnight in 1953 back several minutes prior to the witching hour in the 1970s and 1980s,[76] something profound happened: We became comfortable with the Cold War—comfortable with our enemies, comfortable with the government it created, comfortable with the commander-in-chief, comfortable with the politics of the Cold War itself. Our comfort with the Cold War resulted, I believe, in a hesitancy to see its political underpinnings. This is quite unlike the issue of race relations, where public discomfiture translated into a "white flight" from the Democratic party at the same time blacks sought refuge in it. There is a plethora of books about race yet relatively few about the internal political upheavals the Cold War created in our party system.

It is that comfort with the party system born of the Cold War that has resulted in so much of our present discomfiture and cynicism about politics. Perhaps, in retrospect, we will become uncomfortable with the Cold War and therefore better understand its politics. Whatever happens, we, the survivors of the Cold War, must ask ourselves once more: What does it mean to be an American?

Part One

Cold War Fears and Party Response

chapter one

1945–1946:
Lost Innocence

People react to fear, not love.

—Richard M. Nixon

June 25, 1945

At exactly 2:29 in the afternoon an airplane dubbed *The Sacred Cow* landed in San Francisco to deliver its Very Important Passenger, the thirty-third president of the United States. Harry S. Truman, just ten weeks in office, emerged to the sounds of a twenty-one-gun salute and a band playing "Missouri Waltz." After reviewing an honor guard of 300 soldiers in full battle dress, Truman went to a military hospital to greet wounded survivors from Okinawa and other Pacific battlefields. Then, after consoling the troops, the president clambered aboard an open car for a twenty-five-mile ride through San Francisco's hilly streets to the Fairmont Hotel. An estimated half-million people jammed the sidewalks, waved from open windows, shimmied lampposts, and stood on rooftops (it was still an age of innocence as far as presidential security was concerned). Streamers and confetti flowed from tall buildings as the seventy-five-car motorcade meandered through the choked streets. This crowd did not simply cheer; as one eyewitness put it, "They yell and whistle."[1] Truman was ecstatic at the hero's welcome, standing and waving a tan hat in response to the plaudits. When he finally reached the hotel, several women in the lobby were overcome by "Trumanmania" and screamed, causing the bemused object of their affections to remark: "Well, that wasn't for me. It was for what we stand for. It was for the president of the United States. They were cheering the office, not the man."[2]

There was much to cheer. World War II had ended victoriously in Europe, and newspapers were crammed with pictures of American soldiers jubilantly shaking hands with their Soviet allies at the river Elbe. Twenty-four hours before Truman's arrival in San Francisco, Soviet troops gleefully dragged Adolf Hitler's personal swastika over the cobblestones of Red Square before hurling it into a muddy ditch. On that same day, the golden clocks on the Kremlin's Spasskaya Tower chimed and the great Parade of Victory had begun. Thunderous applause spread throughout the square as the ruling State Committee of Defense emerged from the Kremlin and climbed the stairs of Lenin's Mausoleum. Leading the way was the head of the Soviet empire, Josef Stalin.[3] Meanwhile, war still raged in the Pacific, but the United States possessed a weapon of unparalleled power that would cause the Japanese emperor to sue for peace within two months.

But in San Francisco a new world order was taking shape as Woodrow Wilson's dream of a League of Nations was fast becoming a reality. Senate Republican Arthur H. Vandenberg of Michigan, once an ardent isolationist, expressed his innermost thoughts: "It has been the crowning privilege of my life to have been the author of the San Francisco Charter. It has an excellent chance to save the peace of the world *if* America and Russia can learn to live together and *if* Russia learns to keep her word."[4] At 10:53 P.M., on the very day that Truman triumphantly entered San Francisco, the United Nations Charter was approved, prompting the 3,000 exhausted delegates in San Francisco's fabled Opera House to stand and applaud for a full minute.

In fact, the purpose of Truman's journey was to witness the historic signing of the charter. Following his tumultuous greeting, the chief executive strode into the Opera House on the sixty-third day of the conference to address the delegates assembled from the far corners of the earth. Dozens of crisp United Nations flags hung in a semicircle around a conference table, having been neatly hand-pressed by an ironing woman the week before. A blue cover on the conference table, a dark-blue curtain, and a blue chair accentuated the light-blue flags under which delegates would sign the document.[5] Truman decided to honor the United Nations by wearing a navy blue, double-breasted suit replete with blue shirt, tie, a handkerchief just visible above the breast pocket, and a blue United Nations delegate pin on his left lapel. As he briskly walked onto the stage while the band played "Hail to the Chief," the president was accompanied by conference parliamentarian Charles L. Watkins, naval aide Captain James K. Vardaman, close friend Colonel Harry Vaughn, and the secretary-general of the conference, Alger Hiss.[6]

As Truman began speaking, a euphoria about the peace to come swept the hall. Truman caught the mood and began his address by extemporaneously exclaiming: "Oh, what a great day this can be in history!"—a remark that won the most fervent applause of the entire conference.[7] Truman proposed that future conflicts, instead of being settled by war, be mediated by the United Nations, which he said would be a "solid structure upon which we can build a better world." Watching from his seat in the Opera House was the Soviet ambassador to the United States, Andrei Gromyko, who only the day before raised several last-minute objections to the charter. Gromyko became the object of Truman's lone downbeat note: "Out of this conflict have come powerful military nations, now fully trained and equipped for war. But they have no right to dominate the world. It is rather the duty of those powerful nations to assume the responsibility for leadership toward a world of peace."[8]

But emerging Cold War disputes involving the two superpowers, spreading from war-torn Eastern Europe to the Korean Peninsula, did not escape notice. In 1945, Soviet troops refused to leave the Iranian province of Azerbaijan in defiance of the Iranian government. After the United States took the dispute to the United Nations Security Council, Soviet premier Joseph Stalin relinquished the disputed territory. Foreign Minister Vyacheslav Molotov recalled in chilling detail how Stalin plotted to seize the Dardanelles and Libya and how he even drew up plans for taking Alaska.[9] Marshal Georgi K. Zhukov boasted, "The Soviet state has emerged even more mighty from the grim struggle we waged, and the Red Army [is] the most modern and powerful army in the world."[10] In April, Senator Vandenberg expressed his apprehension in his diary, writing: "There is a general disposition to stop this *Stalinist appeasement*. It *has* to stop *sometime*. Every new surrender makes it more difficult."[11] A cub reporter also saw trouble lurking ahead. In a dispatch from the San Francisco conference, this on-scene correspondent took note of the "tremendous differences" that existed between the two emerging superpowers, writing that they were a "shock to many people who have been lulled into a feeling that all was well by the reports of complete agreement that came out of the conferences at Teheran and Yalta." He charged that the Allies' disputes with the Soviets would reduce the United Nations to "a skeleton," concluding: "It is unfortunate that unity for war against a common aggressor is far easier to obtain than unity for peace. We are commencing to realize how difficult and long the road is ahead. San Francisco is only the beginning."[12] So wrote John F. Kennedy.

That hope-filled day of June 25, 1945, quickly vanished into the mists of time. Bill Clinton, who would one day become only the fourth Democrat to follow Truman into the White House, had not yet been born. John F. Kennedy, still suffering from his war injuries, was on temporary assignment for Chicago's *Herald American*.[13] Lyndon B. Johnson was a young U.S. representative from Texas. Navy Lieutenant Commander Richard M. Nixon was stationed in Maryland, and across the globe Lieutenant (jg) George H.W. Bush prepared with his torpedo bomber group to invade Japan. In California, U.S. Army Second Cavalry Reserve Lieutenant Ronald

W. Reagan was making training films. Joseph R. McCarthy had been elected a Wisconsin circuit court judge. And David Whittaker Chambers was an obscure editor at *Time*. Just five years later the optimism that exuded from San Francisco's Opera House had been dissipated by a "Cold War" that, although different from all other wars, was no less threatening. Americans saw the red specter of Soviet communism encircling the globe, while at home it was feared that the "unseen enemy" of communism had pervaded many minds. The latter apparition became especially vivid on January 21, 1950, when Mrs. Ada Condell, speaking in a quavering and nearly inaudible voice, pronounced a jury's verdict: "Guilty on the first count and guilty on the second."[14] With that, Alger Hiss, the man who stood at Truman's side in San Francisco, was whisked to federal prison. But we are getting ahead of our story.

An Insecure Superpower

Several months before Pearl Harbor, Henry Luce, the *Time-Life* publishing baron, heralded the coming of "The American Century." He described the United States "as the dynamic center of ever-widening spheres of enterprise, America as the training center of the skillful servants of mankind, America as the Good Samaritan, really believing again that it is more blessed to give than to receive, and America as the powerhouse of the ideals of Freedom and Justice." Luce maintained that "out of these elements surely can be fashioned a vision of the 20th century to which we can and will devote ourselves in joy and gladness and enthusiasm."[15] Victory in World War II added more bold colors to Luce's already glorious portrait. Shortly after the war ended, Director of War Mobilization and Reconversion Fred Vinson declared, "The American people are in the pleasant predicament of having to learn to live 50 percent better than they have ever lived before."[16] The Truman administration was not alone in forecasting better days ahead. Hollywood got into the act. The most popular movie of World War II was *This Is the Army* (1943), which starred George Murphy and Ronald Reagan and celebrated the revival of consumerism.

There was every reason to believe that the United States was about to enter a golden age. At the end of World War II it was an unrivaled military superpower, the sole possessor of the atomic bomb. More important, the United States was an economic giant: Half the world's wealth and productivity in addition to nearly two-thirds of all manufacturing was concentrated in its hands. After visiting the United States in the winter of 1948–1949, British historian Robert Payne observed: "There never was a country more fabulous than America. She sits bestride the world like a Colossus; no other power at any time in the world's history has possessed so varied or so great an influence on other nations."[17]

But Americans were not anxious to conquer the world. Rather, they were fixated on picking up the scattered pieces of disrupted lives. The views of a World War I soldier, stuck in Europe and yearning to come home, were echoed by millions of former servicemen a generation later: "As far as we're concerned, most of us don't give a whoop (to put it mildly) whether Russia has a Red Government or no Government and if the King of the Lollypops wants to slaughter his subjects or his Prime Minister it's all the same to us."[18] Captain Harry S. Truman's sentiments in a 1919 letter to cousin Ethel Noland swept the land in the first days of his presidency. Not long after the Japanese surrender, American soldiers organized "I Wanna Go Home" demonstrations. Wives, girlfriends, mothers, and sisters mailed Congress tiny baby boots accompanied by plaintive notes that read, "I miss my Daddy."[19]

These letters did not go unanswered. From 1947 to 1950, the armed forces shrank from 3 million to 1.5 million—*fewer* than the 1.8 million in uniform before Pearl Harbor.[20] In a letter to a critic of such a rapid diminishment of the armed forces, General Dwight Eisenhower admitted that "the present rate of demobilization, while it may have been accelerated beyond that degree desirable for security, still represents the spontaneous expression of the will of the American people."[21] Military budgets also reflected popular nostrums, falling from a wartime high of $90.9 billion to $10.3 billion in 1947. Discharged military personnel were coming home, marrying, and having babies—caring little about the strange lands they left behind. One blue-collar worker sarcastically remarked: "Foreign affairs. That's for people who don't have to work for a living."[22]

That blue-collar man's sentiment that the world could take care of itself gained credence—especially since the United Nations would be the guarantor of world peace. Yet just below the surface there was a sense of unease. Shortly after the war ended, Luce's own *Time* magazine belied its publisher's vision of an American Century: "The knowledge of victory was as charged with sorrow and doubt as with joy and gratitude."[23] A reporter asked a young St. Louis mother what lay ahead: "Oh, things are going along just wonderfully," she burbled. "Harry has a grand job, there's the new baby. . . ." Then a frown overtook her joyous expression and she wondered aloud, "Do you really think it's all going to last?"[24] That question was on many minds, though few had the temerity to express it. Just what kind of country was "Daddy" coming home to?

The America that the returning GIs hoped to find was perhaps best expressed in a film titled *The Best Years of Our Lives:* "A good job, a mild future, and a little house big enough for me and my wife."[25] Everyone longed for "normalcy," but in truth there was no normalcy. A middle-aged American in 1945 had been born in a land that extolled free-enterprise, farming, and old-fashioned virtues. By war's end that same American worked in an economic jumble of capitalism and welfare statism, competed for jobs with newly ascendant immigrants, and often lived some distance away from parents and grandparents. More than *15 million* Americans had left their home towns to work in war plants and shipyards and were no longer living in their state or county of birth.[26] Small-town rural America was fast disappearing. Nervous veterans scoured want ads, fearing that if they did not find work they would be the victims of yet another depression like the one their parents had just experienced. Fortunately, most found jobs—some thanks to the GI bill, which offered many veterans the opportunity to be the first in their family to attend college. Although many returning veterans followed their parents into the factories, many found better opportunities in newfangled, white-collar jobs.

The national landscape was also being reshaped. William Levitt mass-produced homes in new suburban developments much in the same fashion that Henry Ford assembled automobiles. Many returning veterans left their urban neighborhoods and relatives behind to live there: In 1940, 46 percent of American homes were owner-occupied; by 1960, 64 percent were, with most GIs living in nicer homes than their parents had.[27] In addition, the face of the nation was also undergoing a makeover. Since the late nineteenth century, the United States had been teeming with foreign-tongued immigrants who were displacing the old stock—white Anglo-Saxon Protestants. After World War II, WASPs were competing for jobs alongside Irish, Italians, Poles, and others of European stock—with many living next door in formerly gentrified suburbs. Restive blacks, meanwhile, were demanding fulfillment of decades-old promises embodied in the eighteenth century's monumental instruments of civil rights—the Emancipation Proclamation, the Gettysburg Address, and the Fourteenth Amendment. Japanese Americans were freed from various "relocation" centers (to the consternation of some). Add to this ethnic melting pot a rash of labor strikes and a 20 percent inflation rate and one finds all the ingredients for domestic discord. Just two months after V-J Day a somewhat downcast Truman admitted: "We are having our little troubles now—a few of them. They are not serious. Just a blowup after a let-down from war."[28]

Change at home was accompanied by the emergence of a new world order. So quickly did new nations emerge after the collapse of the British and French colonial empires that cartographers could scarcely keep abreast of the redrawn maps and strange-sounding names. Old leaders were quickly discarded. Britons sent Conservative prime minister Winston Churchill packing and elected Labourite Clement Atlee. In the United States, the twelve-year regime of Franklin D. Roosevelt ended with his sudden death from a cerebral hemorrhage. But the office Vice President Harry Truman inherited was itself transformed, as the United States emerged from World War II as the world's unchallenged atomic power. Scholars pinpoint the origins of the modern presidency to Truman's decision to release atom bombs over Hiroshima and Nagasaki. Public opinion was divided about the new nuclear device: Some saw it as a safeguard of world peace; others thought it was the scourge of humankind. Either way, the potential for Armageddon rested with a president who now donned the mantle of Leader of the Free World. Historian Eric Goldman once wrote of the postwar era: "Wherever the American turned, whether to the details of the home or the mores of the presidency, nothing seemed unchanging except change."[29]

"Scaring Hell"

While Americans struggled to cope with these dazzling changes, the Soviet Union remained a troublesome force that would eventually have to be reckoned with. Publicly, Stalin predicted that war was inevitable until communism had conquered capitalism. Politicians from America's two major political parties dismissed Stalin's prophesy as idle chatter. Until his death, Franklin Roosevelt believed his charming persona, coupled with Soviet admission into the "club" of respectable nations, would abate Stalin's edginess and suspicions, resulting in the creation of a new postwar Europe.[30] Senate Republican Robert A. Taft believed Stalin's statements were pure propaganda since the Soviets could "not want war within any reasonable time" given the staggering human and economic toll Germany had just inflicted.[31] Taft added that the "communist army has done more to bring about a German defeat than any other army in the world, and for that Russian aid we shall be eternally grateful." Army Chief of Staff General Dwight D. Eisenhower expressed similar sentiments in an August 14, 1945, declaration: "I see nothing in the future that would prevent Russia and the United States from being the closest possible friends."[32] President Truman also shared Taft's and Eisenhower's views, stubbornly clinging to the conviction that any differences could be amicably settled between himself and "Uncle Joe." In a diary entry dated June 7, 1945, he wrote: "I'm not afraid of Russia. They've always been our friends and I can't see any reason why they shouldn't always be."[33]

Most Americans were less sanguine. In May 1945, 56 percent believed our relations with Russia would be "troublesome for this country in the next few years"—a higher figure than that given to our so-called "enemies," Germany and Japan.[34] There were other troublesome warnings. Shortly after the Yalta Conference, Nazi propaganda chief Joseph Goebbels became the first to use the term "iron curtain" to describe the postwar world: "If the Germans lay down their arms, the whole of eastern and southeastern Europe, together with the Reich, would come under Russian occupation. Behind an iron curtain, mass butchering of people would begin, and all that would remain would be a crude automation, a dull fermenting mass of millions of proletarian and despairing slave animals knowing nothing of the outside world." That prediction worried the Allies. From London, Prime Minister Winston Churchill cabled Truman to warn that an "iron curtain" was being drawn down on the Soviet front, ominously adding: "We do not know what is going on behind."[35] Churchill was later given a unique opportunity to share his concerns with the American public. Presidential aide Colonel Harry Vaughn wangled an invitation from his alma mater, Westminster College, for Churchill to speak and asked Truman to endorse it. He did, appending a personal note promising to accompany Churchill to Fulton, Missouri. Churchill accepted, and the trip was set for March 5, 1946. Aboard the presidential railroad car the atmosphere was jovial as Churchill played poker with the president and his party.[36]

The mood on the train may have been carefree, but the words Churchill uttered were not. His "Iron Curtain" speech envisioned a Soviet empire rising in the East that would menace the West:

> From Stettin in the Baltic to Trieste in the Adriatic, an iron curtain has descended across the continent. Behind that line lie all the capitals of the ancient states of Central and Eastern Europe. Warsaw, Berlin, Prague, Vienna, Budapest, Belgrade, Bucharest, and Sofia, all those famous cities and the populations around them lie in the Soviet sphere and all are subject in one form or another, not only to Soviet influence but to a very high and increasing measure of control from Moscow.[37]

Churchill's warning was something many were unprepared to heed. Years later, Richard Nixon recalled that the force of those words "jolted" him.[38] The effect was equally powerful on Churchill's immediate audience, most of whom sat in stunned silence. Only when Churchill declared, "I do not believe that Soviet Russia desires war," did he receive loud, sustained applause. But even that proved embarrassing as Churchill hastily added: "What they desire are the fruits of war and the indefinite expansion of their powers and doctrines."[39]

Official reaction to Churchill's "Iron Curtain" speech was guarded. Truman refused to endorse it and offered to accompany Stalin to Missouri for a reply. Stalin refused. Truman's Cabinet quarreled over its meaning. Secretary of State James Byrnes argued that the world was about to be divided into "friends" and "enemies."[40] United Nations delegate Adlai E. Stevenson was equally pessimistic: "We must forsake any hope that the Soviet Union is going to lie still and lick her awful wounds. She's not. . . . [S]he intends to advance her aims, many of them objectives of the Czars, to the utmost." Commerce Secretary Henry A. Wallace vehemently disagreed, stoutly maintaining that the Soviets were "offering a race with America in furnishing the needs of the common people without war or business crisis."[41]

The Cabinet squabble was part of a year-long debate within the innermost councils of the government about Soviet intentions. It began before

Churchill's address with the "Long Telegram" sent to the State Department by George F. Kennan on February 22, 1946, from the American embassy in Moscow. Noting the fusion of Soviet nationalism with Marxism, Kennan warned that the result was a messianic state "committed fanatically to the belief that with the U.S. there can be no *modus vivendi*; that it is desirable and necessary that the internal harmony of our society be disrupted, our traditional way of life be destroyed, the international authority of our state be broken, if Soviet power is to be secure."[42] Kennan's communiqué aroused the White House. Staffers Clark Clifford and George Elsey prepared an "eyes only" memorandum for Truman reviewing U.S.-Soviet relations. In unusually frank language, they wrote that the Soviet relationship was "the gravest problem" facing the United States and that the elimination of the tension would be impossible while the Kremlin continued "on a course of aggrandizement designed to lead to eventual world domination." A two-pronged (and somewhat contradictory) approach was recommended: (1) cooperation through cultural, intellectual, and economic interchanges in order to demonstrate that "we have no aggressive intentions and that peaceable co-existence of capitalism and communism is possible"; (2) a military buildup capable of repelling "any attack and sufficient to defeat the U.S.S.R. decisively if a war should start."[43] Only through a fine-tuned policy of openness and firmness would Soviet communism be brought to heel. Clifford and Elsey were especially critical of Wallace's policy of "mutual solidarity": "Adoption of such a policy would . . . only have the effect of raising Soviet hopes and increasing Soviet demands. . . . *The Soviet government will never be easy to get along with*. The American people must accustom themselves to this thought, not as a cause for despair, but as a fact to be faced objectively and courageously" (emphasis added).[44] President Truman read the Clifford-Elsey Report and immediately saw it as a political bombshell. He promptly retrieved all existing copies, placing them in a White House safe. For more than twenty years, the report remained classified as "top secret."[45] But the "containment policy" as outlined by Kennan, Clifford, and Elsey became the cornerstone of American foreign policy during the Cold War.

The containment policy had its first test in Greece. Greek Communists, with Soviet encouragement, were poised in 1947 to seize the birthplace of democracy. Three years earlier a government of national unity was created and its head, Georgios Papandreou, returned to Athens accompanied by British troops after a period in exile. Elections were held in March 1946, resulting in a brief return of the monarchy. Britain, meanwhile, had become economically and militarily drained by World War II and withdrew its large contingent of troops. As it was doing so, the communists began a protracted civil war, and in December 1947 they established a provisional government in the rural mountainside. As Greece came closer to communist rule, pressure mounted on Truman. He conferred with leaders of the Republican-controlled Congress, asking if they would support a massive for-eign assistance program for Greece and neighboring Turkey. Most balked until Undersecretary of State Dean Acheson darkly forecast that if the com-munists captured Greece this "might open three continents to Soviet pene-tration."[46] At this, Vandenberg, chairman of the Senate Foreign Relations Committee, turned to Truman and said: "Mr. President, if that's what you want, there's only one way to get it. That is to make a personal appearance before Congress and scare hell out of the country."[47]

Truman did appear before Congress, demanding a massive infusion of money for the two besieged governments. In his speech he fired a volley of verbal shots aimed at the Soviets. The most important one was his enlarge-ment of the Monroe Doctrine to encompass the entire globe. The "Truman Doctrine" asserted: "It must be the policy of the United States to support free peoples who are resisting attempted subjugation by armed minorities or by outside pressures."[48] A British diplomat observed that the Truman Doctrine was "hardly less than a declaration of war on the Soviet Union."[49] But polls showed Truman scoring with Americans: Nearly two-thirds agreed that if Greece was left unaided it would be in danger of being overrun by the communists.[50] House Democrat John F. Kennedy agreed, warning his colleagues that if Truman failed "the barriers would be down and the Red tide would flow across the face of Europe and through Asia with new power and vigor."[51]

In the ensuing debate on Capitol Hill, Vandenberg became Truman's point man. This was quite a role reversal for the Michigan Republican. En-tering Congress in 1928, he had been an ardent isolationist. But World War II broadened Vandenberg's political horizons. Addressing his Senate col-leagues in early 1945, Vandenberg said Pearl Harbor had "ended isolation-ism for any realist," adding, "Our oceans have ceased to be moats which automatically protect our ramparts."[52] Believing that America's role as Leader of the Free World was both inevitable and indispensable, Vanden-berg encouraged bipartisanship: "[It] united our official voice at the water's edge so that America could speak with maximum authority against those who would divide and conquer us and the free world."[53] Unity became the order of the day, as the Truman aid package won Senate approval by a tally of 67 yeas to 23 nays.

As the Senate vote suggests, most Republicans assented to the new bipar-tisan arrangements—albeit some more reluctantly than others. Robert Taft said "yea" to Greek-Turkish aid but claimed his support should not be seen as "a commitment to any similar policy in any other section of the world."[54] Like so many of his Republican colleagues, Taft knew that op-posing the popularly held maxim that "partisan politics must stop at the water's edge" was fraught with political risks that Democrats would not hesitate to exploit. An internal Democratic National Committee document maintained that bipartisanship would be strengthened when the records of Republican isolationists were exploited: "The public has a right to know which individuals have really supported the objectives of our foreign policy, and which individuals are the backward-looking opponents of these objectives."[55] As the document implies, Democrats could freely criticize Republican isolationists while applauding their "me-too" Republican allies for their statesmanship—a politically untenable proposition if the Republican party was to win back the White House.

But all this was "inside-baseball" politics. As for the voters, the Truman-Vandenberg tactic of "scaring hell" had the desired effect. Sixty-six percent of respondents told pollster George Gallup that communism was a "very serious" or "fairly serious" threat to our form of democratic government.[56] The fact that they should be so spectacularly successful in frightening the public was not surprising given the country's preoccupation with the Red Scare following World War I. In 1919, radicals associated with communists detonated bombs in eight cities, and a year later thirty-three civilians were killed on a New York City street. President Woodrow Wilson likened Bolshevism to a "poison" and gave Attorney General A. Mitchell Palmer the task of finding the antidote.[57] Palmer's Bureau of Investigation swooped down on every alleged communist it could find. Helping him was a twenty-two-year-old special assistant named J. Edgar Hoover. At one point in 1919, Palmer deported 249 aliens to Russia without benefit of trial. Finally, on New Year's Day 1920, "Palmer raids" were staged in thirty-three cities and 4,000 suspected communists were arrested.[58]

Presidential candidate Warren G. Harding made the rise of communism an issue during his successful 1920 campaign—becoming the first of many twentieth-century Republicans to do so. On July 22, 1920, Harding told his supporters: "Humanity is restive, much of the world is in revolution, the agents of discord and destruction have wrought their tragedy in pathetic Russia, have lighted their torches among other peoples, and hope to see America as part of the great Red conflagration."[59] Eventually, the Red Scare subsided, but that did not dampen American hostility toward communism. Gallup polls conducted from 1937 to 1949 showed majorities believed it was worse than fascism, were willing to forego free speech to silence its sympathizers, wanted the U.S. Communist Party abolished and its members subjected to "repressive measures," favored banning communists from government employment, and believed that communism and Christianity were incompatible faiths (see Table 1.1).

Americans saw a direct tie between communist activities in the United States and the Soviet Union. Accordingly, they demanded that their government take the communist threat seriously. Fifty-three percent in a 1939 poll considered it "more important" for the House Committee on Un-American Activities to investigate communist actions in the United States than Nazi

TABLE 1.1
American Attitudes Toward Communism, Selected Gallup Surveys, 1937–1949

Text of Question	Public Response
"If you had to choose between Fascism and Communism which would you choose?" (1937)[a]	
Percentage answering "Fascism"	61
Percentage answering "Communism"	39
"Which do you think is worse, Communism or Fascism?" (1938)[b]	
Percentage answering "Fascism"	42
Percentage answering "Communism"	58
"Do you believe in freedom of speech?" (1938)[c]	
Percentage answering "yes"	97
"Do you believe in it to the extent of allowing communists to hold meetings and express their views in this community?" (1938)[d]	
Percentage answering "yes"	38
"Would you be in favor of doing away with the Communist Party in this country?" (1940)[e]	
Percentage answering "YES!"	55
Percentage answering "yes"	25
Percentage answering "NO!"	8
Percentage answering "no"	12
"If it were up to you to decide, what would you do about the Communist Party in this country?"[f]	
Percentage answering "take repressive measures"	64
Percentage answering "put them in prison"	5
Percentage answering "do nothing"	8
"Should Americans who are members of the Communist Party be forbidden to hold civil service jobs or should they have the same rights as others to hold government jobs?"[g]	
Percentage answering "should be forbidden"	67
Percentage answering "should have same rights"	19
"Do you think a man can be a good Christian and at the same time be a member of the Communist Party?"[h]	
Percentage answering "yes"	11
Percentage answering "no"	77

[a]Gallup poll, April 6, 1937.
[b]Gallup poll, June 21, 1938.
[c]Gallup poll, June 1938.
[d]Gallup poll, June 1938.
[e]Gallup poll, July 1940.
[f]Gallup poll, April 10–15,1941.
[g]Gallup poll, March 28–April 2, 1947.
[h]Gallup poll, July 22–28, 1949.

activities.[60] Reacting to public sentiment Congress passed the Smith Act in 1940, which made it illegal to "advocate, abet, advise, or teach the duty, necessity, desirability, or propriety of overthrowing or destroying any government in the United States by force or violence." The principal targets of the Smith Act were American communists, which won the legislation widespread public approval.[61] A 1940 Gallup survey found 55 percent favored excluding the U.S. Communist Party from radio airwaves.[62] Anticommunism intensified as Soviet adventurism became even more menacing. In 1946, fourteen Canadians were charged with organizing a spy ring whose mission was to swipe American atomic weapons plans.[63] On February 25, 1948, Soviet-backed communists seized power in Prague, adding Czechoslovakia to the growing list of so-called Captive Nations of Eastern Europe. Less than a month later, Jan Masaryk, son of the leader of Czech independence, was found dead on the street after having been pushed from an upper-story window.

Fear of communism pervaded American politics. Truman cited Masaryk's murder as one reason Congress should "speedily complete its action" on the Marshall Plan—a $4 billion program named after Secretary of State George Marshall that would rebuild much of war-torn Western Europe.[64] Soviet foreign minister Vyacheslav Molotov recalled that the Americans "woke up" to the communist threat "only when half of Europe was taken from them."[65] In a strange twist of fate, the Soviets were becoming Truman's most reliable ally in getting his legislative agenda through the Republican-controlled Congress. Early in 1948 Congress approved the Marshall Plan. Foreign aid was never popular, as illustrated in the vehement opposition the Marshall Plan aroused from congressional Republicans. Representative John Taber of New York dubbed it "a fantastic world-wide WPA!" Senator Taft agreed, calling it "futile and dangerous regimentation."[66] But communism was even more politically unpopular with the voters than foreign aid, and a majority of legislators concluded that U.S. dollars would inoculate the war-torn nations of Western Europe against communism.

The extant political climate also managed to boost Truman's legislative agenda. Postwar labor strikes became fused with the growing fear of communism. A 1946 Gallup poll found half believing that there were "many" communists in the United States, with 52 percent agreeing that there was "a great deal" of communist activity in the labor movement.[67] Behind the labor strikes, in the minds of many, lurked the U.S. Communist Party. A year later 58 percent told Gallup that American communists were "loyal to Russia," and nearly two-thirds thought the party took orders from Moscow.[68] The president of General Motors declared, "The problems of the United States can be captiously summed up in two words: Russia abroad and labor at home."[69]

Hollywood, usually a reliable barometer of the popular mood, also began "seeing red." Motion Pictures Association chief Eric Johnston proclaimed his anticommunism, stating: "We'll have no more *Grapes of Wrath*, we'll have no more *Tobacco Roads*. We'll have no more films that show the seamy side of American life. We'll have no pictures that deal with labor strikes. We'll have no pictures that deal with the banker as villain." Johnston, Ronald Reagan (who was then president of the Screen Actors Guild), and Roy Brewer, chief of the International Association of Studio and Stage Employees, distributed *A Screen Guide for Americans* composed by militant anticommunist Ayn Rand. The guide derided New Deal–era movie dialogue about the nobility of the "common man" as the "droolings of weaklings" and proposed a series of "don'ts":

- "Don't Smear the Free Enterprise System"
- "Don't Deify the Common Man"
- "Don't Show That Poverty Is a Virtue . . . and Failure Is Noble."[70]

Thus, less than a year after World War II ended, anticommunist hysteria was on the rise. J. Edgar Hoover, who had become director of the FBI, warned that "at least 100,000 communists were at large in the country." Chamber of Commerce chief John J. Sullivan proposed establishing "firing squads in every good-sized city and town [to] liquidate the Reds and Pink Benedict Arnolds."[71] Actor-singer-dancer George Murphy, who left these jobs for a political career (a path later emulated by his 1943 costar Ronald Reagan), said: "Party labels don't mean anything anymore. You can draw a line right down the middle. On one side are the Americans, on the other are the Communists and Socialists."[72] But despite these belligerent statements many Americans remained unsure of themselves and fearful of the future. A 1946 poll found 49 percent saying communism and capitalism could not peacefully coexist—an ominous finding.[73] A Chicago reporter caught the prevailing mood:

> Cold fear is gripping people hereabouts. They don't talk much about it. But it's just as real and chilling as the current 11-degree weather. Fear of what? Most people don't know exactly. It's not fear of Russia alone. For most think we could rub Joe's [i.e., Stalin's] nose in the dirt. It's not the fear of communism in this country. Few think there are enough commies here to put it over. It's not fear of the atom bomb. For most think we still possess a monopoly. But it does seem to be a reluctant conviction that these three relentless forces are prowling the earth and that somehow they are bound to mean trouble for us. Not many months ago, these forces were something to be thought about only in off moments—like when you tuned in some commentator by mistake. . . . But all winter, confidence in peace has been oozing away. With the Czech coup, it practically vanished.[74]

A new politics based on the old fear of communism was emerging. As more and more Americans were "seeing red," the Republican party began stirring after a long period in exile. At a 1946 Salt Lake City conference, Republican activists urged voters to reject the "alien philosophy" of the Truman administration and to turn instead to it for "tried and true Americanism."[75]

The Republicans: Lost in the Wilderness

A Republican revival was a long time in coming. Ostracized to the political wilderness in 1932 by Franklin Roosevelt, discredited Republicans struggled to come to terms with the Great Depression and the failures of the Hoover administration. Two years after losing the White House, some hidebound Republicans saw a communist tinge to the New Deal and sought to exploit it. Their first chance came in California, where supporters of Governor Frank Merriam, a Republican, tarred his Democratic opponent, Upton Sinclair, as a pro-FDR communist sympathizer. Sinclair was a tempting target. Founder of the End Poverty in California (EPIC) movement, Sinclair wanted the state to seize idle factories and farm warehouses so as to employ the unemployed and house surplus food for the poor. Republicans denounced the idea as communist-inspired. Under a banner headline that screamed "IS THIS STILL AMERICA?" the *Los Angeles Times*, a mouthpiece for the Republican party, editorialized: "What is eating at the heart of America are [*sic*] a maggot-like horde of Reds who have scuttled to [Sinclair's] support. . . . They are termites secretly and darkly eating into the foundations and roof beams of everything that the American heart has held dear and sacred. . . . To this end they rally uncleanly to every sore spot. They drop poison in every bruise." Employing a theme that would eventually become standard Republican boilerplate, the paper continued: "The foe is camouflaged. The Reds are not lined up in solid ranks. Their menace is secret and subtle. Their agent may be your cook or your trusted friend or the movie star whom you admire on the screen."[76] Other Republican "dirty tricksters" pummeled Sinclair. One widely distributed circular read, "WE APPEAL TO THE EXPLOITED MASSES! HELP US SAVE OUR STATE." Below these lines was a caption: "Sponsored by the Young People's Communist League. Vladimir Kosloff, Scty., 234 N. Chicago St., Los Angeles." Of course, there was no Young People's Communist League, nor a Vladimir Kosloff.[77] Sinclair saw the *Times* assault as a partisan diatribe against the New Deal: "Our enemies' efforts to crush this movement by lies and intimidation are not merely an attack upon me in California, they are a preparation for the scrapping of the New Deal at the presidential election of 1936."[78]

When the ballots were finally counted, Merriam won by 259,083 votes in a year marked by additional Democratic gains following Roosevelt's 1932 landslide. Democrats won a 308–104 majority in the House and a 69–25 majority in the Senate. This Democratic dominance enraged GOP activists, prompting most of them to equate the New Deal with communism—just as Sinclair had predicted. Herbert Hoover, for one, took encouragement from Merriam's victory: "There is something to be derived from our experience here in California, where my friends built a bridge with sane Democrats and therefore not only out-flanked the radical Republicans, but brought about the defeat of Sinclair."[79] Others followed Hoover's lead. One party document read thus: "The banner year for the Marxists in America was 1933—the arrival of the New Deal. The Marxists twins [socialism and communism] swarmed into Washington with their sleeves rolled up to make America over," adding that "the most susceptible party had finally been penetrated."[80]

To substantiate their accusation that the New Deal had a communist tinge, Republicans attacked Roosevelt's November 16, 1933, executive order resuming diplomatic ties between the United States and the Soviet Union, characterizing it as "a formal step which three preceding Republican Presidents had refused to take because it would give the Soviet Union the enormous advantage of being able to create listening posts and subversive centers in America with complete diplomatic immunity."[81] Catholics were especially outraged. Roosevelt summoned Father Edmund Walsh to the White House in an attempt to pacify Catholic public opinion. Walsh, dean of Georgetown University and founder of its Foreign Service School, warned Roosevelt that the Soviets would be difficult to work with, to which Roosevelt replied, "Leave it to me, Father; I am a good horse trader."[82]

Adding to the controversy were the pro-Soviet sympathies of some youthful FDR supporters found in the labor movement and on college campuses. In 1933, Walter Reuther and his brother, Victor, paid a visit to the Soviet town of Gorky, where they worked in a large automobile plant. Two years later they returned to the United States marveling about the "atmosphere of freedom and security . . . an inspiring contrast to what we know as Ford wage slaves in Detroit."[83] Many academics agreed. From their ivory towers, students and professors alike openly admired the Soviet "experiment." One was novelist Saul Bellow, who in 1933 was a college student and a self-proclaimed Trotskyite. Sixty years later he ruefully remembered:

The New Deal philosophy of FDR as we heard it in fireside chats generated warmth and confidence. . . . The Popular Front identified itself with this new populism and the CP [U.S. Communist Party] learned for the first time how heady it was to be in the mainstream of national life. The country appeared to be having a great cultural revival. Writers and actors were attracted by well-endowed Front organizations and Fellow-Traveling groups. The Left had struck it rich.[84]

The Saul Bellows of the 1930s gave Republicans a false hope that they could break Roosevelt's hold on the anticommunist "common man." Republicans derided "the reckless atmosphere" generated by the New Deal in which "any radical who could talk Marxian dialectics fluently was regarded as a genius far beyond the average American."[85] In a desperate attempt to regain the White House in 1936, the GOP drew a straight line between the New Deal and communism. Their attacks provoked a blistering response from an outraged Roosevelt: "Partisans, not willing to face realities, will drag out red herrings—as they have always done—to divert attention from the trail of their own weaknesses." The president described the GOP as "desperate in mood, angry at failure, and cunning in purpose," and he firmly rejected communism "or any other 'ism' which would by fair means or foul change our American democracy." Roosevelt defended his New Deal as a patriotic answer to the Great Depression. But in so doing he charged that Republicans had promoted the spread of domestic communism during the ruinous Hoover years: "In their speeches, they deplored it [communism], but by their actions they encouraged it. The injustices, the inequalities, the downright suffering out of which revolutions come—what did they do about these things? Lacking courage, they evaded. Being selfish, they neglected. Being short-sighted, they ignored. When the crisis came—as these wrongs made it sure to come—America was unprepared."[86]

On election night 1936, a confident Roosevelt sat in his mother's dining room at the family estate in Hyde Park awaiting the returns. As the ballots poured into Democratic headquarters, he exclaimed, "It looks as though this sweep has carried every single section of the country."[87] It had. Roosevelt won every state except Maine and Vermont. But 1936 represented more than a personal triumph; it was also a victory for liberalism. *New Republic* gloated, "It was the greatest revolution in our political history." Heywood Broun, writing in *Nation*, could "see no interpretation of the returns which does not suggest that the people of America want the President to proceed along progressive or liberal lines."[88] Others were less enthusiastic. The *Phoenix Republic* warned that Roosevelt's "present position is comparable only with that of Joseph Stalin."[89]

Despite the enormity of Roosevelt's landslide, the communist issue refused to wither away. For the rest of his presidency, FDR felt compelled to disavow any communist backing. In 1938, for instance, he declared: "I have not sought, I do not seek, I repudiate the support of any advocate of communism."[90] One year later he signed legislation making it illegal for communists to be employed by the federal government. In 1940, he rebuked the Soviets once more: "The Soviet Union is run by a dictatorship as absolute as any other dictatorship in the world."[91]

Such protestations did not stop Republicans (and even some Democrats!) from charging that the New Deal was communist-inspired. In 1943, Martin Dies, a Texas Democrat who chaired the House Special Committee on Un-American Activities, asserted that the Roosevelt administration employed "not less than two thousand out-right communists and party-liners"—including Secretary of Labor Frances Perkins, Secretary of the Interior Harold Ickes, and presidential confidant Harry Hopkins.[92] A year later, GOP presidential nominee Thomas E. Dewey maintained communists were "seizing control of the New Deal [in order] to control the Government of the United States."[93] Dewey's running mate, John Bricker, was equally as strident: "First the New Deal took over the Democratic party and destroyed its very foundation; now these Communist forces have taken over the New Deal and will destroy the very foundations of the Republic."[94] These charges were given credence by the domestic activities of the U.S. Communist Party and the controversy swirling around labor union leader Sidney Hillman.

Kansan Earl Browder led the Communist Party of the United States of America. Born on May 20, 1891, Browder was the son of a Methodist minister. He was poorly educated, having left school at age ten after his father became seriously ill. In 1907, Browder joined the Socialist Party, but he became disillusioned with socialism and left the party seven years later. Still, he meandered around the fringes of the radical left, becoming by his own admission an admirer of Soviet leader Vladimir Lenin: "I was a follower of Lenin. I trusted him implicitly."[95] True to his leftist beliefs, Browder opposed American entry into World War I, was arrested for refusing to register for the draft, and spent a year in prison. In 1919, he was jailed again—this time for conspiring to obstruct enforcement of the draft laws. After serving sixteen months behind bars, Browder joined the Communist Party (then known as the Workers' Party), declaring that "communism is twentieth-century Americanism."[96] In 1922, the Workers' Party—led by Browder—went public after a mass arrest following a convention held in the secluded woods near Bridgman, Michigan. By 1924, the Red Scare had abated, and the Workers' Party officially became the U.S. Communist Party. Browder ran for president as the U.S. Communist Party's official candidate in 1936 and again in 1940.

In 1944, Browder addressed 15,000 cheering communists at Madison Square Garden. In his speech, he deemed FDR "one of the three great architects of the new world a-coming"—along with Josef Stalin and Winston Churchill.[97] But this speech was exceptional, since Browder had not always taken kindly to Roosevelt. When the Soviets signed a nonaggression pact with Germany in 1939, Browder issued a vitriolic attack on FDR, accusing him of scheming to get the United States into an "imperialist war" against the Soviet Union.[98] Later he was convicted for unlawful use of a passport, and in March 1941 he was sentenced to four years in prison. After Pearl Harbor, Roosevelt commuted Browder's sentence. Roosevelt's decision came on the eve of a scheduled visit from Soviet foreign minister Molotov. Moreover, Roosevelt wanted to send Stalin a goodwill gesture, still fearing even after the successful Normandy invasion that the Soviet leadership might make another deal with Hitler and withdraw from the war.[99] Still,

Roosevelt's decision drew scorn from Republicans. GOP presidential candidate Thomas E. Dewey thought it a crass political move: A free Browder would ensure the U.S. Communist Party's endorsement of FDR in 1944.[100] Democratic vice presidential nominee Harry S. Truman responded by calling Dewey and Bricker "a couple of fakirs who just want to get into power." Interior's Harold Ickes thought Dewey "an adolescent" who could not resist playing with the fiery issue of communism.[101] Dewey's accusations failed to move the public: In one poll 57 percent firmly rejected Dewey's argument that Roosevelt's reelection would give the communists "more influence in the government than they should have."[102]

But if Dewey was burned by the critics and the public alike, the controversy swirling around union leader Sidney Hillman encouraged the embattled Republican to pursue the communist issue. Born in Lithuania to Jewish parents in 1887, Hillman emigrated to the United States, where he quickly rose to the upper echelons of the labor movement. In 1910, he led 41,000 New York City garment workers on strike and won a favorable settlement. Soon after, the Amalgamated Clothing Workers of America was created, and Hillman was chosen as its president. Initially affiliated with the American Federation of Labor (AFL), Hillman jumped to the more militant Congress of Industrial Organizations (CIO), where he wielded considerable clout in Democratic party affairs. His influence was enhanced in July 1943 when the CIO established the Political Action Committee (PAC). Hillman put $1.5 million into it, and most of the money made its way into Democratic coffers.[103] Dewey accused Hillman of "stalking the country squeezing dollars for the Fourth Term campaign" from labor unions. But Hillman's power was based on more than cold cash. In New York City alone, he had 20,000 "volunteers" who walked the streets in get-out-the-vote drives. Moreover, the CIO distributed political information to 1,500 labor publications and 255 black newspapers—both vital to Democratic success at the polls. [104]

But Hillman also had a past. As a young man he joined the Socialist Party, where he had met and idolized Leon Trotsky. As union president, he collected money and goods for the Soviets. Conservative columnist Westbrook Pegler lashed out at Hillman's pro-Soviet sympathies, writing that they were the product of "naturalized but unassimilated European parasites."[105] Official Republican documents claimed Hillman "had kept his foot in the Marxist camp, having made many trips to Russia and having worked hand-in-hand frequently with communists."[106] But these attacks did not diminish Hillman's power in Democratic circles. When party leaders urged Roosevelt to dump Henry Wallace from the 1944 ticket, the president supposedly said, "Clear it with Sidney."[107] Republicans adopted the slogan "Clear *everything* with Sidney" and let no opportunity pass without recounting Hillman's past Soviet ties.[108] In a guilt-by-association ploy, Republicans distributed palm cards that read thus: "Browder, Hillman, and the Communists will vote. Will you?"[109] Democratic National Chairman Bob Hannegan accused the GOP of "red-baiting and Jew-baiting."[110]

Dewey lost, and in an ironic twist Earl Browder was subsequently expelled from the U.S. Communist Party for favoring alliances with other socialist parties. Browder pleaded with his fellow communists "to maintain the Roosevelt-labor-democratic coalition and to support the Truman administration in all its efforts to that end."[111] At the same time the U.S. Communist Party was engaged in its own fratricide, Roosevelt's New Deal coalition was experiencing its first major fissure over communism and the nascent Cold War. During the presidential campaign, Roosevelt himself saw trouble ahead, telling Secretary of State Cordell Hull, "In regard to the Soviet government, it is true that we have no idea as yet what they have in mind, but we have to remember that in their occupied territory they will do more or less as they wish."[112] The intentions of their ally also troubled Americans. In a 1943 Roper poll, 41 percent believed that the Russians would create communist governments in other European countries; 31 percent thought otherwise.[113] Communism did not die as a domestic political issue with FDR's win in November 1944 and the Allied victory less than one year later. Instead, it had only just begun to cast a pall over the body politic.

Henry Wallace and the Politics of Peace

The first sign of a serious rift in the New Deal coalition came in July 1946, when Secretary of Commerce Henry A. Wallace sent a twelve-page, single-spaced letter to President Truman on U.S.-Soviet relations. Both officials were in an awkward position. Wallace had been unceremoniously dumped from the 1944 Democratic ticket in favor of Truman. Party bosses and southern conservatives knew just how seriously ill FDR was, and they surmised that the three-term incumbent would not last a fourth. In fact, Roosevelt lived less than three months after taking the presidential oath for the last time. Truman was sensitive to Wallace's "might-have-been" status and drew him close to his side after FDR's death, retaining him as commerce secretary.

Henry Agard Wallace's path to power was an unconventional one. Reared a Republican in his native Iowa, he remained a party loyalist until the 1920s. His father was agriculture secretary in the Harding and Coolidge administrations, and Franklin Roosevelt appointed Wallace to the same post in 1933. Wallace's politics was rooted in the progressivism of liberal Republicans Robert LaFollette and Hiram Johnson, and it was from this political lineage that he became an ardent New Dealer. In 1940, a determined FDR put Wallace on the Democratic ticket. As vice president, Wallace took an altruistic view of foreign policy, displaying little use for Metternich's "balance of power" theory. He once urged that after the war ended the U.S. government guarantee "everybody in the world has the privilege of drinking a quart of milk a day."[114] Republicans often quoted this as an illustration of Wallace's fuzzy-minded utopianism.

In his July letter, Wallace pleaded with Truman to see the world from the Soviet vantage point: "How would it look to us if Russia had the atomic bomb and we did not, if Russia had 10,000 mile bombers and air bases within a thousand miles of our coast lines and we did not?" He charged that American actions since the Japanese surrender were provocative: the "large" $13 billion defense budget, the atomic testing on Bikini Atoll, and the production of B-29 and B-36 long-range bombers. Wallace claimed these events looked "as if we were only paying lip service to peace." In his letter, the former vice president excused the Soviet takeover of Eastern Europe, claiming that those nations had never experienced democracy and that in light of the horrors of World War II the Soviet action was understandable. Thus, Wallace maintained that the Soviets would view any Western alliance with the East as "an attempt to reestablish the encirclement of unfriendly neighbors which was created after the last war and which might serve as a springboard of still another attempt to destroy her." He called for a "fresh point of view" about Soviet intentions—a cry echoed by man Democrats in decades to come.[115]

The Wallace letter caused considerable consternation at the White House. Truman tried to reason with its author, noting that getting tough with the Soviet Union was impossible since the United States had only one fully equipped division.[116] Still, Wallace persisted. On September 12, 1946, he traveled to New York to campaign against Governor Thomas E. Dewey's reelection bid. Appearing before an enthusiastic crowd of 20,000 Democrats at Madison Square Garden, Wallace disparaged the Republican party as home to "economic nationalism and political isolationism—and as such is as anachronistic as the dodo and as certain to disappear." But, he added, before the GOP became extinct "it may enjoy a brief period of power during which it can do irreparable damage to the United States and the cause of world peace." Then Wallace gave a reprise of his July letter, rejecting any "get-tough" policy with the Soviets: "'Getting tough' never bought anything real and lasting—whether for school yard bullies or businessmen or world powers. The tougher we get, the tougher the Russians will get."[117]

Although Wallace disavowed what he termed "namby-pamby pacifism," he warned that armed conflict with the Soviets "would hurt the United States many times as much as the last war." In the absence of war, Wallace decried the idea of the atom bomb as a peacekeeper: "He who trusts in the atom bomb will sooner or later perish by the atom bomb—or something worse." Instead, he advocated negotiation and strict neutrality between West and East: "I am neither anti-British nor pro-British—neither anti-

Russian nor pro-Russian." Wallace urged his supporters to work for peace "even though we may be called communists because we dare to speak out." As if that were not forceful enough, he noted that Truman had approved an advance copy of his speech: "And just two days ago, when President Truman read these words, he said they represented the policy of his administration."[118]

Wallace's speech touched off a political firestorm. Arthur Vandenberg observed there could only be one secretary of state at a time, and Wallace was not that man.[119] James Reston opined in the *New York Times*, "Mr. Truman seems to be the only person in the capital who thinks that Mr. Wallace's proposals are 'in line' with Mr. Truman's or Mr. Byrnes'." Truman, who had asked Wallace to make a speech in New York "for its political effect" on liberal Democrats there, was angry.[120] He caustically confided in his diary that Wallace was "100 percent pacifist," adding: "He wants to disband our armed forces, give Russia our atomic bomb secrets and trust a bunch of adventurers in the Kremlin Politburo. I do not understand a 'dreamer' like that. . . . The Reds, phonies, and 'parlor pinks' seem to be banded together and are becoming a national danger."[121] Not surprisingly, eight days after his controversial speech, Wallace tendered his resignation to Truman in an impertinent "Dear Harry" letter that contained an implicit threat: "I shall continue to fight for peace. I am sure that you approve and will join me in that great endeavor."[122]

Truman was not the only Democrat peeved at Wallace. Mayor Hubert H. Humphrey of Minneapolis, once a Wallace fan, begged Wallace to dissociate himself from the U.S. Communist Party.[123] From Boston, John F. Kennedy, a Democrat running for a House seat, condemned Wallace's "irresponsible talk at the Madison Square Garden and the President's casual endorsement of a speech fraught with dangerous possibilities." Kennedy likened Wallace's "neutrality" stand to Dante's contention that "the hottest places in hell are reserved for those who in a period of moral crisis maintain their neutrality."[124]

1946: A Political Armageddon

The Wallace controversy, communism, and postwar inflation punctured New Deal liberalism as no attack by the Republicans ever had. James Loeb Jr., in a letter published in the May 13, 1946, issue of *New Republic*, wrote that liberals "must decide whether it is their conviction that the *sole* objective of the progressive movement is economic security, or whether human freedom, which has historically been a coequal dynamic of progressivism, is still a commendable objective without which 'liberalism' or 'progressivism' or 'radicalism'—call it what you will—must inevitably degenerate into a sterile and self-defeating race for power per se." Loeb argued that liberalism was being linked to communism in the public mind, adding: "Unless these problems are solved in a period where the presence of Franklin D. Roosevelt no longer lends its unifying strength, American liberals will sputter, fume, protest, and denounce, but will get nowhere fast."[125]

Loeb's letter spawned the Americans for Democratic Action (ADA), an organization whose charter rejected "any association with communists or sympathizers with communism."[126] Among the ADA's founding members were Reinhold Niebuhr, Eleanor Roosevelt, Walter Reuther, David Dubinsky, and Hubert Humphrey. Humphrey, in particular, was an ardent ADA enthusiast. After a bruising 1946 fight with communist insurgents in the Democratic-Farmer-Labor Party, Humphrey vowed: "We're not going to let the political philosophy of the Democratic-Farmer-Labor Party be dictated from the Kremlin. You can be a liberal without being a Communist, and you can be a progressive without being a Communist sympathizer, and we're a liberal progressive party out here. We're not going to let this left-wing Communist ideology be the prevailing force, because the people of this state won't accept it, and what's more, it's wrong."[127]

Nationwide, Republicans skillfully exploited the Wallace-Truman bickering, distributing pamphlets depicting a Democratic donkey wearing a turban emblazoned with a Soviet hammer and sickle.[128] Republican National Chairman B. Carroll Reece said the 1946 elections were a "fight basically between communism and Republicanism."[129] Indeed, communism was an issue that was rapidly becoming embedded in the body politic. In an April 1946 poll 73 percent named domestic communism as a "very important issue," with 45 percent forecasting an eventual war with the Soviet Union.[130] Republicans capitalized upon those new fears; at one point Senate Republican Hugh Butler of Nebraska darkly told supporters, "If the New Deal is still in control of Congress after the election it will owe that control to the Communist Party."[131] Taking a cue from Butler, the Republican National Committee distributed 683,000 brochures accusing the Democrats of permitting the "Communist penetration of government" that culminated in the "appeasement" and "cynical betrayal" at Yalta.[132] And while deep inside the heart of Chicago's fabled Democratic machine, a House Republican named Alvin O'Konski beseeched Polish Americans to support the GOP in an emotional speech. In his words:

> The New Deal betrayed and sold down the river Poland, Yugoslavia, Finland, Latvia, Estonia, Lithuania, and other small nations, and the president didn't even blush when he signed their life and liberty away. Our president came back from the Yalta Conference and peddled typical Communist apologies for his actions. Regarding the betrayal of Poland, he said the land didn't belong to the Polish people because there were not enough Polish people living in the area. . . . Poland was not divided by her enemies. She was divided by her allies. So too, will the United States be divided by Communists.[133]

As O'Konski's remarks were greeted with thunderous applause, he blurted: "Don't vote Red—vote red, white, and blue on Election Day! Vote Republican!"[134] Many Democrats understood the Republican strategy of appealing to the New Deal's ethnic constituencies. As early as 1943, Roosevelt told Stalin that he could not take part in any public agreement concerning the redrawing of Poland's boundaries since there were 6 million Polish Americans and that "as a practical man, he did not wish to lose their vote." Two years later, Harry Truman told Stalin that the 6 million Polish Americans would be a lot easier to handle politically if there were free elections in their homeland.[135] But Stalin was not swayed by these entreaties. The Yalta Agreement, initially hailed as a triumph, became an object of scorn. By 1945, two-thirds believed that the agreement was "not fair" to Poland.[136] Senate Republican William E. Jenner of Indiana spoke for many in his party when he declared, "At Yalta, under the influence of Alger Hiss, a dying American President sold Asia down the river."[137] GOP references to the Yalta "sellout" became so numerous that Texas Democrat Tom Connally moaned, "Oh God, Yalta this and Yalta that."[138]

The 1946 elections represented a do-or-die moment for the GOP. After fourteen years of public excoriation, Republicans were angry and desperate. Seeking election to the U.S. Senate from Ohio, John Bricker challenged his Democratic rival to "bring on your New Deal, Communistic and subversive groups. If we can't lick them in Ohio, America is lost anyway."[139] Fellow Ohioan Robert Taft accused the Democrats of being "so divided between communism and Americanism" that they were "dominated by a policy of appeasing the Russians abroad and of fostering communism at home."[140] In Wisconsin, Republican senatorial candidate Joseph R. McCarthy lambasted Truman for his handling of the Soviets: "We retreated mentally and morally in Austria, in Poland, in the Baltic States, in the Balkans, in Manchuria, and today in Iran, and there is no reason to believe that tomorrow we shall not do the same thing in Norway, Sweden and Turkey, which apparently are next on the agenda."[141] McCarthy's attacks were echoed by other, more progressive Republicans. For example, California's Republican governor, Earl Warren, attacked Wallace, saying he was leading the attack of "leftist organizations that are attuned to the Communist movement."[142] But the 1946 race for the seat in California's 12th congressional district best illustrates how Red baiting was used during that election cycle—and how Republicans used such scare tactics for political gain.

Richard M. Nixon: The Making of a Modern Republican

In September 1945, Herman Perry, manager of the Bank of America branch in Whittier, California, sent an airmail letter to Navy Lieutenant Richard

M. Nixon asking if he would be interested in running for a seat in the U.S. Congress. Nixon, then stationed in Maryland, was intrigued and hurried home to his native state. He told Perry that incumbent Democrat Horace Jeremiah ("Jerry") Voorhis could be beaten by a crusade against big government, which Nixon thought would appeal to job-anxious veterans: "I believe the returning veterans, and I have talked to many of them in the foxholes, will not be satisfied with a dole or a government handout. They want a respectable job in private industry where they will be recognized for what they produce, or they want the opportunity to start their own business." Nixon believed Republicans should make concessions to the New Deal by offering a platform of "*practical* liberalism" (his emphasis) as the "antidote" for "New Deal idealism."[143] Another local Republican, Roy Day, was convinced that Nixon could win, repeatedly telling skeptics, "This man is saleable merchandise."[144]

At that time, California had an unusual law allowing Nixon and Voorhis to "cross-file," in effect permitting one to run against the other in their respective party primaries. During the primary season, Nixon focused his attacks on New Deal–style big government:

> If the people want bureaucratic control and domination with every piece of human activity regulated from Washington, then they should not vote for me but for my opponent. The day of reckoning has arrived. The issue is clear. Next Tuesday the people will vote for me as a supporter of free enterprise, individual initiative, and a sound progressive program, or for my opponent who has supported by his votes the foreign ideologies of the New Deal Administration.[145]

But Nixon's assault on the still-popular New Deal failed to produce the desired result. Although he easily won the Republican nomination, when the combined primary votes were tabulated on June 4, Voorhis was ahead 56 percent to 44 percent. Nixon's summer of "practical liberalism" clearly looked like a prescription for defeat in the fall.

But after his initial failure Nixon discovered communism. At first, the issue seemed to be a nonstarter. Voorhis was a member of the House Committee on Un-American Activities and author of the Voorhis Act, which required that the Justice Department be informed of any political organization controlled by a foreign power or engaged in military activities aimed at government subversion.[146] The Voorhis Act prompted the U.S. Communist Party to abandon—at least on paper—its affiliation with Moscow. In addition, Voorhis rejected the ministrations of Henry Wallace (though Wallace rather nonchalantly still included him in a list of endorsements). Thus, Voorhis seemed invulnerable to the charge that he was "soft on communism." But Nixon was undeterred, dwelling on Voorhis's alleged ties to communist sympathizers. The son of a well-to-do businessman, Voorhis was a Yale graduate and founder of a residence for homeless boys.

Social activism led Voorhis to become a Socialist in the 1920s—like so many other college students at the time. In 1934, Voorhis took an active role in Upton Sinclair's gubernatorial campaign, telling a Democratic rally that if the country was to be saved from godless communism, church leaders must "turn a deaf ear to the minions of privilege" and assume their rightful place "at the forefront of the fight for social justice."[147] An announcer in a Nixon radio advertisement solemnly intoned, "Remember, Voorhis is a former registered Socialist and his voting record in Congress is more socialistic and communistic than Democratic."[148]

Nixon's tactics transformed the postprimary campaign dialogue. A September 18 headline in the *Whittier News* read: "Voorhis Raps Wallace for Russ Speech. Takes Stand Squarely in Support of Policy Put Down by Byrnes."[149] Nixon volunteers pedaled a brochure accusing Voorhis of voting "the Moscow-PAC-Henry Wallace line."[150] As the campaign intensified, Nixon flailed away at the communist issue. Speaking to American Legionnaires, he charged that the communists and their fellow-travelers were conspiring to obtain "positions of importance in virtually every federal department and bureau . . . calculated to gradually give the American people a Communist form of government."[151] In yet another guilt-by-association ploy, Nixon noted several "similarities" between the voting records of Voorhis and Vito Marcantonio, a New York representative and a communist sympathizer.[152] The political dirty tricks got even nastier. Nixon biographer Roger Morris writes that GOP boiler rooms telephoned voters with a message: "This is a friend of yours but I can't tell you my name. I just wanted you to know that Jerry Voorhis is a communist." With that, the caller would abruptly hang up.[153]

By election day, communism had become the overriding issue. Although several local newspapers printed editorials proclaiming "Jerry Voorhis Is Not a Communist," these headlines played to Nixon's strategy of keeping the focus on communism.[154] One of the most blatantly demagogic newspapers was the *Los Angeles Times*, published by Norman Chandler. Political columnist Kyle Palmer darkly noted that the socialist "streak" in Voorhis, like Macbeth's spot, "will not rub out." As if this warning was insufficient, the day before the election the front page of the *Times* was blazoned with banner-sized boxes that read: "VOTE AGAINST NEW DEAL COMMUNISM. VOTE REPUBLICAN. VOTE AMERICAN!"[155]

Nixon won 57 percent to Voorhis's 43 percent—transforming his 7,500 primary-vote deficit into a 15,592-vote victory. He even carried Voorhis's hometown of San Dimas. Some years later Nixon admitted that Voorhis was not a communist, but still he justified his campaign tactics, saying: "People react to fear, not love. They don't teach that in Sunday school, but it's true."[156]

Lost Innocence

Across the country other candidates were discovering the potency of the communist issue. Shortly after winning the Democratic congressional nomination, John F. Kennedy found himself on a plane with George Lanigan, a lawyer who had backed one of JFK's primary opponents. Years later Lanigan recalled the conversation:

Kennedy: What's the major problem with the district?

Lanigan: Welfare.

Kennedy: What about communism?

Lanigan: What about communism?[157]

Lanigan recalled, "I'll never forget him saying that—while I'm thinking about putting guys to work and raising their welfare allowances and employment benefits."[158] But Kennedy was an ardent anticommunist, telling a group of intellectual liberals:

> Soviet Russia, internally today, is run by a small clique of ruthless, powerful and selfish men who have established a government which denies the Russian people personal freedom and economic security. Soviet Russia today is a slave state of the worst sort. Soviet Russia today is embarked upon a program of world aggression. The freedom-loving countries of the world must stop Soviet Russia now, or be destroyed. The people in the United States have been far too gullible with respect to the publicity being disseminated throughout the world by the clever and brilliant Moscow propagandists.[159]

These remarks alienated Kennedy's listeners at the time, but they resonated with Boston's profoundly anticommunist Irish Catholics. Burnishing his anticommunist credentials, Kennedy resorted to attacking Truman, decrying the "failure" of U.S. leadership that left an enfeebled United Nations: "We should never have yielded to Russia and allowed the U.N. Charter to embody the principle that a single veto by one of the big powers can stop action by the United Nations."[160]

Kennedy's 1946 congressional election victory was a notable Democratic exception. After all the shouting about communism, Republicans were rejuvenated, winning 246 seats in the U.S. House of Representatives to the Democrats' 188. The GOP gain of fifty-five seats was the party's greatest victory in a congressional election since *1894*—and not equaled until 1994. Thirteen Republicans were added in the Senate, enlarging the party ranks to fifty-one. This was a remarkable reversal of fortune from ten years before when congressional Democrats had to sit alongside Republicans because there were not enough chairs on their side of the aisle. Indeed, the Republican congressional takeover marked the first time since 1930 that the two parties split control of the government. Postwar economic dislocations, coupled with the desire for change after fourteen years of New Dealism, had swelled the Republican numbers. But it was a new kind of Republican that took power in 1946—better educated, more affluent, and living in the suburbs. Richard Nixon was its best representative, but there were many others.

At first, the significance of the election went unappreciated. Initially, the Truman-Vandenberg coalition government resulted in a muted politics with an emphasis on "bipartisanship." If the election meant anything, most pundits agreed that the incoming Republican Congress marked the end of the Truman era. J. William Fulbright suggested that Truman name a Republican to be Secretary of State and then resign his office—prompting Truman to dub the Arkansas Democrat "Senator Half-Bright."[161] Democrats, as Fulbright's advice suggested, were dispirited—but they were far from finished. Neither "bipartisanship" nor an emerging Republican majority were harbingers. Instead, the real meaning of the election was the important role communism played in the reemergence of the Republican party from its political Siberia. Republicans understood the clout communism had with voters. In Chicago, for example, Democratic candidates lost an average of 10 percentage points among Catholic Polish Americans from their 1944 totals.[162] Ethnic Poles and many others were coming to believe that Democrats were too tolerant of communists. For many Republicans, therefore, "scaring hell" became an indispensable part of their political portfolio.

The propulsion of communism to a central place in American politics was accompanied by the discarding of old nostrums about the "American way of life." Thomas Jefferson sketched a portrait of a pastoral nation more than a century before: "Those who labor in the earth are the chosen people of God, if ever He had a chosen people, whose breasts He has made the peculiar deposit for substantial and genuine virtue."[163] Now, practically overnight, that picture was largely erased, a mere memory. In its place was a new "American way of life," one centered in the pristine suburbs, with happy husbands fastening white collars and ties while driving to new, service-sector jobs, as smiling wives waved goodbye and cared for the requisite two children and the dog. The picture seemed perfect, and Republicans were determined to be part of it.

But the picture also contained several dark colors, belying the deep insecurities Americans had about the Cold War. Arthur M. Schlesinger Jr., in a book titled *The Vital Center*, called the postwar era "the age of anxiety." That fear was heightened by what Schlesinger described as the "permanent crisis" between the United States and Soviet Union, one that would "test the moral, political and very possibly the military strength of each side."[164] So as 1946 faded into 1947, Americans were beginning to realize that Schlesinger was right. As the calendar pages kept turning, more Americans became uncomfortably acquainted with the idea of having to live in a permanent war-ready mode.

chapter two

1947–1950:
The New Politics
of Old Fears

Confident people do not become communists.

—Harry S. Truman, September 28, 1948

January 3, 1947

As the 80th Congress convened in Washington, the newly ensconced Republican majority vowed to cleanse the nation of all remaining communists—especially those burrowed in the bureaucracy. In his maiden address as Speaker of the House, Joseph Martin declared that "there is no room in the government of the United States for any who prefer the Communistic system," and he promised to expedite legislation that would discharge any federal employee who did not "believe in the way of life which has made this the greatest country of all time."[1] One tool the Republicans had at their disposal was the expanded powers given to the House Committee on Un-American Activities.

HUAC was created in 1938 to investigate foreign subversion—including communist and Nazi activities.[2] During Franklin Roosevelt's tenure, HUAC investigated suspected communists in New Deal programs such as the Works Progress Administration Arts Project. After World War II, HUAC's anticommunist mission assumed added importance. U.S. Attorney General Tom Clark and FBI Director J. Edgar Hoover warned Truman in 1946 that the U.S. Communist Party had "thousands of invaluable sources of information in various industrial establishments as well as in the departments of the government" and that "every American communist is potentially an espionage agent of the Soviet Government." Truman advisers Clark Clifford and George Elsey took these admonitions seriously, noting that the U.S. Communist Party was "poised to engage in industrial espionage [and] promote left-wing sentiment among soldiers . . . in order to prepare for sabotage in the event of war with the Soviet Union."[3]

Given the temper of the times, the Republican Congress hastily approved a motion by Democrat John Rankin of Mississippi to transform HUAC from a temporary into a permanent committee. With this enhanced stature, HUAC fiercely pursued alleged communists. Motion Picture Association chief Eric Johnston had the following exchange with Rankin that exemplified the committee's interrogations:

Rankin: Mr. Johnston, you say that you would prohibit Communists from holding office.

Johnston: Yes, Mr. Rankin.

Rankin: In Federal, State, or county or municipality?

Johnston: Yes.

Rankin: You would also prohibit them from holding offices in labor unions?

Johnston: Yes.

Rankin: You would also prohibit them from becoming instructors in our educational institutions, I presume?

Johnston: If those are deemed of importance, yes. If those are deemed key positions—and in my opinion they would be.

Rankin: Don't you think it is a key position when a man has the training of the youth of the country?

Johnston: If they are teaching conspiratorial or revolutionary ideas, overthrow of the Government by force, in schools, of course, they should be removed.

Rankin: Would you want to send your children to a school teacher that you knew was in favor [of] and committed to the overthrow of this Government?

Johnston: Why, of course not.

Rankin: All right. Now, then, don't you think that actors who put on plays should also be, who are Communists, should also be banned?

Johnston: If you are performing conspiratorial activities, yes. Mr. Rankin, the difficulty is in labeling everyone who doesn't agree with you a Communist—or agree with me—and that is one of the problems. Many of these people have different points of view.

Rankin: Mr. Johnston, you are so busy with your executive duties that I am afraid you don't read some of these films between the lines, read between the lines, but a great many people—

Johnston: I not only read between the lines, but I get under the sheets, too, Mr. Rankin.

Rankin: What I am driving at, and I think what you are driving at, and all other patriotic Americans are, is, putting a stop to these attempts to undermine and destroy this Government, the American way of life.[4]

Hiss, Chambers, and the Politics of Symbols

The widespread belief that the American way of life was under siege provided the underlying dynamic of what became HUAC's most famous investigation: the Hiss case. It all began on July 31, 1948, when Elizabeth Bentley accused thirty-two government officials of taking part in a Soviet-led spy ring. Bentley, who was the ring's courier, had her sensational testimony corroborated by David Whittaker Chambers on August 3, 1948.

The protagonist in the Hiss case, Whittaker Chambers, was an unusual person. Born in Philadelphia on April 1, 1901, he came from a troubled family, having a father who left home for a male lover, and his only brother committed suicide. From such suffering Chambers came of age in the 1920s when many "bohemian intellectuals" gravitated toward the Communist Party. Chambers was among them, working for the *Daily Worker* and the *New Masses*, two communist publications, before making a complete turnabout to take a job as a senior editor at *Time*.[5] He joined the U.S. Communist Party in 1925 but left thirteen years later, believing it had become an instrument for totalitarianism. His disillusionment intensified after Stalin signed a peace pact with Hitler in 1939. Soon afterwards, Chambers told Assistant Secretary of State Adolf A. Berle Jr. that Hiss had once been a communist and a Soviet spy. Berle promised he would take this information directly to President Roosevelt, but after consulting Dean Acheson and Felix Frankfurter—each of whom vouched for Hiss's loyalty—nothing happened. In 1943, FBI agents visited Chambers at his Westminster, Maryland, farm. Chambers repeated his story and named names. But, once more, nothing happened. Agents contacted Chambers in 1945 and 1947, again with no result.

All that changed when Chambers testified to HUAC that several senior government officials were "fellow-travelers." Those named included the former secretary of the National Labor Relations Board, Nathan Witt, a former attorney for the Labor Department, John Abt, counsel to the Agricultural Adjustment Administration and the Works Progress Administration, Lee Pressman, the creator of the International Monetary Fund and assistant treasury secretary, Harry Dexter White, and the former secretary general of the United Nations Conference, Alger Hiss. Chambers darkly observed that Hiss, the most prominent of those accused, represented "the concealed enemy against which we are all fighting."[6]

The other protagonist in this tale, Alger Hiss, was the polar opposite of Chambers. Born in Baltimore on November 11, 1904, Hiss was handsome, meticulous in his appearance, and a product of privilege. He had graduated from Johns Hopkins University and Harvard Law School and once clerked for U.S. Supreme Court Justice Oliver Wendell Holmes. His first government post was in Henry Wallace's Agriculture Department, where he was assistant general counsel. Later he became counsel to the Senate Committee Investigating the Munitions Industry (the Nye Committee) and was subsequently hired by Solicitor General Stanley F. Reed. In September 1936, Hiss was transferred to the State Department, where he played a crucial role in forming the United Nations. He left public service in 1947 for the presidency of the Carnegie Endowment.

Chambers's testimony incensed Hiss, who vehemently denied ever knowing him ("the name means nothing to me")[7] or having had any contact with the U.S. Communist Party: "I am not and never have been a member of the Communist Party. I am not and have never adhered to the tenets of the Communist Party. I am not and never have been a member of any communist front organization. I have never followed the Communist Party line directly or indirectly. To the best of my knowledge none of my friends is a Communist."[8] But Chambers vehemently refuted these assertions, claiming that he had once lived with Hiss, his wife, Priscilla, and their son, Timothy, and he spoke intimately to the committee members about their lifestyle. Chambers disclosed the couple's affectionate nicknames for each other ("Hilly" and "Dilly"), and he recalled in exquisite detail one day when Hiss (an ardent bird-watcher) came home terribly excited over having spotted a rare prothonotary warbler.

The Hiss-Chambers case was the most listened to national soap opera of its day, and it transformed Richard M. Nixon from an obscure freshman representative into a political comer. Nixon's relentless cross-examination convinced him that Hiss was lying. Chambers recalled Nixon's intense dislike of Hiss: "I have a vivid picture of him, in the blackest hour of the Hiss case, standing by the barn and saying in his quietly savage way (he is the kindest of men): 'If the American people understood the real character of Alger Hiss, they would boil him in oil.'"[9] Almost single-handedly, Nixon shrewdly steered the inquiry away from the sensational charges about Hiss's supposed communist ties to the narrower issue of whether or not the two men knew each other. Nixon's staff uncovered automobile registration records showing Hiss had transferred ownership of a car to Chambers in the 1930s when Chambers was still a communist.

The inconsistencies in Hiss's testimony provided Nixon (and the Republicans) with the evidence they sought. Nixon understood the political implications of the inquiry, and he frequently consulted with the wise men of the Dewey campaign: John Foster Dulles and his brother, Allen, Douglas Dillon, and Christian Herter. Nixon urged the Dewey team to make Hiss the centerpiece of the upcoming presidential campaign. Dulles was noncommittal, having recommended Hiss to head the Carnegie Endowment, and he advised Nixon to proceed cautiously. That did not stop Nixon from writing a four-page letter to Dewey outlining Hiss's guilt.[10]

Eventually, the Hiss case changed venues from committee room to courtroom. Hiss could not be indicted for spying, as the statute of limitations had expired on his alleged communist activities. But he was charged with lying to Congress, and in 1949 he was tried on two counts of perjury. The jury was deadlocked, with eight of twelve supporting a conviction. Hiss was retried in 1950 and sentenced to forty-four months in prison.

After the guilty verdict, Nixon's political stock soared. Former president Herbert Hoover wired his congratulations: "At last the stream of treason that has existed in our government has been exposed in a fashion all may believe."[11] But reaction was far less laudatory at the White House. A reporter asked Truman, "Mr. President, do you think that the Capitol Hill spy scare is a red herring to divert public attention from inflation?" Truman did not equivocate: "Yes, I do."[12] He then raised the political ante by accusing HUAC of causing "irreparable harm to certain people, seriously impairing the morale of federal employees, and undermining public confidence in the government."[13] In response, Senate Republican Karl Mundt of South Dakota mailed thousands of copies of a speech titled "What the Hiss Trial Actually Means." Among its section titles: "Hiss's Job Was to Pervert Policy"; "White House Obstructed Investigation"; "Alger Hiss and the Yalta Conference"; "Alger Hiss and Our China Policy: Today's Political Plotters Must Be Stopped."[14]

One Democrat understood the political importance of the Hiss case and attempted to emulate Nixon's feat. John F. Kennedy sponsored a motion calling for a perjury indictment against Harold Christoffel, president of Local 248 of the UAW-CIO union in Milwaukee. Under questioning by

Kennedy, Christoffel told the House Education and Labor Committee that he was a not communist, adding that he had neither endorsed, supported, nor participated in activities sponsored by the U.S. Communist Party. Louis F. Budenz, an assistant professor of economics at Fordham University, testified to the contrary, claiming Christoffel was an active communist and had agitated a 1941 stoppage at the Allis-Chalmers plant that badly hindered the U.S. defense effort that year. With bipartisan support, Kennedy's resolution passed the House; Christoffel was subsequently convicted of perjury and imprisoned. House Republican Charles J. Kerston likened Kennedy's action to "one of the shots fired at Concord Bridge."[15]

Kennedy notwithstanding, Democrats found themselves on the defensive. The House minority leader, Sam Rayburn, told a reporter in 1948: "There is political dynamite in this [Republican-led] communist investigation. Don't doubt that."[16] Rayburn was prophetic: Not only was a man on trial but the New Deal legacy of the Democratic party as well. Several leading Democrats became enmeshed in the Hiss affair. Dean Acheson, then a law partner of Donald Hiss, Alger's brother, assisted with the early legal planning. Those vouching for Hiss's veracity included Acheson, Adlai Stevenson, and U.S. Supreme Court Justices Stanley F. Reed and Felix Frankfurter. With Hiss's conviction, a generation of New Deal intellectuals was tried in absentia. Leslie Fiedler urged his fellow New Deal liberals in 1951 to make a full "confession" of past errors: "We have desired good, and we have done some! But we have also done great evil. The confession in itself is nothing, but without the confession there can be no understanding, and without the understanding of what the Hiss case tries desperately to declare, we will not be able to move from a liberalism of innocence to a liberalism of responsibility."[17]

The emotions generated by the Hiss case were fierce but brief. However, its political effects endured long after the two protagonists drifted into obscurity. A new politics of "us" and "them" was emerging—one that pitted FDR's "common man" against his former ally, the intellectuals—and the red specter of communism was the bright line that separated the two. After Hiss's conviction, a speech kit prepared by the National Republican Congressional Campaign Committee argued that the New Deal "now stands exposed as the spawning ground of organized communism within the structure of American government." The paper continued: "Under the protective shelter of the New Deal's alphabetical wonderland, communism ceased to be an outlaw, underground movement, and became an active influential force in government."[18] For the first time since the New Deal, conservatives could lay claim to being "one of us"—ordinary folks standing up to the liberal establishment rather than the well-to-do snobs who knew what was best. This new politics became an integral part of one of the greatest political sagas ever written: the 1948 presidential campaign.

1948: The Transitional Election

Harry Truman's rise from the political dead in 1948 is the most celebrated tale of twentieth-century politics in America. The yarn is a familiar one. Faced with a "do-nothing" Republican Congress, Truman took to the stump and "gave them hell." Pollsters and pundits alike were stunned by Truman's come-from-behind victory, and his tenacity became legendary. But what is often overlooked is the importance of communism and the Cold War in Truman's victory. A Roper poll in mid-July 1948 asked the following: "On the whole would you say it is more important this year to elect a president who is especially good at handling domestic affairs here at home, or one who is especially good at handling international affairs and foreign relations?" Forty-nine percent answered international affairs and foreign relations; just 30 percent thought domestic affairs more important.[19] Moreover, 52 percent believed that the United States would be involved in a shooting war with the Soviets, with 49 percent saying a war would start within a year. These results suggest that voters were predisposed to stick with the current commander-in-chief who, unlike Republican Thomas E. Dewey, had already been tested in Greece and Turkey and had resisted these probes of U.S. resolve.

Continued Soviet aggression heightened public fears. On June 24, 1948, the day Thomas E. Dewey was chosen as the Republican standard-bearer, the Soviet Union blockaded Berlin. Dewey supported Truman's massive airlift of goods and material that eventually broke the Berlin Blockade. Presidential adviser James Rowe acknowledged that the escalating Cold War helped Truman politically: "There is considerable political advantage to the Administration in its battle with the Kremlin. In times of crisis the American citizen tends to back up his president."[20] The Hiss case, Soviet adventurism, and the threat of domestic communism made many Americans anxious. Mayor William O'Dwyer of New York City fired 150 municipal employees tagged as security risks—including firefighters, police officers, transit workers, gas inspectors, and washroom attendants.[21] Given these actions, Dewey accurately described the Soviet Union as "a shadow that hangs over us that makes today so troubled and tomorrow so uncertain."[22] But that shadow cast a cloud over Truman's election prospects: public fears about *domestic* communism, and a feeling (encouraged by the Republicans) that Truman was ignoring its potential for danger. Presidential adviser George Elsey warned Truman that domestic communism was becoming his "most vulnerable point," adding: "Our hopes this issue will die are ill-founded. There is paydirt here, and the Republicans have no intention of being diverted by appeals from anguished liberals who see the Bill of Rights transgressed."[23] Many Truman confidants privately acknowledged Elsey's concerns, and they were accentuated by the entry of Henry Wallace into the fray as a third-party candidate.

Henry Wallace's Quixotic Crusade

Henry Wallace began his 1948 campaign by renewing his plea for peace. His quixotic crusade began with his nomination by the Progressive Citizens of America on July 24, 1948. Included among the 3,000 delegates were George McGovern, a graduate student in history at Northwestern University, singer Paul Robeson, and Congressman Vito Marcantonio.[24] Often described as twenty years younger and thirty pounds lighter than their Democratic and Republican counterparts, the Progressives approved a platform that called for antilynching laws, scrapping the Electoral College in favor of a popular tally for president, price controls, and national health insurance. By backing these long-sought liberal measures, the Progressives considered themselves the true heirs of Franklin D. Roosevelt, and they accused Truman of being in cahoots with "machine politicians and Southern Bourbons."[25]

The Progressives' principal complaint, however, was not Truman's domestic agenda but his vociferous anticommunism, which they charged was the by-product of "the dictates of monopoly and the military" and resulted in "preparing for war in the name of peace."[26] To the utopian-minded Progressives, peace was "the prerequisite of survival": "There is no American principle of public interest, and there is no Russian principle of public interest, which would have to be sacrificed to end the Cold War and open up the Century of Peace which the Century of the Common Man demands."[27] Like Wallace, most Progressives dismissed the Soviet Union as a serious national security threat. George McGovern remembered it this way: "The Soviet Union was about 50 percent destroyed in World War II. Half the country was devastated. They were in no position to launch World War III. I always felt that our policy had a big streak of paranoia in that period after World War II, and that we greatly exaggerated the Soviet threat. I think that was true at all points during the Cold War."[28]

Given these views, which were typical of most Wallace supporters, Progressives called for a wholesale reversal in how the government dealt with domestic communism. The party favored eliminating HUAC, claiming it had vilified and prosecuted citizens "in total disregard of the Bill of Rights." They also rejected laws banning the U.S. Communist Party or requiring registration of its members, likening such legislation to the Alien and Sedition Acts.

As the Progressive standard-bearer, Henry Wallace drew large crowds—including many young liberals, blue collars, and blacks. His liberal listeners worried Truman. In a memo dated November 19, 1947, Clark Clifford advised that no effort should be spared to link Wallace with communism: "Every effort must be made *now* jointly and at once and the same time—although, of course, by different groups—to dissuade him [Wallace] and also to identify him in the public mind with the Communists."[29] Wallace's public statements made the task easy. Reflecting on the 1939 Hitler-Stalin pact, he said, "If Stalin were doing it all over again in the light of his present knowledge of Hitler, France, and England, he could hardly act differently than he did."[30] Shortly after the Czechoslovakian coup, Wallace likened the communists to the early Christian martyrs—a comparison that appalled Truman.[31] Later, Wallace argued that the Berlin airlift was misguided, claiming the United States could afford to cede Berlin to the Soviets as a price for peace.[32] The U.S. Communist Party hailed Wallace, claiming he had forged a new alignment of the "people's coalition."[33] In response, Wallace stubbornly refused to renounce communist backing of his candidacy, saying, "I will not repudiate any support which comes to me on the basis of interest in peace."[34] Years later, in March 1951, Wallace regretted the communist involvement in his campaign: "You know, I didn't actually realize how strong the communists were in the Progressive Party. I think now they were out to knife me."[35]

But Wallace's conciliatory statements following communist advances helped Truman make the Progressive Party and the communists one in the public psyche. At various whistle-stops, the Democratic president vowed, "I do not want and I will not accept the political support of Henry Wallace and his communists."[36] In a last-ditch attempt to distance Wallace from the Soviets, Progressive delegate James Hayford, a Vermont farmer, proposed amending the platform to state that it was not the party's intention to endorse the foreign policy of any other nation. The convention rejected the Hayford Amendment, further reinforcing the suspicion that Wallace was procommunist. A Gallup poll taken a month before the Progressive convention found 51 percent agreeing that the Progressive Party was communist-dominated (see Table 2.1). Among those most likely to view Wallace as a communist dupe were Democrats, 57 percent; those sixty years of age or older, 56 percent; and southerners, 62 percent.[37]

As public disdain for Wallace grew, the Progressive Party's vice presidential candidate, Glen H. Taylor, tried to distinguish "pink" communists from "red" communists: "Pink" communists wanted to change the government through evolution; "red" communists wanted revolution.[38] But voters were having none of it. Nearly two-thirds of Wallace's former fellow Democrats had an unfavorable view of him.[39] And one poll made this devastating finding: One-third named Wallace from a list of Roosevelt administration officials as having been "harmful" to the country.[40] Journalist I. F. Stone, who backed Wallace, conceded: "Turn off the white lights and lay off the hotfoot. I admit everything. The Communists are doing a major part of the

TABLE 2.1
Communist Domination of Henry Wallace's Progressive Party, June 1948
(in percentages)

Demographic Category	Agree	Disagree	No Opinion
Nationwide	51	23	25
Party			
Democratic	57	18	26
Republican	53	21	26
Socialist	32	58	10
Independent	43	35	23
Age			
Less than 30	48	28	24
30–44	52	28	25
45–59	50	23	26
60 or older	56	17	26
Region			
New England	56	19	25
Middle Atlantic	49	25	25
East Central	49	24	27
West Central	53	20	28
Southern	62	15	23
Rocky Mountain	49	28	23
Pacific Coast	46	31	23
Sex			
Male	52	27	21
Female	51	19	30

SOURCE: Gallup poll, June 16–23, 1948. Text of question: "Do you think that the Henry Wallace third party is run by Communists?"

work of the Wallace movement, from ringing doorbells to framing platforms. Okay if you want it that way, they 'dominate' the party. So what?"[41]

So what indeed, said Truman, who averred that Wallace was part of "the contemptible communist minority."[42] In a September speech at Gilmore Stadium in Los Angeles, Truman—surrounded by many Hollywood stars, including Ronald Reagan—urged liberals to "think again" and end their dalliance with Wallace: "This is the hour for the liberal forces of America to unite. We have hopes to fulfill and goals to attain. Together we can rout the forces of reaction once again."[43] Ironically, Truman's vitriolic attacks on Wallace put liberalism on the defensive. Historian Arthur M. Schlesinger Jr. wrote that for many Wallace supporters "the USSR keeps coming through as a kind of enlarged Brook Farm community, complete with folk dancing in native costumes, joyous work in the fields, and progressive kindergartens."[44] Some tried to inoculate their liberalism from its most conspicuous messenger. The Congress of Industrial Organizations forbade its members from joining the Progressive Party or even the communist-adverse Americans for Democratic Action. The enormous unpopularity of Wallace's foreign policy stands heightened the liberals' fear of guilt by association with suspected communists. Just 4 percent in one Roper poll thought the United States was being "too tough with Russia"; 76 percent wanted defense spending increased.[45]

Despite Wallace's enormous political shortcomings, he nevertheless was able to influence the election result. When the ballots were counted, Wallace received 1,157,172 votes (slightly more than 2 percent), and half of these were from liberal-dominated New York. This was enough to throw three states to Dewey: New York, Maryland, and Michigan. If Wallace had done somewhat better in California, and had he not been kept off the Illinois ballot, the election could have been decided in the House of Representatives. But such scenarios are the musings of history, and Thomas E. Dewey, who had a few daydreams of his own, was unexpectedly preoccupied by a host of troubles both inside and outside his party.

Thomas E. Dewey: "You Can't Shoot an Idea with a Gun"

In May 1948, Thomas E. Dewey was embroiled in a hotly contested race against Governor Harold Stassen of Minnesota for the Republican presidential nomination. Stassen, in later years, became a laughingstock—a perennial gadfly who won a lone vote at the 1972 Republican National Convention opposing Richard Nixon's renomination. But in 1948 Stassen was no laughing matter. He supported legislation sponsored by Republicans Karl Mundt and Richard Nixon that required communist registration with the government and empowered the Subversive Activities Control Board to investigate any communist-suspected group if requested by the attorney general. The Mundt-Nixon bill also mandated that warning labels be appended to Communist Party radio broadcasts, television programs, and party brochures. Finally, the bill imposed up to a $10,000 fine, ten years in prison, and loss of citizenship if convicted of attempting to overthrow the government.

Mundt-Nixon won strong public backing. Stassen made his support for the bill a principal issue in the crucial Oregon presidential primary: "We must not coddle Communism with legality." Dewey rebuked him, saying, "You can't shoot an idea with a gun."[46] Just four days before the House passed Mundt-Nixon by a vote of 319 to 58, Dewey restated his opposition to communist registration in a radio and television debate with Stassen:

> I am unalterably, wholeheartedly, and unswervingly against any scheme to write laws outlawing people because of their religious, political, social, or economic ideas. I am against it because it is a violation of the Constitution of the United States and of the Bill of Rights, and clearly so. I am against it because it

is immoral and nothing but totalitarian itself. I am against it because I know from a great many years experience in the enforcement of the law that the proposal wouldn't work, and instead it would rapidly advance the cause of Communism in the United States and all over the world. . . . It is a surrender of everything we believe in.[47]

The Oregon balloting was close, with Dewey beating Stassen by fewer than 10,000 votes. But that was enough to secure the nomination. And not wanting to embarrass its presumptive president, the Republican Senate allowed Mundt-Nixon to languish in committee. Supremely confident of victory, Dewey did not want to make communism an issue in the upcoming fall campaign. One reason was that voters did not view him as especially adept at handling Soviet relations. A preconvention Gallup poll found that only one in five Republicans thought Dewey would do the best job of handling Soviet relations, with most giving greater support to Dewey's Republican opponents—especially Vandenberg and Stassen.[48] Dewey also remembered how the communist issue had burned him in 1944, and he did not want to repeat that experience. Finally, Dewey was aware that if he made communism an issue Democrats were prepared to remind voters that his principal foreign policy adviser, John Foster Dulles, had recommended Alger Hiss for the Carnegie Endowment presidency. Poised to make the Democratic charge stick, the FBI possessed some incriminating information concerning Dulles's sister, Eleanor. Back in the 1930s Eleanor Dulles, an economist, belonged to an informal study group committed to a better world. When asked about the organization, she told the FBI: "We felt the world had gone off the track with the Depression and Hitler, and the war. We wanted to put it back."[49] FBI agents discovered that half the group, excluding Eleanor Dulles, had communist ties or belonged to the Communist Party. For all these reasons, Dewey wanted to avoid the communist issue, and he assured his fellow Republicans that if the Democrats attacked him on his stance he would "fleck it lightly."[50]

Dewey tried to "fleck" communism away. In an address at the Hollywood Bowl attended by movie stars Gary Cooper, Jeanette MacDonald, Charles Coburn, Frank Morgan, and Ginger Rogers, Dewey maintained his hands-off approach toward the U.S. Communist Party:

We must neither ignore the communists nor outlaw them. If we ignore them we give them the cloak of immunity they want. If we outlaw them, we give them the martyrdom they want even more. We will keep informed and we'll keep the American people informed—where they are and what they are up to. If they—or if anyone else—break our law against treason, they'll get traitors' treatment. If they engage in sabotage or break any other laws, we'll jail them. If our laws aren't adequate, we'll get ones which are. But in this country we'll have no thought police. We will not jail anybody for what he thinks or believes. So long as we keep the communists among us out in the open, in the light of day, the United States of America has nothing to fear from them within our borders. We know what we have here in America and with everything we have and are, we are dedicated to keeping it. But we can only be sure of keeping it in a world where freedom has a chance.[51]

Dewey's impassioned argument fell by the wayside when his second try for the presidency failed at the polls. For the rest of the Cold War, no Republican presidential nominee ever again tried to "fleck" communism away.

Harry S. Truman: "Scare Hell Out of 'Em, Harry"

Throughout 1948 Truman played two roles. One was the familiar "Give 'Em Hell, Harry" act as Truman lambasted the "do-nothing" Republican Congress. The president delighted in telling audiences that the 80th Congress refused to pass his Fair Deal proposals, artfully coining a new nickname for its GOP leaders—the "Gluttons of Privilege."[52] But the other, less well known role Truman played was "Scare Hell Out of 'Em, Harry." Truman took the communist issue head-on, believing his accomplishments (both domestic and foreign) would inoculate him from the charge that he was "soft on communism." Truman acted boldly—even rashly—to halt the spread of domestic communism. On March 21, 1947, he signed Executive Order 9835 establishing the Federal Employee Loyalty and Security Program, having secured an initial $25 million appropriation from the Republican-controlled Congress. Truman selected Republican lawyer Seth Richardson to chair the Loyalty Review Board, which had total access to FBI and HUAC files. He stoutly defended his order: "I am not worried about the Communist Party taking over the government of the United States, but I am against a person whose loyalty is not to the United States, holding a government job."[53] Wallace attacked Truman's loyalty program, saying it had fostered "an atmosphere of fear and hysteria in government and industry."[54] In fact, many civilians in the federal ranks were accused of disloyalty: By 1951, 3 million had been investigated and 212 were discharged. Years later, Clark Clifford conceded that the Loyalty and Security Program was not based on actual communist infiltration but was politically motivated: "*It was a political problem*. Truman was going to run in '48 and that was it. . . . We never had a serious discussion about a real loyalty problem . . . the president did not attach fundamental importance to the so-called communist scare. He thought it was a lot of baloney. But political pressures were such that he had to recognize it. . . . A problem was being manufactured."[55]

The Loyalty and Security Program caught Truman's opponents by surprise. In a wire dated March 28, 1948, Capitol Hill correspondent Frank McNaughton cabled his editors at *Time*: "The Republicans are now taking

Truman seriously . . . [and his] order to root out subversives from government employment hit a solid note with Congress, and further pulled the rug from under his political detractors. The charge of 'communists in government' and nothing being done about it, a favorite theme of the reactionaries, simply will not stick any longer. . . . The Republicans are beginning to realize Truman is no pushover."[56] Taking note of Truman's obdurate anticommunist stance, the Nationalities Division of the Democratic National Committee organized twenty committees to appeal to those hailing from the so-called Captive Nations of Eastern Europe.[57] Of particular interest were Polish Americans, still smarting over the "sellout" at Yalta. But Truman's most vicious attack on his GOP rivals came at the Oklahoma State Fair at 4:00 P.M. on September 28, 1948.

When the presidential train pulled into Oklahoma City, Truman's campaign coffers were empty. But Truman considered the speech he was about to deliver so important that he ordered the Democratic National Committee to empty its nearly barren treasury to pay for a national radio hookup.[58] When Truman finished speaking, there was no money left to leave the station. (Eventually, enough cash was raised to allow the train to proceed to the next stop.) But his Oklahoma City attack left Republicans reeling. He accused the GOP of "trying to make communism an issue in this election" and warned his listeners: "They are trying to make you think that the Republican Party has a monopoly on patriotism. Don't let them fool you."[59] Truman brazenly argued that it was the *Republicans* who were responsible for the spread of domestic communism. Recalling the "Republican Depression," Truman correlated the support given to the U.S. Communist Party with economic conditions: In 1932 its presidential candidate received 100,000 votes; in 1936, 80,000; in 1940, 46,000. Indeed, a nation that had seen its war veterans enter college and move to the middle-class suburbs had forced the communists to forego offering a presidential candidate and turn to Wallace instead—or so Truman claimed.

Truman's tune that "happy days were here again" was tempered by his assertion that hard times would return if Dewey won. Indeed, the president claimed that Republicans had already endangered the national security by "their failure to deal with the big practical issues of American life such as housing, price control, and education," and he insinuated that the *real* U.S. Communist Party candidate was Dewey: "Could it be that they are counting on a Republican administration to produce another economic crash which would play into the hands of world communism? Think that one over."[60]

Truman plugged his Fair Deal program and chided the GOP-controlled Congress for not passing it: "People who are well-fed, well-clothed, well-housed, and whose basic rights are protected do not become victims of communism."[61] Indeed, by 1948 the New Deal–Fair Deal programs of Roosevelt and Truman were being recast using Cold War terminology. Using unmistakably anticommunist language, the Democratic platform that year advocated an enlarged government: "We shall continue to build [up our] defenses against communism by strengthening the economic and social structure of our own democracy."[62] Truman echoed his party's claim that the economic advancements of the Roosevelt and Truman years were bulwarks against communism, saying, "Confident people do not become communists."[63]

Truman's speech also questioned the patriotism of his Republican critics. In a hard-hitting, artfully worded passage, he laid out a blistering indictment against the GOP:

> I charge that the Republicans have impeded and made more difficult our efforts to cope with communism in this country. . . .
>   I charge that they have not produced any significant information about communist espionage which the FBI did not already have.
>   I charge the Republicans with having impaired our Nation's atomic energy program by their intemperate and unjustified attacks on our atomic scientists.
>   I charge them with having recklessly cast a cloud of suspicion over the most loyal civil service in the world.
>   I charge finally that, in all this, they have not hurt the Communist Party one bit.
>   They have helped it.[64]

To the surprise of nearly everyone—including the voters—Truman won less than 50 percent of the vote to Dewey's 45 percent. In still another shock, Democrats won back the Congress, adding seventy-five seats in the House and nine in the Senate—the highest party gains yet in the twentieth century. Among the new Democratic senators were Hubert H. Humphrey of Minnesota, Lyndon B. Johnson of Texas, Paul Douglas of Illinois, and Estes Kefauver of Tennessee. Especially noteworthy is the fact that nine Democratic House members, two Democratic senators (Humphrey and Douglas), and one governor (Adlai Stevenson of Illinois) belonged to the anticommunist Americans for Democratic Action. Reflecting on these Democratic victories, historian Arthur M. Schlesinger Jr. argued that the nation was still headed left, "but it was categorically a non-communist left." He added that the job of liberalism in the years ahead "was to devote itself to the maintenance of individual liberties and to the democratic control of economic life—and to brook no compromise, at home or abroad, on either of these two central tenets."[65] That proved to be a difficult task. Despite the Truman record, the Democrats' future difficulties were presaged in a 1946 survey in which more than three times as many respondents named the Democrats as the party that would allow the communists to have too much influence in government if they won the presidency in 1948.[66]

For Republicans, Dewey's defeat was an especially bitter blow. National chairman Hugh Scott resigned after being cast as a "symbol of Dewey misrule" and was replaced by Guy Gabrielson, a New Jersey entrepreneur and Taft supporter. Gabrielson proposed a return to the guerrilla tactics of the 1930s—portraying Democrats as the party of "statism" while claiming Republicans stood for "freedom." He acknowledged that this strategy "may turn out to be a failure, but we are going to make a hell of a lot of noise doing it." In spite of such bravado, many Republicans believed they were doomed to permanent minority status. Arthur Summerfield, a member of the Republican National Committee, gave voice to the gnawing pessimism: "There is little dispute in Washington that if the Democrats make any gains whatsoever in the House and the Senate in 1950, there is likely to be a pell-mell rush to get on the socialist bandwagon."[67]

Republicans worried that the communist issue, which they used with devastating effect in 1946, was fading away. In a December 1948 report, Republican members of HUAC took a parting shot at Roosevelt and Truman: "Communist espionage has broken through the security forces of the United States Government and made off with secret information of both military and diplomatic character concerning our national plans, policies, and actions. This espionage system has been carefully developed over *a period of more than fifteen years*, and it has been successful to a degree critical to the welfare and safety of the people of this Republic."[68] Given HUAC's continuing assault on the New Deal, many believed that Truman would either abolish HUAC or substantially weaken it in the incoming Democratic-controlled 81st Congress. Richard Nixon wrote that this prospect "jolted" Whittaker Chambers, "who was deeply depressed by the [election] result."[69] Chambers was right to worry: The Truman Justice Department wanted to indict him for perjury. Thus, in the interregnum between the election and Truman's inauguration, Chambers tried to keep the communist issue alive by giving Nixon the so-called Pumpkin Papers—a set of microfilms purloined from the State Department that Chambers had furtively hidden in his pumpkin patch. The papers purportedly proved that Alger Hiss was a communist.[70]

In hindsight, 1948 was a transitional election. Journalist Samuel Lubell described Truman as the "man who bought time"—for himself and the New Deal–Fair Deal Democratic majority.[71] In so doing, Truman gave the Democrats some much needed breathing space on the communism issue. Moreover, Henry Wallace's poor showing at the polls silenced his most ardent supporters until the Democratic Left, repelled by the Vietnam War, rose from the ashes two decades later. Despite this, 1948 remains an anomaly in terms of the presidential elections that followed it. Although the Cold War was well under way, U.S. draftees had not yet been sent to Western Europe, China had not yet fallen to the Communists, and South Korea had not yet been invaded by North Korea. By 1950, U.S.-Soviet tensions were on the verge of all-out war. Indeed, just two years after Truman prevailed at the polls a new politics was being born.

1949–1950: The New Politics of Old Fears

Harry S. Truman took the oath of office on January 20, 1949, and four of the next five presidents would be members of Congress: John F. Kennedy, Lyndon B. Johnson, Richard M. Nixon, and Gerald R. Ford. This suggests how high a premium voters would give to *national* as opposed to state or local experience when choosing a Cold War president. On the inauguration stand, Truman assumed a very different office than that envisioned by the Founders. Writing in *Democracy in America*, Alexis de Tocqueville noted that the vast Atlantic Ocean kept the presidency weak: "The President of the United States possesses almost royal prerogatives, which he has no opportunity of exercising, and the privileges which he can at present use are very circumscribed. The laws allow him to be strong, but circumstances keep him weak."[72] By 1949, however, the Atlantic had become little more than a pond, helping make Truman the undisputed Leader of the Free World. Truman assumed that mantle in his Inaugural Address, issuing a manifesto addressed to the peoples of the world: "Communism is based on the belief that man is so weak and inadequate that he is unable to govern himself, and therefore requires the rule of strong masters. Democracy is based on the conviction that man has the moral and intellectual capacity, as well as the inalienable right, to govern himself with reason and justice."[73]

Ironically, just one day after Truman was inaugurated, Chinese leader Chiang Kai Shek abdicated and fled to Taiwan. With the fall of China to Mao Zedong's communists, many envisioned rampaging red hordes roaming across Asia. This feeling of vulnerability intensified anticommunism to the point where most Americans were willing to sacrifice their civil liberties in order to ferret out suspected communists at home. Seventy-six percent in a 1950 poll disagreed with the statement "American communists should have the same rights as Democrats, Republicans, or anyone else," and 77 percent in another survey that same year classified containing communism as an important foreign policy objective.[74] Further adding to the emotion was the intertwining of Judeo-Christian values with anticommunism: 77 percent saw communism and Christianity as incompatible concepts, including 81 percent of Catholics and 78 percent of Protestants.[75] FBI Director J. Edgar Hoover reflected these sentiments in speeches given to religious gatherings during this period: "Communism is secularism on the march. It is a moral foe of Christianity. Either it will survive or Christianity will triumph because in this land of ours the two cannot live side by side."[76] The

Christopher Society urged its fellow Catholics to ward off communism by reciting the words, "Savior of the world, save Russia."[77] Anticommunism quickly pervaded all areas of community life, from churches to schools. Nearly three in four people believed that any college professor who was a communist should be summarily fired, and 72 percent wanted all teachers to take an oath forswearing communism.[78]

The emergence of a new Red Scare was reflected in the statements of prominent politicians. Attorney General J. Howard McGrath told Americans in 1949: "There are today many Communists in America. They are everywhere—in factories, offices, butcher stores, on street corners, in private businesses. And each carries in himself the germ of death for our society."[79] And in a startling about-face, Governor Dewey, reversing his 1948 campaign stance, gave the New York State Board of Regents the authority to compile lists of subversive organizations in which membership would result in automatic dismissal from any teaching post.[80] Although these statements reflected the temper of the times, they also belied Truman's belief that "confident people do not become communists." By late 1949, Americans were feeling much less secure than they had a year earlier. Republicans sought to exploit the new political climate. A July Gallup survey (taken before the Chinese communist takeover) found 37 percent saying the GOP was best equipped to handle the problem of communists in the country; 24 percent chose the Democrats.[81]

But it was the fall of China that caused Republicans to redouble their anticommunist campaign. Americans were quite concerned over what a communist-controlled China meant for their country. Seventy-one percent in a 1948 poll said that a communist takeover of China mattered to the United States, and 66 percent persisted in thinking that the Chinese communists took orders from Moscow.[82] Even some *Democrats* were sharply critical of Truman. Congressman John F. Kennedy excoriated Truman's China policy: "The responsibility for the failure of our foreign policy in the Far East rests squarely with the White House and the Department of State. . . . What our young men had saved [during World War II], our diplomats and our President have frittered away."[83] Such bickering within the Democratic ranks gave leading Republicans an opportunity they lost no time in exploiting. One who welcomed the fight over "who lost China" was Senator Robert Taft of Ohio, who faced a tough reelection battle in 1950. Taft's harsh rhetoric allowed him to be perceived as a militant anticommunist (which he was), yet he knew that his attacks on Truman contained little risk in that U.S. troops would most likely not be sent to Asia. Other Republicans followed Taft's example of being rhetorically tough on communism while refraining from deploying U.S. forces overseas. As one Formosan official stationed in the United States observed, "There is *much confusion* among Republicans, and presumably some Democrats, on the whole [China] issue."[84]

The communist takeover of China began a chain of cataclysms that further altered the U.S. political landscape. On September 23, 1949, Truman was notified that the Soviets had detonated an atomic bomb—an event the Pentagon thought was years away. By 1950, the Cold War had become *the* dominant factor of political life. A chronology of some of that year's events helps explain why:

January 10:	The Soviets' United Nations ambassador, Jacob Malik, boycotts the Security Council, stating the Soviet Union would no longer take part in its deliberations until the Nationalist Chinese government was expelled and the Beijing delegation seated.
January 21:	Alger Hiss is convicted of two counts of perjury.
January 31:	Truman announces that he has ordered production of a more powerful hydrogen bomb.
February 2:	Physicist Klaus Fuchs confesses in London to having spied for the Soviets while working on Anglo-American atomic research projects.
February 9:	Joseph McCarthy delivers a Lincoln Day address to the Republican Women's Club in Wheeling, West Virginia, and charges that 205 members of the U.S. Communist Party have infiltrated the State Department.
February 14:	The Soviet Union and the People's Republic of China sign a thirty-year Treaty of Friendship, Alliance, and Mutual Assistance.
June 24:	North Korea invades South Korea.
June 30:	Truman dispatches U.S. troops to Korea.
August 17:	Julius and Ethel Rosenberg are charged with atomic espionage.
September 20:	The Senate, by a vote of 70–7, approves the McCarran Act, which contains many Mundt-Nixon provisions. Truman's veto is overridden and the bill becomes law on September 23.
November 5:	The Chinese enter the Korean War.
November 30:	President Truman causes controversy by publicly stating that the United States is considering using the atomic bomb in Korea. This comment so upsets Prime Minister Clement Atlee of Great Britain that he soon flies to Washington to consult with Truman.

As this chronology suggests, 1950 was a year of trial for Truman. It began with Alger Hiss's conviction, prompting the communist-run *Daily Worker* to editorialize: "There is a new way to spell Franklin D. Roosevelt.

Now they spell it H-I-S-S."[85] Shortly after the verdict, Secretary of State Dean Acheson told reporters, "I should like to make it clear to you that whatever the outcome of any appeal which Mr. Hiss or his lawyers may take in this case I do not intend to turn my back on Alger Hiss."[86] Truman sympathized with Acheson's plight, writing him, "Privately, I refer to [Joseph] McCarthy as a pathological liar and [Senator Kenneth] Wherry as the blockhead undertaker from Nebraska."[87] But with the jury verdict, Hiss managed to turn a prominent member of Truman's Cabinet into a major political liability. *Life* magazine editorialized that Acheson "is the symbol of appeasement of communism and of soft-headed, unrealistic thinking."[88] Republicans concurred. Nebraska's Hugh Butler declared: "I look at that fellow. I watch his smart-aleck manner and his British clothes and that New Dealism, everlasting New Dealism in everything he says and does, and I want to shout, Get out, Get out. You stand for everything that has been wrong with the United States for years." Not to be outdone, Joseph McCarthy chimed in: "He must go. We cannot fight international atheistic communism with men who are hip-deep in their own failures. . . . The chips are down . . . between the American people and the administration Commicrat Party of Betrayal."[89]

McCarthy was a newcomer to the Republican anticommunist cause. In 1936, he made an abortive attempt for political office as a Democrat. Ten years later, a war veteran and a Republican, he won a U.S. Senate seat with the slogan "He and millions of other guys kept you from talking Japanese."[90] But after four years in the Senate, McCarthy had done little and knew it. To prevent his reelection campaign from becoming a referendum on his ineptitude, McCarthy searched for a scapegoat. By February 1950, he found it. In his infamous Lincoln Day address, McCarthy charged that there had been "traitorous actions" in Acheson's State Department: "I have in my hand a list of two-hundred-five who were known to the Secretary of State as being members of the Communist Party and who nevertheless are still working and shaping the policy of the State Department." McCarthy subsequently read into the *Congressional Record* the case files of eighty-one officials whose loyalties he thought compromised. (All had been reviewed and cleared by the Loyalty Review Board years before.)

Truman upbraided McCarthy, deeming him a "Kremlin asset." But the presidential rebuke did not deter the Wisconsin Republican. On March 21, 1950, McCarthy impugned the loyalty of Professor Owen Lattimore of the Johns Hopkins School of International Relations, claiming he was "one of the biggest Soviet espionage agents."[91] A day later the Republican Policy Committee, chaired by Robert Taft, decided not to make Lattimore an issue. But Taft gave McCarthy his imprimatur, advising him to "keep talking and if one case doesn't work out he should proceed with another."[92] By this time, anticommunist hysteria reached fever pitch. A March 1950 Gallup poll found 54 percent believing that McCarthy's charges were true; only 29 percent thought he was "playing politics."[93] Two years later opinion swung overwhelmingly to McCarthy's side: 81 percent agreed there had been "a lot of communists or disloyal people in the State Department," and 58 percent said they had done "serious harm to our country's interests."[94] A 1953 poll found 55 percent stating that "it was more important to find out all the communists in the country, even if some innocent people are accused."[95] Senate Republican Ralph Flanders of Vermont conceded that McCarthy would have had no influence at all "had it not been for the fact that our late, departed saint, Franklin Delano Roosevelt, was soft as taffy on the subject of communism."[96]

By 1950, a new politics based on the old bugaboo of communism had fully emerged. Eisenhower and Nixon biographer Stephen Ambrose writes that "the picture most Americans had of the Soviet Union was that it was led by a madman worse than Hitler, it was bent on world conquest, it had fifth columns all over the world trying to topple free governments, and it was being helped in the U.S. by unwitting dupes and traitors."[97] J. Edgar Hoover noted that although there were just 54,174 members of the U.S. Communist Party, "the fact remains that the party leaders themselves boast that for every party member there are ten others who follow the party line and who are ready, willing, and able to do the party's work."[98] Given such exaggerated fears, Congress passed a variation of the Mundt-Nixon proposal, The Subversive Activities Control Act of 1950, which required members of the U.S. Communist Party to register with the Justice Department. A Gallup poll taken shortly after the Korean War began revealed just how many Americans were predisposed to take extreme measures should war begin with the Soviets (see Table 2.2).

Amid this new Red Scare, worries about an imminent war with the Soviet Union peaked at 4:00 A.M. on June 24, 1950, when North Korea invaded South Korea. Tensions on the Korean Peninsula had been high for some time. After World War II, the superpowers agreed to divide Korea temporarily at the 38th parallel so as to accept the surrender of Japanese troops there.[99] Once the Japanese were removed, it was expected that Korea would reunite. But the Cold War made reunification impossible. Dueling regimes in North and South Korea claimed sovereignty over the entire area. Border skirmishes were commonplace. Thus began North Korea's war for conquest. On June 30, Truman ordered U.S. troops to South Korea under the mandate of the United Nations.

Initially, most Americans supported Truman: 81 percent in a September 1950 poll said that "the United States was right to send troops to stop the communist invasion in Korea." Moreover, 59 percent thought it a "good idea" to tell the Soviet Union that "we will immediately go to war against her with all our power, if any communist army attacks any other coun-

TABLE 2.2
Attitudes Toward Communists in the United States, 1950 (in percentages)

Put them in internment camps	22
Imprison them	18
Send them out of the United States, exile them	15
Send them to Russia	13
Shoot them, hang them	13
Watch them, make them register	4
Nothing, everyone entitled to freedom of thought	1
Miscellaneous	9
No opinion	10

NOTE: Percentages total more than 100 because some respondents gave more than one answer.
SOURCE: Gallup poll, July 30–August 4, 1950. Text of question: "What do you think should be done about members of the Communist Party in the United States in the event we get into a war with Russia?"

try."[100] Although support waned as the Korean War turned into a protracted conflict and casualties mounted, public backing never fell below 55 percent.[101] In September 1953, shortly after an armistice was signed, 64 percent believed that U.S. actions in Korea had been correct.[102]

The 1950 Elections

It was in this atmosphere of war, anticommunist hysteria, and distrust that the 1950 midterm congressional elections took place. Many Democrats were concerned about their fates—especially after the outcome of the party's bitter U.S. Senate primary in Florida. There, George Smathers published a pamphlet titled *The Red Record of Senator Claude Pepper*, shipping nine tons of this small pamphlet to the Miami area alone.[103] In it, Smathers dubbed his opponent and fellow Democrat "Red Pepper," citing his votes against Truman's aid package to Greece and Turkey and quoting Pepper as saying, "Generalissimo Stalin is a man who keeps his promises."[104] In his stump speech, Smathers elaborated on "Red Pepper's" soft spot for communism:

> The leader of the radicals and extremists is now on trial in Florida. Arrayed against him will be loyal Americans, who want to preserve their right to think, to work, and to worship as they please. Standing against us will be certain Northern labor bosses, all the communists, all the Socialists, all the radicals, and the fellow travelers. . . . Surely we will not turn from the noble principles of Jefferson and Jackson to the careermen of communism. . . . Florida will not allow herself to become entangled in the spiraling web of the Red network.

The people of our state will no longer tolerate treason. . . . The outcome can truly determine whether our homes will be destroyed; whether our children will be torn from their mothers, trained as conspirators and turned against their parents, their home, and their church. . . . I stand for election on the principle of the Free State against the Jail State.[105]

Several major press organs backed Smathers. The *New York Times* editorialized that "Red Pepper" had won the praise of Soviet officialdom and its propaganda organ, *Pravda*.[106] The *Saturday Evening Post* told its readers that "the toughest job in Florida politics is knocking over spellbinding pinko Senator Pepper." The *Post* added that for the first time ever, Florida had something resembling the two-party system "with the line drawn between Smathers's conception of a Liberal Democrat and that of the complete New Dealer platform of Senator Pepper."[107] Appeals to reason became smothered in a sea of red: At every Smathers rally the speaker's platform was bedecked in red, white, and blue—the colors of Smathers's alma mater, the University of Florida—as the candidate beguiled rapt audiences with accounts of how Pepper studied law under the "crimson of Harvard."[108] On primary day, May 2, 1950, Pepper succumbed to the relentless assault, winning 46 percent of the vote to Smathers 54 percent.

The Florida result sent Democrats scurrying for political cover. In September 1950, the Democratic-controlled Congress approved the McCarran Act over Truman's veto. It contained many Mundt-Nixon provisions and compelled registration of all communists.[109] Liberal Democrats Hubert H. Humphrey and Paul Douglas attached an amendment requiring communists be sent to detention camps should a national emergency arise. Meanwhile, the Democratic National Committee printed a 100-page document comparing statements made by ten Republican Senators with positions taken by known communists.[110]

But Republicans were not going to abdicate the anticommunism issue to the Democrats without a fight. During the confirmation hearings for Secretary of Defense nominee George C. Marshall, Senator William E. Jenner of Indiana all but called Marshall a traitor:

General Marshall is not only willing, he is eager to play the role of a front man, for traitors. . . . [As a result,] this Government of ours [has been turned] into a military dictatorship, run by the communist-appeasing, communist-protecting betrayer of America, Secretary of State Dean Acheson. . . .

How can the Senate confirm the appointment of General Marshall, and thus turn Dean Acheson into a Siamese twin, in control of two of the most important Cabinet posts in the executive branch of the Government? This is what we are asked to do.

It is tragic, Mr. President, that General Marshall is not enough of a patriot to tell the American people the truth of what has happened, and the terrifying story of what lies in store for us, instead of joining hands once more with this criminal crowd of traitors and communist appeasers who, under the continuing influence and direction of Mr. Truman and Mr. Acheson, are still selling America down the river.[111]

Only a handful of Republicans objected to such bellicose rhetoric. Maine's Margaret Chase Smith criticized her male colleagues for allowing the Senate to have been "debased to the level of a forum of hate and character assassination sheltered by the shield of congressional immunity."[112] The "lady from Maine" continued her "declaration of conscience," saying: "The nation sorely needs a Republican victory. But I do not want to see the Republican party ride to political victory on the four horsemen of calumny—fear, ignorance, bigotry, and smear."[113] But most GOP candidates—and some Democrats—were content to let their charges of treason do their dirty work. U.S. Senate hopeful Prescott Bush, father of the future president, bused hundreds of McCarthyites to Connecticut to campaign against incumbent Democrat William Benton. (Bush lost by 1,000 votes out of 862,000 cast.)

By election day, the midterm campaigns for Congress had degenerated into arenas for rancor and hate. Republicans portrayed themselves as "standing alone" in their fight against the Marxist twins of socialism and communism: "If you are opposed to both forms of Marxism, the Republican party offers you the only militant, fighting organization that is left if you want to save your country. You can do *your part* by *talking Republican, working Republican,* and *voting Republican* to save America."[114] Republicans charged that Democrats had become a threat to national survival by willingly allowing communism to advance:

It was softness toward communism in Washington that made recognition of the Soviet Union possible.

It was softness in Washington that brought about the blundering decisions and secret agreements born out of the Tehran, Yalta, and Potsdam Conferences toward the close of World War II.

It was softness in Washington which allowed the Soviet Union to overrun in two short years after World War II, Poland, Czechoslovakia, Eastern Germany, Estonia, Latvia, Lithuania, Eastern Austria, Bulgaria, Rumania, Albania, Yugoslavia, and Hungary.

It was softness in Washington which could cause the United States to enter into a secret deal at Yalta whereby communist domination of Asia was pledged to the Soviet Union.

It was softness in Washington which could cause President Truman, on December 15, 1945, to announce to the world that unless our faithful ally, China, admitted communists to its government, the United States would cut off aid.

It was softness in Washington which caused the United States not only to cut off aid but to place an embargo on all purchases by the Chinese Government in this country, the better to force the Government of China to accept a truce in its conflict with the Chinese Reds in 1946, thus giving the Reds a precious year to regroup and rearm for their eventual conquest of all China.

It was softness in Washington which caused a nine-months slowdown in delivery of military aid to China which had been ordered by the Republican 80th Congress over Administration protests in 1948, at an hour, though late, that was not too late to turn back the communist onslaught.

It was softness in Washington that caused 50,000 American troops to be withdrawn from South Korea in 1949, despite Republican protests in an official House report which warned that invasion by the North Korean Reds would be hastened and that the withdrawal was being undertaken "at the very instant when logic and common sense both demanded no retreat from the realities of the situation."

It was softness in Washington which enabled Klaus Fuchs and six other communist spies in the United States to steal the secrets of both the atomic and hydrogen bombs and deliver them to Russia.

It was softness in Washington, as much as anything else, that enabled the Soviet Union to expand its domination in five short years from 170,000,000 people to 800,000,000 people, thus making the threat of a third World War more real than ever.[115]

Republican cries that the United States was on the verge of impending doom were raised to new levels when Communist China entered the Korean War just days before the balloting. In a confidential letter dated October 7, 1950, Josef Stalin urged Mao Zedong to help the beleaguered North Koreans, writing that if "war is inevitable" between the communist East and the democratic West, "then let it be waged now" and not years later "when the alliance between Japan and America would be too strong."[116] Many Americans shared Stalin's view that war was inevitable, thereby ensuring that the issue of communism would dominate the 1950 elections. This was especially true of Richard Nixon's 1950 bid for California's open U.S. Senate seat. As Nixon himself put it, "There's no use trying to talk about anything else, because that's all the people want to hear about."[117]

Nixon, who entered the U.S. House of Representatives in 1947, had tired of being a low-ranking member of that body. But the Hiss verdict had cracked open the door to higher office, and Nixon decided to push his way through. A few months after Hiss was jailed, Nixon declared his candidacy for the U.S. Senate, stating: "There is only one way we can win. We must put on a fighting, rocking, socking campaign and carry that campaign directly into every county, city, town, precinct, and home in the state of California."[118]

Nixon did just that, mounting a reprise of his malicious 1946 campaign against Jerry Voorhis. This time his Democratic opponent was Helen Gahagan Douglas (wife of actor Melvyn Douglas), who once had a distinguished career on the Broadway stage before entering politics. Douglas worried about the plight of migrants following publication of John Steinbeck's *The Grapes of Wrath*, and through her efforts she became friends with Eleanor Roosevelt. She won a House seat in 1944 and was a reliable New Deal supporter. As the Democratic standard-bearer in 1950, Douglas thought Nixon might use the communist issue against her, but she naively believed that if she explained the issues and defended her record she would prevail.[119]

Douglas was wrong. Although the U.S. Communist Party denounced her as a "capitalist warmonger,"[120] that did not stop Nixon from dubbing her the "pink lady"—a reference to the 354 times Douglas sided with Vito Marcantonio. The Nixon campaign distributed 500,000 pink-colored fliers smearing Douglas as a communist sympathizer: "Mrs. Douglas Followed the Post-War Communist Platform on China"; the Communist *Daily Worker* hailed Douglas "as a 'hero' of the 80th Congress"; and "Helen Gahagan Douglas . . . was wrong so many times about Russia, about the communists, about our national security, about giving away atomic secrets."[121] Anonymous telephone calls reinforced the content of these fliers by warning of Douglas's supposed communist associations. Postcards also appeared in mailboxes reading: "Vote for Our Helen for Senator. We are with you 100%. The Communist League of Negro Women Voters."[122]

Nixon's virulent anticommunism provided a strong emotional context to the campaign. In March 1950, Joseph McCarthy addressed a Nixon rally that was decorated with red, white, and blue banners reading "Richard Nixon—On Guard for America." McCarthy asserted that Truman headed the "Administration Commicrat Party of Betrayal"; at that Nixon applauded and said, "God give him courage to carry on."[123] Truman badly wanted Nixon beaten, and so most of his Cabinet, along with Eleanor Roosevelt, journeyed to California to attack Nixon, who artfully dubbed them the "foreign legion." Although Democrats like Ronald Reagan were strong Douglas backers, Nixon won other disgruntled Democrats to his cause.[124] George Creel, who headed Woodrow Wilson's propaganda agency and had a prominent role in the Red Scare, chaired Democrats for Nixon. All sixty-three members of this tiny group cited anticommunism as their reason for joining and pleaded with their fellow Democrats to return to the principles of their party's founders. Nixon also gained the tacit support of John F. Kennedy, who sent a note that read thus: "Dick, I know you're in for a pretty rough campaign, and my father wanted to help out. I obviously can't endorse you, but it isn't going to break my heart if you can turn the Senate's loss into Hollywood's gain."[125] Attached was a $1,000 contribution from Kennedy's father, Joe.

Nixon fulfilled Kennedy's wish, winning 2,183,454 votes to Douglas's 1,502,507. Nixon's 680,947 plurality was the largest amassed by any Senate candidate in 1950. Across the country Republicans made a political comeback from the 1948 debacle, adding twenty-eight seats in the House and five in the Senate. Defeated Senate Democrats included Majority Leader Scott Lucas of Illinois and four-term incumbent Millard Tydings of Maryland. Tydings, who had branded McCarthy as a "fraud and a hoax,"[126] was beaten by a Republican who used a doctored photograph placing a smiling Tydings next to former U.S. Communist Party chief Earl Browder. The only major Democratic Senate victories were posted by Herbert Lehman in New York and Thomas Hennings in Missouri, the home states respectively of Roosevelt and Truman. In Chicago, Republican Timothy P. Sheehan won in a heavily Democratic, Polish-dominated district.[127] Even Vito Marcantonio lost.

The Birth of a New Party System

The anticommunist ripples created by this stunning Republican turnaround reached until the end of the Cold War. During Watergate, for example, Richard Nixon told White House counsel John Dean how he would have spun the story: "That [characterization omitted] Hiss would be free today if he hadn't lied. If he had said, 'Yes, I knew Chambers and as a young man I was involved with some communist activities but I broke it off a number of years ago.' And Chambers would have dropped it. If you are going to lie, you go to jail for the lie rather than the crime. So believe me, don't ever lie."[128] The same Watergate transcripts found Nixon saying of Chambers, "The informer [as a role] is not one in our society. . . . That is the one thing people can't survive."[129] But, in 1984, Ronald Reagan presented the presidential Medal of Freedom (posthumously) to the informer, Chambers. Reagan hailed Chambers as a courageous man who "stood alone against the brooding terrors of our age." The citation also included Reagan's interpretation of the Hiss case: "Consummate intellectual, writer of moving majestic prose, and witness to the truth, [Chambers] became the focus of a momentous controversy in American history that symbolized our century's epic struggle between freedom and totalitarianism, a controversy in which the solitary figure of Whittaker Chambers personified the mystery of human redemption in the face of evil and suffering."[130] Reagan's action earned him the enmity of Hiss's son, Tony, who wrote in 1992:

> Terrorism has a horrible effect on countries, but so, in its own way, does a kind of low-grade fearism. From the end of the Second World War until the fall of the Berlin Wall, people in this country were on edge, partly because of the atomic bomb, and partly because we faced an enemy that seemed capable of burrowing inside our minds. Whenever such a situation takes hold of people—and it can happen anywhere—this fear actually does bring about a strange but unnoticed distortion in how people see the world, and see each other. So an honest man can be called, as Alger Hiss was, the Benedict Arnold of the twentieth century, and a self-confessed liar can be given the president's highest honor.[131]

After the withering away of the Soviet state in 1991, the Hiss case returned to the public spotlight. Richard Nixon wrote to General Dmitri Antonovich Volkogonov, head of a Russian commission overseeing disposition of the KGB files, asking if there was any relevant information on Hiss. Hiss himself made a similar inquiry. Volkogonov told both that he had reached "a firm conclusion that Mr. A. Hiss had never and nowhere been recruited as an agent of the intelligence services of the U.S.S.R."[132] Hiss, 87 years old and in failing health, was "overjoyed," telling reporters, "I think J. Edgar Hoover acted with malice trying to please various people who were engineering the Cold War."[133] Volkogonov's statements outraged former Cold Warriors, including conservative columnist William F. Buckley: "There's nothing a Soviet general can say that can upset what was presented. . . . The notion that Hiss has been exonerated is a huge laugh."[134] Buckley was joined by pundit George F. Will, who called believers in Hiss's innocence "childish" and "paranoid."[135] Volkogonov later recanted his statement, claiming he had been pressured by Hiss's lawyer to exonerate a sick, elderly man.

The brief return of Alger Hiss to the headlines in 1992 is only one indication of how poisonous and enduring the anticommunist politics of 1945–1950 was. Arthur M. Schlesinger Jr. once noted that ideology is the curse of public affairs "because it converts politics into a branch of theology and sacrifices human beings on the altar of dogma."[136] This was certainly true during the Cold War. Pronouncing the death sentence in 1953 after Julius and Ethel Rosenberg were found guilty of having given the Soviets the secret of the atom bomb, Judge Irving R. Kaufman said: "This country is engaged in a life and death struggle with a completely different system. This struggle is not only manifested externally between these two forces but this case indicates quite clearly that it also involved the employment by the enemy of secret as well as overt outspoken forces among our own people. All our great democratic institutions are, therefore, directly involved in this great conflict."[137]

But the conformity imposed by the Cold War represents only part of a larger mosaic. More than any other people, Americans demand rigid adherence to a "classical liberal" ideology whose tenets include faith in the individual, a commitment to equality of opportunity, and an unswerving dedication to the preservation of liberty.[138] Thus, only in the United States could there be a House Committee on Un-American Activities, and only in the United States could such a committee be abolished as being itself un-American—as was done in 1975. The rigidity created by classical liberalism causes many Americans, as Richard Hofstadter has observed, to be "tormented by a nagging doubt as to whether they are really and truly and fully American."[139] Thus, questions about "loyalty" elicited an exceptionally emotional response during the Cold War.

Such absolutism distorted our politics. What were essentially political issues in 1945–1950 became questions about patriotism. Like the Salem
Witch Trials or the Alien and Sedition Acts of centuries past, many prefer
not to recall the "unpleasantness" of the period. Postwar baby boomers, for
example, know little about the Hiss case. Instead, it and the HUAC hearings
are incorporated into our absolutist language by the word "McCarthyism,"
which itself is synonymous with being un-American. Those "blacklisted"
became victims of a discredited era—notable, albeit exceptional, examples
of America's intolerance. But Republicans from Dwight Eisenhower to
Robert Taft addressed the communist issue using just as inflammatory language as that of the disgraced McCarthy. Likewise, Democrats ranging from
Harry S. Truman and John F. Kennedy to Hubert H. Humphrey and Lyndon
B. Johnson spoke about communism in vitriolic terms. Most backed legislation that violated basic civil liberties. Governor Allen Shivers of Texas, a Democrat, proposed making membership in the U.S. Communist Party a capital
offense.[140] Later, Senator Humphrey sponsored a 1954 amendment outlawing the U.S. Communist Party and stripping communist-controlled unions of
their right to operate under the National Labor Relations Act. Professing to
be tired of "this talk of twenty years of treason" by Republican
"blowhards," Humphrey said, "The Communist Party isn't really a political
party, it's an international political conspiracy."[141] After challenging his fellow senators "to stand up and to answer whether they are for the Communist Party or against it,"[142] Humphrey's bill was approved 85–0. Columnists
Joseph and Stewart Alsop wrote that Humphrey's ploy was "cleverly con-
ceived, ruthlessly executed, and politically adroit."[143]

Despite Humphrey's attempt to blunt the issue, communism had a delete-
rious impact on Democratic party fortunes. A November 1950 survey
demonstrates just how badly the New Deal coalition was hurt by the Cold
War. When asked which groups were most likely to be communists, those
receiving the most mentions—labor union members, poor people, blacks,
college students, Jews, and New Yorkers—were most likely to be Democrats. Moreover, 18 percent named "people in the government in Washington" as likely communist suspects—an especially significant response since
the Democrats were still the party of government (see Table 2.3).

The fragile state of FDR's New Deal coalition fewer than five years after
his death was ironic, especially since the Democratic majority cracked at a
moment of supreme economic triumph. For all the worries of returning veterans about where to live and what job to take, the vast majority joined the
burgeoning middle class. As Eric Goldman has observed: "In social movement, nothing quite fails like too much success. New Dealism, having la-
bored mightily to lift low-income Americans, found that it had created a
nation of the middle class, shocked at the New Dealism's iconoclasm and
especially annoyed at its insistence on placing the values of change above

TABLE 2.3
Groups Mentioned as Most Likely to Be Communists, 1950 (in percentages)

Group	Public Response
Labor union members	28
Puerto Ricans in the United States[a]	24
Poor people	21
Don't know	19
People in the government at Washington	18
None of them	17
Negroes	14
College students	13
New Yorkers	12
Actors	12
Jews	11
Americans of Italian descent	9
Teachers	8
Americans of Polish descent	7
Catholics	2
Protestants	1

[a]The high response is due to the assassination attempt on President Truman by Puerto Rican nationals on November 1, 1950.

NOTE: Percentages total more than 100 due to multiple responses.

SOURCE: National Opinion Research Center, survey, November 1950. Text of question: "In this country, do you think any of the people listed here are more likely to be communists than others?"

those of standard middle-class thinking."[144] Democratic unity was further weakened as disparate intraparty factions, led by the successors to Wallace and Truman, disagreed about what the struggle against communism meant and about the role the United States should play in world affairs. Amid these internal squabbles, Democrats often found themselves protecting their vulnerable liberal flank from what Dean Acheson called "the attack of the primitives."[145] These attacks left enduring scars. A 1954 poll found 53 percent agreed that there were "some groups of people in this country who are 'soft on communism.'"[146] All too often the phrase "soft on communism" meant liberals. As a result, many Democrats did not want to be seen consorting with "fellow-travelers" and went to great lengths in their "politics of dissociation." Herbert Hoover unwittingly lent his assistance to this effort in 1953 when he created The Committee of One Million Against the Admission of Communist China Into the United Nations. Its roster included conservatives like Whittaker Chambers (no surprise) and more than a few liberals such as Hubert Humphrey, Eugene McCarthy, and Paul Douglas.[147] (Ironically, Richard Nixon was not a member—having no need to seek the "cover" of the Hoover group.)

By the early 1950s, the party system created by Franklin Roosevelt's New Deal coalition had succumbed to a new political order. Republicans, empowered by the communist issue, would from now on enjoy greater success than they had before in presidential contests. An early indication of future Democratic difficulty came in January 1951, when 30 percent thought Russia was winning the Cold War while just 9 percent said the United States was winning—down from 31 percent in 1948.[148] But something deeper than mere dissatisfaction with the status quo was at work: Americans suspected that while both major parties were militantly anticommunist, Republicans really believed their strident rhetoric. In 1950, an internal GOP document declared: "If America is to be preserved, we must start the job by sending to Washington in 1950 a Congress that believes in America. And we must complete the job in 1952 by electing a President whose first interest is the salvation of America."[149] A politics centered on the view that the fate of the nation could not be entrusted to the Democrats—and not one that was centered on different ideas—gave Republicans a sense of mission that undergirded their party for the duration of the Cold War.

This did not mean that Democrats were quiescent. Ardent anticommunists like Kennedy, Johnson, and Humphrey were dominant political figures for much of the Cold War era. But in the new era, neither party would truly reign as Democrats coaxed some additional life out of the New Deal—especially in their advocacy of Social Security and Medicare—helping them to control both houses of Congress continuously from 1954 to 1980. Still, winning the White House in seven of the ten presidential elections held from 1952 to 1988 was something of a political miracle for a party that had been so thoroughly discredited by Franklin D. Roosevelt. Five years after Truman's triumphant visit to San Francisco, newly elected U.S. Senator Richard Nixon visited several GOP headquarters across California—most of which had pianos. An inveterate player, Nixon sat down and plucked a tune. His choice: "Happy Days Are Here Again."[150] As the song suggested, Republicans were poised to win their first Cold War election.

chapter three

1952:
The Transforming Election

Our troubles are all ahead of us.

—Adlai E. Stevenson, July 25, 1952

July 25, 1952

From his rostrum at the Democratic National Convention, Harry S. Truman was the ever-confident president. Though retiring from office, the man from Independence, Missouri, continued to preach from the gospel of American Exceptionalism: "The essence of American belief in the future is faith. We have overcome adversity and triumphed again and again over foes and fears because we are a confident and optimistic people. Our faith will sustain us in the future as it has in the past if we remember to act upon it."[1] But Truman's plea for faith in an "unlimited America" fell on deaf ears. Just 25 percent of his fellow Americans approved of his performance—a record low in the Gallup opinion polls.[2] Instead of echoing Truman, *Cleveland Press* editorial writer Louis B. Seltzer wondered why so many worried about the future since most were "rich beyond the dreams of the kings of old."[3] Indeed, when compared to the Soviet Union, the United States had struck it rich: Steel production was three times that of the Soviets; aluminum, petroleum, and electric power generation showed even greater disparities.[4] A tripling of defense spending from $13 billion in 1950 to $44 billion in 1952 helped fuel the good economic times.[5]

Nonetheless, Seltzer wrote that a bad omen lingered in the air: "Something is not there that should be—something we once had. . . . No one seems to know what to do to meet it. But everybody worries."[6] Seltzer's editorial was reprinted in forty-one newspapers, and strangers stopped him on the street to tell him he got it right. Others shared Seltzer's sense that something was lacking. John Foster Dulles, a member of Dwight Eisenhower's brain trust, wrote in a widely circulated *Life* magazine article: "Looked at in any impartial way, we are the world's greatest and strongest power. The only commodity in which we seem deficient is faith."[7]

As the 1952 presidential election approached, faith in the future was shattered by the specter of spreading communism overseas, communist infiltration of the government here at home, and a foreboding that the United States was losing the Cold War. Richard Nixon charged that in 1946 "there were approximately 1,760,000,000 people on our side and only 180,000,000 on the communist side." By 1952, the math had changed: "Today there are only 540,000,000 people that can be counted on the side of the free nations—our side. There are 800,000,000 people on the Communist side, and there are 600,000,000 that will have to be classified as neutral."[8]

"Six hundred million people lost to the communists" became the Republican rallying cry in 1952. Dwight Eisenhower compiled a list of countries that were either lost or teetering toward communism, including Iran, where nationalization of oil resources resulted in a "dangerous tilt" toward communism; Guatemala, where Ike accused the democratically elected president, Jacobo Arbenz, of creating a communist state in the Western Hemisphere; and Vietnam, where the colonial French were near capitulation to the communist-controlled government in Hanoi.[9] John Foster Dulles conjured an image of a triumphant Kremlin speculating "Which will be the next addition to our camp?" while those in what remained of the free world pondered "Which of us will be the next victim?"[10]

Korea was at the top of foreign concerns. After the Chinese entry into the war in 1950, several inconclusive battles were waged along a bloody front. Republicans charged that "Overnight, young Americans of eighteen and nineteen years have been thrown into battle ill-prepared, ill-equipped, and outnumbered, only to be butchered by hordes of crack communist troops."[11] Secretary of State Dean Acheson bemoaned the Democrats' fate: "If the best minds in the world had set out to find us the worst possible location in the world to fight this damnable war, politically and militarily, the unanimous choice would have been Korea."[12] Negotiations to end the bloodshed were stymied over the prisoner-of-war issue: The United States held approximately 132,000 communist prisoners—75,000 of whom refused to return to their native North Korea or China. Truman would not yield on the communist demand for full repatriation. By March 1952, a majority thought the United States made a mistake going into Korea, and 33 percent (a plurality) thought an immediate cessation of hostilities would mean "a bigger victory for the enemy."[13] As the casualty figures surpassed the 110,000 mark, draft notices became a dreaded reminder of the war's exacting toll. One San Francisco woman put it this way: "They just called my husband back into service. Need I say more?"[14]

Republicans charged that Korea offered "no hope of victory,"[15] and millions considered supporting the GOP ticket for the first time in a generation. By June, 49 percent wanted the Republicans to take charge if the Korean situation worsened, whereas just 32 percent chose the Democrats.[16] One disgruntled former Truman backer said: "I am against this idea that we can go on trading hills in Korea indefinitely. We've got to end it one way or the other."[17] As the U.S. government continued to operate on a warlike footing, Richard Nixon asked, "What then is the end of it all? Are we going to have to remain an armed camp for twenty-five years?"[18] Some thought so. Ernest K. Lindley told *Newsweek* readers that given the rapid Soviet rearmament "by 1952, 1953, or 1954, the Kremlin may be ready for a major war."[19]

Others sounded a similar red alert. Accepting the Nobel Prize for Literature in December 1950, William Faulkner said: "Our tragedy today is a general and universal physical fear so long sustained by now that we can even bear it. There are no longer problems of the spirit. There is only the question: When will I be blown up?"[20] *Time* magazine reported that in hundreds of California backyards "sweating husbands and excited children were blistering their hands and straining their backs burrowing into the ground." Contractors offered a cornucopia of shelters ranging from a $13.50 "foxhole" model to a luxurious $5,500 suite equipped with telephone, escape hatches, bunks, toilets, and Geiger counter. Ruth Calhoun, a divorcée with three children, purchased a deluxe model, saying: "It will make a wonderful place for the children to play in. And it will be a good storehouse, too. I do a lot of canning and bottling in the summer, you know."[21]

While some were digging foxholes to avoid being blown up, others concluded that the communists had already won the Cold War by burrowing into every nook and cranny of American life. Democrat Adlai Stevenson ominously declared, "Communist agents have sought to steal our scientific and military secrets, to mislead and corrupt our young men and women, to infiltrate positions of power in our schools and colleges, in business firms and in labor unions *and in the Government itself*" (emphasis added).[22] Republican Robert Taft maintained that communist agents had infiltrated the labor unions, the publishing and writing fraternities, Hollywood, the teaching profession, as well as the U.S. government: "In these positions, they undertook to make communists if they could, but even more to influence those who were in authority to take a soft attitude toward communism. . . . In this effort the communists were notably successful."[23]

Responding to such charges, Hollywood executives vowed to root out suspected communists by compiling "black lists" of supposed sympathizers. The resultant blacklisting affected the popular culture. For example, on October 5, 1951, the first episode of Jackie Gleason's classic *Honeymoon-*

ers series aired on the Dumont Television Network. Veteran actress Pert
Kelton played Alice Kramden, wife to Gleason's hapless Ralph character.
But Kelton left the show when she was accused of having "subversive con-
nections" to the U.S. Communist Party. Audrey Meadows was quickly substituted, and she has lived on as Alice Kramden in the decades since.[24]
American literature also reflected the obsession with communism. Novelist
Mickey Spillane rewrote the Mike Hammer detective character into a com-
mie-hating hero, selling 2.5 million to 3 million copies of each title in the
series.[25] But the most consequential example of popular literary tastes was
Whittaker Chambers's 1952 autobiography, *Witness*, which reached number one on the *New York Times* best-seller list. Readers, like the youthful
Dan Quayle, recoiled as Chambers chillingly told of a German diplomat
stationed in Moscow who turned against his communist comrades because
"one night—in Moscow—he heard screams . . . five annihilating words:
one night he heard screams."[26] The country was spooked.

Modern Republicanism

George Van Dusen, a student of the post–World War II conservative movement, once observed that the Hiss case "occurred at the right time to fill the
void in conservative thought."[27] Paucities of thought had made the word
"conservative" an epithet. Columnist George Will, for example, described a
man who was arrested in 1950 for creating a public disturbance. According
to Will, an eyewitness told police "He was using abusive language, calling
people conservative and all that."[28] A principal reason for such public
ridicule was that conservative ideologues were mostly isolationists, na-
tivists, protectionists, racists, and anti-Semites. Henry Luce dismissed them
in his 1941 "American Century" editorial: "It is most unfortunate that this
virus of isolationist sterility has so deeply infected an influential section of
the Republican Party. For until the Republican Party can develop a vital
philosophy and program for America's initiative and activity as a world
power, it will continue to cut itself off from any useful participation in this
hour of history."[29]

Old Guard Republicans—marked by their virulent opposition to the New
Deal—denounced Luce. Robert Taft deplored Luce's "American Century" as
embodying the worst excesses of American aggrandizement: "There are a
good many Americans who talk about an American Century in which America will dominate the world. . . . The trouble with those who advocate this
policy is that . . . they are inspired with the same kind of New Deal planned-
control ideas abroad as recent administrations have desired to enforce them
at home."[30] But by 1952 many more conservatives became enamored with
Luce's vision of an "American Century." John Foster Dulles was one, refuting those "who would turn their backs on all the world's problems and wrap

the United States in some magically 'impregnable' isolation."[31] To be sure, some Old Guard Republicans remained staunchly opposed to the North Atlantic Treaty Organization (NATO), the Marshall Plan, and the Korean War. But they were being replaced by a new type of anticommunist conservative best symbolized by Whittaker Chambers, Russell Kirk, William Buckley, Dwight Eisenhower, Richard Nixon, and Barry Goldwater.

Unlike the Old Guard isolationists, Modern Republicans saw the projection of U.S. power overseas as necessary given the Cold War. In a Denver speech on the eve of his presidential nomination, Dwight Eisenhower admonished the Old Guard: "Those who assert that America can retire within its own borders; those who seem to think we have little or no stake in the rest of the world and what happens to it; those who act as though we had no need for friends to share in the defense of freedom—such persons are taking an unjustified gamble with peace."[32] By casting their foreign policy as one that could bring about peace while thwarting communism, Modern Republicans began drawing former supporters of Franklin Roosevelt and Harry Truman who were dissatisfied with the status quo. Many urban and ethnic Catholics, for example, viewed the Democrats as "soft on communism." Most were émigrés from the Captive Nations of Eastern Europe—including Poles, Czechs, Hungarians, and Lithuanians—or had relatives there, making them particularly sensitive to GOP anticommunist appeals. During the 1952 campaign, the Republican National Committee printed thousands of pamphlets aimed at the thirteen nationality groups from Eastern Europe and ran advertisements in their foreign-language newspapers claiming that they had been "betrayed by the Democratic administration during the past decade."[33]

In making these accusations of Democratic perfidy, Republicans found willing allies in the Catholic Church hierarchy. For decades, church leaders had harshly denounced communism. In a 1937 encyclical titled *Atheistic Communism*, Pope Pius XI admonished the faithful that "communism is intrinsically wrong, and no one who would save Christian civilization may collaborate with it in any undertaking whatsoever." From his pulpit, New York's Francis Cardinal Spellman warned that the United States was in imminent danger of "communist conquest and annihilation," noting that security would not be restored "until every communist cell is removed from within our own government."[34]

Modern Republicans made repeated and successful overtures to the Catholic hierarchy. Dwight Eisenhower told Republican delegates that he "admired and respected His Holiness and considered him a great champion in the fight against communism."[35] Appealing to Catholic votes, the 1952 Republican platform accused Truman of abandoning the Captive Nations and leaving them "to fend for themselves against the communist aggression which soon swallowed them."[36] Modern Republicans promised that only their leadership would liberate the Catholic-dominated countries of Eastern Europe from their communist masters. During the 1952 campaign, Dwight Eisenhower promised that if elected "I swear upon my honor and integrity before God to work for the liberation of enslaved nations behind the Iron Curtain."[37] Eisenhower foreign affairs adviser John Foster Dulles believed that continuous repetition of the Republicans' desire for liberation of the Captive Nations would place "heavy new burdens on the jailers."[38] Eisenhower and Dulles proved mistaken, but these expressions of desire paid rich political dividends in Catholic-dominated enclaves.

In addition to making converts of worried Catholics, Republicans learned that suburbs were becoming hospitable Republican territory. The new suburbanites were well educated and were often employed in white-collar jobs—some of them in high-technology defense jobs that were by-products of the Cold War. Thus, they were sensitive to the Republican warnings about Soviet intentions. Moreover, by becoming homeowners more suburbanites saw themselves as taxpayers rather than tax recipients—further diminishing the New Deal in the national memory. One could almost watch the spawning of new Republicans as crowded byways carried refugees from the inner cities (still home to the New Deal) to join the station-wagon set in the suburbs. By the summer of 1952, George Gallup found that the two parties were in a virtual dead heat: Among likely voters there were 22.5 million Democrats, 18.5 million Republicans, and 14 million independents.[39]

All that the Modern Republicans needed was a candidate, and many thought they had one in Dwight Eisenhower. From a humble upbringing in Abilene, Kansas, Eisenhower served as Allied Supreme Commander during World War II and later as Army Chief of Staff. Eisenhower assumed the presidency of Columbia University in 1948, and two years later President Truman asked him to assume command of the Supreme Headquarters Allied Powers Europe (SHAPE). When Eisenhower was summoned back to active military duty in 1950, Truman was in desperate political straits. The Chinese had overrun the U.S. military in Korea, and Truman dispatched four divisions to NATO's European theater to shore up the U.S. position there in case the Chinese move was part of a larger communist plan to attack Western Europe. When congressional Republicans wondered why U.S. troops should defend Europe, Truman responded that he could send troops wherever and whenever he wished. Eisenhower backed Truman, providing invaluable cover from the World War II hero. But if he were to become a candidate, General Eisenhower would have to criticize his former Democratic commanders. That would be awkward: During World War II Eisenhower had dutifully executed FDR's policies, and he supported the 1947 presidential order withdrawing U.S. forces from Korea. After World War II, Eisenhower told a Moscow press conference, "I see nothing in the future that would prevent Russia and the United States from being the closest possible friends."[40] Eisenhower was a staunch supporter of NATO—the linchpin of Truman's containment policy. In addition, Eisenhower was vulnerable to the "who-lost-China" issue, having served as Army Chief of Staff while China was "lost" to the communists. Finally, in a speech at Valley Forge, Pennsylvania, days after the U.S. entry into the Korean War, Eisenhower declared: "The South Koreans' only crime has been the desire to live their own lives as they choose, at peace with the rest of the world. The American decision to assist them was inescapable. The alternative would be another kind of Munich."[41] During the 1952 campaign, when badgered by reporters for his support of the Truman administration's key foreign policy decisions, Eisenhower deftly replied: "Well, some of you men out there were second lieutenants. Did they ask you?"[42]

To many Americans, Eisenhower's management of the burgeoning military establishment made him highly qualified to become the next president. Seventy percent thought Eisenhower would better manage U.S. foreign policy, whereas just 18 percent chose his Republican primary rival, Robert Taft.[43] Among those preferring Eisenhower were Barry Goldwater and a youthful George Bush. To many, Taft was a man of the past. John Franklin Carter, a friend of Thomas E. Dewey's, said of Taft: "I believe he would make a splendid president for a stable prosperous country in an orderly world—say, in 1925. I suspect, however, that as happened to many other able and patriotic men, his political serviceability has been repealed by World War II and the rise of the Third International [that is, Joseph Stalin]."[44] Still, Taft's formidable following among the Old Guard carried considerable weight in the party's presidential selection process. The widespread feeling that it was "Taft's turn" to head the GOP ticket clashed with a sentiment held by other Republicans; that is, after five successive GOP defeats, winning the presidency rather than rewarding a party warhorse was more important. Richard Nixon warned that 1952 would be "the last chance for power for the Republican party."[45] Republicans were near desperation, but most voters thought there was nothing wrong with the party that a good candidate could not fix. When asked after the 1948 debacle what the GOP should do to win the presidency next time, 24 percent—a plurality—said "get better candidates."[46]

The Battle of the Titans: Eisenhower Versus Taft

At first, General Eisenhower seemed a sure bet to capture the Republican nomination. He beat Taft in New Hampshire with 46,661 write-in ballots to Taft's 35,838. Equally impressive was the *tripling* of those requesting a Republican ballot from four years earlier. Although Eisenhower publicly disavowed any presidential ambitions during the early months of 1952, he proved to be a wily politician, writing a friend: "The seeker is never so popular as the sought. People want what they cannot get."[47] The more Ike demurred, the more anxious Republicans became. Henry Cabot Lodge pleaded with him to become an active candidate, believing Taft had little chance of beating Truman. Gallup polls confirmed Lodge's judgment: In a hypothetical matchup, Eisenhower defeated Truman 64 percent to 28 percent; Taft barely edged ahead with 45 percent to Truman's 42 percent.[48]

The "you-can-win" argument resonated with Eisenhower. For twenty years, Republicans had been barred from the White House. Columnist Walter Lippmann warned that if the GOP lost another time, it would be taken over by its "most irreconcilable and ruthless factions."[49] Joseph Alsop agreed, saying he was "constantly blackmailed by the virtual certainty that we shall have a first-class fascist party in the United States if the Republicans don't win."[50] Thus, Eisenhower offered himself not only as one who would rescue the Republican party from itself but as the savior of the two-party system, which he deemed "vital to the ultimate preservation of our national institutions."[51] But in order to save the two-party system, Eisenhower would first have to weaken it.

On February 2, 1952, Citizens for Eisenhower opened its doors in New York City. For the first time since Wendell Willkie's insurgent 1940 candidacy, a Republican had created a campaign apparatus separate from the party organization. One reason was that most party regulars liked Taft. A June 1952 survey of GOP county chairs found 61 percent backing Taft; only 31 percent were for Ike.[52] But those who inhabited the Eisenhower campaign were organization men of a different sort. General Lucius Clay, a key Eisenhower strategist, was a World War II commander; Walter Williams, head of Citizens for Eisenhower, was a mortgage banker; Paul Hoffman, Williams's assistant, was president of the Ford Foundation. To them, Eisenhower's candidacy represented, in their man's words, "a great crusade—for freedom in America and freedom in the world."[53] By putting his crusade above mere politics-as-usual, Eisenhower presented himself as a "nonpartisan" who was simply renting the top slot on the Republican ticket. For their part, voters liked Ike without making a partisan commitment. It was a marriage of convenience. But in this approach to politics— and in other ways both substantive and stylistic—Eisenhower was worlds apart from Taft, who proudly wore the mantle of "Mr. Republican."

Robert A. Taft was the scion of a great political family. His father was a former U.S. president and the chief justice of the Supreme Court. He was elected to the Senate from Ohio in 1938 and 1944, and won his second reelection in 1950 by a landslide 437,000 votes. But Taft possessed little charisma. Richard Nixon remembered a little New Hampshire girl who had asked for an autograph only to be rebuffed as Taft explained "with devastating reasonableness" that it took less time to shake hands than to sign a piece of paper.[54] Nixon confided to *Los Angeles Times* political columnist Kyle Palmer in February 1952 that "Taft would be difficult to elect."[55] Truman agreed, telling confidants before the Republican Convention, "I am afraid that my favorite candidate is going to be beaten."[56] Eisenhower disdained Taft for other reasons, calling him "a very stupid man [with] no intellectual ability, nor any comprehension of the issues of the world."[57] Later, in a frank admission to the traveling press corps, Eisenhower blurted out: "All right, I'll tell you why I'm running for the presidency. I'm running because Taft is an isolationist. His election would be a disaster."[58]

Eisenhower was mistaken on both counts. Although Taft opposed Lend Lease, rejected NATO, only reluctantly supported Truman's aid package for Greece and Turkey, and initially opposed the Marshall Plan, by 1951 the Ohio Republican had considerably distanced himself from his once rock-ribbed Midwest isolationism. In a book titled *A Foreign Policy for All Americans*, Taft wrote that World War III would differ from previous wars insofar as air and sea power (along with the atomic bomb) had shortened the distance between the two superpowers. Thus, Taft favored more military spending—especially for the air force—filling chapters with dramatic subtitles like "The Emphasis in Selecting Military Projects Should Be on Air Power." Taft believed air power would keep the peace: "Not only is an all-powerful air force the best possible defense for the United States, but it is also the best deterrent to war."[59] (His emphasis on technological solutions to the Cold War was later emulated by Ronald Reagan, who proposed the Strategic Defense Initiative, an outer-space "missile shield" that critics dubbed "Star Wars.")

Taft's reliance upon technological means to fight the Cold War permitted him to contrast his "hard" stance against communism with the "soft" one he thought the Democrats took. His harsh rhetoric served another purpose: keeping the remaining isolationists in tow while courting Modern Republicans with his strident anticommunist rhetoric. Taft often was bombastic. Writing that modern warfare is "murder by machine," Taft proposed that it be prosecuted by every available weapon including manned bombers, submarines, aircraft carriers, and even atomic bombs. Politically, Taft knew that the assembly lines that were mass-producing weapons were spawning an unprecedented economic revival. But he realized that public support for protracted land wars involving U.S. troops was quite a different proposition. He demurred from Truman's call that the United States should unilaterally defend other nations against the communists: "I doubt that on principle, we should enter into any definite commitments in advance in time of peace, or undertake the job at all unless we are sure it is well within our capacity and almost certain of success."[60]

Indeed, Taft worried that Truman was becoming "a complete dictator in the entire field of foreign policy."[61] Although he thought stationing troops in South Korea was morally unassailable, Taft attacked Truman's invocation of the United Nations Charter as a grant of war-making authority, saying he was "deluded as to a power which never has existed under the charter." Taft argued that unless the presidency was restrained it would pose a danger to liberty itself: "We cannot afford to destroy at home the very liberty which we must sell to the rest of the world as the basis for progress and happiness."[62] Such sentiments, especially Taft's warnings about a powerful commander in chief, resonated with the Old Guard. Preconvention Gallup polls showed the Ohio Republican with considerably more support among the rank-and-file than independents. In the final Gallup poll before the GOP convention, Eisenhower led by just 9 points among self-described Republicans, but he had an insurmountable 29-point advantage among independents.[63] But soon after his New Hampshire debacle, Taft found his footing. In April he beat Eisenhower in Nebraska on a write-in (76,556 votes to Ike's 61,592) and later won primaries in Wisconsin and Illinois—the latter with 74 percent of the vote. In June he eked out a majority in South Dakota with 50.3 percent to Eisenhower's 49.7 percent. After that, Eisenhower rallied—besting Taft in New Jersey (61 to 36 percent), Massachusetts (70 to 30 percent), Pennsylvania (74 to 15 percent), and Oregon (65 to 7 percent).

Eisenhower's strength in the East was matched by Taft's in the Midwest. Midwest ethnics, including Scandinavian pacifists and German Americans and Irish Americans who disliked the British, liked Taft's perceived isolationism. In addition, many midwesterners resented easterners whom they associated with the corporate values of size and greed, whereas they perceived themselves as supposedly embodying the virtues of small-town America. Newspaper magnate Colonel Robert McCormick described the heartland as "the center of the American spirit."[64] Further, many midwesterners disdained Thomas E. Dewey (an ardent but private Eisenhower backer) as the epitome of Republican failure. From the dais at the 1952 Republican National Convention in Chicago, Senator Everett Dirksen of Illinois caused a near-riot when he shook a finger at Dewey and shouted: "We followed you before, and you took us down the road to defeat. Don't do this to us."[65]

As the Dirksen episode shows, passions were running high when Republicans gathered to select their presidential nominee. In another telling episode, actor John Wayne, an ardent Taft man, jumped out of his cab to confront Ike's old mess sergeant, who was broadcasting from an Eisenhower sound truck: "Why don't you get a red flag?" he hollered.[66] And the founder of the John Birch Society, Robert Welch, wrote that the "betrayal" of Taft was "the dirtiest deal in American political history, participated in if not entirely engineered by Richard Nixon in order to make himself vice president (and to put Earl Warren on the Supreme Court as part of that deal)."[67] The close delegate count fanned these strong emotions: When the convention gavel fell on July 7, 1952, Taft had 530 delegates (including 72 contested delegates from the South)—a mere 74 shy of victory. Eisenhower had 427 delegates (only 21 challenged). Settlement of the disputed southern delegates would determine the nomination. Thanks to some shrewd behind-the-scenes maneuvering and prominent television coverage highlighting a call for "fair play," Dwight D. Eisenhower became the Republican party's twenty-fifth presidential nominee.

Eisenhower's victory was more than a personal triumph. Taft was the last of the Old Guard. And although the two candidates differed over key aspects of foreign policy, it was a nuanced disagreement: Taft emphasized Asia; Eisenhower focused on Europe. On September 12, 1952, Taft endorsed Eisenhower, saying their respective foreign and domestic policies were characterized by mere "differences of degree."[68] What mattered, Taft added, was that they were determined to battle communism "throughout the world."[69] Less than a year later, on July 31, 1953, Taft succumbed to cancer, leaving no immediate political successors. With his death, the Republicans became an internationalist party. Eisenhower's 1952 promise to the delegates became party dogma in the decades hence: "We will so undergird our freedom that today's aggressors and those who tomorrow may rise up to threaten us, will not merely be deterred but stopped in their tracks. Then we will at last be on the road to real peace."[70]

Dispirited Democrats

When the political season opened in January 1952, Democrats were experiencing their own winter of discontent. The Korean War produced an inconclusive standoff; Truman's standing had plunged in the public opinion polls; and there were the "five percenters," a reference to payoffs made to Truman's appointments secretary, naval aide, and treasury secretary in return for political favors. But the problems that beset the Democratic party were far more serious than the Truman administration's peccadilloes. The burdens of the Cold War had sobered the Democrats' rhetoric, and bursting into another chorus of "Happy Days Are Here Again" seemed entirely inappropriate. The 1952 Democratic platform struck a somber tone: "For twenty years, under the dedicated guidance of Franklin Delano Roosevelt and Harry S. Truman, our country has moved steadily along the road which has led the United States of America to world leadership in the cause of freedom. . . . It is our prayerful hope that the people, whom we have so faithfully served, will renew the mandate to continue our service and that Almighty God may grant us the wisdom to succeed."[71]

But the party's services would be terminated in 1952. In the midst of the Korean stalemate, Democrats faced a leadership crisis of profound magnitude. In March, Senator Estes Kefauver of Tennessee defeated Truman in the New Hampshire primary, and the president quickly withdrew from contention. Potential successors were not immediately evident. Vice President Alben Barkley was seventy-four years old; Estes Kefauver was popular among the rank-and-file but had antagonized party leaders with his hearings into organized crime; Senator Richard Russell of Georgia, Senator Robert Kerr of Oklahoma, and Mutual Security Agency Director Averell Harriman rounded out a weak field. Chief Justice Fred Vinson rejected Truman's entreaties to become a candidate. In such circumstances, the governors of New York, Pennsylvania, or California would be likely possibilities, but in 1952 they were all Republicans. Moreover, the governors of Massachusetts and Ohio were Catholics, and Catholicism was taboo after Al Smith's 1928 loss.

That left Adlai Ewing Stevenson II. Stevenson came from a long line of Democratic activists. His namesake grandfather was elected vice president in 1892 and was renominated in 1896. The younger Stevenson had a lengthy résumé: During the first New Deal, he worked in the Agricultural Adjustment Administration; when World War II erupted he assisted Navy Secretary Frank Knox until his death in 1944. Later he joined the State Department, where he served as an adviser at the United Nations conference in San Francisco. In 1948, Stevenson was summoned by Jack Arvey, the Chicago boss, to be the Democratic candidate for governor. Arvey heard of Stevenson from Truman's Secretary of State, Jimmy Byrnes, who called him "a gold nugget."[72]

Stevenson lived up to the billing, winning by 572,067 votes—the largest plurality any Illinois gubernatorial candidate had received to that time. Stevenson was crucial to Truman's Illinois victory (Truman won by only 33,612 votes). Such an impressive performance in a key industrial state gained Stevenson instant notoriety. Truman became one of his fans: "Adlai, if a knuckle-head like me can be president and not do too badly, think what a really educated, smart guy could do in the job."[73] But Stevenson was convinced that 1952 would not be his year, and he preferred to wait. Moreover, he shared Eisenhower's internationalist views and thought the former general would make a good president. In a late-night conversation with *New York Times* reporter James Reston, an agitated Stevenson asked, "What are you trying to tell me? That it's my duty to save Western civilization from Ike Eisenhower?"[74]

But Stevenson reluctantly succumbed to a draft and won the Democratic nomination on the third ballot. In victory, he sounded sorrowful: "I have asked the merciful Father of us all to let this cup pass from me. But from such dread responsibility one does not shrink in fear, in self-interest, or in false humility. So, 'if this cup may not pass away from me, except I drink it, Thy will be done.'"[75] Such maudlin rhetoric matched the convention mood. As the Democratic conclave opened (also in Chicago), newspapers were filled with ominous headlines. A *New York Times* front-page headline read, "Hiss Loses Plea for Another Trial; Court Rejects His 'New Evidence.'"[76] In a welcoming speech, Stevenson noted the "solemn hour" and delivered a grim denouement to the New Deal:

> It was here, my friends, in Chicago just twenty years ago this month that you nominated Franklin Roosevelt; twenty years during which we have fought total depression to victory and have never been more prosperous; twenty years during which we have fought total war to victory, both East and West, and have launched the United Nations, history's more ambitious experiment in international security; twenty years, my friends, that close now in the grim contest with the communist conspiracy on every continent of the globe.[77]

As if this was not pessimistic enough, Stevenson promised "no easy solution, no relief from burdens and anxieties,"[78] and he made a dire prediction: "Our troubles are all ahead of us." He warned that the Cold War would be a "long, patient, costly struggle" with enormous political consequences, most of them bad, for Democrats: "Some will call us appeasers: others will say we are the war party."[79] Richard Nixon observed that Stevenson "gives the American people no hope for safety at home from the sinister threat of communism."[80]

But Stevenson's forecast proved prescient. Communism *had* strained the mystic chords of memory forged by Franklin Roosevelt. The more communism advanced, the more the New Deal became a dim memory. Stevenson acknowledged that when he remembered the Roosevelt years he felt "no exultation, no sense of triumph."[81] Instead, Democrats were reduced to making dire predictions about what would happen to the New Deal's "common man" under a Republican regime. Truman was confident this tactic would pay dividends at the polls: "People are not going to pay any attention to men who've been opposing everything the people have wanted for the last twenty years. They know that the Republican reactionaries have fought against every measure that made our country prosperous at home and powerful abroad."[82] And in a reprise of Truman's 1948 Oklahoma City speech, Stevenson told labor union leaders that it was the Republicans who had promoted communism by opposing first the New Deal and later Truman's containment policy:

> Twenty years ago the most serious threat of communism this country ever faced—a threat arising from poverty and despair, following, as it happens, twelve years of Republican administrations—was stopped by a Democratic administration.
>
> For twenty years my party has helped the people of America to build that economic strength and that faith in freedom which make communism impossible—and every step we have taken has been opposed, ridiculed and sabotaged by the Republican Old Guard.

> For years your Government in Washington has been desperately rallying and strengthening the free peoples of the world against communism, and leading the way in building the collective strength which is the only bulwark against communist expansion—and this, too, over the bitter protest and unrelenting opposition of the Republican Old Guard.
>
> Again, Democratic leadership has built an elaborate internal security system to protect this nation against communist subversion—a system which has put the leaders of the Communist Party in this country where they belong—behind bars.[83]

Although the Democratic attacks had some effect, they did not alter the outcome. When Stevenson claimed he did not want to abandon the New Deal but "merely to freshen it,"[84] he was stating the obvious. Democrats had run out of poor folks, and the growing middle class worried more about communism than unemployment. Moreover, Stevenson's foppishness was ill-suited to deliver the party's message of economic populism. Given these harsh political realities, Stevenson proved no match for what he derisively called "the party of fear,"[85] claiming the Republicans were ruled by "political demagogues, who are hunting for votes much more than for communists."[86]

"The Party of Fear"

After his nomination, Dwight Eisenhower retreated to Denver, Colorado, where he plotted campaign strategy. Eisenhower's strategists concluded that the key to victory was to combine the 20 million loyal Republicans with the estimated 45 million nonaffiliated who rarely voted. To mobilize the stay-at-homes, Robert Humphreys, public relations director at the Republican National Committee, wrote that Eisenhower must stress "an international situation today that causes Americans . . . *to fear for their national security and lives.*"[87] By engaging in the politics of fear, Republicans got a head start on McCarthyism. The party platform accused Truman of treason, charging him with appeasing "communism at home and abroad" and permitting "communists and their fellow travelers to serve in many key agencies and to infiltrate our American life," sanctimoniously adding, "There are no communists in the Republican Party."[88] Privately, Eisenhower admitted that the anticommunist plank was "a bit savage,"[89] but he publicly reiterated its message, claiming his crusade would "get out of the governmental office . . . people who have been weak enough to embrace communism."[90]

But Eisenhower's words were mild compared to those of Joseph R. McCarthy. McCarthy proclaimed the New Deal–Fair Deal years as representing "twenty years of treason," with the result that the communists were everywhere: "I say, one communist in a defense plant is one communist too many. One communist on the faculty of one university is one communist too many. One communist among the American advisers at Yalta was one communist too many. And even if there were only one communist in the State Department there would be one communist too many."[91] In Arizona, Republican Senate candidate Barry Goldwater told voters in McCarthy's presence, "Now is the time to throw out the intellectual radicals and the parlor pinks and the confused and the bumbling." Among those that Goldwater thought confused was Secretary of State Dean Acheson, whom he likened to "the man with the umbrella who went to Munich."[92]

For many Republicans, the State Department was an altogether inviting target. Robert Taft darkly spoke of a "procommunist group in the State Department."[93] Polls showed many Americans had a similar perception: 81 percent agreed that there were "communists or disloyal people" working in the State Department, and 58 percent thought they had done "serious harm" to the national security.[94] Richard Nixon dubbed Acheson "Red Dean" and called Stevenson "Adlai the Appeaser," saying he held a "Ph.D. from Dean Acheson's College of Cowardly Communist Containment." The *Chicago Tribune* branded the Democrats as the "Party of Acheson, Stevenson, and Hiss."[95] In a remark that earned him the enmity of many, Richard Nixon claimed that Truman, Stevenson, and Acheson were "traitors to the high principles in which many of the nation's Democrats believe."[96]

These attacks stung Stevenson. Refuting the charge that Democrats were "soft on communism," he declared that "communism is committed to the destruction of every value which the genuine American liberal holds dear." As president, he promised to "deal sternly and mercilessly with all who would betray their country and their freedom for the sake of manacles and chains."[97] Stevenson believed that a cynical Republican party desperate for votes was manufacturing the communist issue: "Sometimes they call sections of us dupes and fellow travelers—a people without a purpose and without a mind. But at all times they picture us unworthily—scared, stupid and heartless. They thus betray the conquering, hopeful, practical yet deeply moral America which you and I know."[98] Stevenson warned that in the GOP hunt for communists "we must take care not to burn down the barn to kill the rats."[99] Later he mocked those anticipating an Eisenhower victory as "the men who hunt communists in the Bureau of Wild Life and Fisheries while hesitating to aid the gallant men and women who are resisting the real thing in the front lines of Europe and Asia." He sarcastically noted that the Republican party's favorite sport was "prophesying our imminent doom" and described its leaders as "men who seemingly believe we can confound the Kremlin by frightening ourselves to death."[100]

Still, the Republican attacks resonated with the voters. Truman conceded as much when he wrote that Stevenson made a "mistake" by allowing "himself to go on the defensive on the question of so-called communists in government." By accepting the Republican assumption, Stevenson inadvertently helped spread the caricature of an incompetent, bumbling, Democrat all too willing to let communists into sensitive government posts, one that Truman dubbed "the most brazen lie of the century."[101] But whether the accusation was truth or fiction, voters demanded action: 74 percent believed the next president "should do a great deal more to clean out communists in the government"; just 15 percent thought the problem was "well under control."[102]

Communism was so important an issue in 1952 that everything else was refracted through it. That was particularly true for Richard Nixon, for whom 1952 was another in a series of political "crises." He had been tapped for the vice presidency because, in Eisenhower's words, "the question of communist infiltration and proper methods for defeating it in our country had become a burning and widespread issue."[103] After joining the ticket, Eisenhower told Nixon that the Hiss case "was a text from which I could preach everywhere in the country."[104] In a nominating speech, Frank Barrett, Wyoming's Republican governor, praised the putative veep's role in the Hiss affair: "No man did so much as Dick Nixon to put the fear of God in these men who would betray their country."[105]

Yet Nixon quickly stumbled into controversy. While serving in the U.S. Senate Nixon had established a $18,235 fund for his political use.[106] Dana Smith, a Pasadena lawyer who organized the fund, defended it by claiming that the New Deal was "full of commies, men who believe in big government and those who have a backward-looking philosophy—the real reactionaries." Smith added: "Our thinking was that we had to fight selling with selling and for the job Dick Nixon seemed to be the best salesman against socialization available. That's his gift, really—salesmanship."[107] But newspaper publicity about the fund overshadowed the Nixon campaign. At a whistle-stop in Marysville, California, Nixon rebuked a heckler who shouted "Tell them about the [money]":

> You folks know the work that I did investigating communists in the United States. Ever since I have done that work the communists and the left-wingers have been fighting me with every smear that they have been able to do.
>
> Even when I have made—after I received the nomination for the vice presidency, I want you folks to know—and I'm going to reveal it today for the first time—I was warned that if I continued to attack the communists and the crooks *in this government* they would continue to smear me, and, believe me, you can expect that they will continue to do so. . . .
>
> Just let me say this before I leave, let me say this: They have told you, and you can be sure that the smears will continue to come and the purpose of those smears is to make me if possible relent and let up on my attack on the communists and the crooks *in the present administration.*
>
> I'm going to tell you this: As far as I am concerned, they've got another guess coming, because what I intend to do is to go up and down this land, and

the more they smear the more I'm going to expose the communists and the crooks and those that defend them until they throw them all out of Washington (emphases added).[108]

After the tongue-lashing, Nixon campaign manager Murray Chotiner enthused, "Dick, all we've got to do is get you before enough people talking about this fund, and we will win this election in a landslide."[109] Nixon did just that. Under the aegis of the Republican National Committee, Nixon took to the television airwaves to make his case. In an electrifying performance before 58 million Americans, Nixon totaled the fund's receipts and expenses, then did the unexpected by disclosing his modest family finances. But Nixon reserved a large portion of his address for an attack on communism. Dutifully following Eisenhower's advice, he preached from the "gospel" of the Hiss case: "I have no apologies to the American people for my part in putting Alger Hiss where he is today."[110] Nixon cast Eisenhower as "the only man who can save America" from communism. To buttress his case, he reiterated that 600 million people had been "lost" to the communists and another 117,000 had been injured in the Korean War. Nixon blamed Truman and the State Department for these fiascoes.

Reaction to the "Checkers" speech (so named because in denying he used the fund for personal use Nixon identified the lone exception—Checkers, the family dog given as a gift to daughters Trisha and Julie) was immediate and positive. Nixon received more than 2 million letters and telegrams, the vast majority encouraging him to stay put. Among the wires received was one from Congressman Gerald R. Ford of Michigan: "I am in your corner 100 percent. Fight it to the finish just as you did the smears by the communists when you were proving charges against Alger Hiss." Whittaker Chambers agreed: "Attack on you shows how deeply the enemy fears you as he always fears and seeks to destroy a combination of honesty and courage. Be proud to be attacked for all the attackers are the enemies of all of us. To few public figures does this nation owe so much as to you. God help us if we ever forget it."[111] As the plaudits poured in, any inclination Eisenhower may have had to dump Nixon evaporated. At an airport rally in Wheeling, West Virginia, he threw his arm around Nixon, saying, "You're my boy!"[112]

The positive response to the "Checkers" speech left Nixon free to concentrate on Stevenson. Stevenson's actions during the Hiss trial gave Nixon an opening. In court, he had signed a deposition claiming that Hiss's reputation "for veracity, for integrity, and for loyalty was good."[113] Nixon accused the Democratic nominee of "going down the line for the arch traitor of our generation,"[114] and he took to the television airwaves once more to make his case. Declaring that "there is no question in my mind as to the loyalty of Mr. Stevenson," Nixon added a chilling caveat: "But the question is one as to his judgment, and it is a very grave question." He returned to a familiar theme: "In light of the record that we have, there is no question about the danger that we face today. Because we can assume that because of this cover-up of this administration in the Hiss case, that the communists, the fellow-travelers, have not been cleaned out of the executive branch of the Government."[115]

In response, Stevenson denounced Nixon and renounced any ties to Hiss. Characterizing his deposition as something any good citizen would have done, Stevenson claimed he had known Hiss only "briefly"; that "he never entered my house and I never entered his"; that his description of Hiss's reputation as "'good' so far as I had heard from others" did not differ from John Foster Dulles's; and that he "never doubted the verdict of the jury" that convicted Hiss.[116] Although Stevenson promised to "smash the [communist] conspiracy beyond repair,"[117] he warned the GOP to cease its "ugly, twisted, demagogic distortion" that "neither educates nor elevates."[118]

But the Republican attacks were taking a toll. In a nationally broadcast speech, Joseph McCarthy "slipped" twice, stating, "Alger—I mean Adlai"—laughing at his little jokes.[119] Henry Luce's *Life* magazine published an editorial entitled "Softness Toward Communism." In it, Luce wrote, "Many Americans, including Adlai Stevenson, are extremely touchy—and no wonder—about the charge of 'softness toward communism.'" Luce accused "the Acheson faction" in the Democratic party of watching Mao Zedong's victories in China "with feelings ranging from complacency to connivance"; defending "subversives in the U.S. Government with cries of 'red herring' and 'witch hunt'"; and pursuing a foreign policy responsible for enslaving 600 million people to communism. Meanwhile, *Life* charged that "treason was afoot," thereby giving McCarthy and his allies legitimate grounds for "wholesome doubt."[120] But as the Republican sniping continued, Eisenhower was caught in the crossfire.

During the campaign, McCarthy frequently referred to the Acheson-Hiss faction, which he claimed Stevenson was "part and parcel of" and which, in turn, gave "aid to the communist cause."[121] McCarthy demanded that Stevenson "answer those facts."[122] By 1952, McCarthy had become an essential Republican foil. In a candid moment, Senator John Bricker of Ohio gave McCarthy his due: "Joe, you're a real SOB, but sometimes it's useful to have SOBs around to do the dirty work."[123] Already, *McCarthyism* had crept into the lexicon, with McCarthy saying it meant "calling a man a communist who later proves to be one."[124]

In that vein, McCarthy declared that the overriding issue was the "suicidal and criminal direction of our foreign policy [that] was controlled by the communists in our government."[125] He recklessly accused Defense Secretary George Marshall of joining "a conspiracy so immense, an infamy so black, as to dwarf any in the history of man."[126] This charge incensed Eisenhower, who had been tapped by Marshall to become Allied Supreme Commander in World War II. Eisenhower seethed over McCarthy's remark, and he resolved to rebuke the senator in his home state of Wisconsin. In the prepared speech, Eisenhower lauded Marshall "as a man and as a soldier ... dedicated with singular selflessness and the profoundest patriotism to the service of America," adding that McCarthy's indictment constituted "a sobering lesson in the way freedom must *not* defend itself."[127] But when McCarthy saw an advance text of Eisenhower's speech he recognized its importance and begged him not to utter those stinging words. Indianapolis publisher Eugene C. Pulliam advised Eisenhower that it would be "a tragic mistake" to rebuke McCarthy, noting that he "has the confidence of literally millions of people who think he is being directed by God in his campaign."[128] Eisenhower finally acquiesced when campaign adviser Sherman Adams deemed the offending paragraph "an unnecessarily abrupt rebuff to McCarthy." The words were excised, but not before reporters had an advance text. Eisenhower's omission was criticized in a *New York Times* editorial: "Yesterday, could not have been a happy day for General Eisenhower ... nor was it a happy day for many supporters." Publisher Arthur Hays Sulzberger cabled Ike: "Do I need to tell you that I am sick at heart?"[129]

Ironically, what Eisenhower *did* say in that widely criticized speech bordered on McCarthyism. He argued that the loss of China and "the surrender of whole nations" in Eastern Europe were the by-products of communist infiltration in the Truman administration, which "meant—in its most ugly triumph—treason itself."[130] As if to punctuate his remarks, at the end of his speech Eisenhower physically embraced McCarthy.[131]

A Transforming Election

Tuesday, November 4, 1952, dawned cold and wet in some parts of the country. A gas-station attendant in Dennison, Texas, saw the raindrops and exclaimed: "Democratic tears! Eisenhower must be sweeping the country."[132] He was. Eisenhower's victory was sealed less than two weeks before, when he promised, "I shall go to Korea."[133] Democrats called Ike's travel plans "a cheap trick" and claimed he was playing "politics with peace."[134] Stevenson was especially bitter: "There is no greater cruelty, in my judgment, than the raising of false hopes—no greater arrogance than playing politics with peace and war. Rather than exploit human hopes and fears, rather than provide glib solutions and false assurances, I would gladly lose this presidential election."[135] But such protestations fell on deaf ears: In the month prior to the election, 65 percent were choosing Eisenhower as best able to handle Korea; only 19 percent picked Stevenson.[136]

Moreover, three days before the balloting, the United States detonated its first hydrogen bomb, prompting some scientists to reset the figurative Doomsday Clock to just *two minutes* before midnight.[137] The weapon weighed more than ten tons and unleashed the equivalent of 1 million tons of TNT—an unbelievably high figure given that the equivalent of 3 million tons of TNT were used in *all* of the explosives during *all* World War II. The rising mushroom cloud punctuated the Cold War's explosive impact on presidential politics. Eisenhower was not exaggerating when he declared that "this is not just another election, not just another clash of political personalities or political parties." In an election-eve address, he solemnly observed that Americans would choose a president at "a troubled and decisive moment in the history of man's long march from darkness toward light."[138]

Eisenhower's solemnity matched the public mood. Journalist Samuel Lubell reported that many told him that they had "prayed not once, but several times" about their vote. Sixty percent told pollsters that they had given "quite a lot of thought" how they would cast their ballots.[139] By election night, their decision was clear: Eisenhower garnered 55.1 percent of the votes and 39 states to Stevenson's 44.4 percent and 9 states. Turnout rose 26 percent, from 49 million in 1948 to 61.5 million. But the larger turnout did not help the Democrats. Even though Stevenson received 3 *million* more votes than Truman did in 1948 and came within 162,000 votes of surpassing FDR's total vote in 1936, it was not enough to prevent the worst presidential defeat in twenty-six years. Eighteen states that had consistently voted Democratic in every contest since the Roosevelt-Hoover matchup swung to the Eisenhower column. Massachusetts was one: There Ike carried every county except one—including three that had not gone Republican since 1924. In 670 counties spread throughout the northern states that had voted for Roosevelt and Truman, Eisenhower had majorities in one-quarter. Moreover, in Illinois, Indiana, Maryland, and New Mexico, Eisenhower won counties that had *never* voted Republican.[140] Even Cook County, Illinois—that bastion of Democratic machine politics—voted for Eisenhower.

As results were broadcast on election night, Secretary of State Acheson and Supreme Court Justice Frankfurter were commiserating with friends. When they and their government associates received word of the rout, many of the young people present were overcome by "a feeling of despair, almost of panic." Acheson tried to reassure the group: "Most of you are so used to a Democratic Administration and recollect so little of anything else that you think of this state of affairs as normal. But it was not normal."[141] Journalist Samuel Lubell agreed: "From the Eisenhower electoral maps, the proverbial visitor from Mars would never know that Franklin D. Roosevelt had lived."[142] Even John Roosevelt, son of Franklin, had switched parties and voted for Eisenhower.

Acheson's and Lubell's observations that the New Deal could no longer automatically deliver a presidential majority were particularly apt when votes from suburbs, from the South, and among Catholics were analyzed. Eisenhower's popularity in suburbia frequently overcame Democratic big-city tallies. For example, whereas Stevenson won a 160,000 plurality in Philadelphia proper, outlying areas cut the margin to 20,000.[143] And in New York City, Stevenson beat Eisenhower by 10.4 percent while Ike built a 13.8-point lead in four surrounding suburban counties. But even these impressive tallies were overshadowed by Eisenhower's smashing of the once-Democratic "Solid South." Early in 1952, *Life* magazine editorialized, "The new southern middle class and the Republican party need each other."[144] Two top Democrats in Texas thought so, too, as the state's governor and U.S. Senate nominee told voters they liked Ike. But they were not the only "yellow dog" Democrats who jumped ship. In addition to Texas Eisenhower carried Virginia, Tennessee, Florida, and Oklahoma and nearly won Kentucky and South Carolina. Across the Old Confederacy, Eisenhower carried 48.9 percent of the vote and 498 counties—the latter figure tripling the number Dewey posted in 1948.[145] For the first time since its founding nearly 100 years earlier, the GOP became a truly national party thanks to Eisenhower's southern victories in 1952. Not long thereafter, E. E. Schattschneider characterized Eisenhower's demolition of the Solid South as a further extension of the nationalization of U.S. politics that began with the creation of the New Deal in the 1930s.[146]

Eisenhower did even better among Catholics, winning 51 percent of their votes to Stevenson's 49 percent. Long a mainstay of the New Deal coalition, Catholic immigrants and their offspring deserted Stevenson in droves, precipitating a drop of *21 points* from Truman's 1948 Catholic vote (see Table 3.1). Eisenhower's promise that his administration would "never" recognize the "permanence" of Soviet occupation of the Captive Nations had a strong emotional context for millions of Roman Catholics.[147] Historian Richard Hofstadter wrote that the Republican party's anticommunism had caused fundamentalist Protestants and Catholics to subordinate their old feuds and join the Republican crusade against what were called "'godless' elements."[148] One analyst found more than half of Polish Americans sided with Eisenhower.[149] Typifying the feelings of many Catholics was a youthful Patrick J. Buchanan, who admired Eisenhower because he "understood power, and he knew how to deal with [communist] thugs." As for Stevenson, Buchanan derided him as "too wordy, too weak, and too foppish a figure to run the greatest country in the world."[150]

But there were some Democratic bright spots. As Table 3.1 shows, Stevenson scored best among Jews and those with some college education. Stevenson improved on Truman's Jewish vote by 24 percent—partly because Henry Wallace was not a candidate and partly because Jewish voters

TABLE 3.1
Democratic Presidential Vote Compared, 1948 and 1952 (in percentages)

Demographic Category	Stevenson	Truman	Stevenson Minus Truman
Nationwide	44	50	−6
Education			
Less than high school	45	63	−18
High school graduate	36	53	−17
Some College	39	31	+8
Religion			
Protestant	34	48	−14
Catholic	49	70	−21
Jewish	84	60	+24
Union Membership			
Yes	55	73	−18
No	36	49	−13
Age			
Less than 30 years old	47	57	−10
30–44 years old	41	58	−17
45–59 years old	39	51	−12
60 years and older	34	47	−13
Race			
White	39	52	−13
Black	75	77	−2
Sex			
Male	41	53	−12
Female	40	54	−14
Income			
Above Average	29	29	0
Average	36	47	−11
Poor	47	66	−19
Occupation			
Professional	31	38	−7
Farmers	31	42	−11
Business	34	50	−16
Clerical	38	17	+21
Sales Worker	38	46	−8
Skilled Worker	48	63	−15
Unskilled Worker	49	74	−25
Farm Laborer	40	41	−1
Laborers	47	67	−20
Region			
New England	41	45	−4
Mid-Atlantic	40	53	−13
East Central	41	54	−13
West Central	32	55	−23

(continues)

TABLE 3.1   *(continued)*

Demographic Category	Stevenson	Truman	Stevenson Minus Truman
Southern	53	56	−3
Rocky Mountain	36	51	−15
Pacific	39	55	−16

SOURCE: Gallup polls, November 3–8, 1948, and November 14–19, 1952. Text of 1948 question: "Did you vote for Truman, Dewey, Wallace or Thurmond?" Text of 1952 question: "Did you happen to vote for Stevenson or Eisenhower?" Only those who voted were questioned.

perceived Stevenson as a liberal. His 8-point gain among those with some college reflected the Democratic party's newfound popularity among the so-called GI intellectuals.[151] Even at Columbia University, where Eisenhower had been president, Stevenson was preferred. Eric Severeid wrote that Stevenson "excited the passions of the *mind*."[152] That was reflected in print media: Magazines that catered to the "common man" (*Reader's Digest, Saturday Evening Post*) liked Ike; Stevenson won endorsements from more upscale publications (*New Yorker, Harpers, Atlantic Monthly*).[153]

Thus, twenty years before George McGovern became a campus phenomenon, Adlai Stevenson was enticing college students to become Democrats. The results were long-lasting. Val Bjornson, who (unsuccessfully) challenged Hubert Humphrey in his 1954 Senate race, wrote Republican National Chairman Leonard Hall that the "Humphrey machine is a college campus product here in Minnesota," adding that its supply of recruits was "non-ending." Bjornson bemoaned his party's inability to attract "a devoted group of really sharp, intellectual young folks."[154] At Dakota Wesleyan University, Stevenson's candidacy enticed a young history lecturer to enter politics. George McGovern lauded Stevenson's high intelligence, character, and common sense in a series of articles for the *Daily Republic* in Mitchell, South Dakota.[155]

But, Jews and college activists aside, the decline in Democratic totals was both precipitous and prescient. From 1952 to 1988, Democrats lost the White House seven times in ten elections—winning only with John F. Kennedy in 1960; Lyndon B. Johnson in 1964; and Jimmy Carter in 1976. Eisenhower's 1952 win began a Republican presidential era that lasted for the duration of the Cold War.

Still, Eisenhower's victory was incomplete from the GOP's perspective. Nineteen fifty-two gave birth to a new phenomena: ticket-splitting. Republicans thought an Eisenhower-led ticket would produce a Democratic debacle. But voters refused to follow the script. Only four in ten agreed that one "should vote for the same party for president and Congress."[156] One reason was the decidedly mixed strengths of the two parties. Gallup found 50 percent choosing the Democrats as "best for people like yourself"; only 30 percent picked the Republicans.[157] In addition, 48 percent believed there would be more unemployment if Eisenhower won; and 47 percent said they would be better off financially if Stevenson won.[158] But when asked which party was "likely to do the better job of keeping us out of another world war," 43 percent answered Republican; only 24 percent selected the Democrats.[159] For the first time since the New Deal, the electorate had a schizophrenic view of the two parties.

That schizophrenia was reflected in state after state in which voters rendered a mixed verdict. In Florida, for example, Eisenhower got 54.6 percent while the Republican gubernatorial candidate received a paltry 27 percent.[160] In Wisconsin, Ike ran 100,000 votes ahead of Joseph McCarthy, and in Massachusetts Democrat John F. Kennedy wrested a Senate seat away from Republican Henry Cabot Lodge even though Eisenhower swept the state. Likewise, Democratic senatorial candidates Stuart Symington, Mike Mansfield, and Henry Jackson bucked the Eisenhower tide in their respective states—winning in Missouri, Montana, and Washington. Thus, even though some Republican Senate candidates met with success—notably Barry Goldwater in Arizona—they exceeded the Eisenhower totals in only five states.[161]

In Congress, voters gave Republicans the most tenuous of victories. After the balloting, control of the Senate remained uncertain until Wayne Morse deserted the Republicans following the Eisenhower-McCarthy episode, thereby splitting the upper house. Vice President Nixon's vote broke the tie. In the House, Republicans added twenty-two seats to win a razor-thin eight-seat majority. Yet when all the congressional votes were counted, Democrats had 28,715,000, compared to 28,470,000 for the Republicans. Analyzed from a different perspective, Eisenhower got 6 million votes more than his ticket mates—a *10 percent* differential. Speaker of the House Joseph Martin conceded, "I don't think we would have won if Eisenhower had not headed the ticket."[162] Indeed not. Four years later, even though Ike headed the ticket once again, Republicans lost the Congress.

After the campaign, a jubilant John Foster Dulles praised Eisenhower for a "superb campaign," adding that he knew Ike was glad "to have this one behind you and be moving on from the phase of words to the phase of deeds."[163] But Eisenhower's words, and those of his fellow Republicans, had changed electoral maps. Both the outgoing and incoming presidents felt the weight of the Cold War. As the moving vans surrounded the White House, Harry Truman followed the tradition established by George Washington and gave a farewell address. In it, he wrote an epitaph: "I suppose that history will remember my term in office as the years when the 'Cold War' began to overshadow our lives. I have had hardly a day in office that has not been dominated by this all-embracing struggle—this conflict between those who love freedom and those who would lead the world back into slavery and darkness. And always in the background there has been the atomic bomb."[164] For his part, Eisenhower acknowledged the Cold War's political impact: "As we heralded political victory the night of November 4, 1952, it was a far different world from that of May 8, 1945, the day I announced military victory over the Nazis. In place of the exuberance we had felt then, there was now sober thoughtfulness, for the world was caught up in a grim long-range struggle between former associated powers—the Free World on the one hand and Soviet Russia, with the now communized China, on the other."[165]

The new world order that Eisenhower alluded to had set the stage for 1952 to become a transforming election. Adlai Stevenson was among the first to realize this, saying that the globe was "in the torment of transition from an age that has died to an age struggling to be born."[166] Political scientists James MacGregor Burns and Philip Hastings reported that for many voters "Eisenhower served as a symbol of national security much as Roosevelt served as a symbol of economic security."[167] University of Utah Professor Val Jamison went even further: "It's not just that a great man [Stevenson] has been defeated. It's that a whole era is ended, is totally repudiated, a whole era of brains and literacy and exciting thinking."[168] Jamison, one of the new intellectuals attracted to Stevenson, overstated things—but not by much. Eisenhower was the last president to be born in the nineteenth century—but how he handled the Cold War would transform American politics until nearly the end of the twentieth century. Thanks to the eclipse of the isolationists that was accelerated after Taft's defeat, Eisenhower was able to forge an anticommunist "consensus" with Democratic congressional leaders Lyndon Johnson and Sam Rayburn. By 1960, the grand union was so successful that Daniel Bell heralded the "end of ideology."[169]

But politics during the Cold War—although different from that of bygone eras—did not die. Politics involves manipulating emotions, and until the Soviet Union collapsed in 1991 both parties continued to plot their opposition to communism. Their successes and failures in this contest are explored in Chapters 4 and 5.

Part Two

The Cold War Party System

chapter four

The Nationalist Republicans

We must recognize this war as a war . . . and we must win it.

—Barry M. Goldwater, *Why Not Victory?* (1962)

January 20, 1953

On a sunny and unseasonably warm day thousands gathered on the east front of the U.S. Capitol to witness the swearing-in of the thirty-fourth president, Dwight David Eisenhower, and the thirty-sixth vice president, Richard Milhous Nixon. Several luminaries were sprinkled about the crowd, including former presidents Harry S. Truman and Herbert Hoover—the latter attending his first inauguration in twenty years. The newly elected Senator John F. Kennedy, Senate Minority Leader Lyndon B. Johnson, and Congressman Gerald R. Ford were also present. The mood was outwardly festive, especially among the remaining 750,000 onlookers who flocked to the nation's capital to watch the first Republican president in two decades take office. Yet amid the joy of the moment lay an uncertainty about the direction of the Cold War. In his Inaugural Address, Eisenhower struck a somber tone: "We sense with all our faculties that forces of good and evil are massed and armed and opposed as rarely before in history." Eisenhower put the central question thus: "How far have we come in man's long pilgrimage from darkness toward the light? Are we nearing the light—a day of freedom and of peace for all mankind? Or are the shadows of another night closing in upon us?"[1] As if to dramatize his query, the crowd fell silent when, during the Inaugural Parade, an atomic gun rolled down Pennsylvania Avenue on a block-long carriage. Arthur Krock wrote in the *New York Times* that the silence "showed that people were conscious that they live in a dangerous world where deterrent force was the only argument a powerful enemy understood."[2]

Indeed, the problems besetting the new administration derived almost entirely from the Cold War, and their magnitude was daunting, as Eisenhower wrote in his memoirs:

> Two wars, with the United States deeply engaged in one, and vitally concerned in the other, were raging in Eastern Asia; Iran seemed to be almost ready to fall into communist hands; the NATO Alliance had as yet found no positive way to mobilize into its defenses the latent strength of West Germany; Red China seemed increasingly bent on using force to advance its boundaries; Austria was still an occupied country, and Soviet intransigence was keeping it so. European economies were not yet recovered from World War II. Communism was striving to establish its first beachhead in the Americas by gaining control of Guatemala.[3]

But in four short years things would change. On July 27, 1953, the Korean War ended with a signed armistice in Panmunjom. Soviet troops vacated Austria. Iran and Guatemala were no longer teetering toward communism, having been "liberated from Kremlin control"[4] by CIA-inspired coups. Eisenhower boasted in 1963 that his aggressive leadership had reversed the Red tide: "We have seen an end to the old pattern of tragedy: Not a single nation has been surrendered to aggression. We have maintained this defense of freedom without recourse to war."[5] But even as Eisenhower pursued an aggressive anticommunist foreign policy he attempted to place constraints on the Cold War. He introduced the Atoms for Peace Plan, which resulted in agreements with thirty nations for research nuclear reactors and the setting aside of 20,000 kilograms of uranium 235 for sale or lease to friendly nations.[6] Later, he agreed to a July 1955 summit with the Soviet premier, Nikita Khrushchev, in "neutral" Geneva, Switzerland. There Eisenhower bluntly told his Soviet counterpart: "War has failed. The only way to save the world is through diplomacy." Khrushchev, in turn, agreed to seek "an acceptable system of disarmament" and "a progressive elimination of barriers which interfere with free communication and peaceful trade between people."[7] Eisenhower believed these people-to-people programs might contain a possibility that citizens from the two superpowers would voluntarily end the Cold War: "We are beginning to be able—cautiously and with our eyes open—to encourage some interchange of ideas, of books, magazines, students, tourists, artists, radio programs, technical experts, religious leaders and government officials. The hope is that, little by little, mistrust based on falsehoods will give way to international understanding based on truth."[8]

Convinced that war was an anachronism, Eisenhower, in his Acceptance Speech for renomination at the 1956 Republican National Convention, told the enthusiastic throng: "We are in the era of the thermonuclear bomb that can obliterate cities and can be delivered across continents. With such weapons, war has become, not just tragic, but preposterous." Warming up to his peroration, he summoned the "Geneva Spirit," asking voters to give him another term so that he could end the Cold War by bridging "the great chasm that separates us from the peoples under communist rule."[9] In their platform, the party faithful applauded this noble idealism, as well as the leader who provided it: "Nearly four years ago when the people of this Nation entrusted their Government to President Eisenhower and the Republican party, we were locked in a costly and stalemated war. Now we have an honorable peace, which has stopped the bitter toll in casualties and resources, ended the depressing wartime restraints, curbed the runaway inflation, and unleashed the boundless energy of our people to forge forward on the road to progress."[10] Attempting to sell this program of "waging peace," the Republican National Committee distributed 1 million pamphlets showing a wounded veteran in a hospital bed who exclaimed, "Isn't one war in a man's lifetime more than enough?" A woman added: "When Ike flew to Korea in '52 as he promised, I didn't dare let myself believe that he could accomplish anything. But a few months later our wedding bells rang—right after Jim came home from Korea—that was Ike's wedding present to us."[11]

Yet while Republicans were busily "waging peace" they also continued to make war preparations—just in case. Accepting renomination, Eisenhower noted that the nation was ready for war: "The compelling necessities of the moment leave us no alternative to the maintenance of real and respectable strength—not only in our moral rectitude and our economic power, but in terms of adequate military preparedness."[12] In their platform Republicans lauded the military forces being developed by the Pentagon, which included the following: "a jet-powered, long-range strategic air force with a striking capability superior to any other"; "the most effective guided and ballistic missiles"; "a modern navy, with a powerful naval aircraft arm prepared to keep the sea lanes open to meet any assignment"; "an army whose mobility and unit firepower are without equal"; and "bases, strategically dispersed at home and around the world, essential to all these operations."[13] Presiding over this vast military establishment was, in Vice President Nixon's words, "the greatest Commander-in-Chief America has ever had who knows how to maintain the military strength necessary to deter aggression by the men in the Kremlin and Peiping." Nixon derided Eisenhower's hapless 1956 opponent, Adlai E. Stevenson, as "a jittery, inexperienced novice who is eager to have the job but who is utterly unqualified to make the great decisions demanded by the times." The vice president later amplified on his theme of Democratic weakness, telling a Harlem audience that Stevenson was not in Eisenhower's league when it came to dealing with communists: "The butchers of the Kremlin would make mincemeat of Stevenson over a conference table."[14] Republicans agreed, and so widened their broadside to include all Democrats, claiming, "They are still the party that spawned Alger Hiss."[15]

Peace, prosperity, preparedness, and the alleged naïveté of the Democrats proved to be winning themes for Eisenhower and Nixon. More than a year prior to the election, historian Arthur M. Schlesinger Jr. advised Senator John F. Kennedy that foreign policy was a nonstarter as an effective political issue: "The main difference between Eisenhower and the Democrats in foreign affairs will be differences of degree and detail; and these differences will probably not lend themselves to effective political rejection."[16] Schlesinger proved right. When the ballots were counted, Eisenhower beat Stevenson even more decisively than he had four years earlier—winning forty-one states and 57.7 percent of the popular vote. As in 1952, the South proved hospitable to Eisenhower's message of peace through strength. Louisiana voted Republican for the first time since 1876. Kentucky and West Virginia, having supported Stevenson four years earlier, also deserted the Democrat. Maryland cast its largest vote ever for a Republican presidential candidate, giving Eisenhower a 183,311-vote margin.

But the South was not alone in supporting Ike. Every northern state landed in the Eisenhower column, including Stevenson's home state of Illinois. Eisenhower's wins in Connecticut and New Jersey were the largest in those state's histories, and his 1.5 million plurality in New York exceeded Warren Harding's 1920 landslide there. Even Democratic machine–controlled Chicago voted Republican—for the first time since 1928. So, too, did other big cities, including Baltimore, Los Angeles, Milwaukee, San Francisco, Jersey City, and New Haven. The day after the balloting, *New York Times* correspondent James Reston wrote, "Dwight David Eisenhower won yesterday the most spectacular presidential election victory since Franklin D. Roosevelt submerged Alfred M. Landon in 1936."[17] *Newsweek* concluded that millions liked Ike because "he knows how to deal firmly and effectively with the Russians." The *New York Times* agreed: "At home, Dwight David Eisenhower has undergone a remarkable transformation from a hero of a war to hero of an era where there is neither war nor peace. But in that era he is relied upon heavily by most of his countrymen to wage the peace successfully—and in an atmosphere of prosperity and plenty."[18]

But the Democrats were far from vanquished, having hung on to Congress, which they had won back in the 1954 elections. Despite Eisenhower's landslide, Democrats held a 49-to-47 majority in the Senate and a 234-to-201 majority in the House. Never before in history had a party lost the White House by such a large margin and yet won the Congress. The Democrats' appeal was further demonstrated in state races, where they added one governorship, giving them a 28-to-20 advantage—and they occupied nearly all the executive mansions in the large industrial states.

Still, Eisenhower welcomed the outcome, saying "it is a very heartwarming experience to know that your labors, your efforts of four years have achieved that level where they are approved by the United States of America in a vote." Speaking to a room filled with cheering supporters at 1:45 the morning after the election, Eisenhower claimed to have won a mandate for the "principles and ideals" of Modern Republicanism: "I think that Modern Republicanism has now proved itself and America has approved of Modern Republicanism."[19] In asserting a partisan mandate, however flimsy, Eisenhower took his cue from Arthur Larson, a former Rhodes scholar and dean at the University of Pittsburgh who joined the Eisenhower administration as Undersecretary of Labor. Author of a book entitled *A Republican Looks at His Party*, Larson theorized that voters had reached consensus on most fundamental issues. He attributed the resultant formation of the "Authentic American Center" to the Cold War: "Principles that we have always taken for granted as the air we breathe are now flatly denounced and denied over a large part of the world—the principles, for example, of the preeminence and the freedom and the sovereignty of the individual person." The Cold War gave Larson's Authentic Center its staying power: "We are playing for keeps now, with staggering world responsibilities that we cannot escape." Thus, foreign policy agreement sustained the Authentic Center, since "lasting peace cannot come about solely by military strength, but requires that a start be made, however difficult and discouraging, toward the kind of understanding and communication throughout the world which is a necessary foundation on which to build progress toward disarmament and genuine peace."[20]

Not surprisingly, Larson credited Eisenhower with fathering the Authentic Center, since his grudging acceptance of the New Deal, coupled with a strong dose of anticommunism, had forged a "New Republicanism." By occupying the Authentic Center, the GOP was transformed from a bunch of naysayers in the 1930s and 1940s into a patriotic party that spoke for U.S. interests abroad and moderate progressivism at home. As Eisenhower told his fellow Republicans in 1956:

> The Republican party is again the rallying point of Americans of all callings, ages, races, and incomes. They see in its broad, forward-moving, straight-down-the road, fighting program the best promise for their own steady progress toward a bright future. Some opponents have tried to call this a "one-interest party." Indeed it is a one-interest party; and that one interest is the interest of every man, woman, and child in America! And most surely, as long as the Republican party continues to be this kind of one-interest party—a one-universal-interest party—it will continue to be the Party of the Future.[21]

If Eisenhower was correct, the political dividends would be enormous. Larson predicted that by capturing the Authentic Center Republicans would be in "a position of almost unbeatable strength." But to keep the Authentic Center, Larson advised that the word "conservative" be expunged from the party vocabulary: "[If,] as seems unlikely, the Republicans were some day to nominate a candidate for the presidency who was identified with an extreme conservative position, and if, as seems equally unlikely, the Democrats were to seize that moment to choose a nominee who took over the formula of the great middle way, the Democratic candidate would most certainly win, and thereafter it would be difficult indeed for the Republicans to get back in."[22]

Not everyone agreed. Senate Republican Barry Goldwater of Arizona accused Eisenhower of running "a dime-store New Deal."[23] House Republican Noah Mason denounced Ike's New Republicanism as "a form of bribery, a program to buy votes with the voters' own money." Robert T. Mount, a Republican National Committee member from Oregon, agreed: "If we don't get back to fundamental Republicanism we are not men of distinction, but men of extinction."[24] But theirs were distinctly minority views within the GOP ranks. By refurbishing the Republican party into a nonpartisan vehicle acting in the national interest, Eisenhower muted what remained of the give-and-take of politics by presiding over the creation of the national security state. Two landmark laws formed its underpinnings: the National Defense Education Act and the Federal Aid Highway Act. Approved by large bipartisan majorities in both houses of Congress, these measures changed the nation as much as the New Deal and Fair Deal ever had. The $1 billion contained in the National Defense Education Act provided for a fivefold increase in funds for the National Science Foundation; created 5,500 graduate fellowships; established a system of matching grants to allow colleges to expand their graduate programs in the sciences; and allocated federal dollars to the states to employ additional science and math teachers, purchase laboratory equipment, improve testing and guidance programs, and expand foreign-language programs. For good measure, the bill also contained a loyalty-oath provision requiring recipients of federal dollars to pledge that they did not believe in, belong to, or support, any "subversive organization."[25] But the resultant legislation gave the federal government a role in what had heretofore been considered a matter for local and state governments.

In making his pitch for these laws, Eisenhower sold most of the remaining recalcitrant anti–New Deal Republicans on the idea of an enlarged domestic government in the name of national security. At the signing ceremony held on September 2, 1958, Eisenhower noted that the new law would do much "to strengthen our American system of education so it can meet the broad and increasing demands of national security."[26] In fact, Eisenhower had foretold this plan for full-scale citizen participation in the

Cold War in his 1953 Inaugural Address when he declared that "no person, no home, no community can be beyond the reach of this call."[27] Science teachers were only one group drawn into the defense bulwark, as the National Defense Education Act made clear: "The present emergency demands that additional and adequate educational opportunities be made available. The defense of this Nation depends upon the mastery of modern technology developed from complex scientific principles. We must increase our efforts to identify and educate more of the talent of our Nation. This requires programs that will give assurances that no student of ability will be denied an opportunity for higher education because of financial need."[28] A Senate subcommittee agreed: "We have reached a stage of history where defense involves the total effort of a nation."[29]

Joining the new army of Cold Warriors were hard hats—construction workers who were politically and culturally at odds with the New Left. Eisenhower told Congress that a new federally funded interstate highway network was needed to facilitate troop and tank movements should the Soviets attack. When Eisenhower first proposed a massive highway construction bill in 1955, it failed on a vote of 123 to 292 in the House of Representatives. After this overwhelming defeat, Eisenhower changed tactics. Donning his commander-in-chief hat, the Republican president told the Democratic-controlled Congress that constructing an interstate highway system was a national security matter: "Motorists by the millions would read a primary purpose in the signs that would sprout up alongside the pavement: 'In the event of an enemy attack, this road will be closed.'"[30] Congress concurred, and on June 29, 1956, Eisenhower signed the Federal Aid Highway Act into law. From Long Island to Long Beach, a vast network of interconnected highways would provide, literally and figuratively, concrete evidence of the nation's anticommunist resolve.

The political effect of these two laws was to remove the issues in question—education and transportation—from partisanship. Each was put before the public as a life-or-death matter. This made Eisenhower's domestic legacy stylistically and substantively different from Franklin Roosevelt's New Deal or Harry Truman's Fair Deal—each of which was subject to fierce Republican attacks. But by covering domestic issues with a national security blanket, Modern Republicans could not fully capture the Authentic Center, because it had little tolerance for what Eisenhower decried as "the sordid politics of pitting group against group."[31] Thus, the *person* who set atop the national state as president was of grave importance, as the seriousness of the Cold War created a preoccupation with the character of a potential chief executive rather than the party label under which he ran. The center could hold—paraphrasing William Butler Yeats's famous poem *The Second Coming*—but without political parties providing the glue to give issues their partisan tinge.

Samuel Lubell was among the first to understand this reordering of domestic politics. In a prescient 1951 book titled *The Future of American Politics*, he wrote that the Cold War "in a crude sort of way ... has transformed the American economy into a gigantic agency for the redistribution of our national income. So huge are the costs of rearmament that almost every spending action of the government involves taking something from one citizen and giving it to another." In the new politics, Lubell claimed that the burgeoning defense industry had transformed the presidency into "a more glittering prize than ever": "Whoever sits at the levers of power in Washington can decide which groups shall bear the heaviest costs of rearmament and which groups shall escape lightly."[32] This interweaving of political, industrial, and military interests worried Eisenhower. In his memorable 1961 Farewell Address, the outgoing president saw the potential of a "military-industrial complex" to alter existing constitutional arrangements:

> This conjunction of an immense military establishment and a large arms industry is new in the American experience. The total influence—economic, political, even spiritual—is felt in every city, every statehouse, every office of the federal government. We recognize the imperative need for this development. Yet we must not fail to comprehend its grave implications. Our toil, resources and livelihood are all involved; so is the very structure of our society.
>
> In the councils of government we must guard against the acquisition of unwarranted influence, whether sought or unsought, by the military-industrial complex. The potential for the disastrous rise of misplaced power exists and will persist.
>
> We must never let the weight of this combination endanger our liberties or democratic processes. We should take nothing for granted. Only an alert and knowledgeable citizenry can compel the proper meshing of the huge industrial and military machinery of defense with our peaceful methods and goals, so that security and liberty may prosper together.[33]

Despite Eisenhower's admonishments, the "military-industrial complex" grew exponentially. By 1961, the defense establishment employed 3.5 million, and more was spent on military security than the net income of all U.S. corporations. Universities formed an important component of the military-industrial establishment: Eisenhower noted that the enormous sums needed to develop new weaponry meant that "a government contract becomes virtually a substitute for intellectual curiosity."[34]

The result was a military-industrial-labor-university network that had an insatiable craving for bigger, more powerful weapons. To illustrate: In 1953, the Joint Chiefs of Staff advised Eisenhower that if the United States could hit seventy targets inside the Soviet Union, the Red Army would not wage war. Eight years later it raised the stakes tenfold to 700 targets, prompting an exasperated Ike to remark, "Why don't we go completely crazy and plan on a force of 10,000?"[35] By 1974, that target was reached as both sides had 2,500 nuclear missiles, most of them MIRVed, meaning that each weapon could target several independent sites. During his post-presidential years, Eisenhower often warned that the unchecked power of the military-industrial complex made public policy "the captive of a scientific-technological elite."[36] On his deathbed at Walter Reed Army Hospital in 1969, Eisenhower privately informed Nixon that he "totally disapproved" of the Anti-Ballistic Missile system, or ABM, a defense program fiercely supported by the new president—and the first of Nixon's many battles with the Democratic-controlled Congress.[37]

Despite Eisenhower's attempts to achieve a cold peace with the Soviets, there remained a realization that, as he admitted in his Farewell Address, communism was "global in scope, atheistic in character, ruthless in purpose, and insidious in method." "Unhappily," he concluded, "the danger it poses promises to be of indefinite duration."[38] Indeed, the United States was to remain on the precipice of war with the Soviets for decades to come.

Waging Peace

In 1954, the United States exploded a second hydrogen bomb. This one was small enough to be deployed—unlike the H-bomb detonated two years earlier—yet big enough to vaporize a city the size of Pittsburgh. Beacon Wax celebrated the bomb's explosion by taking out newspaper advertisements that read: "The bomb's brilliant gleam reminds me of the brilliant gleam Beacon Wax gives to floors. It's a scientific marvel!"[39] Meanwhile, President Eisenhower sought to reassure the public should the Soviets develop a bomb that could reach America's shores. *Life* magazine published a photograph of a grinning Ike leading his staff to an underground White House shelter.[40]

But instead of allaying fears, the picture frightened many readers. Many remained convinced that the "communist conspiracy" had infiltrated the innermost councils of government. Joseph McCarthy toured the countryside delivering a harangue titled "Twenty Years of Treason." In it, he railed against former president Truman and the U.S. army for not court-martialing a dentist named Irving Peress, a former member of the left-wing American Labor Party. "Who promoted Peress?" became McCarthy's rallying cry. In San Mateo, California, 6,000 paid $1.50 each to hear him attack Truman's "idiocy" and Acheson's "deceit." Privately, McCarthy included Eisenhower on his blacklist of those duped by the communists. Writer Richard Reeves remembered that many believed McCarthy's charges—"at least we did in my house."[41]

Others emulated McCarthy's Red-baiting tactics. The National Republican Congressional Campaign Committee produced a radio commercial that exacerbated voter fears. Over the roar of machinery, a voice exclaimed:

"Those are the printing presses of the Communist Party. Listen to them!" The noise of the presses grew louder, then faded, as the announcer continued: "The date is April 1954. Those printing presses are turning out the official Communist Party line."[42] Congress, Republican-controlled at this time, approved the Communist Control Act of 1954 that made the U.S. Communist Party illegal. Other forms of censorship took place. The U.S. Information Service ordered Henry David Thoreau's *Walden* removed from U.S. embassy shelves because it was "downright socialistic."[43] Other embassies blacklisted Dashiel Hammett's detective classics, including *The Maltese Falcon* and *The Thin Man*, claiming Hammett was a "Fifth Amendment communist" since he refused to testify before HUAC. Another overseas library decided to comply with a State Department order to remove all books by "fellow-travelers" and tossed every work critical of Nationalist China from its bookcases.[44] These missives resonated with the American public: 58 percent agreed with the proposition that "the Republicans have gotten rid of a lot of Reds in the government" was a strong argument for supporting the GOP.[45]

As the hysteria intensified, the Senate voted 85 to 1 to give McCarthy $215,000 to conduct an inquiry into the alleged treachery within the U.S. army. From April 22 to June 17, 1954, millions watched the 187 televised hours of the Army-McCarthy hearings—the nation's first prolonged assembly before their TV screens. One could hardly pass a department-store window without seeing a knot of customers viewing the proceedings. But when McCarthy had clearly, grievously overstepped the bounds of propriety—on June 9, 1954, Army Special Counsel Joseph Welch leveled the famous indictment: "Senator. . . . Have you left no sense of decency?"—Republicans abandoned him in droves. Eisenhower told White House staffers, "I've made up my mind you can't do business with Joe, and to hell with any attempt to compromise." Party chairman Leonard Hall dutifully announced that he could no longer "go along" with McCarthy's sniping at "persons who are fighting communists just as conscientiously as he is." Senate Republican Ralph Flanders of Vermont accused McCarthy of "doing his best to shatter the party whose label he wears." Meanwhile, Adlai Stevenson claimed the GOP was "hopelessly, dismally, fatally, torn and rent . . . divided against itself, half McCarthy and half Eisenhower."[46]

To head off potential division within the Republican ranks, Eisenhower persuaded his reluctant vice president to make a televised response to Stevenson. In it, Nixon denounced the U.S. Communist Party as "a bunch of rats" but instructed his fellow Republicans how to hunt them successfully: "When you go out to shoot rats, you have to shoot straight, because when you shoot wildly it not only means that the rat may get away more easily, but you may also hit someone else who's trying to shoot rats, too." Eisenhower speechwriter William Bragg Ewald recalled that Nixon "appealed to the centrist citizen, the anti-communist man or woman whom he could persuade to desert the McCarthy formula (chemically pure anti-communism diluted by disreputable methods) for the Eisenhower formula (chemically pure anti-communism compounded by fair play and decency)."[47] The U.S. Senate followed the "returns," deciding on December 2, 1954, by a vote of 67 to 22, to "condemn" McCarthy. Among those who dissented were Barry Goldwater, for whom McCarthy had campaigned, and John F. Kennedy, from whom McCarthy had stayed away during his tough 1952 election battle.[48] Goldwater and Kennedy were far from alone in countenancing McCarthy. On the day McCarthy was reprimanded, an armored Brink's truck deposited 1,000,816 pro-McCarthy signatures at the Capitol. But McCarthy was a beaten man. On May 2, 1957, three years after his public disgrace, he died an alcoholic at age forty-eight.

Though McCarthy was gone, the anticommunist fears he exploited remained. Repeated war-scares sustained both the public's hostility toward communism and its fear of another war—thereby greatly enhancing Eisenhower's political standing. Indeed, by their aggressive behavior the communist bloc almost seemed determined to ensure another Eisenhower victory. On August 23, 1956, while leaving his hotel room to accept renomination, Eisenhower received word that China had shot down a navy patrol plane off its coast. Wreckage and a few bodies were spotted in the water. Two months later—on October 29—a more serious crisis developed when the Middle East experienced the first of many eruptions. The ensuing war over the Suez Canal carried the danger that the superpowers might tangle for this vital waterway—a prospect Eisenhower called "somber."[49]

In November another potential flash point occurred: Forty-eight hours before the polls opened, 250,000 Soviet troops invaded Hungary with orders to install a more friendly communist regime there. By election day the Hungarian freedom fighters were crushed, and survivors were fleeing to neighboring Austria. The whole world was watching. Even Adlai Stevenson was more interested in events in Eastern Europe than his own election prospects. Embittered Democrats charged the Russian invasion resulted from a misguided foreign policy. As one Stevenson aide sarcastically told a reporter, "Apparently all you have to do to win elections is to make fatal mistakes in foreign policy."[50]

Whatever the case, the Hungarian and Suez crises clinched Eisenhower's reelection. Americans were not ready to change presidents when war loomed. A November poll found 56 percent saying that the United States would have to fight the Soviet Union "sooner or later," with 23 percent predicting an "all-out" war within two years.[51] Pollster Louis Bean reported that 3.5 million voted for Eisenhower because of the foreign crises, transforming a close election into a landslide.[52] Stevenson campaign manager Jim Finnegan agreed, noting that the Hungarian crisis resulted in a 4–7 percent boost for Eisenhower.[53] Commentator Eric Severeid reported that Eisenhower's victory was more than a single man's triumph: "It was a kind of drawing together of the great majority in a manifestation to a threatening world that we are one people."[54]

Eisenhower's victory did not quell public worries. On October 4, 1957, the communists put a 184-pound satellite into orbit. Less than a month later, another Soviet satellite was launched, this one weighing a half-ton and carrying a live dog. For many Americans, these twin Sputniks turned the sky red. Many looked toward the heavens and saw (or thought they saw) the communist menace flying out of reach. Lyndon Johnson recalled walking with his wife and dinner guests along Texas's Pedernales River, scanning the night sky searching for Sputnik: "As we stood on the lonely country road that runs between our house and the Pedernales River, I felt uneasy and apprehensive. In the open West, you learn to live closely with the sky. It is part of your life. But now, somehow, in some new way, the sky seemed almost alien. I also remember the profound shock of realizing that it might be possible for another nation to achieve technological superiority over this great country of ours."[55]

Johnson later equated the Sputniks with John F. Kennedy's assassination, saying these "two traumatic events shook the nation and created a new climate for action."[56] An editorial note in the *Portland Oregonian* characterized life as "downright terrifying with those Sputniks staring down at us." Writer Eric Goldman caught the fear these hunks of Soviet metal emitted: "Sputniks I and II dramatized as nothing else could have done that the chief thing on which Americans had depended for their national security and for victory in a competitive coexistence with communism—the supremacy of American technical know-how—had been bluntly challenged."[57] One analyst recalled that the orbiting Sputniks had transformed the Russians into "sadists with brains."[58] On January 1, 1959, sadism reached close to America's shores with Fidel Castro's ascension to power in Cuba.

These Soviet thrusts brought cries for retribution. In a July 1959 memo, Vice President Nixon admonished his speechwriters never to mention peaceful coexistence with the communists: "This is the Acheson line in the State Department and I will not put it out!!!!"[59] But Eisenhower understood that retaliation required calibration. In January 1956, Secretary of State John Foster Dulles told *Life* magazine that the administration had perfected a technique for responding to communist threats. Recalling U.S. plans to bomb China during the Korean War, Dulles told how he and Eisenhower chose "specific targets reasonably related to the area. They did not involve massive destruction of great population centers like Shanghai, Peking or Canton." Dulles noted that in making such calibrated responses, the communist must "know in advance that he is going to lose more than he can win. He doesn't have to lose *much* more. It just has to be *something* more."[60] For Dulles, brinkmanship was a risky, but necessary, component for waging peace:

> You have to take chances for peace, just as you must take chances in war. Some say that we were brought to the verge of war. The ability to get to the verge without getting into war is the necessary art. If you cannot master it, you inevitably get into war. If you try to run away from it, if you are scared to go to the brink, you are lost. We've had to look it square in the face on the question of enlarging the Korean War, on the question of Formosa. We walked to the brink and we looked it square in the face.[61]

Dulles thought Eisenhower an expert at this high-wire act. He touted Ike's coolness in the crucible of decisionmaking, telling *Life's* readers: "The president never flinched for a minute on any of these situations. He came up taut."[62] Adlai Stevenson flailed at Dulles, saying he was "shocked that the Secretary of State is willing to play Russian roulette with the life of our nation." Louis Douglas, a prominent Democrat supporting Eisenhower's reelection, said Dulles's remarks "made it difficult for the great mass of independent people, and for the large number who crossed from the shore of our one party to the shore of another in 1952." White House Chief of Staff Sherman Adams agreed, calling the Dulles interview "most unfortunate."[63] But Dulles's intemperate remarks revealed a Cold War axiom: Be willing to go to the verge of war without inadvertently crossing the line. That view was shared by a majority of Americans: 54 percent agreed that the United States "should maintain its dominant position as the world's most powerful nation at all costs, even going to the very brink of war, if necessary."[64]

To espouse war without making it, Republicans believed a strong national defense was needed to back up their bellicose rhetoric. Thus, they belligerently professed their anticommunism while wielding nuclear-tipped weapons. Republicans had no problem identifying who the enemy was and which side they were on. During the Vietnam War, for example, Richard Nixon instructed his staff never to use neutral words such as "the other side"; instead, they were always to say "the enemy," "communist," or "invaders," whenever mentioning the North Vietnamese.[65] To back up their threats, Republicans advocated a "total force policy."[66] Throughout the Cold War, in mantra-like fashion, Republicans chanted that if they won at the polls the United States would remain "number one." The 1960 platform declared: "As long as world tensions menace us with war, we are resolved to maintain an armed power exceeded by no other."[67] To the party faithful, superiority meant keeping "the nation's sword sharp, ready, and dependable."[68] Sixteen years later only the words had changed: "A superior national defense is the fundamental condition for a secure America and for peace in the world. Military strength is the path to peace. A sound foreign policy must be rooted in a superior defense capability, and both must be perceived as a deterrent to aggression and supportive of our national interests."[69]

But in vowing never to "unilaterally disarm America,"[70] Republicans became enthusiastic proponents of U.S. technology as an instrument for winning the Cold War. Barry Goldwater wrote in *Conscience of a Conservative*, "If our objective is victory over communism, we must achieve superiority in all of the weapons—military, as well as political and economic—that may be useful in reaching that goal."[71] Republicans railed against excessive domestic expenditures, but when it came to paring the Pentagon budget many argued there could be "no price ceiling on America's security."[72] The notable exception to such thinking was Dwight Eisenhower, who, as George McGovern observed in an interview, had the credibility to warn against excessive military spending "without being ridden out of town."[73] Modern Republicans promised to enhance two strategic imperatives at any cost: "a second-strike capability that is, a nuclear retaliatory power that can survive surprise attack, strike back, and destroy any possible enemy"; and "highly mobile and versatile forces, including forces deployed, to deter or check local aggressions and 'brush fire wars' which might bring an all-out nuclear war."[74]

In proposing their "total force policy," Republicans received widespread public support. One 1983 survey, for example, found 83 percent backed Ronald Reagan's willingness to dispatch troops into combat situations to signal to the Soviet Union that the United States "will fight to maintain its freedom if it comes to that." The same poll showed 66 percent thinking the Soviets got the message about interfering in the Southern Hemisphere when Reagan ordered troops to Grenada.[75] Likewise, a 1984 CBS News/*New York Times* poll showed that 46 percent agreed that Reagan's military and foreign policies toward the Soviet Union had placed the United States in a "more secure" position than 1980; just 35 percent answered "less secure."[76]

In making their case for "peace through strength," Republicans exploited lingering public suspicions that the Soviets would, as Reagan stated in his first presidential press conference, "reserve unto themselves the right to commit any crime, to lie, to cheat" to advance their position.[77] Thus, in his first year as president, Reagan proposed, and Congress adopted, a whopping 10 percent increase in the Pentagon budget. Reagan accused the Soviets of violating SALT I and SALT II, the Anti-Ballistic Missile Treaty of 1972, the Helsinki Accords, and the Biological and Toxin Weapons Convention of 1972. Never mind that most of these agreements were signed by Richard Nixon during a brief period of détente. Reagan's maxim of "trust but verify" became his watchwords. In fact, Reagan repeated the phrase so often that Mikhail Gorbachev cupped his hands over his ears when he heard it. Like their hero, Reagan's fellow Republicans pledged to be stalwart negotiators: "Soviet intransigence is designed to force concessions from the United States even before negotiations begin. We will not succumb to this strategy."[78]

Given communist duplicity, Republicans believed that "the American people expect that their leaders will assume a national defense posture second to none."[79] Richard Nixon donned this commander-in-chief mantle for his 1972 reelection bid. Campaigning against George McGovern, Nixon ran a television advertisement featuring toy soldiers, planes, and ships. As the announcer hailed U.S. military superiority under Nixon's stewardship, a hand swept the toys away as the commentator issued dire warnings about what would happen in a McGovern administration. The advertisement concluded with Nixon reviewing a U.S. fleet as strains of "Hail to the Chief" echoed in the background.[80]

In 1984, Ronald Reagan reprised Nixon's script. After Reagan's poor performance in the first debate with Walter Mondale, his campaign ran the famous "bear-in-the-woods" ad, reminding voters that the Soviet Union remained a danger. In it, an armed hunter walked in the woods while a bear—symbol for the Soviets—stalked him. An announcer declared: "There is a bear in the woods. For some people, the bear is easy to see. Others don't see it at all. Some people say the bear is tame. Others say it's vicious and dangerous. Since no one can really be sure who's right, isn't it smart to be as strong as the bear—if there is a bear?" As haunting music and a pounding drum of a heartbeat played, the final scene showed the hunter suddenly confronting the bear. Reagan's picture appeared with the slogan "President Reagan: Prepared for Peace."[81] The advertisement tapped into existing concerns: 76 percent said Reagan's ability to deal with the Soviet Union had "a lot of influence" on their voting decision; dealing with communism, 65 percent; military spending, 68 percent; and handling arms control, 69 percent.[82] Fifty-six percent recalled seeing the bear-in-the-woods advertisement, making it the most watched campaign commercial of 1984.[83]

When it suited their interests, Democrats also touted their ability to respond to a crisis. Walter Mondale emphasized Gary Hart's inexperience by running a commercial during the Democratic primaries showing a ringing red telephone. An announcer ominously told viewers: "On Tuesday, you decide between Gary Hart and Walter Mondale for president, the toughest job in the world. A president is tested in a time of crisis. He must make the right decision, under pressure, without much time. It all comes down to knowledge, experience, judgment. He must answer that phone. On Tuesday, vote like our world is at stake. Mondale for President."[84] Mondale's ad was the best-remembered of the Democratic lot, with 57 percent claiming to have seen it.[85] Campaign Manager Bob Beckel claimed the commercial "stopped Hart right in his tracks."[86] Surveys bore out Beckel's assessment: A Louis Harris poll found 58 percent saying Mondale "could be trusted to use sound judgment in a foreign policy crisis."[87]

But it was the Republicans who most often donned the red paint of anti-communism by offering themselves as resolute guardians of America's interests: "Strict reciprocity must govern our diplomatic relations with the Soviet Union" read the 1976 platform.[88] In 1968, Richard Nixon expanded on the reciprocity theme: "No longer will foreign aid activities range free of our foreign policy. Nations hostile to this country will receive no assistance from the United States. . . . Only when communist nations prove by actual deeds that they genuinely seek world peace and will live in harmony with the rest of the world, will we support the expansion of East-West trade."[89]

Such rhetoric led to a nationalism sustained by a profound hatred of communism. In a 1962 book aptly titled *Why Not Victory?* Barry Goldwater proclaimed a "new nationalism," noting its touchstone was "a recognition by the president himself that victory over the communists is a national goal—held by all Americans to be in the vital interest of the country and the Free World"—an objective Goldwater believed President Kennedy did not share. The Arizona Republican wrote that the new nationalism had little room for isolationists: "We cannot . . . isolate ourselves from the rest of the world. What happens in Ghana, or in Vietnam, or in Cuba has a direct bearing on American security."[90]

But merely halting the Red tide was not enough. In his *Life* magazine interview, even Secretary of State John Foster Dulles admitted that containment could not provide victory: "What we need to do is recapture the kind of crusading spirit of the early days of the Republic when we were certain that we had something better than anyone else and we knew the rest of the world needed it and wanted it and that we were going to carry it around the world. The missionaries, the doctors, the educators, and the merchants carried the knowledge of the great American experiment to all four corners of the globe."[91] Republicans found the missing ingredient in the Founders' love of freedom, recalling the Declaration of Independence's assertion of the God-given rights to "life, liberty, and the pursuit of happiness." The party solemnly proclaimed that these were "deathless principles" from which all anticommunists could draw moral strength.[92] By rooting their hatred of communism in the ideas of freedom and individualism, Republicans exploited the ideological passions of the American public. The existence of HUAC makes the point. Historian Daniel Boorstin rhetorically asked, "Who would think of using the word 'un-Italian' or 'un-French' as we use the word un-American?"[93] Since the founding of the Republic, the "American Way of Life" has assumed missionary proportions. In the nineteenth century, Herman Melville compared Americans to the biblical tribes of Israel, claiming they were "the peculiar chosen people . . . the Israel of our time."[94] By the late twentieth century, Ronald Reagan held a similar creationist view: "Think for a moment how special it is to be an American. Can we doubt that only a Divine Providence placed this land, this island of freedom, here as a refuge for all those people in the world who yearn to breathe free?"[95]

Given this rigid stance, it followed that Republicans sought an expanded government role for promoting Americanism abroad—especially in those countries "imprisoned" by communism. Radio Free Europe and Radio Liberty (which beamed signals behind the Iron Curtain), Radio Marti (which broadcast U.S. newscasts into Cuba), and the National Endowment for Democracy (a creation of the Reagan administration with bipartisan support) won strong Republican backing. Even the Peace Corps, an offspring of John F. Kennedy's New Frontier, belatedly received plaudits in the party's 1984 platform: "Because of the importance we place on people-to-people exchange programs, Republicans support the dedicated work of Peace Corps volunteers."[96]

But internationalism had its limits. As Goldwater warned in *Why Not Victory?* the new nationalism "must avoid complete reliance on any organization whose total interest does not coincide with freedom." For Goldwater and his followers, the United Nations was a "politically powerful clique" supported by "a large segment of the press, some professors, the big foundation executives, and some quasi-political associations, all of whom exercise a considerable influence over public opinion in this country."[97] Goldwater proposed downsizing the United Nations in foreign policy calculations: "Let us, then, have done with submitting major policy decisions to a forum where the opinions of the Sultan of Yemen counts equally with ours, where the vote of the United States can be canceled out by the likes of 'Byelorussia.'"[98] Nineteen eighty-eight Democratic presidential candidate Michael Dukakis bitterly recalled Republican accusations of being a "multilaterialist" (a term that he claimed "sounded almost pornographic") because he proposed relying on the United Nations as a peacekeeper.[99]

In short, while waging peace Republicans pledged to conduct a "vigorous, resolute foreign policy—inflexible against every tyrannical encroachment, and mighty in its advance toward our own affirmative goals." Quickly, the promise would assume missionary proportions: "To nullify the Soviet conspiracy is our greatest task."[100] But in making their case, Republicans found that the politics of threatening war was harder to manage than the Cold War itself. Bellicose rhetoric gave birth to the Goldwater movement, which nearly negated Republican claims of being the party that could best calibrate strength with compromise in managing the cold peace.

Barry Goldwater and the Radical Right

For years, right-wing extremists heard the piercing screams in the black of night that Whittaker Chambers so chillingly described in *Witness*. Those cries caused them to shout that the tortured victims of communism were being ignored. As Barry Goldwater penned in *Why Not Victory?* "We still go about our everyday business . . . stubbornly refusing to admit the enormity of the conspiracy which has been created to destroy us."[101] For those on the right, the "communist conspiracy" extended into the highest echelons of the government. Robert Welch, heir to the candy fortune, maintained that Dwight Eisenhower was, in fact, procommunist. As evidence, he cited Eisenhower's acceptance of an invitation from Anna Rosenberg, on behalf of Sidney Hillman, to be the featured speaker at the 1946 CIO convention, which, among other things, placed Ike squarely on "the red fringes of the Democratic party." Later, Welch accused Eisenhower of deliberately ceding the 1954 and 1956 congressional elections to the Democrats: "The communists wanted Eisenhower as president, standing out in single glory above a repudiated Republican party. They wanted, to work with him, a Democratic Congress—the more 'left-wing' the better. And the final blocking of Joe McCarthy by that Democratic Congress was just one of the many objectives they had in mind, to be achieved by the combination."[102] In 1958, Welch founded the John Birch Society (named after an army intelligence officer who was killed the week after World War II ended) to expound his conspiracy theories. The John Birchers eventually grew to 100,000 members, including two members of Congress.

Among those Welch tried to convert was Barry Goldwater. They met in Phoenix, where Welch presented him with an autographed copy of his book, *The Politician.* Goldwater politely received Welch, but he rejected the thesis of his book and the fanaticism of the John Birchers.[103] What conservatism needed, said William F. Buckley, editor of *National Review,* was "a militant, but intelligent anti-communism."[104] Goldwater agreed. In July 1959, Americans for Goldwater had organized chapters in thirty-one states and the District of Columbia. When the Republican National Convention met in Chicago a year later, state delegations representing South Carolina, Louisiana, and Arizona backed Goldwater for president. But the presidential nomination was Nixon's for the asking. Withdrawing his name from contention, Goldwater admonished his supporters: "Let's grow up, conservatives. Let's if we want to, take this party back—and I think we can someday. Let's get to work."[105]

Getting down to work is exactly what Goldwater and his foot-soldiers did, taking their cues from Whittaker Chambers about the nature of the international communist conspiracy, which Chambers called "the deadliest enemy the world has ever known."[106] As Goldwater wrote in 1962:

There are still Americans who do not understand that we have been at war these past sixteen years with an enemy who has never hidden his objective of destroying us and all other people who cherish freedom. As a people we have become like the man who suspects he has cancer but will not see his doctor for fear his suspicion be confirmed. One cannot talk with his fellow Americans—individually or in groups—without sensing the apprehension with which they view today's happenings. But at the same time, one comes to feel that they do not want to know the truth. All of us recognize some symptoms of trouble, but we are dealing with the disease itself. The disease is communism, a cancer that is world-wide and that shows symptoms within our own boundaries.[107]

Goldwater maintained that the Soviet Union was unrelenting in its war against the United States: "If an enemy power is bent on conquering you, and proposes to turn all of his resources to that end, he is at war with you: and you—unless you contemplate surrender—are at war with him. Moreover—unless you contemplate treason—your objective, like his, will be victory. Not 'peace,' but victory."[108] Believing that the Soviet Union was imbued by its own sense of nationalism fueled by ideological communism, Goldwater urged his fellow Americans to wake up: "We must recognize this war as a *war*—not a cold one, but the *Communist* War—and we must win it."[109]

The denunciations Republicans made over the years about the evils of communism inspired Goldwater's call to arms. In 1954, Senator William Knowland of California spoke for many when he likened peaceful coexistence with the Soviet Union to a Trojan horse: "The civilizations that flourished and died in the past had opportunities for a limited period of time to change the course of history. Sooner or later, however, they passed 'the point of no return,' and the decisions were no longer theirs to make."[110] A 1960 House task force chaired by Michigan Republican Gerald R. Ford issued a dire warning: "Survival is not a policy. It is the delusion of a nation marked for social suicide. It is the sure graveyard of human dignity. Captive nations survive, but only in slavery."[111]

Such rhetoric appealed to those on the "mashed potato circuit," but it produced a conundrum that Republican officeholders found difficult to resolve: deal with what Whittaker Chambers called "the focus of concentrated evil"[112] or try to obtain some sort of peaceful coexistence with evil itself. On one side were Republicans who knew war and wanted to avoid it. Dwight Eisenhower was among them. Accepting renomination, he told the Republican delegates: "No one is more aware than I that it is the young who give up years of their lives to military training and service. It is not enough that their elders promise 'Peace in our time'; it must be peace in their time too, and in their children's time; indeed, my friends, there is only one real peace now, and that is peace for all time."[113] The other side opposed peaceful coexistence and instead preferred victory. Writing in *Conscience of a Conservative*, Goldwater claimed, "Our leaders have not made *victory* the goal of American policy." Among those whom Goldwater accused of forestalling victory was Eisenhower, declaring that while the president had "with great sincerity, 'waged' peace" the communists waged war.[114] Although Goldwater did not accuse Eisenhower of treason (unlike Welch), he thought Ike was "misled" at Geneva "into proclaiming the 'dawning of a new day in world relations.'"[115] From Goldwater's perch, Eisenhower's and Nixon's boasts that the communists had not seized additional territory were empty platitudes. Accepting the Republican nomination in 1964, Goldwater stoutly maintained that it was "the cause of Republicanism to restore a clear understanding of the tyranny of man over man in the world at large." In so doing, Goldwater maintained, "It is our cause to dispel the foggy thinking which avoids hard decisions in the delusion that a world of conflict will somehow resolve itself into a world of harmony, if we just don't rock the boat or irritate the forces of aggression—and this is hogwash."[116]

The political paradox Republicans faced was but a reflection of the mixed minds of the voters. A September 1964 Gallup poll neatly captured the dual emotions: Whereas 61 percent thought the United States "should take a firmer stand against the Soviet Union than it has in recent years," 71 percent said we "should continue to negotiate with Russia with a view toward reducing armaments on both sides."[117] But Goldwater had no such cognitive dissonance; instead he repeatedly argued that the United States should immediately wage war, not peace, with the communists. To that end, he was an enthusiastic supporter of the military-industrial complex: "Since we could never match the communists in manpower, our equipment and weapons must more than offset their advantage in numbers."[118] Goldwater's view that the United States should be "masters of the air"[119] reinforced Robert Taft's 1952 opinion and no doubt stemmed from his experience as a World War II fighter pilot and his continued service as a colonel and general in the air force reserves. In arguing for more high-tech weaponry, Goldwater refuted Eisenhower's admonition not to be tempted "to feel that some spectacular and costly action could become the miraculous solution to all current difficulties."[120]

While Goldwater called for a stronger military supplemented by the latest technological advances, he also proposed using diplomatic means to put the Soviets on notice that the United States was hell-bent on winning the Cold War. Goldwater wanted to repeal Franklin Roosevelt's recognition of the Soviet Union, saying that "the Cold War would change for the better the moment we announced that the United States does not regard Mr. Khrushchev's murderous claque as the legitimate rulers of the Russian people or of any other people."[121] Goldwater also favored ending future superpower conclaves, saying, "I have consistently opposed summit meetings on the grounds that the only progress they can produce is progress toward communist domination of the world."[122]

In place of summit conferences, Goldwater proposed more funding for the U.S. Information Agency, Radio Free Europe, and Radio Liberty; establishing a Cuban government-in-exile; opposing admission of "Red China" into the United Nations; and suspending negotiations over the status of Germany until the Berlin Wall was removed. Action, not talk, Goldwater declared, would prevent war: "It is a nation's vacillation, not firmness, that tempts an aggressor into war. It is accommodation, not opposition, that encourages a hostile nation to remain hostile and to remain aggressive."[123] In making his case, Goldwater faulted both parties for failing to devise a Cold War strategy aimed at victory. His attacks on his fellow Republicans were especially salient since Goldwater believed that conservatives, using the Republican party as their instrument, had the responsibility for winning the "Communist War." Accepting the Republican presidential nomination in 1964, Goldwater argued his case: "The Republican cause demands that we brand communism as the principal disturber of peace in the world today. Indeed, we should brand it as the only significant disturber of the peace. And we must make clear that until its goals of conquest are absolutely renounced, and its relations with all nations tempered, communism and the governments it now controls are the enemies of every man on earth who is or wants to be free."[124]

Goldwater imbued his nationalism with a sense of urgency, claiming not only that the United States did not have any plans for victory but that it was actually losing the Cold War—especially in Vietnam, Laos, and Cambodia. In his 1960 book *Conscience of a Conservative*, he wrote, "As long as every encounter with the enemy is fought on his initiative, on grounds of his choosing and with weapons of his choosing, we shall keep on losing the Cold War."[125] Two years later in *Why Not Victory?* he reiterated his view: "If the Communist War were a conventional struggle, the measures we have taken ought to be sufficient to yield some results on the side of freedom. But because this is not a conventional struggle, and because we have not devised a total strategy aimed at victory, we are falling even further behind."[126]

Goldwater was joined by a dedicated cadre of grassroots activists who were imbued with a zealotry that something must be done *NOW!* to save the nation. With this mission, they infiltrated state and local Republican Party organizations to secure delegates pledged to Goldwater at the 1964 convention (including about 100 members of the John Birch Society).[127] Political scientist Aaron Wildavsky noted the Goldwaterites devout anti-communism, dubbing them "purists." Interviewing the Goldwater delegates, their passion overwhelmed Wildavsky—to the point where most were willing to sacrifice party for principle. When they reverently spoke of Goldwater, they were exuberant: "He is frank." "He has courage." "He stands up for what he believes." "He's different from most politicians." "Goldwater speaks about things others avoid." Indeed, unlike supporters of other politicians, the Goldwater "purists" cared more about the righteousness of their cause than winning at the polls. One delegate, asked if the primary qualification of a candidate should be an ability to win votes, replied: "No; principles are more important. I would rather be one against 20,000 and believe I was right. That's what I admire about Goldwater. He's like that."[128] On this point, the Goldwaterites found considerable public backing for their man's warnings about the communist danger: 61 percent thought "communists right here at home" provided "a very great deal" or "a good deal" of danger.[129]

Believing they represented true "American principles," the Goldwaterites methodically went about capturing the Republican nomination for their man—and became the first of the "insurgent" candidacies of the postwar era to do so. Wildavsky worried about the ruthless tactics they employed in outmaneuvering longtime party officials: "Could it be that the United States is producing large numbers of half-educated people with college degrees who have learned that participation (passion and commitment) is good but who do not understand (or cannot stand) the normal practices of democratic politics?"[130] But Wildavsky failed to comprehend how the passion of the Goldwaterites could remake the GOP into a nationalist party. The recollection of Patrick J. Buchanan, one of the Goldwaterites, makes the point: "If there was a single issue that drove the New Conservatism, and the Goldwater campaign, it was this: The United States was in a mortal struggle with the Soviet Empire; the tide was going the other way; we needed leadership that understood the nature of the war we were in, leadership as dedicated to the advance of freedom as our enemies were to the spread of their ideology. Containment was not enough."[131]

Indeed, a mere balance-of-power strategy seemed antiseptic—especially when it came to domestic politics. *Freedom* had a greater resonance: it appealed to people everywhere, and it confirmed an American view that the nation was founded on an idea that could electrify the globe. By standing for freedom, "neutral" nations would surely rally to the American cause in the Communist War. In making his case, Goldwater caustically rejected arguments espoused by liberal Democrats that poverty bred communism: "It does not help to adopt the false notion that communism is spawned by poverty, disease, and other similar social and economic conditions. Communism is spawned by communists, and communists alone."[132] To that end, Goldwater argued that an unyielding faith in freedom, even unto death, was required: "We must—as the first step toward saving American freedom . . . make it the cornerstone of our foreign policy: that we would rather die than lose our freedom."[133] Campaigning in 1964, Goldwater reiterated his "live-free-or-die" stance: "If we have reached the point where we are willing to put our tails between our legs and say to the communists . . . 'We are tired, we are tired of spending money, we are tired of worrying, we will go along with you, we don't mind being slaves.' I don't think I will ever live to see that day in this country. And I will promise you one thing as your president: this country will stay free."[134] Goldwater attempted to arouse public anger by running a commercial depicting American children reciting the *Pledge of Allegiance*. As the schoolchildren repeated the well-known words, Nikita Khrushchev appeared on the television screen, speaking in Russian: "We will bury you. Your children will be communists." At this, Goldwater retorted: "I want American kids to grow up as Americans. And they will, if we have the guts to make our intentions clear—so clear that they don't need translation or interpretation, just respect for a country prepared as no country in all history ever was."[135]

If Goldwater thought Eisenhower lax in prosecuting the Communist War, the Democrats were hopeless vacillators. Accepting the Republican nomination, Goldwater issued a manifesto accusing John F. Kennedy and Lyndon B. Johnson of appeasing communism in Berlin, Cuba, and Southeast Asia: "Failure cements the wall of shame in Berlin; failures blot the sands of shame at the Bay of Pigs; failures marked the slow death of freedom in Laos; failures infest the jungles of Vietnam; and failures haunt the houses of our great alliances and undermine the greatest bulwark ever erected by free nations, the NATO community."[136] Echoing Goldwater, the 1964 Republican platform depicted the Democratic record as one of "disappointment and reverses for freedom" and warned that further appeasement would result in "a potentially fatal parity of power with communism instead of continued military superiority for the United States."[137] Thus, Goldwater personalized his fight against the Democratic ticket, claiming it had done little to stop communist advances in Vietnam. Signs appeared at Republican rallies reading: "Johnson and Humphrey soft on communism."[138] He believed a hardheaded response to communism included using "small, clean nuclear weapons."[139] To that end, Goldwater proposed expanding the Vietnam War using U.S. troops in a military-style invasion of Hanoi replete with low-yield atomic weapons that, he argued, would defoliate the jungles.[140]

But it was by emphasizing their candidate's character that the Goldwaterites turned politics upside-down. Aaron Wildavsky noted the tendency to privatize politics: "The private conscience of the leader rather than his public responsibilities became the focal point of politics."[141] He thought Goldwaterism represented "a retreat from politics through politics."[142] By dwelling on the private conscience of a prospective president, morality became an overriding issue. Goldwaterites thought Johnson amoral because of his love of votes, compromise, bargaining, maneuver, and conciliation. To them, Johnson's character deficiencies were self-evident. In contrast, Goldwater's willingness to "stand up and be counted" was viewed as a test of his character.

But Lyndon Johnson proved that he, too, could engage in personality politics. To him, Goldwater was a godsend—especially for a Texas Democrat unaccustomed to two-party competition. Johnson's joy at Goldwater's nomination was heightened by the anguish so many Republicans felt at

Goldwater's rise. James Reichley, a strategist for Governor William Scranton of Pennsylvania, thought Goldwater signaled the end of the Eisenhower era and, with it, any remaining vestiges of pragmatism left within the GOP. By 1964, pragmatism was regarded by many Republicans as a dirty word. In becoming "me-too" New Dealers and reducing the Cold War to a chess match, Eastern Establishment Republicans led by Nelson Rockefeller and William Scranton deprived their followers of the passion that imbued the Goldwaterites. As Reichley put it:

> Pragmatism failed the moderates and the progressives in the Republican Party in 1964, not only because it prevented them from developing a positive alternative to. . . "Goldwaterism," but also because it prevented their leaders from giving free rein in crucial moments to those moral checks or moral principles which might have enabled them to maintain their supremacy within the party. The argument against Goldwater was based too much on his "electability," too much on the damage that his presence might do to other candidates running on state or local tickets.[143]

Lyndon Johnson agreed, seeking a mandate partially based upon Republican approbation of the expulsion of the Eastern Establishment from their party. Meeting with Democratic strategists shortly after the convention, Johnson declared: "A lot of Republicans in this country ought to be Democrats, but we've never given them a chance to come in. This is the best opportunity we're ever going to get."[144] Goldwater made Johnson's task easy with a string of intemperate remarks about how he would conduct the Cold War if elected. On October 24, 1963, Goldwater announced that he would let NATO commanders decide whether to use atomic weapons.[145] That caused Rockefeller and Scranton to decry Goldwater's abdication of such a vital life-or-death decision to the military. Rockefeller distributed 2 million leaflets to Republican primary voters in California, asking, "Who Do You Want in the Room with the H-Bomb?"[146] Scranton followed with an open letter to the Republican National Convention condemning the personal politics the Goldwaterites had come to embrace:

> You have too often casually prescribed nuclear war as a solution to a troubled world.
>   You have too often allowed the radical extremists to use you.
>   You have too often read Taft and Eisenhower and Lincoln out of the Republican party.[147]

Scranton deplored Goldwater's "ill-advised efforts to make us stand for Goldwaterism instead of Republicanism," adding:

> Goldwaterism has come to stand for nuclear irresponsibility.
>   Goldwaterism has come to stand for keeping the name of Eisenhower out of our platform.

Goldwaterism has come to stand for refusing to stand for law and order in maintaining racial peace.

In short, Goldwaterism has come to stand for a whole crazy-quilt collection of absurd and dangerous positions that would be soundly repudiated by the American people in November.[148]

But Goldwater remained unbowed. Accepting the nomination, he uttered one of the most famous lines in the annals of politics: "I would remind you that extremism in the defense of liberty is no vice! And let me remind you also that moderation in the pursuit of justice is no virtue!"[149] Listening to the address, Richard Nixon said he felt "physically sick."[150] One Democrat watched the proceedings with glee: "My God, he's going to run as Barry Goldwater."[151] Democrats sought to capitalize on their good fortune by running a television advertisement featuring a little girl plucking a daisy. As the petals disappeared one by one, an announcer began a countdown: "Ten, nine, eight. . . ." When zero was finally reached, the camera zoomed in on the girl's face and her eye dissolved as an atom bomb exploded, casting its familiar mushroom cloud over the pastoral scene. Johnson's voice was heard saying, "These are the stakes. To make a world in which all of God's children can live—or to go into the dark. We must either love each other, or we must die." Another Johnson ad also showed an exploding H-bomb, this time as the announcer quoted Goldwater: "On October 24, 1963, Barry Goldwater said of the nuclear bomb—'merely another weapon,'" then cryptically asked, "Merely another weapon?"[152]

Amid the scare tactics was a clear implication: Goldwater would start a war; Johnson would not. Although the "daisy commercial" aired only once, its impact was immediate. As one Goldwater aide recalled: "When I went to bed, . . . I would lie awake asking myself at night, how do you get at the bomb issue? My candidate had been branded a bomb-dropper—and I couldn't figure out how to lick it. And the advertising people, people who could sell anything, toothpaste or soap or automobiles—when it came to a political question like this, they couldn't offer anything either." Signs appeared at Goldwater rallies reading: "Vote for Goldwater and Go to War"; "In Your Guts You Know He's Nuts"; "You Know in Your Heart He's Right—Far Right"; "Welcome Doctor Strangewater"; "Keep Your Atom Bomb in Arizona"; "In Your Heart You Know He Might."[153]

Johnson kept up the pressure. A week after running the "daisy commercial," LBJ authorized another advertisement showing the same little girl, licking an ice-cream cone. A soft, motherly voice observed how radioactive fallout had killed many children, and lauded a treaty that had been signed with the Soviet Union to prevent such future deaths. Then the gloomy voice said one man—Barry Goldwater—voted against the Nuclear Test Ban Treaty. A Geiger counter rose to a crescendo as LBJ's theme appeared: "Vote for President Johnson on November third. The stakes are too high for you to stay home."[154] On the campaign trail, Johnson told voters that "the only real issue in this campaign, the only thing you ought to be concerned about at all, is who can best keep the peace?" Johnson graphically described his Cold War responsibilities: "In the nuclear age the president doesn't get a second chance to make a second guess. If he mashes that button [here Johnson's big thumb mashed and squirmed as it pressed an imaginary button]—that is it."[155]

Public opinion surveys tracked the electorate's discomfiture with the Republican nominee. Asked in October 1964 if Goldwater would get the United States into a war, 51 percent agreed. The same poll found voters evenly split over whether Goldwater was a radical: 45 percent said he was; 45 percent said he was not.[156] Presidential chronicler Theodore H. White concluded that the election was not between peace and war. Rather it was a choice "between peace and *risk* of war."[157]

As expected, Goldwater went down to a crushing defeat. Johnson won 61.1 percent of the popular vote—a margin that remains the largest ever. But, in retrospect, what was especially noteworthy about the Goldwater totals was their southern flavor. Besides winning his native Arizona, Goldwater won five other states—all in the Deep South: Georgia, Alabama, Mississippi, Louisiana, and South Carolina. In assessing how southern politics had changed, it should be remembered that Adlai Stevenson carried each of these states in 1952. Indeed, Goldwater swept 235 southern counties that had never voted for a Republican presidential candidate.[158] This surprising support against a white southerner (Johnson) extended the Republican party's reach into the deepest parts of the South (Goldwater received 87 percent of the vote in Mississippi)—a significant breakthrough in nationalizing the once northern and midwestern Grand Old Party. To be sure, Goldwater's truculent opposition to civil rights swayed the South. Goldwater was the only Republican present to cast his vote against the Civil Rights Act of 1964 (prompting Democratic vice presidential nominee Hubert Humphrey to exclaim that most Democrats and Republicans had supported the measure, "But not Senator Goldwater!"). One year later Johnson signed the Voting Rights Act of 1965 into law—a measure he believed fatal to Democratic southern prospects. After the bill-signing ceremony, Johnson told an aide that he had just "delivered the South into the Republican party for a long time to come."[159]

But the South was also responsive to Goldwater's references to the Communist War and his call for a strong military to win it. The South had long been militaristic: In December 1940, 82 percent were willing to "pay more taxes to meet the costs of the defense program"; just 65 percent of northeasterners agreed. Three months before Pearl Harbor, 11 percent of southerners said Franklin Roosevelt had gone "too far" in aiding Britain; 31 percent of those in the Midwest (home to isolationism) thought FDR overly zealous.

Analyzing these data, political scientists Everett Carll Ladd Jr. and Charles D. Hadley concluded that southern support for Roosevelt "was reinforced by agreement with the thrusts of his interventionist foreign policy, just as it was sustained by relatively high approval of his domestic programs."[160]

In the aftermath of the Civil War, defeated Southerners revered their military heroes, and southern deference to generals increased during the Cold War—especially when so many defense bases were built south of the Mason-Dixon line. A new form of bipartisanship emerged: Republican presidents, in a tacit alliance with Dixiecrat representatives, became enthusiastic sponsors of military bases located in the South, in part because they believed these installations would attract a more friendly, pro-Republican constituency. For their part, the Dixiecrats in Congress were well acquainted with their constituents' antipathy toward communism—especially when so many southerners equated support for civil rights legislation with communism. The result was a newfangled southern one-partyism: Republicans dominated at the presidential level while homespun Dixiecrats, who were Cold War hard-liners, were routinely returned to Congress. At the Dixiecrats' peak in 1955–1956, nearly two-thirds of House Democratic chairs called the South home.[161] And of the seventy-seven national elections in the Old Confederacy from 1968 to 1992 (that is, seven presidential elections in eleven states), Republicans won fifty-five. In 1992, six of George Bush's top-ten vote-getting states were in the South: Mississippi, South Carolina, Alabama, Virginia, North Carolina, and Georgia.[162]

A prototype of the new southern politics was South Carolina Democrat L. Mendel Rivers. The chair of the House Armed Services Committee from 1965 until 1970, Rivers represented Charleston, home to a vast array of defense establishments. Carl Vinson, Rivers's mentor and predecessor as committee chair, once told his protégé, "You put anything else down there in your district, Mendel, it's gonna sink."[163] Vinson was hardly exaggerating. When Rivers died in December 1970, 35 percent of the payrolls in Charleston and its environs were military-related.[164] These included the AVCO Corporation, which repaired and overhauled T-53 helicopter engines; and Blair Algernon, a construction firm that reconstructed part of Charleston's navy facilities. The list of defense installations was unusually long: the Charleston Army Depot (North Charleston), the Marine Corps Air Station (Beaufort), the Marine Corps Recruit Depot (Parris Island), the Charleston Naval Shipyard (Charleston), navy hospitals in Beaufort and Charleston, the Charleston Naval Station, the Naval Supply Center (Charleston), the Naval Weapons Station (Charleston), the Navy Fleet Ballistic Missile Submarine Training Center (Charleston), the Polaris Missile Facility, Atlantic (Charleston), the Charleston Air Force Base (Charleston), and the North Charleston Air Force Station (North Charleston). The expenditures to maintain these facilities totaled more than $385 million per year.[165] On the key question of the day—the Vietnam War—Rivers, like many Dixiecrats, backed Nixon: "Words are fruitless, diplomatic notes are useless. There can be only one answer for America: retaliation, retaliation, retaliation! They say, 'Quit the bombing.' I say, 'Bomb!'"[166] Upon Rivers's death, President Nixon issued a statement saying he had lost a friend who "held unswervingly to a belief that freedom in the modern world is inextricably tied to the military strength of the United States."[167]

Although Rivers represented the district for thirty years—winning his last race with no Republican opposition—South Carolina eventually moved from a one-party Democratic bastion to a Republican-dominated one. The change was substantial. Franklin Roosevelt won 96 percent of South Carolina's votes in 1940—his highest percentage nationwide. That same year, Rivers was first elected to Congress. Chordes Seabrook, an eighth-generation South Carolinian, recalled working a polling booth during the 1960s when only one Republican bothered to vote: "It was like Republicans were from another planet. Nobody had seen one up close, except for Strom [Thurmond]. They used to whisper to each other, 'There goes a Republican.' They thought we had tails."[168]

But by 1964, things began to change. South Carolinians gave Goldwater a majority at the Republican National Convention and voted for him in November. During the 1980s, South Carolina prospered (thanks, in part, to the military), and jobs increased nearly 50 percent.[169] In 1984, Reagan won 63.3 percent of South Carolina's votes. Typical of the new South Carolina Republican was the late Lee Atwater, onetime chairman of the Republican National Committee chairman and Bush's campaign manager in 1988. Rivers's district is currently represented by Republican Marshall Sanford Jr., who first beat Rivers's son, L. Mendel Rivers Jr., in the 1994 GOP primary and later captured 66 percent of the vote against a hapless Democratic opponent.[170] Sanford won reelection in 1996 with 96 percent of the vote against token opposition.

With the new transplants from the North and Midwest—especially those stationed or working near military bases—Republicans prospered in the heart of the Old Confederacy. In 1992, George Bush won 53 percent support in a three-way race against two southerners from Rivers's old district. After its 1994 national sweep, the GOP controlled South Carolina's congressional delegation, holding four of six House seats on 64 percent of the vote. In addition, Republicans captured six of eight state offices in 1994 and elected a speaker in the state legislature. Today, half the state's white voters are Republican; just 7 percent of white males are Democrats.[171] A similar transformation has occurred throughout the South. After the 1994 midterm elections, Republicans—for the first time since Reconstruction— held a majority of southern seats in Congress. Moreover, all the House Republican leaders were southerners or southern transplants: Newt Gingrich

(Georgia, born in Harrisburg, Pennsylvania); Richard Armey (Texas, born in North Dakota); and Tom DeLay (Texas, born in Laredo).

During the Cold War, southerners were motivated by their racial prejudices *and* their anticommunism. As Table 4.1 shows, they were extremely hawkish in their attitudes toward communism. The result was to strengthen the tie between southerners and the GOP. Political scientists Edward G. Carmines and Harold W. Stanley found, for example, that southern whites who favored more money for defense shifted from 52 percent Democratic and 34 percent Republican in 1980 to 49 percent Republican and 38 percent Democratic in 1984.[172] Analysis of the 1984 vote showed a preponderance of southern Cold War hard-liners: 80 percent of southern whites who voted for Reagan thought the United States should "get tougher" with the Russians; just 20 percent of southern whites who backed Walter Mondale agreed. Moreover, 79 percent of southern whites who supported Reagan thought defense spending should be increased—this after the largest peacetime military expenditures in U.S. history.[173] Reagan pollster Richard B. Wirthlin noted that Reagan's hawkishness paid big political dividends in the South: "The South has always been pro–strong preparedness."[174]

Nationalism and Religion: The Reagan Elixir

Dwight Eisenhower, Richard Nixon, and Barry Goldwater were the founders of Cold War Republicanism, but it was Ronald Reagan who completed the transformation. Like the troika of aforementioned Republicans, Reagan professed a profound antipathy toward communism. Although raised a New Deal Democrat—Reagan's father, Jack, worked for the Works Progress Administration—Reagan supported Eisenhower in 1952. Ten years later, Reagan dropped all pretenses of being a nominal Democrat and officially changed his party registration while helping Richard Nixon in his unsuccessful quest for the California governorship. In so doing, Reagan charged that Democrats had forgotten FDR's admonition that budgets should be balanced.

But it was communism and Reagan's distrust of it—a suspicion whose seeds were planted during his years as president of the Screen Actors Guild—that prompted the switch. As Reagan told an interviewer: "Coming out of the cage of the Army [after World War II] . . . a series of hard-nosed happenings began to change my whole view of American dangers. Most of them tied in directly with my own bailiwick of acting. . . . From being an active (though unconscious) partisan in what now and then turned out to be communist causes, I little by little became disillusioned or perhaps, in my case, I should say reawakened."[175] In his autobiography, titled *Where's the Rest of Me?*, Reagan described his hero, Whittaker Chambers, as a "tragic and lonely" figure who believed that in deserting communism he

136

TABLE 4.1
Southerners and the Cold War, 1964–1986

Text of Question	South	Northeast	Midwest	West
"Do you believe it is possible or impossible to reach a peaceful settlement of differences with Russia?"[a]				
Percentage answering "impossible"	39	28	28	30
"It has been suggested that the United States send 100,000 troops to West Germany to remain there until the Russians remove their troops from Czechoslovakia. Do you favor or oppose this proposal?"[b]				
Percentage answering "favor"	40	30	31	32
"Do you think Communist China should or should not be admitted as a member of the United Nations?"[c]				
Percentage answering "should not"	71	56	57	56
"Some people believe that our armed forces are already powerful enough and that we should spend less money for defense. Others feel that military spending should at least continue at the present level. How do you feel—should military spending be cut, or should it continue at least at the present level?"[d]				
Percentage answering "continue at present level"	75	55	57	60
"People are called 'hawks' if they want to step up our military effort in Vietnam. They are called 'doves' if they want to reduce our military effort in Vietnam. How would you describe yourself—as a 'hawk' or a 'dove'?"[e]				
Percentage answering "hawk"	76	66	77	75
"Do you think North Vietnam is sincerely interested in finding a peaceful solution to the war or not?"[f]				
Percentage answering "not interested"	80	67	71	67

(continues)

TABLE 4.1 (continued)

Text of Question	South	Northeast	Midwest	West
"There is much discussion as to the amount of money the government in Washington should spend for national defense and military purposes. Do you think we are spending too much, about the right amount, or too little?"[g]				
Percentage answering "too little"	26	17	20	22
"Would you like to see the United States go ahead with the development of "Star Wars" or not?"[h]				
Percentage answering "no, don't develop"	35	42	37	39
"Do you approve or disapprove of the way Ronald Reagan is handling our relations with the Soviet Union?"[i]				
Percentage answering "approve"	72	68	65	58

[a]AIPO and Michigan surveys, 1964. Cited in Everett Carll Ladd Jr. with Charles D. Hadley, *Transformations of the American Party System* (New York: W. W. Norton, 1975), p. 170.

[b]AIPO and Michigan surveys, 1968. Cited in Ladd with Hadley, *Transformations of the American Party System*, p. 170.

[c]AIPO and Michigan surveys, 1969. Cited in Ladd with Hadley, *Transformations of the American Party System*, p. 170.

[d]CPS Election Study, 1972. Cited in Ladd with Hadley, *Transformations of the American Party System*, p. 170.

[e]AIPO and Michigan surveys, 1969. Cited in Ladd with Hadley, *Transformations of the American Party System*, p. 170.

[f]AIPO and Michigan surveys, 1968. Cited in Ladd with Hadley, *Transformations of the American Party System*, p. 170.

[g]Gallup Organization survey, September 16–19, 1983.

[h]Gallup Organization survey, February 24, 1985. Asked of those who had heard or read about the "Star Wars" proposal.

[i]Decision/Making/Information survey, October 9–10, 1986.

was leaving the winners for the losers. He quoted from *Witness*: "When I took up my little sling and aimed at communism, I also hit at something else. What I hit was the force of the great Socialist revolution which in the name of *liberalism*, spasmodically, incompletely, somewhat formlessly, but always in the same direction, has been inching its ice-cap over the nation for two decades. I had no adequate idea of its extent, the depth of its penetration, or the fierce vindictiveness of its revolutionary temper." Reagan added his own interpretation: "I am too optimistic to agree with his first statement, but I learned for myself the bitter truth of the latter. As my talks gained circulation, they did not go unopposed."[176]

By 1964, Reagan was on the mashed potato circuit campaigning for Barry Goldwater. As his text he used a talk he had given for years to employees of General Electric, sponsor of the television series he hosted (*Death Valley Days*) and a major defense contractor. In advocating Goldwater's candidacy, Reagan railed against communism and claimed that Democratic liberals had become the Neville Chamberlains of their day:

> The specter our well-meaning liberal friends refuse to face is that their policy of accommodation is appeasement, and appeasement does not give you a choice between peace and war, only between fight and surrender. We are told that the problem is too complex for a simple answer. They are wrong. There is no easy answer, but there is a simple answer. We must have the courage to do what we know is morally right, and this policy of accommodation asks us to accept the greatest possible immorality. We are being asked to buy our safety from the threat of the Bomb by selling into permanent slavery our fellow human beings enslaved behind the Iron Curtain. . . .
>
> If we are to believe that nothing is worth the dying, when did this begin? Should Moses have told the children of Israel to live in slavery rather than dare the wilderness? Should Christ have refused the Cross? Should the patriots at Concord Bridge have refused to fire the shot heard 'round the world? Are we to believe that all the martyrs of history died in vain?
>
> You and I have a rendezvous with destiny. We can preserve for our children this the last best hope of man on earth or we can sentence them to take the first step into a thousand years of darkness. If we fail, at least let our children and our children's children, say of us we justified our brief moment here. We did all that could be done.[177]

On October 27, 1964, Reagan reprised his GE speech in a television broadcast for Barry Goldwater. Stephen Hess and David Broder hailed it as "the most successful national political debut since William Jennings Bryan electrified the 1896 Democratic convention with his 'Cross of Gold' speech [which also had been carefully pretested on the lecture circuit] and it made Reagan a political star overnight."[178]

But unlike the libertarian Goldwater, Reagan emphasized Judeo-Christian values as necessary ingredients in the fight against communism. As Reagan himself once noted, the Bible contains "all the answers to the problems that face us today."[179] The result was a powerful elixir of politics and religion. The phrase "godless communism" was first popularized by Harry Truman,[180] and religious leaders often used the words in the same breath. In 1949, for example, evangelist Billy Graham said: "Communism is inspired, directed, and motivated by the Devil himself. America is at a crossroads. Will we turn to the left-wingers and atheists, or will we turn to the right and embrace the cross?"[181] In 1954, during the high point of the Cold War, Congress added the words "under God" to the *Pledge of Allegiance*.[182]

But it was Ronald Reagan, more than any other public figure, who effortlessly sang from the hymnal of "godless communism." Reagan was convinced that communism was antithetical to the will of God, and his midwestern upbringing by a profoundly religious mother made him especially well-suited to place God on the side of anticommunism. The Disciples of Christ Church, home to Nelle Reagan and adopted by son Ronald, rejected communism as "tyrannical, immoral, and anti-Christian."[183] Reagan told television interviewer David Frost in 1968 that Jesus Christ was the historical figure he most admired.[184] Fueled by these religious convictions, Reagan turned foreign policy into an issue of morality—especially when it came to communism. In 1961, he addressed a rally of Dr. Fred Schwarz's Christian Anti-Communism Crusade.[185] Fifteen years later, challenging Gerald R. Ford for the Republican presidential nomination, Reagan inserted into the platform a section titled "Morality in Foreign Policy," which read thus: "Honestly, openly, and with firm conviction, we shall go forward as a united people to forge a lasting peace in the world based upon our deep belief in the rights of man, the rule of law, and guidance by the hand of God."[186] Fueling Reagan's outrage was Ford's refusal to receive Soviet dissident Alexander Solzhenitsyn—a decision Reagan not only decried but thought immoral. Later, at a 1984 Dallas prayer breakfast, Reagan connected politics with morality and religion:

> The truth is, politics and morality are inseparable. And as morality's foundation is religion, religion and politics are necessarily related. . . . Without God there is no virtue, because there's no prompting of the conscience. Without God, we're mired in the material, that flat world that tells us only what the senses perceive. Without God, there is a coarsening of the society. And without God, democracy will not and cannot long endure. If we ever forget that we're one nation under God, then we will be a nation gone under.[187]

But it was in a memorable 1983 address that Reagan fused God with anticommunism. Speaking to the National Association of Evangelicals, Reagan damned the Soviet Union as an "evil empire," saying it was "the focus of evil in the modern world." The speech was designed to prevent the ministers from adopting the Democratic party's call for a "nuclear freeze." But it had a larger purpose. Although Reagan presided over the largest peacetime military expenditures in history, he told the evangelicals that something more than firepower was needed: "I've always maintained that the struggle now going on for the world will never be decided by bombs or rockets, by armies or military might. The real crisis we face today is a spiritual one; at root, it is a test of moral will and faith." Reagan resurrected Whittaker Chambers's view that the "crisis of the Western World exists to the degree in which the West is indifferent to God." He sprinkled his address with allusions to the Almighty, claiming that religious apathy was tantamount to "collusion" with communists. Reagan called communism a counterreligion premised on man rather than God: "[It is] the second oldest faith, first proclaimed in the Garden of Eden with the words of temptation, 'Ye shall be as gods.'" Only God and country could provide victory in the Cold War—an article of faith Reagan thought preordained: "I believe that communism is another sad, bizarre chapter in human history whose last pages even now are being written." Meanwhile, he asked those present to pray for "the salvation of all those who live in that totalitarian darkness."[188]

Reagan's words resonated with most Americans. Seventy-three percent in a December 1983 poll said that the "real problem with communism is that it threatens our religious and moral values."[189] An equal percentage in an earlier survey agreed with this statement: "By sending military aid to countries threatened by communism and by being tough with the Russians, Reagan is sending a message to Moscow that will rebuild respect for the United States in the Kremlin."[190] Christian fundamentalists were especially supportive. For years, they had abhorred communism and shared a belief in a strong military. In 1980, the Moral Majority bought newspaper advertisements that read: "We cannot afford to be number two in defense! But, sadly enough, that's where we are today. Number two. And fading!" Jerry Falwell, founder of the Moral Majority, deplored the "sad fact" that an all-out nuclear exchange with the Soviet Union "would kill 135 million to 160 million Americans, and the United States would kill only 3 to 5 percent of the Soviets."[191]

Thus, Reagan and the evangelicals were in sync on defense matters—and when it came to the satanic aspects of communism. This was especially true when, in 1983, Reagan elevated the plight of seven Soviet Pentecostals who had taken refuge in the U.S. embassy five years earlier. Vice President George Bush told Soviet Ambassador Anatoly Dobrynin, "I may sound bizarre to the Soviet government, but Reagan attaches great significance to the Pentecostals' case."[192] Eventually, the seven were granted exit visas—thanks to Reagan's intervention and a constant barrage of criticism from Christian Americans.

Reagan's overt linking of religion and anticommunism elevated his popularity ratings. But there was another dimension to his appeal. Frequently, he evoked the millenarian sentiments so commonly and passionately felt by the evangelicals. Upon listening to the "evil empire" speech, for example, several born-again Christians thought they were hearing the fulfillment of prophesies found in the Book of Revelations, which heralded the coming of the Anti-Christ. Revelations 13:17 said the Anti-Christ would have "the mark of the Beast" on his forehead—something many took as a reference to Soviet Communist Party chief Mikhail Gorbachev's wine-colored birthmark. Ezekiel 38 and 39 predicted that the final war would come from the north, which many born-agains interpreted as meaning the Soviet Union. Jerry Falwell often made etymological linkages between Russian and biblical names, and Reagan was fascinated to learn that the Russian word for "wormwood" was Chernobyl.[193] Reagan himself believed Armageddon was nigh, telling televangelist Jim Bakker in 1980: "We may be the generation that sees Armageddon."[194] According to Jeffrey K. Hadden and Anson Shupe, "Reagan's first term in office saw evangelicals enjoying unprecedented access to the presidency and the White House, with theological liberals and moderates virtually locked out. Jerry Falwell replaced the more establishment evangelical Billy Graham as the White House's unofficial chaplain."[195] That access reflected the newfound power of the evangelicals: In 1978, 25 Christian ministries regularly broadcast on the tube; by 1989, the number grew to 336.[196]

The linkage Reagan made between anticommunism and religion, coupled with his support for traditional moral values, translated into unprecedented support from the Christian Right.[197] In 1980, Reagan got 61 percent support from white evangelicals; in 1984, 81 percent. Bush also received 81 percent of the born-again vote against his secular opponent, Michael Dukakis, in 1988, and a less impressive but substantial 61 percent backing in 1992.

Catholics, not often associated with the Christian Right, were also inspired by Reagan's rhetoric and remained a key target for GOP strategists. For decades, the Roman Catholic hierarchy had opposed communism as self-avowed atheism. In 1978, that struggle culminated with the election of the cardinal of Krakow, Karol Jozef Wojtyla, to the papacy. Pope John Paul II had spent decades tormenting the communist regime in his native Poland. Like him, many Catholic Americans stood shoulder-to-shoulder with their Eastern European cousins. Patrick Buchanan, a Catholic high school student during the late 1940s, recalled one memorable incident:

> When the Communist regime in Budapest announced in 1948 the coming trial for treason of Josef Cardinal Mindszenty, the Primate of Hungary who had resisted both the Nazis and the communists, there was enormous anguish. Cardinal Mindszenty was constantly in the prayers of the nuns and the school children, and when the newspapers displayed months later, the shocking picture of the drugged and broken prelate as he "confessed" at one of Stalin's ugliest "show trials," the Catholic world was stunned. We did not need any classroom discussion about Marxism to recognize the evil of communism; it was written all over the tortured face of the Catholic priest.[198]

Buchanan recalled that his Catholicism—the church of Cardinals Wyszyski, Stepinac, and Mindszenty, Pope Pius XI, and Pope Pius XII—did not believe in "coexistence with communist regimes." In 1930, the Pope asked Catholic Americans to pray for the reconversion of Russia with a prayer at each Mass that read: "Blessed Michael the Archangel! Defend us in the day of battle! Be our safeguard against the wickedness and snares of the enemy. Rebuke him, O God, we humbly pray! And do thou, O Prince of the Heavenly Host, thrust back into Hell Satan and all other evil spirits who wander through the world seeking the ruin of souls." As Buchanan put it: "This is not the rhetoric of détente." Some years later, watching Soviet schoolchildren being indoctrinated into the Young Octoberists, Buchanan likened the Cold War to "a religious war for control of the soul and destiny of mankind, the outcome of which cannot be arbitrated or negotiated."[199]

The fusion of religion with anticommunism paid enormous political dividends. Catholics, long a mainstay of the New Deal coalition, slowly abandoned their Democratic heritage. Part of that breaking-away resulted from their joining the ranks of the middle class. As they acquired middle-class values, Catholics (like their Protestant brethren) became increasingly critical of excessive federal spending—especially moneys diverted to minority (read: black) programs. Viewing the government through the green eyeshades of middle-class taxpayers, they left the Democratic party in droves. But their political drift had its origins in Republican denunciations of FDR's "sellout" at Yalta. Catholics, remembering the martyrs in the East, lent receptive ears to Republican charges that their sacrifices were made on the altar at Yalta.

Beginning with Dwight Eisenhower's 1952 campaign, Republicans fervently courted Eastern Europeans. Over the years, their appeals intensified. In March 1956, A. B. Hermann, a Republican who worked at the party's national committee, asked Chairman Leonard Hall to reactivate the Republican Nationalities Division. Hermann reminded Hall that 85 percent of voters with antecedents behind the Iron Curtain lived in seventeen states with a total of 302 electoral votes. Hall took Herman's advice, and the Republican Nationalities Division distributed "I Like Ike" buttons in ten languages along with 500,000 pamphlets titled *The Republican Policy of Liberation*.[200]

A shrewd political calculus emerged: Although freeing Eastern Europe was impractical since it could lead to war, Republicans continued to preach the gospel of liberation. The 1956 platform was typical: "We shall continue to seek ... the liberation of the satellite states—Poland, Czechoslovakia, Hungary, Rumania, Bulgaria, Latvia, Lithuania, Estonia and other, once-free countries now behind the Iron Curtain. The Republican party stands firmly with the peoples of these countries in their just quest for freedom. We are confident that our peaceful policies, resolutely pursued, will finally restore freedom and national independence to oppressed peoples and nations."[201] Four years later, during the 1960 presidential race, Republicans tried to neutralize John F. Kennedy's Catholic appeal by stressing their solidarity with the Catholic-dominated nations of Eastern Europe. American Nationalities for Nixon-Lodge printed fliers claiming it was during "the Roosevelt-Truman era when the freedom of millions of people in Europe and Asia was turned over to communist slavery." That same committee distributed 48,000 foreign-language buttons, held freedom rallies in cities with large Polish populations (including Buffalo and Chicago), and printed thousands of postcards showing the famous Nixon-Khrushchev "kitchen debate." Republicans also denounced Kennedy's call to withdraw from the islands of Quemoy and Matsu off the Chinese mainland. GOP National Chairman Thruston Morton depicted Kennedy's stance as "reminiscent of the spirit of Yalta," and American Nationalities for Nixon-Lodge claimed JFK was "part and parcel of the disastrous 'appeasement and retreat' policy advocated for many years by the pro-Soviet Hiss-Acheson clique in the U.S. Department of State."[202]

Nixon was quite ready to play the Catholic card. He declared October 23–29, 1960, "Operation Freedom Week," and he began it by denouncing "Soviet brutality and imperialism," promising never to accept "the status quo of Soviet and communist domination over the people of the Captive Nations." Former Hungarian freedom fighters spoke at these rallies, where audiences watched a film with a voice-over that touted Nixon and Lodge as "fighting for freedom at home and abroad; in Greece, Italy, and even in the heart of communism, the Soviet Union." Speaking to a Polish audience in Michigan, Nixon promised that, if elected, he would visit Eastern Europe "to carry the message of freedom into the communist world." Later, in a television talk forty-eight hours before the balloting, Nixon—in an appeal reminiscent of Eisenhower's pledge to go to Korea—invited leaders from the Captive Nations to visit the United States, and in a dramatic flourish he announced that he would send Eisenhower on a reciprocal visit. Ike replied that he was "ready to go" and suggested that former presidents Truman and Hoover accompany him.[203]

Despite Nixon's big play for Catholics, Kennedy won 78 percent of their votes.[204] One postelection study found Polish voters in Buffalo, Chicago, and Detroit supported Kennedy by margins ranging from two-to-one to nine-to-one.[205] Still, Republicans remained undeterred. In 1964, Barry Goldwater addressed several ethnic gatherings. One memorable occasion was a rally of 6,000 Eastern European mill workers in Hammond, Indiana. When Goldwater pledged that under his administration the Soviet satellites would be freed, the crowd roared its approval. When he insisted that only victory in the Communist War would end communism, they cheered again. Signs sprinkled throughout the crowd read: "Tito killed U.S. flyers"; "Serbian democracy supports Goldwater"; "Tito murderer."[206]

In successive elections, Republicans continued to play the ethnic card. In 1980, Ronald Reagan began his campaign with an "ethnic picnic" at Liberty Park, New Jersey, standing toe-to-toe with the father of Poland's Solidarity leader, Lech Walesa. With the Statue of Liberty serving as a backdrop and the flags of Eastern European nations waving in the breeze, Reagan clasped Walesa's hand and led the crowd in singing "God Bless America."[207] The 1984 GOP platform repeated Reagan's steadfast opposition to Soviet control of Eastern Europe: "The heroic efforts of Lech Walesa and the Solidarity movement in Poland are an inspiration to all people yearning to be free. We are not neutral in their struggle, wherever the flame of liberty brightens the black night of Soviet oppression."[208]

As the years passed, Republican inroads into formerly Democratic Catholic bastions increased. Exit polls from the 1976, 1980, 1984, and 1988 presidential contests showed GOP presidential candidates receiving 44, 50, 54, and 52 percent of Catholic support respectively. With the passage of time, Catholic votes began to draw close to the national totals—a leveling of presidential contests.

A Top-Down Party

As president, Richard Nixon confided to White House Chief of Staff H.R. Haldeman that the American people "are like helpless children yearning for leadership, someone to tell them what to do, and therefore you have to keep doing something in order to satisfy this yearning."[209] Throughout the Cold War, Republican presidents attempted to satisfy this desire for leadership by emphasizing the righteousness of the American cause. In public opinion soundings conducted from 1956 to 1988, Republican candidates frequently out-polled their Democratic counterparts on foreign policy questions, especially when it came to managing the superpower relationship (see Table 4.2). Only Lyndon Johnson in 1964 (not surprisingly) and Jimmy Carter in 1980 (ironically and briefly) were able to neutralize the Republican advantage.

Although voters generally liked tough Republican presidents when it came dealing with communists, the Republican party paid a high price for its presidential victories. Instead of adding more adherents, Eisenhower, Nixon, Reagan, and Bush were "plebiscitary presidents"—winning personal victories at the expense of partisan ones.[210] In so doing, they fulfilled a prophetic warning issued by the American Political Science Association in 1950 at the height of the Cold War:

> When the president's program actually is the sole program, either his party becomes a flock of sheep or the party falls apart. This concept of the presidency disposes of the party system by making the president reach directly for the support of a majority of voters. It favors a president who exploits skillfully the arts of demagoguery, who uses the whole country as his political backyard, and who does not mind turning into the embodiment of personal government.
>
> A generation ago one might have dismissed this prospect as fantastic. At the midway mark of the twentieth century the American people have reason to know better, from recent and current examples abroad, what it does not want.

TABLE 4.2

Perceptions of Presidential Candidates' Ability to Handle Foreign Affairs, Selected Polls, 1956–1988

Text of Question	Public Response
"In general, do you approve or disapprove of the way the present officials in Washington are handling our foreign affairs?"[a] (1956)	
Percentage "approve"	74
"Which of these two men, Nixon or Kennedy, if elected president do you think would do the most effective job of dealing with Russia's leaders?"[b] (1960)	
Percentage answering "Nixon"	43
Percentage answering "Kennedy"	39
"How much trust and confidence would you have in the way Barry Goldwater would handle Khrushchev and relations with Russia?"[c] (1964)	
Percentage answering "a very great deal" or "considerable" confidence in Goldwater	34
"How much trust and confidence would you have in the way Lyndon Johnson and his administration would handle Khrushchev and relations with Russia?"[d] (1964)	
Percentage answering "a very great deal" or "considerable" confidence in Johnson	67
"Agree/Disagree. Richard Nixon knows how to stand up to communists."[e] (1968)	
Percentage answering "agree"	53
"If he were president, who do you think would be better able to negotiate with the Russians and Chinese—Nixon or McGovern?"[f] (1972)	
Percentage answering "Nixon"	70
Percentage answering "McGovern"	11
"Now, if you had to choose, who do you think could do a better job as president on handling relations with Russia—Gerald Ford or Jimmy Carter?"[g] (1976)	
Percentage answering "Ford"	41
Percentage answering "Carter"	30
"I'm going to mention some problems facing the nation today and as I mention each one I would like you to tell me who you thought would do the best job of handling that problem—Gerald Ford or Jimmy Carter. . . . Maintaining a strong national defense."[h] (1976)	
Percentage answering "Ford"	49
Percentage answering "Carter"	29

(continues)

TABLE 4.2 *(continued)*

Text of Question	Public Response
"How would you rate the specific job President Carter has done while in office on handling relations with Russia?"[i] (1980)	
Percentage answering "excellent/pretty good"	26
Percentage answering "only fair/poor"	70
"Regardless of which man you happen to prefer—Carter, Reagan, or Anderson—please tell me which one you, yourself, feel would do a better job of dealing with Russia?"[j] (1980)	
Percentage answering "Reagan"	36
Percentage answering "Carter"	40
Percentage answering "Anderson"	10
"Does the following phrase apply more to Ronald Reagan or to Walter Mondale? . . . More capable of handling relations with the Soviet Union."[k] (1984)	
Percentage answering "Reagan"	69
Percentage answering "Mondale"	20
"Based on what you know about Walter Mondale and Ronald Reagan as a whole, which of the two presidential candidates is likely to maintain our military strength relative to the Soviet Union?"[l] (1984)	
Percentage answering "Reagan"	69
Percentage answering "Mondale"	20
"I'm going to read a list of important issues facing the country that a president must deal with. For each one mention, please tell me whether you feel George Bush or Michael Dukakis would do a better job of handling that particular issue? . . . Guarding against Soviet aggression."[m] (1988)	
Percentage answering "Bush"	62
Percentage answering "Dukakis"	24
"Thinking about the same list of issues, please tell me whether you feel George Bush or Michael Dukakis would do a better job of handling that particular issue. . . . Handling relations with the Soviet Union."[n] (1988)	
Percentage answering "Bush"	67
Percentage answering "Dukakis"	22

[a]National Opinion Research Corporation survey, November 1956.
[b]Gallup poll, October 18–23, 1960.
[c]Gallup poll, October 1964.

(continues)

TABLE 4.2 *(continued)*

[d]Gallup poll, October 1964.
[e]Louis Harris and Associates, survey, September 11–13, 1968.
[f]Opinion Research Corporation, survey, October 20–22, 1972.
[g]Louis Harris and Associates, survey, September 1976.
[h]Robert M. Teeter, National Surveys, November 1976.
[i]ABC News/Louis Harris and Associates, survey, November 7–10, 1980.
[j]Gallup poll, September 12–15, 1980.
[k]Gallup poll, October 21, 1984.
[l]Gordon Black survey for *USA Today*, September 25–26, 1984.
[m]Daniel Yankelovich Group, survey, November 4–7, 1988.
[n]Daniel Yankelovich Group, survey, November 4–7, 1988.

Because Americans are so sure on that score, they cannot afford to be casual about overextending the presidency to the point where it might very well ring in the wrong ending.[211]

But the "wrong ending" is exactly what happened to the Republican party. From 1937 until 1995, Gallup inquiries about partisan affinities found few Republican gains (see Table 4.3). Indeed, the party's base of support was stuck at about one-third of the electorate. That figure was not improved upon, despite the obvious Democratic weaknesses and the singular achievements posted by Republican presidents during the Cold War.

Moreover, as the Cold War droned on, Republican White Houses became staffed by men (and some women) whose party credentials were less than sterling. Most Cabinet officers, for example, had never held elective office. Rather, their expertise lay in managing bureaucracies (William Rogers, Henry Kissinger, Alexander Haig, George Shultz, Caspar Weinberger, James Baker). The few Cold War Democratic presidents followed a similar pattern (see Dean Rusk, Robert McNamara, Cyrus Vance, Harold Brown, Warren Christopher). These White House staffers often were presidential loyalists rather than partisans. As President Johnson once said of Secretary of State Rusk: "I'll always love Dean Rusk, bless his heart. He stayed with me when nobody else did."[212]

The plebiscitary presidency reached its zenith during the Nixon administration. H. R. Haldeman, John Ehrlichman, and the ubiquitous Chuck Colson (who declared he would run over his grandmother, if necessary, to re-elect his boss in 1972) erected a political Berlin Wall separating the president from his party. They were so effective that the word "Republican" was banished from Nixon's television advertisements and campaign brochures. The dreaded R-word never emanated from the presidential lips. Instead, Nixon touted his "new American majority" as an alignment without the party-as-midwife. Accepting renomination in 1972, Nixon told the

TABLE 4.3
Partisan Identification, Selected Gallup Organization Studies, 1937–1995

Year	Democrats	Republicans	Independents
1937	53	32	16
1940	44	36	20
1944	43	39	18
1948	50	30	20
1952	51	29	20
1956	44	35	21
1960	47	29	24
1964	52	25	23
1968	42	28	30
1972	40	28	32
1976	48	24	28
1980	36	32	31
1984	39	35	27
1988	36	32	31
1993	36	30	32
1995	28	31	37

SOURCE: Gallup surveys, 1937–1995. Text of question: "In politics, as of today, do you consider yourself a Republican, a Democrat, or an Independent?"

delegates: "I ask everyone listening to me tonight—Democrats, Republicans, independents, to join our new majority—not on the basis of the party label you wear in your lapel, but on the basis of what you believe in your hearts."[213] Nixon's successor, Gerald Ford, followed a similar strategy in 1976. The Ford campaign plan advised their man to become a stealth candidate when it came to making a case for the Republican party: "The President must not campaign for GOP candidates. This will seriously erode his support among independents and ticket-splitters. The President should not attend any party fundraisers. Any *support* given to a GOP candidate must be done in a manner to *avoid* national media attention. For example, the President can make telephone calls, sign mailers, do videotape endorsements for fundraisers, etc."[214]

The rise of the president as manager removed from any partisan taint reflected a general elevation of expertise throughout American society. As noted earlier, scientists were extolled during the Cold War—especially those engaged in developing the technology used to thwart the Soviets. A 1957 survey found a proclivity to consult experts about nearly everything:

> Experts took the role of psychic healer, but they also assumed a much broader and more important role in directing the behavior, goals, and ideals of normal people. They became the teachers and norm setters who would tell people how to approach and live life. . . . They would provide advice and counsel about rais-

ing and responding to children, how to behave in marriage, and what to see in that relationship. . . . Science moved in because people needed and wanted guidance.[215]

The demand for expertise extended into the realm of politics. Professional campaign managers and pollsters replaced old-time party bosses. The Republican and Democratic National Committees grew from modest circumstances in the 1950s to become the modern bureaucratic moneymaking organizations of the 1990s. But, most notably, the reliance on expertise decoupled the president from party. Presidential elections became referendums on the incumbent, and partisan considerations no longer mattered much. The nationalization of these contests without a reliance on the parties contributed to the rise of landslide elections. As Table 4.4 demonstrates, landslides, once a rarity in the nineteenth century, were commonplace in the late twentieth. By 1992, five of the top ten presidential landslides occurred during the Cold War years, and the Republicans won four.

Political analyst Samuel Lubell termed these landslides "total elections"—ones where presidents exercised nearly complete control of foreign policy and the economy in a manner designed to control the outcome. To wit: In 1968, a fifty-year-old mechanic at the Naval Ordinance Station in Indianhead, Maryland, told Lubell: "I had no use for Nixon when they were going to close our plant down a year ago. We lost a hundred people who weren't replaced." But by election day the mechanic had become a Nixon convert: "Now it looks like they'll keep us open. We got five new contracts to build guns for Vietnam, and they're hiring 800 more men."[216]

The change in the president—from a person of civic virtue in George Washington's day; to Martin Van Buren's partisan leader; to "boss" and commander in chief during the Cold War—was considerable. In a 1963 television interview, columnist Walter Lippmann remarked: "This is a most presidential country. The tone and example set by a president have a tremendous effect on the quality of life in America. The president is like a conductor of a big symphony orchestra."[217] But all too often presidents could not resist playing solos. During the 1960 campaign, John F. Kennedy spoke of the president as one who was "alone at the top."[218] Presidential chronologer Theodore H. White agreed, writing in 1960 that the presidency had become an "entirely personal office. . . . He calls the dance." Indeed, White spoke reverently of "a hush, an entirely personal hush" that surrounded the presidency when it came to the life-or-death issues surrounding the Cold War. White noted that the silence was "deepest in the Oval Office of the West Wing of the White House, where the president, however many his advisers, must sit alone."[219]

And alone they were, especially during times of crisis when nuclear catastrophes hung like swords of Damocles over the globe. Although most

TABLE 4.4
The Rise of "Total Elections": The Top Ten Presidential Landslides in American History

Year	Principal Candidates	Winner's Percentage of the Total Vote Cast	Winner's Margin (in percentage) over the Main Challenger
1964	Johnson, Goldwater	61.1	22.6
1972	Nixon, McGovern	60.8	23.2
1936	F. Roosevelt, Landon	60.8	24.3
1920	Harding, Cox	60.3	26.2
1984	Reagan, Mondale	59.2	18.4
1928	Hoover, Smith	58.2	17.4
1956	Eisenhower, Stevenson	57.4	15.4
1904	T. Roosevelt, Parker	56.4	18.8
1952	Eisenhower, Stevenson	55.1	10.7

SOURCE: Partially derived from Everett Carll Ladd Jr. with Charles D. Hadley, Transformations of the American Party System (New York: W. W. Norton, 1975), p. 279.

commanders in chief adopted the dictum of King Louis XIV—L'état, c'est moi—they did not have the party—or much else—to fall back upon when the inevitable troubles came. Theodore J. Lowi wrote that plebiscitary presidents "must live on appearances and have contingency plans for deceit, yet they are not part of a protective tradition of a ruling class tied by history and religion to the system of governance."[220] Instead, a fickle public seemed disposed to dispatch presidents at will.

Visiting the Oval Office for the final time on the morning of January 20, 1989, Ronald Reagan turned to an aide and said, "I am proud to say I am still an anticommunist."[221] Following Reagan's lead, Republicans pursued a Cold War strategy designed to pick the electoral lock created by Franklin Roosevelt's New Deal: Republicans became a national and patriotic party. Republican pollster Fred Steeper admitted, "We do best against the Democrats when we use nationalism."[222] But by becoming the voice for a superpatriotic nationalism, the base of the party was separated from its leadership. This was a significant change from the nineteenth century, when both parties were mostly local organizations responding to local concerns, worrying about electing friends and neighbors to community offices, and quarreling over the spoils of patronage. Back then, the Democrats were mostly a southern party and the Republicans a northern one. By 1936, the New Deal nationalized the Democratic party to a point where it could compete with the Republicans for the nation's highest office nearly everywhere. The Cold War did much the same for the Republicans. As Chapter 5 will show, a new party system without parties became an enduring legacy of the Cold War.

chapter five

The Divided Democrats

American politics will never be the same again.

—George S. McGovern, July 13, 1972

September 13, 1988

Michael Dukakis was in trouble. Just two months earlier, the Democratic presidential nominee led Republican George Bush by 17 points in the Gallup poll trial heats. But Dukakis's lead evaporated as the warm air of summer turned into the cool, crisp breezes of fall. The Massachusetts Democrat took to the hustings, pleading for support from voters who suspiciously regarded him as a 1960s-style liberal. Meanwhile, George Bush borrowed a phrase from Joseph McCarthy's playbook, calling Dukakis a "card-carrying member" of the much-maligned American Civil Liberties Union.[1] Employing the Red-baiting tactics of the 1950s, Bush maintained that Dukakis was more interested in protecting flag-burners than in protecting the rest of the citizenry from either criminals or communists. When asked why he backed Bush, one Cuban American retorted: "I like the flag. I don't like Jane Fonda, liberals, and communists."[2] Indeed, one-fourth of the electorate still associated the phrase "soft on communism" with liberalism.[3]

Thus, it was in these circumstances that Dukakis traveled to Sterling Heights, Michigan, in mid-September to woo "Reagan Democrats" back to the fold. He had some reason for hope. Bush lacked Reagan's charisma, and Dukakis, taking advantage of Reagan's absence on the ballot, tried to position himself as a different type of Democrat. Sterling Heights was ideally suited to test-market the new strategy. Many of its blue-collar workers were employed by General Dynamic's Land System Division, which manufactured the M-1, dubbed the "most lethal tank in the world."[4]

On his visit, Dukakis told General Dynamic employees that as president he would ensure their jobs by spending more on conventional weapons like

the M-1. Dukakis taunted Bush, recalling how he had once touted the superiority of Soviet tank workers: "Mr. Bush, I'd rather have mechanics from
Michigan."[5] To punctuate his remarks, Dukakis's handlers put their man
into an M-1 tank. In so doing, they copied a tactic from the Bush campaign. A few months before, George Bush had also visited the Sterling
Heights facility and climbed into an M-1 tank to prove that he, too, was
tough on defense. Reminded of Bush's action, Dukakis obliged. Donning a
green tank helmet and gripping the handle of a 7.62-millimeter machine
gun, Dukakis wore his Sly Stallone grin and took aim at ABC News reporter Sam Donaldson, who was watching from a distance.[6] "Rat-a-tat,"
he murmured, as a band played the theme from the movie *Patton*.[7] That
night the evening newscasts poked fun at Dukakis. NBC News correspondent Chris Wallace said the Democrat looked "like Patton on his way to
Berlin." CBS Reporter Bruce Morton called Dukakis a "Massachusetts
Rambo on the prowl."[8] From Bismarck, North Dakota, Republican vice
presidential nominee Dan Quayle derisively dismissed Dukakis as a faker:
"The man from Massachusetts is the most anti-defense candidate on a national level since George McGovern. He's pretending he's had a midnight
conversion on defense, but he didn't just find religion—he found his poll
numbers."[9]

Quayle was right on that last point. When it came to national defense and
foreign policy, voters overwhelmingly preferred Bush: 67 percent said Bush
could best conduct U.S.-U.S.S.R. relations; 64 percent trusted him to negotiate arms control agreements; 62 percent said he could best prevent aggressive Soviet behavior.[10] A plurality thought Bush was likely to *strengthen* national security; Dukakis, by a three-to-one margin, was seen as apt to
weaken it. Moreover, the Republicans had a 33-point advantage as the party
best able to "deal effectively with the Soviet Union."[11] Thus, Bush campaign
manager Lee Atwater was delighted to learn that Dukakis was headed to
Michigan to make national defense his "theme of the week": "If national
defense is the number one topic of the week, that's a loser for him."[12]

Atwater's analysis was astute. Most Americans thought Dukakis had a
lot to learn when it came to conducting the Cold War: 69 percent said he
was "lacking in the foreign policy experience which a candidate should
have";[13] an equal number thought he "still needs to prove he knows
enough foreign policy."[14] Dukakis was not helped by the fact that he had
never met a Soviet leader. Thus, it was not terribly surprising that voters, by
better than a two-to-one margin, named Bush when asked which of the two
candidates could better handle the superpower relationship.[15]

By the fall of 1988, Dukakis was trying to regain momentum in the presidential race by assuming a tough, anti-Soviet posture. Speaking to the
Chicago Council on Foreign Relations, Dukakis argued that he and his fellow Democrats had finally overcome their post-Vietnam timidity: "We must

maintain our military strength, increase our economic strength, preserve our alliances, and reaffirm our willingness to respond to force with force in defense of our vital interests around the world."[16] Then Dukakis took the offensive, claiming that it was Reagan and Bush who were soft on defense:

> In Central Europe today, the most serious danger we face is the two-to-one Warsaw Pact advantage in modern tanks. Yet the Republicans have already cut our tank production and want to slash it almost in half again next year. And after eight years in office, they have still failed to deploy an infantry anti-tank missile that can take out modern Soviet tanks. A recent government report estimated that *up to 85 percent* of the infantry soldiers using today's anti-tank weapons to stop a Soviet tank attack in Europe would be dead after firing a single round! And that round would bounce off the Soviet tank.[17]

Dukakis's tough rhetoric did not persuade even some of his fellow Democrats. Former Carter national security adviser Zbignew Brzezinski declared for Bush, saying Dukakis was "closer to Jesse Jackson and Jane Fonda" when it came to making foreign policy.[18] Such accusations still mattered more than forty years after the Cold War began. Pollster Daniel Yankelovich concluded that "the power of national security issues should not be underestimated in presidential politics," adding that the Cold War "may well have made the difference for George Bush."[19] The polls confirmed his analysis: 63 percent said foreign affairs and national security were very important to them personally; 79 percent saw them as vital to the national well-being.[20] Moreover, 52 percent viewed Soviet aggression as an "extremely serious" or "very serious" threat.[21] Despite the new closeness in superpower relations forged by Ronald Reagan and Mikhail Gorbachev, two-thirds of Americans remained wary of Soviet intentions.[22] In fact, three-fourths wanted the next president to pay as much attention to military matters as to economic concerns.[23]

Republicans saw advantages in the new foreign policy arrangements and highlighted them whenever they could. Forty-three percent of Bush voters characterized foreign policy as a very important issue; only 24 percent of Dukakis voters gave it a high priority, placing it far below the economy, social issues, the environment, and the personal characteristics of the candidates. *Boston Globe* reporters Christine M. Black and Tom Oliphant wrote that the Cold War had become synonymous with Democratic weakness: "In 1988, foreign policy was a metaphor for the personal qualities Americans want their presidents to radiate—stature, readiness, and strength."[24] But by allowing himself to be placed in that tank Dukakis became a caricature of everything the public found distasteful about the Democratic party. After watching Dukakis circle about in the M-1, Bush media adviser Roger Ailes authorized a commercial using Dukakis's own visual—the first time this had been done in presidential politics. Soon afterwards, television sets flickered with the image of the helmeted candidate as a narrator ominously intoned:

> Michael Dukakis has opposed virtually every defense system we developed. He opposed new aircraft carriers. He opposed four missile systems, including the Pershing Two Missile deployment. Dukakis opposed the Stealth bomber and a ground emergency warning system against nuclear attack. He even criticized our rescue mission to Grenada and our strike against Libya. And now he wants to be our Commander-in-Chief. America can't afford that risk.[25]

In fact, several of these claims were false. Dukakis had not opposed "virtually every defense system"; and he rejected two, not four, missile systems—the MX and the Midgetman.[26] But that did not stop Republicans from denouncing Dukakis for being "soft on communism." Bush derided Dukakis, telling voters, "The tank kept veering to the left."[27] Senate Republican Steven Symms of Idaho even accused Kitty Dukakis of burning an American flag at a 1970 Vietnam War demonstration, claiming a photograph existed to support his allegation. None was ever produced, and the charge was absolutely false.[28]

From the Kremlin, Mikhail Gorbachev watched the candidates trade accusations with a wry perspective. In December 1987, Gorbachev gave Bush a lift in his Zil limousine during a summit meeting with President Reagan. As the two men zoomed through the streets of Washington, Bush confided that he would seek the presidency the following year and that he would issue many anti-Soviet statements in order to win. Bush advised Gorbachev to ignore these remarks, saying that when he came to power he would remove the "marginal intellectual thugs" that formulated Reagan's policy toward the Soviet Union. Gorbachev told his Politburo colleagues that this was the "most important talk Bush and I ever had," and he reassured them about the presumptive president: "Don't worry. His heart is in the right place."[29]

Gorbachev's reassurances were valid. Candidate Bush promised: "I will not get rid of the MX, [nor] get rid of the Midgetman. I will not make those unilateral cuts in defense." But President Bush scrapped the MX and Midgetman missiles and halted production of the B-2 stealth bomber. Moreover, in an ironic twist of fate, the M-1 tank proved an essential weapon in the Gulf War when paired against the Soviet-supplied T-62 and T-72 tanks used by Saddam Hussein.[30]

Dukakis tried desperately to respond to Bush's charges. In a hastily-made commercial titled "Counterpunch," the grim, shirt-sleeved candidate was shown watching Bush's tank advertisement. He switched off the television set and said: "I'm fed up with it. George Bush's negative ads are full of lies and he knows it." But by the time "Counterpunch" was first aired on October 21, 1988, the damage was done: Dukakis trailed Bush by 10 points.[31] Moreover, of those who saw Dukakis riding in the tank, 25 percent said they were "less likely" to support him; only 7 percent said they were "more likely" to vote for him.[32]

Years later, Dukakis bitterly recalled how he found himself in an M-1 tank, saying it had become a "political imperative" to counter the widespread view that "Democrats tend to be soft, not willing to engage, not willing to commit force."[33] Dukakis campaign manager John Sasso echoed a similar view: "It is politically dangerous to take for granted that voters will automatically assume the Democratic candidate holds dear the country's basic values: God, patriotism, family, and freedom. In some historically perverse way, Democrats must—at least for now—work hard to prove they are as politically wholesome and decent as Republicans."[34] Even Jane Fonda's then-husband, California state assemblyman Tom Hayden, sought to distance himself from his fellow liberals: "Having lost God, the flag, national defense, tax relief, personal safety, and traditional family values to the conservatives, it becomes more than a little difficult for these liberals to explain why they should be entrusted with the authority to govern."[35] A revealing 1988 survey confirms how modern-day liberalism had become a pariah. When asked if Michael Dukakis was "a liberal in the tradition of Franklin D. Roosevelt, Harry S. Truman, and John F. Kennedy," or "a liberal in the tradition of George McGovern and Walter Mondale," 35 percent cast Dukakis in the McGovern-Mondale mold, whereas just 21 percent saw him as the heir to FDR, Truman, and JFK.[36] The Democrats had come a long way from the last man to be nominated for president from Massachusetts: John F. Kennedy.

John F. Kennedy and the Action Intellectuals

Michael Dukakis once described John Kennedy as a "political child of the Cold War," admiring how his hero had "out-hawked Richard Nixon on national security policy" in 1960.[37] By demonstrating his anticommunist machismo, Kennedy was like many who came of political age during World War II and the Cold War. As a college student, he penned *Why England Slept*, a study of how British unpreparedness and Neville Chamberlain's naïveté paved Hitler's way across Europe. Kennedy had the fiery image of Pearl Harbor emblazoned in his mind, and, like many of his fellow World War II veterans, he was determined never to let the United States be caught unawares again—especially when it came to potential Soviet aggrandizement.

Thus, when it came to measuring Soviet intentions, Kennedy was an unrepentant hawk. In the Foreword to the 1961 edition of *Why England Slept*, Henry Luce wrote that President Kennedy posed a searching question to his fellow Americans: "Will the American of the '60's behave better than the Englishman of the '30's?"[38] Kennedy's fierce anticommunism and his belief, as expressed in *Why England Slept*, that democracies were often ill-prepared to do battle with dictatorships occasionally won him some strange bedfellows. As a Democratic U.S. representative in 1949, Kennedy had blasted Truman for "losing" China. A year later he had tacitly supported Nixon in his quest for California's open Senate seat. In 1952, Joseph McCarthy received $5,000 from Kennedy's father, Joe, for his reelection campaign, and younger brother Bobby went to work for the senator from Wisconsin. Eight years later, Kennedy won plaudits from the conservative-minded Veterans of Foreign Wars when he declared that the United States should always be the world's greatest military superpower: "I do not mean first, but. I do not mean first, and. I do not mean first, if. I mean first—period."[39]

Kennedy's anticommunist credentials were burnished during his congressional tenure. As a member of the House Labor Committee, he won perjury indictments against two United Auto Worker officials who had lied about their membership in the U.S. Communist Party. The *Boston Herald* credited Congressman Kennedy with flushing out these "conspicuous traitors to this country."[40] In the Senate, Kennedy sat on the prestigious Foreign Relations Committee (along with J. William Fulbright), where he became a frequent Eisenhower critic. Senator Kennedy accused Ike of being "wholly unprepared" for the 1956 Hungarian crisis: "One needs little imagination to appreciate the feeling of frustration which overcame the people of Eastern Europe to hear that the United States had never meant the obvious implications of its 'liberation' policy."[41] In 1958, he warned that the United States was about to lose "its superiority in nuclear striking power,"[42] and he chided Eisenhower for voicing "appealing shibboleths" when it came to dealing with communism (an example: "maximum safety at minimum cost").[43] Kennedy maintained that such soothing reassurances masked the harsh realities of the Cold War. He criticized Secretary of State John Foster Dulles's bellicose rhetoric as a poor substitute for global thinking: "We need a new approach to the Russians—one that is just as hard-headed and just as realistic as Mr. Khrushchev's, but one that might well end the current phase—the frozen, belligerent, brink-of-war phase—of the long Cold War."[44]

After an encounter with Kennedy, Cyrus Sulzberger, nephew of the publisher of the *New York Times*, confided in his diary, "He thinks foreign policy will be the main electoral issue in the sense that the Republicans will be attacked for letting the United States slip backward in the power race." Kennedy's handpicked Democratic national chairman, Senator Henry Jackson of Washington, concurred: "National security will be the major issue. The public is going to expect a hard, tough line."[45] Kennedy acted accordingly. In a 1960 campaign tract, he declared that "to sound the alarm is not to panic," but "the sound of the alarm does warn us that time is running out." The Democratic nominee described the 1950s as "the years the locusts have eaten," and he warned that if the status quo were continued the

United States would continue its downhill slide "into dust, dullness, languor, and decay," adding: "If we begin now, we may regain our preeminent position in science by the 1980s or even the 1970s. But the early 1960s are already lost."[46]

Throughout the 1960 campaign, Kennedy relentlessly attacked the Republicans for temerity: "As a substitute for policy, Mr. Eisenhower has tried smiling at the Russians; our State Department has tried frowning at them; and Mr. Nixon has tried both. None have succeeded." More seriously, Kennedy maintained that a lack of presidential leadership had allowed the United States to become "physically, mentally, [and] spiritually soft."[47] He contrasted this soft posture with the Democratic policy of containment:

> I do not say that all was perfection in 1952 under the last Democratic Administration. But we *were* in 1952 the unchallenged leaders of the world in every sphere—militarily, economically, and all the rest. We were building strength and friendships around the world. We were successfully containing the spread of communist imperialism. And we *were* the leaders of a Free World community that was united, dynamic, and growing stronger every day.
>
> And now it is 1959. The Russians beat us into outer space. They beat us around the sun. They beat us to the moon. Half of Indochina has disappeared behind the Iron Curtain. Tibet and Hungary have been crushed. For the first time in history, Russia has its long-sought political foothold in the Middle East—and even an economic foothold in Latin America. And meanwhile we have been forced to abandon the Baghdad Pact, to send our Marines in Lebanon and our fleet to Formosa, to endure our Vice President being spat upon by our former "Good Neighbors," and to forget our plans for a meaningful NATO.[48]

Kennedy's attacks produced squeals of protest. Republican National Chairman Thruston Morton accused Kennedy of "giving aid and comfort to the communists" by decrying U.S. military readiness. Kennedy struck back hard: "It is not naive to call for increased strength. It is naive to think that freedom can prevail without it.... Personal attacks and insults will not halt the spread of communism. Nor will they win the November election."[49] From January 1 (the day he entered the race) to election day, Kennedy repeated his mantra: "It is time to get this country moving again." To do that, Kennedy believed that the president must be the Leader of the Free World. He told the National Press Club that voters "demand a man capable of acting as Commander-in-Chief of the grand alliance, not merely a bookkeeper who feels that his work is done when the numbers on the balance sheet come out even."[50] On the stump, he was even more blunt: "I want a world which looks to the United States for leadership, and which does not always read what Mr. Khrushchev is doing or what Mr. Castro is doing. I want to read what the president of the United States is doing."[51] Still, the Democratic nominee felt that he had to inoculate himself from the charge that he was "soft on communism" by challenging the Republicans to play fair:

> If the 1960 campaign should degenerate into a contest of who can talk toughest to Khrushchev—or which party is the "party of war" or which party is the "party of appeasement"—or which candidate can tell the American voters what they want to hear—or who is "soft on communism" or who can be hardest on foreign aid—then, in my opinion, it makes very little difference who the winners are in July and November—the American people and the whole free world will be the losers.[52]

After a successful campaign that saw JFK repeatedly brandish his anticommunist sword, Larry O'Brien, a member of JFK's "Irish Mafia," told Sulzberger: "The old generation is gone—Mrs. FDR, Truman, Stevenson. Look around you and you will see the new generation that will be running the party."[53] New Deal–like aspirations of helping the disenfranchised were displaced by a new, hardheaded intellectualism. In 1960, Eric Severeid spoke of a "managerial revolution" that was transforming politics. Severeid thought Kennedy its best representative: sharp, ambitious, and opportunistic—quite unlike the young men of the 1930s who "dreamt beautiful and foolish dreams about the perfectibility of man, cheered Roosevelt, and adored the poor."[54] Concomitant with Kennedy's rise to power came the "action intellectuals"—can-do types preoccupied with defending the decency and honor of the United States as a worthy protector of liberty against an enemy they saw as the antithesis of that value. In comparing the "Free World" to the "Iron Curtain," sociologist Nathan Glazer wrote that the action intellectuals had drawn a stark portrait of good against evil.[55] One of them, then-Democrat Irving Kristol, admitted that the picture was designed to remove the red stain of communism from liberal thought. Kristol wryly remarked that one thing Americans understood about Joseph McCarthy was that he, like them, knew there were real communists; many were not so sure about McCarthy's liberal opponents.

To restore liberalism's credibility, the Democratic National Committee established the Democratic Advisory Council (DAC), noting that the nation's "first order of business is to restore the western alliance in a united effort to frustrate the new ambitions and aggressions of Communist Russia."[56] To that end, the DAC established a foreign policy advisory committee headed by Dean Acheson, the former secretary of state. Democratic National Chairman Paul Butler gave Acheson a mandate to "take the lead in constructive criticism of this Republican administration's continuing record of bluff, blunders, and ballyhoo."[57] Accordingly, the Acheson Committee condemned Eisenhower for promoting "unilateral disarmament at the expense of our national security" and cutting defense in the face of "startling Soviet advances in military capability." Other DAC pronouncements decried the "present danger," "our decline in military power," and Soviet "superiority" in strategic weapons. Such hard-line statements drew the ire of some party faithful. Harvard University economist John Kenneth Galbraith accused Acheson of attempting to "out-Dulles John Foster Dulles." Adlai Stevenson, Chester Bowles, Herbert Lehman, and Averell Harriman also tried to cool Acheson's hot rhetoric. During one especially heated session, Stevenson criticized Acheson's "saber-rattling" and Harriman pointedly asked, "Dean, do you want to declare war on the Russians?"[58]

But the 1960 Democratic platform writers ignored such criticisms. Reflecting the thinking of John F. Kennedy's intellectual followers, Democrats claimed that in just eight short years the Republicans had squandered the U.S. advantage: "Our military position today is measured in terms of gaps—missile gap, space gap, limited-war gap." A three-point program was suggested: (1) an enlarged military deterrence so that Soviet and Chinese leaders "will have no doubt that an attack on the United States would surely be followed by their own destruction"; (2) "balanced conventional military forces which will permit a response graded to the intensity of any threats of aggressive force"; and (3) continued modernization of the armed forces "through intensified research and development."[59]

In a bow to the "ban-the-bomb" types, Democrats proposed establishing an Arms Control and Disarmament Agency, claiming that once worldwide disarmament began "it will free vast resources for a new international attack on the problem of world poverty." But all that was in the far-distant future. Meanwhile, Democrats were busy fighting the communists (and the Republicans) on every front. They pledged to "resist the further encroachment of communism on freedom—whether at Berlin, Formosa, or new points of pressure as yet undisclosed." Military might was just one weapon. Another was U.S. government–sponsored shortwave radio programs aired over Voice of America, Radio Free Europe, and Radio Liberty. Democrats asserted that these American voices "must be more than news broadcasts and boastful recitals of *our* accomplishments and *our* material riches. We must find ways to show the people of the world that we share the same goals—dignity, health, freedom, schools for children, a place in the sun— and that we will work together to achieve them." In so doing, Democrats tossed a gauntlet to the Soviet leaders: "We confidently accept your challenge to competition in every field of human effort."[60] In that battle, Democrats remained confident about the outcome:

> We recognize this contest as one between two radically different approaches to the meaning of life—our open society which places its highest value upon individual dignity, and your closed society in which the rights of men are sacrificed to the state.
>
> We believe your communist ideology to be sterile, unsound, and doomed to failure. We believe that your children will reject the intellectual prison in which you confine them, and that ultimately they will choose the eternal principles of freedom.[61]

As the campaign wore on, Kennedy took up his party's promise to defend freedom across the globe—especially in the Western Hemisphere. Fidel Castro's 1959 takeover of Cuba, transforming that nation into a communist base just ninety miles from the U.S. shore, added an exclamation point to Kennedy's claim that the Cold War was being lost. Kennedy called Castro's rise "an incredibly dangerous development to have been permitted by our Republican policymakers."[62] Speaking to an enthusiastic crowd in Johnstown, Pennsylvania, he needled his Republican opponent: "Mr. Nixon hasn't mentioned Cuba very prominently in this campaign. He talks about standing firm in Berlin, standing firm in the Far East, standing up to Khrushchev, but he never mentions standing firm in Cuba—and if you can't stand up to Castro, how can you be expected to stand up to Khrushchev?" Listening to Kennedy talk this way, columnist Joseph Alsop enthused, "Isn't he marvelous! A Stevenson with balls."[63] Yet despite such bravado, 16 percent thought JFK "might be too easy with the Russians"; just 10 percent said the same about Nixon.[64]

The Republican ticket understood the power of Kennedy's anticommunist appeals, and they did not take his attacks lightly. Vice presidential candidate Henry Cabot Lodge tried reassurance: "Now, my friends, no one is going to take over the U.S. and no one is going to take over the world."[65] Nixon tried expertise: "I've been through it—especially in my South American travels and my kitchen debate with Khrushchev."[66] These arguments resonated with voters: In 1958, procommunist sympathizers in Peru and Venezuela had assaulted Nixon during an 18-day vice presidential visit to Latin America; a year later Nixon and Khrushchev had held an impromptu debate in a modern, American-style kitchen at a Moscow exhibition. Each time Nixon referred to his "kitchen debate" with the Soviet premier, audiences cheered: 52 percent named Nixon as better able to handle foreign policy; just 30 percent thought Kennedy better.[67] Moreover, Nixon was preferred (43 percent to 39 percent) as best able to deal with Russia's leaders.[68] One voter neatly captured the prevailing sentiment: "I do not like Nixon, but I am voting for him because of his experience and on account of the foreign situation."[69]

Foreign policy made another incursion into presidential politics when Nikita Khrushchev visited the United States for twenty-five days in September 1960. Senator Albert Gore Sr. of Tennessee advised Kennedy not to be "associated with Khrushchev in criticism of Eisenhower and U.S. policy—allowing Nixon to emerge as the defender of the flag and U.S. honor."[70] Kennedy followed Gore's advice, claiming that "the Democratic program is not one that will please Mr. Khrushchev."[71] As the campaign progressed, it often appeared that Nixon and Kennedy were running against Khrushchev rather than each other. The chairman of Texas Democrats for Nixon accused Kennedy of being a Khrushchev-lover. Anonymous pink cards appeared reading, "One Mr. K. is enough—Vote Republican."[72]

Kennedy dismissed these attacks by reminding voters, "The first living creatures to orbit the earth in space and return were dogs named Strelka and Belka, not Rover or Fido—or Checkers." He told enthusiastic crowds that whereas Nixon boasted of being ahead in producing color televisions during his kitchen debate, he preferred his television in black and white, adding: "I want to be ahead in rocket thrust. Mr. Nixon may be experienced in kitchen debates, but so are a great many other married men I know."[73] By a two-to-one margin, voters agreed with Kennedy that U.S. prestige had plummeted.[74] Moreover, a plurality believed that relations with the Soviet Union would worsen in the next six months.[75] On the campaign trail, Kennedy made his case in classical proportions: "It is our obligation and our privilege to be defenders of the gate in a time of maximum danger. If we fail, freedom fails. Has any people since Athens had a comparable responsibility and opportunity?"[76]

Voter interest in the Kennedy-Nixon contest was high, with 59 percent saying "it is of major importance" that their man win.[77] Turnout reflected the intensity of feelings, with 63 percent of eligible voters trekking to the polls. Kennedy's win was significant: He received 8 million more votes than Stevenson had in 1956, and he delivered states that had not been in the Democratic column since FDR's last race in 1944—including New York, New Jersey, Pennsylvania, and Michigan. Yet despite this Herculean effort Kennedy eked out a mere 118,574-vote plurality, winning just 49.7 percent of the ballots to Nixon's 49.5 percent—a margin of one vote per precinct. What is especially striking is that most states (twenty-seven out of fifty) voted against Kennedy, along with most Protestants, women, whites, business and professional men, college graduates, high-wage earners, farmers, old people, and small-town inhabitants. Thus, it is not surprising that Kennedy lost 228 of the 435 congressional districts. This relatively poor showing contributed to the Democratic loss of twenty-one House seats and two Senate seats.

Many factors were cited as decisive following this, still the closest presidential contest in the twentieth century. Most attributed Kennedy's victory to a large plurality accorded him by his fellow Roman Catholics. But JFK speechwriter Theodore C. Sorensen had another view, citing events that had conspired to deny Nixon the presidency: In May 1960, U-2 pilot Francis Gary Powers was shot down over Soviet airspace. As a result, a scheduled Paris summit between Eisenhower and Khrushchev was canceled. Eisenhower was also forced to cancel planned trips to the Soviet Union and Japan. In a confidential campaign memorandum, Sorensen maintained that these developments, along with fear of a missile gap and communist control of Cuba, had placed Nixon in "a defensive posture on the issue of foreign policy," adding: "By charging forcefully that the Republicans have advocated our standing still with disastrous loss of prestige abroad, Nixon has been forced to protest that all is well, things never were so good. This was

about as convincing as a man shouting that people inhale the clean, sunshine air of Los Angeles in the middle of the smog."[78] Sorensen thought that
instead of "blunting" the traditional Republican foreign policy advantage,
Kennedy had turned it into his favor. Indeed, public dissatisfaction with the
status quo was evident in opinion polls: 80 percent believed that handling
foreign affairs generally and the Russians in particular were the most important qualities the next president should have; and 49 percent wanted a
tougher approach to the Russians "even if it meant taking some risks."[79]

One month into Kennedy's term, Defense Secretary Robert McNamara
concluded that if a missile gap had ever existed with the Soviet Union "it
was in our favor."[80] Republicans were furious. Gerald Ford, leader of the
House Republicans, denounced the so-called missile gap of the 1960 election as a "'political gimmick' designed to frighten our citizens."[81] Senate
Minority Leader Everett Dirksen called for McNamara's scalp and demanded a rerun of the Kennedy-Nixon race. Kennedy took the episode in
stride, telling his beleaguered defense secretary: "Just forget it. It'll blow
over."[82] It did. But the political climate that created the missile gap issue remained unchanged. Thus, during his "thousand-day" tenure as president,
Kennedy continually sought protection from the "soft-on-communism" epithet. In remarks prepared for delivery at the Texas Democratic State Committee on November 22, 1963, Kennedy boasted:

> In the past three years we have increased our defense budget by over 20 per-
> cent; increased the program for acquisition of Polaris submarines from twenty-
> four to forty-one; increased our Minuteman missile purchase program by more
> than 75 percent; doubled the number of strategic bombers and missiles on
> alert; doubled the number of nuclear weapons available in the strategic alert
> forces; increased the tactical nuclear forces deployed in Western Europe by 60
> percent; added five combat ready divisions and five tactical fighter wings to
> our Armed Forces; increased our strategic airlift capabilities by 75 percent;
> and increased our special counter-insurgency forces by 600 percent.

Kennedy added, "We can truly say, with pride in our voices and peace in
our hearts, that the defensive forces of the United States are, without a
doubt, the most powerful and resourceful forces anywhere in the world."[83]

Kennedy biographer Richard Reeves ascribes the buildup and the fear it
engendered not to any looming Soviet threat but to "runaway American
politics, exaggerated threats of communism, misunderstood intelligence, a
few lies here and there, and his own determination never to be vulnerable
to 'soft on communism' charges that Republicans regularly used to dis-
credit Democrats."[84] To blunt potential GOP attacks, Kennedy appointed
several Republicans to his foreign policy team, including McNamara; National Security Council Advisor McGeorge Bundy; Deputy Defense Secretary Roswell Gilpatric; Treasury Secretary Douglas Dillon; and the ambas-

sador to South Vietnam, Henry Cabot Lodge. But these appointments did nothing to stop Republican carping about Kennedy's "no-win" foreign policy. Gerald Ford blamed the Cuban Missile Crisis on Kennedy's ineffectual response at the Bay of Pigs: "Ever since the failure of the Cuban invasion in 1961, ever since the U.S. failed to give air and sea support to Cuban patriots at [the] Bay of Pigs, the military threat to the United States has been growing progressively worse at an alarming rate. . . . A policy of drift, indecision, and appeasement invites trouble."[85] Republicans warned that the consequences of a "no-win" attitude toward the Soviet Union meant that "you will live out your life, and your children will grow into adulthood, with the octopus of communism steadily encircling the United States." [86]

Amid the many crises with the Soviet Union that erupted during his presidency, Kennedy never forgot how important foreign policy was to domestic politics. Following the Bay of Pigs fiasco, he told Nixon: "It really is true that foreign affairs is the only important issue for a president to handle, isn't it. I mean who gives a shit if the minimum wage is $1.15 or $1.25, in comparison to something like this?" During the Cuban Missile Crisis, Treasury Secretary Dillon slipped a note to Kennedy that read: "Have you considered the very real possibility that if we allow Cuba to complete installation and operational readiness of missile bases, the next House of Representatives is likely to have a Republican majority? This would completely paralyze our ability to react sensibly and coherently to further Soviet advances." Kennedy agreed and told Attorney General Robert Kennedy that the Soviet missiles in Cuba meant the end of the 1962 campaign and could result in his impeachment: "This blows it—we've lost anyway. They [the Republicans] were right about Cuba."[87]

Kennedy, of course, was mistaken; Democrats actually *gained* four Senate seats and lost only two House members in the 1962 midterm races. (Included among the incoming House freshmen was former U.S. senator Claude Pepper, who won a predominantly Democratic district in Miami.) According to a November 1962 Gallup poll, 49 percent said what they liked best about Kennedy was his handling of the Cuban Missile Crisis.[88] A little more than a year later Kennedy flew to Dallas.

Lyndon Johnson and the End of the Old Liberalism

On November 22, 1963, President Kennedy told an audience in Fort Worth, Texas, "Because we are stronger our chances for security, our chances for peace, are better than they have been in the past." Earlier that day, Kennedy saw a black-bordered advertisement in the *Dallas Morning News* accusing him of being procommunist. He shook his head and told his wife, Jacqueline, "We're in nut country now."[89] Hours later he was assassinated, and Air Force One transported the shaken new president, Lyndon B.

Johnson, back to the nation's capital. Johnson made a solemn vow on that tragic flight: "I would devote every hour of every day during the remainder of John Kennedy's unfulfilled term to achieving the goals he had set."[90] One of the most pressing problems Kennedy left behind was Vietnam. On November 1, 1963, Ngo Dinh Diem had been killed in a military coup supported by the United States. The situation was dire. Just forty-eight hours after Kennedy's death, Johnson held his first meeting on Vietnam. Although Ambassador Henry Cabot Lodge was optimistic about South Vietnam's prospects, Director of CIA John McCone reported that the Viet Cong were on the move and that the new South Vietnamese government was in a state of chaos with very little popular backing.

Still, Kennedy had made Vietnam a priority, and Johnson saw that faraway country falling within his promise made in the slain president's memory. For years, Kennedy viewed Vietnam as an important Cold War battleground. After the French disaster at Dien Bien Phu, he likened Vietnam to a "finger in the dike" halting the spread of communism.[91] On the last day of his life, Kennedy reasserted his faith in the "domino theory," telling an audience in Austin, Texas: "Without the United States, South Vietnam would collapse overnight. Without the United States, the SEATO alliance would collapse overnight. Without the United States there would be no NATO. And gradually Europe would drift into neutralism and indifference. Without the efforts of the United States in the Alliance for Progress, the communist advance onto the mainland of South America would long ago have taken place."[92]

At the same time, Kennedy understood the limitations of U.S. military power. In a prescient 1954 Senate speech, Kennedy warned that "to pour money, materiel, and men into the jungles of Indochina without at least a remote prospect of victory would be dangerously futile and self-destructive." Kennedy added that "no amount of American military assistance in Indochina can conquer an enemy which is everywhere and at the same time nowhere, 'an enemy of the people' which has the sympathy and covert support of the people."[93] But despite the political realities in South Vietnam, Kennedy bowed to the domestic pressures of the moment. Given his thin margin of victory in 1960 and the political limitations it imposed, Kennedy told Senate Majority Leader Mike Mansfield in December 1962 that he could not withdraw from Vietnam until he had won a solid electoral majority: "If I tried to pull out completely from Vietnam, we would have another Joe McCarthy Red Scare on our hands, but I can do it after I'm reelected. So we had better make damn sure that I am reelected."[94]

But Lyndon Johnson was now president, and he told a joint session of Congress on November 27, 1963, "We will keep our commitments from South Vietnam to West Berlin."[95] Johnson's pledge was more than mere sentiment; it contained an important political truth:

I knew that if we let communist aggression succeed in taking over South Vietnam there would follow in this country an endless national debate—that would shatter my presidency, kill my administration, and damage our democracy. I knew that Harry Truman and Dean Acheson had lost their effectiveness from the day that the communists took over in China. I believe that the loss of China had played a large role in the rise of Joe McCarthy. And I knew that all these problems, taken together, were chickenshit compared with what might happen if we lost Vietnam.[96]

Thus, Johnson often resorted to drastic measures to exorcise the red ghost that haunted the Democratic party. For example, in a desperate gamble to wrest the 1960 nomination away from Kennedy, Johnson accused his rival of being willing to apologize to Khrushchev for the U-2 incident, addressing a joint meeting of the Massachusetts and Texas delegations thus: "I am not prepared to apologize to Mr. Khrushchev—are you?"[97] Predictably, the delegates shouted a vociferous "NO!" Four years later, Johnson offered himself as a staunch anticommunist whose combination of firmness and reasonableness matched the public mood. An October 1964 Gallup survey found 87 percent saying that the United States "should continue to negotiate with the Soviet Union on a broad front in the hope of reaching agreements which would lead to world peace."[98] At the same time, nearly two-thirds wanted the United States to "take a firmer stand against the Soviet Union than it has in recent years."[99]

The 1964 Democratic platform statement on Vietnam paralleled these seemingly contradictory public attitudes by balancing toughness with a willingness to reason together: "Once again power exercised with restraint repulsed communist aggression and strengthened the cause of freedom." Democratic policymakers touted their Cold War successes: "No nation, old or new, has joined the communist bloc since Cuba during the preceding Republican administration. Battered by economic failures, challenged by recent American achievements in space, torn by the Chinese-Russian rift, and faced with American strength and courage—international communism has lost its unity and momentum." Democrats liked to contrast their "responsible leadership" with the reckless Barry Goldwater: "The complications and dangers in our restless, constantly changing world require of us consummate understanding and experience. One rash act, one thoughtless decision, one unchecked reaction—and cities could become smoldering ruins and farms parched wasteland."[100]

Like his fellow partisans, Lyndon Johnson cited Vietnam as the prime example of a calibrated response to communist advances. A few weeks before the Democratic convention, North Vietnamese PT boats attacked U.S. destroyers in the Gulf of Tonkin. Johnson obtained congressional authorization for a retaliatory strike. The Gulf of Tonkin Resolution won unanimous approval in the House and passed with only two Senate dissenters: Wayne

Morse of Oregon and Ernest Greuning of Alaska. Johnson interpreted the measure as a virtual declaration of war. Making his case on television, he told a worried electorate: "The determination of all Americans to carry out our full commitment to the people and to the government of South Vietnam will be redoubled by this outrage. Yet our response, for the present, will be limited and fitting. We Americans know, although others appear to forget, the risks of spreading conflict. We still seek no wider war."[101]

Johnson then co-opted any opposition by announcing that "just a few minutes ago I was able to reach Senator Goldwater and I am glad to say that he has expressed his support of the statement that I am making to you tonight."[102] Thus, Democrats boasted at their 1964 convention: "On the battlefront of the Cold War one engagement after another has been fought and won."[103] These "victories" met with considerable public approbation: 55 percent rejected Goldwater's characterization that LBJ was following "a defeatist 'no win' policy on the international front by appeasing the communists."[104] Johnson calibrated his policy and politics, telling the American Bar Association in August 1964 that the Vietnam War should not be enlarged and that those who wanted to widen the war "call upon us to supply American boys to do the job that Asian boys should do." He concluded, "The South Vietnamese have the basic responsibility for the defense of their own freedom."[105] Johnson repeated this formulation in campaign stops in New Hampshire, Oklahoma, Kentucky, and Ohio. In his postpresidential years, however, Johnson rejected the proposition that he was the "peace candidate" while Goldwater was the "war candidate":

> The American people knew what they were voting for in 1964. They knew Lyndon Johnson was not going to pull up stakes and run. They knew I was not going to go back on my country's word. They knew I would not repudiate the pledges of my predecessors in the presidency. They knew too that I was not going to wipe out Hanoi or use atom bombs to defoliate the Vietnamese jungles. I was going to do what had to be done to protect our interests and to keep our promises. And that is what I did.[106]

Although Johnson was determined to draw the line against communism in Southeast Asia, he also had an aggressive domestic agenda. Passing the Great Society programs was a top priority for the new president. After his landslide victory, Johnson told administration lobbyists to put the Great Society on a fast track:

> I was just elected by the biggest popular margin in the history of the country, fifteen million votes. Just by the natural way people think and because Barry Goldwater scared the hell out of them, I have already lost two of these fifteen and am probably getting down to thirteen. If I get into any fight with Congress, I have already lost another couple of million, and if I have to send any more boys into Vietnam, I may be down to eight million by the end of the summer.[107]

Johnson often drew a straight line between foreign policy and domestic achievements. Behind closed doors, he gave his military advisers a clear directive: "Win the war!"[108] A series of 1964 Gallup polls helps explain Johnson's order: 89 percent said combating world communism was a major concern and 46 percent believed "there is too much communist and left-wing influence in our government these days." Moreover, 61 percent thought the U.S. Communist Party represented a dangerous threat to the country. Interestingly, 46 percent also thought that those organizations pressing for civil rights legislation had been "infiltrated by communists and are now dominated by communist troublemakers."[109] The FBI agreed. In a confidential report to the White House, J. Edgar Hoover concluded, "The communists are not genuinely interested in reforms or improving our society, but only in changes which advance the cause of communism."[110]

To quell these fears, Johnson pledged to

continue the overwhelming supremacy of our strategic nuclear forces; strengthen further our forces for discouraging limited wars and fighting subversion; maintain the world's largest research and development effort which has initiated more than two-hundred new programs since 1961 to ensure continued American leadership in weapons systems and equipment; continue the nationwide Civil Defense program as an important part of our national security; pursue our examination of the Selective Service program to make certain that it is continued only as long as it is necessary and that we meet our military manpower needs without social or economic injustice; attract to the military services the highest caliber of career men and women and make certain they are adequately paid and housed; maintain our cost reduction program to ensure a dollar's worth of defense for every dollar spent, and minimize the disruptive effects of changes in defense spending.[111]

Thus, it is not surprising that 74 percent thought Johnson especially adroit at "maintaining respect for the United States in other countries."[112]

As in the four preceding presidential contests, overseas events made their presence felt in domestic politics. An October Gallup poll found 67 percent saying they had a "very great deal" or "considerable" confidence in Johnson's skill at handling Nikita Khrushchev; just 34 percent expressed confidence in Goldwater's ability to deal with the Russian leader.[113] Almost immediately, LBJ was put to the test. On October 15, 1964, a coup engineered by the Soviet Politburo ousted Khrushchev from power. Leonid Brezhnev became chairman of the Communist Party, and Aleksei Kosygin took over as chairman of the Council of Ministers. Once again, a president's ability to manage the Cold War was foremost in the minds of voters. After the coup, 82 percent voiced "a great deal" or "considerable" worry about relations with the Soviet Union, and 89 percent had similar concerns about combating world communism.[114]

Johnson's landslide victory over the hapless Goldwater gave him a unique political opportunity. In a memo to LBJ dated February 15, 1965, Vice President Hubert H. Humphrey described the potential for intraparty division if Johnson insisted on prosecuting the Vietnam War and proposed an immediate political settlement:

> In the recent campaign, Goldwater and Nixon stressed the Vietnam issue, advocated escalation, and stood for a military solution. The country was frightened by the trigger-happy bomber image which came through from the Goldwater campaign. By contrast we stressed steadiness, staying the course, not enlarging the war, taking on the longer and more difficult task of finding political-military solutions in the South where the war will be won or lost. Already, because of recent decisions on retaliatory bombing, both Goldwater and the Kremlin are alleging that we have bought the Goldwater position of "going North."
>
> In the public mind, the Republicans have traditionally been associated with extreme accusations against Democratic administrations, whether for "losing China," or failing to win the Korean War, or failing to invade Cuba during the missile crisis. By contrast we have had to live with responsibility. Some things are beyond our power to prevent. Always we have sought the best possible settlements short of World War III, combinations of firmness and restraint, leaving opponents some options for credit and face-saving, as in Cuba. We have never stood for military solutions alone, or for victory through air power. We have always stressed the political, economic, and social dimensions. . . . [115]

Humphrey warned of the political traps that would await the Democrats if the war lingered into 1968:

> Politically in Washington, beneath the surface, the opposition [to the Vietnam War] is more Democratic than Republican. This may be even more true at the grassroots across the country. . . . It is always hard to cut losses. But the Johnson Administration is in a stronger position to do so now than any administration in this century. 1965 is the year of minimum political risk for the Johnson Administration. Indeed it is the first year when we can face the Vietnam problem without being preoccupied with the political repercussions from the Republican right. As indicated earlier, our political problems are likely to come from new and different sources (Democratic liberals, independents, labor) if we pursue an enlarged military policy very long. [116]

Johnson ignored Humphrey's memo, believing that negotiations with Ho Chi Minh would commence another Red Scare that would further fracture the New Deal coalition. By way of response to Humphrey's memo, Johnson told Assistant Secretary of State George Ball not to worry about Vietnam War protests from the Democratic heirs of Henry Wallace. Instead, Johnson told Ball to lambaste Republican critics of his administration: "I don't give a damn about those little pinkos on the campuses. The great black beast for us is the right wing. If we don't get this war over soon they'll put enormous heat on us to turn it into an Armageddon and wreck all our other pro-grams."[117] Johnson often referred to the McCarthy era and how, by God, he was not going to be the president who first lost Vietnam, then Congress, and ultimately the White House.

The polls gave some support for Johnson's concerns. Of those who cast a presidential ballot in 1964, 57 percent said "stopping the spread of com-munism throughout the world" had "a great deal" to do with making their final choice for president.[118] While most voters on this issue better liked Johnson, communism remained a threat to Democratic prospects. A Na-tional Opinion Research Center survey found 20 percent classifying for-eign-born Americans as more likely to be card-carrying communists; 17 percent put union leaders in that category; blacks, 14 percent; people in the government in Washington, 12 percent; and college teachers, 8 percent.[119] Each of those groups formed important Democratic voting blocs. Thus, a dozen years after Dwight Eisenhower's election, the Democratic party still could not escape the politics of the 1950s.

The Rise of the New Left

In 1968, the Democratic party was in turmoil, as Humphrey had predicted. By an overwhelming 70 percent to 18 percent, Democrats favored with-drawing from South Vietnam.[120] Eugene McCarthy challenged Johnson's renomination in New Hampshire, and on March 12 he captured 42 percent of the vote to Johnson's 50 percent—a startling showing. On March 31, LBJ withdrew from the race and offered to stop bombing North Vietnam and sit at the peace table in Paris with all parties to the conflict. But it was not enough to stop the anti-Johnson tide. Two days later, McCarthy beat him outright in Wisconsin. Robert Kennedy and Hubert Humphrey soon jumped into the fray, but Kennedy's assassination removed whatever joy there re-mained in politics. Humphrey's nomination in August did nothing to ame-liorate the sadness many Democrats felt over the Vietnam War and their party's responsibility for it. After years of rosy scenarios, the Viet Cong launched the Tet offensive in January 1968—a military and psychological campaign that culminated in the Viet Cong entering the grounds of the U.S. embassy in Saigon. This demonstration of power, along with a grisly photo-graph of the police chief of Saigon putting a bullet into the head of a sus-pected communist, permanently soured U.S. public opinion on the war.

The 1968 platform reflected the uncertainty and self-doubt that gripped the Democratic party. After rejecting a "peace plank" offered by the Mc-Carthy forces, Democrats pledged they would "not turn inward and isolate ourselves from the cares and aspirations of mankind." At the same time, they also promised to "resist the temptation to try to mold the world, or any part of it, in our own image, or to become the self-appointed policeman of the world." The party rhetoric became even more tortured when the platform addressed Vietnam. Claiming that LBJ had "never demanded and does not now demand unconditional surrender by the communists," Democrats clung to the honorable nature of the American cause: "We want no bases in Vietnam; no continued military presence and no political role in Vietnamese affairs. If and when the communists understand our basic commitment and limited goals and are willing to take their chances, as we are, on letting the choice of the postwar government of South Vietnam be determined freely and peacefully by all of the South Vietnamese people, then the bloodshed and tragedy can stop." A bombing halt was possible, they said, only "when this action would not endanger the lives of our troops in the field."[121]

Such awkward formulations failed to satisfy those on the right and the left. Republicans faulted Johnson for breaking faith with voters: "Every citizen bitterly recalls the Democrat campaign oratory of 1964: 'We are not about to send American boys 9–10,000 miles away from home to do what Asian boys ought to be doing for themselves.'" Republicans maintained that the resultant Vietnam policy had failed "militarily, politically, diplomatically, and with relation to our own people."[122] Privately, Richard Nixon deplored Johnson's incessant searches for peace and suggested he would be tougher with the Vietnamese communists. Former governor of Alabama George Wallace also sought to project a "tough-guy" image. Splitting from the Democrats to run as a third party presidential candidate (with U.S.A.F. General [ret.] Curtis LeMay as his running mate), Wallace shared the militarism that characterized so many of his fellow southerners:

> We have been told that strength is weakness and weakness is strength—That is not true.
>
> We have been told that parity rather than superiority in weapons and munitions is sufficient to assume the keeping of the peace and the protection of this country—That is not true.
>
> We have been told a "deterrent" capability is preferable to an offensive capability in maintaining peace and assuring freedom from attack—That is not true.[123]

As if the Vietnam War were not enough, on August 20, 1968, Soviet troops entered Prague and deposed the reform-oriented Czech government. Ironically, Johnson had scheduled a ten-day visit to the Soviet Union October 1–10, 1968, one month before the U.S. presidential balloting. Johnson promptly canceled his trip and consulted with the presidential candidates. During one telephone conversation, Richard Nixon told the president: "The hell with the election. We must all stand firm on this."[124]

By 1968, the view that all politics stop at the water's edge had become passé. A group of McCarthy supporters issued a vitriolic, anti-Humphrey press release: "When a Democrat who bears responsibility for so much tragedy and error is nominated by undemocratic procedures for the presidency . . . the time has come for that faction of the party which won all the major primaries to refuse to be taken for granted. If it does not do so now, it may never do so." A poll commissioned by the Nixon campaign showed just 40 percent of those who supported McCarthy were backing Humphrey. One Humphrey staffer recalled: "The people who were most disenchanted with Humphrey were desperately needed. Not because of their votes—there weren't many of them—but because they are the people who work and write and get active in campaigns: graduate students, young professors, lawyers, upper-middle-class housewives, the elite of the Negro community. They are also the journalists and the people journalists talk to."[125]

These pejoratives contributed mightily to Humphrey's defeat in 1968 against a man many Democratic party professionals disdained—Richard Nixon. Given the many strikes against Humphrey (his unpopular association with Johnson and the lateness and disorganization that permeated his campaign), Humphrey lost by a surprisingly narrow margin: 42.7 percent to Nixon's 43.4 percent. Humphrey also won 191 electoral votes (a high for losing Democrats in the Cold War era) to Nixon's 302 electoral votes. But it was the clamor of those within the Democratic party for an immediate withdrawal from Vietnam that gave Humphrey the most trouble during the fall campaign. Many of those who formed the New Left refused to allow Humphrey to speak on the hustings.

In their protestations, those on the New Left echoed the sentiments of another Democratic voice from the past: Henry Wallace. Although Wallace captured just 2.39 percent of the votes cast in 1948, the Wallace faction never disappeared. In 1956, "ban the bomb" became a popular cause and Adlai Stevenson was its champion. On April 21 of that year Stevenson proposed a unilateral suspension of hydrogen bomb tests, calling it "the most lethal, the most terrible, the most devastating, the most ghastly weapon that has been developed on the face of the earth." Stevenson's proposal met with immediate resistance. Governor Averell Harriman of New York said Stevenson was "soft on communism." Harry Truman told a Detroit crowd: "We should retain our advantage and if that means testing bombs, well okay. We can't possibly quit 'till this Russian business is under control." President Eisenhower brusquely dismissed Stevenson's idea, noting that "the road to surrender is paved with good intentions." He claimed that banning the bomb would make the United States vulnerable to Soviet attack: "We cannot prove wise and strong by any such simple device as suspending unilaterally, our H-bomb tests. Our atomic knowledge and power have formed the saving shield of freedom." Vice President Nixon issued an ominous warning: "It is time that we realize that well-intentioned but mistaken men can be as great a threat to the nation's security as admitted communists or fellow-travelers."[126] Fifty-two percent in a preelection poll disapproved of Stevenson's "ban-the-bomb" position.[127]

The Kennedy-Johnson years provided a brief interlude in the Henry Wallace faction's prominence in Democratic circles. But by 1964, Arkansas Democrat J. William Fulbright took up Wallace's banner. Speaking on the Senate floor, the chairman of the Foreign Relations Committee declared: "The myth is that every communist state is an unmitigated evil and relentless enemy of the Free World. The reality is that some communist regimes pose a threat to the Free World while other pose little or none, and that if we recognize these distinctions, we ourselves will be able to influence events in the communist world in a way favorable to the security of the Free World."[128] Such sentiments earned Fulbright the moniker "Senator Halfbright," first pinned on him by Harry Truman. Barry Goldwater was no less charitable: "Senator Fulbright . . . believes that victory in the Communist War is impossible, that we must coexist with an alien ideological power which is using every device at its command to overwhelm us, and that one of the means toward coexistence is 'aggressive compromise.'"[129] U.S. Senator Christopher Dodd, the recently resigned national chair of the Democratic party, recalled how Fulbright became a lightning rod for the Old Liberalism and the New Left, using his father, the former Connecticut senator Thomas Dodd, as a prime example:

> The old liberal, the old Americans for Democratic Action member, was progressive on health care and workplace issues but fairly conservative on foreign policy. Like Hubert Humphrey, my father was a classic example of the New Deal Democrat—guns and money. But the sixties and seventies defined a new liberalism. Fulbright became a liberal, even though he had signed the Southern Manifesto. My father became a conservative. Vietnam was the event that changed the definition of conservative and liberal.[130]

This split within the Democratic ranks that Christopher Dodd describes led to his father's defeat in a three-way 1970 Senate contest featuring Joseph Duffey, the Democratic nominee, and Republican Lowell Weicker, who ultimately beat them both with just 41.7 percent of the vote.[131] Duffey represented the burgeoning New Left. Son of a West Virginia coal miner, Duffey held a bachelor of arts degree from Marshall University, a doctor of divinity degree from Andover Theological School, a master's degree from Yale Divinity School, and a doctorate from the Hartford Theological Seminary. A Congregational minister, Duffey headed the Connecticut chapter of Americans for Democratic Action, and in June 1969 he became its national president. Throughout his Senate campaign, Duffey emphasized his early opposition to the Vietnam War and his desire to trim military expenditures.

Old Liberals recoiled at Duffey's candidacy. According to analyst Lanny J. Davis, the party establishment "perceived itself to be threatened by a cultural and ideological perspective which it saw as completely alien to its own."[132] As one organization man put it, "Joe Duffey does not appeal to the hard hat."[133] That was evident as Duffey moved across the state. Construction workers held placards reading: "Duffey the Radical," "SDS, Pot, and Duffey Go Together," and "A Vote for Duffey Is a Vote for Khrushchev."[134] In a sarcastic aside, Weicker told his two erstwhile Democratic rivals, "It's the Tom Dodds of this world that create the Joseph Duffeys." Not to be outdone, Vice President Spiro T. Agnew denounced the Americans for Democratic Action as a "nest of radicals," singling out Duffey as a "revisionist Marxist." Duffey, in turn, called Agnew a "cowardly liar."[135]

Nonetheless, Duffey attracted many followers—including a young Arkansan and former Fulbright intern named Bill Clinton. As one Democrat noted, "The people who support Joe Duffey are almost fanatically behind him."[136] Duffey did especially well in the suburban communities and university enclaves. In the Democratic primary, he won 80 percent of the votes cast in Mansfield, Connecticut, home of the University of Connecticut. But Duffey's candidacy and its fracturing of the Connecticut Democratic Party was a precursor for what happened to the Democratic party nationally two years later.

George McGovern: "Come Home, America"

In 1972, the Vietnam War was coming to a close. Draft calls fell from 299,000 in 1968 to 50,000 as Nixon's "Vietnamization" plan took effect.[137] By October, nearly all U.S. ground troops had left South Vietnam. That same month, on the twenty-sixth, National Security Advisor Henry Kissinger announced that the long-awaited peace was "at hand."[138] Kissinger's declaration was premature, but only by a few months. In January 1973, a sullen peace was agreed to in Paris.

But to George McGovern and his supporters, the Vietnam War was more than a bad policy gone awry—it signified a moral lapse. McGovern told his colleagues: "Every Senator in this Chamber is partly responsible for sending 50,000 young Americans to an early grave. This Chamber reeks of blood."[139] McGovern vowed to go to Hanoi to plead on his hands and knees for the safe return of U.S. POWs.[140] A Wisconsin Democratic county chairman expressed the outrage of many McGovernites: "Why am I in politics if they can take my boys and send them off to a war I don't believe in, and I can't do anything about it?"[141] The 1972 Democratic platform blasted Nixon as amoral since he was "continuing the killing of Americans and Vietnamese when our national security is not at stake."[142]

McGovern and his followers saw John Kennedy's anticommunism as an old-fashioned relic of the Cold War. Indeed, most New Politics liberals associated Kennedy with the idealism of the Peace Corps and the Nuclear Test

Ban Treaty. Many forgot (or excused) Kennedy's harsh anticommunism as a political necessity of his time. Illustrative of how much the Democratic party had changed, the 1972 platform proposed reexamining U.S. policy toward Cuba so as to "resolve this Cold War confrontation on mutually acceptable terms."[143] Kennedy would have recoiled at such a statement, and even Bill Clinton has refused to lift the long-standing embargo with this enduring bastion of communism. But to McGovern, the Cold War was an anachronism that distorted foreign policy and thwarted Americans from their better natures: "The war against communism is over. The challenge to the free world from communism is no longer relevant. We're entering a new era, and the Kennedy challenge of 1960 is pretty hollow now. Somehow we have to settle down and live with them. . . . There has to be an easing off of our reliance on power; too much reliance on power weakens a society."[144]

Peaceful coexistence remained a controversial stance in 1972, and McGovern defended it vigorously. Using the slogan "Right from the Start," McGovern piously proclaimed that his early opposition to the Vietnam War could be encapsuled in words that all but said "I told you so." This self-righteous motto also summarized the conviction of this former Wallace supporter that peaceful coexistence with the communists was the only recourse left. McGovern's defense policies were framed accordingly: He would slash $32.5 billion from the Pentagon's budget over a three-year period; reduce the number of navy carriers to six; and trim those in military service from 2.5 million to 1.75 million.[145]

Richard Nixon welcomed McGovern's attacks, confiding to Chief of Staff H. R. Haldeman: "The Democratic administrations of the sixties got us into the war. The Nixon administration is getting us out. If the Democrats want to fight the war issue on a partisan basis, this is the way they're going to have to take it."[146] He told Republican National Chairman Bob Dole to put out this line and woo disgruntled Democrats to his cause. But Nixon need not have worried. During the Democratic primaries, McGovern was weakened by his challengers—especially Hubert Humphrey, who, having come so tantalizingly close to the presidency in 1968, sought his party's nod again in 1972. But this time the former vice president had to compete in intraparty primaries, where his most serious opposition came from McGovern. In June, with the nomination nearly wrested from his grasp, Humphrey made a last stand in California, accusing McGovern of being hopelessly naive when it came to national security:

> I believe Senator McGovern, while having a very catchy phrase . . . "McGovern, Right from the Start," that there are many times you will find that it was not right from the start, but wrong from the start. . . .
>
> He is wrong on defense cuts. I think they will cut into the muscle, into the very fiber of our national security. . . .

> Senator McGovern . . . says halt the Minute Man procurement, halt the Poseidon procurement, halt the B-1 Prototype. Phase out 230 of our 530 strategic bombers. Reduce aircraft carrier forces from 15 to 6. Reduce our naval air squadrons to 80 percent. Halt all naval surface shipbuilding. Reduce the number of cruisers from 230 to 130. Reduce the number of submarines by 11. . . . When you . . . reduce the total number of forces below what we had pre–Pearl Harbor, you're not talking about just removing waste . . . you are cutting into the very fiber and muscle of our defense establishment.[147]

Humphrey proceeded to distinguish McGovern from his Democratic predecessors—Truman, Kennedy, and Johnson—noting that he was proposing cuts in defense "without any similar disarmament agreements from the Russians. It shocks me. No responsible president would think of cutting our defense to the level of a second-class power."[148] This argument was an especially powerful one in a state where defense contractors were the primary employers. After being written off by the pundits before the balloting, Humphrey lost by a surprisingly narrow margin of 39.2 percent to 44.3 percent. In the aerospace community of Burbank, Humphrey bested McGovern two-to-one, and in other defense-minded communities in the Silicon Valley the former vice president garnered impressive two-to-one and three-to-one majorities.[149]

For all of his successes with frightened defense workers, Humphrey's losing effort in California proved to be Old Liberalism's last gasp. Henceforth, the Democratic party would be run by the New Politics types (most of them young), many enticed by McGovern into politics. In New Paltz, New York, for example, Averell Harriman lost his delegate slot to a nineteen-year-old college student. A similar incident occurred in Cambridge, Massachusetts, where Tip O'Neill was denied a place at the party convention. Hearing of his defeat, O'Neill told a reporter: "My God. Do you mean my own district is going against me three-to-one?"[150] As McGovern told the Democratic delegates, his nomination meant that "American politics will never be the same again."[151]

Old Liberals were appalled at the college students who rose to positions of power within the Democratic ranks. Most belonged to the counterculture—something many Old Liberals deplored. In their view, counterculturists adhered to a set of values fundamentally at odds with their own. Stereotypes involved excesses of all sorts, especially drugs and sex. Nixon was reputed to have called the college students "bums,"[152] and his supporters caricatured McGovern as the "AAA candidate," favoring *a*mnesty for draft dodgers, *a*cid (LSD), and *a*bortion on demand. Excepting abortion, none of these positions reflected McGovern's actual views. But that hardly mattered, since the caricature endured for decades to come. Vice President Spiro Agnew described McGovern's world as one "in which the students run the schools, the criminals run the courts and prisons, and the state runs business. There would be amnesty for past crimes. Pot and porn would be super-market items and the commune would replace the family. There would be a 'soak-the-rich-and-the-middle-class' tax system and a free ride for whomever might want it. There would be no need for a draft, or armed forces for that matter, in a dream world in which everyone lived on love."[153] This portrait became deeply embedded in the collective mindset of Nixon and Agnew's "Silent Majority," enduring even after the Cold War ended. The day after the 1994 elections, for example, McGovern recalled that Speaker of the House–designate Newt Gingrich called President Clinton "the worst thing he could think of—a 'counterculture McGovernik.'"[154]

Like Barry Goldwater, McGovern believed politics is inextricably tied to the public morality of a prospective president. For Goldwater, winning the so-called Communist War was the great moral challenge of the Cold War; for McGovern, combating anticommunist hysteria was of equal value. In McGovern's mind, the flag-waving love-it-or-leave-it politics of the Cold War had produced its own moral decay, symbolized by the Vietnam War. McGovern deplored the "senseless bombing" and promised that if elected "there will be no more Asian children running ablaze from bombed-out schools." He pleaded with voters to "turn away from excessive preoccupation overseas" and return to the moral piety that formed the backbone of the nation:

> From secrecy and deception in high places, come home, America.
> From a conflict in Indochina which maims our ideals as well as our soldiers, come home, America.
> From military spending so wasteful that it weakens our nation, come home, America.[155]

As the Democratic presidential nominee, McGovern sought to cast himself as the heir to Wilson, Roosevelt, Truman, and Kennedy by promising to continue the "enlightened internationalism" of these forbears. But when pressed, McGovern shied away from exertion of power abroad. Instead, he sought an immediate withdrawal from Vietnam and spoke of upholding America's "real interests" overseas (loosely defined) without "playing the world's policeman nor abandoning old and good friends." In pursuing his vision of a "newer world," McGovern proposed shrinking the presidency and returning to Congress and the people "a meaningful role in decisions on peace and war."[156]

McGovern's nomination gave Nixon a unique opportunity. The Committee to Re-Elect the President adopted the slogan "Now More than Ever." Behind these words was the suggestion that McGovern would transform the United States into a "pitiful, helpless giant."[157] Nixon warned of dire consequences if this were to happen: "For the United States unilaterally to reduce its strength with the naive hope that other nations would do like-wise would increase the danger of war in the world." But instead of making partisan hay, Nixon placed himself above the fray by linking himself to his Democratic predecessors:

> There have been five presidents in my political lifetime—Franklin D. Roosevelt, Harry Truman, Dwight Eisenhower, John F. Kennedy, and Lyndon Johnson. These five presidents were united in their total opposition to isolation for America and in their belief that the interests of the United States and the interests of world peace require that America be strong enough and intelligent enough to assume the responsibilities of leadership in the world. . . .
>
> But not one of these five men, and no president in our history, believed that America should ask an enemy for peace on terms that will betray our allies and destroy respect for the United States all over the world.[158]

In his Acceptance Speech, Nixon excoriated the New Left and engaged in the politics of "us" versus "them" at which he excelled: "Six weeks ago our opponents at their convention rejected many of the great principles of the Democratic party. To these millions who have been driven out of their home in the Democratic party, we say come home." To make the proposition more enticing to wayward Democrats, Nixon added: "We say come home not to another party, but we say come home to the great principles Americans believe in together." Among these was a belief in the "American system" and a willingness to export it to other, less fortunate nations. By wholeheartedly endorsing American Exceptionalism, Nixon understood that this meant U.S. primacy in world affairs, including continuing the fight against communism with a defense "second to none."[159]

Reflecting on the troubles that have beset the Democratic party since 1972, former New York governor Mario Cuomo maintains that McGovern drove away the lunch-bucket Democrat who "felt alienated by a new Democratic party which he thought neither understood nor related to him." Polls support Cuomo's thesis: A 1972 Louis Harris survey found 56 percent believed McGovern "too radical and too quick to agree to way out ideas." Moreover, by a five-to-three margin respondents saw the Democratic nominee as too closely tied to "radical and protest groups." These became linked in the public consciousness with the New Politics liberals: 54 percent dubbed McGovern an "extreme liberal"; just 26 percent disagreed.[160] McGovern's stance on the Vietnam War put him at an even greater disadvantage: A plurality (47 percent) believed McGovern would end the conflict on dishonorable terms; just 32 percent thought he would win a settlement that would be "honorable and right."[161] By contrast, Nixon held an overwhelmingly positive rating on his ability to handle the Vietnam issue when compared to McGovern (69 percent to 30 percent). His score on handling defense matters was even higher, standing at a record 73 percent. Even *Democrats* rated Nixon positively: 56 percent approved of his handling of the Vietnam War, and 60 percent thought him better suited to be commander in chief.[162] Nixon's foreign policy strengths were accentuated by continued public hand-wringing about the danger of communist expansionism: 54 percent classified this as a "very serious" problem; an additional 25 percent thought it "somewhat serious."[163] What's more, two-thirds believed world tensions were greater in 1972 than they were during the Cuban Missile Crisis![164] Given these concerns, most voters were predisposed to opt for the incumbent. As Gerald Ford challenged in a 1972 television commercial: "Do we vote for surrender—reckless defense cuts—and radical spending by experimenters?"[165]

During his final days of political exile at his Texas ranch, Lyndon Johnson frequently expressed surprise at the outcome of the 1972 presidential election—not so much that Nixon had beaten McGovern, for Johnson's receptive political antennae had detected those signals months before. Rather it was the size of Nixon's victory that caught him off-guard: forty-nine states and 60.7 percent of the popular vote. Johnson remarked to intimates that even Alf Landon—"who was a Republican for Chrissake"—had carried *two* states. Said Johnson of McGovern: "I didn't know they *made* presidential candidates that dumb."[166]

Six weeks later Johnson was dead. But Johnson's embittered feelings were typical of his fellow liberals. The resultant estrangement between the Old Liberalism and the New Left often proved fatal to Democratic prospects. AFL-CIO chief George Meany, an Old Liberal, remained "neutral" in 1972—the first time that organization had failed to endorse a Democrat for president. Many "hard hats"—construction workers who were politically and culturally at odds with the New Left—also backed Nixon. Republican pollster Robert Teeter found that just 22 percent of Nixon's vote came from *Republicans*; the remainder were ticket-splitters or Democrats.[167]

The ignominious end of the Vietnam War in 1975 gave the Democrats a chance to heal old wounds. Political analyst William Schneider outlined the prospective deal: "The regulars would admit their error in Vietnam and accept a less interventionist foreign policy, and the liberals, who came in with no attachment to the old politics, would endorse the big-government, pro-labor, social-welfare liberalism of the party establishment."[168] But the truce Schneider suggested proved only temporary. The base of the Democratic party had changed considerably from John Kennedy's days. A slew of activists—antiwar, pro–civil rights, pro-women, pro-abortion, pro-environmentalist, pro–gay rights—formed the core Democratic constituencies. In short, the New Left posed a substantial threat to Democratic unity and an even greater challenge to governance—as Jimmy Carter was about to discover.

The Carter Interregnum

A successful candidate defines and captures the issues of his times. That maxim held true in 1976. After Vietnam and Watergate, voters sought someone who would affirm such traditional values as freedom, individualism, and equality of opportunity. Jimmy Carter understood this yearning, and in 1976 he sounded less like a politician and more like a preacher: "We have lost some precious things that historically have bound our people and our government together. We feel the moral decay that has weakened the country; that it's crippled by a lack of goals and values and that our public officials have lost faith in us. . . . We want to have faith again. We want to be proud again. We just want the truth again!"[169]

But voters had great difficulty taking Carter's measure. In his campaign autobiography, *Why Not the Best?*, Carter introduced himself this way: "I am a Southerner and an American. I am a farmer, an engineer, a father and a husband, a Christian, a politician and former governor, a planner, a businessman, a nuclear physicist, a naval officer, a canoeist, and, among other things, a lover of Bob Dylan's songs and Dylan Thomas' poetry."[170] No other aspirant, with the possible exception of Thomas Jefferson, could have checked so many occupation boxes on a White House application. In the wee hours of the morning after Carter had won the White House, NBC News correspondent Edwin Newman observed that the former Georgia governor had "spent twenty-three months in pursuit of the presidency . . . and he will embark on that presidency as little-known as any man who has won that office in many, many years."[171]

One reason Americans had so much difficulty assessing Carter was the conflicting signals he sent regarding the Cold War. As a candidate, Carter declared that he was "deeply troubled by the lies our people had been told; our exclusion from the shaping of American political and military policy in Vietnam, Cambodia, Chile, and other countries; and other embarrassing activities of our government, such as the CIA's role in plotting murder and other crimes."[172] He maintained that President Ford and Secretary of State Kissinger clung to antiquated balance-of-power maxims from the nineteenth century instead of promoting traditional American values—especially that of human rights. The 1976 Democratic platform charged Ford and Kissinger with making national security "synonymous with the abuse of power, deceit, and violation of the public trust" and accused them of lacking confidence that American values would ultimately triumph over communism.[173]

Carter promised a foreign policy based "on our nation's commitment to the ideal of individual freedom and justice." In that vein, he proposed cutting military spending—a promise that won grudging consent from the Old Liberals following the Vietnam experience. The prospective Democratic nominee also echoed Eisenhower's warning about the military-industrial complex: "The size of our defense budget should not be dictated by bureaucratic imperatives or the needs of defense contractors but by our assessment of international realities." In that vein, he pledged to eliminate "wasteful, extravagant, and, in some instances, destabilizing military programs."[174]

Few disagreed with these platitudes, but taken together they did not form a strategy for managing the Cold War. However, they did broker a temporary peace between the Democratic party's two warring factions. When Carter echoed the Wilsonian notion of national self-determination and promoted a pro–human rights agenda, Democrats found in their standard-bearer common ground between the Old Liberalism and the New Left. New Left Democrats deplored human rights abuses not only in communist countries but in the oppressive dictatorships (sometimes formed with U.S. assistance) that served to check any threatening Soviet moves. Old Liberals believed in the redemption of mankind, and they viewed human rights as essential to obliterating poverty and restoring social justice. They also deplored human rights abuses in communist countries, and they liked their party's pledge to "continually remind the Soviet Union, by word and conduct, of its commitments in Helsinki to the free flow of people and ideas."[175] In short, both the New Left and the Old Liberals wanted Carter to use the bully pulpit of the presidency on behalf of dissidents across the globe.

The result was a euphoria that gripped the Democratic rank-and-file for the first time since 1964. In a symbolic gesture at the national convention, Democrats celebrated the unity forged by the Civil War when the Georgia and Minnesota delegations tied their standards together to honor the party's standard-bearers, Jimmy Carter and Walter Mondale. The convention hailed the union of black and white, men and women, and those from various ethnic nationalities in time to mark the nation's bicentennial. But a discordant note was struck when it came to the Soviet Union. In a heavily nuanced statement, the Democratic platform flip-flopped between peaceful coexistence and a tough nationalistic approach:

> The United States and the Soviet Union are the only powers who by rivalry or miscalculation, could bring general nuclear war upon our civilization. A principal goal must be the continued reduction of tension with the U.S.S.R. This can, however, only be accomplished by fidelity to our principles and interests and through businesslike negotiations about specific issues, not by the bad bargains, dramatic posturing, and the stress on general declarations that have characterized the Nixon-Ford administration's détente policy.[176]

Republicans denounced this tendency toward "splendid isolation." But they refrained from questioning the anticommunist motivations of the loyal opposition, instead issuing a wistful plea for unity: "Confronted by so many challenges and responsibilities and so many crises, the United States must again speak with one voice, united in spirit and in fact. We reject partisan and ideological quarrels across party lines and urge Democrats to join us to lay the foundations of a true bipartisan spirit." In so doing, Republicans summoned the memory of President Ford's fellow Michigander, Arthur Vandenberg, with whom he had served in Congress.[177]

For the first time since 1952, Republicans did not enjoy a significant foreign policy advantage. This, no doubt, stemmed from the fact that Gerald Ford had become president by a circuitous route. Elected to Congress in 1948, Ford won the post of House minority leader in 1965. In 1973, he was appointed vice president, and the rest was history. Ford's lack of national stature gave him a small platform on which to build public confidence—especially in the waves of cynicism following Vietnam and Watergate. Daniel Yankelovich found 41 percent saying Ford was "too soft on the Russians"; 40 percent disagreed.[178] A CBS News/*New York Times* poll showed 42 percent believing Ford was "more likely to do a better job handling our country's foreign relations"; 36 percent named Carter—a significant but not overwhelming difference.[179] Ford's chief of staff, Richard Cheney, bluntly told the president at the onset of the 1976 campaign that "the key to defeating Carter, very frankly, lies not in trumpeting the achievements of the last two years, but rather in the unwanted havoc that an untested, unknown Carter Presidency would bring."[180]

Ford's political standing had been further debilitated by Ronald Reagan's challenge in the Republican presidential primaries. David Gergen, a member of President Ford's staff, expressed the widely held belief that "a Reagan nomination—representing, as it would, a repudiation of Republican leadership—would split the party so badly that it is very questionable whether the GOP could be put back together again."[181] Still, Reagan persisted, claiming that the Soviet Union "outguns us, out-tanks us, and out-subs us"; and unless defense spending were significantly increased, Reagan warned, "our nation is in great danger, and the danger grows with each passing day."[182] As for Ford, Reagan dismissed him as an ineffective steward steeped in the folkways of bipartisanship:

I do not challenge the President's patriotism. I do not quarrel with the fact that he has asked for more money than this irresponsible Congress has been willing to give. I've never suggested that he share Dr. Kissinger's pessimistic view that you and I, the American people, lack the will and the stamina to keep this country in the number one position. But I do believe that to continue seeking cooperation from Congress gives us a situation that has gone beyond just an imbalance in weapons. I don't believe the people in this country lack the will and the stamina. What we lack is the truth and the information that our government owes us about our situation. I believe a President of the United States should go over the heads of the Congress to the people of the country, tell them what our situation is, and I believe the people in this country will make whatever sacrifice is necessary to keep this country strong.[183]

Reagan's message resonated with Republican primary voters. In a confidential memo to Ford, Vice President Nelson Rockefeller wrote: "The present posture of the Administration in foreign affairs is difficult. Opponents say that 'détente' has produced no visible benefit for the American people, as they would see it, but may be looked upon as a cover used by the Soviets to move communism forward in Southeast Asia, Latin America, Portugal, and to continue turmoil in the Middle East."[184] To counter Reagan's criticism of détente, Ford accused Reagan of being a warmonger. In an infamous pro-Ford television advertisement, a somber female voice warned: "Governor Reagan couldn't start a war. President Reagan could."[185] Another Ford commercial featured a ringing telephone as an announcer ominously declared: "When the Hot Line rings, who do you want to answer? And what do you want him to say? Do you want someone who talks like he wants to start a war or someone who'll stop one? Think about it. You've got 'til Tuesday."[186] These commercials had the desired effect: When asked which one could do a better job of dealing with Russia, respondents preferred Ford by a two-to-one margin.[187]

After defeating Reagan in a close ballot at the Republican National Convention, Ford chose to exploit the Democratic party's traditional Cold War softness by criticizing Carter's oft-repeated promise to pardon Vietnam War draft resisters: "I am against an across-the-board pardon of draft evaders or military deserters." In addition, Ford characterized Carter as a "deceitful fanatic" who was "inexperienced" in foreign affairs.[188] Ford's advisers thought Carter's lack of expertise could be transformed into a major political asset: "Especially in the areas of foreign policy and national defense, there is generally a presumption that the president's position is at least factually correct"; "no-one believes Jimmy Carter knows anything about foreign policy, and his strategists know this is his weak suit. The Commander-in-Chief foreign policy roles are powerful, positive, 'presidential' images which ought to be taken advantage of."[189]

Polls showed Ford's tactics had an impact. By a margin of 49 percent to 29 percent voters thought Ford better able to handle defense issues. Likewise, Ford was preferred to Carter 47 percent to 31 percent in a poll asking which candidate could best manage foreign affairs.[190] But Ford's posturing as an able commander in chief carried little weight in a political environment still fouled by Watergate. Republican pollster Robert Teeter advised Ford to "increase the importance of foreign policy and defense issues," noting that in so doing "there would be a significant increase to the President's vote."[191] Teeter's polls showed that swing voters in particular were especially sensitive to the posture of U.S. defense forces, and he recommended that Ford seize the issue in a manner that would portray him not only as tough on communism but as a defender of traditional American values.[192]

But Reagan's challenge and his own lack of national stature meant that Ford entered the fall campaign from a weak position. His advisers bluntly reported: "*You are not now perceived as being a strong, decisive leader by anywhere near a majority of the American people.*"[193] Ford compounded the problem by committing a major faux pas in a televised debate with Carter. Responding to a question about the Helsinki Accords, which legitimated Soviet influence in the Captive Nations, Ford said, "There is no Soviet domination of Eastern Europe and there never will be under a Ford Administration."[194] Asked to explain, he compounded the blunder:

> I don't believe the Yugoslavians consider themselves dominated by the Soviet Union. I don't believe that the Rumanians consider themselves dominated by the Soviet Union. I don't believe that the Poles consider themselves dominated by the Soviet Union. Each of those countries is independent, autonomous: It has its own territorial integrity and the United States does not concede that those countries are under the domination of the Soviet Union. As a matter of fact, I visited Yugoslavia and Rumania to make certain that the people of those countries understood that the president of the United States and the people of the United States are dedicated to their independence, their autonomy and their freedom.[195]

At this, Carter chuckled and said, "I would like to see Mr. Ford convince the Polish-Americans and the Czech-Americans and the Hungarian-Americans in this country that those countries don't live under the domination and supervision of the Soviet Union behind the Iron Curtain."[196] The Ford White House circulated a statement defending their man:

> It is true that a Republican president has made a slip of the tongue on the status of Eastern Europe, but was it a Republican President who recognized the Soviet Union in 1933?
> Was it a Republican administration that agreed at Tehran to give the Russians a free hand in the Balkans and sacrificed Polish territory east of the Curzon Line to the Soviet Union?
> Was it a Republican administration that agreed to a communist takeover of Eastern Europe in *secret* agreements at Yalta?
> Was it a Republican administration that went to Potsdam and gave East Germany to the USSR and left West Berlin cut off from the rest of the world?
> Was it a Republican administration that sat on its hands when the Berlin Wall was built?
> The record is clear. The people of Eastern Europe have been enslaved not by a slip of the tongue but by the bayonets and hard realities of world politics. And it has been the Republican presidents of the past twenty-five years—not Democratic presidents—who have most steadfastly opposed military domination of those peoples.[197]

Despite Ford's recantation, the 1976 Republican presidential campaign had, in a single moment, temporarily forfeited its traditional anticommunist advantage. Robert Taft, son of the late Ohio Republican and a senator himself, called the White House to express his displeasure.[198] For his part, Jimmy Carter countered that if elected he would be "much tougher" than either Ford or Nixon when it came to the all-important arms control negotiations with the Soviet Union.[199] In an election postmortem, Robert Teeter cited the defection of Eastern European Catholics away from the GOP ticket, noting that Ford won only 41 percent of their votes.[200]

Yet from 1976 onward, Democrats no longer described the Cold War in military-security terms. Instead, they saw it as mutating into a social and economic struggle, one far more suited to the party of Franklin D. Roosevelt. In their view, future superpower summits were likely to focus on trade and other economic concerns. In this new phase of the Cold War, Democrats believed, the Soviets were less overtly aggressive, which gave the East-West conflict a certain predictability. Carter maintained that "too many of our international concerns were being defined almost exclusively by the chronic United States–Soviet confrontation mentality, which seemed to me shortsighted and counterproductive." He noted that such ossified thinking had stalled attempts to normalize relations with the People's Republic of China and halted completion of a new strategic arms limitations agreement with the Soviets.[201] Thus, the president-elect pledged to remove all remnants of the Cold War, including bringing home U.S. ground forces remaining in South Korea.[202]

It was with these moral imperatives that Jimmy Carter took office in January 1977. During his term, President Carter admonished South Korea and the Philippines (loyal allies in the Cold War) for their human rights abuses; cooled relations with the apartheid regime of South Africa; formally recognized the People's Republic of China; canceled the B-1 bomber; and delayed the Cruise Missile, Trident submarine, Trident II missile, MX missile, and the neutron bomb. Speaking to the graduates of Notre Dame University in May 1977, Carter declared that the United States was finally "free of that inordinate fear of communism." He continued: "For too many years, we've been willing to adopt the flawed and erroneous principles and tactics of our adversaries, sometimes abandoning our own values for theirs. We've fought fire with fire, never thinking that fire is better quenched with water. This approach failed, with Vietnam the best example of its intellectual and moral poverty. But through failure we have now found our way back to our own principles and values, and we have regained our lost confidence."[203]

In the same address, Carter announced the arrival of a "new world," one that eschewed colonialism, championed human rights, and controlled the "morally deplorable" arms race. In his new world, Carter said that U.S. foreign policy must be one of "decency" and "optimism."[204] Republicans took aim at these statements in 1980: "Unlike Mr. Carter, we see nothing 'inordinate' in our nation's historic judgment about the goals, tactics, and dangers of Soviet communism."[205] Carter's attempt to assuage fears about communism did little to quell public concerns. At the time of the Notre Dame speech, polls showed Americans were evenly divided on his handling of the Soviet Union: 42 percent gave Carter "excellent" or "pretty good" marks; 43 percent said he was doing "only fair" or "poor."[206]

But Soviet adventurism took its toll on Carter. In mid-1979, Senator Frank Church voiced alarm about a Soviet brigade stationed in Cuba. The Idaho Democrat's warning was motivated by a conservative challenge from the American Conservative Action Coalition, which had targeted him for defeat.[207] Soviet-sponsored clients seized power in Ethiopia, South Yemen, Mozambique, Angola, and Somalia—nations strategically placed around the circumference of Africa. And on December 27, 1979, 80,000 Soviet troops entered Afghanistan, ousting its government and assassinating its president. The Soviet invasion marked the first time since the occupation of Czechoslovakia in February 1948 that it had used its own troops to expand its sphere of influence.

Carter found the Soviet intrusion into a neutral country especially "unsettling"[208] (his word), since it would give the Soviets a wedge between Iran and Pakistan and threaten the Persian Gulf. Shortly after Afghanistan made headlines, the president confided that the invasion had "made a more dramatic change in my opinion of what the Soviets' ultimate goals are than anything else they've done in the previous time I've been in office."[209] Carter imposed several punitive measures: summoning the U.S. ambassador to the Soviet Union home, a grain embargo, suspension of a scheduled Senate vote on SALT II, banning U.S. participation in the International Olympic games scheduled to be held in Moscow, and a postcard-based draft registration system. In his 1980 State of the Union Address, he issued the Carter Doctrine— an explicit warning to the Soviets to stay out of the Persian Gulf: "Let our position be absolutely clear. An attempt by any outside force to gain control of the Persian Gulf region will be regarded as an assault on the vital interests of the United States of America, and such an assault will be repelled by any means necessary, including military force."[210]

But Carter's tough talk won him few admirers. Republicans criticized the Olympic boycott and grain embargo—the latter being especially unpopular in the electoral vote–rich farm states. More broadly, Republicans dubbed Carter a modern-day Neville Chamberlain: "The evidence of the Soviet threat has never been more stark and unambiguous, nor has any president been more oblivious to this threat and its potential consequences."[211] This touched a public nerve: The proportion of those who thought the United States was militarily inferior to the Soviet Union rose 20 percent between 1976 and 1980.[212] In addition, those who had a highly unfavorable view of the Soviets grew from 21 percent in 1973 to 62 percent in 1980.[213] Finally, those who viewed communism as the "worst kind of government" increased from 47 percent in 1973 to 57 percent in 1980.[214]

Americans wanted decisive presidential action—a sentiment that John Kennedy exploited in 1960 and Ronald Reagan tapped into twenty years later. The 1980 Republican platform proposed "a major upgrading of our military forces, a strengthening of our commitments to our allies, and a resolve that our national interests be vigorously protected." It continued: "Ultimately, those who practice strength and firmness truly guard the peace."[215]

While Republicans called for swift retaliation the Soviet invasion of Afghanistan renewed the rift between the Old Liberalism and the New Left. Jeane Kirkpatrick, one of the Old Liberals, penned an influential article titled "Dictatorships and Double-Standards" that caught Reagan's eye. In it, she excoriated Carter: "In Jimmy Carter—egalitarian, optimist, liberal, Christian—the tendency to be repelled by frankly non-democratic rulers and hierarchical societies is almost as strong as the tendency to be attracted to the idea of popular revolution, liberation, and progress. Carter is, *par excellence*, the kind of liberal most likely to confound revolution with idealism, change with progress, optimism with virtue." To this former Humphrey adviser Carter's naïveté was downright dangerous: "Having moved past what the President calls our 'inordinate fear of communism,' identified by him with the Cold War, we should, we are told, now be capable of distinguishing Soviet and Cuban 'machinations,' which anyway exist mainly in the minds of cold warriors and others guilty of oversimplifying the world, from evolutionary changes which seem to be the only kind that actually occur." Kirkpatrick argued that the real foe remained Soviet-style communism: "Since Moscow is the aggressive expansionist power today, it is more often than not insurgents, encouraged and armed by the Soviet Union, who challenge the status quo."[216]

The divisions within the Democratic ranks were apparent by 1980. Having suffered through a divisive primary battle between President Carter and Massachusetts Senator Edward M. Kennedy, Democrats were timid when discussing foreign affairs: "In its third century, America faces great challenges and an uncertain future." The Carter forces argued that their man sought to reconcile principle with power, sometimes sending confusing messages in the process: "A foreign policy which seeks to blend our ideals and our strength does not easily reduce itself to simple statements." Such was the case with the Cold War. Democrats noted that their hope of reducing tensions had been tossed aside: "It was the Democratic party's greatest hope that we could, in fact, reduce our military effort. But realities of the world situation, including the unremitting buildup of Soviet military forces, required that we begin early to reverse the decade-long decline in American defense efforts."[217]

As if to counter Kirkpatrick's charges directly, Democrats claimed that they, too, were communism's fierce critics: "We note in particular that many of the communist-dominated countries are persistent violators of the most basic human freedoms—the right to free speech, the right to religious freedom, the right to travel and emigrate, and the right to be free from arbitrary harassment."[218] But the Democratic penchant for a nuanced foreign policy paled in comparison to Reagan's thundering about the danger posed by Soviet adventurism. Republicans accused Carter of "misleading the American people about Soviet policies and behavior" and argued that he had championed human rights everywhere except the Soviet Union.[219] Reagan's trouncing of Carter at the polls and the U.S. military buildup that followed had major consequences for future Democratic presidential candidates. By 1984, it was as if the Carter presidency had never happened.

The Triumph of the New Left

In 1984, the Democrats had taken a decidedly leftward lurch. This left turn was a direct result of Ronald Reagan's hard-line anticommunism. During his first term, Reagan presided over the largest peacetime military buildup in history—bigger, even, than Kennedy's. Among the exotic weapons Reagan wanted to construct was a laser defense system that would deter incoming Soviet missiles. The Strategic Defense Initiative, which cynics immediately dubbed "Star Wars," cost the taxpayers $38 billion by 1993.[220] The arms buildup, of which strategic defense was a part, did not produce immediate results. Reagan was the first president in twenty years who did not sign an arms control agreement with the Soviets, and he was the first in fifty years not to meet with a Soviet leader. Superpower tensions were exacerbated when Reagan called for renegotiation of SALT II and when he approved a covert plan to aid the Nicaraguan Contras. Democratic presidential nominee Walter Mondale accused Reagan of shouting at the Soviets through "megaphones" and called for annual superpower summits "in order to reduce tensions and explore possible formal agreements."[221]

Reagan's foreign policy met with nearly uniform disapproval from Democrats. Their 1984 platform accused him of using "easy and abusive anti-Soviet rhetoric as a substitute for strength, progress, and careful use of power." Democrats made passing references to the "dangerous behavior" and "totalitarian nature" of the Soviet empire, but they glossed over these unpleasantries, believing that the Soviet Union wanted to avoid a nuclear war at all costs. This premise guided the "nuclear freeze" movement that had won widespread backing among Democrats during the early 1980s. In 1984, Democrats advocated a "mutual and verifiable freeze on the testing, production, and deployment of all nuclear weapons." Several New England communities considered the nuclear freeze proposal during their annual town meetings, and in New York City 4,000 people took part in eleven "neighborhood" meetings to debate the issue. By 1984, Democrats took the nuclear freeze idea one step further by promising in their platform to adhere to a "no-first-use" policy—an idea resisted by previous Democratic presidents. Moreover, Democrats wanted a mutual withdrawal of nuclear weapons from the European front lines in order to avoid a Hobson's choice of "use 'em or lose 'em" should war erupt there. Finally, Democrats favored scrapping the draft registration system created by Carter.[222]

Other examples of Democratic activists recoiling at Reagan's military policies abound. In the university enclave of Amherst, Massachusetts, local Democrats collected signatures for a "Pledge of Resistance," a 1985 document banning nuclear weapons in the Bay State. In upstate New York, members of the New Left formed the Central American Peace Project, a "teach-in" designed to highlight awareness of the Reagan administration's policies in Central America. National Democrats proposed establishing a peace academy, which would "study the disciplines and train experts in the arts of waging peace."[223]

The 1984 platform reflected the virulent anti-Reaganism that was rampant throughout the Democratic ranks. The document was not a catalog of grievances against Reagan; instead it expressed moral outrage, claiming Reagan had poisoned children's minds with fears about a nuclear holocaust, and promised that if Mondale won "children will dream of better days ahead." But, Democrats warned, if they lost, Armageddon might be in the offing:

> Under Mr. Reagan, the nuclear arms race would continue to spiral out of control. A new generation of destabilizing missiles will imperil all humanity. We will live in a world where the nuclear arms race has spread from earth into space. . . . Can America afford the irresponsibility of a president who undermines confidence in our deterrent with misleading allegations of Soviet nuclear 'superiority' and whose administration beguiles the American public with false claims that nuclear war can be survived with enough shovels?[224]

One reason for such harsh rhetoric was the demise of the so-called Dixiecrats, southern Democrats who were Republican buddies on most military matters. By 1984, many Democratic House leaders and committee chairs were northern liberals: House Majority Leader Thomas P. "Tip" O'Neill (Massachusetts), Ways and Means Committee Chair Dan Rostenkowski (Illinois), Banking, Finance, and Urban Affairs Chair Fernand St. Germain (Rhode Island), Energy and Commerce Chair John Dingell (Michigan), Education and Labor Chair Augustus Hawkins (California), and Judiciary Chair Peter Rodino (New Jersey). Northern Democrats also ran key party committees in the House, including the Democratic Congressional Campaign Committee (Tony Coehlo, California), the Democratic Personnel Committee (Joe Moakley, Massachusetts), and the Democratic Steering and Policy Committee (Tip O'Neill, Massachusetts). In the Senate, the minority Democrats held leading positions: Joseph Biden (Judiciary), Claiborne Pell (Foreign Relations), and William Proxmire (Banking, Housing, and Urban Affairs). (Democrats regained their Senate majority in 1986.) Unlike Richard Nixon, who was able to forge coalitions with the likes of L. Mendel Rivers, there were few southern conservatives in whom Reagan could confide (Senator Sam Nunn of Georgia being a notable exception). Most either had died or had become Republicans. Thus, Reagan preferred making crucial foreign policy decisions in secret—a preference that resulted in the Iran-Contra affair.

Democratic liberals also prevailed in winning their party's presidential nomination. From 1968 to 1988, four of them held the top slot: Hubert Humphrey, George McGovern, Walter Mondale, and Michael Dukakis. Moreover, liberals held important positions in these campaigns, including Mondale, who cochaired Humphrey's unsuccessful 1968 effort. But Mondale was far removed from Humphrey's strident anticommunism. That was reflected in the 1984 platform drafted by the Mondale forces: "While not underestimating the Soviet threat, we can no longer afford simply to blame all of our troubles on a single 'focus of evil,' for the sources of international change run even deeper than the sources of superpower competition. . . . A Democratic President will reverse the automatic militarization of foreign policy and look to the causes of conflict to find out whether they are internal or external, whether they are political or primarily social and economic."[225]

Instead of making communist containment the overriding objective of U.S. foreign policy, the Democrats made racial and gender pluralism, along with environmental protection, primary goals of their foreign policy: "In the 1980s and beyond, America must not only make the world safe for diversity; we must learn to thrive on diversity." Thus, a "no-first-use" nuclear policy was proposed to ensure planetary survival, and gender equality in the military was supported in the name of diversity. In making their case for a policy that substituted anticommunism for progressivism, Democrats sought alliances with "leaders of grass-roots, civic, women's, labor, business, religious, and professional groups, including scientists, lawyers, and educators."[226]

But this approach won few converts: 65 percent of registered voters said communism would have "a lot" of influence in deciding whom they would choose to be president; the Soviet Union, 72 percent; arms control, 69 percent; military spending, 68 percent.[227] Surveys found Reagan ahead of Mondale (52 percent to 39 percent) as the one better able to handle foreign policy; 52 percent also supported Reagan's hard line toward the Soviets.[228] In addition, by a margin of 44 percent to 38 percent, voters wanted Reagan, not Mondale, to negotiate any nuclear arms agreements with the Soviets.[229] Moreover, 60 percent said that such an agreement should be a top priority the "government should concentrate on in the next several years."[230] A narrow 43 percent plurality was more concerned about a communist takeover in Central America than with any potential U.S. involvement in a war there, and most were willing to prop up military dictatorships to thwart the spread of communism there.[231] Regarding a unilateral suspension of nuclear testing, 50 percent believed the Soviets would take advantage of that situation, and 70 percent were satisfied that Reagan would make a real effort to negotiate an arms control agreement in a second term.[232] Finally, just 54 percent believed the United States was "doing all it can to keep peace in the world," whereas 81 percent said the Soviet Union was acting in just the opposite manner.[233] And in a revealing poll, a tiny 7 percent said the Soviet Union sought "only to protect itself against the possibility of attack by other countries"; 28 percent maintained it wanted "to compete with the United States for more influence in different parts of the world"; 38 percent said it desired "global domination, but not at the expense of starting a major war"; and 20 percent believed it wanted "global domination and will risk a major war to achieve that domination if it can't be achieved by other means."[234]

Given these lingering suspicions, Democrats were easily cast as weaklings by nationalist Republicans. Democrat Jeane Kirkpatrick told the 1984 Republican convention that her party had abandoned the Cold War policies of Harry Truman, John Kennedy, and Lyndon Johnson. According to her, these presidents extolled "our democratic government, our economic system, our great natural resources," adding: "That's the way Democratic presidents and Democratic candidates used to talk about America. . . . They were not afraid to be resolute nor ashamed to speak of America as a great nation. They didn't doubt that we must be strong enough to protect ourselves and to help others. They didn't imagine that America should depend for its very survival on the promises of adversaries. They happily assumed the responsibilities of freedom." Noting that foreign policy remained a life-or-death concern, Kirkpatrick likened the "San Francisco Democrats" (the Democrats had held their 1984 convention in the city, home to many gay activists) to ostriches that bury their heads in the sand every time the Soviet Union threatens to upset the status quo. Such behavior, she argued, would trigger a series of falling dominoes if the Democrats won the White House:

> Ask yourself: what would become of Europe if the United States withdrew? What would become of Africa if Europe fell under Soviet domination? What would become of Europe if the Middle East fell under Soviet control? What would become of Israel if surrounded by Soviet client states? What would become of Asia if the Philippines or Japan fell under Soviet domination? What would become of Mexico if Central America became a Soviet satellite? What then could the United States do?[235]

Then, Kirkpatrick took dead aim at the patriotism of the "San Francisco Democrats":

> When the Soviet Union walked out of arms control negotiations, and refused even to discuss the issues, the San Francisco Democrats didn't blame Soviet intransigence. They blamed the United States. But then, they always blame America first.

When Marxist dictators shoot their way into power in Central America, the San Francisco Democrats don't blame the guerrillas and their Soviet allies, they blame United States policies of one-hundred years ago. But then, they always blame America first.[236]

Kirkpatrick's assertions were repeated in the GOP platform: "We reject the notions of guilt and apology which animate so much of the foreign policy of the Democratic party." As in 1972, the New Left had given the Republicans an opportunity to cast themselves as the nationalist party. Quoting from the GOP platform: "We believe American foreign policy can only succeed when it is based on unquestioned faith in a single idea: the idea that all human beings are created equal, the founding idea of democracy." This was in sharp contrast to the two-headed monster nicknamed Carter-Mondale, which held the "illusion that the Soviet leaders share our ideals and aspirations"; covered up Soviet violations of the SALT II and ABM treaties; weakened the nation's defenses and commanded a "hollow army" whose service families often lived below the poverty level; and consigned the ship-building industry to near extinction. Republicans argued that in spite of Democratic intransigence and Soviet belligerence Reagan had established "an effective margin of safety."[237]

Kirkpatrick's arguments resonated with an electorate uneasy about Soviet intentions and believing that the end of the Cold War was still a long way off. But her arguments carried weight only in the presidential contest. Mondale won one state (his home state of Minnesota, by just 3,761 votes out of 2 million cast) and captured only 40.6 percent of the popular vote. Despite the Reagan landslide, however, many other Democrats won—just as they had always done. In Nebraska, for example, Reagan won 71 percent of the ballots, yet Democratic Senate candidate James Exon won with *twice* as many votes as Mondale. New Jersey voters awarded Reagan 71 percent of their ballots, but the Republican Senate candidate polled *even fewer* votes than Mondale. Nationally, 44 percent of the congressional districts selected a presidential candidate of one party (mostly Republican) and a congressional candidate of the other (mostly Democratic).[238] Thus, Republicans added just fifteen seats in the House; given "normal" landslide conditions, the party should have expected to gain three times that number.[239]

These split-tickets frustrated GOP activists. In Massachusetts, conservative Republican Ray Shamie, who lost his Senate bid to Democrat John Kerry, exclaimed: "Why would somebody vote for President Reagan and then vote for John Kerry? It doesn't make any sense."[240] The answer to Shamie's lament lies in the words of Marxist writer Antonio Gramsci: "The crisis consists precisely in the fact that the old is dying and the new cannot be born; in this interregnum a great variety of morbid symptoms occurs."[241] By 1984, the New Deal coalition was dead. But the Cold War also masked what was political and prevented both parties from forming new, enduring majorities. Instead of transforming the anticommunist struggle into a partisan cause, Republican presidents donned their nonpartisan commander-in-chief hats. Meanwhile, congressional Democrats managed to distance themselves from their party's presidential candidates. Thus, by the mid-1980s, both parties had become permanent minorities. The morbid conditions described by Gramsci had metastasized.

An Uneasy Coexistence

On August 12, 1956, the Sunday before the Democratic convention opened in Chicago, President Eisenhower summoned congressional leaders to discuss the Suez crisis. Twenty-two representatives came to the White House, including nine Democrats who flew from Chicago to attend the meeting. After hearing from the president, Senate Majority Leader Lyndon Johnson stepped onto the White House lawn and told assembled reporters, "Politics stop at the water's edge when the security of our country is at stake."[242] Johnson's view that politics ends at the water's edge was a widely held one until the mid-1960s. In large measure, it was a manifestation of the crisis atmosphere engendered by the Cold War—sometimes real, sometimes manufactured.

Two of the Cold War's landslide losers stepped into the uncharted waters that Johnson had so assiduously avoided: Barry Goldwater and George McGovern. By centering their politics on public morality (namely, their own moral code), they altered politics in America permanently. Henceforth, candidates would accentuate their character (public and personal), often at the expense of detailed policies. This, too, placed the candidate above party and weakened the parties institutionally. But the Goldwater and McGovern candidacies altered voter perceptions of the two parties for the duration of the Cold War. As described in Chapter 4, Republicans became the nationalist party, summoning God and country in the battle against communism. Goldwater rhetorically carried things a bit too far, but the GOP never surrendered the defense issue to the Democrats. McGovern, too, altered public attitudes about the Democrats, but in a far more damaging fashion. His revulsion against the Vietnam War and his followers' links to the counterculture contributed to a view that the Democrats were pantywaists—too easily led astray by shrewd Soviet negotiators, far more interested in government social programs at the expense of national defense, and uncertain trumpeters of old-fashioned patriotism. Henceforth, liberalism became a dirty word. Several years later, Barney Frank, Democratic congressman from Massachusetts, described a self-imposed gag order that gravely hurt liberalism:

> Until very recently many on the left argued that we were not-sa-posta point
> out that the American government was morally superior to the Soviet govern
> ment by every relevant criterion or that America's role in the world has been a

positive one over the last forty-five years. The risk was that such sentiments could be used by Republicans to justify more military spending and foreign interventions. Variations of these arguments are now used to discourage liberals from noting that George Bush is morally superior to a variety of third-world dictators, or that America today continues to be one of the places in the world where political and artistic expression is the freest.[243]

A November 1988 survey conducted by Louis Harris and Associates gives ample evidence to Frank's assertions. In an open-ended question, 25 percent associated the phrase liberalism with "soft on communism."[244] Henry Wallace and his New Left successors left a dubious legacy: Pending only the most anomalous conditions (read: Watergate), Democrats were all but excluded from the presidency during the Cold War. Ironically, a widespread perception that Democrats would be especially apt to keep the United States out of World War III contributed to the party's growing electoral liabilities. A survey of polls conducted by George Gallup from 1952 to 1992 makes the point. During the Eisenhower years, Republicans held the advantage when people were asked, "Which party, the Republican or the Democratic, is most likely to keep the United States out of World War III?" In 1956, for example, 46 percent answered "Republican"; just 21 percent said "Democratic." But during the Reagan era, Democrats held comfortable leads as the party most likely to avoid World War III. For example, in 1980, 45 percent maintained that the Democrats could keep the nation out of war; less than 25 percent said the same of the Republicans.[245] The New Left had turned a potential strength into a political liability: More and more Americans came to the conclusion that Democrats would acquiesce to communist advances—from Africa and Southeast Asia to Central and Southern America. The "peace issue" had became an albatross around the necks of Democratic presidential aspirants.

But the Democratic party was not bereft. Ever since the New Deal, congressional Democrats excelled at the "politics of redistribution." The Cold War was no exception. When demanding constituents asked "What have you done for me lately?" Democratic incumbents proudly pointed to a stream of Social Security checks for the elderly, Medicare coverage for the sick, Great Society programs for the poor, and defense contracts for the middle class. The latter was especially important. During the Cold War, the federal government spent *$2 trillion* on nuclear warheads, *$1 trillion* to control and defend these weapons, *$375 billion* for plutonium and uranium, and *$20 billion* to keep these things secret.[246] Congress authorized the purchase of 4,000 bombers at a cost of more than $200 billion. Moreover, $371 billion was spent building some 67,500 missiles capable of delivering these weapons.[247] The result was the construction of a vast network of industrial facilities housing the research, production, and testing of nuclear weapons. This "nuclear-industrial complex" constituted 120 million square feet of buildings and 2.3 million acres of land—an area larger than Delaware, Rhode Island, and the District of Columbia combined.[248]

Thus, money flooded congressional districts, many of them represented by Democrats eager to have their share of the federal bomb-making pie. Former Democratic congressman Tino Roncalio recently recalled, "I was a believer that you better bring home the bacon or you're not going to stay in Congress very long." To keep voters satisfied, Roncalio won a spot on the coveted Joint Atomic Energy Committee, from which he steered federal dollars to his Wyoming constituency. Bob Barker of the Lawrence Livermore National Laboratory remembered, "I was told to think of the budget as two pieces: delivering a specific weapon and pursuing research into the possible."[249] Often, vast spending for solely *domestic* programs was justified under the cloak of national security. For example, in 1952, the Democratic platform advocated more federal spending for day care, citing the Cold War as the primary reason: "Since several million mothers must now be away from their children during the day, because they are engaged in defense work, facilities of adequate day care of these children should be provided and adequately financed."[250] A few years later, arguing for more government involvement in the arts, President Kennedy told the *New York Times*, "I think it is tremendously important that we regard music not just as part of our arsenal in the Cold War, but as an integral part of a free society."[251] In 1972, George McGovern advised his fellow Democrats in a similar vein: "National security includes schools for our children as well as silos for our missiles, the health of our families, as much as the size of our bombs, the safety of our streets and the condition of our cities and not just the engines of war. And if we someday choke on the pollution of our own air, there will be little consolation in leaving behind a dying continent ringed with steel."[252]

But the Cold War rationale resulted in vast expenditures and warped priorities for an entire generation. Only Social Security consumed a larger share of the national budget than defense during the Cold War.[253] In 1958, Yale economist James Tobin pronounced this truism: "Had the Cold War never existed, the United States would not have spent more money on social programs; it would have spent less."[254] An uneasy social peace ensued—poor citizens would be better able to make ends meet and not be prone to riot in the streets. The middle class would receive its own form of welfare by making bombs in government-subsidized defense plants. Ironically, both groups did not see their common benefactor. The middle class was as likely to view their impoverished compatriots as "welfare queens" who, in the vernacular, were "getting something for nothing." A tax revolt that questioned virtually every government program, except defense, followed.

All of this social spending, however, reinforced the New Deal perception that the Democratic party was "best able to keep the country prosperous."

Gallup polls taken from 1960 to 1980 show Democrats with a fairly consistent advantage on this issue. When respondents were asked during the Kennedy-Nixon contest to name the party that was "best able to keep the country prosperous," 47 percent named the Democrats; just 31 percent named the Republicans. It was not until the Reagan years, when the national economy was fueled by the largest peacetime military expansion in history, that the Republicans finally took this issue away from their erstwhile rivals. Asked during the 1984 Reagan-Mondale contest which party could best handle the economy, 49 percent identified the Republicans; 33 percent identified the Democrats.[255]

The separation of presidential politics from congressional politics remains one of the permanent legacies of the Cold War. Republican capture of the Authentic Center on national security and foreign policy issues helped them win the White House time and again. Yet these same issues did not count for much in congressional races. In 1984, *1 percent* mentioned foreign policy as the single most important reason why they voted for their party's congressional candidate.[256] Because presidential and congressional candidates posed different questions to voters, divided control of the government became a staple of the Cold War. The resultant division—Republican White House and Democratic Congress—prompted Senate Majority Leader Lyndon Johnson to speak of a "qualified mandate" after the ballots were counted in 1956:

> A political party at a national convention draws up a program to present to the voters. The voters can either accept it by giving the party full power, reject it by taking the party completely out of power, or give it qualified approval by giving one party the Congress and the other party the Presidency. And when we in the Congress have been given a qualified mandate, as we were in 1956, it means that we have a solemn responsibility to cooperate with the President and produce a program that is neither his blueprint nor our blueprint but a combination of the two. It is the politician's task to pass legislation, not to sit around saying principled things.[257]

In the four decades that have passed since Johnson uttered these words, one or the other party controlled the White House and Congress simultaneously for a mere fourteen years—about one-third of the time. Parties have continuously clamored for total responsibility, but the weakened condition of the two-party system—a condition that the Cold War exacerbated—left voters suspicious. Bill Clinton understood this. In June 1992, as he was about to capture the Democratic presidential nomination, he told the *New York Times* that since 1968 "the Democrats have had a lot of trouble," adding:

> The American people have voted for Republican presidents and Democratic congresses, a situation which has given us gridlock and quadrupled our investments and our economic potential. But I think largely on something like this,

you know [voters say]: "Republicans would be better presidents because they manage the economy better, keep taxes low, stick up for the country abroad, but the Congress should be Democratic because they care more about the people that really need help."[258]

In 1992, it would be up to Clinton to attempt to reverse these public perceptions about his party. The end of the Cold War gave him that opportunity.

Part Three

Diminished Parties
in Search of
a New Politics

chapter six

High Anxiety: Post–Cold War Politics

We won the Cold War, and now they're saying here's a pink slip.

—Charlie Witt Jr., shipyard worker, March 29, 1992

The White House, Christmas Night, 1991

A satisfied George Bush appeared on television to announce that the Cold War was won: "This is a victory for democracy and freedom. It's a victory for the moral force of our values. Every American can take pride in this victory, from the millions of men and women who have served our country in uniform to millions of Americans who supported their country and a strong defense under nine presidents."[1] Earlier that day, Soviet president Mikhail Gorbachev walked from his Kremlin office and entered a room decorated with pecan-colored woodwork, light-green damask wall coverings, and marquise curtains. There a television crew was waiting. As the camera lights blazed, Gorbachev took to the airwaves and announced, "I hereby discontinue my activities at the post of President of the Union of Soviet Socialist Republics." With that, Soviet communism was no more.[2]

The disintegration of the Soviet Union was preceded by a series of earth-shattering events: The Berlin Wall fell; Germany was reunited; the Captive Nations were set free; and Soviet hard-liners, anxious to preserve their crumbling empire, staged an abortive coup. Six months after the Soviet Union lurched into oblivion, Russian president Boris Yeltsin addressed the U.S. Congress and gave communism its final epitaph: "The idol of communism, which spread everywhere social strife, animosity and unparalleled brutality, which instilled fear in humanity has collapsed. It has collapsed never to rise again. I am here to assure you, we will not let it rise again in our land." At this, the legislators cheered. It was the applause many longed to give when Winston Churchill delivered his famous "Iron Curtain" speech forty-six years earlier. Now Yeltsin said what many waited decades to hear: "Freedom and communism are incompatible."[3] The peace that eluded Truman, Churchill, and Stalin at the close of World War II was at hand.

As these momentous events came cascading one after the other, George Bush wrapped himself in the robes of a Great Conqueror. Accepting renomination for a second term, he told the assembled Republican delegates, "This convention is the first at which an American president can say the Cold War is over, and freedom finished first."[4] Bush had much to crow about. In 1989, American forces invaded Panama and forcibly seized dictator Manuel Noriega. Two years later, U.S. troops, many of them stationed in Europe poised to fight World War III, were rushed to Saudi Arabia to liberate Kuwait. As Bush became presider-in-chief over the triumphant close of the Cold War, Republicans paid him homage. A campaign brochure boasted, "Today, this year, for the first time since December 1941, the United States is not engaged in a war, hot or cold."[5] This was no idle boast: For the first time since 1936, foreign policy would not figure as a major issue in a presidential contest.

Years ago, John F. Kennedy observed that victory has many fathers while defeat is an orphan. The months following the twin victories in the Cold War and Persian Gulf provided ample proof that Kennedy's maxim still held. Bush received a 91 percent approval rating after the triumphant ejection of Saddam Hussein's forces from Kuwait, and nearly three-fourths approved of his Soviet policy—with 58 percent saying he was better than Reagan on this issue.[6] Not wanting to be left orphaned, the Republican party claimed a starring role in the Cold War's triumphant end: "Only the naive believe that history is an inevitable tide or a series of accidents. Our crusade of a half-century to champion freedom and civilization against the dark tide of totalitarianism is now victorious."[7] For decades, Republicans had stuck to the adage of "peace through strength." After the Cold War, they found vindication in their steadfastness: "Peace through strength was more than a slogan. It was the calculated Republican plan for first, the survival and then, the triumph of America."[8] To punctuate the point, a large slab of the Berlin Wall stood outside Houston's Astrodome when the GOP convened for its quadrennial convention.

Democrats retorted that "peace through strength" was an irrelevant political dogma. Vice presidential candidate Al Gore stated his party's case: "George Bush taking credit for the Berlin Wall coming down is like the rooster taking credit for the sunrise."[9] Nevertheless, Republican platform writers brushed aside Gore's criticism, preferring to link the Democrats with the old bugaboo of communism:

We Republicans saw clearly the dangers of collectivism: not only the military threat, but the deeper threat to the souls of people bound in dependence. Here at home, we warned against Big Government because we knew concentrated decision-making, no matter how well-intentioned, was a danger to liberty and prosperity. Republicans stood at the rampart of freedom, defending the individual against the domineering state. While we did not always prevail, we always stood our ground, faithful to our principles and confident of history's ultimate verdict.[10]

Such claims led to an inescapable conclusion: If the United States and the Republican party were victors in the Cold War, the Democrats were its losers. Republicans charged that the Loyal Opposition was wrong about nearly everything during the long conflict—from creating bloated bureaucracies at home to capitulating to communism abroad. Senator Phil Gramm of Texas tossed some red meat to hungry GOP delegates: "Don't you know the Democrats are lonely tonight! In all the world, only in Cuba and North Korea and in the Democratic Party in America do we still have organized political groups who believe that the answer to every problem is more government."[11] Evangelist Pat Robertson also engaged in some political hyperbole: "The people of Eastern Europe got rid of their left-wingers; it is time we in America got rid of our left-wingers."[12] Ronald Reagan reminded delegates he had seen the "evil empire" and deserved credit for its downfall: "I heard those speakers at the other convention saying 'we won the Cold War'—and I couldn't help wondering, just who exactly do they mean by 'we'?"[13] These were the smug statements of a political party whose crusade against communists and their fellow-travelers was over. But in victory, the Republicans were about to suffer their first presidential defeat in sixteen years.

The Republicans: "Walking the Edge of Anarchy"

In his address, Boris Yeltsin told the Congress: "Every man is a man of his own time. No exception is made for anyone, whether an ordinary citizen or the president."[14] When he spoke in June 1992, Yeltsin was the man of the hour, and Bush hoped voters would see him the same way on election day less than five months hence. But Bush's résumé—the best since Dwight Eisenhower's—was tailored for prosecuting the Cold War: congressman, U.N. ambassador, CIA director, envoy to China, vice president. Each job gave credence to his 1988 claim that he was "Ready on Day One to Be a Great President." Four years later, Bush maintained that the Cold War's successful outcome made him the right man for the times. A Republican television advertisement featured a female newscaster saying, "President Bush said today that he reassured Mr. Yeltsin the United States would stand by democracy." In a voice-over, an announcer intoned, "In a world where we're just one unknown dictator away from the next major crisis, who do you most trust to be sitting in this chair?"[15] Voters took notice, choosing Bush over rivals Bill Clinton and Ross Perot by 63 percent to 24 percent and 7 percent respectively when asked which one "would do the best job of handling an international crisis."[16]

But with the Cold War over, Bush had the powers of the presidency while lacking purpose. One voter put it this way: "Now that the Cold War is over, we don't need a world leader."[17] A Cold War president without the Cold War, Bush floundered. Howard Baker, former senator from Tennessee and Reagan chief of staff, sensed that a "major opportunity"—to remake the GOP into a full-scale majority party in the wake of the Cold War—was being squandered: "There's an opportunity in all this bedlam as we move out of the warm glow of stability and walk the edge of anarchy, with dozens of small problems instead of one big confrontation. . . . But I'm not seeing it yet, in the Congress or the White House, from the Republicans or the Democrats. Nobody's talking fundamentals, nobody's laying out goals."[18] Most Americans sensed the GOP lassitude, and they vented their anger at Bush. A mere *1 percent* cited foreign policy as an important issue in making a presidential pick.[19] Even Bush's sterling résumé became a liability, as he acknowledged: "My opponents say I spend too much time on foreign policy."[20] The Republican platform tacitly agreed. Apart from a preamble touting Bush's overseas achievements, foreign policy was relegated to page fifty-six, after planks on enterprise zones, capital gains tax cuts, the environment, D.C. statehood (against), Puerto Rican statehood (for), and even the Mining Law of 1872![21]

Democrats coined the phrase "George Bush doesn't get it." What Bush did not understand were domestic worries about unemployment and health care that had become breeding grounds for middle-class insecurities. When asked to name "the single most important thing Bush had accomplished as president," a June 1992 CBS News/*New York Times* survey found 39 percent saying "Nothing!" Even those who mentioned the Persian Gulf (29 percent) were stumped to cite another milestone; 18 percent answered "I don't know." Together, an astounding *57 percent* thought Bush a do-nothing president, and just 4 percent credited him for ending the Cold War.[22]

Battered by the relentless opposition from the Democrats and his fall from grace in the public polls, Bush plaintively sought plaudits for the Cold War's success: "I hope every Mother and Dad out there says, 'Hey, we ought to give this president a little credit out there for the fact that our little kids don't worry so much about nuclear war.' Isn't that important?"[23] It was important, and voters gave Bush and Reagan kudos for the Soviet Union's demise: 56 percent said both "helped speed the end of communism in Russia."[24] But Bush's argument failed to energize his flagging candidacy. Bush pollster Fred Steeper advised: "It is important that you describe your own role in reducing the threat of nuclear war. People do not respond the way we want when you simply say 'kids go to bed at night without the fear of nuclear war.'. . . The lesson is that, if you do not give yourself direct credit, people assume that the reduction of the nuclear threat just happened on its own or because the Soviets unilaterally backed off."[25] Facing an uncertain future in an ill-defined world, the electorate looked for a visionary and did not find one in their beleaguered president. Forty-nine percent answered negatively when asked whether Bush had a "vision for the future of the country."[26]

Seeing an opportunity, Democrats seized it. In 1991, Pennsylvania senatorial candidate Harris Wofford adopted the slogan "It's time to take care of our own."[27] Wofford beat Republican Dick Thornburgh in a race that had been characterized as a David-versus-Goliath contest, with Wofford cast as David. Wofford's win assumed mythical proportions, as Democrats discovered that with the country turned inward more Americans than ever before were willing to give them a hearing. Sixty-five percent said they would be more likely to support a Democratic presidential candidate because that person "would spend more time here at home and less time on foreign policy."[28] Democratic House Leader Richard Gephardt saw opportunities in the new political climate:

> [The end of the Cold War] has the potential to change the partisan balance, probably in our favor, because one of the themes [the Republicans] raised, especially in presidential campaigns and often with considerable success, is that they were better able to deal with the Kremlin. But what we have now is a world with economics and foreign policy intertwined, where our embassies will have to deal with economics more than geopolitical questions, and where politicians will have to help in organizing here for economic success worldwide.[29]

Bill Clinton presented a worldview far different from that of Bush *or* those of Democratic predecessors. Instead of focusing on old questions of containment, Clinton changed the subject entirely, telling the Democratic convention, "Just as we have won the Cold War abroad, we are losing the battles for economic opportunity and social justice here at home."[30] Clinton saw new enemies in the emerging economic superpowers, particularly Germany and Japan. He reminded audiences that whereas in 1980 the United States had the highest wages in the world it now ranked thirteenth—behind the Germans and the Japanese.[31] The Democratic platform derided the Reagan-Bush years as "a nightmare of Republican irresponsibility and neglect."[32] As David Halberstam succinctly observed, "The Cold War is over: Japan won."[33] Such sentiments contributed to a feeling of queasiness. Exit polls found 69 percent saying Bush had left the country in worse shape than he found it in 1988.[34] Harold Mixner, a Republican from Sherman Oaks, California, was exasperated with Bush: "I don't understand what happened to him. I want to shake him."[35] Mixner's desire to rattle his party's leader reflected an underlying pessimism that was seeping into the body politic. Francis Fukuyama, author of *The End of History*, prophesied the end of the American Century: "As with a star that has gone supernova, the light emanating from the United States continues to shine brightly at the periphery of the universe, where it is observed by various Russians, Chinese, Lithuanians, and the like; but the energy at the core is rapidly extinguishing."[36]

The Anxious Middle

Ironically, victory in the Cold War generated a crisis of confidence in the U.S. government that had successfully prosecuted it. For decades, Republicans told voters that government was virtually useless except for fighting communism. With the Cold War finished, Republicans lost a theme; more important, the federal government lost much of its raison d'être. Still, policymakers soldiered on, almost as if nothing had happened. Political scientist Theodore J. Lowi noted that the federal bureaucracy was still immersed in the Cold War: "The Cold War Culture is the widely inculcated belief that your adversary is prepared for war and is ready to commit aggressive and hostile acts the moment your guard is down. If war doesn't happen, that is proof that your preparations prevented it."[37] The third principal presidential candidate in 1992, Texas billionaire Ross Perot, expressed a similar view in a "town meeting" hosted by CBS News anchor Dan Rather:

> Perot: The whole thing that jumps against you, Dan, is that our whole government is still organized to fight the Cold War against Russia. It's over. And I'm not just talking defense. Everything is structured for the Cold War. I would restructure everything to give the proper priority now to rebuilding our country.

> Rather: Including intelligence agencies?

> Perot: Everything. . . . If we let our economy continue to deteriorate we, like Russia, will no longer be a superpower. And Russia is living proof that if you're broke you're not a superpower. We almost went broke in the Cold War. . . . We've got to turn that around now with the highest priority. We've got to reorganize our government from the top down. That's going to take hard-minded thinking and action. Talk won't do it.[38]

Perot instinctively understood what *Washington Post* columnist E. J. Dionne Jr. has called "the Anxious Middle."[39] According to Dionne, the Anxious Middle is thoroughly disaffected with the status quo, pragmatic in its expectations of what government can and cannot do, and longing for successes—both economic and patriotic—that defined the United States during the heyday of World War II and the Cold War. Unlike the Authentic Center of which Arthur Larson spoke, the Anxious Middle was willing to publicly question assumptions that Americans had previously taken for granted. These included doubts that the American Dream could persist much longer. An October 1992 CBS News/*New York Times* survey found 44 percent thinking that future generations would not be better off than their parents; just 26 percent said they would.[40] The belief that "my kids will not have it as good as I did" formed a leitmotif to the 1992 campaign. The Anxious Middle, which had given life to the American Dream, now seemed to be falling victim to stagnation, unemployment, and a belief that the country's best days were behind it.

But the Anxious Middle had something in common with the Authentic Center—an eschewing of "traditional politics" in its search for solutions to national problems. As described in Chapter 3, the Authentic Center muted politics by cloaking most issues under the guise of national security. The Anxious Middle had its own form of new politics—it smothered potential controversies with a nonideological sugarcoating and believed, like Michael Dukakis, that competence, not ideology, was the most important prerequisite in solving the country's problems. Those belonging to the Anxious Middle also held the conviction that neither the Democrats nor the Republicans had shown themselves capable of solving the country's problems and they were willing to eschew both of them if the right outsider could be found.

The Anxious Middle had other, less endearing qualities. It questioned things it once widely accepted, and a peevishness set in that corroded faith in government. In March 1992, a scant 5 percent held federal agency officials in "high regard"; Congress, 4 percent; politicians, 3 percent.[41] A grassroots campaign to limit congressional terms gathered momentum. Perot touched a responsive chord when he chastised government bureaucrats and members of Congress: "Those people work for you and me, but they don't act like our servants. Close the barber shop, the gym, the parking lot. Make them pay for it. Ground every airplane for federal officials except Air Force One. Let 'em fly commercial, get in line, wait three hours, get their baggage lost. We're going broke, and they're flying around in our airplanes."[42] Filmmakers also played to the cynical public mood. One of the most-watched films of 1992 was Oliver Stone's *JFK*. In it, Stone questioned official accounts of the Kennedy assassination and claimed that Lyndon Johnson, the FBI, the Warren Commission, and a host of others lied about what really happened. Near the end of his life Richard Nixon warned, "At a time when we should be celebrating victory, many observers are wallowing in pessimism, as if we had suffered a defeat."[43] Nixon advised that the president must create a new nationalism to achieve greatness in the history books:

> No one would say that war is good for a country, but it is undeniable that the United States has been at its best when confronted with aggression or some other significant international challenge (our space effort after the shock of

Sputnik is a case in point). Most of our greatest presidents were war presidents. Our greatest bursts of increased productivity and scientific advancement have occurred during war. To meet the challenges we face in the post–Cold War era, we must marshal the same resources of energy, optimism, and common purpose that thrive during war and put them to work at home and abroad during an era when our enemy will be neither communism nor Nazism but our own self-defeating pessimism. . . . Without a great cause to galvanize America, the very unity of our nation will be at risk as we struggle to meet the challenges of the coming century.[44]

Among the first to fall victim to the nation's disunity was the Republican party that Nixon helped transform into an anticommunist instrument. Having no great national purpose, post–Cold War Republicans were in imminent danger of being redefined by their marginal constituencies. The candidate who became the repository for the collective anxieties of the party's rank-and-file was conservative commentator Patrick J. Buchanan. A staunch anticommunist, Buchanan once dubbed Lenin's party "a war party" bent on destroying the West: "The very existence of a free, prosperous, powerful democratic Republic halfway around the world [from the Soviet Union] is not only the last obstacle to Soviet global hegemony, it is a vast mirror in which mankind can see the immense depth of communist duplicity, deceit, and failure. The United States is mankind's most eloquent statement that Marxism and Leninism are squalid, self-serving lies."[45]

Buchanan's anticommunism drew him into the Republican ranks—first as a special assistant to President Nixon and later as President Reagan's White House communications director. But with communism nearly defunct, Buchanan borrowed a line from onetime nemesis George McGovern and urged America to "come home." Buchanan predicted that "the old Cold warriors, Catholics, and others who saw communism as evil and a threat against our country will go back to our familiar point of view—let's tend to our own affairs."[46] Embellishing on his isolationist paradigm, Buchanan cast Bush as a man of yesteryear: "He is yesterday and we are tomorrow. He is a globalist and we are nationalists. He believes in some *Pax Universalis*; we believe in the Old Republic. He would put America's wealth and power at the service of some vague New World Order; we will put America first." In Buchanan's view, communism's demise offered Republicans an opportunity to rethink first principles: "All the institutions of the Cold War, from vast permanent U.S. armies on foreign soil, to old alliances against communist enemies that no longer exist, to billions in foreign aid, must be reexamined." With his usual rhetorical flourish, Buchanan asserted that Republicans could not be captives of history: "With a $4 trillion debt, with a U.S. budget chronically out of balance, should the United States be required to carry indefinitely the full burden of defending rich and prosperous allies who take America's generosity for granted as they invade our markets?" Buchanan called for a "new patriotism"—one that would not "trade our sovereignty for a cushion seat at the head table of anybody's New World Order."[47]

Bush vehemently took issue with Buchanan. Recalling World War II, Bush thought it a dreadful error to "pull back into some isolationistic sphere listening to the siren call of 'America First,'"[48] adding: "I learned that lesson as a young kid just at the beginning of World War II. I don't want to see this country go back to 'America First' and to protection that will shrink markets and throw people out of work."[49] Brookings Institution scholar Stephen Hess noted that Bush is "the only candidate who is really trying to hold back the tide from the left and the right that is turning the country rapidly inward."[50] But Buchanan's message had resonance—especially with the Anxious Middle that Bush never understood. One survey found 40 percent saying they would be "much more likely" to back a candidate who "favors a major reduction in U.S. foreign aid and less U.S. involvement in foreign affairs."[51] Buchanan's "America First!" rallying cry signaled the return of the old isolationist-internationalist cleavage that cut across the liberal-conservative divide before Pearl Harbor.

Like Clinton, Buchanan saw Germany and Japan as potential new enemies. In trade negotiations with these nations, Buchanan's "tough-guy" approach dictated that the U.S. government should always seek "advantage and victory for the United States."[52] But while Germany and Japan constituted new enemies from without, Buchanan saw liberalism as a pernicious enemy from within that was undermining traditional "Judeo-Christian" values. In a strident speech at the 1992 Republican National Convention, Buchanan likened the emerging "cultural war" between liberals and conservatives to the Cold War: "There is a religious war going on in this country for the soul of America. It is a cultural war, as critical to the kind of nation we shall be as the Cold War itself, for the war is for the soul of America."[53]

Buchanan received an astonishing 37 percent of the primary vote in New Hampshire (his best showing in any state), holding Bush to just 53 percent. After that, Buchanan took 36 percent of the Georgia ballots, 32 percent in Rhode Island and Florida, and 30 percent in Colorado and Maryland. In thirteen other states, Buchanan won between 20 and 27 percent of the vote.[54] But these tallies did not represent a "pro-Buchanan" mandate—rather they were a sound repudiation of the Cold War Republican establishment. Buchanan's candidacy symbolized the GOP difficulties in the post–Cold War era. As Christian conservatives and evangelicals flocked to the Buchanan tent, members of the Anxious Middle became even more alienated from the GOP. Michael Deaver, a deputy White House chief of staff under Reagan, fretted that the Republicans were toying with extinction: "For years the Republican party suffered from [the comparison with] Herbert Hoover. Reagan tried to repair that, but now Bush has made us the party not only of Herbert Hoover but Billy Sunday."[55] But more than a Grand Old Coalition was dissolving. The Authentic Center had been morphed into the Anxious Middle. Yet unlike Richard Nixon's Silent Majority (another euphemism for the Authentic Center) the Anxious Middle was no longer content to be either centrist or silent.

Enter the Perotistas

By the time the Soviet Union dissolved, the Republican and Democratic parties had weakened because they had foregone the traditional give-and-take of politics for which they were designed in favor of appeals to the Authentic Center and acquiescence to an "imperial presidency." By 1992, the parties had no "normal" politics to which they could return. Instead of engaging in the art of compromise that characterized ordinary politics, Republicans tried to construct a "leave-us-alone" coalition filled with middle-class angst against big government (which, ironically, had won the Cold War) and high taxes. Meanwhile, Democrats were suspiciously viewed as unreliable stewards of government—an enduring legacy of the Cold War era. But something more than mere disillusionment was at work. What Hubert Humphrey had once called "the politics of joy" now seemed like an oxymoron. To many Americans, politics had become a nasty game of media-positioning and name-calling. In that devastating 1960s phrase, politics had become part of the problem, not part of the solution.

Enter Ross Perot. The Texas billionaire castigated Democratic and Republican activists as little more than do-nothing political aficionados: "Everybody has detailed positions. Nobody implements them."[56] It was with colloquialisms like these that Perot tapped into a well-spring of anti-party resentment. When ten registered voters in Phoenix were asked what the two parties meant to them, two shouted "Corruption!"; others used words like "rich," "self-serving," "good-old-boy networks," "special interests," "bunch of lost causes," "lost sheep," "immorality," "going whatever way is on top," and "liars" in their word-association game.[57] Eighty-five percent believed that political action committee (PAC) money had more influence on the parties than they did; an equal number said money bought a candidate's loyalty. Sixty-four percent were angry with Bush, but 72 percent were unhappy with the Democratic Senate, and 69 percent were dissatisfied with the Democratic House; 56 percent said neither party was any good.[58] Pamela Lopez, a Phoenix paralegal, captured the antipathy toward the two-party system: "We're living in a feudal system—they are at the top and we're outside."[59]

These profound antiparty sentiments became a full-throated cry for a political revolution: 82 percent said "both parties are pretty much out of touch with the American people";[60] 81 percent blamed the early 1990s recession on Democrats and Republicans in Congress;[61] 58 percent said the country "needs a new political party to compete with the Democratic and Republican parties in offering the best candidates for political office." Strikingly, 54 percent of Democrats and 53 percent of Republicans agreed that another party was needed.[62] Republican pollster Gordon Black found that support for a new reform party would make it *"the largest political party in the United States,"* with a voter pool that "starts at 30 percent of the electorate and could go over half of the electorate as a voting bloc." Black added that "not since the founding of the Republican party in 1854 has there been this much potential to create a full scale national party."[63] Ed Rollins, Ronald Reagan's 1984 campaign manager who briefly hitched his star to Ross Perot's, claimed that both parties were in trouble:

> The parties do not stand for anything. The parties try to cover all bases. You have everyone from Congresswoman Maxine Waters to Senator Howell Heflin—that's the full range of politics in the Democratic party. In my [Republican] party, you have everyone from Congressman Chris Shays, one of the most liberal, to Strom Thurmond [one of the most conservative]. That covers the whole game. So everybody is covering all issues. I think what the American electorate is saying, "Tell me you stand for something. Show me some convictions. And I'll either accept you or reject you."[64]

Public anger was one thing—finding consensus another. Nearly a century before, in his masterpiece *The American Commonwealth*, James Bryce wrote: "In a country so full of change and movement as America, new questions are always coming up and must be answered. New troubles surround a government and a way must be found to escape from them; new diseases attack the nation, and have to be cured. The duty of a great party is . . . to find answers and remedies."[65] One hundred years after Bryce penned those words, new questions and troubles abounded. Unfortunately, neither party seemed capable of coping. Republican pollster Richard Wirthlin found that on a thermometer scale ranging from zero to 100 degrees, the GOP dropped from a temperate 63 degrees in 1984 to a chilly 49 degrees by 1992 while the Democratic temperature rose just slightly, from 55 degrees to 58 degrees.[66] But the warmer Democratic reading and cooler Republican one reflected more neutrality than real passions, either hot or cold.

For years, advocates of stronger political parties have pushed for laws that would ensure their existence. Some campaigned for campaign finance reforms that would give them a greater role in the collection and distribution of monies to congressional candidates. Others sought protection from the courts, claiming that parties have a "right of association" that permits them to organize with little interference from the state.[67] Theodore J. Lowi believes that such laws and court decisions have kept the major parties "alive by artificial respiration, through state laws protecting them from third parties, and by artificial insemination, with federal subsidies and other so-called campaign reforms." Lowi maintains that "if all the tubes were pulled and all the IV's cut," both parties would "collapse in an instant."[68]

The reality is that although the two-party system is ingrained in the code books, many voters have long disliked them and, thanks to television, have ignored them. The diminished party-in-the-electorate, coupled with the resentment directed at the status quo, contributed to what Lowi calls "the radicalization of the moderates."[69] This radicalization of the Anxious Middle had its genesis on February 20, 1992, when Ross Perot appeared on *Larry King Live* and told viewers that "if you're that serious [about my running for president]—you, the people . . . register me in fifty states."[70] With that order to his legions of volunteers, the quixotic Perot candidacy began.

Ross Perot had never sought elective office, aside from a successful 1952 campaign for the senior class presidency at the U.S. Naval Academy (Perot was later summoned to the White House to shake hands with President Eisenhower). Forty years later, Perot was running for president again—initially with good prospects of success. After his startling announcement on the King program, thousands of volunteers manned card tables at shopping malls, beauty parlors, and grocery stores collecting signatures from registered voters to put Perot's name on state ballots. Many more telephoned a toll-free 800 number Perot had established in his Dallas headquarters—often overloading Perot's vaunted computerized telephone system. Together, 5.5 million registered voters signed petitions to put Perot on state ballots.

Perot struck a responsive chord because, as Yeltsin told the Congress, he seemed to be a man of his time. Growing up in modest circumstances in Texarkana, Texas—fewer than fifty miles from Clinton's native Hope, Arkansas—Perot enlisted in the navy, where in 1953 he boarded the ship *Sigourney* bound for Korea. Near the end of Eisenhower's second term, he joined the computer revolution—taking a job with International Business Machines. By 1962, Perot's knack for salesmanship allowed him to complete his IBM yearly sales quota in just nineteen days. In 1968, Perot left IBM and founded his own company, Electronic Data Systems (EDS). The company grew from 300 employees in 1968 to 1,800 two years later—largely on the strength of government subsidies. As the firm expanded, so did Perot's fortune. In 1984, Perot sold EDS to General Motors for $2.5 billion. By 1992, Perot's net worth was estimated at $3 billion—more than the entire federal budget for 1930, the year he was born.

Bored with his computer business and rich beyond measure, the Texas billionaire took up politics, spurred by his conviction that the American Century was coming to a close. On March 29, 1992, Perot told the *New York Times*: "We've got a patient whose heart has stopped beating and has broken fingers and toes, and all the politicians want to talk about is the fingers and toes. I want to go straight to the heart."[71] For Perot and his followers, the gargantuan federal deficits were a metaphor for a nation out of control. Perot likened the debt to "a crazy aunt that we keep in the basement. Everybody knows she's there but nobody talks about her. But one day she's going to get loose and kill a neighbor."[72] Jim Ash, chairman of Wright Ashphal, liked Perot's antideficit talk: "I'm fed up with what's going on in Washington. My grandchildren are going to have serious problems unless something is done with the deficit."[73] Ash was joined by Margaret Rich, a secretary who backed Michael Dukakis in 1988 but now preferred Perot: "I'm tired of the bozos that are up there in both Congress and the White House. Our generation is being screwed by the nation's $4 trillion debt."[74]

As Ash and Rich attest, Perot's support ranged from the boardroom to the front office. In May, the Texas billionaire led in several national polls. Nestor Valdez, a Perot volunteer in Ventura, California, captured the prevailing sentiments of many Perot backers: "I think the two-party system will fall just like the Berlin Wall. I love this country. It's provided me with an excellent life. But there has come a time when people who are managing this country have fallen into corruption—into not addressing problems. Everyone has forgotten the word 'united' in United States."[75]

Perot and his people saw the president as resembling a chief mechanic who would, in Perot's words, get "under the hood working on fixing the old car to get it back on the road."[76] The analogy appealed to many. So, too, did another analogy: the president as boss. Thousands donned "Ross for Boss" buttons, believing that Perot's background made him best suited to be America's "boss" in the post–Cold War world. But instead of leading a true third-party effort, Perot had become a "Rorschach candidate"— someone upon whom voters could project their dreams of what the United States could be—and someone, too, who would mirror their cynicism and resentment. To win, Democrats realized that Perot's potential supporters— not Bush's—had to be their primary targets.

The Democrats: "It's the Economy, Stupid!"

Throughout the Cold War, presidential elections were frequently fought over the corpse of the Democratic party. In those elections where Democrats seemed especially weak in meeting the communist challenge, assertive Republicans always captured the prize, as Richard Nixon's 1972 landslide win against George McGovern, Ronald Reagan's 1980 rout of Jimmy Carter, and George Bush's comfortable 1988 win over Michael Dukakis attest. Throughout the Cold War, Republicans delighted in exploiting the Democrats' weaknesses in foreign policy, defense, and handling the superpower relationship. These issues formed the "legs" upon which GOP strategists built a stool. As Tables 6.1 and 6.2 show, those "legs" remained sturdy supports in 1992. On every aspect of foreign policy—from trade to the

TABLE 6.1
Foreign Policy Issues, by Party, 1991–1992 (in percentages)

Text of Question	Republicans	Democrats
"Which political party do you trust to do a better job in handling foreign affairs?"[a]	56	33
"Which political party, the Republican or the Democratic, do you think would do a better job of dealing with relations with the Soviets?"[b]	66	17
"Regardless of how you intend to vote, do you think the Republican party or the Democratic party is better able to deal with foreign economic competition?"[c]	51	30
"When it comes to the policies and goal of the Democratic [Republican] party on foreign policy do you strongly agree, mainly agree, have mixed feelings, mainly disagree, or do you strongly disagree with the parties policies and goals?"[d]		
Strongly agree/mainly agree	52	34

[a]ABC News/*Washington Post,* survey, January 30–February 2, 1992. Both equally (volunteered), 4 percent; neither (volunteered), 3 percent; don't know/no opinion, 4 percent.

[b]Gallup, survey, September 5–8, 1991. No difference (volunteered)/no opinion, 16 percent.

[c]CBS News/*New York Times,* survey, October 2–4, 1992. Both (volunteered), 3 percent; neither (volunteered), 4 percent; don't know/no answer, 13 percent.

[d]Hart and Breglio Research Companies, survey, December 12–15, 1992.

former Soviet Union—respondents favored the Republicans generally and Bush in particular. Moreover, a 1991 Gallup poll found 50 percent saying the Democrats "are too weak on foreign policy and national defense."[77]

Bill Clinton used his considerable political skills to defuse foreign policy as a defining presidential issue, as Michael Dukakis recalled: "Even after the Cold War had ended Clinton set a pretty hard line on foreign policy and national defense. I think he did it because he understood that he could not afford to be undermined, or hurt, or wounded as I had been and every other Democratic nominee had been."[78] Clinton was the only Democratic contender in 1992 who supported adding another Seawolf submarine (at $2.4 billion apiece) to the U.S. arsenal. The Seawolf was vital to maintaining the viability of the Groton, Connecticut, Electric Boat shipyard, yet few could find a rationale for building another vessel whose purpose was to counter the Soviet buildup during the 1980s.[79] In a 1996 interview, George

TABLE 6.2

George Bush and Potential Democratic Presidents Compared on Foreign Policy Issues, 1992 (in percentages)

Text of Question	Bush	Democrats
"Who's more likely do a better job of handling U.S. foreign policy—George Bush or a Democratic president?"[a]	61	17
"Who's more likely to see to it that the United States is respected by other countries—George Bush or a Democratic president?"[b]	58	26
"Who do you think would do the best job of making wise decisions about the new situation in East Europe and Russia, George Bush or a Democratic candidate for president?"[c]	61	25

[a]CBS News/*New York Times,* survey, October 15–18, 1992. Both, 2 percent; neither, 1 percent; don't know/no answer, 19 percent.

[b]CBS News/*New York Times,* survey, January 22–25, 1992. Both (volunteered), 3 percent; neither (volunteered), 3 percent; don't know/no answer, 10 percent.

[c]Princeton Survey Research Associates, survey, January 3–7, 1992. Not sure, 14 percent.

McGovern expressed his "disappointment" with Clinton, noting that he had "supported things like the Seawolf submarine that has no use for anybody in this world or the next."[80]

Even when Clinton took exception with Bush on a foreign policy matter, such as the incumbent's timid response to the ethnic cleansing in Bosnia or his tepid protestations of human rights violations in communist China, Clinton cast the disagreement in a way that made himself appear *tougher.*[81] But this political posturing did not stop Republicans from trying to instill fear of a Clinton presidency. GOP strategists warned that Clinton was a carbon copy of Jimmy Carter and would re-create the "hollow military" of the Carter years.[82] Yet these accusations fell flat. For the first time since 1964, Democrats were united on foreign policy, as John D. Issacs of the Council for a Livable World explained: "The old ideological divide—'Scoop' Jackson versus George McGovern—is not a conflict that exists within the Democratic party anymore. It's not a matter of reducing the military budget, but how fast and how far. It's not a question of withdrawing troops from overseas, but how fast and how many. Who are the hawks left?"[83]

The lack of hawks also gave Democrats a unique opportunity as the once-comfortable became profoundly uncomfortable. Those who had prospered from the Cold War were suddenly thrown into the future without a safety net. At the Pentagon, a new term crept into the military lexicon: "involuntary separation"—a reference to those terminated against their will from military service. In 1990, just after the Berlin Wall collapsed, there were 314,000 U.S. troops in Western Europe; by 1995, 150,000. But more than defense layoffs were at work. The military-industrial-labor complex that Dwight Eisenhower warned against was slowly but surely being disassembled. Charlie Witt Jr., a shipyard worker at Electric Boat in Groton, expressed the frustrations of his coworkers: "We won the Cold War, and now they're saying here's a pink slip."[84] By December 1992, 4,200 had been laid off at the facility.

The story of the Grumman Corporation in Salisbury, Maryland—a small town of 17,000 along the state's Eastern Shore—is illustrative how dependent ordinary Americans had become on their government for employment. Grumman, one of the nation's premier aircraft companies, opened the Salisbury plant in 1985 with construction orders for forty-eight combat aircraft. Quickly, the facility grew to 480 employees and an annual payroll of $5.3 million. But by 1993 production slowed to a trickle, with only four planes on order from the Pentagon. Management decided to close the gates. Company vice president John Harrison expressed his condolences: "You people who helped us win the Cold War are going to have your lives disrupted. But we have to do what we have to do to keep the corporation alive. I personally want to apologize. It has nothing to do with you. It has to do with the defense business."[85]

Employees were stunned. Most had been deboners for Perdue Chicken, farm workers, or on the dole. Barbara Savage, a stockroom employee and former waitress, said of Grumman, "It was the best job I ever had." Milton Rodriguez, a young father of two, thought he could find work elsewhere but fretted about his older colleagues: "I am worried about the people who've worked for Grumman for twenty or thirty years, and know nothing besides defense contracting. What are they supposed to do? They're expendable. . . . It was supposed to be a company you could retire with." Savage was among those Rodriguez was concerned about. Now in her fifties, she wondered what was next: "When I fill out a job application and they look at my age, I don't stand a chance."[86]

The Grumman closure affected everyone in Salisbury—especially when the local Campbell Soup Company facility cut its workforce by 800. Unemployment climbed to 8.5 percent, and in some surrounding counties it rose to a depression-level 12 percent. The 400 positions at the new Wal-Mart store helped Salisbury, but these were low-paying, low-skill jobs with few benefits. When Grumman desperately tried to secure a Pentagon contract that would save the Salisbury plant, company officials telephoned eighty former employees asking if they were available for work. Seventy-nine said they could start in two weeks. When a local mall advertised fifty part-time employment positions for the 1991 Christmas season, *2,000* applied.[87]

Salisbury's tale was retold in hundreds of other towns. In Webster, Texas, and Great River, New York, Grumman plants were slated for closure.[88] Pink slips piled up in once secure Republican states. In California, 200,000 were unemployed because of defense-related layoffs. In Florida, unemployment climbed to 8.9 percent; in wealthy Naples, a community along the Gulf Coast, it was 13 percent.[89] Helen Thayer, a Miami grandmother, expressed her dismay at what was happening to her family: "My godson is a lawyer and can't get work. A lawyer! Nobody's taking on new people. He's got a family. People are hurting."[90]

People were hurting. Democrats charged that Bush "has given America the slowest economic growth, the slowest income growth, and the slowest jobs growth since the Great Depression."[91] They were right: Gross domestic product grew at a paltry 2.5 percent; jobs increased by just 0.7 percent (a far cry from the 15 million Bush promised in 1988); industrial production shrank by 0.4 percent; hourly wages also fell by 1.7 percent. Median family incomes dropped from $37,062 in 1988 to $35,939 in 1991.[92] And, in a significant shift, more Americans for the first time in 1992 worked in government than in manufacturing.[93] Anxiety grew.

With the economy in the doldrums, Republicans tried to change the subject. Instead of having the election focus on the economy, they tried to make it a referendum on the 1960s counterculture. Dan Quayle portrayed Democratic liberals "joking about how much Republicans must be missing all those communists who had folded their tents." Still, he wondered: "Who will be our enemy now? What great cause was there for us to champion?" Quayle's answer: "The enemy was ourselves: the spiritual decay we'd allowed to rot us, the poverty of values we were too afraid to challenge for fear of appearing 'unsophisticated.'"[94] Voters seemed to agree: by a 57 percent to 37 percent margin, they chose family values as a more important issue than foreign policy.[95] For his part, Quayle pledged to renew the GOP's commitment to "our Judeo-Christian values," including "family, hard work, integrity, and personal responsibility."[96] In that vein, he castigated the television character Murphy Brown (played by forty-something actress Candice Bergen) for having an out-of-wedlock baby, which, Quayle argued, mocked "the importance of fathers by bearing a child alone and calling it just another lifestyle choice."[97]

Others followed Quayle on a search for new enemies. Pat Robertson sent a fund-raising letter claiming that the feminist movement "encourages women to leave their husbands, kill their children, practice witchcraft, destroy capitalism, and become lesbians." Newt Gingrich accused Democrats of advocating "a multi-cultural nihilistic hedonism that is inherently destructive of a healthy society."[98] Pat Buchanan told convention delegates that the duo of "Clinton & Clinton"—a reference to the Democratic nominee and his wife, Hillary—were former hippies bent on undermining family values: "The agenda Clinton & Clinton would impose on America—abortion on demand, a litmus test for the Supreme Court, homosexual rights, discrimination against religious schools, women in combat—that's change, all right. But it is not the change America wants. . . . It is not the kind of change we can tolerate in a nation that we still call God's country."[99]

As the first of the "flower children" to win a major party nomination for president, Clinton was subjected to a series of personal inquiries that gave Republicans an opportunity. First, he acknowledged that he had experimented "a time or two" with marijuana although he "didn't inhale."[100] Then, in a *60 Minutes* interview, Clinton tacitly admitted that he had not always been faithful to his wife. Finally, Clinton had avoided military service during the Vietnam War by winning a student deferment—like many of his generation. Floyd Brown, who produced the infamous "Willie Horton" advertisement that appeared during Bush's 1988 campaign, wrote that Clinton's opposition to the Vietnam War while studying at Oxford was "under the aegis and support of one of the most notorious Communist front organizations in Europe." When Bush staffers were asked why they were so curious about Clinton's student days at Oxford, one cracked, "You mean Red Willie?"[101] The issue came to a head in the presidential debates, where Bush insinuated that Clinton may have forged some communist ties on a trip to the Soviet Union during his Oxford years:

> Bush: I said something the other day where I was accused of being like Joe McCarthy, because I questioned—I put it this way: I think it's wrong to demonstrate against your own country or organize demonstrations against your own country on foreign soil. I just think it's wrong. . . . Some say you're a little old-fashioned. Maybe I am, but I just don't think that's right.

> Clinton: You have questioned my patriotism. You even brought some right-wing Congressmen into the White House to plot how to attack me for going to Russia in 1969–1970 when over 50,000 other Americans did. Now I honor your service in World War II. . . . But when Joe McCarthy went around this country attacking people's patriotism, he was wrong. He was wrong. And a Senator from Connecticut stood up to him named Prescott Bush. Your father was right to stand up to Joe McCarthy. You were wrong to attack my patriotism. I was opposed to the [Vietnam] War, but I love my country and we need a president who will bring this country together, not divide it. We've got enough division. I want to lead a unified country.[102]

Clinton's reference to Prescott Bush caught the president off guard. But Bush's innuendo had some effect. Whereas 51 percent were satisfied with Clinton's explanation of his 1969 Moscow trip, 31 percent said the journey left them with "major doubts" about having Clinton serve as president.[103] But the GOP playbook for winning elections was rapidly becoming outdated. Referring to Clinton's draft avoidance, one World War II veteran said: "I was in World War II. Who cares? That was forty-five years ago. Who cares what Clinton did twenty years ago as a young man? Let's talk about the homeless and unemployment, Mr. President. What are you going to do about those?"[104] According to exit polls, 80 percent said Clinton's draft status and antiwar protests were "not important" in making their voting decision.[105] Moreover, nearly two-thirds thought too much attention had been paid to the issue.[106]

For the first time in twelve years, values politics failed the GOP. During the Reagan-Bush years, the Republican party chanted a litany consisting of the words "family, work, neighborhood, peace, and freedom."[107] But given the economic hard times, those value-laden phrases had become devoid of meaning. Clinton adviser Mandy Grunwald explains:

> There are a lot of issues that I consider "luxury issues." I mean luxury in the sense that if you can put food on your table and pay your health care bills, and you [aren't] worried about whether you have a job, then you have the luxury to think about whether or not Michael Dukakis furloughed some guy and you can think about whether this guy [Clinton] dodged the draft twenty-three years ago. What was so unusual about [1992] was that people didn't have that luxury. And they had a very clear sense of what the problems were and they were really single-minded about keeping focus on those problems, because it mattered deeply to their lives what the state of the election was. I think that fundamental fact influenced everything, from viewership of the debates ... to the dismissing of issues like the draft or his [Clinton's] trip to Moscow or any of that.[108]

Kansas farmer Orville Mitchell captured Bush's difficulty in exploiting these "luxury issues": "You can talk about family values and military service and all that stuff. But when it gets down to the bottom line, it's how the economy is going. The economy is in trouble. We had a heck of a time getting Bush to even admit it was in trouble. Now he knows it's in trouble because he's in trouble."[109] A well-known sign tacked to the wall at Clinton's campaign headquarters in Little Rock summarized the Democrats' strategy: "It's the economy, stupid!"

But Clinton and the Democrats failed to capture the public imagination. Old suspicions lingered: Democrats were "soft on communism," their only mission to "tax and spend, tax and spend." Democrats tacitly acknowledged these Republican shibboleths by reinventing themselves into "new kinds of Democrats." The New Democrats proposed an amalgam of liberal and conservative solutions that were touted as the antidote to the old New Deal liberalism:

> We offer a new social contract based neither on callous, do-nothing Republican neglect, nor an outdated faith in programs as the solution to every problem. We favor a third way beyond the old approaches—to put government back on the side of citizens who play by the rules. We believe that by what it

says and how it conducts its business, government must once again make responsibility an instrument of national purpose. Our future as a nation depends upon the daily assumption of personal responsibility by millions of Americans from all walks of life—for the religious faiths they follow, the ethics they practice, the values they instill, and the pride they take in their work.[110]

Such platitudes did not reassure voters. An election-eve poll found 46 percent describing Clinton as a "typical" Democratic presidential candidate; 44 percent saw him as different.[111] And although Bush lacked the Cold War as an energizing political force, Clinton and the Democrats failed to come up with an equally large mission. Clinton offered his twelve years as governor (the longest tenure in the nation) and his intellectual prowess as his entrée to the White House. But voters believed that neither Bush nor Clinton could give them what they really wanted: a different, purposeful presidency.

Marking Time

In the summer of 1992, George Bush confidently told a reporter: "In the final analysis, people are going to say, 'Who do you want sitting at that desk? Who has the temperament? Who has the experience? Who do we trust?'" Bush rose from his wing chair, thrust a gold-trimmed pen into his shirt pocket, adjusted his glasses, and said: "That's why I'm going to win this election. You watch."[112] Throughout 1992, Bush believed that voters would not reject him in favor of "a failed governor of a small state."[113] But as exit polls confirmed Clinton's electoral landslide, Bush gathered his campaign team around him and asked, "Do you think we've been kidding ourselves?"[114] As state after state fell into the Clinton column, network television screens were bathed in a sea of Democratic red. Clinton won 370 electoral votes to Bush's 168 (none for Perot). As the candidate of the minority presidential party, Clinton had replicated Dwight Eisenhower's feat of forty years before: win in all parts of the nation, including the Republican-dominated South.

The Cold War–based, race-based Republican presidential coalition was finished. Nationally, the 1992 GOP vote fell 16 points from 1988. Not since 1968, when Hubert H. Humphrey saw his party's support plummet by 18 percent from the prior election, had a major party suffered such a steep decline. Among certain demographic groups, Bush went into free-fall: White Protestants posted a 20-point decline; college graduates, 21 points; those with some college exposure, 20 points; men, 19 points; westerners, 18 points; independents, 23 points; and Republicans, 18 points. Recriminations in GOP circles were widespread. Looking back, Dan Quayle recalled, "This was the most poorly planned and executed incumbent presidential campaign in this century."[115] Bush called 1992 "the most unpleasant year of my life."[116]

Clinton's victory was a tribute not only to Republican ineptitude and his enormous political skill but also to the end of the Cold War. Fewer than one in ten voters leaving the ballot box mentioned foreign policy as an important issue.[117] Ethnic Catholics—including Poles, Lithuanians, and other refugees from Eastern Europe—gave Clinton crucial victories in Illinois, Ohio, and Michigan—allowing him to become only the second Democrat since 1936 to win this "trifecta." One Clinton aide remarked, "A lot of these people are middle class, and now that the Cold War is over they're ready to support a Democrat."[118]

The election was also a referendum on the economy and George Bush's stewardship of it. Exit polls found one-third of the voters, a plurality, described their economic plight as "worse" than it was in 1988, and they divided their ballots as follows: Clinton, 61 percent; Perot, 25 percent; Bush, 14 percent. Overall, 89 percent of Perot's backers and 94 percent of Clinton's supporters described national economic conditions as "not good" or "poor"—significantly higher than the 57 percent of Bush voters who judged the economy to be in terrible shape.[119] Reagan Democrats, many of them Catholics and blue-collar workers, flocked to the Clinton-Gore ticket. Like Charlie Witt, many found a pink slip attached to their time cards—or feared having one in the not-too-distant future. Of the 1988 so-called Bush Democrats, 54 percent returned to their native party. With Clinton's win, many forecasted a resurrection of the old New Deal coalition—as economics returned to the fore of voters' concerns. Joe Lyons, a Democratic party precinct captain in Chicago, enthused, "There is a God: a Democrat can be president again."[120]

But Clinton's win hardly represented a Democratic resurgence. As Table 6.3 indicates, Clinton added little to the Democratic vote and often fell below the percentages posted by Michael Dukakis. Only among those aged sixty or older, college and postcollege graduates, Jews, and southerners did Clinton contribute to the Dukakis coalition—and the South remained largely Bush country.

Moreover, in the House of Representatives Democrats lost ten seats—marking the third time in this century (the others being 1916 and 1960) that Democrats won the presidency while losing seats in Congress. Portending the difficulties he would confront as president in 1994, Clinton ran behind all but *five* members of Congress in 1992. Nick Niederlander, a librarian in Richmond Heights, Missouri, captured the tentativeness of many Clinton backers: "I want to like Clinton more than I like him."[121] In a startling finding, 58 percent told pollsters on election day that they were "concerned" or "scared" at the prospect of a Clinton presidency.[122] Clinton pollster Stanley Greenberg told the Democratic National Committee after Clinton's inauguration, "We need to understand that the Republican coalition collapsed in 1992, but we have not yet formed a new Democratic coalition."[123]

TABLE 6.3

Two-Party Presidential Vote Compared, 1988 and 1992 (in percentages)

Demographic Category	Clinton Minus Dukakis	Bush '92 Minus Bush '88
Nationwide	−3	−16
Sex		
Men	0	−19
Women	−3	−13
Race		
Whites	−1	−18
Blacks	−4	−1
Hispanics	−7	−5
Age		
18–29 years old	−3	−18
30–44 years old	−3	−16
45–59 years old	−1	−17
60 and older	+1	−12
Income		
Under $15,000	−3	−14
$15,000–$29,999	−5	−14
$30,000–$49,999	−3	−18
$50,000–$74,999	−2	−14
$75,000 and over	−1	−14
Education		
Less than high school	−1	−15
High school graduate	−6	−14
Some college	0	−20
College graduate	+3	−21
Postgraduate	+1	−14
Region		
East	−2	−15
Midwest	−5	−15
South	+1	−15
West	−2	−18
Religion		
White Protestant	0	−20
Catholic	−3	−16
Jewish	+14	−23
Party		
Democrats	−5	−7
Republicans	+2	−18
Independents	−5	−23
Philosophy		
Liberal	−13	−4
Moderate	−2	−18
Conservative	−1	−15

SOURCE: Voter Research and Surveys, exit poll, November 3, 1992, and CBS News/*New York Times,* exit poll, November 8, 1988.

The collapse of the Republican coalition and the outstanding weaknesses of the Democrats were evident in the unusually large vote for Ross Perot. Perot won 19 percent of the vote—the best performance for a third-party candidate since Theodore Roosevelt in 1912 and Robert LaFollette in 1924. Besides the 30 percent he accumulated in Maine (his best showing) and the 27 percent he won in Kansas, Perot's best states were out West: Utah (29 percent), Idaho (28 percent), Alaska (27 percent), Montana (26 percent), Nevada (26 percent), Wyoming (26 percent), Oregon (25 percent), Oklahoma (25 percent), and Arizona (24 percent). But Perot remained a vehicle for expression of voter anxiety rather than a third force in American politics. Fifty-six percent answered "no" when asked if Perot could cause "the kind of change the country needs."[124] Instead of producing a real revolution in 1992, voters were marking time. Examining the entrails of the election, E. J. Dionne Jr. wrote, "It is not clear what was being born, but an old politics—the politics of American triumph in World War II and the Cold War—was in the process of dying."[125]

The Half-Term President

Fewer than two months after becoming president, Bill Clinton traveled to Hyde Park, the estate of his hero, Franklin Delano Roosevelt. Along the route were signs reading "Get the U.S. Fit," "I Want to Give Something to My Country," "Shake 'Em Up, Bill," "Give Bill a Chance," "Turn the Country Around," "I've Got a B.A. and No Job," and most tellingly, "Just Do Something."[126] Senator Daniel Patrick Moynihan of New York, accompanying Clinton, saw a military officer in the presidential party holding a briefcase. "See that man?" Moynihan asked. "He's carrying the football." As a student of the Cold War, Moynihan knew that the "football" referred to the military codes that would unleash the U.S. nuclear arsenal in case of a Soviet attack. Moynihan then noticed that the officer brought up the rear of the Clinton entourage. "Ah," he said, "the Cold War is over."[127]

Indeed it was. Clinton, a child of the Cold War, had won the first post–Cold war presidential election. Two days after the balloting the president-elect told ABC's Diane Sawyer: "I felt like the dog that chased the pickup truck. I got it; now what am I going to do?"[128] Clinton voters knew the answer—concentrate on the economy: 50 percent said the economy and jobs were a top priority; 30 percent cited health care; and just 18 percent named reducing the federal deficit.[129] Clinton agreed, promising to focus "like a laser beam" on the economy.[130]

But in his first two years in office things went awry. Instead of zeroing in on the economy and behaving like a New Democrat, Clinton governed like an Old Liberal. He advocated a "don't ask, don't tell" policy of identifying suspected gays in the military. The gays-in-the-military issue reminded voters why they disliked the Democratic party in the first place. During the

1972 campaign, Richard Nixon tagged George McGovern as the "AAA candidate" who represented *a*mnesty, *a*cid, and *a*bortion. Nixon's caricature stuck, and it tarred the Democratic party.[131] Twenty years later, Clinton assiduously portrayed himself as someone who understood the Anxious Middle's yearning for a restoration of traditional values. For example, when discussing abortion, Clinton professed that he wanted the procedure to be safe, legal, and *rare*. He also was a strong proponent of the death penalty, even signing a 1992 execution warrant for a brain-damaged convict.[132] Such posturing neutralized the Republican values advantage: Voters chose Bush over Clinton by a remarkable 39 percent to 33 percent margin as the candidate who "would do the most to strengthen traditional American values."[133]

By becoming mired in the social and cultural divisions of the past, Clinton gave Republicans a splendid opportunity to make political hay. Republicans resumed their cultural war, begun by Buchanan two years earlier, by devising a simplistic slogan: "God, Guns, and Gays." In this political shorthand, Clinton was depicted as antireligious; his support of the Brady Bill made him antigun; and his military induction policy made him progay. Such characterizations energized the GOP base. House Democrat David Price of North Carolina, who was defeated in his 1994 reelection bid by a mere 1,215 votes, described the "extraordinary local Republican mobilization that included conservative Christian groups, anti-tax groups, and those who listen to conservative talk radio shows that blanket eastern North Carolina."[134]

As Table 6.4 shows, the "God, guns, and gays" message resonated with many voters. Majorities of those who were "born again," married, National Rifle Association supporters, parents of children under age eighteen, weekly churchgoers, and full-time employees sided with the Republicans. Democrats, meanwhile, won the backing of those who had no health insurance, belonged to a labor union, or had a proclivity toward homosexual behavior. A new "us-versus-them" politics was emerging—one fraught with considerable danger for the Democratic party.

While Republicans seemed intent on building a values coalition, Clinton seemed unsure of himself—and voters sensed his discomfiture. Congress exploited his political weakness. David Price observed that the "malaise" that overcame the Democratic caucus after the health care debacle was "deep seated and rooted in years of divided government and party decline."[135] Clinton's failure to enact health care reform subjected him to ridicule, as legislators no longer feared the president. Inaction on other issues contributed to the malaise. Paul Tsongas, Clinton's erstwhile 1992 primary opponent, wrote after the 1994 balloting:

> The Democrats claim they lost because they did not "communicate" effectively. The truth is that the Democrats lost because they communicated all too effectively. The health care bill, the inertia on political and congressional re-

TABLE 6.4
The Republican "Values Majority," 1994 Congressional Vote (in percentages)

Voter Description	Democrat	Republican
Born again/evangelical Christian	39	61
Married	46	54
Without health insurance	56	44
Support the National Rifle Association	34	66
Someone in household in a labor union	63	37
Parent of a child under 18	47	53
Attend religious services once a week	47	53
Gay/lesbian/bisexual	60	40
Employed full-time	48	52

SOURCE: Voter Research and Surveys, exit poll, November 8, 1994. Text of question: "Do any of the following apply to you?"

form, opposition to the line item veto and the balanced budget amendment—all of these positions were well understood by the voters. Throw in such sidebar matters involving the Clintons as Paula Jones, Whitewater, and the commodities futures, and you have a problem. All the polling data and focus groups and spin doctors could not save the Democrats from their own convictions—or lack thereof.[136]

By September 1993, the malaise had produced a corrosive result: 68 percent told pollsters Peter Hart and Robert Teeter that they were "not confident" that life for their children's generation will be better than it had been for them.[137] The rationale for Clinton's 1992 candidacy had disappeared, and he was, in effect, a half-term president. Clinton acknowledged his failure: "Everybody knows all is not well with America."[138] This was especially true of the Anxious Middle whom Clinton accurately characterized as thinking thus: "I'm doing everything I can—I'm working a longer work week; I can't afford a vacation anymore; I'm paying more for health care; I may lose my job tomorrow; my kid could get shot on the way to school; and all my money is going to people who misbehave."[139] Pollster Gordon Black saw a renewed opportunity for a third political party to enter the fray. He warned that the Anxious Middle was "becoming radicalized among people who believe the two parties as now constituted are threatening the security of their children."[140] The U.S. Census Bureau confirmed the growing feeling of high anxiety: After the economic "recovery" of 1993–1994, the median household income was still 6 percent below what it had been in 1989.[141]

Clinton's difficulties presented Republicans with an opportunity to make political gains, and Newt Gingrich pursued the task with relish. Gingrich told a meeting of interest-group lobbyists that the Clinton administration was the "enemy of normal Americans."[142] But Gingrich knew that merely opposing Clinton would not give Republicans a map for governance. Believing new ideas were needed to substitute for the Republican party's historic anticommunism, Gingrich proposed the Contract With America—a document signed by all but four Republican House contenders in a flashy Capitol Hill ceremony in the fall of 1994. The Contract With America promised that if the Republicans won Congress, party leaders would schedule votes during the first 100 days of the new Congress on such issues as term limits, a line-item veto for the president, and a balanced budget amendment. Although only one voter in eight said they knew much about the Contract With America, and seven in ten had never heard of it, Republicans were winning the war of ideas.[143] Addressing the Democratic Leadership Council (DLC), Clinton acknowledged the growing Republican idea advantage: "We've got to engage the Republicans in a spirit of genuine partisanship and say, you have some new ideas; we do, too; let's have a contest of ideas."[144]

But Clinton's plea was too little, too late. For the first time in forty years, Republicans won control of the Congress, gaining fifty-two seats in the House and eight in the Senate. More significantly, Republicans captured most state legislatures—the first time that had happened since the Supreme Court issued its "one person, one vote" ruling in 1962.[145] The GOP rout was complete when no Republican incumbent—either House member, senator, or governor—was denied reelection. A perennial question was asked once more: Had realignment arrived? Walter Dean Burnham, a prominent scholar on the issue of party realignment, contended that it had, writing that the 1994 election was "the most consequential off-year election in (exactly) one hundred years."[146]

Bill Clinton disagreed, likening himself to Harry Truman, who had suffered a monumental setback in the midterm elections of 1946. But the two Democratic presidents could not have been more different. Truman, though weakened personally, headed the nation's majority party. In 1946, the New Deal coalition still commanded the loyalties of most voters. In 1994, these ties bound some voters to the Democrats: Blacks cast 88 percent of their ballots for Democratic House candidates; Hispanics, 70 percent; liberals, 82 percent; Jews, 80 percent; and those earning less than $15,000, 62 percent. But Franklin Roosevelt's polyglot of white southerners, Catholics, ethnics, blacks, and low-income voters is a shadow of its former self. Al From, then president of the DLC, declared: "The old New Deal coalition is gone. It's dead. It's Humpty Dumpty."[147] Exit polls confirmed From's diagnosis. In congressional races, 54 percent of white Catholics cast their ballots for Republican candidates, as did 55 percent of southerners.[148] Especially telling was incumbent Mario Cuomo's paltry 45 percent showing in the New York race for governor. More than any other contemporary political figure, Cuomo was a direct descendent of FDR's New Deal, yet in Roosevelt's home state the New Deal no longer commanded a majority. Across the globe the old Socialist parties of the left fell into disrepute during the post–Cold War period. By 1994, that fact had caught up with the Democrats. The "L-word," a jingoistic term coined by George Bush in 1988 to denounce mushy-headed liberalism, remained the scarlet letter of American politics.

The post–Cold War Republican party retained some ties to its Cold War past. In the 1994 House races, the Christian Right, which hated communism and loved Ronald Reagan and constituted 13 percent of the total electorate—equaling the percentage of blacks who voted—cast 80 percent of their ballots for GOP candidates. Southerners, cut loose from their Democratic moorings, voted for Republican congressional candidates 55 percent of the time. Realignment had arrived south of the border, as the following examples illustrate:

- In 1990, Georgia Republicans fielded, for the first time this century, a complete congressional slate of candidates, with meager results—less than 40 percent of the statewide vote and just one winner (incumbent Newt Gingrich). Two years later they did somewhat better, winning 45 percent of the ballots and electing four members. But the payoff came in 1994, when Republicans took 55 percent of the Georgia vote and captured seven of eleven seats.[149] The remaining white Democrat, Nathan Deal, bolted to the Republicans in 1995.
- Prior to the 1994 election, Democrats held fifty-one House seats in southern districts twice won by Bush. But in 1994 Democrats lost twenty-seven of these seats. For the first time since Reconstruction, Republicans held most of the southern congressional districts.[150]
- All the Republican leaders in the 104th Congress called the South home: Newt Gingrich (Speaker, Georgia), Richard Armey (Majority Leader, Texas), and Tom DeLay (Majority Whip, Texas).

But in the rest of the country the predisposition to back Republicans had a tentative quality to it. GOP congressional candidates won just 51.3 percent of the votes cast in 1994. Moreover, an NBC News/*Wall Street Journal* poll taken immediately after the balloting found many answering "no difference" or "not sure" when asked whom they trusted, President Clinton or the Republican-controlled Congress, to handle important issues. As Table 6.5 shows, except in the cases of taxes, the federal deficit, and welfare reform, slightly more than one-third chose the GOP, about the same share preferred the Democrats, and one-quarter was uncertain.

These were hardly ringing endorsements for what some called the new majority party. Democratic pollster Peter Hart discovered voters had their own, nonpartisan explanation for the election outcome: 53 percent said people wanted change in Washington; 19 percent thought the Republicans

TABLE 6.5
Party Preference by Issue, November 1994 (in percentages)

Issue	Clinton	Republicans	No Difference/Not Sure
Foreign affairs	36	37	27
Health care	36	39	25
Jobs and economic growth	30	44	26
Social Security and Medicare	29	42	29
Welfare reform	26	48	26
The budget deficit	23	46	18
Crime	18	38	44
Taxes	17	55	28

SOURCE: NBC News/*Wall Street Journal*, survey, November 9, 1994. Text of question: "For each of the following issues, please tell me if you think that President Clinton or the Republicans in Congress generally will have the better approach to this issue, or if there will not be much difference."

won because people voted against Clinton and his agenda; 12 percent claimed voters wanted a more conservative Congress; and just 9 percent said the GOP had better candidates.[151] In short, Republicans held a "masquerade majority." One postelection survey provided a glimpse into the future: 31 percent of those who voted said they were "fed up" with both political parties.[152]

Republicans still had to find an agenda to replace that of the Cold War. Newt Gingrich recognized this would be an awesome task. Shortly after the election, he admitted that Republicans "will have to think through what are the deeper underlying meanings of being American and how do we reassert them."[153] It was Gingrich's singular failure to redefine Americanism that set the stage for the Clinton-Dole contest. Egged on by the Republican House freshmen, of whom only *twenty-six* of seventy had any prior legislative experience, the budget hawks in Congress forced two government shutdowns in late 1995 and early 1996. These acts gave Clinton an opening. Behind closed doors, Clinton plotted his return to the political stage that gave new meaning to his well-deserved nickname, the Comeback Kid.

Déjà Vu: The Cold War Returns

It seemed like old times. On election day 1996, events in Russia made headlines as Boris Yeltsin entered a Moscow hospital for emergency heart bypass surgery. The state of the Russian president's health underscored the fragile condition of his country's nascent democracy. Although the news from Russia did not have nearly the same earth-shattering import as did the bulletins of the Soviet invasion of Hungary on election day 1956, there was a sense of déjà vu about the Clinton-Dole contest—not only at its final denouement but also when the curtain rose a year earlier. A slew of GOP hopefuls, still savoring their 1994 victories, took aim at knocking Clinton from his presidential perch. One of them, Richard Lugar, stole a page from his party's Cold War bible. Stressing his foreign policy expertise as a senior member of the Senate Foreign Relations Committee, Lugar made his pitch: "The Republican candidate for President who has the best chance to win the election is somebody who has experience in foreign policy and speaks to those issues constantly."[154] To buttress his claim, Lugar ran a television commercial whose theme echoed Lyndon Johnson's "daisy commercial" and Ronald Reagan's "bear-in-the-woods" advertisements:

Narrator: A rogue terrorist group has threatened to explode three nuclear bombs in the United States.

Little girl (getting ready for bed): Mommy.

Mother: What honey?

Little girl: Won't the bomb wake everybody up?

Announcer: They're waiting outside, Mr. President. We need a decision.

Television screen reads: Lugar for President. To be continued.[155]

Although this was a powerful message, Republicans were not interested in the promised sequel, jettisoning Lugar after the first round of primaries. But that did not stop the other contenders from making foreign policy an issue. The Republican front-runner, Senate Majority Leader Robert J. Dole, followed the Cold War maxim that Democrats were "soft on communism." Planting himself firmly in the footsteps of his mentor, Richard Nixon, Dole accused President Clinton of "coddling communists" in North Korea after that country refused to let inspectors visit areas suspected of shielding nuclear weapons–producing facilities. The entry of former Democratic president Jimmy Carter as a negotiator with North Korea's then-communist dictator, Kim Il Sung, reinforced Dole's battle cry. Dole promised, if elected, to keep North Korea isolated until there had been a full accounting of the POWs and MIAs from the Korean War.

Having dispensed with this communist target, Dole turned his attention to another one: Vietnam. Having finally won the GOP nomination, the prize he had sought for so long, Dole startled convention delegates with his critique of the *Johnson administration's* conduct of the Vietnam War: "For those who might be sharply taken aback in thinking of Vietnam, think again, for in Vietnam the long gray line did not fail us, we failed it in Vietnam. The American soldier was not made for the casual and arrogant treatment that he suffered there, where he was committed without clear purpose or resolve, bound by rules that prevented victory, and kept waiting in the valley of the shadow of death for ten years while the nation debated the un-debatable question of his honor."[156] Finally, Dole aimed at a target closer to home—chiding Cuba's Fidel Castro for shooting down a private U.S. airplane in international waters and promising never to waver in his determination to restore democracy to that imprisoned island.

As these examples illustrate, Dole was still a Cold War captive. Once, speaking at a convention of automobile dealers, the Republican candidate momentarily forgot that the hammer and sickle had been ripped from the Kremlin towers. Believing that the evil empire still threatened Lugar's made-for-TV little girl, Dole proposed a return to Ronald Reagan's beloved Strategic Defense Initiative: "What would you want the president to do if he were informed in the middle of the night or the middle of the day . . . that there was an incoming missile, maybe from the Soviet Union? You may say, 'Shoot it down.' But we can't shoot it down."[157] While still in the Senate (he later left to pursue the campaign full-time), Dole proposed the Defend America Act of 1996, which would require a national defense system for all fifty states by 2003.

But more than having a strong defense motivated Dole. In many ways, Dole believed that his opponent was not Bill Clinton but George McGovern. In Dole's view, Clinton was the spoiled child of the 1960s "who never grew up, never did anything real, never sacrificed, never suffered, and never learned." Using rhetoric reminiscent of his days as Republican national chairman under Nixon, Dole maintained that Clinton clung to all the misconceptions once held by McGovern and his ilk about national defense and its importance: "We are the party whose resolve did not flag as the Cold War dragged on, we did not tremble before a Soviet giant that was just about to fall, and we did not have to be begged to take up arms against Saddam Hussein"—implying that it was the *Democrats* who were "soft" on all counts. In Dole's view, this "softness" had resulted in Clinton's going AWOL in performing his constitutional responsibility as commander-in-chief: "He believes it is acceptable to ask our military forces to do more with less. I do not. He defends giving a green light to a terrorist state, Iran, to expand its influence in Europe, and he relies on the United Nations to [find] Libyan terrorists who murdered American citizens. I will not. And he believes that defending our people and our territory from missile attack is unnecessary. I do not."[158] Dole thought Clinton derelict in his Pentagon budgets, which, Dole observed, proposed a "devastating" reduction of the armed forces from eighteen to ten divisions, the trimming fighter wings from twenty-five to thirteen, and the mothballing of 200 navy ships. Altogether, defense spending during Clinton's first term had been trimmed by $112 billion—and Dole promised that if elected he would plug in the Cold War machine, including more money for B-2 bombers.[159] Dole thought this would be welcome news in vote-rich, defense-poor southern California—home to the 1996 Republican National Convention—but Dole left the most stinging attacks to Republican platform writers who all but called Clinton a traitor:

> Clinton slashed the funding budgeted by past presidents for missile defense and even violates the law by slowing down critical theater missile defenses. He has pursued negotiations to actually expand the outdated ABM Treaty, further tying America's hands, and hobbling our self-defense. He now seeks new limitations that will hinder the United States from developing and deploying even theater ballistic missile defenses to protect our troops abroad.
>
> In a peaceful world, such limitations would be impudent. In today's world, they are immoral. The danger of a missile attack with nuclear, chemical, or biological weapons is the most serious threat to our national security. Communist China has mocked our vulnerability by threatening to attack Los Angeles if we stand by our historic commitment to the Republic of China on Taiwan.[160]

For Republicans, the lessons of the Cold War still applied: "Because this is a difficult and dangerous world, we believe that peace can be assured only through strength, that a strong national defense is necessary to protect America at home and secure its interests abroad, and that we must restore leadership and character to the presidency as the best way to restore America's leadership and credibility throughout the world."[161] Reacting to the Republicans' mantra-like invocation of "peace through strength," Democrats dryly observed that Dole was "locked in a Cold War mentality" without a "coherent strategy to nurture and strengthen the global progress toward peace and democracy."[162] But Republicans clung to the old anticommunist script. The GOP-controlled 104th Congress, for example, proposed building a privately funded international memorial dedicated to those who once lived in the former Captive Nations who constituted the "100 million victims of communism." Meanwhile, in lieu of concrete ideas, Republicans relied on their words to summon the ghosts of the Cold War past. Vice presidential candidate Jack Kemp paid homage to Ronald Reagan: "Make no mistake about it. Communism came down not because it fell but because he pushed it."[163] Even Bill Clinton could not resist the nostalgia for Reagan, telling the *New York Times*, "I think the 'Evil Empire' meant more afterward than it did before because it was the end of the Cold War."[164]

As Clinton's comment suggests, Cold War déjà vu was not limited to the Republicans. Recalling how foreign policy attacks had hurt previous Democratic presidential aspirants, Clinton was determined to inoculate himself from them by responding in kind. Clinton even sat in the White House theater to watch old videotapes of the Gipper saluting the troops. Almost before the films ended, Clinton counterattacked. Countering Dole's charge that he was soft on defense, Clinton noted that he had proposed spending

$1.6 *trillion* on defense between 1996 and 2002—a difference of less than 1 percent between his budget and the Republican alternative.[165] As Bob Bischak of the National Commission for Economic Conversion and Disarmament observed, "There's just about a dime's worth of difference between Bob Dole and Bill Clinton."[166] By maintaining much of the Cold War arsenal, Clinton echoed his Republican predecessors' claims that the United States was still number one, with the "best-trained, best-equipped and best-prepared fighting force on Earth."[167] Clinton also hewed to a tough anti-Castro line—supporting the Republican-sponsored Helms-Burton measure that further tightened the U.S. embargo of that last western isle of communism. Clinton also touted his North Korean policy, claiming that his State Department had "secured an agreement that not only froze North Korea's nuclear program, but ensured it would be dismantled under international monitoring."[168]

But Clinton reserved most of his self-proclaimed kudos for his handling of Russian relations. Echoing George Bush, who bragged in 1992 that not one Soviet missile was pointed at American children, Clinton indulged in some similar political hyperbole: "There are no nuclear missiles pointed at the children of the United States tonight and have not been in our administration for the first time since the dawn of the nuclear age."[169] Like Bush, Clinton sought credit for having brought the Cold War to a successful conclusion:

> When I became President, the dissolution of the Soviet Union created four nuclear powers—Russia, Belarus, Kazakhstan, and Ukraine—where once there had been just one. I saw it as my highest responsibility to continue the work of my predecessors to reduce the threat from Russia and to eliminate it entirely from the other three newly independent states. Today, for the first time in decades, not a single Russian nuclear missile is aimed at an American city. We are cutting Russian and American arsenals by two-thirds from their Cold War height. And soon, there will not be a single nuclear missile left in Ukraine, Belarus, or Kazakhstan.[170]

Granted a second term, Clinton promised to "complete the unfinished business of the Cold War," telling ethnic Americans that by 1999 the former Warsaw Pact countries would be granted admission to NATO.[171] Bob Dole saw the political appeal of Clinton's promise and could only respond that the president was dragging his feet: "It is an outrage that the patriots who threw off the claims of Soviet bondage have been told by Bill Clinton that they must wait to join the NATO alliance."[172] But Clinton's partisans maintained that he was best equipped to lead the nation into the post–Cold War era. Senator Edward M. Kennedy of Massachusetts reminded Democratic delegates of John F. Kennedy's brief encounter with the youthful Clinton: "Thirty-three years ago this summer, a young man from Boys Nation stood in the Rose Garden and shook the hand of a young President. That day, Bill Clinton took my brother's hand, and now he is the young President who has taken up the fallen standard: the belief that America can do better. And we will do better, with President William Jefferson Clinton leading us into the next American century."[173]

But to most voters, the Cold War–like rhetoric had a musty smell to it—as if the two parties were rummaging around in their attics looking for their "greatest hits." Several news headlines punctuated the prevailing public mood by underscoring the fact that the Cold War was finally over. In September, Spiro Agnew, Richard Nixon's disgraced vice president whose colorful alliterations of Vietnam War protesters included such gems as "nattering nabobs of negativism" and "pusillanimous pussy-footers with the vicars of vacillation," died.[174] Ten days after Clinton's reelection, Alger Hiss, aged ninety-two, met his Maker. Hiss's death prompted another public airing of the Hiss case, with defenders and detractors debating Hiss's and liberalism's collective guilt or innocence. The day after Hiss's death, the Emergency Broadcast System, established by President Kennedy in 1963, announced it was curtailing the long shrill tone used in television warnings about a potential nuclear attack and followed by the disclaimer "This is a test of the Emergency Broadcast System—this is *only* a test." Instead of the long whine, which scared many children and annoyed most adults, a few short buzzes would be substituted.[175] These events punctuated the public perception that the Cold War was over and that both parties had better come to grips with that fact. Former Clinton strategist Dick Morris detected the voters' collective impatience and complained that his client had become "too focused on foreign policy and he needs to move back to domestic."[176] But neither Clinton nor Dole could abandon the political psyches that had shaped their respective parties' pasts.

Clinton Redux: Back to the Future

Following the 1994 Democratic debacle, Clinton issued an order to his political advisers: "I want my presidency back."[177] At the time, the likelihood that Clinton's edict could be implemented seemed bleak. At an April 1995 news conference, a forlorn Clinton told the assembled reporters that he was still "relevant" to the goings-on in Washington: "The Constitution gives me relevance. The power of our ideas gives me relevance.... The president is relevant here, especially an activist president."[178] Clinton's assertion that Speaker of the House Newt Gingrich and his band of followers would eventually have to deal with him seemed like wishful thinking. But the next day Clinton's hope for yet another political resurrection from the dead materialized when a bomb exploded in the Alfred P. Murrah Federal Office Building in Oklahoma City. Clinton took center stage, consoling victims' families and healing a grieving nation. Recalling how the bomb's detonation, in Clinton's words, "broke the spell in the country" and ended the "bitter, bitter rhetoric," senior adviser George Stephanopoulous observed that the president's soothing voice stole the political center away from the Republicans and created a new one.[179]

Clinton's comeback received an immeasurable boost by a relatively robust economy. On the campaign trail, Clinton often repeated lines from Ronald Reagan's playbook: "Four years ago, you took me on faith. Now there's a record: ten-and-a-half million more jobs, rising incomes, falling crime rates and welfare rolls, a strong America at peace. We are better off than we were four years ago. Let's keep it going."[180] Dole tried to toss aside Clinton's reprise of Reagan's famous "are-you-better-off" question with a sarcastic quip: "Well, he's better off than he was four years ago. Saddam Hussein is probably better off than he was four years ago."[181] Later, Dole admitted that economic conditions were good, but could be better still. In a campaign monograph titled *Trusting the People*, Dole and Kemp claimed that the country was experiencing "the slowest expansion of our economy in more than a century," and they wondered if the United States had become a "'Grow Slow' society, content to let government spend our earnings for us, make our decisions for us, and let our wages stagnate and dreams fall away."[182] The Republican platform painted an even gloomier picture: "For millions of families, the American Dream is fading. Our goal is to revive it, renew it, and extend it to all who reach for it."[183]

Among those for whom the American Dream was dimming were laid-off defense workers. Dole acknowledged their plight, telling a partisan gathering in California—a state that had seen more than its share of defense cutbacks—that Clinton's Pentagon budget had eliminated 500,000 defense jobs there. Seeking to contrast his jaunty optimism with Dole's dour recitation of economic statistics, Clinton retorted, "If you believe that the California economy was better in 1992 than it is today, you should vote for Bob Dole."[184] Clinton's optimism was shared by a majority: 55 percent of those leaving the voting booths rated the economy as "excellent" or "good"; 43 percent thought it was "not good" or "poor." Of those who rated the economy positively, two-thirds backed Clinton. The rising consumer confidence gave renewed meaning to the Clinton campaign's 1992 slogan "It's the economy, stupid!" The good-times feeling shared by most Americans—as evidenced in the fact that 53 percent thought the country was on the "right track"—meant that Dole's third try for the presidency was stillborn.[185]

But Clinton did not rest his case for reelection on the economic laurels garnered by his administration. Instead, he cast the seventy-three-year-old Dole as a prisoner of the past. Dole gave Clinton's argument an inadvertent boost as he fondly recalled his service during World War II and the myths shrouded in the years after it: "Age has its advantages. Let me be the bridge to an America that only the unknowing call myth. Let me be the bridge to a time of tranquillity, faith, and confidence in action. And to those who say it was never so, that America has not been better, I say, you're wrong, and I know, because I was there. And I have seen it. And I remember."[186] Clinton derided Dole's longing for the *Leave It to Beaver* era: "The real choice is whether we will build a bridge to the future or a bridge to the past, about whether we believe our best days are still out there or our best days are behind us; about whether we want a country of people all working together or one where you're on your own."[187] Fifteen times during his Acceptance Speech and ten times in the first televised debate with Dole, Clinton repeated his mantra of building a "bridge to the twenty-first century." Voters got the picture: 89 percent of those who said that their candidate was "in touch with the 1990s" pulled the Clinton-Gore lever.[188]

But Clinton's bridge seemed more like that engineered by Franklin D. Roosevelt than one designed to move the nation (and the Democratic party) into the next century. For six decades, Democratic candidates have pledged to protect the New Deal, Fair Deal, New Frontier, and Great Society from Republican-inspired efforts to dismantle what FDR's backers called "the humanizing policies of the federal government." In 1936, the Democratic platform boasted: "We have built foundations for the security of those who are faced with the hazards of unemployment and old age; for the orphaned, the crippled, and the blind. On the foundation of the Social Security Act, we are determined to erect a structure of economic security for all our people, making sure that this benefit shall keep step with the ever-increasing capacity of America to provide a high standard of living for all its citizens."[189]

Although the 1996 Clinton campaign was nearly as far removed in time from Roosevelt's bid for a second term as the New Deal was from the Civil War, the contemporary Democratic *reportoraire* still began with a hymn of praise to FDR followed by a reprise to help those who have yet to benefit from its benevolence. Back in 1964, for example, Lyndon Johnson promised a Great Society that included Medicare for the elderly; Medicaid for the poor; food stamps for the hungry; legal assistance for the indigent; economic revitalization plans for distressed areas; research and care for victims of heart disease and cancer. Campaigning on a Providence, Rhode Island, street corner, Johnson gave this grand summation of his governing strategy: "We're in favor of a lot of things and we're against mighty few."[190] Thus it was that Johnson, momentarily acting more as a prime minister than a Cold War president, engineered congressional passage of the Civil Rights Act of 1964, the Voting Rights Act of 1965, a highway beautification program, the Corporation for Public Broadcasting, a food stamp program, and the Model Cities program. Even LBJ's successor, Richard Nixon, enlarged the New Deal by signing into law the Occupational Safety and Health Act of 1970, the Clear Air and Clean Water Acts of 1971, and the Environmental Protection Agency, which was added to the growing multitude of federal bureaucracies.

But it was Johnson's crowning achievement to place into law the long-sought Democratic objective of health care for the elderly. In 1935, opposition from the American Medical Association forced Franklin Roosevelt to remove medical coverage from the Social Security Act. Roosevelt promised to return to the issue, and in 1943 he issued a plan for national health insurance. But World War II was still raging, and the time was not ripe for reform. At war's end, Harry Truman promulgated an "economic bill of rights," which included "health security for all regardless of residence, station, or race." Seeking to return to the White House in 1948, Truman made health care a major issue. After his upset victory over Republican Thomas Dewey, Truman wanted to fulfill the last unkept promise of his predecessor. Opposing him were the American Medical Association, the U.S. Chamber of Commerce, the American Farm Bureau, and even the social welfare arm of the Roman Catholic Church, who together spent an estimated $4 million to guarantee that Truman's health care bill died in Congress.[191]

The health care issue remained dormant until 1960, when House Democrat Aime Forand of Rhode Island proposed adding Social Security coverage for hospital and nursing-home care. Presidential candidate John F. Kennedy carried the banner for "Medicare," as Forand's plan became popularly known. Speaking to an enthusiastic crowd at Madison Square Garden, Kennedy declared: "This is not a campaign against doctors. The people of the United States recognize that this is a problem whose solution is long overdue." But Kennedy's narrow plurality over Richard Nixon (and GOP gains in Congress) stymied any prospects for congressional action.[192]

There matters rested until Lyndon Johnson's rout of Barry Goldwater in 1964. During the campaign, Johnson told the large crowds that came to greet him that Medicare would be "at the top of my list" of proposals he would submit to the new Congress. The Johnson landslide brought seventy-one new Democratic members to the House—enough to overcome the animus of the powerful American Medical Association. Most of these newly elected Democrats supported Medicare, leading Johnson to conclude that "the voters of America passed the law."[193] One of the twelve House members who voted "no" was Bob Dole, the three-term congressman from Kansas. Thirty years later, Dole proudly recounted his opposition to the Republican faithful: "I was right then; I knew it wouldn't work."[194] But Dole's recalcitrance was not enough to overcome the groundswell for Medicare, and Johnson traveled to Independence, Missouri, Harry Truman's hometown, to sign the bill. Truman and his wife, Bess, were to be the first beneficiaries. When Johnson finished scrawling his signature, the only New Deal objective left unfilled was universal health care—a goal that eluded Bill Clinton three decades later. Admirers saw Clinton's proposal as fulfilling a long-standing Democratic legacy, whereas detractors denounced it as an overgrown government boondoggle and hooted Clinton supporters with cries of "Go back to Russia!"[195]

The success of Clinton's foes in blocking his health care proposal nearly doomed his presidency, but it cemented the Democratic advantage as the party that "cares more about people like you." Ever since the Great Depression, Democrats have been viewed as more compassionate, whereas Republicans have been depicted as cruel, heartless louts. Back in 1932, former president Calvin Coolidge inadvertently added a few more brushstrokes to his party's unflattering portrait: "The charge is made that the Republican party does not show solicitude for the *common run of people* but is interested only in promoting the interests of a few favored individuals and corporations. . . . All this is a question of method. . . . We have advocated strengthening the position of the employer that he might pay better wages to his employees" (emphasis added).[196] But it was the "common run of people" who greeted Roosevelt along the campaign trail in 1936 with cries of "He saved my job! He saved my home!"[197]

Roosevelt's portrait of the caring Democrat and the coldhearted Republican persisted throughout the Cold War—and thereafter. Republicans responded by painting Democrats as bleeding-heart liberals, but their attempt to equate liberalism with do-goodism never could erase their unsympathetic image. It was a golden oldie Democrats used whenever they were in trouble. In 1968, for example, Hubert Humphrey recalled how his party had stood by Roosevelt's "common man": "Our Republican friends have fought every piece of social legislation that has benefited this country. They have fought against Social Security, they have been against all forms of federal aid to education, they have been against Medicare for our senior citizens. They have been against minimum wages. . . . Why you just name it, and I'll guarantee you that you will have found a majority of them in Congress against it."[198] Humphrey's rhetoric soared as he claimed that "Democrats have been responsible for every piece of constructive legislation that has passed Congress in these last thirty-five years" over the nays of Richard Nixon and his Republicans: "When did you start to get so progressive, Mr. Nixon? All your life you stood there and resisted and fought. You called my party the 'Party of Treason'—and he did. He fought Harry Truman. He fought Roosevelt. He fought Kennedy and Stevenson. He fought Lyndon Johnson. And he fought me. . . . Mr. Republican is saying he's a friend of the workingman. Now that's news for you, I'll guarantee you that—if he is a friend of the workingman, Scrooge is Santa Claus."[199]

Humphrey's portrait matched the perception held by most voters—even as they elected Republican presidents to cope with the Soviet menace. A 1951 Gallup poll found that most respondents would tell a new voter that the Democratic party stood for "the working man" and that the Republican party promoted the "privileged few."[200] Other Gallup surveys added texture to the party pictures. A 1948 poll found a plurality depicting the GOP as being "run by a few big businessmen," and a 1955 majority maintained that Republicans best served the interests of "professional and business groups" but that Democrats cared more for "skilled" and "unskilled" workers.[201] In 1996, the Roosevelt portrait was still intact: 65 percent named the Republicans as being "concerned with the needs of business and powerful groups"; just 19 percent thought the Democrats were concerned.

It was against this chapter in Republican party history—replete with several new pages added by Newt Gingrich—that Clinton would campaign for reelection in a manner Franklin Roosevelt would have understood. Chastising those who wanted to return to Coolidge's vision of a dwarfed federal government, Clinton admonished, "We must not go back to an era of 'every man for himself.'"[202] That era was vigorously defended by the Republicans in 1936 when they nominated another Kansan, Alf Landon, for president:

> America is in peril. The welfare of the American men and women and the future of our youth are at stake. We dedicate ourselves to the preservation of their political liberty, their individual opportunity, and their character as free citizens, which today for the first time are threatened by government itself. . . . We pledge ourselves to maintain the American system of Constitutional and local self-government [and] to preserve the American system of free enterprise, private competition, and equality of opportunity, and to seek its constant betterment in the interests of all.[203]

In order to accomplish these goals, Republicans promised to "stop the folly of uncontrolled spending [and] balance the budget—not by increasing taxes but by cutting expenditures, drastically and immediately."[204] Gingrich and his colleagues took up Alf Landon's forgotten cause of shrinking government and balancing the budget by proposing to slash $270 *billion* in projected Medicare costs. The effects of such an action, Gingrich hoped, would allow the Democrats' beloved Medicare entitlement to "wither on the vine."[205] Gingrich's promise to redeem the ancient, pre–Cold War pledges of the Republican party united the notoriously fractured Democrats. Democrats and independents, who once took Medicare and Social Security for granted, came to have a renewed appreciation of these programs even as they did not want the federal government to enlarge much further. Democrats seized on the prevailing public attitudes by running a series of television advertisements denouncing the "Dolegingrich" Medicare cuts. By a 45 percent to 26 percent margin, Americans said the Democrats were better able than the Republicans to deal with the problems posed by the Medicare trust fund's shortfall.[206] The lopsided pro-Democratic Medicare margins spelled bad news for Gingrich: 59 percent held an unfavorable opinion of him, including 68 percent of Clinton's voters. Moreover, 52 percent disapproved of the actions of the Republican-controlled Congress during its two years in power.[207]

Gingrich's hostility to the New Deal was quite different from the critique of government advanced by Ronald Reagan. Reagan had grown up to admire FDR, and his father, Jack, had been an unemployed shoe salesman who was hired by Roosevelt's Federal Emergency Relief Administration. Instead of criticizing Roosevelt, Reagan reserved his ire for the "have-nots" who had benefited from Lyndon Johnson's Great Society.[208] Reagan never tired of describing the "welfare queen" who had used the system at the expense of everyone else. But Gingrich's assault on the New Deal gave Democrats the sword they would use to emasculate Gingrich and his coterie:

> We are proud the president forced Congressional Republicans to abandon their wrongheaded and mean-spirited efforts to punish the poor. Republicans wanted to eliminate the guarantee of health care for the poor, the elderly, and the disabled. They were wrong and we stopped them. Republicans wanted to destroy the food stamp and school lunch programs that provide basic nutrition to millions of working class families and poor children. They were wrong, and we stopped them. Republicans wanted to cut off young-unwed mothers—because they actually thought their children would be better off living in an orphanage. They were dead wrong, and we stopped them. The bill Republicans passed last year was values-backward—it was soft on work and tough and children, and we applaud the president for stopping it.[209]

Like Roosevelt Democrats of the 1930s, Clinton Democrats told voters that a Republican restoration would result in a Robin Hood–like role reversal as the GOP would give "a massive tax break to the wealthiest Americans, and [pay] for it by raising taxes on ordinary Americans and slashing health care for the elderly."[210] Each time Clinton charged that Republicans would have seniors paying $270 more per year in medical bills, Dole replied, "There you go again, Mr. President, talking about a Medicare cut." Throughout his ill-fated candidacy, Dole complained that Democrats were engaged in political demagoguery: "I think if I were a senior citizen I'd be a little fed up with all these ads scaring seniors, scaring veterans, and scaring students about education. When you don't have any ideas, when you don't have any agenda, and all you have is fear, that's all you can use."[211] Dole pledged never to "touch" Social Security, recalling how his late mother would admonish him "All I've got is my Social Security; don't touch it."[212]

But Dole was trapped by a Republican establishment determined to scale back government. In 1994, Grover G. Norquist, a conservative, antitax Republican activist, wrote that the sine qua non of Dole's presidential candidacy "will be Dole's ability to block any government-run health care system."[213] Dole's success boosted his chances among Republicans but ran afoul of the general electorate. Of the 15 percent who named Medicare as the most important factor in their voting decision, 67 percent supported Clinton. Moreover, 42 percent named the Republicans as "more likely" to cut Medicare; just 17 percent thought Democrats would attack this holy grail of American politics. Finally, of the 9 percent who said that compassion was an important factor in determining their presidential vote, 72 percent chose Clinton.[214]

In addition to the Medicare issue, Clinton made his case for reelection by resurrecting yet another Democratic legacy: education. Ever since Jimmy Carter told the National Education Association that he would establish a Department of Education—a promise he fulfilled in 1979—Democrats have made education a priority. They received an added boost in 1983, when the Reagan-appointed National Commission on Excellence in Education issued a report titled *A Nation at Risk*. Using the language of the Cold War, the commission sounded an alarm about declining educational standards:

> If an unfriendly foreign power had attempted to impose on America the mediocre educational performance that exists today, we might well have viewed it as an act of war. As it stands, we have allowed this to happen to ourselves. We have even squandered the gains in student achievement made in the wake of the Sputnik challenge. Moreover, we have dismantled essential support systems which helped make those gains possible. We have, in effect, been committing an act of unthinking, unilateral educational disarmament.[215]

In the years since, public opinion polls have consistently shown a large Democratic advantage as the party best able to handle the education issue. A Gallup poll conducted in October 1996 gave the Democrats a 29-point advantage as the party best able to deal with the education issue.[216] Republicans compounded their problem by advocating elimination of the Department of Education, slashing slated increases in federally sponsored school lunch programs, and jettisoning the Corporation for Public Broadcasting, which funded such popular children's television programs as *Sesame Street*. Dole parroted the party line in an unsuccessful attempt to cast the National Education Association into a political pariah: "The teachers' unions nominated Bill Clinton in 1992, they are funding his reelection now, and they, his most reliable supporters know he will maintain the status quo. I say this not to the teachers, but to their unions: If education were a war, you would be losing it. If it were a business, you would be driving it into bankruptcy. If it were a patient, it would be dying."[217] Democrats shrugged off Dole's attacks, drawing on the country's Cold War experience to defend their stance: "Cutting education as we move into the twenty-first century would be like cutting defense spending at the height of the Cold War. We must do more to expand educational opportunity—not less."[218] Clinton used Dole's education plank as a means to place the former senator firmly in the past: "Senator Dole voted against student loans, against Head Start, against creating the Department of Education. If he gets elected president, we'll start the new century without anyone in the Cabinet of the president representing education and our children."[219] Democrats added to Dole's dilemma by equating education with traditional GOP heartlessness: "The Republican budget tried to take Big Bird away from five-year-olds, school lunches away from ten-year-olds, summer jobs away from fifteen-year-olds, and college loans away from twenty-year-olds."[220]

But Clinton's vision of being a modern-day Roosevelt was mired in continued public distrust of government. Fifty-two percent believed the federal government should do less; just 41 percent said there was more for government to do.[221] Thus, voters came to a judgment: They wanted a president who would preserve the best of the New Deal, Fair Deal, and Great Society while not enlarging the federal establishment much beyond it. The Democratic platform, for example, advised parents to "help their children with their homework, to read to them, to know their teachers, and above all, to teach their children right from wrong, set the best example, and teach children how to make responsible decisions."[222] The document also published a toll-free 800 number for battered spouses who needed to find shelter and report their abusive partners to the authorities. While promising a reinvented government that would instill the values of opportunity, community, and responsibility, Clinton's New Democratic party described its mission for the next century:

> Today's Democratic party knows that the era of big government is over. Big bureaucracies and Washington solutions are not the real answers to today's challenges. We need a smaller government . . . and we must have a larger national spirit. Government's job should be to give people the tools they need to make the most of their own lives. Americans must take the responsibility to use them, to build good lives for themselves and their families. Personal responsibility is the most powerful force we have to meet our challenges and shape the future we want for ourselves, for our children, and for America.[223]

But Clinton's forward-looking rhetoric contained much still mired in the New Deal past. Although touting V-chips that would control children's access to television, promoting the wearing of school uniforms and family leave, launching a war on teenage smoking, continuing the ban against assault weapons, teaching every eight-year-old to read and every twelve-year-old to use the Internet, and extending some college education to every eighteen-year-old were noble goals, they did not constitute a vision upon which future Democratic presidents could build. Bill Clinton's dilemma was to move his administration and his party away from Franklin Roosevelt's and Lyndon Johnson's domestic victories and to give Democrats a mission that would energize them in the years to come. But instead of presenting a grand vision during the campaign, Clinton proposed what could only be called a "New Deal lite" platform of promises.

The Last Warrior

October 21, 1996

It was a gorgeous day on the campaign trail. Stumping in the battleground state of Michigan, Bob Dole appealed for support from his native midwesterners. In the village of Chelsea a large crowd gathered, entertained by the obligatory high school band. But even in small-town America, Dole could not escape his underdog status. As he mounted the stage the band played the theme from *Mission Impossible*, and Clinton supporters held aloft Dole's "15%" signs (referring to Dole's pledge to cut taxes 15 percent) that had been altered to read "15% behind."[224] These incidents illustrated the problems that bedeviled the Dole team. As the general election campaign began in earnest after Labor Day, Dole and his handlers were still searching for a theme.

It wasn't supposed to be like this. When Dole announced his candidacy in 1995, he was well positioned to base his campaign on the danger of unbalanced federal budgets. Throughout his thirty-five years in Congress, Dole maintained that government had grown too big—taking, he said, a lesson from the Cold War: "Just as we rolled back the Soviet Empire in the 1980s, we're going to roll back the empire of liberal, big spending special interests and big government in the latter half of the 1990s."[225] In order to shrink the enlarged federal bureaucracy, Dole backed the balanced budget amendment—the one proviso of Gingrich's Contract With America with which he was truly comfortable. Like most budget-balancers, however, Dole still wanted a relatively large federal government. For example, during the 1960s he cosponsored the food stamp program with South Dakota's George McGovern. In the 1980s, Dole teamed with New York's Daniel Patrick Moynihan to save Social Security. Although his commitment to a balanced budget did not prevent him from working with Democrats, Dole was decidedly uncomfortable with the supply-side advocates who formed the core of the Reagan revolution. Sardonically, Dole liked to tell the tale of a bus filled with supply-siders that had gone over a cliff. The tragedy, Dole quipped, was that there were three empty seats. But with the Cold War finished and Reagan long gone, the time seemed ripe for an old-fashioned, balance-the-budget midwestern conservative to lead the GOP. In keeping with Alf Landon's Kansas-style Republicanism, Dole preached the gospel of self-reliance: "We must rein in our runaway government, return power to the people, reduce the tax burden, put parents back in charge of our schools, untie the hands of our police, restore justice to our courts, and put our faith once again in the basic goodness, wisdom, and self-reliance of our people."[226] Back in 1936, Republicans decried the "vast multitude of new offices" and the "centralized bureaucracy" from which "swarms of inspectors" swooped over the countryside to "harass our people."[227] Sixty years later, Dole spoke in a similar fashion, pledging to revive the dormant Tenth Amendment to the Constitution.

Dole's cryptic references to the Tenth Amendment failed to register with the public ("The powers not delegated to the United States by the Constitution, nor prohibited by it to the States, are reserved to the States respectively, or to the people"). Behind in the polls and needing to jump-start his lagging campaign, Dole turned to the sure-fire Reagan gimmick of tax cuts. To emphasize his conversion to the supply-side theory, Dole selected one of its founders, Jack Kemp, to join him on the Republican ticket. The move was presaged months earlier, when Dole told the Republican National Committee, "I'm willing to be another Ronald Reagan, if that's what you want."[228] Candidate Dole appropriated much of the Reagan tax-cut script, promising a 15 percent reduction in federal taxes over a three-year period. Adopting the slogan "It's your money," Dole attempted to square his conversion to the supply-side religion with his orthodox conservatism: "The principle involved here is time-honored and true, and that is, it's your money. You shouldn't have to apologize for wanting to keep what you earn. To the contrary, the government should apologize for taking too much of it."[229] Dole argued that his tax cut would not "blow a hole in the deficit" as Clinton claimed: "The president wants to spend 20 percent more over the next six years. I want to spend 14 percent more and give that 6 percent back to the people."[230] At the same time, Dole pledged to protect veterans, Medicare and Social Security beneficiaries, and the Pentagon from the budget ax. But given the $3 *trillion* increase in the federal debt since 1980, voters were not buying Reaganomics II. Two-thirds maintained that Dole could not reduce taxes and balance the budget.[231] Tax cuts, absent the Soviet menace, were not enough to buy entrée into the White House.

By election day, the one thing Dole had left was his persona—and Dole had a compelling tale of courage and perseverance to tell. In the closing days of World War II, while serving in the U.S. Army Tenth Mountain Division in Italy, Dole was grievously wounded and left for dead. Only through sheer force of will did he recover—albeit not completely. For the rest of Dole's life his right arm would hang uselessly at his side, and he usually is seen grasping a pen with his hand to ease the pain he still felt.[232] Though Dole never talked much about his war wound, it became an integral part of his story once he became a presidential candidate. Dole realized that American presidents convey moral lessons to voters unlike any other public official. As presidential scholar Clinton Rossiter once wrote, "The final greatness of the presidency lies in the truth that it is not just an office of incredible power but a breeding ground of indestructible myth."[233] Seeking reelection in 1864 with the Civil War not yet won, Abraham Lincoln was depicted in several "popular life" biographies as an example of what a poor American boy can achieve if he wants to "climb the heights."[234] Ever since, the presidency has become "a living symbol" for the values that Americans hold dear. By immersing his story in the mythology of the presidency, Dole hoped to plant himself firmly in the Lincoln tradition.

Dole's real-life biography only accentuated public doubts about Clinton. Throughout his tenure, Clinton had been tinged by the whiff of scandal. There was "Filegate" (the collection of FBI documents on former Reagan and Bush officials by a rogue Clinton White House staffer), "Travelgate" (the firing of the White House Travel Office staff allegedly at the behest of the first lady), and Whitewater (a controversial land deal involving the Clintons and their Arkansas cronies back when Clinton was governor). Only one-third of those leaving the polls believed that Clinton had told the truth about Whitewater; 60 percent thought he was hiding something. Most devastatingly, 54 percent said Clinton could not be trusted—a quality heretofore believed essential for a prospective president.[235] Thus, the Republican candidate attempted to capitalize on these personal differences. "It's your money" gave way to another theme: "Trust Dole." Dole asked voters to trust in his character as he would, in turn, trust them. This one was lifted from his former running mate, Gerald R. Ford, who told voters twenty years before: "It's not enough for anyone to say, 'Trust me.' Trust must be earned."[236] But a superlative character alone could not make Dole president: By a margin of 58 percent to 38 percent, issues trumped character as the more important factor in picking a president.[237]

It was in a final act of desperation that Dole attempted to reclaim another traditional Republican issue: values. Ever since Ronald Reagan promised voters in 1980 that he would restore traditional American values of "family, work, neighborhood, peace, and freedom" to their rightful place, politicians from both parties have recognized the power of the so-called values issues.[238] As a candidate in 1992 Clinton used the phrase "New Covenant" to package his product: "In the end, the New Covenant simply asks us all to be Americans again. Old-fashioned Americans for a new time. Opportunity. Responsibility. Community. When we pull together, America will pull ahead."[239] Although Clinton dropped that phrase, the value-laden buzzwords *opportunity*, *community*, and *responsibility* laced every major address Clinton made as president. Republican pollster Richard Wirthlin believed that Clinton had "cleaned their clocks" in appropriating these values to himself, and Republicans were determined to retake the lost ground.[240] As Dole told the U.S. Conference of Mayors: "To put it simply: values count, not just in our lives, but in our society. . . . We must speak, not just for innovative policies, but for the enduring values like family, work, responsibility, and tolerance. I decided that I must use the bully pulpit to discuss these issues if I am to lead."[241] Dole's belief that prospective presidents must, in David Kusnet's phrase, "speak American"[242] was correct, but it did not provide sufficient grounding for a successful campaign. Instead of listening to a president talk about values, voters believed that their realization rested with them. A 1996 Hart-Teeter survey found 81 percent saying that "strengthening families" should be left to individuals; just 4 percent thought government had a role to play. Likewise, 73 percent said "improving the moral climate of the country" should be an individual goal; only 5 percent thought this was government's job.[243] Put simply, most Americans thought presidents had better things to do than be the moralist in chief.

That left Dole with one last weapon: the L-word. By the end of the Cold War, Republicans had transformed liberalism from the ennobling philosophy espoused by Franklin D. Roosevelt into an epithet. Conservatives spat the word from their lips, knowing voters had first equated liberalism with being "soft on communism" and later associated it with a kind of cultural hedonism. By 1996, just one in five voters called themselves liberal.[244] Cognizant of liberalism's decline, a confident Dole told *Washington Post* reporter Bob Woodward, "Once Clinton's perceived as a liberal, the election's over."[245] Dole subsequently took to the hustings with a full-throated cry of "liberal, liberal, liberal Bill Clinton!"[246] Dole sought to tie Clinton's liberalism with his opposition to a 15 percent tax cut, his support for health care reform, and his proposed "don't ask, don't tell" policy concerning gays in the military. Clinton was having none of it: "You know, this 'liberal' charge, that's what their party always drags out when they get in a tight race. It's sort of their 'golden oldie,' you know. It's a record they think they can play that everybody loves to hear. And I just don't think that dog will hunt this time."[247]

Clinton was right. By reiterating his New Democratic philosophy, Clinton had inoculated himself from any susceptibility to the old liberalism. A frustrated Dole admitted, "He's not perceived as a liberal."[248] In fact, Clinton's stated objective for a second term was balancing the budget by 2002. It was as if Clinton was quoting the famous line from the 1936 Democratic platform: "Our retrenchment, tax and recovery programs thus reflect our firm determination to achieve a balanced budget and the reduction of the national debt at the earliest possible moment."[249] By campaign's end, Dole lamented to CNN's Candy Crowley: "I'm baffled. I'm really baffled. It seems to me, and I'm not trying to be judgmental, but if the American people really care and they're really concerned about who's in charge, something ought to get their attention sooner or later. . . . Maybe the electorate doesn't have any interest this year."[250]

But even before the Dole campaign's final denouement, Republicans were engaging in piranha politics as they devoured their own. Wisconsin's Republican governor, Tommy Thompson, told reporters in late October, "I thought George Bush's campaign was probably the poorest run presidential campaign—and I think this is a close second."[251] Conservative activist William Kristol likened the Dole campaign to the old Soviet Politburo: "No one's willing to bring bad news to the boss—they report cheerfully that steel production is up 400 percent. It is ultimately the Brezhnev campaign."[252] Even conservative icon Barry Goldwater had his doubts about Dole: "I would first vote for Dole if he was the only one running, but. . . ." Goldwater praised the Clintons: "I think he's a good president and he has a very good wife."[253] Don Sipple, a media strategist fired by Dole, told *Newsweek*:

> This is a very good, very decent man. Noble. But my inescapable conclusion is that his clock stopped in the late 1950s or early 1960s. He is a man not of this time. . . . He thought the presidency was a reward system and he was next in line for the ring.
>
> I don't think he would be a particularly good president. There's the lack of communication skills, the indecisiveness, the obsession with self-reliance.[254]

At campaign's end, Dole traveled with Gerald Ford and George Bush—forming a trio of World War II's remaining soldiers (excluding Jimmy Carter and Ronald Reagan) either to serve or seek the presidency. Accompanying them was Arizona Senator John McCain, himself a Vietnam War hero, who dubbed Dole "the last warrior." But the Dole caravan only emphasized their man as a candidate of the past. As Simon Rosenberg of the centrist New Democrat Network observed, "For a newer, younger America, Bob Dole was always a black and white movie in a color age."[255] When voters went to the polls on election day, they faced a conundrum: Clinton had been unable to adequately define change as Dole had proved incapable of resisting it.

Republican Disarray

The Dole experience may prove emblematic for the Republican party's prospects in the post–Cold War era. Throughout the Cold War, presidential contests were fought over the corpse of the Democratic party. Now the same thing seems to be happening to the Republicans. In an age when voters want more than self-congratulatory kudos for beating communism, Republicans may find that success poses the greatest danger a political party can face. Just as the success of the New Deal created a strong middle class that benefited from the largess of government but came to believe as taxpayers the government wasted vast sums of revenue, so too the Republican party's Cold War victory enabled Clinton to become the first Democrat since Franklin D. Roosevelt to renew his White House lease. Steve Merrill, former Republican governor of New Hampshire, perceptively observed: "It is time for reflection in our party. The losses we've suffered at the presidential level should cause us to reflect that we really have not explained our vision of the future as well as we should have."[256]

It is these losses that should give the Republicans pause. By any measure, George Bush's 38 percent showing and Bob Dole's 41 percent showing are devastating. One need only look back to the Democratic defeats in 1980 (Carter) and 1984 (Mondale) to find a bigger pair of losers. Republicans like to blame their two defeats on Ross Perot, but exit polls indicate that Dole's vote would have risen by just 2 points had Perot not run.[257] As Table 6.6 shows, the striking feature in comparing the 1992 and 1996 Republican votes is that it resembles the plains found in Bob Dole's native Kansas. From the first election to the next, a flat line can be drawn in nearly every demographic category.

Thus, the 2000 Republican ticket faces a daunting task: To win it must outperform Dole by 9 points. Recent history shows this to be nearly impossible. Only Dwight Eisenhower in 1952 following the Korean stalemate and Jimmy Carter in 1976 after the Watergate disaster were able to do so. The Republican dilemma is also compounded by the fact that there is no obvious heir apparent. The last time the GOP faced a leadership crisis was in 1964—when the Goldwater forces engineered their takeover. Today's Republican party has at least four factions that would like to control it: (1) Libertarians—socially liberal and economically conservative and led by Christine Todd Whitman and William Weld; (2) old-fashioned, balance-the-budget conservatives whose leader was Bob Dole; (3) supply-siders, whose leading spokespersons are Jack Kemp and Steve Forbes; and (4) the religious right, led by Pat Robertson, Ralph Reed, and Dan Quayle. Of these, born-agains have the most potential to wrest control away from the other groups. Already, the Christian Right has won control in such key states as Texas and Pennsylvania. Ralph Reed notes that they are well on their way to achieving their final objective: "Our ambition is to be larger and more effective than both political parties combined."[258] David Durenberger, a former senator from Minnesota, described the GOP's "Mondale problem":

> We are suffering currently from what is [known as] "leadership" in the Republican party. What is it? Is it going to be known by what you're against or what you're for? It's so much easier to say you're *against* employer mandates and you're *against* large government and you're *against* taxes. Then what are you *for*? . . . Dole is *for* whatever the people are at the moment. Dole's problem is basically the Mondale problem. You can't get to be president unless you go through that damn convention, and if you go through that damn convention you probably won't be president. That's the bad news. And the good news is

TABLE 6.6

Two-Party Presidential Vote Compared, 1992 and 1996 (in percentages)

Democratic Category	Clinton '96 Minus Clinton '92	Dole Minus Bush
Nationwide	+6	+3
Sex		
Men	+2	+6
Women	+9	+1
Race		
Whites	+4	+6
Blacks	+1	+2
Hispanics	+11	−4
Age		
18–29 years old	+10	0
30–44 years old	+7	+3
45–59 years old	+7	+1
60 and older	−2	+6
Income		
Under $15,000	+1	+5
$15,000–$29,999	+8	+1
$30,000–$49,999	+7	+2
$50,000–$74,999	+5	+4
$75,000 and over	+5	+3
Education		
Less than high school	+5	0
High school graduate	+8	−1
Some college	+7	+3
College graduate	+5	+5
Postgraduate	+2	+4
Region		
East	+8	−1
Midwest	+6	+4
South	+5	+3
West	+5	+6
Religion		
White Protestant	+3	+6
Catholic	+9	+2
Jewish	−2	+5
Party		
Democrats	+7	0
Republicans	+3	+7
Independents	+5	+3
Philosophy		
Liberal	+10	−3
Moderate	+10	+2
Conservative	+2	+7

SOURCE: Voter Research and Surveys, exit poll, November 3, 1992, and Voter News and Surveys, exit poll, November 5, 1996.

that the Democrats have the same problem we have. It's a helluva problem when the parties have moved so far from the middle that there's no room left for real leadership.[259]

Although Durenberger's analysis of the perils that Democrats face still holds, the problems that beset the Republican party in post–Cold War presidential contests seem especially large. As this book has detailed, Republican presidents rested on a three-legged stool of the economy, foreign policy, and defense throughout the long Cold War. By 1996, the economy was no longer so reliant on Eisenhower's military-industrial complex, foreign policy no longer mattered much in presidential contests, and Clinton's Pentagon budgets represented only differences in degree from Republican proposals. As Table 6.7 indicates, Dole did quite well among the small number of voters still trapped in the Cold War rubric—especially the *4 percent* of those who said foreign policy mattered most. But it was Clinton's agenda that most voters responded to, and it seems likely to remain important four years hence. For Clinton backers, education, Medicare, and the economy were all-important; in contrast, Dole won the largest vote share from those who said taxes, foreign policy, and deficit reduction mattered most. Of these, deficit reduction and taxes are likely to remain important considerations. But the difficulties that Clinton and the 105th Congress face on entitlement issues also mean that the old Democratic standbys of Medicare and Social Security are likely to remain high on the voters' list of priorities. In Florida, exit polls showed that the top issue for most voters were Medicare and Social Security—no surprise in the retirement haven. Among those who named these issues as important, Clinton captured 62 percent to Dole's 33 percent.[260] Florida, which sided with Bush in 1992, proved crucial in Clinton's 1996 victory. Telephoning friends after the networks colored the Sunshine State red for Clinton, the president exulted, "It's over."[261]

Add education and the environment (not asked in the 1996 exit polls) to the post–Cold War issues mix and Democrats are well poised to walk across Bill Clinton's famous bridge to the twenty-first century. The altered set of issues, dubbed by White House strategists as "M^2E^2" (shorthand for Medicare, Medicaid, education, and the environment) appeal to female voters—especially single mothers dependent on the social safety nets provided by government. Exit polls showed that the gender gap that first appeared with Ronald Reagan's election in 1980 had been transformed into a canyon. Clinton had a 16-point lead among women, winning 54 percent of their ballots; Dole scored better with men, capturing 44 percent of their votes.[262] For the first time in history, the sexes were on opposite sides of the presidential balloting. Men are more sensitive to the traditional GOP concerns about taxes, deficit reduction, and crime. But as long as women are responsive to the Clinton's M^2E^2 agenda, women will continue to put Democrats in the White House. House Republican Marge Roukema observed

TABLE 6.7
Issue Concerns and Candidate Preferences, 1996 (in percentages)

Issue Concern	Clinton Voters	Dole Voters	All Voters
Taxes	19	73	11
Medicare	67	26	15
Foreign policy	35	56	4
Federal deficit	27	52	12
Economy/jobs	61	27	21
Education	78	16	12
Crime/drugs	40	50	7

SOURCE: Voter News and Surveys, exit poll, November 5, 1996.

that unless Republicans consciously addressed these issues they would be "a long time coming back."[263]

The changing issues mix has also altered the chosen path prospective candidates take to the White House. Instead of underemployed vice presidents and senators who emphasize their foreign policy expertise, as was the case during the Cold War, our next group of presidential candidates are likely to be underemployed vice presidents and *governors* who emphasize their familiarity with domestic concerns. This represents a return, in part, to an earlier era. Throughout much of the nineteenth century and well into the twentieth, governors trod a well-worn path to the presidency. Franklin Pierce, Rutherford B. Hayes, Grover Cleveland, William McKinley, Theodore Roosevelt, Woodrow Wilson, Warren G. Harding, Calvin Coolidge, and Franklin D. Roosevelt were among those who made the leap from the statehouse to the White House. But the Cold War contributed to the corrosion of federalism. As one governor lamented, "We don't have sovereign states anymore. All we have are a bunch of provinces. . . . We are becoming conveyor belts for policies signed, sealed, and delivered in Washington."[264] By the late 1990s, a new post–Cold War consensus had formed: The states, not the federal government, would have primary responsibility for social welfare. The new thinking was amply illustrated in the welfare reform enacted in 1996, which repealed that part of the 1935 Social Security Act dealing with children. In this and in other areas, governors will have to make executive decisions and execute them. Senators, lacking a foreign policy crisis, will continue to talk about decisions largely made by others. The fact that foreign policy no longer really matters much is illustrated by the fact that seats on the once coveted Senate Foreign Relations Committee now go begging. Michael Dukakis and Bill Clinton constitute the first wave of gubernatorial aspirants to capture the Democratic presidential nomination, and they are likely to be joined in 2000 by a group of equally ambitious Republican governors who aspire to be president.

Clinton's joining the ranks of Thomas Jefferson, James Madison, James Monroe, Andrew Jackson, Woodrow Wilson, and Franklin Roosevelt as two-term Democratic presidents was no fluke: It demonstrates that the vaunted "electoral lock" secured by the Republicans during the 1980s has been broken. Twenty-nine states and the District of Columbia with a total of 346 electoral votes (far more than the 270 needed for victory) have *twice* sided with Clinton. Even Whiteside County, Illinois, which contains Ronald Reagan's hometown of Tampico, has twice backed Clinton—the first time a Democrat has twice won there since the founding of the Republican party. Clinton's ability to color the electoral maps red (television's preferred color for Democrats) was evident in the returns from the ten largest industrial states—eight of which backed Clinton. An even closer look shows that although Clinton won an outright majority only in his native Arkansas in 1992, voters in twenty-one states, including California, Illinois, Michigan, New Jersey, and New York, joined Arkansas in 1996 to give Clinton majority backing.[265] By contrast, Dole's best states were the usual Republican bastions of Kansas, Utah, Nebraska, and Idaho followed by Alabama, Alaska, South Carolina, Wyoming, Mississippi, North Carolina, and Texas. Altogether, Dole received just 159 electoral votes to Clinton's 379—the worst Republican showing since Barry Goldwater in 1964. The southern tinge to the pro-Dole states attests to the realignment that has taken place in the Old Confederacy. Given Dole's poor national showing, the Old Confederacy has become the GOP's base in presidential contests. Other races also point to the Republican party's strength in the region. While Dole was losing Florida, Republicans captured both houses of that state's legislature for the first time ever.[266]

The Vital Center

Republicans breathed a sigh of relief when they held on to the House and Senate—making for the first back-to-back GOP Congresses in sixty-eight years. In the wee hours of the morning after election day, a relieved Newt Gingrich told reporters, "It's pretty amazing, a truly historic moment."[267] Indeed it was. The power of incumbency certainly helped the GOP keep its hold on power—just as it did during the long years of Democratic domination. Ninety-five percent of House members from both parties who sought reelection won—including 83 percent of the Republican class of 1994. Likewise, the Republican "incumbent party" prevailed in the Senate, where ninety-three-year-old Strom Thurmond won an eighth term and Jesse Helms was reelected to his fifth. Only South Dakota's Larry Pressler lost to a Democratic challenger.

The House results were especially intriguing. Only twelve of the seventy Republican freshmen elected in 1994 were defeated. One of them was Frederick K. Heineman, beaten by North Carolina Democrat David Price in a rematch for this contested House seat. But Price's win, occurring as it did well below the Mason-Dixon line, was unusual since the election returns reaffirmed the South as a bastion of conservative Republicanism. In the states that once formed the Old Confederacy, Republicans won eight House seats and lost only three for a net gain of five. Republicans captured Democratic-held seats in Texas, Oklahoma, Mississippi, Alabama, and even Bill Clinton's native Arkansas. Partisan control of the Alabama and Mississippi delegations switched from Democratic to Republican, further underscoring the Republican realignment in the Deep South that began with Barry Goldwater in 1964. Even the Senate was not immune to the Republicans' southern accent. After Dole's departure, Republicans selected Trent Lott of Mississippi to be majority leader. The rise of southern Republicanism contains a bundle of post–Cold War ironies. As Michael Lind has observed, it is hard to imagine "Dwight Eisenhower supporting congressional witchhunts against federal law enforcement agents, or Robert Taft cultivating votes by denouncing abortion, premarital sex, and homosexuality."[268] The Republican southern "firewall," as the late Lee Atwater liked to call it, will continue to withstand the pro-Democratic tide on both the Atlantic and Pacific coasts that is likely to mark post–Cold War politics.

Elsewhere in the country there was a small Democratic resurgence as Democrats gained six seats in the Northeast (now the most reliably Democratic region of the country), four in the Midwest, and two in the West. In Massachusetts, the two lone Republican representatives, Peter Blute and Peter Torkildsen, were defeated—producing the first all-Democratic delegation in decades. Republican incumbents were ousted in Maine, Connecticut, New York, New Jersey, California, and Washington, and Democrats wrested control of the California, Connecticut, Maine, Washington, and Wisconsin delegations away from the Republicans. These returns show continued Democratic gains in the Northeast, upper and industrial Midwest, and West Coast that partially offset the rising tide of southern Republicanism. The result was a Democratic gain of nine seats, making them the largest minority in the House since 1953: 207 Democrats to 227 Republicans.[269] In the post–Cold War era, control of the House will remain hotly contested and uncertain.

But just as presidential contests have transformed since the end of the Cold War, so too have congressional races. Most House members, for example, have won their seats since the Berlin Wall collapsed of its own weight in 1989. In the new post–Cold War Congress, successful candidates—Democratic and Republican—must make their pitches to self-described independents who hold the balance of power. Republican pollster Frank Luntz maintains that 1996 "may be the last election in which partisan affiliation counts for much," adding: "The only people who express strong party loyalty are those over age fifty-five. Few under age thirty-two have any allegiances at all."[270] Most independents like the new division of power they have created between a Democratic president and a Republican Congress. By a margin of 49 percent to 44 percent, voters leaving the polls expressed a preference for a Republican Congress if Clinton were to win again.[271] Aware of this, Republican strategists cobbled together an election night television advertisement for viewing on the West Coast that abandoned Dole: "Remember the last time Democrats ran everything? The largest tax increase in history. Government-run health care. More wasteful spending. Who wants that again? Don't let Oregon down. Don't let the media stop you from voting. And don't hand Bill Clinton a blank check. The polls close at eight."[272] Some credit the advertisement with helping Republican Gordon Smith win a close Senate race over Democrat Tom Bruggere.

Independents are renowned for their cognitive dissonance when it comes to the role of government. In 1967, social scientists Lloyd Free and Hadley Cantril observed a dichotomy between the public's preference for "ideological conservatism" and its penchant for "programmatic liberalism."[273] Voters wanted the federal government in the abstract to be kept to a minimum, but when asked about specific programs they voiced strong support for a more involved bureaucracy. Today, the contradictions maintain their conventional partisan overtones, with Republicans cast in the role of the "ideological conservatives" and Democrats acting as the "programmatic liberals." Delivering his 1996 State of the Union Address, Bill Clinton tried to reconcile the "ideological conservatives" and the "programmatic liberals": "We know big government does not have all the answers. There is not a program for every problem. We know we need a smaller, less bureaucratic government in Washington—one that lives within its means."[274] But the elevation of such issues as tax cuts, entitlements, and deficit reduction coupled with education and the environment has created a divided government decidedly different from its predecessors, one that appeals to American sensibilities. Americans have never bought the concept of unified party government as either desirable or necessary to make government work. Back in 1944, pollster Elmo Roper found only 37 percent saying split-party control of the presidency and Congress would be "bad because it has made it impossible to work on solutions to the important problems facing the country."[275] Today, voters do not trust either major party, preferring the extraconstitutional check that divided ballots have created. Questioning Clinton and Dole at their second debate, schoolteacher Sharon MacAfee spoke for many when she quoted the sentiments of a sixth-grader:

> If I were president, I would think about Abraham Lincoln and George Washington and what they did to make our country great. We should unite the white and black people and people of all cultures. Democrats and Republicans should

unite also. We should all come together and think of the best ways to solve the economic problems of our country. I believe that when we are able to come together and stop fighting amongst ourselves, we will get along a lot better.[276]

After the election, both parties got the message. Speaking to an enthusiastic crowd of supporters, Bill Clinton sounded like Thomas Jefferson in eschewing partisanship:

> The challenges we face, they're not Democratic or Republican challenges. They're American challenges. What we know from the budget battles of the last two years and from the remarkable success of the last few weeks of the Congress is the lesson we have learned for the last 220 years—what we have achieved as Americans of lasting good, we have achieved by working together. So let me say to the leaders of my Democratic party and the leaders of the Republican party, it is time to put country ahead of party.[277]

Newt Gingrich agreed: "Our goal is to find common ground [with Clinton]. . . . We don't have to live in a world of confrontation. We ought to work with him and give him a chance to lead in the direction he campaigned on."[278]

The American desire for a fusion between the two parties rather than gridlock is a dominant characteristic of the post–Cold War era. As Daniel Bell prematurely postulated in 1960, Americans may be witnessing the "end of ideology."[279] If so, it also means an end to the politics of passion—for passion is what gives ideology its force. That seems to suit the electorate just fine. In 1996, Americans had settled down from the dizzying changes that characterized elections immediately following the end of the Cold War. A grand settlement was reached: Voters said NO! to any new big agendas from either party—preferring that government give tax cuts that would empower them to do more for themselves, protect middle-class entitlements such as Social Security and Medicare, and provide an enhanced federal role in such vital twenty-first century concerns as education and the environment. Like Dwight Eisenhower before him, Bill Clinton took note of the emerging public consensus and placed himself squarely in favor of it. Whereas Eisenhower had found solace in the Authentic Center, whose consensus rested in the fight against communism, Bill Clinton told supporters on election night that "the vital American center is alive and well."[280] Clinton subsequently put it thus: "The ground has shifted beneath our feet, but we have clearly created a new center, not the lukewarm midpoint between overheated liberalism and chilly conservatism, but instead, a place where throughout our history, people of good will have tried to forge new approaches to new challenges."[281] Like Eisenhower's Authentic Center, the Vital Center eschews parties—preferring that the president and Congress get under the hood of the American engine of government to fix whatever is wrong. Clinton interpreted the voters' collective thinking on election night: "They are sending us a message: Work together. Meet our challenges. Put aside the politics of division and build America's community together."[282] Whether or not Clinton's Vital Center will hold without the communist challenge to the American way of life remains to be seen. But it is clear that the Authentic Center and the Anxious Middle have been morphed into the Vital Center. Its staying power will be tested in the years to come.

chapter seven

The Collapse of the Old Order

Gosh, I miss the Cold War.

—Bill Clinton, October 12, 1993

When the Cold War ended with a whimper in December 1991, former KGB general Oleg Kalugin was astonished that the Soviet Union should have fallen so quickly.[1] A different sentiment prevailed in U.S. military circles. An army officer told William Odum, former director of the National Security Agency, that the intelligence community was "madder than hell" that the Soviets should have quit so abruptly.[2] Indeed, the stunning fall of communism was no panacea, as one senior cartographer at the Central Intelligence Agency explained: "Suddenly everything we had produced was out of date—hundreds, thousands of maps, all out of date."[3] Although the CIA continued to spy on assorted terrorists, drug traffickers, and other "international criminals," the agency missed the glamour and single-minded purpose it had when combating communists.[4] Throughout the layers of the federal bureaucracy a similar soul-searching has occurred. As the years pass since the collapse of the Soviet empire, it is obvious that the U.S. government planned for every Cold War contingency except one: victory.

Shortly after the Cold War ended, Richard Nixon wrote, "We live in a new world—a world we helped create."[5] But in this "new world" much that was once familiar has disappeared: the old arrangements; the old way of doing things; indeed, the old order itself has collapsed. In Moscow, for example, guardians of Lenin's tomb no longer rely on the Communist Party to pay the bills and have instead turned to a department store located across from Lenin's remains to defray the rent. In effect, Russia's burgeoning capitalists are now preserving the corpse of the communist founder.[6] Meanwhile, in faraway Kansas, 300 Russian troops march—not as invaders but in a joint training exercise with U.S. soldiers for a peacekeeping mission in strife-torn Bosnia. While the former enemies posed for souvenir snapshots in front of a nattily dressed Russian color guard, Colonel Gennadi M. Averyanov declared: "In the past, we could never imagine that we would one day conduct combined operations on American soil. Every day brings something new." The ironic scene also struck a Russian veteran of Soviet occupation in Hungary and East Germany: "Here, land can be private property. Everywhere there are fences marking people's property."[7]

These fences were not only literal but figurative. After the Cold War, many recalled with renewed fervor George Washington's ancient admonition that the United States "steer clear of permanent Alliances with any portion of the foreign world." Washington maintained in his 1796 Farewell Address that such "entangling alliances" would inevitably lead to "overgrown Military establishments, which under any form of Government are inauspicious to liberty and which are to be regarded as particularly hostile to Republican Liberty."[8] NATO, the permanent alliance created by the Cold War, grappled with the new post–Cold War world by creating the Partnership for Peace program with the former communist nations of Eastern Europe. Yet most Americans professed not to care about the fate of those still living in the former Soviet empire. President Clinton was aware of the prevailing public sentiments while reminding fellow citizens that the absence of the Soviet Union had not eliminated the need for American leadership: "The disintegration of the former Soviet Union eliminated the preeminent threat but exposed many others: an increasingly tangled and dangerous web of international terrorism, crime, and drug trafficking; the aggression of rogue states and vicious ethnic and religious conflicts; the spread of dangerous weapons, including nuclear, biological, and chemical ones, and transnational threats like disease, overpopulation, and environmental degradation. . . . Just as fascism and then communism attacked the one clear and true idea that defines us and embodies the promise we represent to the world, today's threats attack the idea of a safe and open society of a free people."[9] Clinton's 1996 rival for the White House, former senator Bob Dole, agreed that Americans needed to stay involved in world affairs:

We are an insular people by historical predisposition and natural inclination. Somewhere in the pantheon of instructive American slogans must be an honored place for the one that says: "You mind your business, and I'll mind mine." We like to think of minding our own business as a virtue. Like other virtues, it isn't practiced much, but it's there in the grain anyway. And it touches on our role as a power among nations. We have never liked that role. In the past twenty-five years, most—not all, but most—of our difficulties have come from those foreign entanglements President Washington warned us against. Yet we

could not find a more dangerous time than the present to kneel to the tempta-
tions of isolationism. Nothing could be more irresponsible than to feed the
false hopes that we can lock our doors and close our minds to the world.[10]

But these bipartisan warnings fell on largely deaf ears. Dole's Republican
opponent for the 1996 presidential nomination, Patrick J. Buchanan, advocated a new foreign policy that "pulls up all the trip wires laid down by the
Cold War to involve American soldiers in wars that are none of America's
business."[11] Meanwhile, a host of foreign difficulties, many having no locus
in the Cold War, caused policymakers to choose sides in ways the old Cold
War could hardly have forecast. The crisis in Bosnia was a case in point.
Senate Republican John McCain, a "hawk" on the Vietnam War and a former POW there, was a "dove" on Bosnia. Clinton, who avoided the draft
during the Vietnam War and protested against it, was a "hawk" on Bosnia.
Washington Post columnist E. J. Dionne Jr. wrote: "Barely four years after
the fall of the Berlin Wall, the seemingly solid foreign policy coalitions that
set in during the Vietnam War had been disrupted beyond recognition."[12]

Reminded that John Kennedy won broad public backing for his activist
foreign policy, Clinton half-joked, "Gosh, I miss the Cold War," adding: "I
envy Kennedy having an enemy. The question now is how to persuade people they should do things when they are not immediately threatened."[13]
Clinton's lament was understandable since the Cold War offered American
presidents a useful enemy in communism. As one White House chief of
staff said, "You tell [Congress] that they're helping no one but Brezhnev by
their stubbornness, and they cave fast."[14] But ethnic hatreds in Bosnia, the
generals' coup in Haiti, and tribal conflicts between Tutsis and Hutus in
Rwanda lack a similar compelling moral appeal. Janell Mullin, a black
postal worker in Chicago, spoke for many when asked about Clinton's plan
to send U.S. troops to Bosnia: "I think they should stop worrying about
Bosnia. If they want to send the troops somewhere, they should send them
to the South Side of Chicago."[15] Pat Buchanan agreed, espousing a return
to the pre–World War II "America First" isolationism: "Every nation to rise
to industrial power in modern times did so by first protecting the home
market. Perhaps [cities are in crisis] because the good jobs that were once
there have been exported to Mexico, Taiwan, Korea, and China."[16]

The desire for a respite from world affairs is not surprising. Political scientist Louis Hartz has noted that the United States, with its universalistic commitment to classical liberalism, is especially susceptible to an "absolutist nationalism," which either embraces the globe in a belief that it can be won
over to American ideas, or withdraws from the rest of the world believing it
to be alien to the American way of thinking. Thus, Woodrow Wilson and
Warren G. Harding are distinctly "American" thinkers since each represents
a response to these twin impulses.[17] Wilson's global democratic dream was

replaced after World War I by Harding's plea for "normalcy." Addressing the Republican convention in 1920, Senator Henry Cabot Lodge used phrases since resurrected by Buchanan: "We must be now and ever for Americanism and Nationalism, and against Internationalism!"[18] Unfortunately, Lodge's advice was heeded, thus setting conservatives on a long isolationist path abandoned only in response to World War II and the advancement of Soviet-style communism that followed. After the Cold War, historian Arthur M. Schlesinger Jr. used language reminiscent of the 1920s: "[The Cold War] distorted our politics, and foreign policy became the obsessive concern of our presidents, and that is going to return to normal now."[19]

But what is "normal"? Americans seemed to be rushing backward and forward simultaneously: backward into an age of heightened nationalism, old-fashioned conservatism, and an evocation of "traditional values"; and forward into an era where the global economy makes a mockery of nationalism and where computers link the individual to a vast panoply of data on the information superhighway. Political analyst Michael Barone saw "normalcy" in a return to Tocqueville's America, where the United States was even more egalitarian, individualistic, decentralized, religious, property-loving, and lightly governed.[20] Similarly, Bob Dole found "normalcy" in a rejuvenated Tenth Amendment—that part of the Constitution that says that "the powers not delegated to the United States by the Constitution, nor prohibited by it to the States, are reserved to the States respectively, or to the people." Although Woodrow Wilson once observed that the Tenth Amendment had been among the "least effectual" elements of the Constitution,[21] Dole staked his campaign on its restoration, telling President Clinton in their first debate: "I carry a little card around in my pocket called the Tenth Amendment. Where possible, I want to give power back to the states and back to the people. That's my difference with the president."[22] The 1996 Republican platform proposed to carry out Dole's stated objective by eliminating the Departments of Commerce, Housing and Urban Development, Education, and Energy. Republicans also advocated the defunding or privatization of agencies that had become, in their view, obsolete. Among these were the National Endowment for the Humanities, the Corporation for Public Broadcasting, and the Legal Services Corporation. In addition, some Republican congressmen backed a measure that would require proponents of proposed federal legislation to cite the specific constitutional authority for the proposal.[23]

Others saw "normalcy" in a resurgent Congress and a weakened presidency. During the Cold War, political scientists extolled the presidency—even as they decried the excessive burdens that the atomic bomb and its accompanying threat to people placed on the office. Clinton Rossiter, in his book *The American Presidency* (penned long before the Watergate scandal), celebrated it as an "office of freedom" in the struggle against communism:

The presidency is a standing reproach to those petty doctrinaires who insist that executive power is inherently undemocratic; for, to the exact contrary, it has been more responsive to the needs and dreams of giant democracy than any other office or institution in the whole mosaic of American life. . . . The vast power of this office has not been "poison," as Henry Adams wrote in scorn; rather, it has elevated often and corrupted never, chiefly because those who held it recognized the true source of the power and were ennobled by the knowledge.[24]

Yet Rossiter acknowledged that the Cold War had extracted an enormous toll on each White House occupant. In an epigraph, Rossiter borrowed lines from William Shakespeare's *The Tragedy of Macbeth*: "Methought I heard a voice cry 'Sleep no more!'" A few days before John Kennedy's assassination, Rossiter sent the president an autographed copy of his work. Kennedy replied that he enjoyed the book but thought the epigraph wrong. Kennedy suggested using lines from *Henry the Fourth*, in which Glendower boasts, "I can call spirits from the vasty deep," to which the reply is given:

Why, so can I, or so can any man;
But will they come when you do call for them?[25]

The Cold War gave American presidents many opportunities to summon spirits from the "vasty deep." As Woodrow Wilson noted in *Congressional Government*, when it came to foreign policy matters, congressional supremacy inevitably yielded to presidential authority: "When foreign affairs play a prominent part in the politics and policy of a nation, its Executive must of necessity be its guide: must utter every initial judgment, take every first step of action, supply the information upon which it is to act, suggest and in large measure control its conduct."[26] Aside from foreign affairs, Wilson saw the Congress—especially its committees—controlling much of what happened inside Washington. Yet just thirteen years after Wilson published *Congressional Government*, William McKinley's successful war against Spain in 1898 made Wilson's picture of congressional supremacy, in his words, "hopelessly out of date."[27]

Following the Cold War, Wilson's portrait of Congress as the first among equals has been refurbished. After the demise of the Soviet Union, columnist George Will presciently wrote, "Peace is going to be hell for presidents, at least for those not reconciled to the restoration of what is, when viewed against the sweep of American history, normal: congressional supremacy."[28] Issues such as health care, welfare reform, and the state of the economy encroached on precious committee provinces. The president had become, in effect, the governor of the United States—leading, but responsive to, legislative assertions of authority. This was not an especially exciting role, however. Confiding to his staff late one evening in January 1995, Clinton lamented that there was no longer an air of crisis surrounding the

White House: "I would have much preferred being president during World War II. I'm a person out of my time."[29]

Nonetheless, Clinton sought to reclaim his precious powers by finding a new "enemy" in Congress itself—no matter which party controlled it. Presidential pollster Stanley Greenberg found that respondents were not measuring Clinton by his management of foreign affairs or how he played the commander-in-chief role but whether or not he could tame Congress. In an August 1993 report titled *The Presidential Project*, Greenberg advised Clinton that the *Democratic* Congress had become "the new Soviet Union," adding that John Kennedy, Richard Nixon, and Ronald Reagan had made opposing communism the "moral imperative of their presidencies" and that Clinton should make controlling Congress his moral imperative.[30] In other words, Clinton should restrain Congress while also peacefully coexisting with it—that is, a domestic Soviet-style containment recipe with a dash of détente. But Clinton believed managing Congress could not be "the sum and substance of this presidency."[31] Instead, he relied on amorphous references to traditional values such as "opportunity, community, and responsibility" to be his guides.

Clinton's public ruminations about the nature of the post–Cold War presidency did not prevent Congress from asserting its "traditional" peacetime powers. Speaker of the House Newt Gingrich observed that a succession of chief executives, including Clinton, had become excessively dependent on the first-person personal pronoun: "We'll try to educate the president and his staff that the use of 'I' is not helpful," adding that the presidency was no longer "towering over the land."[32] Following in the footsteps of Henry Cabot Lodge and Robert Taft, Gingrich advocated a return to the Wilsonian idea of "congressional government." In his book titled *To Renew America*, Gingrich declared: "With the end of the Cold War, the case for a strong central government has been dramatically weakened. The time has come for a reversion to first principles. In America, one of those first principles is that power resides first and foremost with the individual citizen."[33] Many of Gingrich's fellow Republicans said they were "citizen-politicians," sent to Washington for a short period before returning home.[34] But Gingrich's idea of a Congress populated with "citizen-politicians" contains a profound irony: Congress's ceding of much of its legislative authority, from welfare reform to health care, to the states in the form of block grants.

Thus, in the intrigues between the president and Congress following the Cold War, there is evidently no "normalcy" to which to return. Faced with such profound philosophical and institutional revisionism, an exasperated Bill Clinton declared: "We are debating things now we thought were settled for decades. We are back to fundamental issues that were debated like this fifty, sixty, seventy years ago."[35] In many ways, the end of the Cold War recalls Abraham Lincoln's famous words during the dark days of the Civil War: "The dogmas of the past are inadequate to the stormy present. The occasion is piled high with difficulty, and we must rise with the occasion. As our case is new, so we must think anew and act anew. We must disenthrall ourselves, and then we shall save our country."[36] As with Lincoln, disenthralling ourselves from first principles often follows a prolonged conflict (or can occur during wartime, as during Lincoln's tenure). Turning back the pages of history, one discovers that after the Revolutionary War Americans directed their energies to first principles: nation-building and creating the necessary constitutional arrangements to sustain these efforts. Likewise, after the War of 1812, taming a big country (substantially larger thanks to the Louisiana Purchase) provided a sense of "manifest destiny." Economic expansion and the creation of a party system also tapped into these energies, especially after the collapse of the Federalists. The post–Civil War years saw the reconstruction of the Old Confederacy and the assembling of a great industrial engine that resulted in what Herbert Croly aptly called "the promise of American life."[37] In 1907, an energetic President Theodore Roosevelt bragged that the United States had become "the mightiest republic on which the sun ever shone."[38] But following World War I the country wandered aimlessly until TR's jaunty cousin Franklin restored America's mission and confidence.

From the mid-twentieth century to 1991, war and near-war gave Americans a fixed sense of who the enemy was and who we were. Ever since 1941, the United States has been on war footing—either in general armed conflict, such as World War II, or on the brink of World War III, as at various times during the Cold War. The fall of Soviet communism may mark the "end of history" of a kind. But in reality the 1990s represent a caesura as one era closes and another opens. Historian Eric Hobsbawm has noted that the war-filled and state-enhancing "short twentieth century" that began in 1914 ended in 1991 has become part of the history books. On all planes, he argues, "we are moving into a radically different twenty-first century a decade early."[39] But it is a journey of ironic twists and turns. In 1995, the former communist Aleksander Kwasniewski emulated Clinton's 1992 bus tour and narrowly beat Solidarity's Lech Walesa, who had waged a vigorous anti-communist campaign, in the race for the Polish presidency.[40] In the nearby Czech Republic, President Vaclav Havel likened the dismemberment of the Soviet empire to the fall of the Romans: "To build a new world on the ruins of communism might be as extended and complex a process as the creation of a Christian Europe—after the great migration—once was."[41]

"We Haven't Got the Rhythm Right"

The collapse of the old order in the East has been accompanied by an end to the old arrangements in the West—military, economic, and political. After the fall of the Soviet Union, the United States has signed treaties committing itself to disassembling 20,000 hydrogen bombs at a cost of $200–300 billion until the year 2070.[42] In Amarillo, Texas, five hydrogen bombs are dismantled each day at the Pantax weapons plant. Technicians unscrew the wires and crack open the blue or antique rose–speckled plastic explosive. The broken pieces are taken outside, placed on an open grate, doused with fuel oil, and burned. Training supervisor Dave Daves, whose interest in nuclear weaponry was sparked by the Boy Scouts atomic energy merit badge program, says "it feels great to be part of history."[43] But Dean Long, a former auto mechanic, has a different perspective. He likens the task to "taking an old Model T apart" adding: "There's no tension. But I'd rather be building hobby horses."[44] Long may get his wish: By the year 2000 it is expected that the workforce at the Texas facility will be cut in half.[45]

In a 1994 speech to the National Baptist Convention, President Clinton voiced the question so many Americans had kept to themselves: "If I'm so rich, why am I not happy?"[46] With the end of the Cold War, the United States stood as the world's lone superpower—a military colossus and, more important, economically stronger than its Western allies. But the collapse of communism has produced considerable economic dislocation. In the new economic order, real median wages for blue-collar workers fell 8 percent from 1988 to 1995.[47] George Nowosielski, president of Pipe Fitters Local 620 at Electric Boat in Groton, noted that the Connecticut facility "has been a grandfather, a father, a son place. Generations have worked on the line here." But after the Cold War, he lamented, "We win the war and we are the losers."[48] Despite Clinton's promise to protect defense jobs, thousands left Electric Boat's gates dismayed over careers cut short.

Other manufacturers once central to the military-industrial complex have also fallen on hard times. In November 1995, Bethlehem Steel extinguished its last blast furnace at its Bethlehem, Pennsylvania, facility. The mill, which had been making steel since the Civil War, sent its remaining 1,800 workers home. Local 2599 union boss Danny Mills observed, "There was a time when we were unbeatable." But American invincibility had long subsided: Of the 31,000 employed in the steel plants during the 1960s, only 1,200 remain. Larry Brandon, a furnace operator, described their fate: "There's nothing here for them anymore. Just a town looking over a graveyard."[49] In his 1996 bid for the Republican presidential nomination, Pat Buchanan vied for votes from northeastern and midwestern factory workers who had lost, or feared losing, their jobs: "We have a government that is frozen in the ice of its own indifference, a government that does not listen anymore to the forgotten men and women who work in the forges and factories and plants and businesses of this country. We have instead a government that is too busy taking phone calls from lobbyists for foreign countries and the corporate contributors of the *Fortune 500*."[50]

It is not simply disgruntled hard hats who are being displaced. At the Los Alamos laboratory in New Mexico, 12 percent of the workforce has been eliminated since the Cold War ended. Director Sig Hecker: "It used to be so simple. The comfort and security are gone."[51] Aerospace workers, too, were hit hard by the fall of communism. In California, for example, there were 707,000 aerospace and high-technology employees in 1988; by 1996, the figure had fallen to 473,000. Cities such as Torrence and Long Beach— mainstays of the defense industry—were awash in "For Sale" signs.[52] Defense industry workers also felt the effects of the Cold War's end. Rockwell International, the nation's fourteenth largest defense contractor, sold its defense and aerospace units to Boeing for $3.2 billion. Texas Instruments, number twenty-two among defense contractors, also placed its business up for sale. Lockheed announced in late November 1996 that it was laying off 1,600 defense workers. Altogether, some 1 million employees in the defense industry have lost their jobs. Lawrence Korb, a former assistant secretary of defense in the Reagan administration, put it thus: "Stealth technology isn't making it in conversion."[53]

For many Americans, the Cold War provided a strange economic benefit. During the Cold War's zenith, median take-home pay grew at an annual rate of 2 percent in constant dollars.[54] A prosperous economy translated into good news for incumbents. In those presidential elections when the economy grew, incumbents—or members of their party—were reelected. (The sole exception to this "iron law" of politics occurred in 1968 amid considerable dissension over the Vietnam War.) But even this old rule, like so much else in the post–Cold War period, has been cast aside. George Bush presided over modest economic growth in 1992, but he lost anyway. Likewise, Bill Clinton saw the economy expand slightly during his first two years in office—but that did not stop the Republican takeover of Congress in 1994. One reason for the profound public anxiety over the economy was that from 1975 to 1995, median real wages grew by a mere 1 *percent!*[55] Moreover, the high-powered mergers that dominated the business pages added a new phrase to the lexicon: "corporate downsizing." The 1995 merger of Chase Manhattan and Chemical Banks, for example, resulted in a loss of 12,000 jobs.[56] The result in this and other well-publicized cases were leaner, meaner companies—but often at the expense of longtime employees. The number of jobs lost was staggering: from 1992 to 1996, fifteen giant corporations, many of which were once mainstays of the Cold War, "downsized" their workforces, resulting in layoffs ranging from 18,000 to 123,000 (see Table 7.1).

By late 1996, layoff announcements from corporate boardrooms had become so widespread that 49 percent of Americans told pollsters that they were "very worried" or "somewhat worried" that they or someone in their household "might be out of work and looking for a job for any reason."[57] These concerns were eminently justified. By November 1996, the number of layoffs announced by major companies had increased 14 percent. In fact,

TABLE 7.1
The Downsizing of Corporate America, 1992–1996

Company	Jobs Lost	Percent of Workforce
AT&T	123,000	30
IBM	122,000	35
General Motors	99,400	29
Boeing	61,000	37
Sears, Roebuck	50,000	15
Digital Equipment	29,800	26
Lockheed Martin	29,100	17
Bell South	21,000	23
McDonnell Douglas	21,000	20
Pacific Telesis	19,000	19
Delta Airlines	18,800	14
GTE	18,400	14
NYNEX	17,400	33
Eastman Kodak	16,800	13
Baxter International	16,600	23

SOURCE: Louis Uchitelle and N. R. Klienfield, "On the Battlefields of Business, Millions of Casualties," *New York Times,* March 3, 1996, p. A-1.

since 1980, nearly three-quarters of all American households saw a family member, friend, relative, or neighbor lose a job.[58]

The front pages of many newspapers gave rise to their concerns. Less than a week after reporting a 1995 quarterly profit of $636 million, Mobil fired 4,700 people (9 percent of its worldwide workforce).[59] In January 1996, AT&T, one of the industry giants, announced that it was eliminating 40,000 jobs. Chairman Robert E. Allen expressed sympathy but observed that "our people now realize that the contract [the implied promise of lifetime job security in exchange for hard work and loyalty] does not exist anymore."[60] One AT&T worker expressed her dismay: "When I was hired for the phone company I thought, 'This is it! I'm going to retire with this company.' Now I don't know what's going to happen tomorrow."[61] Clinton's first-term labor secretary, Robert Reich, worried about the impact of these layoffs on the American psyche: "All the old bargains, it seems, have been breached," he said. "The economic bargain was that if you worked hard and your company prospered, you would share the fruits of success. There was a cultural bargain, too, echoing the same themes of responsibility and its rewards: live by the norms of your community—take care of your family, obey the law, treat your neighbors with respect, love your country—and you'll feel secure in the certainty that everyone else would behave that way."[62]

But one by one the "old bargains" were being torn asunder in the post–Cold War era. From 1992 to 1996, an estimated 12 million Americans had been subjected to "corporate restructuring."[63] Personnel officers masked the bad news by referring to planned layoffs as a "payroll adjustment," "personnel surplus reduction," "job separation," "reduction-in-force," "redundancy elimination," "refocusing of the skill mix," "resource reallocation," "reorganization," "right-sizing," or a "workforce imbalance correction." The newly unemployed also had their own special terminology, calling themselves "bumped," "decruited," "dehired," "deselected," "destaffed," "discontinued," "disemployed," "dislocated," "displaced," "downsized," "involuntarily separated," "nonretained," "nonrenewed," "severed," "surplussed," or "vocationally relocated."[64] But the euphemisms did not hide a harsh reality. As one graphics designer said: "Downsizing—I hate that word. You just blew my life away, and you're telling me I was downsized."[65] A black state representative from Ohio observed that "downsizing" was the language of white America: "Downsizing—that's a middle-class term. Now it's affected the white middle-class management where no one ever thought it would go."[66]

Downsizing has not been limited to corporate America. Within the halls of government, many mid-level managers have seen their jobs disappear. The emergence of a global economy has meant that national governments—including that of the United States—are losing control over their financial destinies and are no longer able to honor the old bargains. Most present-day government bureaucracies were patterned after the corporate model, and like their big business brethren they are having trouble meeting the demands of the post–Cold War era. Since 1993, the federal civilian workforce has been trimmed by 272,900 employees—making it the smallest since John Kennedy was president. Nearly $58 billion has been cut from the federal payroll, and 16,000 pages of rules and regulations have been excised from the *Federal Register*, thanks to Vice President Al Gore's "reinventing government" initiatives.[67] These cuts, although politically popular, have contributed to what Robert Reich sees as an "anxious middle class":

> In an astonishingly short period of time, the old middle class has splintered. The erosion of a sense of shared prospects poses what may be our nation's most critical challenge of the post–Cold War era. Broad trends that have converged and accelerated since the middle 1970s have split the old middle class into three new groups. An underclass largely trapped in center cities, increasingly isolated from the core economy; an overclass of those who are positioned profitably to ride the wave of change; and in between, the largest group, an anxious class, most of whom hold jobs but are justifiably uneasy about their own standing and fearful for their children's future.[68]

Those who remain at the top of the corporate ladder contrast with the anxious class. After AT&T fired 40,000 workers, the New York Stock Exchange added $6 billion to the company's stock value.[69] AT&T chairman Allen, who held many shares of AT&T stock, made more than $5 million after the layoffs were announced.[70] A survey of seventy-six of the nation's largest corporations found that in 1995 the total compensation package for chief executives (including stock options) rose 31 percent to nearly $5 million, increasing the ratio between the typical worker and executive—once 30 to 1 in the 1960s—to more than 100 to 1, the largest gap between workers and managers in the industrialized world.[71] Economist Lester Thurow attributes the growing disparity to the end of the Cold War. According to Thurow, corporate executives were reluctant to raise their salaries after World War II because they were "scared to hell" over communism: "If you had done this twenty-five years ago, the Communists would have been winning elections in France and Italy. The socialist parties would have been doing well in places like Germany and England. And in the United States, the Democrats would have been moving very quickly to the left." Now, says Thurow, "with socialism and communism gone—with the Democrats depending on the same financial sources as the Republicans for political funds—as a capitalist CEO, I don't have anything to worry about."[72]

The collapse of socialism and communism as political alternatives to free-market capitalism means that political leaders have few weapons left in their arsenals. President Clinton can admonish corporate executives to exercise more community responsibility, as he did in 1996: "No one should lose a job for short-term considerations that are not necessary for the long-term well-being of the profitable enterprise. People my age, fifty-year-old men, are being told they're not important anymore: 'Thank you very much for the last twenty-five years, you figure out how to send your kids to college.'"[73] But apart from using the presidency as a bully pulpit, Clinton has done little more than give corporate heads a slap on the wrist.

As many discover that their "lifetime" jobs are no more, a widespread insecurity has taken hold. Most of those laid-off—both within the government and in the large corporations—had some college exposure. Unlike steelworkers from Bethlehem, who became inured to the inevitable layoffs and rehires, only 35 percent of these newly unemployed find better jobs than the ones they lost. Many despair for the future, as historian David Herbert McDonald has observed:

> It is important to recall that throughout American history, discontent has always had less to do with material well-being than with expectations and anxiety. You read that 40,000 people are laid-off at AT&T and a shiver goes down your back that says, "That could be me," even if the fear is exaggerated. What we are reacting against is the end of a predictable kind of life, just as the people who left the predictable rhythms of the farm in the 1880s felt such a loss of control once they were in the cities.[74]

Expectations of some brighter future are at the heart of the American Dream. James Truslow Adams coined the phrase "American dream" in describing the life of President John Quincy Adams. Historian Adams wrote that the sixth president believed his country stood for opportunity, "the chance to grow into something bigger and finer, as bigger and finer appealed to him."[75] For nearly two centuries, the American Dream has gone unchallenged. But upon leaving their polling booths in 1996, Americans no longer accepted the American Dream as an entitlement: 33 percent said "life for the next generation will be worse than it is today"; just 29 percent answered "better," and 35 percent said "about the same."[76] A voter from Mason City, Iowa, spoke for many: "I'm starting to wonder if the American Dream still exists." A fellow Iowan who fretted about his children echoed this concern: "There's no future for them. There's nothing there. No job. The American Dream just doesn't exist for them."[77]

Public worry about whether the American Dream remains viable is a new phenomena. Historian Oscar Handlin once wrote that even during the Great Depression "there was a sense of hope that a better society of some sort, a new twentieth century society, would emerge."[78] Although the economic dislocations of the late 1990s bear no resemblance to the enormity of the Great Depression, the widespread belief that the American Dream may be dying is a shocking phenomena that worries most politicians. Of those personally laid-off or who had a family member lose a job, 69 percent were "angry at both political parties."[79] Taking note of these figures, President Clinton posed three challenges to those in Congress: "How do we make the American Dream of opportunity a reality for all who are willing to work for it? How do we preserve our old and enduring values as we move into the future? And how do we meet these challenges together, as one America?"[80]

But many Americans found these tasks especially daunting. Diane Ortel spoke of her family's plight to an inquiring journalist while seated at a picnic table at the 1994 Illinois State Fair:

> Everybody wants to cut things, so they all get up and say, "I'll cut, cut, cut." Well, one of those jobs they cut was my husband's. And we found out he was losing his job the same week I found out I was pregnant with my third child.
>
> I'd like these politicians to know what these cuts mean—to real people with real families. My husband has a master's degree, and I'm a registered nurse. And we're struggling, man. We're driving an '87 van with 150,000 miles on it. And college money for my kids? Not even in my dreams. We just don't have it.[81]

Clinton seemed to have taken Ortel's pulse, telling a gathering of Baptist ministers, "We still haven't quite got the rhythm right."[82] Part of the national arrhythmia is due to the letdown following the Cold War. After surveying the carnage at Waterloo in 1815, Lord Wellington remarked that there is "only one thing worse than winning a battle, and that was losing it."[83] Clinton has expressed similar sentiments, noting that the post–Cold War world is "unsettling," adding that in a period of profound change "we are vulnerable to getting out of our rhythm."[84] The public "funk" (Clinton's word)[85] is evident in the historical revisionism that has followed the Cold War: 77 percent tell pollsters that "nobody" won the Cold War—ignoring the large slabs of the Berlin Wall on display at presidential libraries from Boston to California.[86] Since the Cold War ended without so much as a gunshot—let alone the launching of nuclear missiles—it is astounding that so many should be so pessimistic. According to one 1995 poll, 53 percent characterized the country's troubles as "deep and serious"; only 40 percent believed they were "no worse than at any other time in recent years."[87] Bill Clinton fretted about these numbers: "When I ran for this job I said I wanted to restore the American Dream and to bring the American people together. I have now come to the conclusion, having watched this drama unfold here in the last two-and-a-half-years, that I cannot do the first unless we can do the latter. We can't restore the American Dream unless we can find some way to bring the American people closer together. Therefore, how we resolve our differences is as important as what specific position we advocate."[88]

But instead of coming together, nations across the globe split apart as ideological conflicts gave way to ethnic rivalries and nationalistic desires. In the former Soviet Union, citizens in Chechnya took to the streets in a revolution against Russian rule. In Eastern Europe, a bloody battle of "ethnic cleansing" raged in the remnants of the former Yugoslavia. After a short period of postcommunist unity, the Czechs and Slovaks called it quits, as nationalism proved too powerful a tug to keep the two peoples together. In Canada, dissolution was narrowly (and perhaps only temporarily) averted in 1995 following the defeat of the separatist referendum in Quebec. Meanwhile, in another corner of the globe, Hutus and Tutsis in Rwanda were busy slaughtering each other after that country's president was assassinated. By late 1996, a half-million had been killed in this most recent outbreak of genocide.

In the United States, old racial divisions and new ethnic ones replaced the spirit of *e pluribus unum*. In the wake of the not-guilty verdict in the O. J. Simpson trial, the conclusions drawn by the Kerner Commission in 1968 were given renewed force: "Our nation is moving toward two societies, one black, one white—separate and unequal."[89] During a 1995 House debate over welfare reform, Cynthia McKinney, a black Democrat from Georgia, read a letter from a white man in Texas that referred to "Negro females who pop out bastard Negro children like monkeys in the jungles." Florida Republican John Mica responded by holding a sign reading "Don't feed the alligators." A Wyoming Republican subsequently drew a parallel between wayward wolves and welfare recipients. An exasperated Sam Gibbons, a Florida Democrat, exclaimed: "We have a millionaire from Florida comparing children to alligators, and a gentlewoman in red has compared children to wolves. That tops all!"[90]

A large dose of anger has added to the undercurrent of racial hatred that dominates virtually every arena of public discourse—often reducing it to a new form of "entertainment" as one combatant screams at another. Shouting has created several well-known public personas such as John McLaughlin, Pat Buchanan, Robert Novak, Eleanor Clift, and Fred Barnes. Absenting himself from the presidential fray in 1996, retired general Colin Powell took note of the blistering attacks from some of his conservative fellow Republicans: "When you move away from just disagreeing with somebody's views and you move into ad hominem attacks to destroy character, you're adding to the incivility that exists in our political life right now and which we ought to do something about."[91] Not surprisingly, Bill Clinton agreed, telling a Democratic gathering after the 1996 campaign, "We cannot afford to continue the politics of personal destruction and division that have taken too much of the lifeblood of this country."[92]

Lacking a common communist enemy, many Democrats and Republicans have found one in each other. Bipartisanship, once a hallmark of the Cold War, has given way to an extreme form of partisan attack. Denouncing Bill Clinton's 1994 anticrime legislation, Newt Gingrich said: "I don't want my daughter and wife raped and killed. I don't want to see my neighborhood destroyed. People like me are what stands between us and Auschwitz. I see evil around me every day."[93] Political scientist Clyde Wilcox reports that Gingrich advised Republican congressional candidates to use "contrast words" such as "decay," "failure," "shallow," "traitors," "pathetic," "corrupt," "cheat," "steal," "devour," "self-serving," "criminal rights," "incompetent," and "sick" in labeling their Democratic opponents.[94] Joseph Gaylord, a Gingrich aide, advised his client that "important issues can be of limited value." Citing Willie Horton as illustrative of how a "minor detail" can be exaggerated, Gaylord told Gingrich to "go negative" early and "never back off."[95] The tactic worked, helping long-frustrated Republicans win a congressional majority. Forgoing another Senate term in 1996, Nebraska Democrat James J. Exon cited "the ever-increasing vicious polarization of the electorate, the us-against-them mentality," adding: "The traditional art of workable compromises for the ultimate good of all, the essence of democracy, has demonstrably eroded. The hate level fueled by attack ads has unfortunately become the measure of a successful campaign. As long as money and plenty of it continues to pour in, absent campaign spending limits, the deterioration will continue."[96]

Many other public officials joined Exon at the exits. In 1996, twelve senators (including Bill Bradley, Sam Nunn, Paul Simon, and Mark Hatfield) retired—the largest number since the Seventeenth Amendment (which allowed for direct election of senators) was adopted in 1913. In the House, a record forty-one members (twenty-six Democrats and fifteen Republicans) called it quits. Jean Bethke Elshtain described some of these retiring members as victims of the "politics of displacement" that has "two trajectories": "In the first, everything private—from one's sexual practices to blaming one's parents for a lack of 'self-esteem' becomes grist for the public mill. In the second, everything public—from the grounds on which politicians are judged to health policies to gun regulations—is itself privatized, the playing out of a psychodrama on a grand scale. That is, we fret as much about a politician's affairs as his foreign policy."[97]

One of the battle-scarred survivors of the "politics of displacement," Bill Clinton, has admonished both parties: "Our civic life is suffering in America today. Citizens are working together less and shouting at each other more. The common bonds of community, which have been the great strength of our country from its very beginning, are badly frayed." A 1995 survey of residents in Dallas and Fort Worth, Texas, showed just how badly torn those bonds had become: 72 percent said folks "seem angrier than they used to be"; one-half said crime made them angry, and 49 percent said they got mad watching the news at least once a week. Most expressed their anger by yelling, cursing, crying, or praying.[98] Similar results were posted in a *New York Times* poll that found 53 percent saying that their workplaces had become "more angry" in recent years.[99] As Elshtain has observed: "All human lives are lived on the edge of quiet desperation. We must all be rescued from time to time of fear and sorrow."[100]

It is ironic that Americans should be so profoundly discouraged, since it was their steadfastness that sustained them and their presidents during the long Cold War. In 1960, political scientist E. E. Schattschneider wrote:

> Today our view of politics is greatly modified by the fact that the United States is involved in a titanic struggle for survival. Burdens that were inconceivable a few years ago seem to have become a permanent part of the public function. The primacy of foreign policy calls for a new kind of politics involving a wholly new calculus. The government now needs above everything else the steady support of the public, and this support cannot be had without a new scale of public involvement in public life. This is the modern problem of democratic government. The price of support is participation. The choice is between participation and propaganda, between democratic and dictatorial ways of *changing consent into support because consent is no longer enough.*[101]

Harry Truman reflected on the importance of public consent in his 1953 Farewell Address:

> As I have thought about our worldwide struggle with the communists these past eight years—day in and day out—I have never once doubted that you, the people of our country, have the will to do what is necessary to win this terrible fight against communism. I know the people of this country have that will and determination, and I have always depended on it. Because I have been sure of that, I have been able to make necessary decisions even though

they called for sacrifices by all of us. And I have not been wrong in my judgment of the American people.[102]

Truman's Democratic successor, Bill Clinton, had no such assurances. In 1995, Clinton described an anxious public that feels "like they're lost in the fun house, they're in a room where something can hit them from any direction at anytime."[103] In many ways, Clinton's "fun house" was a metaphor for his presidency. During his first term, 10 million jobs were created—an expansion greater than the go-go eighties. But Clinton found that voters were not applauding his "huge amount of success" because "too many of our people are still working harder for less and less." Clinton noted that "too many of our people still can't be sure of having a job next year or next month." Looking ahead, Clinton said his job is to "get people out of their funk about it."[104]

But the churlishness expressed by hard-pressed Americans is only part of the problem. The other is the absence of a clearly defined enemy. Enemies define politics and give nationalism its meaning—thereby sharpening the sense of national purpose. This is especially true during wartime. But when the conflict ceases, anomie results. Following the success of the Revolutionary War, Richard Henry Lee bemoaned his new country's plight: "Unhappily for us, immediately after our extrication from a cruel and unnatural war, luxury and dissipation overran the country, banishing all that economy, frugality, and industry which had been exhibited during the war. I fear it is more vicious manners, than mistakes in form, that we must seek for the causes of the present discontent."[105] Scholar William James observed that war was "the romance of history" and searched, unsuccessfully, for "the moral equivalent of war." James observed that "war has been the only force that can discipline a whole community, and until an equivalent discipline is organized, I believe that war must have its way."[106] Winston Churchill voiced similar sentiments following World War I:

> Why should war be the only purpose capable of uniting us in comradeship? Why should war be the only cause large enough to call forth really great and fine sacrifice? Look at the wonderful, superb things people will do to carry on a war and win a victory. Look at what they will give up. Look at what toil they achieve—what risks, what suffering, what marvelous ingenuity, what heroic and splendid qualities they display. All for war. Nothing is too good for war! Why cannot we have some of it for peace? Why is war to have all the splendors, all the nobleness, all the courage and loyalty? Why should peace have nothing but the squabbles and selfishness and the pettiness of daily life? All the arts and science that we use at war are standing by us now ready to help us in peace. Only one thing do we require—a common principle of action, a plain objective that everyone can understand and work for.[107]

Other nations have had similar experiences following great victories. Charles DeGaulle once observed that France "was never her true self unless she was engaged in a great enterprise."[108] The Cold War was a "great enterprise," but now that it is over the United States seems adrift. Richard Nixon rightly noted that the demise of the Soviet Union had several unintended consequences: "Historically there is always a period of exhaustion after a military victory. Victory in the Cold War was not just military. It was a complex ideological, political, and economic triumph. Our exhaustion is therefore felt in all these dimensions simultaneously."[109]

Who's "Us"? Who's "Them"?

One day in 1971, Treasury Secretary John Connally, still a Democrat, visited his Republican boss, President Nixon. As Connally struggled to make his way past the Vietnam War demonstrators outside the White House, he told Nixon that in politics having enemies was not necessarily bad—especially when they were an obnoxious but small minority. Nixon, a master at the "us-versus-them" invective, liked to tell this story. According to his account, Connally told Nixon how another master at "us-versus-them" politics, Franklin D. Roosevelt, once advised a gathering of the Young Democrats that if a leader did not have enemies he had better create them.[110] As Vice President Al Gore noted in accepting renomination in 1996, "You can judge a president by the enemies he is willing to make."[111]

Brooks Adams once quipped that American politics consists of the systemic organization of hatreds.[112] Indeed, the politics of divide and conquer is as old as the history books. Since the founding of the republic, partisans have aroused passions by urging potential supporters to become "one of us." The Constitution, for example, opened with the audacious phrase, "We, the people," a claim to which opposition leader Patrick Henry took special offense: "What right had they to say, *We, the People*? My political curiosity, exclusive of my anxious solicitude for the public welfare, leads me to ask, who authorized them to speak the language of *We, the People*, instead of *We, the states*?"[113] Following the Civil War, passions flared anew as Republicans and Democrats sought to demonize each other. In 1866, Oliver P. Morton, Indiana's Republican governor, delivered a blistering attack on the so-called Loyal Opposition:

> Every unregenerate rebel . . . calls himself a Democrat. Every bounty jumper, every deserter, every sneak who ran away from the draft. Every man . . . who murdered Union prisoners . . . who contrived hellish schemes to introduce into Northern cities the wasting pestilence of yellow fever, calls himself a Democrat. Every wolf in sheep's clothing . . . everyone who shoots down Negroes in the streets, burns Negro school-houses and meeting-houses, and murders women and children by the light of their flaming dwellings, calls himself a Democrat. . . . In short, the Democratic party may be described as a common sewer and loathsome receptacle, into which is emptied every element of trea-

son North and South, and every element of inhumanity and barbarism which has dishonored the age.[114]

During the New Deal, the mental pictures of "us" and "them" were so sharply redrawn that they endured throughout the Cold War and lingered after it. Seeking reelection in 1936, Franklin Roosevelt portrayed his Republican opponents as more concerned with corporate profits than the general welfare, using pejorative words such as "princes of privilege" and "economic royalists" to describe them. Speaking before a large gathering at Madison Square Garden a few days before the balloting, Roosevelt said of his enemies: "Never before in all our history have those forces been so united against one candidate as they stand today. They are unanimous in their *hate* for me—*and I welcome their hatred*." The crowd applauded, but the president was not finished: "I should like to have it said of my first administration that in it the forces of selfishness and of lust for power met their *match*." At this Democrats lustily cheered, but Roosevelt cried, "Wait a moment!"—as he did not want the audience stepping on his best line: "I should like to have it said of my second administration that *in it these forces met their master*." Roosevelt biographer James MacGregor Burns described the response as a "raucous, almost animal-like roar [that] burst from the crowd, died away, and then rose again in wave after wave."[115]

The Cold War created new voter images, which are described at length in this book. Republicans successfully portrayed themselves as patriotic nationalists better able to defend the United States against tough Soviet adversaries, whereas Democrats were caricatured as muddleheaded in combating the "communist conspiracy." This new "us-versus-them" mental image was placed alongside the pictures drawn by Franklin Roosevelt. With the end of the Cold War, some Americans have found it hard to jettison the old scrapbook. Warren Christopher, former secretary of state under Clinton, warned: "Americans have a deeply ingrained sense of fear of Russia. It's a virus that has not been conquered. It still lies there in the body politic, waiting to be stirred up by some politician or other."[116] Texas Republican Richard Armey painted one of the most vivid reminders of the Cold War portraits. In 1993, Armey likened Hillary Rodham Clinton's Health Care Security Act to the ideas of Karl Marx. Ominously, the future House majority leader included the first lady's staff in his guilt-by-association charge, saying, "All her friends are Marxists." Democratic Congressional Campaign Committee head Vic Fazio issued a vehement rejoinder: "Attacking the First Lady as a communist is absolutely despicable. The Cold War is over and the Republicans have run out of enemies, so they have turned to pathetic red-baiting and old smear tactics of decades ago." Armey apologized, noting he had "crossed the line."[117] But that did not stop his incendiary rhetoric. After the 1994 election, Armey compared Franklin Roosevelt, John Kennedy, and Lyndon Johnson to Stalin and Mao Zedong: "Behind our New Deals and

New Frontiers and Great Societies, you will find, *with a difference only in power and nerve*, the same sort of person who gave the world its Five Year Plans and Great Leaps Forward—the Soviet and Chinese counterparts."[118]

Other Republicans also saw red. In 1994, a House candidate from Vermont named John Carroll maintained that his incumbent opponent, the socialist Bernie Sanders, enjoyed support from "a small band of fellow-travelers" who, he claimed, subscribed to a "gloomy, angry vision of class struggle."[119] Sanders, meanwhile, summoned Franklin Roosevelt from the dead, claiming he was "a fighter for working people" and that his GOP opponent favored "big money interests."[120] Sanders, one of the most liberal members of Congress with a perfect score from the Americans for Democratic Action, defied the Republican juggernaut, capturing 50 percent of the vote to Carroll's 47 percent.[121] One year later, Randy "Duke" Cunningham, a Republican congressman from California, assailed the "socialist tendencies" of the Democrats and castigated the party's "communist supporters," singling out then-Labor Secretary Robert Reich for special attention: "He goes along with Karl Marx in many of his writings."[122] In 1996, Socialist Sanders and Republican Cunningham won easy reelection victories.

Despite Republican efforts to paint Democrats red by association, the Cold War no longer remains an organizing image in American politics. Its fading portrait poses a significant challenge for the GOP. Just as the successes of the New Deal contributed to the Democrats' downfall during the 1960s, Republican boasts of how they mobilized voters against the Soviets (and the Democrats) have created problems at a much quicker pace. Former defense secretary James Schlesinger observed that the end of the Cold War deprives conservatives of "the stark simplicity" and "remarkable clarity" that battling communism once provided.[123] Schlesinger's point was given renewed emphasis in 1993, when President Clinton said of his Russian counterparts, "We are partners and future allies."[124] Sixty-three percent in a 1993 poll said Russia either was only a "minor threat" or was "not a threat at all."[125] The Republican maxim of "peace through strength" now has the musty aura of an ancient Model-T. New enemies must be found.

Clearly, the United States (and the Republican party) do, not lack potential adversaries. Iraq's Saddam Hussein remains a tempting target. Libya's Colonel Muammar Gadhafi also continues to make mischief, and Iran is still viewed as a threat. Muslim extremists, especially after the 1993 bombing of the World Trade Center in New York, give many Americans pause for concern. Three years later, Americans were further startled when a terrorist bomb killed nineteen U.S. service personnel stationed in Saudi Arabia. But the desperate acts of small bands of international terrorists are not the only potential threats to U.S. security. Nuclear terrorism from a foreign source constitutes the single greatest danger to U.S. shores in the twenty-first century. Communist regimes in North Korea and China—not to mention Cuba—still have the capacity to make mischief that can galvanize public opinion, and Republicans claimed Clinton ignored these potential Soviet-like bears in the woods: "Terrorist states have made a comeback during Bill Clinton's administration. . . . The governments of North Korea, Iran, Syria, Iraq, Libya, Sudan, and Cuba must know that America's first line of defense is not our shoreline, but their own borders. We will be proactive, not reactive, to strike the hand of terrorism before it can be raised against Americans."[126] As the Republican platform writers suggest, rogue states can be useful political enemies. To vigorous applause at the Republican National Convention, Bob Dole said: "On my first day in office, I will put terrorists on notice: If you harm one American, you harm all Americans. And America will pursue you to the ends of the earth. In short, don't mess with us if you're not prepared to suffer the consequences."[127]

At home, the FBI gave increased attention to the activities of small militia groups following the April 1995 bombing of the federal building in Oklahoma City. As domestic and foreign terrorist activities kept intelligence agencies occupied, former CIA director James Woolsey observed that although the United States had "slain a large [Soviet] dragon . . . we now live in a jungle filled with a bewildering variety of poisonous snakes, and in many ways the dragon was easier to keep track of."[128]

Others suggest that our real enemies are not religious militants or maniacal leaders but emerging economic giants. The end of the Cold War has given way to a new international struggle that involves a heightened competition for trade and for protecting high-technology secrets. The losers of World War II, Germany and Japan, are often singled out for special attention, as is the People's Republic of China. Germany and Japan run large trade imbalances with the United States, and China, which has quickly attained a favorable trade balance with the United States, seems determined to enter the twenty-first century by stealing as many high-tech secrets from the United States as possible. Various national security apparatuses have pursued those engaged in economic and technical espionage. Meanwhile, many fretted about another kind of economic war—the loss of jobs to Third World nations. Many agreed with Ross Perot that the North American Free Trade Agreement, known as NAFTA, would emit "a giant sucking sound" of American jobs being consumed by low-wage, unskilled Mexicans. During the 1996 Republican presidential primaries, Pat Buchanan carried Perot's banner: "When I am elected president of the United States, there will be no more NAFTA sellouts of American workers. There will be no more GATT deals done for the benefit of Wall Street bankers. And there will be no more $50 billion bailouts of Third World Socialists, whether in Moscow or Mexico City."[129]

A return to a pre–World War I "Fortress America" nationalism has been a significant theme of the post–Cold War era. During the Cold War, Americans welcomed refugees from the Captive Nations. After the Cold War, refugees either escaping the terror of despotic rulers or wanting to stake their claim to the American Dream lost their cachet with voters (except those fleeing Castro's Cuba). The arrival of the greatest number of immigrants since the wave of eastern, central, and southern European ethnics in 1901–1910 caused anti-immigrant fervor to spread.[130] Passions ran high in vote-rich states such as California, Florida, New Jersey, Texas, Illinois, New York, and California. During the 1994 midterm elections, Californians ratified Proposition 187, which banned all state spending on illegal immigrants and required police to report suspected illegals to the California Department of Justice and the U.S. Immigration Service. Television sets flickered with pictures of illegal Mexicans swarming across the border as an announcer intoned, "They just keep coming."[131] As the campaign escalated, Republicans Jack Kemp and William Bennett denounced the measure, claiming it was "politically unwise and fundamentally at odds with the best tradition and spirit of our party."[132] Despite their protestations, Proposition 187 won handily, 59 percent to 41 percent. But whereas whites gave it 64 percent backing, 69 percent of Hispanics disapproved—a sharp delineation of the new "us-versus-them" politics.[133] Pete Wilson, the GOP governor who made the ballot initiative a cornerstone of his reelection bid, won by a nearly equal vote of 55 percent to 41 percent. Two years later, Kemp realigned his immigration stance once he was chosen by Bob Dole to be the 1996 Republican vice presidential nominee.

Immigration is an old issue in American politics. In the late eighteenth century, the anti-Federalists railed against the open-door policies of some states: "To what purpose have you expended so freely the blood and treasures of this country? To have a government with unlimited powers administered by foreigners?"[134] With the coming of the Irish in the 1840s and the Europeans in the late nineteenth century, immigration became a vibrant issue and gave renewed meaning to the "us-versus-them" politics that characterizes much of American political history. In 1854, Protestant militants used gunpowder to destroy a Catholic church in Boston. That same year, the Know-Nothing Party, an anti-immigrant, anti-Catholic coalition, captured all the statewide offices in Massachusetts and won impressive numbers in the U.S. Congress. Three-quarters of a century later, ethnicity remained an organizing force in American politics. The *Springfield Republican* reported that when voters discussed politics in the 1928 contest between Catholic Alfred E. Smith and Quaker Herbert Hoover they talked in "terms of French, Irish, Pole, and Yankee or Catholic and non-Catholic." The paper concluded, "Votes will undoubtedly be cast on other issues, particularly prohibition and prosperity, but when you get down to the ground there's dirt!"[135]

By the late 1990s, immigration once again divided Americans into new categories of "us" versus "them." A *Time*/CNN poll found a 10-point increase from 1985 to 1994 in those who wanted to "strictly limit immigration."[136] The issue had a special resonance among those affected by layoffs: 74 percent wanted the number of immigrants cut.[137] Pat Buchanan attempted to exploit the growing anti-immigrant sentiment: "I think God made all people good. But if we had to take a million immigrants in, say, Zulus, next year, or Englishmen, and put them in Virginia, which group would be easier to assimilate and would cause less problems for the people of Virginia?"[138] Buchanan proposed building a doubled security fence along the most porous section of the border with Mexico and advocated a nationwide Proposition 187.[139] The 1996 Republican platform highlighted the immigration issue, noting that illegal immigration had reached "crisis proportions": "Illegal aliens should not receive public benefits other than emergency aid, and those who become parents while illegally in the United States should not be qualified to claim benefits for their offspring."[140] But legal immigrants were not spared the Republican party's wrath, as congressional Republicans attached a provision in the 1996 welfare reform bill denying benefits to them. Alfredo Alvarez, a legal immigrant from Honduras, became a naturalized citizen because of such GOP-led hostility: "I love this country, but I feel unwanted. I feel like unless I am a true American, the government could one day knock on my door and tell me, 'Alfredo, go back to Honduras!'"[141] Such reactions notwithstanding, the Republican-controlled House of Representatives responded by passing legislation that doubled the number of U.S. Border Patrol agents to 10,000 and speeding the deportation of immigrants who use false documents. Yielding to White House pressure, however, Republicans dropped provisions that would have prevented states from providing free public education to children of illegal immigrants, deported legal immigrants who use more than twelve months of public assistance in a seven-year period, and barred both legal and illegal immigrants who are HIV-positive or have AIDS from enrolling in federally financed treatment programs.[142] Such harsh proposals hurt the Dole-Kemp ticket—especially among Hispanics. Clinton's support among that strategically placed immigrant group rose 11 percent from his 1992 score. Even staunchly pro-Republican Cubans cast aside their hatred of communism and Fidel Castro to give Clinton 40 percent of their votes, support that proved crucial in Clinton's victory in vote-rich Florida. First-time voter Jesse Henriquez, a forty-eight-year-old immigrant from El Salvador, captured the sentiments of many Hispanics: "The only way we can tell the people that we are working hard and that Latinos should not be blamed for all the country's problems is to register and vote. . . . Little by little, we are telling people, 'No more Proposition 187s.'"[143]

A related issue that enhanced the new immigrant-based "us-versus-them" politics was a proposed federal law that would have made English the official language of the United States. Republicans strongly favored the measure, and twenty-two states (including Clinton's Arkansas) had already passed it.[144] The 1996 Republican platform strongly urged the adoption of English as the official national language: "The use of English is indispensable to all who wish to participate fully in our society and realize the American dream."[145] The Republican platform writers reflected the position of their presidential candidate. In 1995, Bob Dole told a gathering of American Legionnaires, "We must stop the practice of multilingual education as a means of instilling ethnic pride, or as a therapy for low self-esteem, or out of elitist guilt over a culture built on the traditions of the West."[146] His erstwhile rival for the 1996 Republican presidential nomination, Pat Buchanan, agreed, suggesting that all federal funding for bilingual education be stopped forthwith.[147] Whether immigration will remain a defining issue for the vast majority of Americans remains an open question. Asked about Pete Wilson's support of Proposition 187 in the 1994 California governor's race, a San Francisco man told a pollster: "It's not an issue. It's a red herring. It's an issue Wilson created." Another respondent agreed: "These are all red herrings—about foreign aid and all that stuff."[148] Even *Republican* 1996 presidential primary voters had a similar view: 51 percent believed the United States should welcome some immigrants; 42 percent said the country could not afford any new immigrants.[149]

But other so-called wedge issues remain that generally favor Republicans. Crime is one: The GOP "tough-guy" approach to criminals (revenge, not rehabilitation) remains popular. Ever since George Bush faulted Michael Dukakis for being a "card-carrying member of the ACLU"—code words for "soft on crime"—Republicans have resisted any encroachment on this sacred turf. When it came to battling crime, the 1996 Republican platform took its inspiration from the Cold War: "Making Americans safe again will be a tremendous undertaking, in its own way as heroic as was the liberation of Europe from a different kind of criminal half a century ago."[150] Thus, Republicans were angered when President Clinton proposed a tough crime bill in 1994 that would add 100,000 police officers to the streets. Congressional leaders denounced the measure, claiming that Clinton was coddling criminals by including money for such items as midnight basketball. For his part, Bob Dole sought to portray himself as tough on crime, telling a cheering Republican National Convention: "As our many and voracious criminals go to bed tonight, at, say six in the morning, they had better pray that I lose the election. Because if I win, the lives of violent criminals are going to be hell."[151]

Other Republicans find a meaningful "us-versus-them" politics in the roiling cultural upheavals of the 1960s. Bob Dole tried to make Bill Clinton's veto of a Republican-sponsored ban on late-term abortions a touchstone during the 1996 presidential campaign. Pat Buchanan likened the sexual revolution that liberalized the nation's abortion laws to the "evil empire" of communism.[152] On the political hustings, Buchanan maintained that the Department of Education is populated with bureaucrats clad in "sandals and beads."[153] He took special aim at the National Endowment for the Arts, which during the Bush administration awarded grants to one artist who embalmed the cross of Christ in a jar of urine and another who liked to perform nude while smeared in chocolate. Echoing George Wallace, Buchanan promised that if he was elected "the first week [in office] I'm going to walk out of that White House down to the National Endowment for the Arts. I'm going to padlock the place and fumigate it."[154] Bob Dole castigated filmmakers in a much publicized Hollywood speech, noting that they posed "one of the greatest threats to American family values," adding: "Our music, movies, television and advertising regularly push the limits of decency, bombarding our children with destructive messages of casual violence and even more casual sex."[155] Colin Powell called for a restoration of "a sense of shame in our society."[156]

Dole and Powell have been joined in their critique by William Bennett, who was education secretary under Reagan, and Senator Joe Lieberman, Democrat from Connecticut, who are leading a "revolt of the revolted" to take the "trash" out of daytime talk shows. As Lieberman put it: "A growing number of Americans are sickened by the morass of sex, vulgarity, and violence that increasingly dominates our electronic media; and they are disgusted by what they see as the entertainment industry's abandonment of basic standards of decency, as if anything goes. The result is an increasingly debased culture that rejects, rather than reflects, the basic values that most Americans share."[157]

Others target their cultural warfare on liberals, homosexuals, and others who are not "like us." Responding to Clinton's 1996 State of the Union Address, Dole likened liberals to the post–Cold War equivalent of political subversives: "It's as though our government, our institutions, and our culture have been hijacked by liberals and are careening dangerously off course."[158] Neoconservative intellectual Irving Kristol agreed:

> There is no "after the Cold War" for me. So far from having ended, my cold war has increased in intensity, as sector after sector of American life has been ruthlessly corrupted by the liberal ethos. It is an ethos that aims simultaneously at political and social collectivism on the one hand, and moral anarchy on the other. . . . Now that the other "Cold War" is over, the real cold war has begun. We are far less prepared for this cold war, far more vulnerable to our enemy, than was the case with our victorious war against a global communist threat. We are, I sometimes feel, starting from ground zero, and it is a conflict I shall be passing on to my children and grandchildren. But it is a far more interesting cold war—intellectually interesting, spiritually interesting—than the cold war we have recently won, and I rather envy those young enough for the opportunities they will have to participate in it.[159]

Beside liberals, new-found enemies of Republicanism include homosexuals. In 1995, Bob Dole returned a $1,000 contribution from a gay Republican group, saying he did not want to create "the perception that we were buying into some special rights for any group, whether it is gays or anyone else."[160] Republicans often use the new "values politics" to object to homosexuals on cultural and political grounds—arguing that gays should not be given "special treatment" when it comes to protecting their job security, health care, or housing. In 1996, GOP lawmakers, sensing a political opportunity, passed the Defense of Marriage Act. This law precluded the states from recognizing gay marriages, defined marriage as the union between a man and a woman, and prohibited gay couples from receiving federal benefits. Not wanting to transform gay rights into a political liability for his reelection bid, President Clinton quietly signed the measure in a 12:50 A.M. ceremony at the White House.

But sensing that so-called values issues would not produce consistent victories, Republicans still searched for that big idea that would illuminate the post–Cold War era. Some suggested that an "empowerment agenda" was the answer. In 1993, Jack Kemp, Vin Weber, William Bennett, and Jeane Kirkpatrick formed Empower America, which cast itself as a "shadow government" that would "reshape the terms of our national political debate." Funded by GOP presidential contender Steve Forbes and listing former Tennessee governor Lamar Alexander and Speaker of the House Newt Gingrich as board members, Empower America promised to abide by three principles:

- Champion the advancement of freedom and democratic capitalism around the world through strong international leadership.
- Implement economic policies which encourage economic growth, entrepreneurship, job creation, and expanded opportunity for all people through lower taxes, sound money, and less government spending and regulation.
- Pursue new approaches to cultural and social issues such as education, poverty, crime, and health care and promote policies which empower families and people rather than government bureaucracies.[161]

Founding member Vin Weber maintains that "empowerment encompasses a principled approach to government activism that Republicans can feel comfortable with."[162] But Dick Darman, director of the Office of Management and Budget during the Bush years, has argued that empowerment is not a recipe for political success: "As far as I can tell, it adds up mostly to a slogan. It's like motherhood. You're for it. I'm for it. Who isn't for it?" Darman believed that Republicans could not become a majority party "by simply aggregating the alienated." Instead, he argued, the GOP must have a positive approach to society's problems and "slogans alone won't do it."[163]

But Democrats also lacked ideas during the 1990s. As mentioned in the previous chapter, Franklin Roosevelt gave his party a mission during the 1930s when New Dealers raised high the banner of big government. The emergence of the so-called Dixiecrat coalition (conservative southern Democrats and their Republican allies) following the defeat of Roosevelt's 1937 court-packing proposal actually helped the stymied Roosevelt and his Democratic successors, since none of them had any difficulty addressing what George Bush once called "the vision thing." Truman and Kennedy, for example, offered a domestic program based on completing the "unfinished business" of the New Deal. National health insurance, civil rights, and Medicare were depicted as uncompleted portions of the New Deal that would be realized by electing a Democratic president.

Lyndon Johnson solved the Democrats' "problem." But his solution left many Democrats troubled. Addressing a Liberal Party dinner in New York City in 1971, Senator Edmund Muskie of Maine said: "The blunt truth is that liberals have achieved virtually no fundamental change in our society since the end of the New Deal. We should talk to the country—to hard-hats and housewives and clerks—to men and women who will support liberal principles if those principles give them programs they can trust."[164] Indeed, the very successes of the New Deal in lifting millions of disadvantaged Americans from poverty became a liability. Instead of seeing themselves as recipients of government services, entrants into the ranks of the middle class watched their government through the green eyeshades worn in their newfound roles as taxpayers—and they did not like what they saw. A new battle cry emerged: "No more something for nothing!" This prevalent attitude gave Republicans new opportunities to make inroads among those Democrats whose party ties the New Deal's successes had loosened. By 1995, 72 percent believed that the federal government "creates more problems than it solves," and 67 percent thought it "spent too much money on the wrong things."[165] One government report found the Defense Department owned more than $40 billion in "unnecessary supplies."[166] A report by the General Accounting Office was even more disturbing, claiming that Pentagon officials deliberately misled the public and Congress in assessing Soviet military capacity. Former Reagan defense secretary Caspar Weinberger responded to the allegation: "In the end, we won the Cold War, and if we won it by too much, if it was overkill, so be it."[167]

Bill Clinton, like his Democratic forebears, promised to enact the last remaining piece of the New Deal that many believed required attention: national health care. The new president bestrode the House podium in 1993 and told Congress that every American, as a matter of right, was entitled to a "health security card" that would guarantee universal medical care in times of emergency. Republicans attacked the plan as another government boondoggle, and Clinton's proposal went down in flames. After that, Clinton searched for other ways to redefine "us" and "them," but the task proved difficult. Historian James Patterson wrote after the 1994 elections: "President Clinton, stripped of the electoral coalition that had elevated FDR and elected Truman, cannot seek refuge behind the flag. Instead, he confronts a different kind of yearning—that he do something to solve the formidable social problems at home. This has always been a demanding assignment. From this perspective, Clinton (and his successors) seem more fated than ever to encounter frustrations on Capitol Hill, whatever party may control it."[168]

Clinton's persona also proved an obstacle. By nature, Clinton was a southern charmer not given to making enemies. This quality was exhibited in spades throughout the Clinton presidency. Addressing the Congressional Black Caucus during the 1996 campaign, Clinton denounced the Republican tactic of creating wedge issues on such questions as race, affirmative action, crime, and communism: "Well, let me tell you something folks, those wedge issues nearly did us in. We've had about all the wedge issues we need. I'd like them to take those wedge issues and go someplace else."[169] Still, Clinton's advisers counseled their client to create his own set of wedge issues in order to ensure a partisan victory. James Carville, for example, recommended that Clinton demonize absent fathers who refused to pay for child support.[170] In 1992, Clinton promised to "end welfare as we know it" but demurred when it came to condemning parental irresponsibility in using the language of "us" versus "them." Instead, Clinton staked his presidency on passage of the 1993 deficit reduction measures and the North American Free Trade Agreement. In so doing, Clinton unwittingly transformed the battle into one that pitted Eisenhower Republicans (Clintonites) against Reagan Republicans (everyone else). During a particularly contentious moment when all seemed lost, Clinton lashed out at his staff: "Where are all the Democrats? I hope you're all aware we're all Eisenhower Republicans. We're Eisenhower Republicans here, and we are fighting the Reagan Republicans. We stand for lower deficits and free trade and the bond market. Isn't that great?" Clinton realized that abandoning his party base in this way meant that congressional Democrats were certain to lose in 1994: "Congress thinks it can run in '94 on this budget, plus GATT and NAFTA. They're crazy."[171]

As public disillusionment with big government hardened, the Clinton administration bowed to reality. After Republicans assumed control of Congress in 1994, Clinton adopted a "triangulation" strategy—separating himself from liberal Democrats *and* conservative Republicans. In January 1996, Clinton gave a foretaste of his reelection campaign: "The American people don't think it's the president's business to tell them what ought to happen in a congressional election." Clinton seldom pressed the case for a Democratic-controlled Congress: "A president has to be careful how he makes these arguments to the American people because a lot of time in our history, they would prefer having a president of one party and the Congress the other."[172] Only a single line in Clinton's Acceptance Speech at the 1996 Democratic National Convention was devoted to appealing to voters for unified party control of the federal government.[173] Instead of updating the liberal vision of the New Deal, Clinton sought to recast its role—sometimes sounding like a Republican in the process. In 1996, Clinton echoed Ronald Reagan's famous line that "government is not the solution to our problem; government is the problem,"[174] telling the nation matter-of-factly: "The era of big government is over."[175] At the same time, Clinton argued that government cannot abandon its role in the polity altogether. Rather than resting on the laurels of success in combating the Great Depression, World War II, and the Cold War, Clinton proposed a role for the government not nearly so grand as that advocated by presidents during previous crises, but in keeping with what voters want. Fifty-two percent told pollsters on election day 1996 that they wanted the federal government to "do less"; 41 percent thought government should "do more." In keeping with the public mood, Clinton told voters that by the time he left office he wanted a country where every eight-year-old can read, every twelve-year-old can log on to the Internet, and every eighteen-year-old can have access to a college education.[176] Other presidents, too, have had their wish lists, but what set the great presidents apart from mediocre ones has been their ability to immerse their visions in the mythology of America. Unlike dreams, myths acquire their staying power because they are already fulfilled in our collective imaginations. George Washington's cherry tree, Lincoln's log cabin, and Franklin Roosevelt's supposed lifting himself out of a wheelchair to get the nation back on its feet—all gave renewed life to the American Dream from which citizens and government could draw important moral lessons. As it edged closer to the turn of the century, America found itself in need of an uplifting vision once more, but Clinton's goals, while laudable, seemed cramped.

The Lonely Public Square

Addressing delegates to the New York state convention called to ratify the U.S. Constitution in 1788, Federalist leader Alexander Hamilton said: "The confidence of the people will easily be gained by good administration. This is the true touchstone."[177] But "good administration" has not been the antidote for true civic-mindedness. By the late 1990s, the concerns of the anti-Federalists—who feared the large republic envisioned by Hamilton and his Federalist brethren—had finally come to pass. Opposing passage of the Constitution, anti-Federalists argued that in a large republic the people "will have no confidence in their legislature, suspect them of ambitious views, be jealous of every measure they adopt, and will not support the laws they pass."[178] As historian Ralph Ketcham has written: "Anti-Federalists saw mild, grass roots, small-scale governments in sharp contrast to the splendid edifice and overweening ambitions implicit in the new Constitution. . . . The first left citizens free to live their own lives and to cultivate the virtue (private and public) vital to republicanism, while the second soon entailed taxes and drafts and offices and wars damaging to human dignity and thus fatal to self-government."[179]

A profound cynicism has taken hold of the nation's body politic—corroding everything it touches. Jean Bethke Elshtain describes a disturbing conversation she had with a member of "Generation X": "If you have a thought that doesn't seem cynical, you have to get cynical about your own non-cynicism, so you can be safely cynical again and not seem like a dweeb or optimist of some sort."[180] Harvard sociologist Robert D. Putnam found that the number of Americans who had attended a public meeting on town or school affairs fell from 22 percent in 1973 to 13 percent twenty years later. Likewise, the number of associational memberships declined by 25 percent over the last quarter-century. A nation of joiners has become a nation of loners. To emphasize the point, Putnam noted that memberships in bowling leagues have plummeted while the number of bowlers increased 10 percent from 1980 to 1993. Americans are, says Putnam, "bowling alone."[181]

Cynicism and the American penchant for "standing alone," as Tocqueville once put it, are nothing new. After visiting the United States in 1842, Charles Dickens spoke admirably of Americans in his incisive book *American Notes*. On a journey that carried him from Boston to Virginia and Philadelphia to St. Louis, Dickens wrote that Americans were by nature "frank, brave, cordial, hospitable, and affectionate." But Dickens saw "one great blemish in the popular mind of America . . . Universal Distrust." Casting himself in the role of the stranger, Dickens described the "ruin" such distrust created:

"You carry," says the stranger, "this jealousy and distrust into every transaction of public life. By repelling worthy men from your legislative assemblies, it has bred up a class of candidates for the suffrage, who, in their every act, disgrace your Institutions and your people's choice. It has rendered you so fickle, and so given to change, that your inconstancy has passed into a proverb; for you no sooner set up an idol firmly, than you are sure to pull it down and dash it into fragments: and this, because directly you reward a benefactor, or a public servant, you distrust him, merely because he *is* rewarded; and immediately apply yourselves to find out, either that you have been too bountiful in your acknowledgments, or he remiss in his deserts. Any man who attains a high place among you, from the President downwards, may date his downfall from that moment; for any printed lie that any notorious villain pens, although it militate directly against the character and conduct of a life, appeals at once to your distrust, and is believed. You will strain at a gnat in the way of trustfulness and confidence, however fairly won and well deserved; but you will swallow a whole caravan of camels, if they be laden with unworthy doubts and mean suspicions. Is this well, think you, or likely to elevate the character of the governors or the governed, among you?"

The answer is invariably the same: "There's freedom of opinion here, you know. Every man thinks for himself, and we are not to be easily overreached. That's how our people come to be suspicious."[182]

But the "freedom of opinion" must be tempered by mediating institutions that can translate opinion from the masses into policies carried out by national leaders. Without such institutions, governments cannot function. As Publius wrote in supporting the new U.S. Constitution, "A NATION without a NATIONAL GOVERNMENT, is, in my view, an awful spectacle."[183] Transmitting the Constitution to the Congress, George Washington saw the need for the "consolidation of our Union."[184] After the Cold War, the need for consolidation seems equally great. Before and during much of the Cold War, political parties were the repositories of big ideas that gave life to our politics: the New Deal, Great Society, and Reaganism. Woodrow Wilson once noted the unique role political parties play as national unifiers: "There is a sense in which our parties may be said to have been our real body politic. Not the authority of Congress, nor the leadership of the president, but the discipline and zest of parties, has held us together, has made it possible for us to form and to carry out national programs."[185] But the end of the Cold War has placed both Republicans and Democrats in a feeble state. As Clark Clifford wrote in his memoirs, "In America, both the Left, with its readiness to accept communism as inevitable, and the Right, which searched for the enemy within and advocated a swollen and wasteful American military establishment, had been wrong."[186]

As Americans deal with the legacy of the Cold War and its lessons for the future, they would do well to remember the advice given by George Washington more than two centuries ago. Taking leave of the Revolutionary Army, Washington noted that Americans had two choices—"whether they will be respectable and prosperous, or contemptible and miserable as a nation." Given the interstate rivalries and challenges facing the new country, Washington was not altogether sure which path his fellow citizens would take. While taking pride in the fact that his role in the just-completed war had reached a satisfactory outcome, Washington observed that if Americans "should not be completely free and happy, the fault will be entirely their own."[187] After the Cold War, Americans still had their freedom, but they seemed profoundly dissatisfied. Capturing the public mood, an aged Richard Nixon said in his final public appearance, "The Soviets have lost the Cold War, but the United States has not yet won it."[188] Another president, in a another age, issued a dire warning about America's future. In a review of James Bryce's masterpiece, *The American Commonwealth*, Woodrow Wilson wrote:

America is now sauntering through her resources and through her mazes of her politics with easy nonchalance; but presently there will come a time when she will be surprised to find herself grown old—a country crowded, strained, perplexed—when she will be obliged to pull herself together, adopt a new regimen of life, husband her resources, concentrate her strength, steady her methods, sober her views, restrict her vagaries, trust her best, not her average members. That will be the time of change.[189]

That time of change has arrived. As in 1945, Americans in the 1990s are realizing that the current crisis lies within themselves, within ourselves. Issues such as term limits and the balance budget amendment say much about our mutual distrust—be it to vote out of office those members of Congress who have overstayed their welcome, or take the hard steps necessary to bring the federal ledgers into balance. Many seem more interested in following the popular culture than in participating in the public square. Still, there are some encouraging signs: The anger that has characterized the post–Cold War political contests is beginning to ebb, and a greater sense of personal and public responsibility is gradually emerging. We are only just beginning to realize that our problems lie within ourselves. Once more, Americans must answer the question, "Who are we?" The answer will shape much of the politics of the twenty-first century.

Notes

Introduction

1. Cited in David Remnick, *Lenin's Tomb: The Last Days of the Soviet Empire* (New York: Random House, 1993), p. 18.

2. See Oleg Kalugin with Fen Montaigne, *The First Directorate: My Thirty-Two Years in Intelligence and Espionage Against the West* (New York: St. Martin's Press, 1994), p. 74.

3. Oleg Kalugin, lecture, Catholic University of America, Washington, D.C., March 18, 1995.

4. Kalugin with Montaigne, *The First Directorate*, pp. 110, 111.

5. Anatoly Dobrynin, *In Confidence* (New York: Times Books, 1995), p. 176.

6. See Kalugin with Montaigne, *The First Directorate*, p. 112.

7. Quoted in Michael Dobbs, "Panhandling the Kremlin: How Gus Hall Got Millions," *Washington Post*, March 1, 1992, p. A-1.

8. See Michael Dobbs, "Revelations from the Communist Files," *Washington Post*, February 8, 1992, p. A-14.

9. *Final Report: Advisory Committee on Human Radiation Experiments* (Washington, D.C.: U.S. Government Printing Office, 1995), p. 245.

10. Ibid., pp. 320, 792.

11. See Ted Gup, "The Doomsday Blueprints," *Time*, August 10, 1992, pp. 32–35.

12. Ibid., p. 37.

13. Ibid.

14. Quoted in Joel Brinkley, "U.S. Looking for a New Path as Superpower Conflict Ends," *New York Times*, February 2, 1992, p. A-1.

15. Gallup poll, July 2–7, 1954. Text of question: "Do you think the time will come when we can live peacefully with communist Russia, or do you think it is only a matter of time until we will have to fight it out?" Live peacefully, 16 percent; fight it out, 72 percent; no opinion, 12 percent.

16. See Gup, "The Doomsday Blueprints," p. 34.

17. Quoted in Elaine Tyler May, "Explosive Issues: Sex, Women, and the Bomb," in *Recasting America: Culture and Politics in the Age of Cold War*, ed. Lary May (Chicago: University of Chicago Press, 1988), p. 161.

18. Quoted in Richard Bernstein, "Long Conflict Deeply Marked the Self-Image of Americans," *New York Times*, February 2, 1992, p. 11.

19. Cited in Brinkley, "U.S. Looking for a New Path," p. A-1.

20. Gallup poll, July 13–16, 1984. Text of question: "Assuming that both were equally well qualified for the job, do you think that a *MALE* president or a *FEMALE* president of the United States would do a better job of handling our relations with the Soviet Union?" Male better, 57 percent; female better, 11 percent; no difference (volunteered) 25 percent; no opinion, 7 percent.

21. Bernstein, "Long Conflict," p. 11.

22. Cited in May, "Explosive Issues," p. 166.

23. United Press wire report, "South Korean Unit, Bayoneting Reds, Regains Key Peak," *New York Times*, October 10, 1952, p. 1. Thomas J. Hamilton, "Work Completed on U.N. Buildings," *New York Times*, October 10, 1952, p. 1. James Reston, "Stevenson Taunts Rival for Backing McCarthy, Dirksen," *New York Times*, October 10, 1952, p. 1. Felix Belair, Jr., "U.S. to Give France $525,000,000 in Aid and Hints at More," *New York Times*, October 10, 1952, p. 1.

24. ABC News/*Washington Post*, survey, June 15–19, 1989. Text of question: "In your view, is communism dying out or not?" Yes, 31 percent; no, 67 percent; don't know/no opinion, 2 percent.

25. Murray Kempton, "Notes from Underground," *New York Review of Books*, July 13, 1995, p. 29.

26. Gallup poll, January 27-February 5, 1989. Text of question: "Communists are responsible for a lot of the unrest in the United States today." Completely agree, 18 percent; mostly agree, 34 percent; mostly disagree, 28 percent; completely disagree, 12 percent; don't know, 8 percent.

27. Arthur M. Schlesinger, *The Vital Center* (Boston: Houghton Mifflin, 1949), p. 244.

28. See Louis Hartz, *The Liberal Tradition in America* (New York: Harcourt Brace Jovanovich, 1955).

29. Alexis de Tocqueville, *Democracy in America*, ed. Richard D. Heffner (New York: New American Library, 1956), pp. 117–118.

30. Quoted in Everett Carll Ladd, *The American Ideology: An Exploration of the Origins, Meaning, and Role of American Political Ideas* (Storrs, Connecticut: The Roper Center for Public Opinion Research, 1994), p. 32.

31. Quoted in John Gerring, "A Chapter in the History of American Party Ideology: The Nineteenth Century Democratic Party (1828–1892)," paper presented at the Northeastern Political Science Association, Newark, New Jersey, November 11–13, 1993, pp. 36–37. Cass made these remarks on September 2, 1852.

32. See Roy P. Basler, ed., *The Collected Works of Abraham Lincoln* (New Brunswick, New Jersey: Rutgers University Press, 1953), p. 323.

33. Cited in Seymour Martin Lipset, "Why No Socialism in the United States?" in *Radicalism in the Contemporary Age*, ed. Seweryn Bailer and Sophia Sluzar (Boulder: Westview Press, 1977), p. 40.

34. *The World Book Encyclopedia* (Chicago: Field Enterprises Educational Corporation, 1964), p. 724b.

35. "Text of the Address by President Roosevelt at Dinner of the Foreign Policy Association Here," *New York Times*, October 22, 1944, p. 34. The incident is recounted in Doris Kearns Goodwin, *No Ordinary Time: Franklin and Eleanor Roosevelt, The Home Front in World War Two* (New York: Simon and Schuster, 1994), pp. 550–551.

36. Yankelovich, Skelly, and White, survey, June 27–29, 1983. Text of question: "I'm going to read you a list of statements that some Americans believe describe life in a communist country. For each statement, please tell me whether you believe it to be true or not true." (a) "You only hear the news the government wants you to hear." True, 92 percent; not true, 5 percent; don't know, 2 percent. (b) "If you speak your mind you risk going to jail." True, 91 percent; not true, 6 percent; don't know, 3 percent. (c) "Life for the average person is pretty much the same as in the United States." True, 12 percent; not true, 84 percent; don't know, 4 percent. (d) "You can't move or relocate without permission from the government." True, 80 percent; not true, 10 percent; don't know, 10 percent. (e) "You always have to be afraid of the police." True, 75 percent; not true, 19 percent; don't know, 6 percent. (f) "You can't pick your own job

or change jobs, the government decides for you." True, 75 percent; not true, 16 percent; don't know, 8 percent. (g) "There is no freedom of religion." True, 69 percent; not true, 27 percent; don't know, 4 percent. (h) "There's less stress and tension for the average person." True, 24 percent; not true, 65 percent; don't know, 10 percent. (i) "You can't get a fair trial." True, 61 percent; not true, 23 percent; don't know, 16 percent. (j) "Men and women are treated equally." True, 27 percent; not true, 60 percent; don't know, 13 percent.

37. H. R. Haldeman, *The Haldeman Diaries* (New York: G. P. Putnam's Sons, 1994), p. 577.

38. ABC News/Louis Harris, survey, March 26–30, 1980. Text of question: "Now let me read you some statements. For each, tell me if you tend to agree or disagree. . . . A candidate for president who says his opponent is soft on communism is probably a hypocrite because, if elected, he will soon be sitting down in Moscow and Peking to work out agreements with communist leaders." Agree, 50 percent; disagree, 42 percent; not sure, 8 percent.

39. "Democratic Platform, 1952," in Kirk H. Porter and Donald Bruce Johnson, *National Party Platforms: 1840–1968* (Urbana: University of Illinois Press, 1970), p. 480.

40. Cited in John Kenneth White, *The New Politics of Old Values* (Hanover, New Hampshire: University Press of New England, 1990), p. 63.

41. "Best Lines Slung from Tongues in '88," *Providence Journal*, January 3, 1989, p. B-4.

42. Lloyd Free and Hadley Cantril, *The Political Beliefs of Americans* (New Brunswick, New Jersey: Rutgers University Press, 1967), pp. 175–177.

43. William J. Clinton, "Remarks by the President on Responsible Citizenship and the American Community," Georgetown University, Washington, D.C., July 6, 1995.

44. CBS News/*New York Times*, survey, May 9–11, 1989. Text of question: "Suppose you had to make the decision between fighting an all-out nuclear war or living under communist rule. How would you decide?" Fight an all-out nuclear war, 47 percent; live under communist rule, 32 percent; don't know/no answer, 21 percent.

45. Gallup poll, May–July 1954. Text of question: "Do you think a man can believe in communism and still be a loyal American, or not?" Yes, 5 percent; qualified yes (volunteered), 2 percent; no, 87 percent; don't know, 7 percent.

46. See Seymour Martin Lipset, *Political Man: The Social Bases of Politics* (Garden City, New York: Anchor Books, 1963), p. 171. Sixty percent of "nineteenth-century liberals" said they favored McCarthy's methods.

47. "Forty Years Ago in *Time*: The Sexy Schoolteacher Gap," *Time*, May 29, 1995, p. 17.

48. "Report Card," *Time*, May 30, 1955, p. 46.

49. See William Booth, "Florida Senate Unveils Records of Probe Styled on McCarthyism," *Washington Post*, July 3, 1993, p. A-3. Among those voting for the Johns Committee was then State Senator Lawton Chiles, the current governor of Florida.

50. Cited in Herbert Parmet, *Richard Nixon and His America* (Boston: Little, Brown, 1990), p. 213.

51. Quoted in Samuel P. Huntington, *American Politics: The Promise of Disharmony* (Cambridge: Harvard University Press, 1981), p. 25.

52. Hartz, *The Liberal Tradition in America*, pp. 10–11.

53. Quoted in Huntington, *American Politics*, p. 25.

54. John F. Kennedy, "Some Elements of the American Character," Independence Day Oration, 1946. In John F. Kennedy prepresidential files, Box 94, John F. Kennedy Library.

55. Survey conducted by the Roper Organization, December 1939. The results are taken among "whites only." There are no dollar definitions as to what constitutes "poor" in this survey.

56. Dwight D. Eisenhower, *Waging Peace, 1956–1961* (Garden City, New York: Doubleday, 1965), p. 627. In 1993, President Clinton ordered the radio transmissions of these two

agencies to cease in order to save scarce federal dollars. See Steven A. Holmes, "Clinton Turns Off Cold War Voice," *New York Times*, February 2, 1993, p. 13.

57. Quoted in Thomas G. Paterson, *Meeting the Communist Threat: Truman to Reagan* (New York: Oxford University Press, 1988), p. vii.

58. Peter J. Boyer, "Gore's Dilemma," *New Yorker*, November 28, 1994, pp. 108–109.

59. Ibid., p. 109.

60. Quoted in Carl E. Prince, *Brooklyn's Dodgers: The Bums, the Borough, and the Best of Baseball, 1947–1957* (New York: Oxford University Press, 1996), p. 24.

61. See Richard Reeves, "1954," *American Heritage*, December 1994, p. 36.

62. Brinkley, "U.S. Looking for a New Path," p. A-1.

63. Eric Hoffer, *The True Believer* (New York: Harper and Row, 1951), p. xi.

64. Parmet, *Richard Nixon and His America*, p. 120.

65. Garry Wills, "Late Bloomer," *Time*, April 23, 1990, p. 29.

66. John F. Kennedy, "Remarks to Delegates to the 18th Annual American Legion 'Boys Nation,'" July 24, 1963, in *Public Papers of the Presidents of the United States: John F. Kennedy* (Washington, D.C.: U.S. Government Printing Office, 1964), p. 598.

67. David Maraniss, "Bill Clinton and Realpolitik U.," *Washington Post*, October 25, 1992, p. F-6.

68. Quoted in Lou Cannon, *President Reagan: The Role of a Lifetime* (New York: Simon and Schuster, 1991), p. 524.

69. Quoted in Reeves, "1954," p. 34.

70. Richard Reeves, *President Kennedy* (New York: Simon and Schuster, 1993), p. 354.

71. John F. Kennedy, "Radio and Television Report to the American People on Civil Rights," June 11, 1963, in *Public Papers of the Presidents of the United States: John F. Kennedy*, p. 468. Michael Lind argues that the Cold War precipitated the rapid dismantling of white supremacy. See Michael Lind, *The Next American Nation: The New Nationalism and the Fourth American Revolution* (New York: Free Press, 1995), pp. 105–106.

72. Brinkley, "U.S. Looking for a New Path," p. A-1.

73. Quoted in Samuel Lubell, *The Future of American Politics* (New York: Harper Colophon Books, 1965 ed. [first published 1952]), p. 236.

74. Quoted in Brinkley, "U.S. Looking for a New Path," p. A-1.

75. Robert Pear, "Shake-Up Over Agency's Secret Money," *New York Times*, September 25, 1995, p. A-11.

76. See "How Many Minutes to Midnight 50 Years After the A-Bomb's Birth?" *New York Times*, December 3, 1995, p. E-7.

Chapter One

1. Charles Raudebaugh, "500,000 Crowd S.F. Streets to Welcome Their President," *San Francisco Chronicle*, June 26, 1945, p. 1.

2. John H. Crider, "Truman Acclaimed on Arrival by Air to Close Parley," *New York Times*, June 26, 1945, p. 1.

3. See Erich Fromm, *Inside the Kremlin's Cold War: From Stalin to Khrushchev* (Cambridge, Massachusetts: Harvard University Press, 1996), p. 1.

4. Arthur H. Vandenberg Jr., *The Private Papers of Senator Vandenberg* (Boston: Houghton Mifflin, 1952), p. 216.

5. Lawrence E. Davies, "Historic Plenary Session Approves World Charter," *New York Times*, June 25, 1945, p. 1.

6. John H. Crider, "Truman Closes United Nations Conference with Plea to Translate Charter into Deeds," *New York Times*, June 27, 1945, p. 1.

7. Charles Raudebaugh, "Truman's Conference Address," *San Francisco Chronicle*, June 27, 1945, p. 1.

8. Harry S. Truman, "Address in San Francisco at the Closing Session of the United Nations Conference," in *Public Papers of the Presidents of the United States: Harry S. Truman* (Washington, D.C.: Government Printing Office, 1946), p. 138.

9. Cited in Jacob Heilbrunn, "The Revision Thing: Who Is to Blame for the Cold War? A New Quarrel," *New Republic*, August 15, 1994, p. 34.

10. Eddy Gilmore, "Russia Welcomes Her Generals," *San Francisco Chronicle*, June 25, 1945, p. 1.

11. Vandenberg, *Private Papers*, p. 161.

12. Quoted in Nigel Hamilton, *JFK: Reckless Youth* (New York: Random House, 1992), p. 699. Kennedy's sentiments are echoed in a newly published diary. In an entry dated July 10, 1945, he wrote that the United Nations "suffered from inadequate preparation . . . and an unfortunate Press which praised it beyond all limit," adding that "democracies have to go through a gradual disillusionment in their hopes of peace." See John F. Kennedy, *Prelude to Leadership: The European Diary of John F. Kennedy* (Washington, D.C.: Regnery Publishing, 1995), pp. 5, 7.

13. Kennedy was recruited by the executive editor of the Chicago *Herald American*, who wanted him to cover the U.N. conference "from the point of view of the ordinary G.I." See Hamilton, *JFK: Reckless Youth*, p. 687.

14. Eric Goldman, *The Crucial Decade—And After: America, 1945–1960* (New York: Alfred A. Knopf, 1966), p. 134.

15. Henry R. Luce, "The American Century," editorial, *Life*, February 17, 1941.

16. Quoted in Goldman, *The Crucial Decade—And After*, p. 14.

17. David Halberstam, *The Fifties* (New York: Villard Books, 1993), p. 116.

18. See David McCullough, *Truman* (New York: Simon and Schuster, 1992), p. 138.

19. See Goldman, *The Crucial Decade—And After*, p. 28.

20. See Michael Barone, *Our Country: The Shaping of America from Roosevelt to Reagan* (New York: Free Press, 1990), p. 230.

21. General Dwight D. Eisenhower to Mrs. A. H. Nickless, letter dated December 19, 1945, quoted in Democratic National Committee, "Statements of General Eisenhower on National Issues," August 23, 1952. In John F. Kennedy prepresidential papers, Box 101, 1952 campaign files, John F. Kennedy Library.

22. Thomas Paterson, *Meeting the Communist Threat* (New York: Oxford University Press, 1988), p. 80.

23. Quoted in Roger Morris, *Richard Milhous Nixon: The Rise of an American Politician* (New York: Henry Holt, 1990), p. 264.

24. Quoted in Goldman, *The Crucial Decade—And After*, p. 15

25. Quoted in William Strauss and Neil Howe, *Generations: The History of America's Future, 1584–2069* (New York: William Morrow, 1991), p. 272.

26. Cited in Doris Kearns Goodwin, *No Ordinary Time: Franklin and Eleanor Roosevelt, The Home Front in World War Two* (New York: Simon and Schuster, 1994), p. 624.

27. See Strauss and Howe, *Generations*, p. 268.

28. Quoted in Goldman, *The Crucial Decade—And After*, pp. 20–21.

29. Ibid., p. 119.

30. See George F. Kennan and John Lukacs, "From World War to Cold War," *American Heritage*, December 1995, pp. 50, 52.

31. Quoted in A. James Reichley, *The Life of the Parties* (New York: Free Press, 1992), p. 295.

32. Quoted in "The Issue in 1950: Communism vs. Democracy," *New Republic Election Supplement*, October 9, 1950, p. 10.

33. Quoted in David Fromkin, *In the Time of the Americans: FDR, Truman, Eisenhower, Marshall, MacArthur—the Generation That Changed America's Role in the World* (New York: Alfred A. Knopf, 1995), p. 490.

34. Roper poll, May 1945. Text of question: "Which of the things on that list do you think are going to be troublesome for this country in the next few years?" Our relations with Russia, 56 percent; unemployment, 59 percent; handling of Germany, 52 percent; handling of Japan, 50 percent. The results add to more than 100 percent due to multiple responses given.

35. Quoted in Hamilton, *JFK: Reckless Youth*, p. 695. This is the first use of the term "iron curtain."

36. See Goldman, *The Crucial Decade—And After*, p. 37.

37. Winston S. Churchill, "The Sinews of Peace," address at Westminster College, Fulton, Missouri, March 5, 1946.

38. Richard M. Nixon, *RN: The Memoirs of Richard Nixon* (New York: Grosset and Dunlap, 1978), p. 45.

39. Churchill, "The Sinews of Peace."

40. Quoted in Clark Clifford with Richard Holbrooke, *Counsel to the President: A Memoir* (New York: Anchor Books, Doubleday, 1991), p. 110, and Paterson, *Meeting the Communist Threat*, p. 31.

41. Adlai E. Stevenson, *The Major Campaign Speeches of Adlai E. Stevenson, 1952* (New York: Random House, 1953), p. 182.

42. Quoted in Ernest R. May, ed., *American Cold War Strategy: Interpreting NSC 68* (Boston: Bedford Books of St. Martin's Press, 1993), p. 5.

43. Cited in Clifford with Holbrooke, *Counsel to the President*, pp. 125–126.

44. Ibid., p. 126.

45. Ibid., p. 128. Truman never even mentioned it in his memoirs.

46. Quoted in Barone, *Our Country*, pp. 204–205.

47. Quoted in Goldman, *The Crucial Decade—And After*, p. 59.

48. Quoted in Barone, *Our Country*, p. 207.

49. Quoted in Stephen Ambrose, *Nixon: The Education of a Politician, 1913–1962* (New York: Simon and Schuster, 1987), p. 148.

50. National Opinion Research Center, survey, April 1947. Text of question: "If it doesn't get help, do you believe the present government in Greece is in danger of being overthrown by the communists?" Yes, 64 percent; no, 12 percent; don't know, 24 percent.

51. John F. Kennedy, "Aid for Greece and Turkey," *Congressional Record*, April 1, 1947. In John F. Kennedy prepresidential papers, Box 94, John F. Kennedy Library.

52. Paterson, *Meeting the Communist Threat*, p. 79.

53. Quoted in David R. Kepley, *The Collapse of the Middle Way: Senate Republicans and the Bipartisan Foreign Policy, 1948–1952* (Westport, Connecticut: Greenwood Press, 1988), p. 2. One of Vandenberg's protégés was Gerald R. Ford, who defeated a Republican isolationist in a 1948 primary. As for Vandenberg, he died from lung cancer on April 18, 1951. By then, bipartisanship had given way to an extreme form of partisanship.

54. See Reichley, *The Life of the Parties*, p. 296.

55. "Questions and Answers on Foreign Policy," Democratic National Committee, 1952, p. 4. In John F. Kennedy prepresidential papers, John F. Kennedy Library.

56. Gallup poll, May 23–28, 1947. Text of question: "As things stand right now, how serious a threat do you think communism is to our form of democratic government—a very serious threat, a fairly serious threat, or no threat at all?" Very serious, 32 percent; fairly serious, 34 percent; no threat, 23 percent; no opinion, 11 percent.

57. Quoted in Louis Hartz, *The Liberal Tradition in America* (New York: Harcourt Brace Jovanovich, 1955), p. 300.

58. Arthur M. Schlesinger Jr., *The Vital Center* (Boston: Houghton Mifflin, 1949), p. 195.

59. Quoted in John Gerring, *Party Ideology in America, 1828–1992*, unpublished manuscript, 1996, p. 77.

60. Gallup poll, December 24–29, 1939. Asked of the 74 percent who had heard of the Dies Committee: "Which of the following do you consider more important for the Dies Committee to investigate—Communist activities in this country, or Nazi activities in this country?" Communist activities, 53 percent; Nazi activities, 23 percent; no opinion, 25 percent.

61. In 1951, the U.S. Supreme Court upheld the constitutionality of the Smith Act in a case involving eleven members of the U.S. Communist Party. A decade later the Court ruled "active membership" in the U.S. Communist Party was illegal, claiming that these individuals had a "specific intent" to bring about the downfall of the U.S. government.

62. Gallup poll, September 22–27, 1940. Text of question: "Do you think Communist party candidates should be allowed any time on the radio?" Yes, 32 percent; no, 55 percent; no opinion, 13 percent.

63. See Richard Norton Smith, *Thomas E. Dewey and His Times* (New York: Simon and Schuster, 1982), p. 463.

64. Quoted in Kepley, *The Collapse of the Middle Way*, p. 13. The Marshall Plan was signed into law on April 3, 1948.

65. Quoted in Fromkin, *In The Time of the Americans*, p. 476.

66. Quoted in "The Issue in 1950: Communism vs. Democracy," p. 11.

67. Gallup poll, June 14–19, 1946. Text of question: "Would you say that there are many or only a few communists in the U.S. today?" Many, 50 percent; few, 29 percent; no opinion, 21 percent.

68. Gallup poll, October 24–29, 1947. Text of first question: "In general, do you think most American citizens who belong to the Communist Party in this country are loyal to America or to Russia?" America, 22 percent; Russia, 58 percent; no opinion, 20 percent. These responses were consistent with a November 1939 Gallup poll that asked: "Which of these statements best describes your opinion of the Communist Party in the United States? 1. The Communist Party in the country takes orders directly from Russia [26 percent]; 2. the policies of the Communist Party in the United States are decided on by Communists in this country in consultation with Russia [28 percent]; 3. the policies of the American Communist Party are decided entirely by the Communists in the United States [9 percent]; 4. know nothing about the Communist Party [37 percent]." Text of second question: "Do you think the communists in this country actually take orders from Moscow?" Yes, 62 percent; no, 13 percent; no opinion, 25 percent.

69. Quoted in Morris, *Richard Milhous Nixon*, p. 265.

70. Lary May, "Movie Star Politics: The Screen Actors' Guild, Cultural Convention, and the Hollywood Red Scare," in Lary May, ed., *Recasting America: Culture and Politics in the Age of the Cold War* (Chicago: University of Chicago Press, 1988), p. 145.

71. Quoted in Morris, *Richard Milhous Nixon*, pp. 326, 266.

72. Halberstam, *The Fifties*, p. 10.

73. Gallup poll, August 16–21, 1946. Text of question: "Do you think countries under the capitalistic system and countries under the communistic system can get along peacefully?" Yes, 35 percent; no, 49 percent; no opinion, 15 percent.

74. Quoted in Goldman, *The Crucial Decade—And After*, pp. 78–79.

75. Quoted in Tom Wicker, *One of Us: Richard Nixon and the American Dream* (New York: Random House, 1991), p. 38.

76. Quoted in Greg Mitchell, *The Campaign of the Century: Upton Sinclair's Race for Governor of California* (New York: Random House, 1992), p. 32. The Communist Party had just 300 registered Californians in 1934. Ibid., p. 264.

77. Ibid., pp. 130–131.

78. Ibid., p. 23. Sinclair thought communism "the wrong way for this country." Ibid., p. 264.

79. Quoted in Clyde P. Weed, *The Nemesis of Reform: The Republican Party During the New Deal* (New York: Columbia University Press, 1994), p. 77.

80. "1951 Speech Kit, Republican Congressional Campaign Committee," In Gerald R. Ford congressional papers, Box G-1, Gerald R. Ford Library.

81. Ibid.

82. Quoted in Richard Gid Powers, *Not Without Honor: The History of Anticommunism* (New York: Free Press, 1995), p. 113.

83. Quoted in Alan Brinkley, "Last of His Kind," review of Nelson Lichtenstein, *The Most Dangerous Man in Detroit: Walter Reuther and the Fate of American Labor*, in *New York Times Books Review*, December 17, 1995, p. 9.

84. Saul Bellow, "Writers, Intellectuals, Politics," *National Interest*, No. 31 (Spring 1993), pp. 125–126. Bellow was subsequently employed by the WPA Writer's Project.

85. "1951 Speech Kit, Republican Congressional Campaign Committee."

86. Franklin D. Roosevelt, "Address at the Democratic State Convention," Syracuse, New York, September 29, 1936.

87. Quoted in Alan Brinkley, *The End of Reform: New Deal Liberalism and War* (New York: Alfred A. Knopf, 1995), p. 15.

88. Ibid., p. 16.

89. Quoted in "Editorial Comment of Representative Newspapers on Vote Outcome," *New York Times*, November 5, 1936, p. 4.

90. Schlesinger, *The Vital Center*, p. 164.

91. Quoted in Robert A. Taft, *A Foreign Policy for All Americans* (Garden City, New York: Doubleday, 1951), p. 51.

92. Cited in Brinkley, *The End of Reform*, p. 141.

93. Quoted in McCullough, *Truman*, p. 332.

94. Quoted in Wicker, *One of Us*, p. 38.

95. "Earl Browder, Ex-Communist Leader, Dies at 82," *New York Times*, June 28, 1973, p. 50.

96. Ibid.

97. Quoted in Smith, *Thomas E. Dewey and His Times*, p. 410.

98. Ibid.

99. See Kennan and Lukacs, "From World War to Cold War," p. 50.

100. See Smith, *Thomas E. Dewey and His Times*, pp. 433–434.

101. Ibid.

102. National Opinion Research Center, survey, November 26-December 3, 1944. Text of question: "Some people said that if Roosevelt were reelected [president] the communists would have more influence in the government than they should have. Do you think the communists will have more influence in the government than they should have, or not?" More influence, 30 percent; not more influence, 57 percent; none (volunteered) 1 percent; don't know, 13 percent.

103. See Smith, *Thomas E. Dewey and His Times*, pp. 409–410.

104. Ibid., pp. 433–434.

105. Ibid., pp. 409–410, 433–434.

106. "1951 Speech Kit, Republican Congressional Campaign Committee."

107. Dewey responded by running radio advertisements promising to clear everything only with Congress and the American people. See Smith, *Thomas E. Dewey and His Times*, p. 410.

108. See Bruce L. Felknor, *Political Mischief: Smear, Sabotage, and Reform in the United States* (Westport, Connecticut: Greenwood Press, 1992), p. 82.

109. Ibid.

110. Smith, *Thomas E. Dewey and His Times*, p. 433.

111. Quoted in Schlesinger, *The Vital Center*, pp. 114–115.

112. Quoted in Fromkin, *In the Time of the Americans*, p. 476.

113. Roper poll, March 22–April 5, 1943. Text of question: "After the war, do you think Russia will or will not try to bring about communist governments in other European countries?" Will, 41 percent; will not, 31 percent; don't know, 28 percent.

114. Quoted in Reichley, *The Life of the Parties*, p. 292.

115. Quoted in Clifford with Holbrooke, *Counsel to the President*, p. 114.

116. Halberstam, *The Fifties*, p. 27.

117. Henry A. Wallace, *The Price of Vision: The Diary of Henry A. Wallace, 1942–1946* (Boston: Houghton Mifflin, 1973), pp. 661–664, passim.

118. Ibid., pp. 661–668, passim. The White House issued a clarification in Truman's name: "It was my intention to express the thought that I approved the right of the Secretary of Commerce to deliver the speech. I did not intend to indicate that I approved the speech as constituting a statement of the foreign policy of this country." See Clifford with Holbrooke, *Counsel to the President*, p. 119.

119. See McCullough, *Truman*, p. 515.

120. Quoted in Clifford with Holbrooke, *Counsel to the President*, p. 118–119. Byrnes was an important figure in Democratic councils, as he was crucial to obtaining Southern support.

121. Quoted in McCullough, *Truman*, p. 517.

122. Reproduced in Clifford with Holbrooke, *Counsel to the President*, p. 120.

123. Carl Solberg, *Hubert Humphrey: A Biography* (New York: W. W. Norton, 1984), p. 115.

124. John F. Kennedy, "Speech to Business and Professional Women," Lynn, Massachusetts, October 21, 1946, and John F. Kennedy, "Radio Speech on Russia," October 21, 1946. In John F. Kennedy prepresidential papers, 1945–1952, Box 94, John F. Kennedy Library.

125. James Loeb Jr., "Progressives and Communists," *New Republic*, May 13, 1946, p. 699.

126. Charles Krauthammer, "How Conservatism Can Come Back," *Time*, January 18, 1993, p. 68.

127. Hubert H. Humphrey, *The Education of a Public Man: My Life in Politics* (Garden City, New York: Doubleday, 1976), p. 106.

128. Morris, *Richard Milhous Nixon*, p. 265.

129. Quoted in Wicker, *One of Us*, p. 39.

130. This was a confidential poll taken for the Psychological Corporation. Cited in Smith, *Thomas E. Dewey and His Times*, p. 462.

131. Quoted in Halberstam, *The Fifties*, p. 57.

132. Parmet, *Richard Nixon and His America*, p. 107.

133. Quoted in Robert D. Ubriaco Jr., "Bread and Butter Politics at the Factory Gate: Class Versus Ethnicity in the Polish-American Community During the 1946 Congressional Elections," unpublished paper.

134. Ibid.

135. Paterson, *Meeting the Communist Threat*, p. 186.

136. Cited in James S. Pula, *Polish Americans: An Ethnic Community* (New York: Twyane Publishers, 1995), p. 105.

137. Quoted in "The Issue in 1950: Communism vs. Democracy," p. 12.

138. Quoted in Goldman, *The Crucial Decade—And After*, p. 34.

139. Quoted in Parmet, *Richard Nixon and His America*, p. 107.

140. Quoted in Morris, *Richard Milhous Nixon*, p. 265.

141. Quoted in Richard Gid Powers, *Not Without Honor*, p. 237.

142. Quoted in Wicker, *One of Us*, p. 39.

143. Quoted in Nixon, *RN: The Memoirs of Richard Nixon*, p. 35.

144. Quoted in Jonathan Aitken, *Nixon: A Life* (Washington, D.C.: Regnery Publishing, 1993), p. 116.

145. Quoted in Jerry Voorhis, *The Strange Case of Richard Milhous Nixon* (New York: Popular Library, 1973), p. 15.

146. Ibid., p. 13.

147. Quoted in Mitchell, *Campaign of the Century*, pp. 313–314.

148. Otto Friedrich, "'I Have Never Been a Quitter,'" *Time*, May 2, 1994, p. 45.

149. See Voorhis, *The Strange Case of Richard Milhous Nixon*, p. 15.

150. Parmet, *Richard Nixon and His America*, p. 113.

151. An October 18, 1946, speech quoted in Ambrose, *Nixon: The Education of a Politician*, p. 136.

152. Among the votes that Nixon considered communist-inspired were Voorhis's support for the Reciprocal Trade Agreements, a wartime loan to Britain, abolition of the poll tax, establishment of the school lunch program, unemployment insurance for federal workers, travel pay for war workers compelled to relocate, separating the Reconstruction Finance Corporation from the Department of Commerce, abolishing certain price subsidies, and establishing limits on the cost of homes sold to returning veterans. See Voorhis, *The Strange Case of Richard Milhous Nixon*, p. 16.

153. Morris, *Richard Milhous Nixon*, p. 332.

154. Parmet, *Richard Nixon and His America*, p. 113.

155. Morris, *Richard Milhous Nixon*, p. 333.

156. Quoted on PBS broadcast, "Nixon: The American Experience," September 24, 1992.

157. Quoted in Hamilton, *JFK: Reckless Youth*, p. 774.

158. Ibid.

159. John F. Kennedy, "Radio Speech on Russia," October 21, 1946. In John F. Kennedy prepresidential papers, Box 94, John F. Kennedy Library.

160. John F. Kennedy, "1946 Platform." In John F. Kennedy prepresidential campaign files, Box 99, John F. Kennedy Library.

161. Quoted in James Patterson, "Not So Fast, Newt," *New Republic*, January 23, 1995, p. 27.

162. Cited in Ubracio, "Bread and Butter Politics at the Factory Gate."

163. Quoted in Ted Morgan, *FDR: A Biography* (New York: Simon and Schuster, 1985), p. 38.

164. Schlesinger, *The Vital Center*, pp. 9–10.

Chapter Two

1. Quoted in Clark Clifford with Richard Holbrooke, *Counsel to the President: A Memoir* (New York: Anchor Books, Doubleday, 1991), p. 178.

2. The Un-American Activities Committee of the House of Representatives was created in 1938 as a temporary investigating committee. It was often referred to as the "Dies Committee," after its chairman, Martin Dies. In January 1945, it was made a permanent committee and named the House Committee on Un-American Activities. See Robert K. Carr, *The House*

Committee on Un-American Activities, 1945–1950 (Ithaca, New York: Cornell University Press, 1952), pp. 1, 19.

3. Ibid., p. 177.

4. Eric Johnston, Testimony before the House Committee on Un-American Activities, March 26, 1947, pp. 301–305. Johnston's comment about getting "under the sheets" was a jibe at Rankin's associations with the Ku Klux Klan.

5. See John Judis, "The Two Faces of Whittaker Chambers," in *New Republic*, April 16, 1984, pp. 26–27.

6. Quoted in Richard M. Nixon, *RN: The Memoirs of Richard Nixon* (New York: Grosset and Dunlap, 1978), p. 65.

7. Chambers had a penchant for using aliases, among them "David Breen," "Lloyd Cantwell," "Charles Adams," "Arthur Dwyer," "Harold Phillips," "Carl Carlson," and "George Crosley."

8. Quoted in Richard M. Nixon, *Six Crises* (New York: Warner Books, 1962 and 1979), pp. 7, 8.

9. Whittaker Chambers, *Witness* (New York: Random House, 1952), p. 793 (note).

10. Richard Norton Smith, *Thomas E. Dewey and His Times* (New York: Simon and Schuster, 1982), p. 507.

11. Quoted in Nixon, *RN: The Memoirs of Richard Nixon*, p. 69.

12. Quoted in Clifford with Holbrooke, *Counsel to the President*, p. 230. Truman tried to hamper HUAC's investigation by prohibiting federal agencies from releasing personnel information to Congress.

13. Quoted in Smith, *Thomas E. Dewey and His Times*, p. 506.

14. Allen Weinstein, *Perjury: The Hiss-Chambers Case* (New York: Alfred A. Knopf, 1978), p. 510.

15. "The Christoffel Case—Factual Background." In John F. Kennedy prepresidential papers, Box 98, John F. Kennedy Library.

16. Quoted in David McCullough, *Truman* (New York: Simon and Schuster, 1992), p. 652.

17. Ibid., p. 516.

18. "1951 Speech Kit: Republican Congressional Campaign Committee." In Gerald R. Ford congressional papers, Box G-1, Gerald R. Ford Library.

19. Roper poll, July 19–26, 1948. Don't know, 19 percent; no answer, 2 percent.

20. McCullough, *Truman*, p. 648.

21. Smith, *Thomas E. Dewey and His Times*, p. 558. Most belonged to the communist-dominated American Labor Party.

22. "Text of Dewey Speech at the Hollywood Bowl," *New York Times*, September 25, 1948, p. 2.

23. Clifford with Holbrooke, *Counsel to the President*, p. 230.

24. McGovern did not vote for Wallace, however, because Wallace was not listed on the South Dakota ballot where McGovern maintained a residence. But in an interview, McGovern claimed he would have voted for Wallace if he had a chance to vote. Author's interview with George S. McGovern, Washington, D.C., January 4, 1996.

25. "Progressive Party Platform, 1948," in Kirk H. Porter and Donald Bruce Johnson, *National Party Platforms: 1840–1968* (Urbana: University of Illinois Press, 1970), p. 438.

26. Ibid., p. 437.

27. Ibid., p. 439.

28. Author's interview with McGovern.

29. Quoted in Thomas G. Paterson, *Meeting the Communist Threat: Truman to Reagan* (New York: Oxford University Press, 1988), p. 84.

30. Quoted in Arthur M. Schlesinger Jr., *The Vital Center* (Boston: Houghton Mifflin Company, 1949), p. 49 ff.

31. Clifford, with Holbrooke, *Counsel to the President*, p. 234.

32. McCullough, *Truman*, p. 646.

33. Quoted in V. O. Key, *Politics, Parties, and Pressure Groups*, 5th ed. (New York: Thomas Y. Crowell, 1964), p. 272.

34. Quoted in Clifford with Holbrooke, *Counsel to the President*, p. 224.

35. Quoted in Steven M. Gillion, *Politics and Vision: The ADA and American Liberalism, 1947–1985* (New York: Oxford University Press, 1987), p. 51.

36. Quoted in A. James Reichley, *The Life of the Parties* (New York: Free Press, 1992), p. 297.

37. A September Roper poll found an even higher percentage thinking Wallace was controlled by the communists. Of the 84 percent who had heard or read about Wallace's Progressive Party, 61 percent said the communists were behind it.

38. McCullough, *Truman*, p. 645.

39. Gallup poll, May 23–28, 1947. Sixty-three percent of the Democrats had an unfavorable view of Wallace, whereas just 22 percent were favorable.

40. Roper poll, September 13–20, 1948. Text of question: "Here is a list of people who held important positions during the Roosevelt administrations. Are there any on the list you think were harmful to the country?" Wallace led with 37 percent mentioning him; just 12 percent said Wallace did a "good job for the country."

41. I. F. Stone, *The Truman Era* (New York: Random House, 1973), pp. 67–68.

42. Quoted in Smith, *Thomas E. Dewey and His Times*, p. 509.

43. Harry S. Truman, "Address at the Gilmore Stadium in Los Angeles," September 23, 1948, in *Public Papers of the Presidents of the United States: Harry S. Truman* (Washington, D.C.: Government Printing Office, 1949), pp. 559, 610.

44. Schlesinger, *The Vital Center*, p. 37.

45. Roper poll, July 19–26, 1948. Text of question: "Here are several statements that might be made in campaign speeches and we'd like to know for each one whether you would agree or disagree with a candidate making the statement. . . . We are being too tough with Russia." Agree, 4 percent; disagree, 87 percent; don't know, 8 percent; no answer, 1 percent. From the same poll, "Our present military strength is sufficient and it should not be increased." Agree, 12 percent; disagree, 76 percent; don't know, 11 percent; no answer, 1 percent.

46. Quoted in Smith, *Thomas E. Dewey and His Times*, pp. 487, 493.

47. Ibid., p. 493.

48. Gallup poll, May 28–June 2, 1948. Text of question: "I'd like to ask you which one of the four leading Republican candidates—that is, Dewey, Vandenberg, Taft, or Stassen—would you say would do the best job of dealing with Russia?" Dewey, 20 percent; Vandenberg, 25 percent; Taft, 8 percent; Stassen, 24 percent; no opinion, 24 percent.

49. Quoted in Smith, *Thomas E. Dewey and His Times*, p. 463.

50. Ibid., p. 507. Dewey complained that he was tired of campaigning as a prosecutor and did not want to assume that role in attacking domestic communism.

51. "Text of Dewey Speech," *New York Times*, September 25, 1948, p. 2.

52. See Sean J. Savage, "The Party Leadership Styles of Roosevelt and Truman," paper presented at the annual meeting of the Midwest Political Science Association, Chicago, April 17, 1993, p. 6.

53. Quoted in McCullough, *Truman*, p. 552. Years later Truman privately called the Loyalty and Security Program "terrible." Ibid., p. 553.

54. "Progressive Party Platform, 1948," in Porter and Johnson, *National Party Platforms*, p. 437.

55. Ibid., pp. 552–553.

56. Ibid., p. 553.

57. James S. Pula, *Polish Americans: An Ethnic Community* (New York: Twayne Publishers, 1995), p. 108.

58. McCullough, *Truman*, p. 680.

59. Harry S. Truman, "Address in Oklahoma City," September 28, 1948, in *Public Papers of the Presidents of the United States: Harry S. Truman*, p. 613.

60. Ibid., pp. 609, 613.

61. Ibid., p. 611.

62. "Democratic Party Platform, 1948," in Porter and Johnson, *National Party Platforms: 1840–1968*, pp. 435–436.

63. Truman, "Address in Oklahoma City," in *Public Papers of the Presidents of the United States: Harry S. Truman*, p. 610.

64. Ibid., p. 609.

65. Schlesinger, *The Vital Center*, p. 169.

66. Roper poll, December 1–16, 1946. Text of question: "If the Democrats [Republicans] are elected in 1948, do you think they will or will not . . . allow the communists to have too much influence?" Democrats: Will, 21 percent; will not, 55 percent; don't know, 24 percent. Republicans: Will, 6 percent; will not, 71 percent; don't know, 23 percent.

67. Quoted in David R. Kepley, *The Collapse of the Middle Way: Senate Republicans and the Bipartisan Foreign Policy, 1948–1952* (Westport, Connecticut: Greenwood Press, 1988), p. 58.

68. "1951 Speech Kit: Republican Congressional Campaign Committee."

69. Nixon, *Six Crises*, p. 53.

70. One of the microfilms in the Pumpkin Papers was titled "Portable Carbon Dioxide Fire Extinguishers—Painting Of."

71. Samuel Lubell, *The Future of American Politics* (New York: Harper Colophon Books, first published 1952, 1965 ed.), p. 26.

72. Alexis de Tocqueville, *Democracy in America* (New York: Mentor Books, 1956), p. 81.

73. Quoted in Clifford with Holbrooke, *Counsel to the President*, p. 251. In his Inaugural Address, Truman introduced his "Point IV" program—a proposal to extend technical and financial help to underdeveloped regions of the world in order to prevent further communist advances.

74. National Opinion Research Center, survey, November 1950. Text of question: "Here is a statement that people have a different opinion about, and I'd like to know whether you agree or disagree with it. American communists should have the same rights as Democrats, Republicans, or anyone else." Agree, 15 percent; disagree, 76 percent; don't know, 9 percent. National Opinion Research Center, survey, January 1950. Text of question: "In general, how important do you think it is for the United States to try to stop the spread of communism in the world—very important, only fairly important, or not important at all?" Very important, 77 percent; only fairly important, 10 percent; not important at all, 5 percent; don't know, 8 percent.

75. Gallup poll, July 23–29, 1949. Text of question: "Do you think a man can be a good Christian and at the same time be a member of the Communist Party?"

76. Richard Gid Powers, *Not Without Honor* (New York: Free Press, 1995), p. 254.

77. Ibid., p. 255.

78. Gallup polls, July 22–28, 1949 and July 2–7, 1949. Text of questions: "Some people say that, as long as the Communist Party is permitted by law in the United States, college and university teachers should be allowed to belong to the party and to continue teaching. Do you agree or disagree?" Agree, 15 percent; disagree, 73 percent, no opinion, 12 percent. Text of

question: "The University of California recently said it would require all its teachers to take an oath that they are not communists. Some other colleges oppose this idea because they feel it is an insult to teachers to require them to take such an oath. How do you, yourself, feel about this?" Agree with oath, 72 percent; disagree with oath, 22 percent; no opinion, 6 percent.

79. Quoted in Paterson, *Meeting the Communist Threat*, p. 103.

80. See Smith, *Thomas E. Dewey and His Times*, p. 558.

81. Gallup poll, July 2–7, 1949. Text of question: "As you feel today, which political party—the Republican or Democratic—can handle each of these problems best? Handling the communists in this country." Republican, 37 percent; Democratic, 24 percent; no difference, 28 percent; no opinion, 12 percent. Interestingly, 45 percent of southerners chose the Democrats as the party best able to handle this problem.

82. National Opinion Research Center, survey, November 1948. Text of question: "Do you think it makes much difference to the United States whether China goes Communist or not?" Yes, 71 percent; no, 17 percent; don't know, 12 percent. Gallup poll, November 26-December 3, 1948. Text of question: "Do you think the Chinese Communists take their orders from Moscow, or not?" Yes, 66 percent; no, 12 percent; no opinion, 22 percent.

83. Extracted from John F. Kennedy, "Statement on the Floor of the House of Representatives," January 25, 1949. In John F. Kennedy prepresidential papers, Box 98, John F. Kennedy Library, and John F. Kennedy, "China—Statement of Honorable John F. Kennedy, of Massachusetts," *Congressional Record*, February 21, 1949. In John F. Kennedy prepresidential papers, Box 95, John F. Kennedy Library.

84. See Kepley, *The Collapse of the Middle Way*, p. 63.

85. Quoted in Weinstein, *Perjury*, p. 513.

86. Quoted in Dean Acheson, *Present at the Creation: My Years in the State Department* (New York: W. W. Norton, 1969), p. 360.

87. Ibid., p. 76.

88. Quoted in "The Issue in 1950: Communism vs. Democracy," *New Republic Election Supplement*, October 9, 1950, p. 13.

89. Quoted in Eric Goldman, *The Crucial Decade—And After: America, 1945–1960* (New York: Alfred A. Knopf, 1966), pp. 125, 219.

90. See Smith, *Thomas E. Dewey and His Times*, p. 557.

91. Quoted in Kepley, *The Collapse of the Middle Way*, pp. 71–72, 74.

92. Quoted in Acheson, *Present at the Creation*, p. 364.

93. Gallup poll, March 26–31, 1950. Text of question: "U.S. Senator Joseph McCarthy, Republican of Wisconsin, claims there are communists in the State Department of our government. Do you think this is true—or do you think it's just a case of playing politics?" True, 54 percent; playing politics, 29 percent; no opinion, 17 percent.

94. National Opinion Research Center, survey, December 1952. Text of question: "As you know, there has been a lot of talk about communists in the State Department in Washington. Do you think there is any truth in these charges or not?" Yes, 81 percent; no, 19 percent. Follow-up question: "Do you think such people (communists or disloyal people in the State Department) have done serious harm to our country's interests, or not?" Asked of those who thought there was truth to the charges: Have, 58 percent; have not, 28 percent; don't know, 14 percent.

95. National Opinion Research Center, survey, May 1953. Text of question: "In your opinion, is it more important to find out all the communists in the country, even if some innocent people are accused—or is it more important to protect people who might be innocent, even if some communists are not found out?" Find out about communists, 55 percent; protect innocent people, 37 percent; don't know, 8 percent.

96. Quoted in Patrick J. Buchanan, *Right from the Beginning* (Boston: Little, Brown, 1988), p. 93.

97. Stephen Ambrose, *Nixon: The Education of a Politician, 1913–1962* (New York: Simon and Schuster, 1987), p. 215.

98. "1951 Speech Kit: Republican Congressional Campaign Committee."

99. The demarcation line was chosen by two young colonels in the War Department, Dean Rusk and Charles Bonesteel. They chose the 38th parallel because it was a narrow little neck. This offer was made to the Soviets and, to the surprise of U.S. officials, it was accepted. See David Halberstam, *The Fifties* (New York: Villard, 1993), p. 63.

100. National Opinion Research Center, survey, September 1950. Text of question: "As things stand now, do you think the United States was right or wrong to send American troops to stop the communist invasion in Korea?" Right, 81 percent; wrong, 13 percent; don't know, 6 percent. Second question: "Do you think it would be a good idea or a bad idea for the United States to tell Russia now that we will immediately go to war against her with all our power, if any communist army attacks any other country?" Good idea, 59 percent; bad idea, 31 percent; don't know, 11 percent.

101. A December 1951 National Opinion Research survey showed support at 55 percent; a year later it was 56 percent; in June 1952 it was back at a steady 55 percent.

102. National Opinion Research Center, survey, September 1953. Text of question: "As you look back on the Korean war, do you think the United States did the right thing in sending troops to stop the communist invasion, or should we have stayed out of it entirely?" U.S. should have stayed out, 28 percent; U.S. did the right thing, 64 percent; don't know, 8 percent.

103. Claude Denson Pepper with Hays Gorey, *Pepper: Eyewitness to a Century* (New York: Harcourt Brace Jovanovich, 1987), p. 205. The authors cite an unpublished Ph.D. dissertation written by Richard D. Hutto, "Political Feud in the Palmettos: A Chronology and Analysis of the 1950 Florida Senatorial Campaign."

104. Ralph McGill, "Can He Purge Senator Pepper?" *Saturday Evening Post*, April 22, 1950, p. 33.

105. Quoted in Pepper with Gorey, *Pepper*, p. 198.

106. Paterson, *Meeting the Communist Threat*, p. 105.

107. McGill, "Can He Purge Senator Pepper?," pp. 32–33.

108. Pepper with Gorey, *Pepper: Eyewitness to a Century*, p. 203.

109. The Supreme Court later overturned the McCarran Act, saying it violated the Fifth Amendment's protection against self-incrimination.

110. Herbert Parmet, *Richard Nixon and His America* (Boston: Little, Brown, 1990), p. 195

111. Quoted in Acheson, *Present at the Creation*, p. 365.

112. Quoted in Richard Pearson, "Margaret Chase Smith Dies; GOP Senator from Maine," *Washington Post*, May 30, 1995, p. B-6.

113. Quoted in Acheson, *Present at the Creation*, pp. 364–365.

114. "1951 Speech Kit: Republican Congressional Campaign Committee."

115. Ibid.

116. See Walter Pincus, "Papers Show Mao Wary of Korean War," *Washington Post*, December 20, 1995, p. A-27. The letter was found in a search of the Soviet archives.

117. Quoted in Parmet, *Richard Nixon and His America*, p. 190.

118. Quoted in Nixon: *RN: The Memoirs of Richard Nixon*, p. 73.

119. See Richard I. Miller, "Resident Remembers Richard M. Nixon," *Lexington Minuteman*, April 28, 1994, letter to the editor. Miller was chairman of Students for Douglas.

120. John Herbers, "In Three Decades, Nixon Tasted Crisis and Defeat, Ruin and Revival," *New York Times*, April 24, 1994, p. 30.

121. Quoted in Janice Mathews, "On the Paper Trail of the Assassins," *Extensions*, Spring 1994, p. 16.

122. Parmet, *Richard Nixon and His America*, p. 215.

123. Ibid., p. 199.

124. At the time, Reagan had a moderate position on domestic communism. Testifying before the House Un-American Activities Committee, Reagan opposed outlawing the U.S. Communist Party: "As a citizen I would hesitate, or not like, to see any political party outlawed on the basis of its political ideology. . . . I detest, I abhor their philosophy, but I detest more than that their tactics, which are those of the fifth column, and are dishonest, but at the same time I never as a citizen want to see our country become urged, either by fear or resentment of this group, that we ever compromise with our democratic principles through that fear or resentment. I still think that democracy can do it."

125. Quoted in Jonathan Aitken, *Nixon: A Life* (Washington, D.C.: Regnery Publishing, 1993), p. 184.

126. Quoted in Michael Barone, *Our Country: The Shaping of America from Roosevelt to Reagan* (New York: Free Press, 1990), p. 240.

127. See Pula, *Polish Americans: An Ethnic Community*, p. 111.

128. *The Presidential Transcripts* (New York: Dell Publishing, 1974), p. 435.

129. Ibid., p. 56.

130. Ronald Reagan, "Announcement of the Recipients of the Presidential Medal of Freedom," February 21, 1984, in *Public Papers of the Presidents of the United States: Ronald Reagan* (Washington, D.C.: Government Printing Office, 1985), p. 415.

131. Tony Hiss, "My Father's Honor," *New Yorker*, November 2, 1992, p. 106.

132. Dmitri A. Volkogonov to John Lowenthal, *Cold War International History Project Bulletin*, Woodrow Wilson International Center for Scholars, Washington, D.C., Fall 1992, p. 33. In an interview, former KGB general Oleg Kalugin repeatedly asserted that Hiss was "never a Soviet KGB agent." Author's interview with Oleg Kalugin, Washington, D.C., March 18, 1995.

133. Jeffrey A. Frank, "Stalin Biographer Offers Latest Twist in Hiss Case," *Washington Post*, October 31, 1992, p. A-3.

134. Ibid.

135. George F. Will, "'Exoneration' of Alger Hiss," *Newsweek*, November 1, 1993, p. 66.

136. Arthur M. Schlesinger Jr., *The Cycles of American History* (Boston: Houghton Mifflin, 1986), p. 67.

137. Quoted in Powers, *Not Without Honor*, p. 266. After the Cold War, it was revealed that a CIA-led team of code-breakers verified that Julius and Ethel Rosenberg were part of a spy ring that give the blueprints of the atomic bomb to the Soviets. See Tim Weiner, "Code-crackers Reveal World War II Secret," *Denver Post*, July 12, 1995, p. 12A.

138. See especially Louis Hartz, *The Liberal Tradition in America* (New York: Harcourt Brace Jovanovich, 1955).

139. Richard Hofstadter, "The Pseudo-Conservative Revolt (1955)," in Daniel Bell, ed., *The Radical Right* (Garden City, New York: Anchor Books, Doubleday, 1964), p. 90.

140. Powers, *Not Without Honor*, p. 244.

141. Carl Solberg, *Hubert Humphrey: A Biography* (New York: W. W. Norton, 1984), p. 158, and "Statement of Senator Humphrey of Minnesota," *Congressional Record*, April 24, 1952, p. 4446.

142. Quoted in Charles L. Garrettson III, *Hubert H. Humphrey: The Politics of Joy* (New Brunswick, New Jersey: Transaction Publishers, 1993), p. 281.

143. Solberg, *Hubert Humphrey: A Biography*, p. 158. Eisenhower disapproved of the measure and the Republican Senate negated the Humphrey amendment by removing the penalties for joining the U.S. Communist Party. The final bill became the Communist Control Act of 1954.

144. Goldman, *The Crucial Decade—And After*, p. 237.

145. Acheson, *Present at the Creation*, pp. 354–370.

146. National Opinion Research Center, survey, November 1954. Text of question: "It has been said that there are some groups of people in this country who are 'soft on communism.' Do you agree or disagree?" Agree, 53 percent; disagree, 26 percent; don't know, 21 percent.

147. Parmet, *Richard Nixon and His America*, p. 209.

148. Gallup polls November 3–8, 1948, and January 1–5, 1951. Text of question: "In general, who do you think is winning the Cold War—the United States or Russia?" 1948 responses: U.S., 31 percent; Russia, 28 percent; neither, 30 percent; no opinion, 11 percent. 1951 responses: U.S., 9 percent; Russia, 30 percent; neither, 12 percent; no opinion, 4 percent.

149. "1951 Speech Kit: Republican Congressional Campaign Committee."

150. Recounted in Ambrose, *Nixon: The Education of a Politician*, p. 223.

Chapter Three

1. "Text of President's Address Presenting Stevenson to Convention," *New York Times*, July 26, 1952, p. 4.

2. Gallup poll, January 20–25, 1952. Text of question: "Do you approve or disapprove of the way Harry Truman is handling his job as President?" Approve, 25 percent; disapprove, 62 percent; no opinion, 13 percent.

3. Quoted in Eric F. Goldman, *The Crucial Decade—And After: America, 1945–1960* (New York: Alfred A. Knopf, 1966), p. 218.

4. Cited in John Foster Dulles, "A Policy of Boldness," *Life*, May 19, 1952, p. 146.

5. Cited in Michael Barone, *Our Country: The Shaping of America from Roosevelt to Reagan* (New York: Free Press, 1990), p. 238.

6. Quoted in Goldman, *The Crucial Decade—And After*, p. 218.

7. Dulles, "A Policy of Boldness," p. 146.

8. Quoted in Stephen E. Ambrose, *Nixon: The Education of a Politician, 1913–1962* (New York: Simon and Schuster, 1987), p. 227.

9. Dwight D. Eisenhower, *Mandate for Change* (Garden City, New York: Doubleday, 1963), p. 83.

10. Dulles, "A Policy of Boldness," p. 146.

11. "1951 Speech Kit: Republican Congressional Campaign Committee." In Gerald R. Ford congressional papers, Box G-1, Gerald R. Ford Library.

12. Quoted in David Halberstam, *The Fifties* (New York: Villard, 1993), p. 62.

13. Gallup poll, February 28-March 5, 1952. Text of question: "Do you think the United States made a mistake in going into the war in Korea, or not?" Yes, 51 percent; no, 35 percent; no opinion, 14 percent. Gallup poll, February 28-March 3, 1952. Text of question: "Suppose that a truce settlement is reached in Korea. As matters stand today, which side—ours or the enemy's—do you think will have won the bigger victory?" Our side, 30 percent; enemy, 33 percent; neither, 23 percent; no opinion, 14 percent.

14. Quoted in Malcolm Moos, *The Republicans: A History of Their Party* (New York: Random House, 1956), p. 490.

15. "Republican Platform, 1952," in Kirk H. Porter and Donald Bruce Johnson, *National Party Platforms: 1840–1968* (Urbana: University of Illinois Press, 1970), p. 497.

16. Gallup survey, June 15–20, 1952. Text of question: "Suppose that between now and the [1952] election the war situation begins to look worse. In that case, would you prefer to have the Republicans in office or the Democrats?" Republicans/qualified Republicans, 49 percent; Democrats/qualified Democrats, 32 percent; no difference, 13 percent; no opinion, 6 percent.

17. Quoted in Moos, *The Republicans*, p. 490.

18. Quoted in Ambrose, *Nixon: The Education of a Politician*, p. 243.

19. Ernest K. Lindley, "Is There Real Danger of War?" *Newsweek*, May 15, 1950, p. 27.

20. Quoted in Allen Freeman, "Echoes of the Cold War," *Historic Preservation*, January/February 1994, p. 86.

21. "Wonderful to Play In," *Time*, February 5, 1951, p. 12.

22. Cited in John Gerring, *Party Ideology in America, 1828–1992*, unpublished manuscript, 1996, p. 239.

23. Robert A. Taft, *A Foreign Policy for All Americans* (Garden City, New York: Doubleday, 1951), pp. 118–119.

24. Tom Shales, "Golden Glow of the First 'Honeymooners,'" *Washington Post*, April 19, 1993, p. C-1.

25. Cited in Halberstam, *The Fifties*, p. 59.

26. Whittaker Chambers, *Witness* (New York: Random House, 1952), p. 14. Garry Wills describes how *Witness* was regarded as a "kind of bible in the Quayle family." See Garry Wills, "Late Bloomer," *Time*, April 23, 1990, p. 29.

27. Quoted in Allen Weinstein, *Perjury: The Hiss-Chambers Case* (New York: Alfred A. Knopf, 1978), p. 518.

28. Quoted from the "Foreword" by George F. Will in Clinton Rossiter, *Conservatism in America* (Cambridge, Massachusetts: Harvard University Press, 1982 ed.), p. v.

29. Henry R. Luce, "The American Century," *Life*, February 17, 1941.

30. Taft, *A Foreign Policy for All Americans*, p. 17.

31. Dulles, "A Policy of Boldness," p. 146.

32. Quoted in "Statements of General Eisenhower on National Issues," Democratic National Committee, August 23, 1952. In John F. Kennedy prepresidential papers, Box 101, 1952 campaign files, John F. Kennedy Library.

33. Quoted in Robert A. Divine, *Foreign Policy and U.S. Presidential Elections* (New York: New Viewpoints, 1974), p. 55. See also James S. Pula, *Polish Americans: An Ethnic Community* (New York: Twayne Publishers, 1995), p. 113.

34. Quoted in Goldman, *The Crucial Decade—And After*, pp. 130, 131.

35. Eisenhower, *Mandate for Change*, p. 37.

36. "Republican Platform, 1952," in Porter and Johnson, *National Party Platforms*, p. 497.

37. Democratic National Committee, "Foreign Policy: Diplomacy by Slogan Weakens Free World," 1956. In Robert F. Kennedy preadministration files, Box 1, John F. Kennedy Library.

38. Dulles, "A Policy of Boldness," p. 154.

39. Gallup poll, July 25–30, 1952.

40. Quoted in Rudolph L. Treuenfels, ed., *Eisenhower Speaks: Dwight D. Eisenhower in His Messages and Speeches* (New York: Farrar Straus, 1948), p. 46.

41. Quoted in Democratic National Committee, "Statements of General Eisenhower on National Issues," August 23, 1952.

42. Quoted in Divine, *Foreign Policy and U.S. Presidential Elections*, pp. 28–29.

43. Gallup poll, January 20–25, 1952. Text of question: "Senator Robert Taft and General Dwight Eisenhower are two of the candidates for the Republican nomination. Which one do you think would handle this country's foreign policy better?" Eisenhower, 70 percent; Taft, 18 percent; no opinion, 12 percent.

44. Quoted in Halberstam, *The Fifties*, p. 205.

45. Quoted in Roger Morris, *Richard Milhous Nixon: The Rise of an American Politician* (New York: Henry Holt, 1990), p. 667.

46. Gallup poll, December 10–15, 1948. Text of question: "What do you yourself think the Republican party will have to do between now and 1952 in order to win the presidential elec-

tion that year?" Nothing—people will get tired of the Democrats, 2 percent; get better candidates, good men, new men, need strong candidates, new blood, 24 percent; work harder, get more people to vote, fight to gain the confidence of labor, agriculture, and poor people, 11 percent; reorganize the platform, change policies, become more liberal, 17 percent; general do a lot of changing, wake up, 3 percent; cooperation—between the two parties with the present government, 1 percent; derogatory—they'll never win again, 8 percent.

47. Quoted in Halberstam, *The Fifties*, p. 209. Eisenhower admitted to being a Republican, telling reporters at a 1952 press conference: "In 1948 I voted the Republican ticket and there were two special elections in New York, one in 1949 and then for Governor in 1950, and I voted the Republican ticket and that is my entire voting record." Press conference, Abilene, Kansas, June 5, 1952.

48. Gallup poll, March 14–19, 1952. Earlier surveys taken by the Gallup organization revealed Eisenhower's popularity: In January 1948 Eisenhower beat Truman 47 percent to 40 percent while Taft lost by 51 percent to 31 percent. See Gallup poll, January 2–7, 1948.

49. Quoted in Moos, *The Republicans*, p. 489.

50. Quoted in Halberstam, *The Fifties*, pp. 235–236.

51. Quoted in Eisenhower, *Mandate for Change*, p. 17.

52. Gallup poll, June 1952. Others and no opinion responses totaled 8 percent.

53. Eisenhower, *Mandate for Change*, p. 46.

54. Richard M. Nixon, *RN: The Memoirs of Richard Nixon* (New York: Grosset and Dunlap, 1978), p. 82.

55. Ambrose, *Nixon: The Education of a Politician*, p. 231.

56. Moos, *The Republicans*, p. 476.

57. Quoted in Halberstam, *The Fifties*, p. 209.

58. Quoted in Divine, *Foreign Policy and U.S. Presidential Elections*, p. 31.

59. Taft, *A Foreign Policy for All Americans*, pp. 74, 77.

60. Ibid., pp. 12, 81.

61. Ibid., pp. 21, 23, 43, 102.

62. Ibid., p. 102.

63. Gallup poll, June 15–20, 1952. Text of question: "Here is a list of men who have been mentioned as possible presidential candidates this year for the Republican Party. Which one would you like to see nominated as the Republican candidate for president?" Republicans: Eisenhower, 44 percent; Taft, 35 percent. Independents: Eisenhower, 48 percent; Taft, 19 percent.

64. Quoted in Halberstam, *The Fifties*, p. 214.

65. Quoted in Herbert Brownell with John P. Burke, *Advising Ike* (Lawrence: University of Kansas Press, 1993), p. 117.

66. Quoted in Halberstam, *The Fifties*, p. 212.

67. Quoted in Garry Wills, *Reagan's America: Innocents at Home* (Garden City, New York: Doubleday, 1987), p. 286.

68. Quoted in Democratic National Committee, "Statements of General Eisenhower on National Issues," Research Division, Supplement A, September 17, 1952. In John F. Kennedy prepresidential papers, Box 101, 1952 campaign files, John F. Kennedy Library.

69. Quoted in John Bartlow Martin, *Adlai Stevenson of Illinois* (Garden City, New York: Anchor Books, Doubleday, 1977), p. 676.

70. "Text of Eisenhower and Nixon Addresses to the Convention," *New York Times*, July 12, 1952, p. 4.

71. "Democratic Platform, 1952," in Porter and Johnson, *National Party Platforms*, p. 473.

72. Quoted in Halberstam, *The Fifties*, p. 219.

73. Ibid., p. 222.

74. Martin, *Adlai Stevenson of Illinois*, pp. 523–524.

75. "Text of Stevenson's Speeches of Acceptance," *New York Times*, July 26, 1952, p. 5.

76. "Hiss Loses Plea for Another Trial; Court Rejects His 'New Evidence,'" *New York Times*, July 23, 1952, p. 1.

77. "Text of Stevenson Speech of Welcome to Convention," *New York Times*, July 22, 1952, p. 12.

78. Adlai E. Stevenson, "Korea," in *Major Campaign Speeches of Adlai E. Stevenson, 1952* (New York: Random House, 1953), p. 188.

79. "Text of Stevenson Speech of Welcome to Convention," *New York Times*, July 22, 1952, p. 12.   •

80. Quoted in Herbert Parmet, *Richard Nixon and His America* (Boston: Little, Brown, 1990), p. 261.

81. "Text of Stevenson's Speeches of Acceptance," p. 5.

82. "Text of President's Address Presenting Stevenson to Convention," p. 4.

83. Stevenson, "Safeguards Against Communism," in *Major Campaign Speeches of Adlai E. Stevenson, 1952*, p. 214.

84. Quoted in Moos, *The Republicans*, p. 488.

85. "Stevenson Calls Republicans 'Party of the Past and of Fear,'" *New York Times*, September 12, 1952.

86. Stevenson, "Safeguards Against Communism," in *Major Campaign Speeches of Adlai E. Stevenson, 1952*, p. 214.

87. See Divine, *Foreign Policy and U.S. Presidential Elections*, p. 43.

88. "Republican Platform, 1952," in Porter and Johnson, *National Party Platforms*, p. 500.

89. Quoted in Divine, *Foreign Policy and U.S. Presidential Elections*, p. 35.

90. Quoted in Tom Wicker, *One of Us: Richard Nixon and the American Dream* (New York: Random House, 1991), p. 85.

91. Quoted in Parmet, *Richard Nixon and His America*, p. 237.

92. Quoted in Michael Lind, "The Myth of Barry Goldwater," *New York Review of Books*, November 30, 1995, p. 24.

93. Quoted in Clark Clifford with Richard Holbrooke, *Counsel to the President: A Memoir* (New York: Anchor Books, Doubleday, 1991), p. 142.

94. National Opinion Research Center, survey, December 1952. Text of first question: "As you know, there has been a lot of talk about communists or disloyal people in the State Department in Washington. Do you think there is any truth in these charges, or not?" Yes, 81 percent; no, 19 percent. Second question: "Do you think such people (communists or disloyal people in the State Department) have done any serious harm to our country's interests, or not?" Have, 58 percent; have not, 28 percent; don't know, 14 percent.

95. Martin, *Adlai Stevenson of Illinois*, p. 477.

96. Quoted in Clifford with Holbrooke, *Counsel to the President*, p. 142.

97. Stevenson, "The Threat of Communism," in *Major Campaign Speeches of Adlai E. Stevenson, 1952*, p. 129.

98. Stevenson, "On Liberty of Conscience," in *Major Campaign Speeches of Adlai E. Stevenson, 1952*, p. 246.

99. Stevenson, "The Nature of Patriotism," in *Major Campaign Speeches of Adlai E. Stevenson, 1952*, p. 20.

100. Stevenson, "Faith in Liberalism," in *Major Campaign Speeches of Adlai E. Stevenson, 1952*, p. 32.

101. Harry S. Truman, "A Candid Analysis of the '52 Election," *Life*, February 20, 1956, p. 122.

102. Opinion Research Corporation, survey, September 4–17, 1952. Text of question: "Should they (the next administration) do a great deal more to clean out communists in the government or is that pretty well under control?" Yes, should do more, 74 percent; under control, 15 percent; no opinion, 10 percent.

103. Eisenhower, *Mandate for Change*, pp. 46–47.

104. Quoted in Nixon, *RN: The Memoirs of Richard Nixon*, p. 88.

105. Quoted in Morris, *Richard Milhous Nixon*, p. 734.

106. Ibid., p. 795. Adlai Stevenson had an even larger fund from which he supplemented the salaries of Illinois state employees. Nixon claimed the fund totaled $16,000.

107. Quoted in Morris, *Richard Milhous Nixon*, pp. 759–760.

108. Ibid., pp. 769, 772–774.

109. Quoted in Stephen E. Ambrose, *Eisenhower: Soldier and President* (New York: Simon and Schuster, 1990), p. 279.

110. Quoted in Morris, *Richard Milhous Nixon*, p. 833.

111. Quoted in Nixon, *RN: The Memoirs of Richard Nixon*, pp. 101–102.

112. Quoted in Nixon, *Six Crises* (New York: Warner Books, 1979 rep.), p. 144.

113. Quoted in Parmet, *Richard Nixon and His America*, p. 228.

114. Quoted in Morris, *Richard Milhous Nixon*, p. 859.

115. William R. Conklin, "Nixon Criticizes Stevenson in Hiss Trial," *New York Times*, October 14, 1952, p. 1.

116. Adlai E. Stevenson, "The Hiss Case," in *Major Campaign Speeches of Adlai E. Stevenson, 1952*, pp. 271, 272.

117. Weinstein, *Perjury*, p. 512.

118. Quoted in Martin, *Adlai Stevenson of Illinois*, p. 705.

119. Divine, *Foreign Policy and U.S. Presidential Elections*, p. 80.

120. Quoted in Martin, *Adlai Stevenson of Illinois*, p. 741.

121. Ibid., p. 744.

122. Weinstein, *Perjury*, p. 511.

123. Quoted in Halberstam, *The Fifties*, p. 250.

124. "Anti-Communist Voices of Yesterday," audio cassette, 1951–1952. Published by 123 Audio Forum.

125. Ibid.

126. Quoted in Ambrose, *Eisenhower: Soldier and President*, p. 269. McCarthy described Marshall as "a man steeped in falsehood." Quoted in Martin, *Adlai Stevenson of Illinois*, p. 712 n.

127. Quoted in Ambrose, *Eisenhower: Soldier and President*, pp. 269, 276, 282.

128. Quoted in Divine, *Foreign Policy and U.S. Presidential Elections*, p. 60.

129. Quoted in Ambrose, *Eisenhower: Soldier and President*, pp. 283, 284.

130. Ibid., p. 283.

131. Eisenhower later regretted his embrace of McCarthy: "Indeed, if I could have foreseen this distortion of the facts, a distortion that even led some to question any loyalty to General Marshall, I would never have acceded to the staff's arguments, logical as they sounded at the time." See Eisenhower, *Mandate for Change*, p. 318.

132. Moos, *The Republicans*, p. 485.

133. Eisenhower, *Mandate for Change*, p. 72.

134. Moos, *The Republicans*, p. 491.

135. Quoted in Divine, *Foreign Policy and U.S. Presidential Elections*, p. 79.

136. Gallup poll, October 9–14, 1952. Text of question: "Which presidential candidate—Stevenson or Eisenhower—do you think could handle the Korean situation best?" Eisenhower, 65 percent; Stevenson, 19 percent; no difference (volunteered), 8 percent; no opinion, 8 percent.

137. See "How Many Minutes to Midnight 50 Years After the A-Bomb's Birth?" *New York Times*, December 3, 1995, p. E-7.

138. "Text of Eisenhower's Speech Ending Campaign with Appeal for Unity," *New York Times*, November 4, 1952, p. 23.

139. Quoted in Moos, *The Republicans*, p. 487. See Gallup poll, October 17–22, 1952. Text of question: "How much thought have you given to the coming (1952) election for President—quite a lot, or only a little?' Quite a lot, 60 percent; some (volunteered), 19 percent; only a little, 19 percent; none (volunteered), 3 percent.

140. Cited in Moos, *The Republicans*, p. 486.

141. Dean Acheson, *Present at the Creation: My Years in the State Department* (New York: W. W. Norton, 1969), p. 693.

142. Ibid., p. 485.

143. Ibid., p. 500.

144. Quoted in *Life*, editorial, "The Republicans and the South," May 19, 1952, p. 34.

145. Cited in Moos, *The Republicans*, pp. 485, 507.

146. E. E. Schattschneider, "1954: The Ike Party Fights to Live," *New Republic*, February 23, 1953, pp. 16–17.

147. Quoted in Ambrose, *Eisenhower: Soldier and President*, p. 275.

148. Richard Hofstadter, "The Pseudo-Conservative Revolt," in Daniel Bell, ed., *The Radical Right* (Garden City, New York: Doubleday, 1963), p. 80, note 8.

149. See Pula, *Polish Americans: An Ethnic Community*, p. 114.

150. Patrick J. Buchanan, *Right from the Beginning* (Boston: Little, Brown, 1988), p. 220.

151. Quoted in Halberstam, *The Fifties*, p. 234.

152. Brownell, *Advising Ike*, pp. 131, 235.

153. In September 1952, Stewart Alsop told his brother, John, that among those with whom he was associated, Stevenson was doing well. John Alsop responded: "Sure, all the eggheads are for Stevenson, but how many eggheads are there?" See Halberstam, *The Fifties*, p. 235. Eisenhower worried about Stevenson's appeal to the intelligentsia. Watching Stevenson's Acceptance Speech on television, Ike noted his polished phrasing and contrasted it with his mangled syntax. George Allen reassured him: "He's too accomplished an orator; he'll be easy to beat." Ibid., p. 234.

154. Quoted in Moos, *The Republicans*, pp. 512–513. Still, as Murray Kempton said of the 1952 outcome: "The knuckleheads have beaten the eggheads." See Divine, *Foreign Policy and U.S. Presidential Elections*, p. 82.

155. Quoted in George McGovern, *Grassroots: The Autobiography of George McGovern* (New York: Random House, 1977), p. 50.

156. Cited in Lawrence Fuchs, *John F. Kennedy and American Catholicism* (New York: Meredith Press, 1967), p. 161.

157. Gallup poll, October 17–22, 1952. Text of question: "Looking ahead for the next few years, which political party—the Republican or Democratic—do you think will be best for people like yourself?"

158. Gallup poll, July 25–30, 1952. Text of question: "Do you think there will or will not be more unemployment if the Republicans win the election in November?" Will, 48 percent; will not, 34 percent; no opinion, 18 percent. Gallup poll, September 11–16, 1952. Text of question: "Just making your best guess about the next few years, do you think you will be better off financially if the Republicans or the Democrats win in November (1952)? (If no differ-

ence or no opinion ask:) Well, if you have to make up your mind today on whether you would likely be better off in a money way if the Republicans or the Democrats win in November, which party would you choose?" Republicans, 25 percent; lean Republican, 12 percent; Democrats, 37 percent; lean Democratic, 10 percent; no difference/no lean, 3 percent; no opinion/still no opinion, 14 percent.

159. Gallup poll, August 31-September 5, 1952. Text of question: "Which candidate—the Republican or Democratic—do you think would most likely do the best job of keeping us out of another world war?" Republican, 43 percent; Democratic, 24 percent; no difference (volunteered) 22 percent; no opinion, 11 percent.

160. Cited in Moos, *The Republicans*, p. 486.

161. Those were Vermont, New York, Minnesota, Delaware, and California. Goldwater's defeat of Ernest McFarland by 6,275 votes set the stage for Lyndon Johnson to become Senate majority leader in 1953.

162. Quoted in Moos, *The Republicans*, p. 493.

163. Quoted in Divine, *Foreign Policy and U.S. Presidential Elections*, p. 81.

164. Harry S. Truman, "Farewell Address," Washington, D.C., January 15, 1953.

165. Eisenhower, *Mandate for Change*, p. 76.

166. "Text of Stevenson Speech of Welcome to Convention," p. 12.

167. Quoted in Divine, *Foreign Policy and U.S. Presidential Elections*, p. 83.

168. Quoted in Goldman, *The Crucial Decade—And After*, p. 235.

169. Daniel Bell, *The End of Ideology* (Glencoe, Illinois: Free Press, 1960).

Chapter Four

1. Dwight D. Eisenhower, "Inaugural Address," Washington, D.C., January 20, 1953.

2. Arthur Krock, "Mighty Pageant Is Proof," *New York Times*, January 21, 1953, p. 1.

3. Dwight D. Eisenhower, *Mandate for Change, 1953–1956* (Garden City, New York: Doubleday, 1963), p. 3.

4. "Republican Party Platform, 1956," in Kirk H. Porter and Donald Bruce Johnson, *National Party Platforms: 1840–1968* (Urbana: University of Illinois Press, 1970), p. 546.

5. Quoted in Robert A. Divine, *Foreign Policy and U.S. Presidential Elections, 1952–1960* (New York: New Viewpoints, 1974), p. 134.

6. Dwight D. Eisenhower, "Acceptance Speech," Republican National Convention, San Francisco, August 23, 1956, and Republican Congressional Campaign Committee, "Republican Speech Kit, 1956." In Gerald R. Ford congressional papers, "1956 Campaign Speech Kit," Box G-3, Gerald R. Ford Library.

7. Eisenhower, *Mandate for Change*, pp. 518, 527.

8. Eisenhower, "Acceptance Speech," Republican National Convention, August 23, 1956.

9. Ibid.

10. "Republican Party Platform, 1956," in Porter and Johnson, *National Party Platforms*, p. 545.

11. Quoted in Divine, *Foreign Policy and U.S. Presidential Elections, 1952–1960*, p. 134. Eisenhower used the phrase "Waging Peace" for volume two of his memoirs. See Dwight D. Eisenhower, *Waging Peace, 1956–1961* (Garden City, New York: Doubleday, 1965).

12. Eisenhower, "Acceptance Speech," Republican National Convention, August 23, 1956.

13. "Republican Platform, 1956," in Porter and Johnson, *National Party Platforms*, p. 558.

14. Quoted in Divine, *Foreign Policy and U.S. Presidential Elections, 1952–1960*, p. 172.

15. Republican Congressional Campaign Committee, "1956 Speech Kit."

16. Arthur M. Schlesinger Jr. to John F. Kennedy, letter dated January 10, 1955. In Theodore Sorensen papers, 1953–1960, Box 11, John F. Kennedy Library.

17. James Reston, "Eisenhower by a Landslide," *New York Times*, November 7, 1956, p. 1.

18. "Eisenhower, the Leader," *New York Times*, November 7, 1956, p. 12.

19. "Speeches by Eisenhower, Nixon," *New York Times*, November 7, 1956, p. 12.

20. Arthur Larson, *A Republican Looks at His Party* (New York: Harper and Brothers, 1956), pp. 14, 15, ix.

21. Eisenhower, "Acceptance Speech," Republican National Convention, August 23, 1956.

22. Larson, *A Republican Looks at His Party*, p. 19.

23. Barry M. Goldwater with Jack Casserly, *Goldwater* (New York: Doubleday, 1988), p. 109.

24. Cited in Democratic National Committee, press release, May 17, 1957. In Theodore Sorensen papers, 1953–1960, Box 10, John F. Kennedy Library.

25. Cited in John F. Kennedy, *The Strategy of Peace* (New York: Harper and Brothers, 1960), p. 176.

26. Dwight D. Eisenhower, "Statement by the President Upon Signing the National Defense Education Act," September 2, 1958. In *Public Papers of the Presidents of the United States: Dwight D. Eisenhower* (Washington, D.C.: U.S. Government Printing Office, 1959), p. 224.

27. Eisenhower, "Inaugural Address," Washington, D.C., January 20, 1953.

28. Quoted in Kennedy, *The Strategy of Peace*, p. 178.

29. Quoted in Lyndon B. Johnson, *The Vantage Point: Perspectives on the Presidency, 1963–1969* (New York: Holt, Rinehart, and Winston, 1971), p. 275.

30. Eisenhower, *Mandate for Change*, p. 549.

31. Eisenhower, "Acceptance Speech," Republican National Convention, August 23, 1956.

32. Samuel Lubell, *The Future of American Politics* (New York: Harper and Row, 1965 ed.), p. 231.

33. Dwight D. Eisenhower, "Farewell Address," Washington, D.C., January 17, 1961.

34. Ibid.

35. Quoted in Stephen E. Ambrose, *Nixon: Ruin and Recovery, 1973–1990* (New York: Simon and Schuster, 1991), p. 366.

36. Eisenhower, "Farewell Address," January 17, 1961.

37. See H.R. Haldeman, *The Haldeman Diaries: Inside the Nixon White House* (New York: G. P. Putnam's Sons, 1994), p. 39. Eisenhower sent his message on March 13, 1969, and died fifteen days later.

38. Eisenhower, "Farewell Address," January 17, 1961.

39. Quoted in Richard Reeves, "1954," *American Heritage*, December 1994, p. 32.

40. Ibid.

41. Ibid., pp. 32–33.

42. See Bruce L. Felknor, *Political Mischief: Smear, Sabotage, and Reform in U.S. Elections* (New York: Praeger, 1992), p. 35.

43. Reeves, "1954," p. 33.

44. Cited in Fred I. Greenstein, *The Hidden-Hand Presidency: Eisenhower As Leader* (New York: Basic Books, 1982), p. 175.

45. Gallup poll, August 26–31, 1954. Text of question: "During the next few months, you will be hearing various reasons why you should vote for one political party or the other. Please tell me which of the following reasons would help you to make up your mind to vote Republican or Democratic. Let's take first the arguments which the Republicans are using against the Democrats. The Republicans are saying that . . . the Republicans have gotten rid of a lot of

Reds in the government. In your case, is that a strong or a weak argument to get you to vote Republican?" Strong, 58 percent; weak, 32 percent; no opinion, 10 percent.

46. Quoted in Greenstein, *The Hidden-Hand Presidency*, pp. 200, 189, 195, 194.

47. Quoted in Herbert Parmet, *Richard Nixon and His America* (Boston: Little, Brown, 1990), p. 260. Ironically, Nixon's speech was broadcast the same week as Edward R. Murrow's famous indictment of McCarthy on his CBS program "See It Now."

48. Kennedy was recuperating from a serious back operation at the time of the censure vote.

49. Quoted in John Bartlow Martin, *Adlai Stevenson and the World* (Garden City, New York: Anchor Books/Doubleday, 1978), p. 385.

50. Harrison Salisbury, "Stevenson Lays Defeat to Crisis," *New York Times*, November 8, 1956, p. 1.

51. National Opinion Research Center, poll, November 1956. Text of question: "Do you expect the United States to get into an all-out war with Russia during the next two years?" (If "no" or "don't know," ask:) "Do you think we can avoid a big war with Russia entirely, or will we have to fight them sooner or later?" Yes, all-out war in the next two years; 23 percent; can avoid big war, 34 percent; have to fight sooner or later, 33 percent; don't know, 8 percent.

52. See Divine, *Foreign Policy and U.S. Presidential Elections, 1952–1960*, p. 178.

53. Salisbury, "Stevenson Lays Defeat to Crisis," p. 1.

54. Quoted in Divine, *Foreign Policy and U.S. Presidential Elections, 1952–1960*, p. 178.

55. Quoted in Johnson, *The Vantage Point*, p. 272.

56. Ibid., pp. 70–71.

57. Quoted in Eric Goldman, *The Crucial Decade—And After: America, 1945–1960* (New York: Alfred A. Knopf, 1966), pp. 313, 310.

58. ABC News, "The Missiles of October," broadcast, 1992.

59. Quoted in David Halberstam, *The Fifties* (New York: Villard, 1993), p. 723.

60. James R. Shepley, "How Dulles Averted War," *Life*, January 16, 1956, p. 78.

61. Ibid.

62. Ibid.

63. Quoted in Divine, *Foreign Policy and U.S. Presidential Elections, 1952–1960*, pp. 96, 97.

64. Gallup poll, October 1964.

65. Cited in Haldeman, *The Haldeman Diaries*, p. 448.

66. "Republican Platform, 1976," in Porter and Johnson, *National Party Platforms*, p. 987.

67. "Republican Platform, 1960," in Porter and Johnson, *National Party Platforms*, p. 606.

68. "Republican Platform, 1964," in Porter and Johnson, *National Party Platforms*, p. 689.

69. "Republican Platform, 1976," in Porter and Johnson, *National Party Platforms*, p. 986.

70. "Republican Platform, 1964," in Porter and Johnson, *National Party Platforms*, p. 689.

71. Barry M. Goldwater, *The Conscience of a Conservative* (New York: MacFadden Books, 1964 ed.), p. 113.

72. "Republican Platform, 1960," in Porter and Johnson, *National Party Platforms*, p. 608.

73. Author's interview with George S. McGovern, Washington, D.C., January 4, 1996.

74. "Republican Platform, 1960," in Porter and Johnson, *National Party Platforms*, p. 608.

75. Louis Harris and Associates, survey, October 28–31, 1983. Text of question: "Now I want to read to you some statements about the way President Reagan has been handling foreign and defense policy. For each, tell me if you agree or disagree. . . . In his willingness to send U.S. troops into actual combat situations, he is right in warning the Russians that this country will fight to maintain freedom if it comes to that." Agree, 83 percent; disagree, 13 percent; not sure, 4 percent. Text of question: "He was right in ordering the invasion of Grenada because it sent a message to the Russians that we will stop their subversion in this hemisphere, even if we have to lose the lives of our fighting men in the process." Agree, 66 percent; disagree, 28 percent; not sure, 6 percent.

76. CBS News/*New York Times*, poll, October 23–25, 1984. Text of question: "Have Ronald Reagan's military and foreign policies toward the Soviet Union and other communist countries made us more secure or less secure than we were four years ago?" More secure, 46 percent; less secure, 35 percent; no difference (volunteered), 6 percent; don't know/no answer, 13 percent.

77. Ronald Reagan, press conference, January 29, 1981.

78. *Republican Platform, 1984* (Washington, D.C.: Republican National Committee, 1984), p. 28.

79. "Republican Platform, 1976," in Porter and Johnson, *National Party Platforms*, p. 986.

80. Al Kamen, "A Campaign with No Bear in the Woods," *Washington Post*, March 15, 1992, p. C-5.

81. *Campaigns and Elections*, "The Classics of Political TV Advertising, I," Washington, D.C., 1986 video.

82. Yankelovich, Skelly, and White, survey, September 11–13, 1984. Text of question: "Next I'm going to ask you some questions about the issues in the campaign. As the 1984 election draws closer, some issues will matter to you much more than others. How much influence would a presidential candidate's stand on each of the following issues have on your decision to support that candidate? A LOT of influence, A LITTLE influence, or NO influence?" Dealing with communism: a lot, 65 percent; a little, 25 percent; no, 7 percent; not sure, 3 percent. Dealing with the Soviet Union: a lot, 76 percent; a little, 18 percent; no, 4 percent; not sure, 2 percent. Handling military spending: a lot, 68 percent; a little, 26 percent; no, 4 percent; not sure, 2 percent. Handling arms control: a lot, 69 percent; a little, 24 percent; no, 5 percent; not sure, 3 percent.

83. Decision/Making/Information, mail survey, November 16–December 13, 1984.

84. *Campaigns and Elections*, "The Classics of Political TV Advertising, I."

85. Decision/Making/Information, mail survey, November 16–December 13, 1984.

86. Kamen, "A Campaign with No Bear in the Woods," p. C-5.

87. Louis Harris and Associates, poll, October 12–14, 1984. Text of question: "Now let me read you some statements about Walter Mondale. For each, tell me if you tend to agree or disagree. If president, he could be trusted to use sound judgment in a foreign policy crisis." Agree, 58 percent; disagree, 34 percent; not sure, 8 percent.

88. "Republican Platform, 1976," in Porter and Johnson, *National Party Platforms*, p. 992.

89. "Republican Platform, 1968," in Porter and Johnson, *National Party Platforms*, p. 759.

90. Barry M. Goldwater, *Why Not Victory? A Fresh Look at American Foreign Policy* (New York: McGraw-Hill, 1962), p. 130.

91. Shepley, "How Dulles Averted War," p. 80.

92. "Republican Platform, 1960," in Porter and Johnson, *National Party Platforms*, p. 621.

93. Daniel J. Boorstin, *The Genius of American Politics* (Chicago: University of Chicago Press, 1953), p. 14.

94. Quoted in Thomas E. Cronin, *The State of the Presidency* (Boston: Little, Brown, 1980), p. 161.

95. Remarks by the president and first lady in a national television address on drug abuse and prevention, Washington, D.C., September 14, 1986.

96. *Republican Platform, 1984*, p. 27.

97. Goldwater, *Why Not Victory?* pp. 130–131.

98. Goldwater, *Conscience of a Conservative*, p. 116.

99. Author's interview with Michael S. Dukakis, Boston, Massachusetts, June 29, 1994.

100. "Republican Platform, 1960," in Porter and Johnson, *National Party Platforms*, p. 605.

101. Goldwater, *Why Not Victory?* p. 27.

102. Robert Welch, *The Politician* (Belmont, Massachusetts: Belmont Publishing, 1964), pp. 97, 108, 114, 116.

103. See Goldwater with Casserly, *Goldwater*, p. 126.

104. Quoted in Patrick J. Buchanan, *Right from the Beginning* (Boston: Little, Brown, 1988), p. 218. In a similar vein, Russell Kirk published *The Conservative Mind* in 1953, which gave the movement its name. In 1955, William F. Buckley founded *National Review*.

105. Goldwater with Casserly, *Goldwater*, p. 119.

106. Cited in Goldwater, *Why Not Victory?* p. 84.

107. Ibid., p. 22.

108. Goldwater, *Conscience of a Conservative*, p. 91.

109. Goldwater, *Why Not Victory?* p. 36.

110. Quoted in Goldman, *The Crucial Decade—And After*, p. 284.

111. "American Strategy and Strength: A Special Task Force Report Prepared by the Republican Policy Committee, U.S. House of Representatives." In Gerald R. Ford congressional papers, "1960 Campaign," Box G-17, Gerald R. Ford Library.

112. Quoted in John Judis, "The Two Faces of Whittaker Chambers," *New Republic*, April 16, 1984, p. 30.

113. Eisenhower, "Acceptance Speech," Republican National Convention, August 23, 1956.

114. Goldwater, *Conscience of a Conservative*, pp. 91, 92.

115. Goldwater, *Why Not Victory?* p. 24.

116. Barry M. Goldwater, "Acceptance Speech," Republican National Convention, San Francisco, July 16, 1964.

117. Gallup poll, September 1964. Text of question: "The U.S. should take a firmer stand against the Soviet Union than it has in recent years." Agree, 61 percent; disagree, 27 percent; don't know, 13 percent. Text of question: "In particular, the U.S. should continue to negotiate with Russia with a view toward reducing armaments on both sides." Agree, 71 percent; disagree, 18 percent; don't know, 10 percent.

118. Goldwater, *Conscience of a Conservative*, p. 91.

119. Ibid., p. 92.

120. See Goldwater, *Why Not Victory?* p. 42, and Eisenhower, "Farewell Address," January 17, 1961.

121. Goldwater, *Conscience of a Conservative*, p. 109. Goldwater thought Franklin Roosevelt's recognition of the U.S.S.R. a "dreadful mistake," saying in 1964: "We know less about the Soviet Union today than when we recognized her." Theodore H. White, *The Making of the President, 1964* (New York: Signet Books, 1966), p. 132.

122. Goldwater, *Why Not Victory?* p. 65.

123. "Republican Platform, 1964," in Porter and Johnson, *National Party Platforms*, pp. 687–688.

124. Goldwater, "Acceptance Speech," Republican National Convention, July 16, 1964.

125. Goldwater, *Conscience of a Conservative*, p. 97.

126. Goldwater, *Why Not Victory?* p. 166.

127. Michael Lind, "The Myth of Barry Goldwater," *New York Review of Books*, November 30, 1995, p. 25.

128. See Aaron Wildavsky, "The Goldwater Phenomenon: Purists, Politicians, and the Two-Party System," in Norman L. Zucker, ed., *The American Party Process: Readings and Comments* (New York: Dodd, Mead, 1968), pp. 445–446.

129. Gallup poll, September 1964. Text of question: "How much danger do you think the communists right here in America are to this country at the present time—a very great deal, a good deal, not very much, or none at all?" A very great deal, 26 percent; a good deal, 35 percent; not much, 30 percent; none at all, 4 percent; don't know, 6 percent.

130. Wildavsky, "The Goldwater Phenomenon," pp. 447, 460.

131. Buchanan, *Right from the Beginning*, p. 290.

132. Goldwater, *Why Not Victory?* p. 171.

133. Goldwater, *Conscience of a Conservative*, pp. 93, 90.

134. Quoted in White, *The Making of the President, 1964*, p. 389.

135. *Campaigns and Elections,* "The Classics of Political TV Advertising I."

136. Goldwater, "Acceptance Speech," Republican National Convention, July 16, 1964.

137. "Republican Platform, 1964," in Porter and Johnson, *National Party Platforms*, pp. 679–680.

138. White, *The Making of the President, 1964*, p. 391.

139. Goldwater, *Conscience of a Conservative*, p. 122.

140. Goldwater with Casserly, *Goldwater*, p. 168.

141. Wildavsky, "The Goldwater Phenomenon," p. 449.

142. Ibid., p. 451.

143. Robert D. Novak, *The Agony of the G.O.P., 1964* (New York: Macmillan, 1965), p. 469.

144. Quoted in Carl Solberg, *Hubert Humphrey: A Biography* (New York: W. W. Norton, 1984), p. 259.

145. See White, *The Making of the President, 1964*, p. 129.

146. Goldwater with Casserly, *Goldwater*, p. 171.

147. Novak, *Agony of the G.O.P., 1964*, p. 456.

148. Ibid., pp. 456–457.

149. Goldwater, "Acceptance Speech," Republican National Convention, July 16, 1964.

150. Lind, "The Myth of Barry Goldwater," p. 25.

151. White, *The Making of the President, 1964*, p. 262.

152. *Campaigns and Elections*, "The Classics of Political TV Advertising, I."

153. See White, *The Making of the President, 1964*, pp. 393, 358, 391.

154. See Goldwater with Casserly, *Goldwater*, pp. 198–199.

155. Quoted in White, *The Making of the President, 1964*, pp. 444–445.

156. Cited in Everett Carll Ladd Jr. with Charles D. Hadley, *Transformations of the American Party System* (New York: W. W. Norton, 1975), p. 283.

157. White, *The Making of the President, 1964*, p. 358.

158. Samuel Lubell, *The Hidden Crisis in American Politics* (New York: W. W. Norton, 1971), p. 46.

159. Quoted in Thomas Byrne Edsall with Mary D. Edsall, *Chain Reaction: The Impact of Race, Rights, and Taxes on American Politics* (New York: W. W. Norton, 1992), p. 37.

160. See Ladd with Hadley, *Transformations of the American Party System*, p. 133.

161. See Jack Bass and Walter DeVries, *The Transformation of Southern Politics: Social Change and Political Consequence Since 1945* (New York: Basic Books, 1976), p. 383.

162. The top ten Bush states were Mississippi, 50.1 percent; South Carolina, 48.3 percent; Alabama, 47.9 percent; Nebraska, 46.8 percent; Utah, 45.5 percent; Virginia, 45.3 percent; North Dakota, 44.5 percent; North Carolina, 43.5 percent; Indiana and Idaho (tie), 43.1 percent; Georgia, 43.0 percent.

163. "Representative L. Mendel Rivers Is Dead; Powerful Military Affairs Chief," *New York Times*, December 29, 1970, p. 1.

164. Michael Barone and Grant Ujifusa, *The Almanac of American Politics, 1972* (Boston: Gambit, 1972), pp. 738, 739.

165. Ibid., p. 739.

166. "Representative L. Mendel Rivers Is Dead," p. 1.

167. Richard M. Nixon, "Statement on the Death of Representative L. Mendel Rivers of South Carolina," December 28, 1970. In *Public Papers of the Presidents of the United States: Richard Nixon* (Washington, D.C.: U.S. Government Printing Office, 1971), p. 1160.

168. William Booth, "Southern Officials Switching Sides," *Washington Post*, March 16, 1995, p. A-1.

169. See Michael Barone and Grant Ujifusa, *The Almanac of American Politics, 1994* (Washington, D.C.: National Journal, 1993), p. 1149.

170. See Michael Barone and Grant Ujifusa, *The Almanac of American Politics, 1996* (Washington, D.C.: National Journal, 1995), pp. 1202–1204.

171. Booth, "Southern Officials Switching Sides," p. A-1.

172. Cited in Thomas B. Edsall, "Key November Voters Sitting Out Primaries," *Washington Post*, March 23, 1992, p. A-1.

173. Reported in Alexander P. Lamis, *The Two-Party South* (New York: Oxford University Press, 1990), p. 245.

174. Author's interview with Richard Wirthlin, McLean, Virginia, March 22, 1995.

175. Quoted in Lary May, "Movie Star Politics: The Screen Actors Guild, Cultural Conversion, and the Hollywood Red Scare," in Lary May, ed., *Recasting America: Culture and Politics in the Age of the Cold War* (Chicago: University of Chicago Press, 1989), p. 125.

176. Ronald Reagan with Richard G. Hubler, *Where's the Rest of Me?* (New York: Karz-Segil Publishers, 1981), p. 268.

177. Ibid., pp. 311–312.

178. Stephen Hess and David Broder, *The Republican Establishment: The Present and Future of the GOP* (New York: Harper and Row, 1967), pp. 253–254.

179. Quoted in A. James Reichley, *Religion in American Public Life* (Washington, D.C: The Brookings Institution, 1985), p. 325.

180. Garry Wills, lecture, National Archives, Washington, D.C., May 17, 1994.

181. Quoted in Reichley, *Religion in American Public Life*, pp. 313–314.

182. See Michael Lind, *The Next American Revolution: The New Nationalism and the Fourth American Revolution* (New York: Free Press, 1995), p. 219.

183. Cited in Steven Vaughn, "The Moral Inheritance of a President: Reagan and the Dixon Disciples of Christ," *Presidential Studies Quarterly*, Winter 1995, p. 115.

184. See Lou Cannon, *President Reagan: The Role of a Lifetime* (New York: Simon and Schuster, 1990), p. 288.

185. Garry Wills, *Reagan's America: Innocents at Home* (Garden City, New York: Doubleday, 1987), p. 287.

186. "Republican Platform, 1976," in Porter and Johnson, *National Party Platforms*, p. 986. James Reichley writes that the plank was a tactical move by Reagan and that Ford out-

witted him by directing his supporters to accept it. Reichley to the author, letter dated May 25, 1995.

187. Ronald Reagan, "Remarks at an Ecumenical Prayer Breakfast in Dallas, Texas," August 23, 1984.

188. Ronald Reagan, "Remarks at the Annual Convention of the National Association of Evangelicals," Orlando, Florida, March 8, 1983.

189. Yankelovich, Skelly, and White, survey, December 6–8, 1983. Text of question: "The real problem with communism is that it threatens our religious and moral values." Agree, 73 percent; disagree, 23 percent; not sure, 4 percent.

190. Harris survey, March 27–April 2, 1981. Text of question: "Let me read you some statements about the new Reagan foreign policy. For each, tell me if you agree or disagree. . . . By sending military aid to countries threatened by communism and being tough with the Russians, Reagan is sending a message to Moscow that will rebuild respect for the United States in the Kremlin." Agree, 73 percent; disagree, 22 percent; not sure, 5 percent.

191. Quoted in Reichley, *Religion in American Public Life*, p. 326.

192. Quoted in Anatoly Dobrynin, *In Confidence: Moscow's Ambassador to America's Six Cold War Presidents* (New York: Times Books, 1995), p. 530.

193. See Garry Wills, *Under God: Religion and American Politics* (New York: Simon and Schuster, 1990), p. 150.

194. Quoted in Cannon, *President Reagan: The Role of a Lifetime*, p. 289.

195. Jeffrey K. Hadden and Anson Shupe, *Televangelism: Power and Politics on God's Frontier* (New York: Henry Holt, 1988), p. 35.

196. Haynes Johnson, *Sleepwalking Through History: America in the Reagan Years* (New York: W. W. Norton, 1991), p. 196.

197. But that support did not extend to more traditional Protestant elements. The National Council of Churches consistently opposed Reagan, saying he represented an older vision of "America as private opportunity and empire." Walter Mondale thought Reagan was "out to lunch" when it came to the Christian's responsibility to provide for social justice. See Reichley, *Religion in American Public Life*, pp. 274, 1.

198. Buchanan, *Right from the Beginning*, pp. 66–67.

199. Ibid., pp. 67, 65.

200. Divine, *Foreign Policy and U.S. Presidential Elections, 1952–1960*, p. 114.

201. "Republican Platform, 1956," in Porter and Johnson, *National Party Platforms*, p. 557.

202. Quoted in Divine, *Foreign Policy and U.S. Presidential Elections, 1952–1960*, pp. 275–277.

203. Ibid.

204. See Michael Barone, *Our Country: The Shaping of America from Roosevelt to Reagan* (New York: Free Press, 1990), p. 335.

205. See Divine, *Foreign Policy and U.S. Presidential Elections*, p. 284.

206. See White, *The Making of the President, 1964*, p. 387.

207. See Howell Raines, "Carter and Reagan Open Fall Race with Praise for the Polish Workers," *New York Times*, September 2, 1980, p. A-1.

208. *Republican Platform, 1984*, p. 24.

209. Haldeman, *The Haldeman Diaries*, p. 476.

210. The term is not mine but Theodore J. Lowi's. See Theodore J. Lowi, *The Personal President: Power Invested, Promise Unfulfilled* (Ithaca, New York: Cornell University Press, 1985), especially pp. 97–133.

211. Committee on Political Parties, *Toward a More Responsible Two-Party System* (New York: Rinehart, 1950), p. 94.

212. Cited in Lowi, *The Personal Presidency*, p. 166.

213. Richard Nixon, "Acceptance Speech," Republican National Convention, Miami Beach, August 23, 1972.

214. President Ford Committee, "Ford Campaign Strategy Plan," August 1976, p. 70. Courtesy of Gerald F. Ford Library.

215. Quoted in Elaine Tyler May, "Explosive Issues: Sex, Women, and the Bomb," in Lary May, ed., *Recasting America*, p. 156.

216. See Samuel Lubell, *The Future While It Happened* (New York: W. W. Norton, 1973), especially pp. 30–45.

217. Quoted in Richard Reeves, *President Kennedy: Profile of Power* (New York: Simon and Schuster, 1993), p. 480.

218. John F. Kennedy, "The Presidency and Foreign Policy," speech to the California Democratic Clubs Convention, February 12, 1960, Fresno, California. In Theodore Sorensen campaign files, 1959–1960, Box 26, John F. Kennedy Library.

219. Theodore H. White, *The Making of the President, 1960* (New York: Atheneum House, 1961), pp. 409, 415.

220. Lowi, *The Personal Presidency*, p. 174.

221. Quoted in Richard Gid Powers, *Not Without Honor: The History of American Anti-Communism.* (New York: Free Press, 1995), p. x.

222. Quoted in Peter Goldman, Thomas DeFrank, Mark Miller, Andrew Muir, Tom Mathews, *Quest for the Presidency, 1992* (College Station: Texas A & M University Press, 1994), p. 639.

Chapter Five

1. Dukakis's first formative political experience was watching the Army-McCarthy hearings on television, prompting the Massachusetts Democrat to join the American Civil Liberties Union. See Sidney Blumenthal, *Pledging Allegiance: The Last Campaign of the Cold War* (New York: HarperCollins, 1990), p. 294.

2. Quoted in Maureen Dowd, "Bush, in Reagan Style, Drops Script and Assails Dukakis's Foreign Policy," *New York Times*, September 13, 1988, p. D-25.

3. Louis Harris and Associates, survey, November 2–4, 1988. Text of (open-ended) question: "Now I am going to read you some phrases that some people associate with those candidates for public office who are liberals. Which two or three would you associate with liberals?" Soft on communism, 25 percent.

4. Quoted in Bernard Weintraub, "Loaded for Bear and then Some," *New York Times*, September 14, 1988, p. A-1.

5. Quoted in Kathleen Hall Jamieson, *Dirty Politics: Deception, Distraction, and Democracy* (New York: Oxford University Press, 1992), p. 8.

6. See Christine M. Black and Thomas Oliphant, *All by Myself: The Unmaking of a Presidential Campaign* (Chester, Connecticut: Globe Pequot Press, 1989), p. 233.

7. See Weintraub, "Loaded for Bear," p. A-1.

8. Quoted in Jamieson, *Dirty Politics*, p. 3.

9. Quoted in B. Drummond Ayres Jr., "Quayle Using Jokes and Jabs, Assails Dukakis on Military," *New York Times*, September 14, 1988, p. A-1.

10. Black and Oliphant, *All by Myself*, p. 322.

11. Yankelovich, Clancy, Shulman, survey, October 25–26, 1988. Text of question: "Now with regard to the parties, do you feel the Democratic party or the Republican party can do a better job in dealing effectively with the Soviet Union, or don't you think there's any difference between them?" Democratic party, 20 percent; Republican party, 53 percent; no difference, 17 percent; not sure, 11 percent.

12. Quoted in Jack W. Germond and Jules Witcover, *Whose Broad Stripes and Bright Stars? The Trivial Pursuit of the Presidency, 1988* (New York: Warner Books, 1989), p. 408.

13. Louis Harris and Associates, survey, October 14–17, 1988. Text of question: "Let me read you some statements about Governor Michael Dukakis of Massachusetts. For each, tell me if you tend to agree or disagree. . . . Because he has always served at the state government level, he's lacking in the foreign policy experience which a candidate should have." Agree, 69 percent; disagree, 29 percent; not sure, 2 percent.

14. Gallup poll, September 3–8, 1988. Text of question: "Now I will mention some questions about the image of the candidates. Which candidate, George Bush or Michael Dukakis, still needs to prove he knows enough foreign policy?" Bush, 12 percent; Dukakis, 69 percent; both (volunteered), 10 percent; neither (volunteered), 4 percent; don't know/refused, 5 percent.

15. Daniel Yankelovich Group, survey, September 30–October 4, 1988. Text of question: "I'm going to read a list of important issues facing the country that a President must deal with. For each one I mention, please tell me whether you feel George Bush or Michael Dukakis would do a better job of handling that issue. . . . Handling relations with the Soviet Union." Bush, 58 percent; Dukakis, 22 percent; both, 5 percent; neither, 4 percent; not sure, 11 percent.

16. Quoted in Andrew Rosenthal, "Dukakis Suggests Caution on U.S.S.R.," *New York Times*, September 14, 1988, p. A-1.

17. Quoted in Jamieson, *Dirty Politics*, p. 7.

18. Quoted in Dowd, "Bush, in Reagan Style, Drops Script," p. D-25.

19. Quoted in Black and Oliphant, *All by Myself*, p. 322.

20. Daniel Yankelovich Group, survey, September 30–October 4, 1988. Text of question: "How important are the issues of foreign affairs and national security to you personally?" Very important, 63 percent; somewhat important, 30 percent; of little importance, 5 percent; not at all important, 1 percent; not sure, 1 percent. Second question: "How important do you think issues of foreign affairs and national security are to the nation?" Very important, 79 percent; somewhat important, 17 percent; of little importance, 3 percent; not at all important, 1 percent.

21. Market Opinion Research, survey, September 7–18, 1988. Text of question: "I'm going to read a list of several foreign policy issues and developments. Thinking about the next five years or so, please tell me whether you feel each issue I mention poses an extremely serious, very serious, somewhat serious, or not very serious threat to our country's national security interests. Remember, I'm not asking how important the issue is, but how serious a threat it is to our national security. . . . Soviet aggression around the world." Extremely serious/very serious, 52 percent; somewhat serious, 31 percent; not very serious, 14 percent; don't know/refused, 2 percent.

22. Daniel Yankelovich Group, survey, November 4–7, 1988. Text of question: "During this presidential campaign, there has been a lot of discussion about national defense. I'd like to read you several positions the candidates have taken. For each, please tell me whether you strongly approve, somewhat approve, somewhat disapprove, or strongly disapprove of that position?. . . . Seek to make progress with the Soviets, but proceed very cautiously in order to test their real intentions." Strongly approve, 64 percent; somewhat approve, 28 percent; somewhat disapprove, 3 percent; strongly disapprove, 2 percent; not sure, 2 percent.

23. Black and Oliphant, *All by Myself*, p. 323.

24. Ibid., pp. 322–323.

25. Quoted in Germond and Witcover, *Whose Broad Stripes and Bright Stars?* p. 411.

26. See Jamieson, *Dirty Politics*, p. 5.

27. Quoted in Blumenthal, *Pledging Allegiance*, p. 301.

28. In a letter to the author dated October 16, 1995, Dukakis wrote: "Steve Symms not only couldn't produce the photographs he claimed existed, the charge was absolutely false."

29. Quoted in Michael R. Beschloss and Strobe Talbott, *At the Highest Levels: The Inside Story of the End of the Cold War* (Boston: Little, Brown, 1993), p. 4.

30. Quoted in Jamieson, *Dirty Politics*, pp. 8–9.

31. Quoted in Black and Oliphant, *All by Myself*, pp. 233, 256.

32. WBZ-TV/*Boston Herald*, poll, October 1988.

33. Author's interview with Michael S. Dukakis, Boston, Massachusetts, June 29, 1994.

34. John Sasso, "Speech to the World Trade Center Club," Boston, Massachusetts, January 19, 1989.

35. Quoted in Hugh Heclo, "The Emerging Regime," in Richard A. Harris and Sidney M. Milkis, eds., *Remaking American Politics* (Boulder: Westview Press, 1989), p. 313.

36. KRC Communications poll for the *Presidential Campaign Hotline*, November 1–3, 1988. Text of question: "Would you describe Michael Dukakis as a liberal in the tradition of Franklin D. Roosevelt, Harry S. Truman, and John F. Kennedy, or would you describe him as a liberal in the tradition of George McGovern and Walter Mondale?" Thirty-five percent answered "McGovern-Mondale," 21 percent said "Roosevelt-Truman-Kennedy."

37. Author's interview with Dukakis.

38. John F. Kennedy, *Why England Slept* (New York: Wilfred Funk, 1940; rep. 1961), p. x.

39. Quoted in Robert A. Divine, *Foreign Policy and U.S. Presidential Elections, 1952–1960* (New York: New Viewpoints, 1974), p. 242.

40. Quoted in Herbert Parmet, *Richard Nixon and His America* (Boston: Little, Brown, 1990), p. 121.

41. John F. Kennedy, *The Strategy of Peace* (New York: Harper and Brothers, 1960), p. 84.

42. Quoted in Divine, *Foreign Policy and U.S. Presidential Elections*, pp. 191–192.

43. Kennedy, *The Strategy of Peace*, p. 40.

44. Ibid., p. 7.

45. Quoted in Divine, *Foreign Policy and U.S. Presidential Elections*, pp. 191, 211.

46. Kennedy, *The Strategy of Peace*, pp. 41, 4, 168. Kennedy also described 1946–1950 as the "Locust Years." See John F. Kennedy, "Remarks in the House of Representatives," April 9, 1952. In John F. Kennedy prepresidential papers, Box 96, John F. Kennedy Library.

47. Kennedy, *The Strategy of Peace*, pp. 4, 200.

48. Ibid., p. 194.

49. Quoted in Theodore C. Sorensen, *Kennedy* (New York: Bantam Books, 1966), p. 209.

50. Quoted in Divine, *Foreign Policy and U.S. Presidential Elections*, p. 192.

51. Quoted in Sorensen, *Kennedy*, p. 207.

52. Kennedy, *The Strategy of Peace*, p. 3.

53. Ibid., p. 218.

54. Quoted in Arthur M. Schlesinger Jr., *A Thousand Days: John F. Kennedy in the White House* (New York: Fawcett Books, 1965), p. 67.

55. Nathan Glazer, "Did We Go Too Far?" *National Interest*, Spring 1993, p. 137.

56. Democratic National Committee, press release, November 27, 1956. In Theodore Sorensen files, Box 9, John F. Kennedy Library.

57. Democratic National Committee, press release, June 13, 1957. In Theodore Sorensen files, 1953–1960, Box 9, John F. Kennedy Library. Among those invited to join the Democratic Advisory Council were John F. Kennedy, Lyndon B. Johnson, and Hubert H. Humphrey. Only Humphrey accepted. Kennedy declined the invitation, writing Butler: "I must stand for re-election next year, and the interests of my state do not always coincide with national party views on some issues of most concern to the Advisory Committee." John F. Kennedy to Paul M. Butler, letter dated February 7, 1957. In Theodore Sorensen files, 1953–1960, Box 9, John F. Kennedy Library.

58. See Philip A. Klinkner, *The Losing Parties: Out-Party National Committees, 1956–1993* (New Haven: Yale University Press, 1994), pp. 27, 28.

59. "Democratic Party Platform, 1960," in Kirk H. Porter and Donald Bruce Johnson, *National Party Platforms: 1840–1968* (Urbana: University of Illinois Press, 1970), p. 575.

60. Ibid., pp. 576, 580.

61. Ibid.

62. Quoted in Richard Reeves, *President Kennedy: Profile of Power* (New York: Simon and Schuster, 1993), pp. 388–389.

63. Quoted in David Halberstam, *The Fifties* (New York: Villard Books, 1993), p. 729.

64. Roper Organization, survey, October 22–24, 1960. Text of question: "Here is a list of phrases that have been used to describe candidates in elections from time to time. Would you go down the list and first call off those you feel describe Kennedy/Nixon?"

65. Quoted in Divine, *Foreign Policy and U.S. Presidential Elections*, p. 244.

66. Ibid., p. 222.

67. Ibid., p. 251.

68. Gallup poll, October 18–23, 1960. Text of question: "Which of these two men, Nixon or Kennedy, if elected president do you think would do the most effective job of dealing with Russia's leaders?" Nixon, 43 percent; Kennedy, 39 percent; no difference, 10 percent; no opinion, 8 percent.

69. Quoted in Divine, *Foreign Policy and U.S. Presidential Elections*, p. 251.

70. Fred Dutton to Ted Sorensen, memorandum, September 13, 1960. In Theodore Sorensen campaign files, 1959–1960, Box 21, John F. Kennedy Library.

71. John F. Kennedy foreign policy speech, in Theodore Sorensen, 1959–1960 campaign files, John F. Kennedy Library.

72. Sorensen, *Kennedy*, p. 236.

73. Ibid., p. 206.

74. Gallup poll, October 18–23, 1960. Text of question: "In the last year, would you say that respect for the U.S. in other countries around the world has increased or decreased?" Increased, 22 percent; decreased, 44 percent; stayed the same (volunteered), 23 percent; no opinion, 10 percent.

75. Gallup poll, September 28-October 2, 1960. Text of question: "Do you think relations between the U.S. and Russia will get better or worse in the next six months?" Better, 21 percent; worse, 34 percent; about the same (volunteered), 30 percent; don't know, 14 percent.

76. Quoted in Sorensen, *Kennedy*, p. 201.

77. Roper Organization, survey, October 22–24, 1960. Text of question: "Of course, there have been times in our history when it has seemed particularly important that one side wins an election and other times when it hasn't made much difference. How do you feel about this election—that it is of major importance that the candidate you prefer wins, or that it would just generally be better if the candidate you prefer wins, or that it actually won't make too much difference one way or the other?" Major importance, 59 percent; generally better, 23 percent; not too much difference, 15 percent; has no side (volunteered), 1 percent; don't know, 2 percent.

78. Theodore Sorensen, "Memorandum on Basic Positive Kennedy Approach in Foreign Policy," September 22, 1960. In Robert F. Kennedy preadministration political files, "1960 Campaign and Transition," Box 36, John F. Kennedy Library.

79. Gallup poll, October 22–24, 1960. Text of question: "Now regardless of who may get elected in 1960, which two or three of those descriptions would you select as the most important for our next President to have?" Would handle our foreign affairs well, 50 percent; would be good at handling the Russians, 30 percent. Roper Organization, survey, October 22–24, 1960. Text of question: "There has been a good deal of discussion about what we should do about Russia. In which of these directions do you believe the next administration should go in dealing with Russia?" Adopt an even tougher policy of dealing with the Russians than we

have to up now—even if it means taking some risks, 49 percent; keep on with about the same degree of toughness we have been pursuing in the last two to three years, 22 percent; try a somewhat friendlier approach in the hope that the Russians will in time learn to play fair when they know more about us and what we believe in, 20 percent; don't know, 9 percent.

80. Robert S. McNamara with Brian VanDeMark, *In Retrospect: The Tragedy and Lessons of Vietnam* (New York: Times Books, 1995), p. 21.

81. Gerald R. Ford, television advertisement, 1964. In Gerald R. Ford congressional papers, "1964 Campaign—Public Relations, Television Advertising," Box G-11, Gerald R. Ford Library.

82. McNamara with VanDeMark, *In Retrospect*, p. 21.

83. John F. Kennedy, "Remarks Intended for Delivery to the Texas Democratic State Committee in the Municipal Auditorium in Austin," November 22, 1963, in *Public Papers of the Presidents of the United States: John F. Kennedy* (Washington, D.C.: U.S. Government Printing Office, 1964), p. 898.

84. Reeves, *President Kennedy*, p. 230.

85. Ford television response on WOOD-TV, 6:10–6:15 P.M., October 24, 1962. In Gerald R. Ford congressional papers, "1962 Campaign—Public Relations," Box G-9, "Ford Reactions to Cuban Missile Crisis," Gerald R. Ford Library.

86. See Gerald R. Ford congressional papers, "1962 Campaign Speech Material," Box G-9, Gerald R. Ford Library.

87. Reeves, *President Kennedy*, pp. 100, 381, 385.

88. Gallup survey, November 16–21, 1962. Text of (open-ended) question: "Which things has Kennedy done that you like best?" Approve of his handling of the Cuban situation, 49 percent.

89. Sorensen, *Kennedy*, pp. 840, 844.

90. Lyndon B. Johnson, *The Vantage Point: Perspectives on the Presidency, 1963–1969* (New York: Holt, Rinehart, and Winston, 1971), p. 42.

91. Thomas G. Paterson, *Meeting the Communist Threat: Truman to Reagan* (New York: Oxford University Press, 1988), p. 198.

92. John F. Kennedy, "Remarks at the Breakfast of the Fort Worth Chamber of Commerce," November 22, 1963, in *Public Papers of the Presidents of the United States: John F. Kennedy*, p. 889.

93. John F. Kennedy, press release, April 6, 1954. In Robert F. Kennedy preadministration political files, Box 1, John F. Kennedy Library.

94. Quoted in Reeves, *President Kennedy*, p. 444.

95. Johnson, *The Vantage Point*, p. 43.

96. Quoted in James G. Richter, "Perpetuating the Cold War: Domestic Sources of International Patterns of Behavior," *Political Science Quarterly*, Summer 1992, p. 291.

97. Quoted in Divine, *Foreign Policy and U.S. Presidential Elections*, p. 210.

98. Gallup poll, October 1964. Text of question: "The United States should continue to negotiate with the Soviet Union on a broad front in the hope of reaching agreements which would contribute to world peace." Agree, 87 percent; disagree, 5 percent; don't know, 8 percent.

99. Gallup poll, October 1964. Text of question: "The U.S. should take a firmer stand against the Soviet Union than it has in recent years." Agree, 61 percent; disagree, 27 percent; don't know, 13 percent.

100. "Democratic Party Platform, 1964," in Porter and Johnson, *National Party Platforms*, pp. 642, 643.

101. Lyndon B. Johnson, "Radio and Television Report to the American People Following Renewed Aggression in the Gulf of Tonkin," August 4, 1964, in *Public Papers of the Presi-*

dents of the United States: Lyndon B. Johnson (Washington, D.C.: U.S. Government Printing Office, 1965), p. 927.

102. Ibid., p. 928.

103. "Democratic Party Platform, 1964," in Porter and Johnson, *National Party Platforms*, p. 644.

104. Gallup organization, September 1964. Text of question: "President Johnson and his administration have been following a defeatist 'no win' policy on the international front by appeasing the communists." Agree, 26 percent; disagree, 55 percent; don't know, 19 percent.

105. Lyndon B. Johnson, "Remarks Before the American Bar Association," New York City, August 12, 1964, *in Public Papers of the Presidents of the United States: Lyndon B. Johnson* (Washington, D.C.: U.S. Government Printing Office, 1964), p. 953.

106. Johnson, *The Vantage Point*, p. 68.

107. Quoted in Roland Evans and Robert D. Novak, *Lyndon B. Johnson: The Exercise of Power* (New York: New American Library, 1968), pp. 514–515.

108. Quoted in McNamara, *In Retrospect*, p. 147.

109. First survey, Gallup organization, October 1964. Text of question: "I'd like to find out how worried or concerned you are about each of the problems I am going to mention. If you don't really feel very much concerned about some of them, don't hesitate to say so. Are you concerned about combating world communism?" A great deal, 65 percent; considerable, 24 percent; not very much, 7 percent; not at all, 1 percent; don't know, 3 percent. Second survey, Gallup poll, September 1964. Text of question: "Here are several statements that people critical of the government sometimes make. Just tell me whether, in general, you agree or disagree. There is too much communist and left-wing influence in our government these days." Agree, 46 percent; disagree, 31 percent; don't know, 22 percent. Third survey, Gallup poll, September 1964. Text of question: "How much danger do you think the communists right here in America are to this country at the present time—a very great deal, a good deal, not very much, or none at all?" A very great deal, 26 percent; a good deal, 35 percent; not very much, 30 percent; none at all, 4 percent; don't know, 6 percent. Fourth survey, Gallup poll, September 1964. Text of question: "Most of the organizations pushing for civil rights have been infiltrated by the communists and are now dominated by communist trouble-makers. Do you agree with the statement or not?" Agree, 46 percent; disagree, 35 percent; don't know, 19 percent.

110. Federal Bureau of Investigation, "The Communist Party Line," in "White House Central Files," Box 694, John F. Kennedy Library.

111. "Democratic Party Platform, 1964," in Porter and Johnson, *National Party Platforms*, p. 642.

112. Gallup poll, October 1964. Text of question: "The U.S. should maintain its dominant position as the world's most powerful nation at all costs, even going to the brink of war if necessary." Agree, 54 percent; disagree, 33 percent; don't know, 13 percent. Text of second question: "Let's look at some specific problems. How much trust and confidence would you have in the way Lyndon Johnson and his administration would handle each of these problems—a very great deal, considerable, not very much, or none at all? . . . Maintaining respect for the U.S. in other countries?" A very great deal, 31 percent; considerable, 43 percent; not very much, 15 percent; none at all, 5 percent; not sure or don't know, 7 percent.

113. Gallup poll, October 1964. Text of question: "How much trust and confidence would you have in the way Lyndon Johnson and his administration would handle each of these problems—a very great deal, considerable, not very much, or none at all? . . . Handling Khrushchev and relations with Russia?" A very great deal, 24 percent; considerable, 43 percent; not very much, 17 percent; none at all, 5 percent; not sure or don't know, 11 percent.

114. Gallup poll, October 1964. Text of questions: "I'd like to find out how worried or concerned you are about each of the problems I am going to mention. If you don't really feel very much concerned about some of them, don't hesitate to say so. Are you concerned about these problems a great deal, considerable, not very much, or not at all?. . . . Relations with Russia . . . Combating world communism." First question: great deal, 45 percent; considerable, 37 percent; not very much, 14 percent; not at all, 2 percent; don't know, 3 percent. Second question: great deal, 65 percent; considerable, 24 percent; not very much, 7 percent; not at all, 1 percent; don't know, 3 percent.

115. Quoted in Charles L. Garrettson III, *Hubert Humphrey: The Politics of Joy* (New Brunswick, New Jersey: Transaction Publishers, 1993), p. 324.

116. Ibid., p. 325.

117. George Ball, "The Rationalist in Power," *New York Review of Books*, April 22, 1993, p. 34.

118. Opinion Research Corporation, survey, November 4–8, 1964. Text of question: "Here are some of the issues that were discussed in the (1964) presidential campaign. How much did each of these have to do with your final choice of which presidential candidate to vote for?. . . . Stopping the spread of communism throughout the world." Great deal, 57 percent; fair amount, 29 percent; little or nothing, 9 percent; no opinion, 5 percent.

119. National Opinion Research Center, survey, October 1964. Text of question: "In this country, do you think any of the people on this card are more likely than other Americans to be communists?" None, 38 percent; union leaders, 17 percent; Negroes, 14 percent; Jews, 3 percent; college teachers, 8 percent; foreign-born, 20 percent; people in the government in Washington, 12 percent; don't know, 13 percent. Adds to more than 100 percent due to multiple responses.

120. See Nelson W. Polsby, *Consequences of Party Reform* (New York: Oxford University Press, 1983), p. 20.

121. "Democratic Party Platform, 1968," in Porter and Johnson, *National Party Platforms*, pp. 723, 725, 726.

122. "Republican Party Platform, 1964," p. 761.

123. "American Independent Party Platform, 1968," Porter and Johnson, *National Party Platforms*, p. 716.

124. Quoted in Johnson, *The Vantage Point*, p. 489.

125. Quoted in Klinkner, *The Losing Parties*, pp. 91, 92.

126. Quoted in Divine, *Foreign Policy and U.S. Presidential Elections*, pp. 198, 109, 142, 157, 140, 138.

127. National Opinion Research Center, survey, November 1956. Text of question: "As you may know, Adlai Stevenson proposed that the United States take the lead in offering to stop any further hydrogen bomb tests, assuming Russia and England would do the same. In general, do you approve or disapprove of this idea?" Approve, 42 percent; disapprove, 52 percent; don't know, 6 percent.

128. Quoted in "J. W. Fulbright, Outspoken Senator-Scholar, Dies," *Washington Post*, February 10, 1995, p. A-1.

129. Barry M. Goldwater, *Why Not Victory? A Fresh Look at American Foreign Policy* (New York: McGraw-Hill, 1962), pp. 149–150.

130. Quoted in William Schneider, "JFK's Children: The Class of '74," *Atlantic Monthly*, March 1989, p. 40.

131. Weicker captured 41.7 percent of the vote to Duffey's 33.8 percent and Dodd's 24.5 percent.

132. Lanny J. Davis, *The Emerging Democratic Majority: Lessons and Legacies from the New Politics* (New York: Stein and Day, 1974), p. 61.

133. "Opponents See Duffey's Victory as a Benefit to Them in November," *New York Times*, August 21, 1970, p. 25.

134. Quoted in David Maraniss, *First in His Class: A Biography of Bill Clinton* (New York: Simon and Schuster, 1995), p. 231.

135. Quoted in Lowell P. Weicker Jr., *Maverick: A Life in Politics* (Boston: Little, Brown, 1995), pp. 37, 232.

136. "Bailey Sees Senatorial Primary in Connecticut on Wednesday as a Close Contest," *New York Times*, August 16, 1970, p. 29.

137. Cited in Michael Barone, *Our Country: The Shaping of America from Roosevelt to Reagan* (New York: Free Press, 1990), p. 508.

138. Quoted in Herbert Parmet, *Richard Nixon and His America* (Boston: Little, Brown, 1990), p. 625.

139. Quoted in George McGovern, *Grassroots: The Autobiography of George McGovern* (New York: Random House, 1977), p. 167.

140. Quoted in Barone, *Our Country*, p. 508.

141. Quoted in Theodore H. White, *The Making of the President, 1972* (New York: Atheneum Publishers, 1973), p. xv.

142. "Democratic Party Platform, 1972," in Porter and Johnson, *National Party Platforms*, p. 811.

143. Ibid., p. 816.

144. Quoted in White, *The Making of the President, 1972*, p. 116.

145. Ibid., p. 117.

146. H. R. Haldeman, *The Haldeman Diaries* (New York: G. P. Putnam's Sons, 1994), p. 251.

147. Quoted in White, *The Making of the President, 1972*, pp. 127–128.

148. See Gerald R. Ford, "Five Minute Statement for Telecast on WKZO-TV," October 10, 1972. In Gerald R. Ford congressional papers, "1972 Campaign—Public Relations," Box G-23, Gerald R. Ford Library.

149. White, *The Making of the President, 1972*, p. 128.

150. Ibid., p. 111.

151. George S. McGovern, "Acceptance Speech," Democratic National Convention, Miami Beach, July 13, 1972.

152. Richard M. Nixon, *RN: The Memoirs of Richard Nixon* (New York: Grosset and Dunlap, 1978), p. 456.

153. Spiro T. Agnew, "Address by the Vice President to the Jaycees National Convention," Atlanta, Georgia, June 19, 1972. In Gerald R. Ford congressional papers, "1972 Campaign Speech Material," Box G-23, Gerald R. Ford Library.

154. Quoted in Sidney Blumenthal, "Ghosts in the Machine," *New Yorker*, October 2, 1995, p. 41.

155. McGovern, "Acceptance Speech," Democratic National Convention, July 13, 1972.

156. "Democratic Party Platform, 1972," in Porter and Johnson, *National Party Platforms*, pp. 782. 812.

157. The phrase was Richard Nixon's. See Richard M. Nixon, "Address to the Nation," Washington, D.C., August 15, 1971.

158. Richard M. Nixon, "Acceptance Speech," Republican National Convention, Miami Beach, August 23, 1972.

159. Ibid.

160. Quoted in Fred Barnes, "Meet Mario the Moderate," *New Republic*, April 8, 1985, p. 19.

161. Louis Harris and Associates, survey, October 17–19, 1972. Text of question: "Do you think the kinds of terms Senator McGovern would agree to in settling the Vietnam War would

be honorable and right for the U.S. to accept, or do you think he would agree to terms the U.S. would be wrong to accept?" Honorable and right, 32 percent; wrong to accept, 47 percent; not sure, 21 percent.

162. Robert Teeter and Associates, survey, September 5–16, 1972. Nixon's ratings on Vietnam were 69 percent positive and 30 percent negative; on defense those ratings were 73 percent positive and 20 percent negative.

163. Peter D. Hart Research Associates, survey, October 12–22, 1972. Text of question: "Here is a list of various world problems that have been mentioned by people like yourself. How serious do you consider each problem—very serious, somewhat serious, or not serious at all? If you think it is a problem, just say so. . . . Communism." Very serious, 54 percent; somewhat serious, 25 percent; not serious, 11 percent; not a problem, 4 percent; not sure, 6 percent.

164. Peter D. Hart Research Associates, survey, October 12–22, 1972. Text of question: "I would like to ask you if you think that tension in the world is greater than it was ten years ago, about the same, or has world tension eased during the last ten years?" Greater, 67 percent; about the same, 18 percent; eased, 13 percent; not sure, 2 percent.

165. Ford, "Five-Minute Statement for Telecast on WKZO-TV."

166. Quoted in Merle Miller, *Lyndon: An Oral Biography* (New York: Ballantine Books, 1980), p. 673.

167. See Robert M. Teeter, Barbara E. Bryant, Frederick P. Currier, and Frederick T. Steeper, "Reslicing the American Political Pie," unpublished manuscript in Robert Teeter papers, Box 6, Gerald R. Ford Library.

168. Schneider, "JFK's Children: The Class of '74," p. 40.

169. Jimmy Carter, "Acceptance Speech," Democratic National Convention, New York City, July 15, 1976.

170. Jimmy Carter, *Why Not the Best?* (New York: Bantam Books, 1976), p. 4.

171. Edwin Newman, NBC News, November 3, 1976, author's personal tape recording.

172. Quoted in Jimmy Carter, *Keeping Faith* (New York: Bantam Books, 1982), p. 143.

173. See "Democratic Party Platform, 1976," in Porter and Johnson, *National Party Platforms*, p. 937.

174. Ibid., pp. 941, 937.

175. Ibid., p. 942.

176. Ibid.

177. "Republican Party Platform, 1976," in Porter and Johnson, *National Party Platforms*, pp. 985, 989.

178. Yankelovich, Skelly, and White, survey, October 16–19, 1976. Text of question: "What about some of the things people say about Gerald Ford—will you tell me for each of the following whether you agree or disagree with this statement—or aren't you sure?. . . He is too soft on the Russians." Agree, 41 percent; disagree, 40 percent; not sure, 19 percent.

179. CBS News/*New York Times*, survey, November 4–8, 1976. Text of question: "Which presidential candidate do you think is more likely to do a better job handling our country's foreign relations?" Ford, 42 percent; Carter, 36 percent; someone else (volunteered), 1 percent; no one, 1 percent; don't know/no answer/refused, 10 percent.

180. Richard B. Cheney, "Memorandum for the President," August 27, 1976. In Richard B. Cheney papers, "Campaign Strategy," Box 16, Gerald R. Ford Library.

181. David Gergen to Jack Marsh, memorandum, June 11, 1976. In James Reichley files, Box 5, Gerald R. Ford Library.

182. See Reagan advertisement, WCBS-TV, New York, April 28, 1976. Ronald Reagan, television speech, March 31, 1976. In Michael Raoul Duval, "Reagan, Ronald," Box 23, Gerald R. Ford Library.

183. Ronald Reagan, "Speech to the Detroit Economic Club," Detroit, Michigan, May 14, 1976.

184. Nelson A. Rockefeller, "Memorandum for the President from the Vice President," May 8, 1975. In Richard B. Cheney papers, "Rockefeller, Nelson," Box 19, Gerald R. Ford Library.

185. President Ford Committee, "Rhodesia," XXPF, June 4, 1976. Tape provided courtesy of the Gerald R. Ford Library. Text of commercial: "If you've been waiting for this presidential campaign to become a little clearer so that you can make a choice, it's happened. Last Wednesday, Ronald Reagan said he would send American troops to Rhodesia. Thursday he clarified that. He said they could be observers or advisors. What does he think happened in Vietnam? Or was Governor Reagan playing with words? A president of the United States can't play with words. When you vote Tuesday remember: Governor Reagan couldn't start a war, President Reagan could."

186. President Ford Committee, "Hot Line," television text, May 15, 1976. Courtesy of the Gerald R. Ford Library.

187. Louis Harris and Associates, poll, July 16–19, 1976. Text of question: "Between Gerald Ford and Ronald Reagan, who do you think could do a better job on handling relations with Russia?" Ford, 54 percent; Reagan, 27 percent; not sure, 19 percent.

188. Cited in President Ford Committee, "Ford Campaign Strategy Plan," August 1976, p. 25. Courtesy of Gerald R. Ford Library.

189. Ibid., p. 31.

190. See Robert M. Teeter papers, "National Surveys—Post-Election Analyses, November 1976," Box 62, Gerald R. Ford Library. Text of questions: "Now I am going to mention some problems facing the nation today and as I mention each one I would like you to tell me who you think would do the best job of handling that problem—Gerald Ford or Jimmy Carter. . . . Maintaining a strong national defense. . . . Handling our foreign affairs." Defense: Ford, 49 percent; Carter, 29 percent; both, 7 percent; neither, 2 percent; don't know, 13 percent. Foreign affairs: Ford, 47 percent; Carter, 31 percent; both, 4 percent; neither, 3 percent; don't know, 15 percent.

191. Ibid.

192. "Ford Campaign Strategy Plan, 1976," p. 46.

193. Ibid., p. 7.

194. Quoted in Sidney Kraus, ed., The Great Debates: Carter vs. Ford, 1976 (Bloomington: Indiana University Press, 1979), p. 482.

195. Ibid.

196. Ibid.

197. A. James Reichley, draft statement, in David R. Gergen files, "Debates," Box 3, Gerald R. Ford Library.

198. Cited in Jack Marsh to Dick Cheney, memorandum, October 7, 1976. In Richard B. Cheney papers, "Debates," Box 16, Gerald R. Ford Library.

199. See Albuquerque Journal, September 2, 1976.

200. Cited in Robert M. Teeter papers, "National Surveys—Post-Election Analyses," November 1976, Box 62, Gerald R. Ford Library.

201. Quoted in Carter, Keeping Faith, p. 188.

202. See "Democratic Party Platform, 1976," in Porter and Johnson, National Party Platforms, p. 945.

203. Jimmy Carter, "Commencement Address," Notre Dame University, South Bend, Indiana, May 22, 1977.

204. Ibid.

205. Republican Party Platform, 1980 (Washington, D.C.: Republican National Committee, 1980), p. 36.

206. Louis Harris and Associates, survey, May 31–June 5, 1977. Text of question: "Now let me ask you about some specific things President Carter has done. How would you rate him on his handling of relations with Russia—excellent, pretty good, only fair, or poor?" Excellent/pretty good, 42 percent; only fair/poor, 43 percent; not sure, 15 percent.

207. See Richter, "Perpetuating the Cold War," *Political Science Quarterly*, p. 297. Church lost to Republican Steven Symms in November. The Soviet brigade had been in Cuba since 1963 and did not violate the Kennedy-Khrushchev understanding.

208. Jimmy Carter, "Address to the Nation," Washington, D.C., January 14, 1980.

209. Quoted in Barone, *Our Country*, p. 591.

210. Quoted in Carter, *Keeping Faith*, p. 483.

211. *Republican Party Platform, 1980*, p. 30.

212. William G. Mayer, *The Changing American Mind: How and Why American Public Opinion Changed Between 1960 and 1988* (Ann Arbor: University of Michigan Press, 1992), pp. 49–50.

213. Ibid., p. 47.

214. Ibid.

215. *Republican Party Platform, 1980*, p. 4.

216. Jeane Kirkpatrick, "Dictatorships and Double Standards," *Commentary*, November 1979, pp. 42, 38, 41.

217. *Democratic Party Platform, 1980* (Washington, D.C.: Democratic National Committee, 1980), pp. 1, 17.

218. Ibid., p. 19.

219. *Republican Party Platform, 1980*, p. 37.

220. See Stephen I. Schwartz, "Atomic Audit: What the U.S. Nuclear Arsenal Has Cost," *Brookings Review*, Fall 1995, p. 16.

221. *Democratic Party Platform, 1984* (Washington, D.C.: Democratic National Committee, 1984), p. 47.

222. Ibid., pp. 45, 51, 47, 48, 49.

223. Ibid., p. 49.

224. Ibid., pp. 1, 44.

225. Ibid., p. 50.

226. Ibid., pp. 43, 48.

227. Yankelovich, Skelly, and White, survey, September 11–13, 1984. Text of question: "Now I'm going to ask you some questions about the issues in the campaign. As the 1984 election draws closer, some issues will matter to you much more than others. How much influence would a presidential candidate's stand on each of the following issues have on your decision to support that candidate? A LOT of influence, A LITTLE influence, or NO influence? ... Communism ... Dealing with the Soviet Union ... Military spending ... Arms Control." Communism: a lot, 65 percent; a little, 25 percent; no influence, 7 percent; not sure, 3 percent. Dealing with the Soviet Union: a lot, 76 percent; a little, 18 percent; no influence, 4 percent; not sure, 2 percent. Military spending: a lot, 68 percent; a little, 26 percent; no influence, 4 percent; not sure, 2 percent. Arms control: a lot, 69 percent; a little, 24 percent; no influence, 5 percent; not sure, 3 percent.

228. ABC News/*Washington Post*, survey, October 22–23, 1984. Text of question: "Which one (as President) would you trust more in handling foreign policy, overall?" Reagan, 52 percent; Mondale, 39 percent; neither (volunteered), 2 percent; don't know/no opinion, 7 percent. Gallup poll, November 30-December 3, 1984. Text of question: "Now let me ask you about some specific foreign and domestic problems. As I read off each problem, would you tell me whether you approve or disapprove of the way President Reagan is handling that problem? ... Relations with the Soviet Union." Approve, 52 percent; disapprove, 36 percent; no opinion, 12 percent.

229. Gordon Black for *USA Today*, survey, September 25–26, 1984. Text of question: "Based on what you know about Walter Mondale and Ronald Reagan as a whole, which of the two presidential candidates is likely to try to do the most to resolve each of the following problems? Which is likely to do the most—Mondale or Reagan—to negotiate a successful nuclear arms agreement with the Soviet Union?" Reagan, 44 percent; Mondale, 38 percent; same (volunteered), 2 percent; neither (volunteered), 8 percent; don't know/refused, 9 percent.

230. Gordon Black for *USA TODAY*, survey, November 27–29, 1984. Text of question: "First, I would like you, as a private citizen, to help set the priorities for our government during the coming year (1985) I will read a list of things that various people have said are problems the government needs to do something about. For each thing that I mention, please tell me in which of the three categories of importance you would place the problem. The three categories are: (a) one of the two or three most important problems you would like to see the government concentrate on during the next several years; (b) an important problem which the government should continue to work on, but not one of the two or three most important problems; (c) or, that you either don't see it as a problem, or that you don't think it is a problem the government ought to be involved with. . . . Negotiating nuclear arms limitations or reductions with the Soviet Union." Two or three most important, 60 percent; important, 29 percent; not important, 8 percent; don't know/refused, 3 percent.

231. CBS News/*New York Times*, survey, October 14–17, 1984. Text of question: "When it comes to the situation in Central America, are you more worried about the United States getting involved in a war there, or more worried about a communist takeover in that area?" War, 38 percent; communists, 43 percent; both (volunteered), 4 percent; neither (volunteered), 4 percent; don't know/no answer, 11 percent. Second question: "Do you think the United States should do whatever is necessary to stop the spread of communism in Central America, even if that means supporting military dictatorships?" Yes, 40 percent; no, 36 percent; don't know/no answer, 24 percent.

232. CBS News/*New York Times*, survey, October 14–17, 1984. Text of question: "After the election suppose the next president announced that the United States would stop testing all nuclear and space weapons. Do you think that would lead the Soviet Union to take advantage of our new policy, or would they be more likely to start negotiating seriously about arms control?" Take advantage, 50 percent; negotiate seriously, 30 percent; don't know/no answer, 19 percent. CBS News/*New York Times*, survey, November 8–14, 1984. Text of question: "Do you think Ronald Reagan will make a real effort to negotiate a good arms control agreement with the Soviet Union?" Yes, 70 percent; no, 20 percent; no opinion, 10 percent.

233. Gallup poll, November 26-December 9, 1984. Text of question: "Do you think the U.S. is or is not doing all it can to keep peace in the world?" Yes, 54 percent; no, 40 percent; no opinion, 6 percent. Second question: "Do you think the U.S.S.R. (Union of Soviet Socialist Republics) is or is not doing all it can to keep peace in the world?" Yes, 10 percent; no, 81 percent; no opinion, 9 percent.

234. Roper Organization, survey, September 15–22, 1984. Text of question: "In your opinion, which of the following best describes Russia's primary objective in world affairs? (A) Russia seeks only to protect itself against the possibility of attack by other countries (7 percent); (B) Russia seeks to compete with the U.S. for more influence in different parts of the world (28 percent); (C) Russia seeks global domination, but not at the expense of starting a major war (38 percent); (D) Russia seeks global domination and will risk a major war to achieve that domination if it can't be achieved by other means (20 percent); don't know (8 percent)."

235. Jeane J. Kirkpatrick, "Text of Jeane J. Kirkpatrick's Remarks at the Republican National Convention," *New York Times*, August 21, 1984, p. A-22.

236. Ibid.

237. *Republican Party Platform, 1984* (Washington, D.C.: Republican National Committee, 1984), pp. 22–23, 28–29.

238. See John Kenneth White, *The New Politics of Old Values* (Hanover, New Hampshire: University Press of New England, 1990), p. 75.

239. See Newt Gingrich, *To Renew America* (New York: HarperCollins, 1995), p. 235.

240. Quoted in Dennis Hale and Marc Landy, "Are Critical Elections Extinct?" *Boston College Bi-Weekly*, November 15, 1984.

241. Quoted in Walter Dean Burnham, *The Current Crisis in American Politics* (New York: Oxford University Press, 1982), p. 14.

242. Quoted in Divine, *Foreign Policy and U.S. Presidential Elections*, p. 120.

243. Barney Frank, *Speaking Frankly* (New York: Times Books, 1992), p. 36.

244. Louis Harris and Associates, survey, November 2–4, 1988. Text of (open-ended) question: "Now I am going to read you some phrases that some people associate with those candidates for public office who are liberals. Which two or three would you associate with liberals?" Soft on communism, 25 percent.

245. Gallup polls, 1956 and 1980. Text of question: "Which party, the Republican or Democratic, is most likely to keep the United States out of World War III?" 1956 responses: Republican, 46 percent; Democrats, 21 percent; no difference, 18 percent; no opinion, 15 percent. 1980 responses: Republicans, 24 percent; Democrats, 45 percent; no difference, 20 percent; no opinion, 11 percent.

246. Figures cited in Jim Carrier, "Bomb Blues," *Denver Post*, July 13, 1995, p. A-1. The Energy Department still houses 280 million pages of classified information. See Stephen I. Schwartz, "Atomic Audit: What the U.S. Nuclear Arsenal Has Cost," *Brookings Review*, Fall 1995, p. 17.

247. See Schwartz, "Atomic Audit," p. 15.

248. U.S. Department of Energy Office of Environmental Management, *Estimating the Cold War Mortgage* (Springfield, Virginia: U.S. Department of Commerce, Technology Administration, National Technical Information Service, 1995), p. ii.

249. Carrier, "Bomb Blues," p. A-1.

250. "Democratic Party Platform, 1952," in Porter and Johnson, *National Party Platforms*, p. 485.

251. Quoted in Reeves, *President Kennedy*, pp. 475–476.

252. McGovern, "Acceptance Speech," Democratic National Convention, July 13, 1972.

253. Cited in Frank, *Speaking Frankly*, p. 92.

254. Quoted in Jacob Heilbrunn, "The Revision Thing: Who Is to Blame for the Cold War? A New Quarrel," *New Republic*, August 15, 1994, p. 38.

255. Gallup polls, 1960 and 1984. Text of question: "Which party, the Republican or the Democratic, do you think would do the better job of keeping the country prosperous?" 1960 results: Republicans, 31 percent; Democrats, 47 percent. 1984 results: Republicans, 49 percent; Democrats, 33 percent.

256. CBS News/*New York Times*, survey, November 4, 1984. Text of question: "What is the single most important reason you are for the (Republican/Democratic) candidate for the U.S. House of Representatives in your district? (open-ended)" Ideology, 35 percent; party affiliation, 25 percent; Reagan/Mondale, 4 percent; experience/done a good job, 19 percent; just like him/her, 6 percent; economy, 9 percent; domestic issues, 15 percent; foreign policy, 1 percent; other, 3 percent; don't know/no answer, 15 percent.

257. Quoted in Doris Kearns, *Lyndon Johnson and the American Dream* (New York: New American Library, 1976), pp. 146–147.

258. "Excerpts from Interview with Clinton on Goals for Presidency," *New York Times*, June 28, 1992, p. 17.

Chapter Six

1. George Bush, "Address to the Nation on the Commonwealth of Independent States," Washington, D.C., December 25, 1991.

2. See "Text of Gorbachev's Farewell Address," *New York Times*, December 26, 1991, p. A-1, and Jack F. Matlock Jr., *Autopsy of an Empire* (New York: Random House, 1995), p. 1.

3. "Russian President's Address to Joint Session of Congress," *Washington Post*, June 18, 1992, p. A-36.

4. George Bush, "Acceptance Speech," Republican National Convention, Houston, Texas, August 20, 1992.

5. George Bush, *Agenda for American Renewal* (Washington, D.C.: Bush-Quayle Campaign Committee, 1992), p. 1.

6. See Louis Harris and Associates, survey, February 2–6, 1990. Text of question: "If you had to choose, who would you say was better on handling relations with Russia—Ronald Reagan or George Bush?" Reagan, 33 percent; Bush, 58 percent; both equal, 5 percent; neither, 1 percent; not sure, 3 percent.

7. *Republican Party Platform, 1992* (Washington, D.C.: Republican National Committee, adopted August 17, 1992), p. 57.

8. Ibid., p. 67.

9. "Excerpts from the Debate Among Quayle, Gore, and Stockdale," *New York Times*, October 14, 1992, p. A-21.

10. *Republican Party Platform, 1992*, p. 1.

11. Quoted in Garry Wills, "The Born-Again Republicans," *New York Review of Books*, September 24, 1992, p. 9.

12. Ibid., p. 9.

13. Quoted in Wills, "The Born-Again Republicans," p. 10.

14. "Russian President's Address to Joint Session of Congress," p. A-36.

15. "Bush: Playing the Crisis Card," *New York Times*, October 24, 1992, p. 10.

16. Yankelovich, Clancy, Shulman, survey, October 20–22, 1992. Text of question: "Which candidate—Bush, Clinton, or Perot—do you think would do the best job handling an international crisis?" Bush, 63 percent; Clinton, 24 percent; Perot, 7 percent; none (volunteered), 1 percent; not sure, 5 percent.

17. Quoted in Peter Goldman, Thomas M. DeFrank, Mark Miller, Andrew Murr, and Tom Mathews, *Quest for the Presidency, 1992* (College Station: Texas A & M University Press, 1994), p.672.

18. R. W. Apple Jr., "White House Race Is Recast: No Kremlin to Run Against," *New York Times*, February 6, 1992, p. A-1.

19. Associated Press, survey, June 10–14, 1992. Text of question: "I'm going to name some issues and ask which one is most important to you in deciding who you would vote for this year for President?" Economy, 39 percent; education, 13 percent; health care costs, 13 percent; crime 8 percent; environment, 7 percent; drug abuse, 6 percent; civil rights, 4 percent; foreign policy, 1 percent; other (volunteered), 4 percent; don't know, 4 percent; refused 1 percent.

20. Bush, "Acceptance Speech," Republican National Convention, August 20, 1992.

21. *Republican Party Platform, 1992*, p. 56.

22. CBS News/*New York Times*, survey, June 17–20, 1992.

23. George Bush, interview, CNN, June 15, 1992.

24. Princeton Survey Research Associates, survey, October 31-November 10, 1991. Text of question: "The policies of Ronald Reagan and George Bush helped speed the end of commu-

nism in Russia." Completely agree, 18 percent; mostly agree, 38 percent; mostly disagree, 19 percent; completely disagree, 14 percent; don't know, 11 percent.

25. Goldman et. al., *Quest for the Presidency, 1992*, pp. 729–730.

26. ABC News/*Washington Post*, survey, October 4, 1992. Text of question: "I'm going to read you some statements. After each please tell me whether or not each applies to each candidate. How about he has a vision of the future of the country. Does it apply to George Bush [Bill Clinton, Ross Perot] or not?" Bush: yes, 48 percent; no, 49 percent; don't know/no opinion, 4 percent. Clinton: yes, 70 percent; no, 25 percent; don't know/no opinion, 5 percent. Perot: yes, 47 percent; no, 42 percent; don't know/no opinion, 12 percent.

27. E. J. Dionne Jr., "Age of Conservatism in the White House Has Come to a Close," *Washington Post*, November 4, 1992, p. A–21. The election occurred after the death of Republican U.S. Senator John Heinz in a 1991 helicopter crash.

28. Hickman-Brown Research, survey, December 16–19, 1991. Text of question: "Here are some of the reasons people have given for supporting a Democrat over (George) Bush in the (1992) election for President. Regardless of your current intentions, for each of the following, tell me if that reason makes you more or less likely to vote for a Democrat, of if it makes no difference at all to you. . . . A Democrat would spend more time here at home and less time on foreign policy." More likely, 65 percent; less likely, 14 percent; no difference, 18 percent; don't know, 2 percent.

29. Apple, "White House Race Is Recast," p. A-1.

30. Bill Clinton, "Acceptance Speech," Democratic National Convention, New York, July 16, 1992.

31. "Transcript of First TV Debate Among Bush, Clinton, and Perot," *New York Times*, October 12, 1992, p. A–14.

32. *The Democratic Party Platform, 1992* (Washington, D.C.: Democratic National Committee, 1992), p. 1.

33. Quoted in Don Oberdorfer, "Democrats Offer Broad Themes for U.S. Role in Post–Cold War Era," *Washington Post*, March 15, 1992, p. A-20.

34. Gallup poll for *Newsweek*, September 10–11, 1992.

35. Jeffrey Schmalz, "Americans Are Sadder and Wiser, but Not Apathetic," *New York Times*, November 1, 1992, p. E-1.

36. Quoted in John B. Judis, "The End of Conservatism," *New Republic*, August 31, 1992, p. 30.

37. Theodore J. Lowi, "Cross-Roads 1992: And All Lights Stuck on Red," The Spencer T. and Ann W. Olin Address, Cornell University, Ithaca, New York, June 5, 1992.

38. CBS News, "National Town Meeting," broadcast, June 2, 1992.

39. See E. J. Dionne Jr., *They Only Look Dead: Why Progressives Will Dominate the Next Political Era* (New York: Simon and Schuster, 1996), p. 86.

40. CBS News/*New York Times*, survey, October 27–28, 1992. Nineteen percent answered "same."

41. Roper Organization, survey, March 17–24, 1992.

42. Tony Chiu, *Ross Perot: In His Own Words* (New York: Warner Books, 1992), pp. 180–181.

43. Richard Nixon, *Beyond Peace* (New York: Random House, 1994), p. 5.

44. Ibid., pp. 9–10.

45. Patrick J. Buchanan, *Right from the Beginning* (Boston: Little, Brown, 1988), pp. 364–365.

46. Quoted in Dionne, *They Only Look Dead*, p. 166.

47. Patrick J. Buchanan, "Announcement Speech," Concord, New Hampshire, December 10, 1991.

48. James M. Perry, "Buchanan Launches Presidential Bid, Says Bush Has Abandoned GOP Tenets," *Wall Street Journal*, December 11, 1991, p. A–18.

49. E. J. Dionne Jr., "Buchanan Challenges Bush with 'America First' Call," *Washington Post*, December 11, 1991, p. A-1.

50. Apple, "White House Race Is Recast," p. A-1.

51. Hart and Breglio Research Companies, survey, February 28–March 2, 1992. Text of question: "If a candidate favors a major reduction in U.S. foreign aid and less U.S. involvement in foreign affairs, would this make you more likely, somewhat more likely, or much less likely to support this candidate?" Much more likely, 40 percent; somewhat more likely, 28 percent; somewhat less likely, 20 percent; much less likely, 8 percent; not much difference (volunteered), 1 percent; not sure, 3 percent.

52. Patrick J. Buchanan, "Announcement Speech," Concord, New Hampshire, December 10, 1991.

53. Wills, "The Born-Again Republicans," p. 9.

54. Those states were California, 26 percent; Connecticut, 22 percent; Illinois, 22 percent; Indiana, 20 percent; Louisiana, 27 percent; Massachusetts, 27 percent; Michigan, 25 percent; Minnesota, 24 percent; Oklahoma, 27 percent; Pennsylvania, 23 percent; South Carolina, 26 percent; Tennessee, 22 percent; Texas, 24 percent.

55. R. W. Apple Jr., "Faltering Economy, Fallen President," *New York Times*, November 4, 1992, p. A-1.

56. E. J. Dionne Jr., "Voters' Attraction to Perot May Signal that Party Labels Are Now Liabilities," *Washington Post*, May 21, 1992, p. A-17.

57. See Richard Morin and E. J. Dionne Jr., "Majority of Voters Say Parties Have Lost Touch," *Washington Post*, July 8, 1992, p. 1.

58. These data are found in Gordon S. Black, "American Discontent Reaches Unprecedented Levels," executive summary, June 1992.

59. Morin and Dionne, "Majority of Voters Say Parties Have Lost Touch," p. 1.

60. ABC News/*Washington Post*, survey, June 24–28, 1992. Text of question: "Do you agree or disagree with the following statement: Both political parties are pretty much out of touch with the American people." Agree, 82 percent; disagree, 15 percent; no opinion, 3 percent.

61. CBS News/*New York Times*, survey, February 26–March 1, 1992. Text of question: "Is it mainly the Republicans in Congress who are to blame for the recession, or is it the Democrats in Congress, or is it both parties in Congress?" Republicans, 7 percent; Democrats, 10 percent; both parties, 81 percent; don't know/no answer, 2 percent.

62. CBS News/*New York Times*, survey, June 17–20, 1992. Text of question: "Some people say the country needs a new political party to compete with the Democratic and Republican parties in offering the best candidates for political office. Do you agree or disagree?" Agree, 58 percent; disagree, 36 percent; don't know, 6 percent. Democrats: agree, 54 percent; disagree, 40 percent; don't know, 6 percent. Republicans: agree, 53 percent; disagree, 43 percent; don't know, 4 percent. Independents: agree, 67 percent; disagree, 25 percent; don't know, 8 percent.

63. Black, "American Discontent Reaches Unprecedented Levels."

64. Ed Rollins, interview, *MacNeil/Lehrer NewsHour*, PBS, broadcast, May 21, 1992.

65. Quoted in Arthur M. Schlesinger Jr., "Faded Glory," *New York Times Magazine*, July 12, 1992, p. 14.

66. Cited in David S. Broder, "Politicians on Probation," *Washington Post*, December 6, 1992, p. C–7.

67. See *Republican Party v. Tashjian*, 599 F. Supp. 1228, 1238 (1983).

68. Theodore J. Lowi, "Yes—It's Time for a Third Major Party in American Politics," in Gary L. Rose, ed., *Controversial Issues in Presidential Selection*, 2d ed. (Albany: State University of New York Press, 1994), p. 248.

69. Theodore J. Lowi, address, C-SPAN, broadcast, June 3, 1992.

70. Jack W. Germond and Jules Witcover, *Mad As Hell: Revolt at the Ballot Box, 1992* (New York: Warner Books, 1993), p. 221.

71. Chiu, *Ross Perot: In His Own Words*, p. 171.

72. Ibid., p. 48.

73. Quoted in Carolyn Barta, *Perot and His People* (Fort Worth, Texas: The Summit Group, 1993), p. 50.

74. Bert Solomon, "Politics of Protest," *National Journal*, May 9, 1992, p. 1101.

75. Ibid.

76. "Transcript of Third TV Debate Between Bush, Clinton, and Perot," *New York Times*, October 20, 1992, p. A-23. Still, his lack of experience hurt. An ABC News/*Washington Post* October 4, 1992, survey found just 18 percent saying Perot had "the right kind of experience to be President," whereas 73 percent thought Bush qualified and 56 percent said Clinton was qualified.

77. Gallup poll, April 25–28, 1991. Thirty-eight percent disagreed and 12 percent had no opinion.

78. Author's interview with Michael S. Dukakis, Boston, Massachusetts, June 29, 1994.

79. See Dana Priest and John Mintz, "Sub Has More Friends Than Enemies," *Washington Post*, October 13, 1995, p. A-4.

80. Author's interview with George S. McGovern, Washington, D.C., January 4, 1996.

81. See Dionne, *They Only Look Dead*, pp. 59–60.

82. *Republican Party Platform, 1992*, p. 68.

83. David C. Morrison, "Home Front Politics," *National Journal*, September 5, 1992, p. 2007.

84. NBC News, *Sunday Today*, broadcast, March 29, 1992.

85. John Mintz, "Defense Cuts Exact Human Toll in Maryland." *Washington Post*, May 7, 1993.

86. Ibid.

87. Ibid.

88. Ibid.

89. R. W. Apple Jr., "In Formerly Safe Florida, It's Nip and Tuck for Bush," *New York Times*, October 15, 1992, p. A-22.

90. Schmaltz, "Americans Are Sadder and Wiser," p. E-1.

91. *The Democratic Party Platform, 1992*, p. 2.

92. See Schmaltz, "Americans Are Sadder and Wiser," p. E-1.

93. See David Fromkin, *In the Time of the Americans* (New York: Alfred A. Knopf, 1995), p. 513.

94. Quayle, *Standing Firm* (New York: HarperCollins, 1994), p. 247.

95. Gallup poll, August 21, 1992. Text of question: "How important will family values be in deciding your vote for president compared with other key issues? Will family values be more important or less important than foreign policy?" More important, 57 percent; less important, 37 percent; same (volunteered), 3 percent; don't know/refused, 4 percent.

96. Quayle, *Standing Firm*, p. 247.

97. Dan Quayle, "Address to the Commonwealth Club of California," San Francisco, California, May 19, 1992.

98. Quoted in Norman Mailer, "By Heaven Inspired," *New Republic*, October 12, 1992, pp. 24, 30.

99. E. J. Dionne Jr., "Buchanan Heaps Scorn on Democrats," *Washington Post*, August 18, 1992, p. A-18.

100. Germond and Witcover, *Mad As Hell*, p. 273.

101. Anthony Lewis, "The Two Faces of George," *New York Times*, September 21, 1992, p. A-17.

102. "Transcript of First TV Debate Among Bush, Clinton, and Perot," p. A-14.

103. Hart and Breglio Research, survey, October 20–21, 1992. Text of question: "Regardless of how you will vote, when you just consider Bill Clinton's explanation of his trip to Moscow in 1969 would you say you feel satisfied or do you have major doubts about having him as President?" Satisfied, 51 percent; major doubts, 31 percent; not sure, 18 percent.

104. Schmaltz, "Americans Are Sadder and Wiser," p. E-1.

105. Voter Research and Surveys, exit poll, November 3, 1992. Text of question: "Were any of the items below very important in making your presidential choice?. . . . Clinton's draft status and anti-war protests during Vietnam." Yes, 20 percent; no, 80 percent.

106. Yankelovich Clancy Shulman, survey, September 22–24, 1992. Text of question: "Do you feel there has been too much attention paid to Bill Clinton's draft record during this campaign, too little attention, or the right amount of attention?" Too much, 62 percent; too little, 6 percent; right amount, 25 percent; not sure, 7 percent.

107. See John Kenneth White, *The New Politics of Old Values* (Hanover, New Hampshire: University Press of New England, 1990).

108. Germond and Witcover, *Mad As Hell*, p. 512.

109. Orville Mitchell, interview, *MacNeil/Lehrer NewsHour*, PBS, September 25, 1992.

110. *The Democratic Party Platform, 1992*, p. 7.

111. CBS News/*New York Times*, survey, October 31-November 1, 1992. Text of question: "Do you think Bill Clinton and Al Gore are different from Democratic presidential candidates in previous years, or are they typical Democratic candidates?" Different, 44 percent; typical, 46 percent; both (volunteered), 2 percent; don't know/no answer, 9 percent.

112. Andrew Rosenthal with Joel Brinkley, "Old Compass in New World: A President Sticks to Course," *New York Times*, June 25, 1992, p. A-1.

113. Ann Devroy, "The Nation Changed but Bush Did Not," *Washington Post*, January 17, 1993, p. 1.

114. Quayle, *Standing Firm*, p. 356.

115. Ibid., p. 355.

116. Ann Devroy, "Domestic Perils Sink President Bush," *Washington Post*, November 4, 1992, p. A-21.

117. Voter Research and Surveys, exit poll, November 3, 1992. Text of question: "Which one issue mattered most in deciding how you voted?" Foreign policy, 8 percent.

118. Elizabeth Drew, "High Noon," *New Yorker*, October 19, 1992, p. 54.

119. The preceding data are taken from Voter Research and Surveys, exit poll, November 3, 1992.

120. Francis X. Clines, "Civics 101: Cultivating Grass Roots the Old Way," *New York Times*, November 4, 1992, p. B-1.

121. Schmaltz, "Americans Are Sadder and Wiser," p. E-1.

122. Voter Research and Surveys, exit poll, November 3, 1992. Text of question: "If Bill Clinton wins today, what best describes your feeling about what he will do as President?" Excited, 15 percent; optimistic, but not excited, 25 percent; concerned, but not scared, 30 percent; don't know/no answer, 2 percent.

123. Quoted in George C. Edwards III and Tami Swenson, "The Limits of the Public Presidency," *Polling Report*, September 26, 1994, p. 6.

124. CBS News, survey, November 2, 1992. Text of question: "Do you think reelecting [electing] George Bush [Bill Clinton, Ross Perot] in November would bring about the kind of change the country needs or not?" Bush: yes, 26 percent; no, 65 percent; don't know/no answer, 9 percent. Clinton: yes, 41 percent; no, 45 percent; don't know/no answer, 14 percent. Perot: yes, 29 percent; no, 56 percent; don't know/no answer, 15 percent.

125. Dionne, *They Only Look Dead*, p. 75.

126. See William J. Clinton, "Remarks on the Economic Program in Hyde Park, New York," in *Public Papers of the Presidents of the United States: William J. Clinton* (Washington, D.C.: U.S. Government Printing Office, 1994), p. 138.

127. Sidney Blumenthal, "Rendezvousing with Destiny," *New Yorker*, March 8, 1993, p. 40.

128. Dan Balz, "Can Clinton Bring Discipline to Policy?" *Washington Post*, January 17, 1993, p. 1.

129. Voter Research and Surveys, exit poll, November 3, 1992.

130. Bill Clinton, interview with Ted Koppel, *ABC News*, "Seventy-Two Hours to Victory," broadcast, November 4, 1992.

131. See White, *The New Politics of Old Values*, pp. 82–83.

132. The convict, Rickey Ray Rector, killed a police officer and then turned the gun on himself, destroying a portion of his brain.

133. Louis Harris and Associates, survey, October 30–November 1, 1992. Text of question: "Which one of the three candidates—Bush, or Clinton, or Perot—would do the most to strengthen traditional American values?" Bush, 39 percent; Clinton, 33 percent; Perot, 19 percent.

134. Quoted in Clyde Wilcox, *The Latest American Revolution? The 1994 Elections and Their Implications for Governance* (New York: St. Martin's Press, 1995), pp. 16–17.

135. Quoted in Helen Dewar, "Congress Nervously Eyes Challenge of Handling Health Care Reform," *Washington Post*, November 6, 1993, p. A-4.

136. Paul Tsongas, *Journey of Purpose: Reflections on the Presidency, Multiculturalism, and Third Parties* (New Haven: Yale University Press, 1995), pp. 81–82.

137. Peter D. Hart and Robert M. Teeter, survey, September 1993. Text of question: "Do you feel confident or not confident that life for our children's generation will be better than it has been for us?" Confident life will be better, 25 percent; not confident, 68 percent; not sure, 7 percent.

138. Bill Clinton, "Address to the Nation," Washington, D.C., December 15, 1994.

139. Bill Clinton, "Speech to the Democratic Leadership Council," Washington, D.C., December 15, 1994.

140. Quoted in Dan Balz, "Independence a Trait," *Washington Post*, August 29, 1994, p. 1.

141. Cited in Dionne, *They Only Look Dead*, p. 44.

142. Quoted in John Kenneth White, "Reviving the Political Parties: What Must Be Done?" in John Kenneth White and John C. Green, eds., *The Politics of Ideas* (Lanham, Maryland: Rowman and Littlefield, 1995), p. 21.

143. Guy Molyneux, "The Big Lie," *Rolling Stone*, December 29, 1994, p. 154.

144. Clinton, "Speech to the Democratic Leadership Council," December 15, 1994.

145. See *Baker v. Carr*, 369 U.S. 186 (1962).

146. Walter Dean Burnham, "Realignment Lives: The 1994 Earthquake and Its Implications," in Colin Campbell and Bert A. Rockman, eds., *The Clinton Presidency: First Appraisals* (Chatham, New Jersey: Chatham House Publishers, 1996), p. 363.

147. Rhodes Cook, "President Defends Record, Concedes Mistakes," *Congressional Quarterly Weekly Report*, December 10, 1994, p. 3516.

148. Voter Research and Surveys, exit poll, November 8, 1994.

149. See Rhodes Cook, "Democrats' Congressional Base Shredded by November Vote," *Congressional Quarterly Weekly Report*, December 10, 1994, p. 3518.

150. See Dionne, *They Only Look Dead*, p. 81.

151. See Molyneux, "The Big Lie," p. 154.

152. Cited in Wilcox, *The Latest American Revolution?* p. 31.

153. Quoted in Dionne, *They Only Look Dead*, p. 271.

154. Quoted in R. W. Apple Jr., "Post–Cold War Candidates Find No Place Like Home," *New York Times*, February 20, 1996, p. A-14.

155. CNN, *Inside Politics*, December 19, 1995.

156. Robert J. Dole, "Acceptance Speech," Republican National Convention, San Diego, August 15, 1996.

157. "Dole Won't Confirm Reports He Will Urge Drug Tests for All on Welfare," *Boston Globe*, May 21, 1996, p. 3.

158. Dole, "Acceptance Speech," Republican National Convention, August 15, 1996.

159. See "Transcript of the Second Presidential Debate," *Washington Post*, October 17, 1996, p. A-12.

160. *The Republican Platform, 1996: Restoring the American Dream* (Washington, D.C.: Republican National Committee, 1996), p. 78.

161. Ibid., p. 4.

162. *The 1996 Democratic National Platform* (Washington, D.C.: Democratic National Committee, 1996), p. 32.

163. Jack Kemp, "Acceptance Speech," Republican National Convention, San Diego, August 15, 1996.

164. Todd S. Purdum, "What Kind of Democrat?" *New York Times Magazine*, May 19, 1996, p. 77.

165. "Transcript of the Second Presidential Debate," p. A-12.

166. "Defense Cuts Are Likely During Next Presidential Term," *Hartford Courant*, October 7, 1996.

167. Bill Clinton, *Between Hope and History: Meeting America's Challenges for the 21st Century* (New York: Times Books, 1996), p. 148.

168 Ibid., p. 153.

169. "Transcript of the First Presidential Debate," *Washington Post*, October 7, 1996, p. A-8.

170. Clinton, *Between Hope and History*, p. 154.

171. See Bill Clinton, "Speech to the Democratic Leadership Council," Washington, D.C., December 11, 1996, and John F. Harris, "Clinton Vows Wider NATO in Three Years," *Washington Post*, October 23, 1996, p. A-1.

172. *The Republican Platform, 1996*, p. 75.

173. "Text of Kennedy's Speech: 'If We Stand Our Ground, We Can Prevail,'" *New York Times*, August 30, 1996, p. A-13.

174. See William Safire, *Before the Fall: An Inside View of the Pre-Watergate White House* (New York: Ballantine Books, 1977), pp. 416–417.

175. "Shrill Emergency Broadcast Test Soon to Be a Cold War Relic," *New York Times*, November 17, 1996, p. 29.

176. John F. Harris, "Unsolicited Advice from an Erstwhile Confidant," *Washington Post*, September 20, 1996.

177. Alison Mitchell, "Stung by Defeats in '94 Clinton Regrouped and Co-opted GOP Strategies," *New York Times*, November 7, 1996, p. B-1.

178. Office of the Press Secretary, "Transcript of Press Conference by the President," Washington, D.C., April 18, 1995.

179. Mitchell, "Stung By Defeats," p. B-1.

180. "Transcript of the First Presidential Debate," p. A-8.

181. Ibid.

182. Bob Dole and Jack Kemp, *Trusting the People: The Dole-Kemp Plan to Free the Economy and Create a Better America* (New York: HarperCollins, 1996), pp. 41, xi.

183. *The Republican Platform, 1996*, pp. 6–7.

184. "Excerpts from the Second Televised Debate Between Clinton and Dole," *Washington Post*, October 18, 1996.

185. Voter News and Surveys, exit poll, November 5, 1996. Text of questions: "Do you think the condition of the nation's economy is excellent, good, not so good, or poor?" Excellent, 4 percent; good, 51 percent; not so good, 36 percent; poor, 7 percent. "Do you think things in this country today are generally going in the right direction or are seriously off on the wrong track?" Right direction, 53 percent; wrong track, 43 percent.

186. Dole, "Acceptance Speech," Republican National Convention, August 15, 1996.

187. Bill Clinton, "Acceptance Speech," Democratic National Convention, Chicago, August 29, 1996.

188. Voter News and Surveys, exit poll, November 5, 1996. Text of question: "Which one candidate quality mattered most in deciding how you voted for president?" He shares my view of government, 20 percent; he stands up for what he believes in, 13 percent; he cares about people like me, 9 percent; he is honest and trustworthy, 20 percent; he is in touch with the 1990s, 10 percent; he has a vision for the future, 16 percent.

189. "Text of Democratic Platform," reprinted in *New York Times*, June 26, 1936, p. 1.

190. Theodore H. White, *The Making of the President, 1964* (New York: New American Library, 1965), p. 366.

191. See Haynes Johnson and David S. Broder, *The System: The American Way of Politics at the Breaking Point* (Boston: Little, Brown, 1996), p. 66.

192. Ibid., pp. 65–67.

193. Lyndon Baines Johnson, *The Vantage Point: Perspectives of the Presidency, 1963–1969* (New York: Holt, Rinehart, and Winston, 1971), p. 213.

194. Clinton quoting Dole, "Transcript of the Second Presidential Debate," p. A-12.

195. Johnson and Broder, *The System*, p. 473.

196. Quoted in Stefan Lorant, *The Presidency: A Pictorial History of Presidential Elections from Washington to Truman* (New York: Macmillan, 1951), p. 591.

197. Ted Morgan, *FDR* (New York: Simon and Schuster, 1985), p. 40.

198. Quoted in Theodore H. White, *The Making of the President, 1968* (New York: Atheneum Publishers, 1969), p. 359.

199. Ibid.

200. Gallup poll, August 3–8, 1951. Text of question: "Suppose a young person, just turned 21, asked you what the Republican party (Democratic party) stands for today—what would you tell them?" The number-one Republican response, 16 percent, was "for the privileged few, moneyed interests." The number-one Democratic response, 19 percent, was "for the working man, for the public benefit, for the common man."

201. Gallup poll, June 18–23, 1948. Text of question: "Do you think the Republican party is run by a few big businessmen of the country?" Yes, 47 percent; no, 37 percent; no opinion, 16 percent. Gallup poll, January 20–25, 1955. Text of question: "Which political party—the

Democratic or the Republican—do you think serves the interests of the following groups best?" Professional and business: Republicans, 57 percent; Democrats, 21 percent. Skilled workers: Republicans 21 percent; Democrats, 53 percent. Unskilled workers: Republicans, 15 percent; Democrats, 61 percent.

202. Clinton, *Between Hope and History*, p. 90.

203. Quoted in Kirk H. Porter and Donald Bruce Johnson, *National Party Platforms: 1840–1968* (Urbana: University of Illinois Press, 1970), pp. 365–366.

204. Ibid., p. 369.

205. Quoted in *The 1996 Democratic National Platform*, p. 11.

206. NBC News/*Wall Street Journal*, survey, May 10–14, 1996. Reported in *Public Perspective*, October/November 1996, p. 31.

207. Voter News and Surveys, exit poll, November 5, 1996. Text of questions: "Is your opinion of Newt Gingrich favorable or unfavorable?" Favorable, 32 percent; unfavorable, 59 percent. "In general, do you approve or disapprove of what the Republicans in Congress have done in the last two years?" Approve, 42 percent; disapprove, 52 percent.

208. See Samuel H. Beer, "Ronald Reagan: New Deal Conservative?" *Society*, January/February, 1983, pp. 40–44.

209. *The 1996 Democratic National Platform*, p. 21.

210. Ibid., p. 6.

211. "Transcript of the Second Presidential Debate," p. A-12.

212. Ibid., p. A-15.

213. Quoted in Johnson and Broder, *The System*, p. 384.

214. Voter News and Surveys, exit poll, November 5, 1996. Text of questions: "Which one issue mattered most in deciding how you voted for President?" Foreign policy, 4 percent; Medicare/Social Security, 15 percent; taxes, 11 percent; crime/drugs, 7 percent; economy/jobs, 21 percent; education, 12 percent; federal budget deficit, 12 percent.

215. National Commission on Excellence in Education, *A Nation At Risk: The Imperative for Educational Reform* (Washington, D.C.: Superintendent of Documents, U.S. Government Printing Office, 1983), p. 5

216. Gallup poll, October 26–29, 1996.

217. Dole, "Acceptance Speech," Republican National Convention, August 15, 1996.

218. *The 1996 Democratic National Platform*, p. 8.

219. "Transcript of the First Presidential Debate," p. A-8.

220. *The 1996 Democratic National Platform*, p. 6.

221. Voter News and Surveys, exit poll, November 5, 1996. Text of question: "Which comes closer to your view: government should do more to solve problems or government is doing too many things better left to businesses and individuals?" Should do more, 41 percent; should do less, 52 percent.

222. *The 1996 Democratic National Platform*, p. 40.

223. Ibid., p. 17.

224. Thomas B. Edsall, "Dole Accentuating the Positive," *Washington Post*, October 22, 1996, p. A-12.

225. Dole and Kemp, *Trusting the People*, p. 126.

226. Katherine Q. Seelye, "Dole Says President Defends Old Elites Seeking Largesse," *New York Times*, January 24, 1996, p. A-1.

227. "Republican National Platform, 1936," in Porter and Johnson, *National Party Platforms*, p. 365.

228. Samuel G. Freedman, "Why Bob Dole Can't Be Reagan," *New York Times*, October 27, 1996, p. E-4.

229. Dole and Kemp, *Trusting the People*, p. 1.

230. "Transcript of the Second Presidential Debate," p. A-14.

231. Voter News and Surveys, exit poll, November 5, 1996. Text of question: "Do you think Bob Dole would be able to reduce the federal budget deficit and cut taxes by 15 percent at the same time?" Yes, 30 percent; no, 66 percent.

232. For a fuller rendition see Richard Ben Cramer, *Bob Dole* (New York: Vintage Books, 1992).

233. Clinton Rossiter, *The American Presidency* (New York: New American Library, 1960), p. 103.

234. Cited in Carl Sandburg, *Abraham Lincoln*, vol. 3, *The War Years* (New York: Dell, 1954), p. 661.

235. Voter News and Surveys, exit poll, November 5, 1996. Text of questions: "In explaining Whitewater and other matters under investigation, do you think Bill Clinton has told the truth or not told the truth." Told the truth, 33 percent; not told the truth, 60 percent. "Regardless of how you voted today, do you think Bill Clinton is honest and trustworthy?" Yes, 41 percent; no, 54 percent.

236. Gerald R. Ford, *A Time to Heal* (New York: Harper and Row, 1979), p. 413.

237. Voter News and Surveys, exit poll, November 5, 1996. Text of question: "Which was more important in your vote for President: His position on the issues or his personal character and values." Issue positions, 58 percent; character and values, 38 percent.

238. See White, *The New Politics of Old Values*, especially pp. 37–55.

239. Bill Clinton, "Acceptance Speech," Democratic National Convention, July 19, 1992.

240. Richard B. Wirthlin, lecture, Catholic University of America, September 29, 1992.

241. Robert J. Dole, "Speech to the U.S. Conference of Mayors," Miami, Florida, June 17, 1995.

242. David Kusnet, *Speaking American: How the Democrats Can Win in the Nineties* (New York: Thunder's Mouth Press, 1992).

243. Hart-Teeter, survey, March 16–18, 1995. Text of question: "Now I'm going to read a list of goals. For each one, please tell me which of the following groups you think has the greatest responsibility for achieving that goal—government, businesses, community leaders, or individuals?" Government responses only: Controlling immigration, 90 percent; providing income assistance to the needy, 57 percent; improving education, 44 percent; creating more jobs and strengthening the economy, 43 percent; reducing crime, 39 percent; reducing air and water pollution, 31 percent; improving opportunities for racial and ethnic minorities, 22 percent; promoting culture through museums and concerts, 15 percent; improving moral values, 5 percent; strengthening families, 4 percent.

244. Voter News and Surveys, exit poll, November 5, 1996. Text of question: "On most political matters, do you consider yourself to be liberal, moderate, or conservative?" Liberal, 20 percent; moderate, 47 percent; conservative, 33 percent.

245. Bob Woodward, *The Choice* (New York: Simon and Schuster, 1996), p. 420.

246. Edward Walsh, "Dole's New Battle Cry: Clinton Is an Elitist 'Liberal, Liberal, Liberal,'" *Washington Post*, September 29, 1996, p. A-12.

247. "Transcript of the First Presidential Debate," p. A-11.

248. Quoted in Woodward, *The Choice*, p. 420

249. "Democratic Platform, 1936," in Porter and Johnson, *National Party Platforms*, p. 363.

250. Blaine Harden, "Dole Woos California," *Washington Post*, October 29, 1996, p. A-1.

251. Richard L. Berke, "GOP Leaders Doubtful that Dole Can Close Gap," *New York Times*, October 20, 1996, p. 1.

252. Quoted in Michael Crowley, "Party Line," *New Republic*, November 4, 1996, p. 9.

253. "GOP Conservative Goldwater Says Clinton Makes a Good President," *Boston Globe*, August 5, 1996, p. A-7.

254. Quoted in Jonathan Alter, "A Man Not of His Time," *Newsweek*, November 4, 1996, p. 30.

255. Evan Thomas, "The Small Deal," *Newsweek*, November 18, 1996, p. 127.

256. David S. Broder, "Factions, Competing Ideologies Challenge Coalition Builders," *Washington Post*, November 7, 1996.

257. Voter News and Surveys, exit poll, November 5, 1996. Text of question: "If there were only two presidential candidates on the ballot today, who would you have voted for?" Clinton, 50 percent; Dole, 43 percent; would not vote, 5 percent.

258. Laurence I. Barrett, "Fighting for God and the Right Wing," *Time*, September 13, 1993, p. 60.

259. Quoted in Johnson and Broder, *The System*, p. 445.

260. William Booth, "From Florida Voters, a Mixed Verdict," *Washington Post*, November 7, 1996, p. A-25.

261. Evan Thomas, "Bridge to 2000," *Newsweek*, November 18, 1996, p. 125.

262. Voter News and Surveys, exit poll, November 5, 1996. Men: Clinton, 43 percent; Dole, 44 percent; Perot, 10 percent. Women: Clinton, 54 percent; Dole, 38 percent; Perot, 7 percent.

263. Broder, "Factions, Competing Ideologies Challenge Coalition Builders," p. A-23.

264. Quoted in Larry Sabato, *Goodbye to Good-time Charlie: The American Governorship Transformed* (Washington, D.C.: Congressional Quarterly, 1983), p. 160.

265. Dan Balz, "Republicans Sound Conciliatory Tone," *Washington Post*, November 7, 1996, p. A-1.

266. The Florida State Senate contained 23 Republicans to 17 Democrats and the State House had 61 Republicans and 59 Democrats.

267. Richard L. Berke, "Clinton Preparing for Second Term with Shuffle of Top Officials," *New York Times*, November 7, 1996, p. A–1.

268. Michael Lind, "The Southern Coup," *New Republic*, June 19, 1995, p. 29.

269. Bernard Sanders, the Vermont Socialist, is the lone "independent." Missouri Representative-elect Jo Ann Emerson, who ran as an independent due to ballot access restrictions, is listed among the Republicans.

270. Quoted in Joe Klein, "Plain Vanilla or Rain Forest Crunch?" *Newsweek*, July 18, 1994, p. 38.

271. Voter News and Surveys, exit poll, November 5, 1996. Text of question: "If Bill Clinton is reelected, would you rather have the U.S. Congress controlled by the Democrats or the Republicans?" Democrats, 44 percent; Republicans, 49 percent.

272. Warren P. Strobel, "President Improves on His 1992 Showing," *Washington Times*, November 6, 1996, p. A-1.

273. Lloyd Free and Hadley Cantril, *The Political Beliefs of Americans* (New Brunswick, New Jersey: Rutgers University Press, 1967).

274. Bill Clinton, "State of the Union Address," Washington, D.C., January 23, 1996.

275. Cited in Everett Carll Ladd, "Public Opinion and the 'Congress Problem,'" *Public Interest*, Summer 1990, p. 66.

276. "Transcript of the Second Presidential Debate," p. A-12.

277. Bill Clinton, "Victory Speech," Little Rock, Arkansas, November 5, 1996.

278. Quoted in Adam Clymer, "Top Republicans Say They Seek Common Ground with Clinton," *New York Times*, November 7, 1996, p. A-1.

279. Daniel Bell, *The End of Ideology* (Glencoe, Illinois: Free Press, 1960).

280. Clinton, "Victory Speech," November 5, 1996.

281. Clinton, "Speech to the Democratic Leadership Council," December 11, 1996.

282. Clinton, "Victory Speech," November 5, 1996.

Chapter Seven

1. Author's interview with Oleg Kalugin, Washington, D.C., March 18, 1995.

2. Author's interview with William Odum, Washington, D.C., March 18, 1995.

3. Quoted in Thomas L. Friedman, "Cold War Without End," *New York Times Magazine*, August 22, 1993, p. 30.

4. See Pat M. Holt, "Spying Out New Roles for Central Intelligence Agency," *Christian Science Monitor*, October 5, 1995, p. 19.

5. Richard Nixon, *Beyond Peace* (New York: Random House, 1994), p. 4.

6. See David Remnick, "America: Love It or Loathe It," *New York Times Magazine*, June 6, 1995, p. 27.

7. Quoted in James Brooke, "Russians Have Landed in Kansas! But They've Come to Make Peace," *New York Times*, October 27, 1995, p. A-14.

8. George Washington, "Farewell Address," September 19, 1796.

9. Bill Clinton, *Between Hope and History: Meeting America's Challenges for the 21st Century* (New York: Times Books, 1996), pp. 143, 144.

10. Robert J. Dole, campaign speech, quoted in the *Washington Post*, June 13, 1987.

11. Patrick J. Buchanan, "Buchanan on the Issues," campaign brochure, 1996.

12. E. J. Dionne Jr., *They Only Look Dead: Why Progressives Will Dominate the Next Political Era* (New York: Simon and Schuster, 1996), p. 56.

13. Quoted in Ann Devroy and Jeffrey Smith, "Clinton Reexamines Foreign Policy Under Siege," *Washington Post*, October 17, 1993, p. 1, and Richard Reeves, *Running in Place: How Bill Clinton Disappointed America* (Kansas City: Andrews and McMeel, 1996), p. 94.

14. Quoted in R. W. Apple Jr., "White House Race Is Recast: No Kremlin to Run Against," *New York Times*, February 6, 1992, p. A-1.

15. Dirk Johnson, "Voices from the Grass Roots: Anger Over Partisan Politics," *New York Times*, August 27, 1994, p. A-1.

16. Quoted in George F. Will, "Buchanan's Nonsense," *Washington Post*, November 5, 1995, p. C-7.

17. See Louis Hartz, *The Liberal Tradition in America* (New York: Harcourt Brace, 1955), p. 286.

18. Quoted in Stefan Lorant, *The Presidency* (New York: MacMillan, 1951), p. 543.

19. Quoted in Apple, "White House Race Is Recast," p. A-1.

20. Michael Barone, "The Restoration of the Constitutional Order and the Return to Tocquevillian America," in Michael Barone and Grant Ujifusa, *The Almanac of American Politics, 1996* (Washington, D.C.: National Journal, 1995), p. xxvi. See also Michael Barone, "The Road Back to Tocqueville," *Washington Post*, January 7, 1996, p. C-1.

21. Woodrow Wilson, *Congressional Government* (Gloucester, Massachusetts: Peter Smith, 1973 reprint), p. 34. Originally published in 1885.

22. "Transcript of the First Presidential Debate," *Washington Post*, October 7, 1996.

23. *Republican Platform, 1996: Restoring the American Dream* (Washington, D.C.: Republican National Committee, 1996), p. 21.

24. Clinton Rossiter, *The American Presidency* (New York: Harcourt, Brace, and World, 1960), pp. 261–262. This was written prior to Nixon's presidency and Watergate.

25. The Kennedy-Rossiter anecdote is found in Everett Carll Ladd, *The American Polity* (New York: W. W. Norton, 1987), p. 167.

26. Wilson, *Congressional Government*, p. 23.

27. Ibid., p. 24.

28. George F. Will, "Peace Is Hell," *Washington Post*, May 30, 1993, p. C-7.

29. Quoted in Bob Woodward, *The Choice* (New York: Simon and Schuster, 1996), p. 65.

30. Bob Woodward, *The Agenda: Inside the Clinton White House* (New York: Simon and Schuster, 1994), p. 268.

31. Ibid., p. 315.

32. Stephen Engelberg, Jeff Gerth, and Katherine Q. Seelye, "Files Show How Gingrich Laid a Grand GOP Plan," *New York Times*, December 3, 1995, p. A-1, and "The Contract Is Working Perfectly," *Washington Post*, October 20, 1994, p. A-27.

33. Newt Gingrich, *To Renew America* (New York: HarperCollins, 1995), p. 102.

34. "Gingrich Advises GOP to Stress Community," *Boston Globe*, March 13, 1996, p. 16. The term "citizen-politician" was coined by James Q. Wilson. See James Q. Wilson, "A Guide to Reagan Country: The Political Culture of Southern California," *Commentary*, May 1967.

35. Bill Clinton, "Remarks by the President on Responsible Citizenship and the American Community," Georgetown University, Washington, D.C., July 6, 1995.

36. Abraham Lincoln, "Second Annual Message to Congress," December 1, 1862.

37. Herbert Croly, *The Promise of American Life* (New York: Archon Books, reprint, 1963).

38. Quoted in Edmund Morris, *The Rise of Theodore Roosevelt* (New York: Coward, McCann, and Geoghegan, 1979), p. 13.

39. Quoted in Walter Dean Burnham, "Realignment Lives: The 1994 Earthquake and Its Implications," in Bert A. Rockman, ed., *The Clinton Presidency* (Chatham, New Jersey: Chatham House, 1996), p. 390.

40. See Jane Perlez, "Media-Wise Walesa Foe Copies Style of Clinton," *New York Times*, November 19, 1994, p. 4.

41. Vaclav Havel, "The Post-Communist Nightmare," *New York Review of Books*, May 27, 1993, p. 10.

42. U.S. Department of Energy, Office of Environmental Management, *Estimating the Cold War Mortgage* (Springfield, Virginia: U.S. Department of Commerce, National Technical Information Service, 1995), p. xiv.

43. Quoted in Thomas W. Lippman, "Tearing Down Remnants of Cold War Leaves Amarillo Holding the Pits," *Washington Post*, October 29, 1994, p. A-3.

44. Cited in Jim Carrier, "Bomb Blues," *Denver Post*, July 13, 1995, p. A-1.

45. Ibid.

46. Bill Clinton, "Remarks by the President in Speech to National Baptist Convention," New Orleans, Louisiana, September 9, 1994.

47. Robert Wright, "Who's Really to Blame?" *Time*, November 6, 1995, p. 34.

48. Quoted in Thomas B. Edsall, "Democrats Look to Factories, Faculties," *Washington Post*, May 21, 1994, p. A-1.

49. Associated Press, "Town Built on Steel Industry Resigns Itself to End of Era," *New York Times*, November 19, 1995, p. 27.

50. Buchanan speech reprinted on his home page on the World Wide Web, spring 1996.

51. Quoted in Carrier, "Bomb Blues," p. A-1.

52. Rick Brace, "Big Holes Where the Dignity Used to Be," *New York Times*, March 5, 1996, p. A-1.

53. See Jack Egan with Dana Coleman, "Get Bigger or Get Out," *U.S. News and World Report*, December 2, 1996, pp. 50–56, and Richard Bierck, "How Golf Saved a Defense Supplier," *U.S. News and World Report*, December 2, 1996, p. 56.

54. Wright, "Who's Really to Blame?" p. 34.

55. Ibid.

56. Ibid., p. 36.

57. *New York Times*, survey, December 8–11, 1996. Text of question: "How concerned are you that in the next two or three years someone else in your household might be laid off?" Very concerned, 16 percent; somewhat concerned, 33 percent.

58. Steve Lohr, "Though Upbeat on the Economy, People Still Fear for Their Jobs," *New York Times*, December 29, 1996, p. 1.

59. Wright, "Who's Really to Blame?" p. 36.

60. Cited in George J. Church, "Disconnected," *Time*, January 15, 1996, p. 45.

61. Harwood Group, *America's Struggle Within: Citizens Talk About the State of the Union* (Washington, D.C.: Pew Center for Civic Journalism, 1996), p. 8.

62. Quoted in Dionne, *They Only Look Dead*, p. 90.

63. Louis Uchitelle and N. R. Kleinfield, "On the Battlefields of Business, Millions of Casualties," *New York Times*, March 3, 1996, p. A-1.

64. Cited in N. R. Kleinfield, "The Company as Family No More," *New York Times*, March 4, 1996, p. A-1.

65. Sara Rimer, "A Hometown Feels Less Like Home," *New York Times*, March 6, 1996, p. A-1.

66. Ibid.

67. See Bill Clinton, "Speech to the Democratic Leadership Council," Washington, D.C., November 13, 1995, and Al Gore, *Common Sense Government* (New York: Random House, 1995), p. 14.

68. See Dionne, *They Only Look Dead*, p. 89.

69. Allan Sloan, "For Whom Bell Tolls," *Newsweek*, January 15, 1996, p. 44.

70. See Allan Sloan, "The Hit Men," *Newsweek*, February 26, 1996, p. 46.

71. Louis Uchitelle, "1995 Was Good for Companies and Better for a Lot of CEO's," *New York Times*, March 29, 1996, p. A-1.

72. Randall Richard, "MIT Economist: Hard Times Ahead for Middle Class," *Providence Journal*, March 31, 1996, p. A-1.

73. CNN/*Time*, All Politics, "Clinton Questions Corporate Layoffs," Internet, http://www.allpolitics.com, March 4, 1996.

74. Quoted in Uchitelle and Kleinfield, "On the Battlefields of Business, Millions of Casualties," p. A-1.

75. See James Truslow Adams, *The Epic of America* (Boston: Little, Brown, 1935), p. 174.

76. Voter News and Surveys, exit poll, November 5, 1996. Text of question: "Do you expect life for the next generation of Americans to be (1) better than life today, (2) worse than life today, (3) about the same." Better, 29 percent; worse, 33 percent; about the same, 35 percent.

77. See Harwood Group, *America's Struggle Within*, p. 9.

78. Quoted in Patrick H. Caddell, "Crisis of Confidence—Trapped in a Downward Spiral," *Public Opinion*, October/November 1979, p. 55.

79. *New York Times*, survey, December 3–6, 1995. Text of question: "Do you agree with this statement: I am angry at both political parties." Agree, 49 percent; of those hard-hit by layoffs, 69 percent.

80. Bill Clinton, "State of the Union Address," Washington, D.C., January 23, 1996.

81. Quoted in Dirk Johnson, "Voices from the Grass Roots: Anger Over Partisan Politics," *New York Times*, August 27, 1994, p. A-1.

82. Clinton, "Remarks by the President in Speech to National Baptist Convention."

83. Quoted in Nixon, *Beyond Peace*, p. 8.

84. Clinton, "Remarks by the President in Speech to National Baptist Convention."

85. Todd S. Purdum, "Clinton Plans to Lift Public Out of 'Funk,'" *New York Times*, September 24, 1995, p. A-1.

86. CBS News/*New York Times*, poll, January 13–15, 1990. Text of question: "Who won the Cold War? Did the United States and its allies win, or did the Soviet Union and its allies win, or did neither side really win?" United States and its allies, 14 percent; Soviet Union and its allies, 5 percent; neither side, 77 percent; don't know, 4 percent.

87. Yankelovich Partners for *Time* and CNN, survey, January 11–12, 1995. Text of question: "In commenting on how things are going in the country, some people tell us that the problems we face are no worse than at any other time in recent years. Others say the country is in deep and serious trouble today. Which comes closest to your own feelings?" Country is in deep and serious trouble, 53 percent; problems are no worse, 42 percent; not sure, 5 percent.

88. Clinton, "Remarks by the President on Responsible Citizenship and the American Community."

89. *Report of the National Advisory Commission on Civil Disorders* (New York: Bantam Books, 1968), p. 1.

90. Dialogue cited in Burnham, "Realignment Lives," p. 386.

91. "Excerpts from General Powell's News Conference on Political Plans," *New York Times*, November 9, 1995, p. B-13.

92. Bill Clinton, "Speech to the Democratic Leadership Council," Washington, D.C., December 11, 1996.

93. Quoted in Clyde Wilcox, *The Latest American Revolution? The 1994 Elections and Their Implications for Governance* (New York: St. Martin's Press, 1995), p. 44.

94. Ibid., p. 46. See also Connie Bruck, "The Politics of Perception," *New Yorker*, October 9, 1995, p. 62.

95. See Dionne, *They Only Look Dead*, p. 22.

96. Quoted in Burnham, "Realignment Lives," p. 386.

97. Jean Bethke Elshtain, *Democracy on Trial* (New York: Basic Books, 1995), p. 38.

98. *Dallas Morning News*, survey, March 2–18, 1995. The survey was based on 1,001 telephone interviews conducted in Dallas, Tarrant, Collin, and Denton Counties. Text of questions: (a) "Based on what you've been and heard, do you think people, in general, seem angrier than they used to be?" Yes, 72 percent. (b) "Now I'm going to read you a list of subjects that may or may not make you really angry when you think about them or discuss them with others. . . . Crime." Those who were "really angry" about crime totaled 55 percent. (c) "Some settings more than others may influence your level of anger. Please tell me about how often you get angry in the following settings." Those responding that got angry "at least once a week watching or reading the news" totaled 49 percent. (d) "How often do you do these things when you are angry?" Percentage answering "often or sometimes": "scream or yell," 46 percent; "cry," 44 percent; "pray," 76 percent; "swear or curse," 57 percent.

99. *New York Times*, survey, December 3–6, 1995. Text of question: "Compared to the way things used to be, do you think the mood at many workplaces today has become more angry or more friendly?" More angry, 53 percent; friendlier mood, 8 percent.

100. Elshtain, *Democracy on Trial*, p. 20.

101. E. E. Schattschneider, *The Semi-Sovereign People* (Hinsdale, Illinois: Dryden Press, 1975), p. 109.

102. Harry S. Truman, "Farewell Address," Washington, D.C., January 15, 1953.

103. Quotations taken from John F. Harris, "After Season of Doubt, Clinton Charging Up for '96 Campaign," *Washington Post*, September 24, 1995, p. A-1, and Purdum, "Clinton Plans to Lift Public Out of 'Funk,'" p. A-1.

104. Ibid.

105. Quoted in Herbert J. Storing, *What the Anti-Federalists Were For* (Chicago: University of Chicago Press, 1981), p. 26.

106. William James, *The Moral Equivalent of War and Other Essays* (New York: Harper and Row, 1971 edition), p. 14. James's essay, "The Moral Equivalent of War," was first published in *McClure's Magazine*, August 1910. Jimmy Carter borrowed James's phrase "the moral equivalent of war" in an unsuccessful attempt to rally the country in support of his energy policy.

107. Quoted in Nixon, *Beyond Peace*, p. 13.

108. Ibid., p. 10.

109. Ibid., p. 8.

110. Cited in Richard M. Nixon, *In the Arena: A Memoir of Victory, Defeat, and Renewal* (New York: Simon and Schuster, 1990), p. 245.

111. Al Gore, "Acceptance Speech," Democratic National Convention, Chicago, Illinois, August 28, 1996.

112. Quoted in James MacGregor Burns, *The Deadlock of Democracy: Four-Party Politics in America* (Englewood Cliffs, New Jersey: Prentice-Hall, 1963), p. 51.

113. Quoted in Storing, *What the Anti-Federalists Were For*, p. 12.

114. Quoted in Milton Viorst, *Fall From Grace* (New York: Simon and Schuster, 1968), p. 64.

115. Quoted in James MacGregor Burns, *Roosevelt: The Lion and the Fox* (New York: Harcourt, Brace, and World, 1956), p. 283.

116. Quoted in Thomas Oliphant, "U.S. Fear Could Set Back Change in Russia, Christopher Warns," *Boston Globe*, January 23, 1996, p. 15.

117. Quoted in Thomas B. Edsall, "Armey's Line on Hillary and 'Marxists,'" *Washington Post*, June 6, 1993, p. A–21. During the 1995 budget impasse, when Armey denounced statements coming from the White House as "lies," Clinton remembered Armey's attacks on his wife, saying, "I never, ever have and never expect to criticize your wife or members of your family." Quoted in John E. Yang, "Underlying Gingrich's Stance Is His Pique About President," *Washington Post*, November 16, 1995, p. A-1.

118. Quoted in Dionne, *They Only Look Dead*, p. 286.

119. "Republican Seeks to Make House Less Independent," *Washington Post*, October 12, 1994, p. A-8.

120. Ibid.

121. Sanders is only the third Socialist elected to the House. Victor Berger of Milwaukee (1911–1913, 1923–1929) and Meyer London of New York City (1915–1923) were the other two. Sanders aligns himself with the Democrats.

122. Quoted in Bruck, "The Politics of Perception," p. 74.

123. Quoted in E. J. Dionne Jr., *Why Americans Hate Politics* (New York: Touchstone Books, 1991), p. 362.

124. "Excerpts from Clinton-Yeltsin News Conference," *Washington Post*, April 5, 1993, p. A-16.

125. Market Strategies and Greenberg Research, poll, March 23-April 4, 1993. Text of question: "Now that the Cold War has ended, how much of a threat would you say the former republics of the Soviet Union are to the United States these days—a very serious threat, a minor threat, or not a threat at all?" Very serious threat, 7 percent; serious threat, 28 percent; minor threat, 46 percent; not a threat at all, 17 percent; don't know, 2 percent.

126. *Republican Platform, 1996*, p. 82.

127. Robert J. Dole, "Acceptance Speech," Republican National Convention, San Diego, August 15, 1996.

128. Quoted in Robert A. Divine, "The Cold War As History," in *Reviews in American History*, Volume 21, number 3, September 1993, p. 530.

129. Buchanan, "Buchanan on the Issues."

130. Data found in "Immigration," *Time/CNN*, All Politics, Internet, March 25, 1996.

131. Quoted in Barone and Ujifusa, *The Almanac of American Politics, 1996*, p. 81.

132. Quoted in Dick Kirschten, "Second Thoughts," *National Journal*, January 21, 1995, p. 150.

133. See Everett Carll Ladd, *America at the Polls, 1994* (Storrs, Connecticut: Roper Center for Public Opinion Research, 1995), p. 124.

134. Quoted in Storing, *What the Anti-Federalists Were For*, p. 20.

135. Quoted in J. Joseph Huthmacher, *Massachusetts: People and Politics, 1919–1933* (New York: Atheneum, 1969), p. 162.

136. *Time/CNN*, selected surveys, May 1985-September 1994. Text of question: "Some people feel that America should keep its doors open to people who wish to immigrate to the United States because that is what our heritage is all about. Others feel that this philosophy is no longer reasonable and we should strictly limit the number of people who should immigrate. Which of these positions comes closest to your opinion?" May 1985 responses: keep doors open, 27 percent; strictly limit immigration, 67 percent; not sure, 5 percent. September 1994 responses: keep doors open, 20 percent; strictly limit immigration, 77 percent; not sure, 3 percent.

137. *New York Times*, survey, December 3–6, 1995. Text of question: "Do you think immigrants into the United States should be increased, decreased, or kept about the same?" Decreased, 64 percent; asked of those already hard-hit by a layoff, 74 percent.

138. Cited in "Pat Speaks," *New Republic*, March 18, 1996, p. 17.

139. See Associated Press, "Buchanan Calls for Tougher Border Control," *Washington Post*, May 9, 1995, p. A-15.

140. *Republican Platform, 1996*, p. 37.

141. William Booth, "In a Rush, New Citizens Register Their Political Interest," *Washington Post*, September 26, 1996, p. A-1.

142. See Eric Schmitt, "Bill Tries to Balance Concerns on Immigration," *New York Times*, September 29, 1996, p. 28, and Eric Pianin and Helen Dewar, "Immigration, Budget Agreement Reached," *Washington Post*, September 29, 1996, p. A-1.

143. William Claiborne, "Democrats Don't Have Lock on Hispanic Vote, Latino Leaders Say," *Washington Post*, November 24, 1996, p. A-12.

144. In 1987, Governor Bill Clinton signed legislation making English the official language of Arkansas, but congressional Democrats have been reluctant to support a similar measure.

145. *Republican Platform, 1996*, p. 38.

146. Robert J. Dole, "Address to the American Legion Convention," Indianapolis, Indiana, September 4, 1995.

147. See David S. Broder, "Dole Backs Official Language," *Washington Post*, September 5, 1995, p. A-1.

148. Harwood Group, *America's Struggle Within*, p. 18.

149. Voter News Service, exit poll, March 26, 1996. Text of question: "Which comes closer to your view? The United States should welcome some immigrants. The United States can't afford any new immigrants." Welcome, 51 percent; can't afford, 42 percent; don't know, 7 percent.

150. *Republican Platform, 1996*, p. 45.

151. Dole, "Acceptance Speech," Republican National Convention, August 15, 1996.

152. Quoted in Adam Nagourney, "Buchanan Vows, if Elected, to Put an End to Abortions," *New York Times*, February 24, 1996, p. A-1.

153. Quoted in Jeffrey H. Birnbaum, "The Pat Solution," *Time*, November 6, 1995, p. 29.

154. Ibid.

155. Robert J. Dole, "Remarks by Senator Bob Dole," Los Angeles, California, May 31, 1995.

156. "Excerpts from Colin L. Powell's News Conference," *Washington Post*, November 9, 1995, p. A-14.

157. Joe Lieberman, "Statement of Joe Lieberman, Talk Show Campaign News Conference," Washington, D.C., October 26, 1995.

158. Robert J. Dole, "State of the Union: The Republican Response," Washington, D.C., January 23, 1996.

159. Irving Kristol, *Neoconservatism: The Autobiography of an Idea* (New York: Free Press, 1995), p. 486.

160. Robert J. Dole, transcript, *This Week with David Brinkley*, ABC News broadcast, September 17, 1995.

161. Empower America brochure.

162. Quoted in Dan Balz, "Darman Warns GOP Not to Rely on Slogans," *Washington Post*, June 8, 1994, p. A-6.

163. Ibid.

164. Quoted in R. W. Apple Jr., "Edmund S. Muskie, 81, Dies; Maine Senator and a Power on the National Scene," *New York Times*, March 27, 1996, p. D-21.

165. Hart-Teeter survey for the Council for Excellence in Government, March 16–18, 1995. Text of questions: 1. "Which of the following statements do you agree with more—(a) the *federal* government creates more problems than it solves or (b) the *federal* government solves more problems than it creates." Creates more problems than it solves, 72 percent; solves more problems than it creates, 21 percent; not sure, 7 percent. 2. Agree/Disagree: Statement A: "The federal government spends too much money on the wrong things. It could reduce spending considerably and still take care of essential needs if it were managed better." Statement B: "In reality, the federal government provides many essential services, and spending probably can't be reduced a lot without cutting some of those services and hurting large numbers of people." Statement A/federal government spends too much, 67 percent; Statement B/federal government provides essential services, 29 percent; some of both (volunteered), 3 percent; not sure, 1 percent.

166. See Vice President Gore, *Creating a Government That Works Better and Costs Less: The Gore Report on Reinventing Government* (New York: Times Books, 1993), p. 1.

167. Tim Weiner, "Military Accused of Lies Over Arms," *New York Times*, June 28, 1993, p. A-10.

168. James Patterson, "Not So Fast, Newt," *New Republic*, January 23, 1995, p. 28.

169. Peter Baker, *Washington Post*, "Clinton Embraces Affirmative Action, Accuses GOP of Making It 'Wedge Issue,'" September 15, 1996, p. A-16.

170. See Woodward, *The Agenda*, p. 35.

171. Ibid., p. 165.

172. David S. Broder, "Does Clinton Want to Govern?" *Washington Post*, February 4, 1996, p. C-7.

173. "We could have the right kind of balanced budget with a new Congress—a Democratic Congress." See Clinton, "Acceptance Speech," Democratic National Convention, Chicago, August 29, 1996.

174. Ronald Reagan, "Inaugural Address," Washington, D.C., January 20, 1981.

175. Clinton, "State of the Union Address," January 23, 1996.

176. Bill Clinton, "Victory Speech," Little Rock, Arkansas, November 5, 1996.

177. Quoted in Storing, *What the Anti-Federalists Were For*, p. 42.

178. Ibid., p. 16.

179. Quoted in Elshtain, *Democracy on Trial*, p. 9.

180. Ibid., p. 21.

181. Robert D. Putnam, "Bowling Alone: America's Declining Social Capital," *Journal of Democracy*, January 1995, pp. 68–72.

182. Charles Dickens, *American Notes and Pictures from Italy* (New York: Oxford University Press, 1957 reprint), p. 245.

183. Quoted in Storing, *What the Anti-Federalists Were For*, p. 10.

184. Ibid.

185. Wilson, *Constitutional Government in the United States* (New York: Columbia University Press, 1908), p. 218.

186. Clark Clifford with Richard Holbrooke, *Counsel to the President: A Memoir* (New York: Anchor Books, Doubleday, 1991), p. 661.

187. George Washington, "Circular to the States," June 14, 1783, in W. B. Allen, *George Washington: A Collection* (Indianapolis: Liberty Classics, 1988), p. 241.

188. Quoted in Robert J. Dole, "Speech to the Nixon Center for Peace and Freedom," March 1, 1995.

189. Quoted in Arthur Schlesinger, "Faded Glory," *New York Times Magazine*, July 12, 1992, p. 52.

Bibliography

Selected Books

Acheson, Dean. *Present at the Creation: My Years in the State Department*. New York: W. W. Norton, 1969.

Adams, James Truslow. *The Epic of America*. Boston: Little, Brown, 1935.

Aitken, Jonathan. *Nixon: A Life*. Washington, D.C.: Regnery Publishing, Inc., 1993.

Allen, W. B. *George Washington: A Collection*. Indianapolis: Liberty Classics, 1988.

Ambrose, Stephen. *Eisenhower: Soldier and President*. New York: Simon and Schuster, 1990.

_____. *Nixon: Ruin and Recovery, 1973–1990*. New York: Simon and Schuster, 1991.

_____. *Nixon: The Education of a Politician, 1913–1962*. New York: Simon and Schuster, 1987.

Barone, Michael. *Our Country: The Shaping of America from Roosevelt to Reagan*. New York: Free Press, 1990.

Barone, Michael, and Grant Ujifusa. *The Almanac of American Politics, 1996*. Washington, D.C.: National Journal, 1995.

_____. *The Almanac of American Politics, 1994*. Washington, D.C.: National Journal, 1993.

Barta, Carolyn. *Perot and His People*. Fort Worth, Texas: The Summit Group, 1993.

Bass, Jack, and Walter DeVries. *The Transformation of Southern Politics: Social Change and Political Consequence Since 1945*. New York: Basic Books, 1976.

Bell, Daniel. *The End of Ideology*. Glencoe, Illinois: Free Press, 1960.

_____. *The Radical Right*. Garden City, New York: Doubleday, 1963.

Beschloss, Michael R., and Strobe Talbott. *At the Highest Levels: The Inside Story of the End of the Cold War*. Boston: Little, Brown, 1993.

Bialer, Seweryn, and Sophia Sluzar, eds. *Radicalism in the Contemporary Age*. Boulder: Westview Press, 1977.

Black, Christine M., and Thomas Oliphant. *All by Myself: The Unmaking of a Presidential Campaign*. Chester, Connecticut: The Globe Pequot Press, 1989.

Blumenthal, Sidney. *Pledging Allegiance: The Last Campaign of the Cold War*. New York: HarperCollins, 1990.

Boorstin, Daniel J. *The Genius of American Politics*. Chicago: University of Chicago Press, 1953.

Brinkley, Alan. *The End of Reform: New Deal Liberalism in Recession and War*. New York: Alfred A. Knopf, 1995.

Brownell, Herbert, with John P. Burke. *Advising Ike*. Lawrence: University of Kansas Press, 1993.

Buchanan, Patrick J. *Right from the Beginning*. Boston: Little, Brown, 1988.

Burnham, Walter Dean. *The Current Crisis in American Politics*. New York: Oxford University Press, 1982.

Burns, James MacGregor. *Roosevelt: The Lion and the Fox*. New York: Harcourt, Brace, and World, 1956.

Burns, James MacGregor. *The Deadlock of Democracy: Four-Party Politics in America*. Englewood Cliffs, New Jersey: Prentice-Hall, 1963.

Bush, Barbara. *Barbara Bush: A Memoir*. New York: Charles Scribner's Sons, 1994.

Bush, George. *Agenda for American Renewal*. Washington, D.C.: Bush-Quayle Campaign Committee, 1992.

Cannon, Lou. *President Reagan: The Role of a Lifetime*. New York: Simon and Schuster, 1991.

Carr, Robert K. *The House Committee on Un-American Activities, 1945–1950*. Ithaca, New York: Cornell University Press, 1952.

Carter, Jimmy. *Keeping Faith*. New York: Bantam Books, 1982.

_____. *Why Not the Best?* New York: Bantam Books, 1976.

Chambers, Whittaker. *Witness*. New York: Random House, 1952.

Chesterton, Gilbert K. *What I Saw in America*. New York: Dodd, Mead, 1922.

Chiu, Tony. *Ross Perot: In His Own Words*. New York: Warner Books, 1992.

Clifford, Clark, with Richard Holbrooke. *Counsel to the President: A Memoir*. New York: Anchor Books, Doubleday, 1991.

Clinton, Bill. *Between Hope and History: Meeting America's Challenges for the 21st Century*. New York: Times Books, 1996.

_____. *Putting People First: A National Economic Strategy for America*. Little Rock, Arkansas: Clinton for President Committee, 1992.

Colby, Peter W., and John K. White, eds. *New York State Today*. Albany: State University of New York Press, 1989.

Committee on Political Parties. *Toward a More Responsible Two-Party System*. New York: Rinehart, 1950.

Cramer, Richard Ben. *Bob Dole*. New York: Vintage Books, 1992.

Croly, Herbert. *The Promise of American Life*. Reprint, New York: Archon Books, 1963.

Cronin, Thomas E. *The State of the Presidency*. Boston: Little, Brown, 1980.

Cuomo, Mario M. *Diaries of Mario M. Cuomo*. New York: Random House, 1984.

Davis, Lanny J. *The Emerging Democratic Majority: Lessons and Legacies from the New Politics*. New York: Stein and Day, 1974.

De Tocqueville, Alexis. *Democracy in America*. New York: Mentor Books, 1956.

Dickens, Charles. *American Notes and Pictures from Italy*. Reprint, New York: Oxford University Press, 1957.

Dionne, E. J. Jr. *They Only Look Dead: Why Progressives Will Dominate the Next Political Era*. New York: Simon and Schuster, 1996.

_____. *Why Americans Hate Politics*. New York: Touchstone Books, 1991.

Divine, Robert A. *Foreign Policy and U.S. Presidential Elections, 1952–1960*. New York: New Viewpoints, 1974.

Dobrynin, Anatoly. *In Confidence*. New York: Times Books, 1995.

Dole, Robert J., and Jack Kemp. *Trusting the People: The Dole-Kemp Plan to Free the Economy and Create a Better America*. New York: HarperCollins, 1996.

Economic Report of the President, February 1994. Washington, D.C.: U.S. Government Printing Office, 1994.

Edsall, Thomas Byrne, with Mary D. Edsall. *Chain Reaction: The Impact of Race, Rights, and Taxes on American Politics*. New York: W. W. Norton, 1992.

Edwards, George C., and Stephen J. Wayne. *Presidential Leadership: Politics and Policy Making*. New York: St. Martin's Press, 1994.

Eisenhower, Dwight D. *Mandate for Change, 1953–1956*. Garden City, New York: Doubleday, 1963.

_____. *Waging Peace, 1956–1961*. Garden City, New York: Doubleday, 1965.

Elshtain, Jean Bethke. *Democracy on Trial*. New York: Basic Books, 1995.

Evans, Roland, and Robert D. Novak. *Lyndon B. Johnson: The Exercise of Power*. New York: New American Library, 1968.

Federici, Michael P. *The Challenge of Populism: The Rise of Right-Wing Democratism in Postwar America*. Westport, Connecticut: Praeger, 1991.

Felknor, Bruce L. *Political Mischief: Smear, Sabotage, and Reform in the United States*. Westport, Connecticut: Greenwood Press, 1992.

Ford, Gerald R. *A Time to Heal*. New York: Harper and Row, 1979.

Frank, Barney. *Speaking Frankly*. New York: Times Books, 1992.

Free, Lloyd, and Hadley Cantril. *The Political Beliefs of Americans*. New Brunswick, New Jersey: Rutgers University Press, 1967.

Fromkin, David. *In the Time of the Americans: FDR, Truman, Eisenhower, Marshall, MacArthur—the Generation That Changed America's Role in the World*. New York: Alfred A. Knopf, 1995.

Fromm, Erich. *Inside the Kremlin's Cold War: From Stalin to Khrushchev*. Cambridge, Massachusetts: Harvard University Press, 1996.

Fuchs, Lawrence. *John F. Kennedy and American Catholicism*. New York: Meredith Press, 1967.

_____. *The Political Behavior of American Jews*. Glencoe, Illinois: Free Press, 1956.

Galambos, Louis. *The Papers of Dwight David Eisenhower: NATO and the Campaign of 1952*. Baltimore: Johns Hopkins University Press, 1989.

Garrettson, Charles L. III. *Hubert H. Humphrey: The Politics of Joy*. New Brunswick, New Jersey: Transaction Publishers, 1993.

Germond, Jack W., and Jules Witcover. *Mad as Hell: Revolt at the Ballot Box, 1992*. New York: Warner Books, 1993.

_____. *Whose Broad Stripes and Bright Stars? The Trivial Pursuit of the Presidency, 1988*. New York: Warner Books, 1989.

Gillon, Steven M. *Politics and Vision: The ADA and American Liberalism, 1947–1985*. New York: Oxford University Press, 1987.

Gingrich, Newt. *To Renew America*. New York: HarperCollins, 1995.

Goldman, Eric. *The Crucial Decade—And After: America, 1945–1960*. New York: Alfred A. Knopf, 1966.

Goldman, Peter, Thomas DeFrank, Mark Miller, Andrew Murr, and Tom Mathews. *Quest for the Presidency, 1992*. College Station: Texas A&M University Press, 1994.

Goldwater, Barry M. *The Conscience of a Conservative*. New York: MacFadden Boosk, 1964 ed.

_____. *Why Not Victory? A Fresh Look at American Foreign Policy*. New York: McGraw-Hill, 1962.

Goldwater, Barry M., with Jack Casserly. *Goldwater*. New York: Doubleday, 1988.

Goodwin, Doris Kearns. *No Ordinary Time: Franklin and Eleanor Roosevelt, The Home Front in World War Two*. New York: Simon and Schuster, 1994.

Gore, Al. *Common Sense Government*. New York: Random House, 1995.

_____. *Creating A Government That Works Better and Costs Less: The Gore Report on Reinventing Government*. New York: Times Books, 1993.

Graebner, Norman A., ed. *The Cold War: Ideological Conflict or Power Struggle?* Lexington, Massachusetts: D. C. Heath, 1963.

Greenstein, Fred. *The Hidden-Hand Presidency: Eisenhower As Leader*. New York: Basic Books, 1982.

Hadden, Jeffrey K., and Anson Shupe. *Televangelism: Power and Politics on God's Frontier.* New York: Henry Holt, 1988.

Halberstam, David. *The Fifties.* New York: Villard Books, 1993.

Halderman, H. R. *The Haldeman Diaries: Inside the Nixon White House.* New York: G. P. Putnam's Sons, 1994.

Hamilton, Nigel. *JFK: Reckless Youth.* New York: Random House, 1992.

Harris, Richard A., and Sidney M. Milkis. *Remaking American Politics.* Boulder: Westview Press, 1989.

Hartz, Louis. *The Liberal Tradition in America.* New York: Harcourt Brace Jovanovich, 1955.

Harwood Group. *America's Struggle Within: Citizens Talk About the State of the Union.* Washington, D.C.: Pew Center for Civic Journalism, 1996.

Hess, Stephen, and David Broder. *The Republican Establishment: The Present and Future of the GOP.* New York: Harper and Row, 1967.

Hoffer, Eric. *The True Believer.* New York: Harper and Row, 1951.

Huntington, Samuel P. *American Politics: The Promise of Disharmony.* Cambridge, Massachusetts: Harvard University Press, 1981.

Humphrey, Hubert H. *The Education of a Public Man: My Life in Politics.* Garden City, New York: Doubleday, 1976.

Huthmacher, J. Joseph. *Massachusetts: People and Politics, 1919–1933.* New York: Atheneum, 1969.

James, William. *The Moral Equivalent of War and Other Essays.* New York: Harper and Row, 1971.

Jamieson, Kathleen Hall. *Dirty Politics: Deception, Distraction, and Democracy.* New York: Oxford University Press, 1992.

Johnson, Haynes. *Divided We Fall.* New York: W. W. Norton, 1994.

_____. *Sleepwalking Through History: America in the Reagan Years.* New York: W. W. Norton, 1991.

Johnson, Haynes, and David S. Broder. *The System: The American Way of Politics at the Breaking Point.* Boston: Little, Brown, 1996.

Johnson, Lyndon Baines. *The Vantage Point: Perspectives on the Presidency, 1963–1969.* New York: Holt, Rinehart, and Winston, 1971.

Kallenbach, Jessamine S. *American State Governors, 1776–1976.* Dobbs Ferry, New York: Oceana Publications, 1977.

Kalugin, Oleg, with Fen Montaigne. *The First Directorate: My Thirty-Two Years in Intelligence and Espionage Against the West.* New York: St. Martin's Press, 1994.

Kearnes, Doris. *Lyndon Johnson and the American Dream.* New York: New American Library, 1976.

Kennedy, John F. *Prelude to Leadership: The European Diary of John F. Kennedy, Summer 1945.* Washington, D.C.: Regnery Publishing, 1995.

_____. *The Strategy of Peace.* New York: Harper and Brothers, 1960.

_____. *Why England Slept.* New York: Wilfred Funk, 1940.

Kepley, David R. *The Collapse of the Middle Way: Senate Republicans and the Bipartisan Foreign Policy, 1948–1952.* Westport, Connecticut: Greenwood Press, 1988.

Key, V. O. *The Responsible Electorate: Rationality in Presidential Voting, 1936–1960.* New York: Vintage Books, 1966.

Klehr, Harvey, John Eary Haynes, and Fridrikh Igorevich Firsov. *The Secret World of American Communism.* New Haven: Yale University Press, 1995.

Klein, Patricia A. *1992 Presidential Primary Election Results.* Washington, D.C.: Federal Election Commission, 1992.

Klinkner, Philip A. *The Losing Parties: Out-Party National Committees, 1956–1993.* New Haven: Yale University Press, 1994.

Kraus, Sidney, ed. *The Great Debates: Carter vs. Ford, 1976.* Bloomington: Indiana University Press, 1979.

Kristol, Irving. *Neoconservatism: The Autobiography of an Idea.* New York: Free Press, 1995.

Kusnet, David. *Speaking American: How the Democrats Can Win in the Nineties.* New York: Thunder's Mouth Press, 1992.

Ladd, Everett Carll. *America at the Polls, 1994.* Storrs, Connecticut: The Roper Center for Public Opinion Research, 1995.

_____. *The American Ideology: An Exploration of the Origins, Meaning, and Role of American Political Ideas.* Storrs, Connecticut: The Roper Center for Public Opinion Research, 1994.

Ladd, Everett Carll, with Charles D. Hadley. *Transformations of the American Party System.* New York: W. W. Norton, 1975.

Lamis, Alexander P. *The Two-Party South.* New York: Oxford University Press, 1990.

Larson, Arthur. *A Republican Looks at His Party.* New York: Harper and Brothers, 1956.

Levering, Ralph B. *The Public and American Foreign Policy, 1918–1978.* New York: William Morrow, 1978.

Lind, Michael. *The Next American Revolution: The New Nationalism and the Fourth American Revolution.* New York: Free Press, 1995.

Link, Arthur S., and William B. Catton. *American Epoch: A History of the United States Since 1900.* New York: Alfred A. Knopf, 1980.

Lippmann, Walter. *The Cold War: A Study in U.S. Foreign Policy.* New York: Harper and Brothers, 1947.

_____. *U.S. Foreign Policy: Shield of the Republic.* Boston: Little, Brown, 1943.

Lipset, Seymour Martin. *Political Man: The Social Bases of Politics.* Garden City, New York: Anchor Books, 1963.

Lorant, Stefan. *The Presidency.* New York: The MacMillan Company, 1951.

Lowi, Theodore J. *The Personal President: Power Invested, Promise Unfulfilled.* Ithaca: Cornell University Press, 1985.

Lubell, Samuel. *The Future of American Politics.* New York: Harper Colophon Books, 1965 (first published 1952).

_____. *The Future While It Happened.* New York: W. W. Norton, 1973.

_____. *The Hidden Crisis in American Politics.* New York: W. W. Norton, 1971.

Maraniss, David. *First in His Class: A Biography of Bill Clinton.* New York: Simon and Schuster, 1995.

Martin, John Bartlow. *Adlai Stevenson and the World.* Garden City, New York: Anchor Books, Doubleday, 1978.

_____. *Adlai Stevenson of Illinois.* Garden City, New York: Anchor Books, Doubleday, 1977.

Matlock, Jack F. Jr. *Autopsy of an Empire: The American Ambassador's Account of the Collapse of the Soviet Union,* New York: Random House, 1995.

May, Ernest R., ed. *American Cold War Strategy: Interpreting NSC 68.* Boston: Bedford Books of St. Martin's Press, 1993.

May, Lary, ed. *Recasting America: Culture and Politics in the Age of the Cold War.* Chicago: University of Chicago Press, 1989.

Mayer, William G. *The Changing American Mind: How and Why American Public Opinion Changed Between 1960 and 1988.* Ann Arbor: University of Michigan Press, 1992.

McCullough, David. *Truman.* New York: Simon and Schuster, 1992.

McGovern, George. *Grassroots: The Autobiography of George McGovern.* New York: Random House, 1977.

McNamara, Robert S., with Brian VandeMark. *In Retrospect: The Tragedy and Lessons of Vietnam.* New York: Times Books, 1995.

Miller, Merle. *Lyndon: An Oral Biography.* New York: Ballantine Books, 1980.

Mitchell, Greg. *The Campaign of the Century: Upton Sinclair's Race for Governor of California.* New York: Random House, 1992.

Moore, Jim, with Rick Idhe. *Clinton: Young Man in a Hurry.* Fort Worth, Texas: The Summit Group, 1992.

Moos, Malcolm. *The Republicans: A History of Their Party.* New York: Random House, 1956.

Morgan, Ted. *FDR: A Biography.* New York: Simon and Schuster, 1985.

Morris, Edmund. *The Rise of Theodore Roosevelt.* New York: Coward, McCann, and Geoghegan, 1979.

Morris, Roger. *Richard Milhous Nixon: The Rise of an American Politician.* New York: Henry Holt, 1990.

Nixon, Richard M. *Beyond Peace.* New York: Random House, 1994.

_____. *In the Arena: A Memoir of Victory, Defeat, and Renewal.* New York: Simon and Schuster, 1990.

_____. *RN: The Memoirs of Richard Nixon.* New York: Grosset and Dunlap, 1978.

_____. *Six Crises.* New York: Warner Books, 1962 and 1979.

_____. *The Real War.* New York: Warner Books, 1981.

Novak, Robert D. *The Agony of the G.O.P., 1964.* New York: Macmillan, 1965.

Oberdorfer, Don. *The Turn: From the Cold War to a New Era, the United States and the Soviet Union, 1983–1990.* New York: Poseidon Press, 1991.

Parmet, Herbert. *Richard Nixon and His America.* Boston: Little, Brown, 1990.

Paterson, Thomas G. *Meeting the Communist Threat: Truman to Reagan.* New York: Oxford University Press, 1988.

Pepper, Claude, with Hays Gorey. *Pepper: Eyewitness to a Century.* New York: Harcourt Brace Jovanovich, 1987.

Polsby, Nelson W. *Consequences of Party Reform.* New York: Oxford University Press, 1983.

Porter, Kirk H., and Donald Bruce Johnson. *National Party Platforms: 1840–1968.* Urbana: University of Illinois Press, 1970.

Powell, Colin L., with Joseph E. Persico. *My American Journey.* New York: Random House, 1995.

Powers, Richard Gid. *Not Without Honor: The History of American Anticommunism.* New York: Free Press, 1995.

Prince, Carl E. *Brooklyn's Dodgers: The Bums, the Borough, and the Best of Baseball.* New York: Oxford University Press, 1996.

Pula, James S. *Polish Americans: An Ethnic Community.* New York: Twayne Publishers, 1995.

Quayle, Dan. *Standing Firm.* New York: HarperCollins, 1994.

Reagan, Ronald, with Richard G. Huebler. *Where's the Rest of Me?* New York: Duell, Sloan, and Pearce, 1965.

_____. *An American Life*. New York: Simon and Schuster, 1990.

Reeves, Richard. *President Kennedy: Profile of Power*. New York: Simon and Schuster, 1993.

_____. *Running in Place: How Bill Clinton Disappointed America*. Kansas City: Andrews and McMeel, 1996.

Reich, Emil. *Success Among the Nations*. New York: Harper and Brothers, 1904.

Reichley, A. James. *Religion in American Public Life*. Washington, D.C.: The Brookings Institution, 1985.

_____. *The Life of the Parties*. New York: Free Press, 1992.

Remnick, David. *Lenin's Tomb: The Last Days of the Soviet Empire*. New York: Random House, 1993.

Report of the National Advisory Commission on Civil Disorders. New York: Bantam Books, 1968.

Rockman, Bert, ed. *The Clinton Presidency*. Chatham, New Jersey: Chatham House, 1996.

Rose, Gary. *Controversial Issues in Presidential Selection*. Albany: State University of New York Press, 1994.

Rossiter, Clinton. *Conservatism in America*. Cambridge, Massachusetts: Harvard University Press, 1982 edition.

_____. *The American Presidency*. New York: Harcourt, Brace, and World, 1960.

Rovere, Richard H. *Senator Joe McCarthy*. New York: Harper and Row, 1959.

Sabato, Larry. *Goodbye to Good-time Charlie: The American Governorship Transformed*. Washington, D.C.: Congressional Quarterly, 1983.

Safire, William. *Before the Fall: An Inside View of the Pre-Watergate White House*. New York: Ballantine Books, 1977.

Scammon, Richard M., and Ben J. Wattenberg. *The Real Majority*. New York: Coward-McCann, 1970.

Schantz, Harvey. *Presidential Elections Through the Years*. Albany: State University of New York Press, 1996.

Schattschneider, E. E. *The Semi-Sovereign People*. Hinsdale, Illinois: The Dryden Press, 1975.

Schlesinger, Arthur M. *The Cycles of American History*. Boston: Houghton Mifflin, 1986.

_____. *The Vital Center*. Boston: Houghton Mifflin, 1949.

Skowronek, Stephen. *The Politics Presidents Make*. Cambridge, Massachusetts: Harvard University Press, 1993.

Smith, Richard Norton. *Thomas E. Dewey and His Times*. New York: Simon and Schuster, 1982.

Solberg, Carl. *Hubert Humphrey: A Biography*. New York: W. W. Norton, 1984.

Sorensen, Theodore C. *Kennedy*. New York: Bantam Books, 1966.

Stevenson, Adlai E. *Major Campaign Speeches of Adlai E. Stevenson, 1952*. New York: Random House, 1953.

Storing, Herbert J. *What the Anti-Federalists Were For*. Chicago: University of Chicago Press, 1981.

Strauss, William, and Neil Howe. *Generations: The History of America's Future: 1584–2069*. New York: William Morrow, 1991.

Stone, I. F. *The Truman Era*. New York: Random House, 1973.

Taft, Robert A. *A Foreign Policy for All Americans*. Garden City, New York: Doubleday, 1951.

Treuenfels, Rudolph L. *Eisenhower Speaks: Dwight D. Eisenhower in His Messages and Speeches*. New York: Farrar, Straus, 1948.

Tsongas, Paul. *Journey of Purpose: Reflections on the Presidency, Multiculturalism, and Third Parties.* New Haven: Yale University Press, 1995.

The Presidential Transcripts. New York: Dell Publishing, 1974.

U.S. Department of Energy. *Estimating the Cold War Mortgage.* Springfield, Virginia: U.S. Department of Commerce, National Technical Information Service, 1995.

Vandenberg, Arthur H. Jr. *The Private Papers of Senator Vandenberg.* Boston: Houghton Mifflin, 1952.

Viorst, Milton. *Fall from Grace.* New York: Simon and Schuster, 1968.

Voorhis, Jerry. *The Strange Case of Richard Milhous Nixon.* New York: Popular Library, 1973.

Wallace, Henry A. *The Price of Vision: The Diary of Henry A. Wallace, 1942–1946.* Boston: Houghton Mifflin, 1973.

Wattenberg, Martin P. *The Decline of Political Parties, 1952–1988.* Cambridge, Massachusetts: Harvard University Press, 1990.

Weed, Clyde P. *The Nemesis of Reform: The Republican Party During the New Deal.* New York: Columbia University Press, 1994.

Weicker, Lowell P. *Maverick: A Life in Politics.* Boston: Little, Brown, 1995.

Weinstein, Allen. *Perjury: The Hiss-Chambers Case.* New York: Alfred A. Knopf, 1978.

Welch, Robert. *The Politician.* Belmont, Massachusetts: Belmont, 1964,

White, John Kenneth. *The Fractured Electorate: Political Parties and Social Change in Southern New England.* Hanover, New Hampshire: University Press of New England, 1983.

_____. *The New Politics of Old Values.* Hanover, New Hampshire: University Press of New England, 1990.

White, John Kenneth, and Jerome M. Mileur, eds. *Challenges to Party Government.* Carbondale: Southern Illinois University Press, 1992.

White, John Kenneth, and John C. Green, eds. *The Politics of Ideas.* Lanham, Maryland: Rowman and Littlefield, 1995.

White, Theodore H. *The Making of the President, 1960.* New York: Atheneum House, 1961.

_____. *The Making of the President, 1964.* New York: New American Library, 1965.

_____. *The Making of the President, 1968.* New York: Atheneum Publishers, 1969.

_____. *The Making of the President, 1972.* New York: Atheneum Publishers, 1973.

Wicker, Tom. *One of Us: Richard Nixon and the American Dream.* New York: Random House, 1991.

Wilcox, Clyde. *The Latest American Revolution? The 1994 Elections and Their Implications for Governance.* New York: St. Martin's Press, 1995.

Wills, Garry. *Inventing America.* New York: Vintage Books, 1978.

_____. *Reagan's America: Innocents at Home.* Garden City, New York: Doubleday, 1987.

_____. *Under God: Religion and American Politics.* New York: Simon and Schuster, 1990.

Wilson, Woodrow. *Congressional Government.* Reprint Gloucester, Massachusetts: Peter Smith, 1973 (originally published in 1885).

_____. *Constitutional Government in the United States.* New York: Columbia University Press, 1908.

Wolforth, William, ed. *Witness to the End of the Cold War.* Balitmore: Johns Hopkins University Press, 1996.

Woodward, Bob. *The Agenda: Inside the Clinton White House.* New York: Simon and Schuster, 1994.

_____. *The Choice.* New York: Simon and Schuster, 1996.

Selected Articles

Alter, Jonathan. "A Man Not of His Time." *Newsweek*, November 4, 1996.

Apple, R. W. Jr. "Edmund S. Muskie, 81, Dies; Maine Senator and a Power on the National Scene." *New York Times*, March 27, 1996.

_____. "Faltering Economy, Fallen President." *New York Times*, November 4, 1992.

_____. "In Formerly Safe Florida, It's Nip and Tuck for Bush." *New York Times*, October 15, 1992.

_____. "Post-Cold War Candidates Find No Place Like Home," *New York Times*, February 20, 1996.

_____. "Prudent Meets Timid." *New York Times*, October 15, 1989.

_____. "White House Race Is Recast: No Kremlin to Run Against." *New York Times*, February 6, 1992.

Associated Press, "Buchanan Calls for Tougher Border Patrol." *Washington Post*, May 9, 1995.

_____. "Town Built on Steel Industry Resigns Itself to End of Era." *New York Times*, November 19, 1995.

Ayres, B. Drummond Jr. "Quayle Using Jokes and Jabs, Assails Dukakis on Military." *New York Times*, September 14, 1988.

_____. "Tips for Young Politician in the Making," *New York Times*, October 24, 1992.

"Bailey Sees Senatorial Primary in Connecticut on Wednesday As a Close Contest." *New York Times*, August 16, 1970.

Ball, George. "The Rationalist in Power." *New York Review of Books*, April 22, 1993.

Balz, Dan. "Can Clinton Bring Discipline to Policy?" *Washington Post*, January 17, 1993.

_____. "Darman Warns GOP Not to Rely on Slogans." *Washington Post*, June 8, 1994.

_____. "Independence a Trait." *Washington Post*, August 29, 1994.

_____. "Perot Unifies California's Disaffected." *Washington Post*, May 22, 1992.

_____. "Republicans Sound Conciliatory Tone." *Washington Post*, November 7, 1996.

Barnes, Bart. "J. W. Fulbright, Outspoken Senator-Scholar, Dies." *Washington Post*, February 2, 1995.

Barnes, Fred. "Meet Mario the Moderate." *New Republic*, April 8, 1985.

Barone, Michael. "The Road Back to Tocqueville." *Washington Post*, January 7, 1996.

Barrett, Laurence I. "Fighting for God and the Right Wing." *Time*, September 13, 1993.

Beer, Samuel. "Ronald Reagan: New Deal Conservative?" *Society*, January/February, 1983.

Behrens, Earl C. "S.F. Charter Signing: Senator Vandenberg Pledges to Lead GOP Fight in Senate for Its Ratification." *San Francisco Chronicle*, June 26, 1945.

Belair, Felix. "U.S. to Give France $525,000,000 in Aid and Hints at More." *New York Times*, October 10, 1952.

Bellow, Saul. "Writers, Intellectuals, Politics." *National Interest*, Spring 1993.

Berke, Richard L. "Clinton Preparing for Second Term with Shuffle of Top Officials." *New York Times*, November 7, 1996.

_____. "GOP Leaders Doubtful That Dole Can Close Gap." *New York Times*, October 20, 1996.

Bernstein, Richard. "Long Conflict Deeply Marked the Self-Image of Americans." *New York Times*, February 2, 1992.

"Best Lines Slung from Tongues in '88." *Providence Journal*, January 3, 1989.

Birnbaum, Jeffrey H. "The Pat Solution." *Time*, November 6, 1995.

Blumenthal, Sidney. "Ghosts in the Machine." *New Yorker*, October 2, 1995.

———. "Rendezvousing with Destiny." *New Yorker*, March 8, 1993.

———. "Tomorrow Belongs to Me." *New Republic*, January 6 and 13, 1992.

Booth, William. "Florida Senate Unveils Records of Probe Styled on McCarthyism." *Washington Post*, July 3, 1993.

———. "From Florida Voters, a Mixed Verdict." *Washington Post*, November 7, 1996.

———. "In a Rush, New Citizens Register Their Political Interest." *Washington Post*, September 26, 1996.

———. "Southern Officials Switching Sides." *Washington Post*, March 16, 1995.

Boyer, Peter J. "Gore's Dilemma." *New Yorker*, November 28, 1994.

Brace, Rick. "Big Holes Where the Dignity Used to Be." *New York Times*, March 5, 1996.

Branigin, William. "Conferees Agree on Immigration Bill." *Washington Post*, September 25, 1996.

Breindel, Eric. "Hiss's Guilt." *New Republic*, April 15, 1996.

Brinkley, Alan. "Last of His Kind." *New York Times Book Review*, December 17, 1995.

Brinkley, Joel. "U.S. Looking for a New Path as Superpower Conflict Ends." *New York Times*, February 2, 1992.

Broad, William J. "In Space and in East-West Politics, It's a Very Long Voyage to Mars." *New York Times*, February 5, 1992.

———. "Swords That Have Been Sheathed by Plowshares Lack Design." *New York Times*, February 5, 1992.

Broder, David S. "Does Clinton Want to Govern?" *Washington Post*, February 4, 1996.

———. "Dole Backs Official Language." *Washington Post*, September 5, 1995.

———. "Factions, Competing Ideologies Challenge Coalition Builders." *Washington Post*, November 7, 1996.

———. "First Baby Boom President Faces Huge Task." *Washington Post*, November 4, 1992.

———. "Politicians on Probation." *Washington Post*, December 6, 1992.

———. "Trouble for Incumbents." *Washington Post*, March 22, 1992.

———. "Where's Bush's Beef?" *Washington Post*, June 21, 1992.

Brooke, James. "Russians Have Landed in Kansas! But They've Come to Make Peace." *New York Times*, October 27, 1995.

Brown, David. "Study Details the Culture That Drove Experiments." *Washington Post*, October 4, 1995.

Bruck, Connie. "The Politics of Perception." *New Yorker*, October 9, 1995.

Bush, George. "Excerpts of Interview with President Bush on His First Term." *New York Times*, June 25, 1992.

"Bush: Playing the Crisis Card." *New York Times*, October 24, 1992.

Caddell, Patrick H. "Crisis of Confidence—Trapped in a Downward Spiral." *Public Opinion*, October/November 1979.

Carrier, Jim. "Bomb Blues." *Denver Post*, July 13, 1995.

Church, George J. "Disconnected." *Time*, January 15, 1996.

Claiborne, William. "Democrats Don't Have Lock on Hispanic Vote, Latino Leaders Say." *Washington Post*, November 24, 1996.

Clines, Francis X. "Civics 101: Cultivating Grass Roots the Old Way," *New York Times*, November 4, 1992.

"Clinton Questions Corporate Layoffs." CNN/*Time*, All Politics, Internet, March 4, 1996.

Clymer, Adam. "Top Republicans Say They Seek Common Ground with Clinton." *New York Times*, November 7, 1996.

Cohen, Jacob. "Innocent After All?" *National Review*, January 18, 1993.

Conklin, William R. "Nixon Criticizes Stevenson on Deposition in Hiss Trial." *New York Times*, October 14, 1952.

Crider, John H. "Truman Acclaimed on Arrival by Air to Close Parley." *New York Times*, June 26, 1945.

Crowley, Candy. "Dole, Buchanan Campaign in California Ahead of Tuesday's Vote." *CNN/Time*, All Politics, Internet, March 24, 1996.

Crowley, Michael. "Party Line." *New Republic*, November 4, 1996.

Davies, Lawrence E. "Historic Plenary Session Approves World Charter." *New York Times*, June 26, 1945.

"Defense Cuts Are Likely During Next Presidential Term." *Hartford Courant*, October 7, 1996.

"Defense Officials End Lease on Secret Bunker in West Virginia." *Baltimore Sun*, October 6, 1995.

Devroy, Ann. "Domestic Perils Sink President Bush." *Washington Post*, November 4, 1992.

_____. "The Nation Changed but Bush Did Not." *Washington Post*, January 17, 1993.

Devroy, Ann, and Jeffrey Smith. "Clinton Reexamines Foreign Policy Under Siege." *Washington Post*, October 17, 1993.

Devroy, Ann, and John F. Harris. "'The President is Relevant': Clinton Asserts His Role in Political Debate." *Washington Post*, April 19, 1995.

Dionne, E. J. Jr. "A Philosophical Bush Outlines Vision for Second Term." *Washington Post*, October 27, 1992.

_____. "Age of Conservatism in the White House Has Come to a Close." *Washington Post*, November 4, 1992.

_____. "Buchanan Challenges Bush with 'America First' Call," *Washington Post*, December 11, 1991.

_____. "Buchanan Heaps Scorn on Democrats." *Washington Post*, August 18, 1992.

_____. "Voters' Attraction to Perot May Signal That Party Labels Are Now Liabilities." *Washington Post*, July 8, 1992.

Divine, Robert A. "The Cold War as History." *Reviews in American History*, September 1993.

Dobbs, Michael. "Panhandling the Kremlin: How Gus Hall Got Millions." *Washington Post*, March 1, 1992.

_____. "Revelations from the Communist Files." *Washington Post*, February 8, 1992.

"Dole Won't Confirm Reports He Will Urge Drug Tests for All on Welfare." *Boston Globe*, May 21, 1996.

Dowd, Maureen. "Bush, in Reagan Style, Drops Script and Assails Dukakis's Foreign Policy." *New York Times*, September 13, 1988.

Drew, Elizabeth. "High Noon." *New Yorker*, October 19, 1992.

Dulles, John Foster. "A Policy of Boldness." *Life*, May 19, 1952.

"Earl Browder, Ex-Communist Leader, Dies at 82." *New York Times*, June 28, 1973.

Edsall, Thomas B. "Armey's Line on Hillary and 'Marxists.'" *Washington Post*, June 6, 1993.

_____. "Democrats Look to Factories, Faculties." *Washington Post*, May 21, 1994.

_____. "Dole Accentuating the Positive." *Washington Post*, October 22, 1996.

_____. "Key November Voters Sitting Out Primaries." *Washington Post*, March 23, 1992.

Edwards, George C. III, and Tami Swenson. "The Limits of the Public Presidency." *The Polling Report*, September 26, 1994.

"Eisenhower, the Leader." *New York Times*, November 7, 1956.

Engelberg, Stephen, Jeff Gerth, and Kathryn Q. Seelye. "Files Show How Gingrich Laid a Grand GOP Plan." *New York Times*, December 3, 1995.

"Excerpts from Clinton-Yeltsin News Conference." *Washington Post*, April 5, 1993.

"Excerpts from Colin L. Powell's News Conference." *Washington Post*, November 9, 1995.

"Excerpts from General Powell's News Conference on Political Plans." *New York Times*, November 9, 1995.

"Excerpts from Interview with Clinton on Goals for Presidency." *New York Times*, June 28, 1992.

"Excerpts from the Debate Among Quayle, Gore, and Stockdale." *New York Times*, October 14, 1992.

Ewald, William Bragg Jr. "Ike's First Move." *New York Times Sunday Magazine*, November 14, 1993.

Fineman, Howard. "Knowing When the Party's Over." *Newsweek*, November 16, 1992.

"Foreign Roots on Native Soil." *U.S. News and World Report*, July 7, 1986.

"Forty Years Ago in *Time*: The Sexy Schoolteacher Gap." *Time*, May 29, 1995.

Frank, Jeffrey A. "Stalin Biographer Offers Latest Twist in Hiss Case." *Washington Post*, October 31, 1992.

Freedman, Samuel G. "Why Bob Dole Can't Be Reagan." *New York Times*, October 27, 1996.

Freeman, Allen. "Echoes of the Cold War." *Historic Preservation*, January/February 1994.

Friedman, Thomas L. "Bush's Roles on the World Stage: Triumphs, but Troubles, Too." *New York Times*, June 26, 1992.

_____. "Cold War Without End." *New York Times Magazine*, June 6, 1995.

Friedrich, Otto. "'I Have Never Been A Quitter.'" *Time*, May 2, 1994.

Gerstenzang, James. "Richard Nixon Dead at 81." *Providence Journal*, April 23, 1994.

Gilmore, Eddy. "Russia Welcomes Her Generals." *San Francisco Chronicle*, June 25, 1945.

"Gingrich Advises GOP to Stress Community." *Boston Globe*, March 13, 1996.

Glazer, Nathan. "Did We Go Too Far?" *National Interest*, Spring 1993.

"GOP Conservative Goldwater Says Clinton Makes a Good President." *Boston Globe*, August 5, 1996.

Gup, Ted. "The Doomsday Blueprints." *Time*, August 10, 1992.

Hale, Dennis, and Marc Landy. "Are Critical Elections Extinct?" *Boston College Bi-Weekly*, November 15, 1984.

Hall, Charles W. "U.S. Military's Next Casualty: Jobs." *Washington Post*, February 23, 1992.

Hallow, Ralph Z. "Buchanan Cries 'America First' As He Joins Race." *Washington Times*, December 11, 1991.

_____. "Richard Nixon Dies at 81 in New York City." *Washington Times*, April 23, 1994.

Hamilton, Thomas J. "Work Completed on U.N. Buildings." *New York Times*, October 10, 1952.

Harden, Blaine. "Dole Woos California." *Washington Post*, October 29, 1996.

Harris, John F. "Clinton Vows Wider NATO in Three Years." *Washington Post*, October 23, 1996.

_____. "Unsolicited Advice from an Erstwhile Confidant." *Washington Post*, September 20, 1996.

Harris, John R. "After Season of Doubt, Clinton Charging Up for '96 Campaign." *Washington Post*, September 24, 1995.

Havel, Vaclav. "The Post-Communist Nightmare." *New York Review of Books*, May 27, 1993.

Hedley, John Hollister. "Truman's Trial and Error with the CIA." *Christian Science Monitor*, September 22, 1995.

Heilbrunn, Jacob. "Curious George." *New Republic*, August 23 and 30, 1993.

_____. "The Revision Thing: Who Is to Blame for the Cold War? A New Quarrel." *New Republic*, August 15, 1994.

Herbers, John. "In Three Decades, Nixon Tasted Crisis and Defeat, Ruin and Revival." *New York Times*, April 24, 1994.

Hilts, Philip J. "Panel Urges U.S. to Apologize for Radiation Testing and Pay Damages." *New York Times*, October 3, 1995.

"Hiss Loses Plea for Another Trial; Court Rejects His 'New Evidence.'" *New York Times*, July 23, 1952.

Hiss, Tony. "My Father's Honor." *New Yorker*, November 2, 1992.

Hockstader, Lee. "Russian General Dmitri Volkogonov Dies; Wrote of Soviet Repression." *Washington Post*, December 7, 1995.

Hoffman, Dennis E. "Watchdog on Crime." *Chicago History*, Spring 1994.

Holmes, Steven A. "Clinton Turns Off Cold War's Voice." *New York Times*, February 2, 1993.

_____. "White House to Suspend a Program for Minorities." *New York Times*, March 8, 1996.

Holt, Pat M. "Spying Out New Roles for Central Intelligence Agency." *Christian Science Monitor*, October 5, 1995.

"How Many Minutes to Midnight 50 Years After the A-Bomb's Birth?" *New York Times*, December 3, 1995.

"Immigration." CNN/*Time*, All Politics, Internet, March 25, 1996.

"Interview: An 'Americanologist' Looks Back on the Cold War." *Boston Globe*, September 20, 1992.

"J. W. Fulbright, Outspoken Senator-Scholar, Dies." *Washington Post*, February 10, 1995.

Johnson, Dirk. "Voices from the Grass Roots: Anger Over Partisan Politics." *New York Times*, August 27, 1994.

Judis, John. "The End of Conservatism." *New Republic*. August 31, 1992.

_____. "The Two Faces of Whittaker Chambers." *New Republic*, April 16, 1984.

Kamen, Al. "A Campaign with No Bear in the Woods." *Washington Post*, March 15, 1992.

Kempton, Murray. "Notes from Underground." *New York Review of Books*, July 13, 1995.

Kennan, George F. "The Sources of Soviet Conduct." *Foreign Affairs*, July 1947.

Kennan, George F., and John Lukacs. "From World War to Cold War." *American Heritage*, December 1995.

Kirkpatrick, Jeane. "Dictatorships and Double Standards." *Commentary*, November 1979.

Kirschten, Dick. "Second Thoughts." *National Journal*, January 21, 1995.

Klein, Joe. "Plain Vanilla or Rain Forest Crunch?" *Newsweek*, July 18, 1994.

Kleinfield, N. R. "The Company As Family No More." *New York Times*, March 4, 1996.

Krauthammer, Charles. "After the Battle." *Washington Post*, November 18, 1994.

_____. "How Conservatism Can Come Back." *Time*, January 18, 1993.

Krock, Arthur. "Mighty Pageant Is Proof." *New York Times*, January 21, 1953.

Ladd, Everett Carll. "Public Opinion and the 'Congress Problem.'" *Public Interest*, Summer 1990.

Lee, Gary. "Clinton Apologizes for U.S. Radiation Tests, Praises Panel Report." *Washington Post*, October 4, 1995.

_____. "Panel Urges Compensation for Radiation Subjects." *Washington Post*, October 3, 1995.

_____. "Prisoner Irradiation Probed." *Washington Post*, November 20, 1994.

Lewis, Anthony. "The Two Faces of George." *New York Times*, September 21, 1992.

"Liberal Tag Hurts Dukakis, Times-Mirror Survey Finds." *Times-Mirror*, press release, September 22, 1988.

Lind, Michael. "The Myth of Barry Goldwater." *New York Review of Books*, November 30, 1995.

_____. "The Southern Coup." *New Republic*, June 19, 1995.

Lindley, Ernest K. "Is There Real Danger of War?" *Newsweek*, May 15, 1950.

Lippman, Thomas W. "Tearing Down Remnants of Cold War Leaves Amarillo Holding the Pits." *Washington Post*, October 29, 1994.

Lipset, Seymour Martin. "The Significance of the 1992 Election." *PS*, March 1993.

Loeb, James Jr. "Progressives and Communists." *New Republic*. May 13, 1946.

Lohr, Steve. "Though Upbeat on the Economy, People Still Fear for Their Jobs." New York Times, December 19, 1996.

Luce, Henry R. "The American Century." *Life*, February 17, 1941.

Mailer, Norman. "By Heaven Inspired." *New Republic*. October 12, 1992.

Maraniss, David. "Bill Clinton and Realpolitik U." *Washington Post*, October 25, 1992.

Mathews, Janice. "On The Paper Trail of the Assassins." *Extensions*, Spring 1994.

McGill, Ralph. "Can He Purge Senator Pepper?" *Saturday Evening Post*, April 22, 1950.

McGovern, George S. "The Last Nixon." *Rolling Stone*, June 16, 1994.

Mencken, H. L. "In Praise of Gamaliel." *New Republic*, October 18, 1920.

Miller, Richard I. "Resident Remembers Richard M. Nixon." *Lexington Minuteman*, April 28, 1994.

Mintz, John. "Defense Cuts Exact Human Toll in Maryland." *Washington Post*, May 7, 1993.

Mitchell, Alison. "Stung By Defeats in '94 Clinton Regrouped and Co-opted GOP Strategies." *New York Times*, November 7, 1996.

Morgan, Dan, and Walter Pincus. "When Defense Conferees Meet, Frugal Trend Ends." *Washington Post*, October 13, 1995.

Morin, Richard, and E. J. Dionne Jr. "Majority of Voters Say Parties Have Lost Touch." *Washington Post*, July 8, 1992.

Morrison, David C. "Home Front Politics." *National Journal*, September 5, 1992.

Nagourney, Adam. "Buchanan Vows, if Elected, to Put an End to Abortions." *New York Times*, February 24, 1996.

Oberdorfer, Don. "Democrats Offer Broad Themes for U.S. Role in Post–Cold War Era." *Washington Post*, March 15, 1992.

Oliphant, Thomas. "U.S. Fear Could Set Back Change in Russia, Christopher Warns." *Boston Globe*, January 23, 1996.

"Opponents See Duffey's Victory as a Benefit to Them in November." *New York Times*, August 21, 1970.

"Pat Speaks." *New Republic*, March 18, 1996.

Patterson, James. "Not So Fast, Newt." *New Republic*, January 23, 1995.

Pear, Robert. "Shake-Up Over Agency's Secret Money." *New York Times*, September 25, 1995.

Pearson, Richard. "Margaret Chase Smith Dies; GOP Senator from Maine." *Washington Post*, May 30, 1995.

Perlez, Jane. "Media-Wise Walesa Foe Copies Style of Clinton." *New York Times*, November 19, 1994.

Perry, James M. "Buchanan Launches Presidential Bid, Says Bush Has Abandoned GOP Tenets." *Wall Street Journal*, December 11, 1991.

Pincus, Walter. "Papers Show Mao Wary of Korean War." *Washington Post*, December 20, 1995.

"Portrait of the Electorate." *New York Times*, November 5, 1992.

Priest, Dana, and John Mintz. "Sub Has More Friends Than Enemies." *Washington Post*, October 13, 1995.

Purdum, Todd S. "Clinton Plans to Lift Public Out of 'Funk.'" *New York Times*, September 24, 1995.

_____. "What Kind of Democrat?" *New York Times Magazine*, May 19, 1996.

Putnam, Robert D. "Bowling Alone: America's Declining Social Capital." *Journal of Democracy*, January 1995.

Raines, Howell. "Carter and Reagan Open Fall Race with Praise for Polish Workers." *New York Times*, September 2, 1980.

Raudebaugh, Charles. "500,000 Crowd S.F. Streets to Welcome Their President." *San Francisco Chronicle*, June 26, 1945.

_____. "Truman's Conference Address." *San Francisco Chronicle*, June 27, 1945.

Reeves, Richard. "1954." *American Heritage*, January 1995.

Reichard, Gary W. "Seeing Red: Eisenhower, the Republicans, and the Anti-Communist Consensus." *Reviews in American History* 21 (1993).

Remnick, David. "America: Love It or Loathe It." *New York Times Magazine*, June 6, 1995.

"Report Card." *Time*, May 30, 1955.

"Representative L. Mendel Rivers Is Dead; Powerful Military Affairs Chief." *New York Times*, December 29, 1970.

"Republican Seeks to Make House Less Independent." *Washington Post*, October 12, 1994.

Reston, James. "Eisenhower by a Landslide." *New York Times*, November 7, 1956.

_____. "Stevenson Taunts Rival for Backing McCarthy, Dirksen." *New York Times*, October 10, 1952.

Richard, Randall. "MIT Economist: Hard Times Ahead for Middle Class." *Providence Journal*, March 31, 1996.

Richter, James G. "Perpetuating the Cold War: Domestic Sources of International Patterns of Behavior." *Political Science Quarterly*, Summer 1992.

Rimer, Sara. "A Hometown Feels Less Like Home." *New York Times*, March 6, 1996.

Rosenthal, Andrew. "Dukakis Suggests Caution on U.S.S.R." *New York Times*, September 14, 1988.

Rosenthal, Andrew, with Joel Brinkley. "Old Compass in a New World: A President Sticks to Course." *New York Times*, June 25, 1992.

Royko, Mike. "Tales from a Target of the Red Squad." *Denver Post*, July 9, 1995.

Salisbury, Harrison. "Stevenson Lays Defeat to Crisis." *New York Times*, November 8, 1956.

Schattschneider, E. E. "1954: The Ike Party Fights to Live." *New Republic*, February 23, 1953.

Schlesinger, Arthur M. "Faded Glory." *New York Times Magazine*, July 12, 1992.

Schmaltz, Jeffrey. "Americans Are Sadder and Wiser, but Not Apathetic." *New York Times*, November 1, 1992.

Schmidt, Eric. "Bids to Cut Legal Immigration Are Dropped from House Bill." *New York Times*, March 22, 1996.

Schmidt, Maria. "The Hiss Dossier." *New Republic*, November 8, 1993.

Schneider, William. "JFK's Children: The Class of '74." *Atlantic Monthly*, March 1989.

Schwartz, Stephen I. "Atomic Audit: What the U.S. Nuclear Arsenal Has Cost." *Brookings Review*, Fall 1995.

Scott, Janny. "U.S. Communist Party Has Little Appeal." *Providence Journal*, December 24, 1994.

"Security Charter Approved by United Nations Parley." *Los Angeles Times*, June 26, 1945.

Seelye, Katherine Q. "Dole Says President Defends Old Elites Seeking Largesse." *New York Times*, January 24, 1996.

"Senate Takes Up Immigration Debate." CNN/*Time*, All Politics, Internet, March 22, 1996.

Shales, Tom. "Golden Glow of the First 'Honeymooners.'" *Washington Post*, April 19, 1993.

Shepley, James R. "How Dulles Averted War." *Life*, January 16, 1956.

"Shrill Emergency Broadcast Test Soon to Be a Cold War Relic." *New York Times*, November 17, 1996.

Sloan, Allan. "For Whom the Bell Tolls." *Newsweek*, January 15, 1996.

_____. "The Hit Men." *Newsweek*, February 26, 1996.

Solomon, Bert. "Politics of Protest." *National Journal*, May 9, 1992.

"South Korean Unit, Bayoneting Reds, Regains Key Peak." *New York Times*, October 10, 1952.

"Speeches by Eisenhower, Nixon." *New York Times*, November 7, 1956.

Stanley, Alessandra. "Dmitri Volkogonov, 67, Historian Who Debunked Heroes, Dies." *New York Times*, December 7, 1995.

"Stevenson Calls Republicans 'Party of the Past and of Fear.'" *New York Times*, September 12, 1952.

Strobel, Warren P. "President Improves on His 1992 Showing." *Washington Times*, November 6, 1996.

Tanenhaus, Sam. "Hiss Case 'Smoking Gun?'" *New York Times*, op-ed, October 15, 1993.

"Ten World Statesmen Hail the Work on UNICO." *San Francisco Chronicle*, June 26, 1945.

"Text of Kennedy's Speech: 'If We Stand Our Ground, We Can Prevail.'" *New York Times*, August 30, 1996.

"Text of the Address by President Roosevelt at Dinner of the Foreign Policy Association Here." *New York Times*, October 22, 1944.

"The People and Ross Perot." *Washington Post*, June 2, 1992.

"The Republicans and the South." *Life*, editorial, May 19, 1952.

Thomas, Evan. "Bridge to 2000." *Newsweek*, November 18, 1996.

_____. "The Small Deal." *Newsweek*, November 18, 1996.

"Transcript of First TV Debate Among Bush, Clinton, and Perot." *New York Times*, October 12, 1992.

"Transcript of Second Debate Between the Presidential Candidates." *New York Times*, October 17, 1992.

"Transcript of the First Presidential Debate." *Washington Post*, October 7, 1996.

"Transcript of the Second Presidential Debate." *Washington Post*, October 17, 1996.

"Transcript of Third TV Debate Between Bush, Clinton, and Perot." *New York Times*, October 20, 1992.

Truman, Harry S. "A Candid Analysis of the '52 Election." *Life*, February 20, 1956.

Uchitelle, Louis. "1995 Was Good for Companies and Better for a Lot of CEO's." *New York Times*, March 29, 1996.

Uchitelle, Louis, and N. R. Kleinfield. "On the Battlefields of Business, Millions of Casualties." *New York Times*, March 3, 1996.

Vaughn, Steven. "The Moral Inheritence of a President: Reagan and the Dixon Disciples of Christ." *Presidential Studies Quarterly*, Winter 1995.

Wallace, Henry A. "The People Talk." *New Republic*, February 2, 1948.

Walsh, Edward. "Dole's New Battle Cry: Clinton Is an Elitist 'Liberal, Liberal, Liberal.'" *Washington Post*, September 29, 1996.

Watson, Bruce. "We Couldn't Run, So We Hoped We Could Hide." *Smithsonian*, April 1994.

Weiner, Tim. "Code-Crackers Reveal World War II Secret." *Denver Post*, July 12, 1995.

_____. "Military Accused of Lies Over Arms." *New York Times*, June 28, 1993.

Weintraub, Bernard. "Loaded for Bear and Then Some." *New York Times*, September 14, 1988.

White, William S. "Internationalist Inaugural Acclaimed in Both Parties." *New York Times*, January 21, 1953.

White, William S. "Sweep in Congress: Democrats Obtain 54–42 Margin in Senate by Winning 9 GOP Seats." *New York Times*, November 4, 1948.

Wildavsky, Aaron. "The Goldwater Phenomenon: Purists, Politicians, and the Two-Party System." Reprinted in *The American Party Process: Readings and Comments*, ed. Norman L. Zucker. New York: Dodd, Mead, 1968.

Will, George F. "Buchanan's Nonsense." *Washington Post*, November 5, 1995.

_____. "'Exoneration' of Alger Hiss." *Newsweek*, November 1, 1993.

_____. "Peace Is Hell." *Washington Post*, May 30, 1993.

Wills, Garry. "Clinton's Hell Raiser." *New Yorker*, October 12, 1992.

_____. "Clinton's Troubles." *New York Review of Books*, September 22, 1994.

_____. "Late Bloomer." *Time*, April 23, 1990.

_____. "The Born-Again Republicans." *New York Review of Books*, September 24, 1992.

_____. "The Power of the Savior." *Time*, June 22, 1992.

Wilson, James Q. "A Guide to Reagan Country: The Political Culture of Southern California." *Commentary*, May 1967.

"Wonderful to Play in." *Time*, February 5, 1951.

Wright, Robert. "Who's Really to Blame?" *Time*, November 6, 1995.

Yang, John E. "Underlying Gingrich's Stance Is His Pique About President." *Washington Post*, November 16, 1995.

Selected Polls

ABC News/Louis Harris and Associates, 1980.

ABC News/*Washington Post*, 1984–1996.

Associated Press, 1992.

Blum and Weprin Associates, 1992.

CBS News/*New York Times*, 1984–1996.

Dallas Morning News, 1995.

Decision/Making/Information, 1984.

Gallup Organization, 1937–1994.

Gordon Black, 1984.

Hart and Breglio Research Companies, 1992.

Hickman-Brown, 1991.

KRC Communications, 1988

Los Angeles Times, 1992.

Louis Harris and Associates, 1976–1990.

Market Opinion Research, 1988.

National Opinion Research Center, 1944–1994.

Opinion Research Corporation, 1952–1994.

Peter D. Hart Research Associates, 1972.

Princeton Survey Research Associates, 1992.

Roper Organization, 1948–1994.

Voter Research and Surveys (exit polls), 1992, 1994, and 1996.

Daniel Yankelovich Group, 1988–1996.

Yankelovich, Clancy, Shulman, 1988–1992.
Yankelovich, Skelly and White, 1983–1984.

Selected Speeches

Buchanan, Patrick J. "Announcement Speech." Concord, New Hampshire, December 10, 1991.

Bush, George. "Acceptance Speech." Republican National Convention, New Orleans, August 18, 1988.

_____. "Acceptance Speech." Republican National Convention, Houston, August 20, 1992.

_____. "Address to the Nation on the Commonwealth of Independent States," Washington, D.C., December 25, 1991.

Carter, Jimmy. "Acceptance Speech." Democratic National Convention, New York City, July 15, 1976.

_____. "Address to the Nation." Washington, D.C., January 14, 1980.

_____. "Commencement Address." Notre Dame University, South Bend, Indiana, May 22, 1977.

Clinton, William J. "A New Covenant for American Security." Georgetown University, Washington, D.C., December 12, 1991.

_____. "A New Covenant for Economic Change." Georgetown University, Washington, D.C., November 20, 1991.

_____. "Acceptance Speech." Democratic National Convention, New York, July 16, 1992.

_____. "Acceptance Speech." Democratic National Convention, Chicago, August 29, 1996.

_____. "Address to the Nation." Washington, D.C., December 15, 1994.

_____. "Clinton's Words on Mission to Bosnia: 'The Right Thing to Do.'" *New York Times*, November 28, 1995.

_____. "Remarks by the President in Speech to National Baptist Convention." New Orleans, September 9, 1994.

_____. "Remarks by the President on Responsible Citizenship and the American Community." Georgetown University, Washington, D.C., July 6, 1995.

_____. "Remarks on the Economic Program in Hyde Park, New York." Hyde Park, New York, February 19, 1993.

_____. "Speech to the Democratic Leadership Council." Washington, D.C., November 13, 1995.

_____. "Speech to the Democratic Leadership Council." Washington, D.C., December 15, 1994.

_____. "Speech to the Democratic Leadership Council." Washington, D.C., December 11, 1996.

_____. "State of the Union Address." Washington, D.C., January 23, 1996.

_____. "The New Covenant: Responsibility and Rebuilding the American Community." Georgetown University, Washington, D.C., October 23, 1991.

_____. "Victory Speech." Little Rock, Arkansas, November 5, 1996.

Churchill, Winston S. "The Sinews of Peace." Address at Westminster College, Fulton, Missouri, March 5, 1946.

Dewey, Thomas E. "Text of Dewey Speech at the Hollywood Bowl." *New York Times*, September 25, 1948.

Dole, Robert J. "Acceptance Speech." Republican National Convention, San Diego, August 15, 1996.

_____. "Address to the American Legion Convention." Indianapolis, Indiana, September 4, 1995.

_____. "Address to the U.S. Conference of Mayors." Miami, Florida, June 17, 1995.

_____. "Announcement Speech." Russell, Kansas, April 10, 1995.

_____. "Remarks by Senator Bob Dole." Los Angeles, California, May 31, 1995.

_____. "Remarks for Delivery." Denver, Colorado, April 11, 1995.

_____. "Speech to the Nixon Center for Peace and Freedom." March 1, 1995.

_____. "State of the Union: The Republican Response." Washington, D.C., January 23, 1996.

Douglas, Paul. "Digest of Senator Douglas's Address on Korean War at Democratic Convention." *New York Times*, July 25, 1952.

Dukakis, Michael S. "Acceptance Speech." Democratic National Convention, Atlanta, July 21, 1988.

Eisenhower, Dwight D. "Acceptance Speech." Republican National Convention, San Francisco, August 23, 1956.

_____. "Farewell Address." Washington, D.C., January 17, 1961.

_____. "Inaugural Address." Washington, D.C., January 20, 1953.

_____. "Text of Eisenhower and Nixon Addresses to the Convention." *New York Times*, July 12, 1952.

_____. "Text of Eisenhower's Speech Ending Campaign with Appeal for Unity." *New York Times*, November 4, 1952.

Goldwater, Barry M. "Acceptance Speech." Republican National Convention, San Francisco, July 16, 1964.

Gorbachev, Mikhail. "Text of Gorbachev's Farewell Address." *New York Times*, December 26, 1991.

Gore, Al. "Acceptance Speech." Democratic National Convention, Chicago, August 28, 1996.

Kemp, Jack F. "Acceptance Speech." Republican National Convention, San Diego, August 15, 1996.

Kennedy, John F. "Radio and Television Report to the American People on Civil Rights." June 11, 1963. *Public Papers of the Presidents of the United States: John F. Kennedy.* Washington, D.C.: U.S. Government Printing Office, 1964.

_____. "Remarks at the Breakfast of the Fort Worth Chamber of Commerce," November 22, 1963. *Public Papers of the Presidents of the United States: John F. Kennedy.* Washington, D.C.: U.S. Government Printing Office, 1964.

_____. "Remarks Intended for Delivery to the Texas Democratic State Committee in the Municipal Auditorium in Austin," November 22, 1963. *Public Papers of the Presidents of the United States: John F. Kennedy.* Washington, D.C.: U.S. Government Printing Office, 1964.

_____. "Remarks to Delegates to the 18th Annual American Legion 'Boys Nation,'" July 24, 1963. *Public Papers of the Presidents of the United States: John F. Kennedy.* Washington, D.C.: U.S. Government Printing Office, 1964.

Kepley, David R. "Robert Taft's Legacy." Speech to the Robert A. Taft Honors Fellows, Catholic University of America, June 14, 1993.

Kirkpatrick, Jeane J. "Address to Republican National Convention." Dallas, August 20, 1984.

Lowi, Theodore J. "Cross-Roads 1992: And All Lights Stuck on Red." The Spencer T. and Ann W. Olin Address, Cornell University, Ithaca, New York, June 5, 1992.

Johnson, Lyndon B. "Radio and Television Report to the American People Following Renewed Aggression in the Gulf of Tonkin," August 4, 1964. *Public Papers of the Presidents of the United States: Lyndon B. Johnson.* Washington, D.C.: U.S. Government Printing Office, 1965.

Lincoln, Abraham. "Second Annual Message to Congress," December 1, 1862.

McGovern, George S. "Acceptance Speech." Democratic National Convention, Miami Beach, July 13, 1972.

Nixon, Richard M. "Acceptance Speech." Republican National Convention, Chicago, July 28, 1960.

_____. "Acceptance Speech." Republican National Convention, Miami Beach, August 23, 1972.

_____. "Address to the Nation." Washington, D.C., August 15, 1971.

_____. "Statement on the Death of Representative L. Mendel Rivers of South Carolina." December 28, 1970.

_____. "Text of Eisenhower and Nixon Addresses to the Convention." *New York Times*, July 12, 1952.

Quayle, Dan. "Address to the Commonwealth Club of California." San Francisco, May 19, 1992.

Reagan, Ronald. "Announcement of the Recipients of the Presidential Medal of Freedom." Washington, D.C., February 21, 1984.

_____. "Farewell Address." Washington, D.C., January 11, 1989.

_____. "Inaugural Address." Washington, D.C., January 20, 1981.

_____. "Remarks at an Ecumenical Prayer Breakfast in Dallas, Texas." August 23, 1984.

_____. "Remarks at the Annual Convention of the National Association of Evangelicals." Orlando, Florida, March 8, 1983.

_____. "Remarks at Eureka College in Eureka, Illinois, February 6, 1984." *Public Papers of the Presidents of the United States: Ronald Reagan*. Washington, D.C.: Government Printing Office, 1985.

_____. "Remarks by the President and First Lady in a National Television Address on Drug Abuse and Prevention." Washington, D.C., September 14, 1986.

Roosevelt, Franklin D. "Address at the Democratic State Convention." Syracuse, New York, September 29, 1936.

_____. "Inaugural Address." Washington, D.C., March 4, 1933.

Sasso, John. "Speech to the World Trade Center Club." Boston, Massachusetts, January 19, 1989.

Stevenson, Adlai E. "Text of Stevenson Speech of Welcome to Convention." *New York Times*, July 22, 1952.

_____. "Text of Stevenson's Speeches of Acceptance." *New York Times*, July 26, 1952.

_____. "Text of Truman, Stevenson Addresses Ending Democratic Campaign." *New York Times*, November 4, 1952.

Truman, Harry S. "Address in San Francisco at the Closing Session of the United Nations Conference," June 26, 1945. *Public Papers of the Presidents of the United States: Harry S. Truman*. Washington, D.C.: Government Printing Office, 1946.

_____. "Address at the Gilmore Stadium in Los Angeles," September 23, 1948. *Public Papers of the Presidents of the United States: Harry S. Truman*. Washington, D.C.: Government Printing Office, 1949.

_____. "Address in Oklahoma City," September 28, 1948. *Public Papers of the Presidents of the United States: Harry S. Truman*. Washington, D.C.: Government Printing Office, 1949.

Truman, Harry S. "Farewell Address." Washington, D.C. January 15, 1953.

Truman, Harry S. "Text of President's Address Presenting Stevenson to Convention." *New York Times*. July 26, 1952.

Truman, Harry S. "Texts of Truman, Stevenson Addresses Ending Democratic Campaign." *New York Times*, November 4, 1952.

Washington, George. "Farewell Address." September 19, 1796.

Yeltsin, Boris. "Russian President's Address to Joint Session of Congress." *Washington Post*, June 18, 1992.

Other Printed Matter

A Nation at Risk. Washington, D.C.: Superintendent of Documents, U.S. Government Printing Office, 1983.

Black, Gordon S. "American Discontent Reaches Unprecedented Levels." Executive summary, June 1992.

Buchanan, Patrick J. "Buchanan on the Issues." 1996 campaign brochure.

Bush, George. CNN interview, June 15, 1992. Transcript provided by CNN.

Democratic National Committee, *Democratic Platform, 1980*. Washington, D.C.: DNC, 1980.

Democratic National Committee, *Democratic Platform, 1984*. Washington, D.C.: DNC, 1984.

Democratic National Committee, *Democratic Party Platform, 1992*. Washington, D.C.: DNC, 1992.

_____. *The 1996 Democratic National Platform*. Washington, D.C.: DNC, 1996.

Dole, Robert J. "Bob Dole for President." 1996 campaign brochure.

_____. *Conversations with David Frost*. PBS broadcast, April 3, 1995.

_____. Transcript, *This Week with David Brinkley*. ABC News broadcast, September 17, 1995.

Empower America. Brochure, 1995.

Final Report: Advisory Committee on Human Radiation Experiments. Washington, D.C.: U.S. Government Printing Office, October 1995.

Gerring, John. "A Chapter in the History of American Party Ideology: The Nineteenth Century Democratic Party (1828–1892)." Paper presented at the Northeastern Political Science Association, Newark, New Jersey, November 11–13, 1993.

_____. *Party Ideology in America: 1828–1992*. Unpubished manuscript, 1996.

Johnston, Eric. Testimony Before the House Committee on UnAmerican Activities, March 26, 1947.

Lieberman, Joe. "Statement of Joe Lieberman, Talk Show Campaign News Conference." Washington, D.C., October 26, 1995.

Memoranda and speeches from the Gerald R. Ford Library, Ann Arbor, Michigan.

Memoranda and speeches from the John F. Kennedy Library, Boston, Massachusetts.

Office of the Press Secretary. "Transcript of Press Conference by the President." White House, Washington, D.C., April 18, 1995.

Republican National Committee, *Republican Platform, 1980*. Washington, D.C.: RNC, 1980.

Republican National Committee, *Republican Platform, 1984*. Washington, D.C.: RNC, 1984.

Republican National Committee, *Republican Platform, 1992*. Washington, D.C.: RNC, 1992.

_____. *The Republican Platform, 1996: Restoring the American Dream*. Washington, D.C.: RNC, 1996.

Rollins, Ed. Interview, *MacNeil/Lehrer NewsHour*, PBS broadcast, May 21, 1992. Transcript of interview provided by PBS.

Savage, Sean J. "The Party Leadership Styles of Roosevelt and Truman." Paper presented at the annual meeting of the Midwest Political Science Association, Chicago, April 17, 1993.

Ubriaco, Robert D. Jr. "Bread and Butter Politics at the Factory Gate: Class Versus Ethnicity in the Polish-American Community during the 1946 Congressional Elections." Unpublished paper.

Volkogonov, Dmitri A. Letter to John Lowenthal. Reprinted in *Cold War International History Project Bulletin*, Woodrow Wilson International Center for Scholars, Washington, D.C., Fall 1992.

Videocassettes/Cassette Tapes

ABC News. "Seventy-Two Hours to Victory." Videocassette, originally broadcast on November 4, 1992.

ABC News. "The Missiles of October." Videocassette, originally broadcast in 1992.

"Anti-Communist Voices of Yesterday." Audio Cassette, 1951–1952. Published by 123 Audio Forum.

Lowi, Theodore J. C-SPAN, broadcast address, June 3, 1992.

MacNeil/Lehrer NewsHour, PBS broadcast, September 25, 1992.

NBC News, "Sunday Today," broadcast March 29, 1992.

Perot, Ross. *Conversations with David Frost*. PBS broadcast, April 24, 1992.

"The Classics of Political TV Advertising, 1." Video produced by *Campaigns and Elections* magazine.

Author's Interviews

Dukakis, Michael S. Boston, Massachusetts, June 29, 1994.

Kalugin, Oleg. Washington, D.C., March 18, 1995.

McGovern, George S. Washington, D.C., January 4, 1996.

Odum, William. Washington, D.C., March 18, 1995.

Wirthlin, Richard B. McLean, Virginia, March 22, 1995.

About the Book
and Author

In *Still Seeing Red,* John Kenneth White explores how the Cold War molded the internal politics of the United States. In a powerful narrative backed by a rich treasure trove of polling data, White takes the reader through the Cold War years, describing its effect in redrawing the electoral map as we came to know it after World War II. The primary beneficiaries of the altered landscape were reinvigorated Republicans who emerged after five successive defeats to tar the Democrats with the "soft on communism" epithet. A new nationalist Republican party—whose Cold War prescription for winning the White House was copyrighted to Dwight Eisenhower, Richard Nixon, Barry Goldwater, and Ronald Reagan—attained primacy in presidential politics because of two contradictory impulses embedded in the American character: a fanatical preoccupation with communism and a robust liberalism. From 1952 to 1988 Republicans won the presidency seven times in ten tries. The rare Democratic victors—John F. Kennedy, Lyndon B. Johnson, and Jimmy Carter—attempted to rearm the Democratic party to fight the Cold War. Their collective failure says much about the politics of the period. Even so, the Republican dream of becoming a majority party became perverted as the Grand Old Party was recast into a top-down party routinely winning the presidency even as its electoral base remained relatively stagnant.

In the post–Cold War era, Americans are coming to appreciate how the fifty-year struggle with the Soviet Union organized thinking in such diverse areas as civil rights, social welfare, education, and defense policy. At the same time, Americans are also more aware of how the Cold War shaped their lives—from the "duck and cover" drills in the classrooms to the bomb shelters dug in the backyard when most baby boomers were growing up. Like millions of those same baby boomers, Bill Clinton can truthfully say, "I am a child of the Cold War."

With the last gasp of the Soviet Union, Americans are learning that the politics of the Cold War are hard to shed. As the electoral maps are being redrawn once more in the Clinton years, landmarks left behind by the Cold War provide an important reference point. In the height of the Cold War, voters divided the world into "us" noncommunists versus "them" communists and reduced contests for the presidency into battles of which party would be tougher in dealing with the Evil Empire. But in a convoluted post–Cold War era, politics defies such simple characteristics and presidents find it harder to lead. Recalling how John F. Kennedy could so easily rally public opinion, an exasperated Bill Clinton once lamented, "Gosh, I miss the Cold War."

John Kenneth White is professor of politics at the Catholic University of America and author of *The Fractured Electorate* and *The New Politics of Old Values*. He serves as cochair of the Committee for Party Renewal and as vice president of the Center for Party Development.

Index

TRANSFORMING AMERICAN POLITICS

Lawrence C. Dodd, Series Editor

Dramatic changes in political institutions and behavior over the past three decades have underscored the dynamic nature of American politics, confronting political scientists with a new and pressing intellectual agenda. The pioneering work of early postwar scholars, while laying a firm empirical foundation for contemporary scholarship, failed to consider how American politics might change or recognize the forces that would make fundamental change inevitable. In reassessing the static interpretations fostered by these classic studies, political scientists are now examining the underlying dynamics that generate transformational change.

Transforming American Politics brings together texts and monographs that address four closely related aspects of change. A first concern is documenting and explaining recent changes in American politics—in institutions, processes, behavior, and policymaking. A second is reinterpreting classic studies and theories to provide a more accurate perspective on postwar politics. The series looks at historical change to identify recurring patterns of political transformation within and across the distinctive eras of American politics. Last and perhaps most important, the series presents new theories and interpretations that explain the dynamic processes at work and thus clarify the direction of contemporary politics. All of the books focus on the central theme of transformation—transformation in both the conduct of American politics and in the way we study and understand its many aspects.

FORTHCOMING TITLES

Revolving Gridlock, David Brady and Craig Volden

The Parties Respond: Changes in American Parties and Campaigns,
Third Edition, edited by Sandy L. Maisel

New Media in American Politics, Richard Davis and Diana Owen

Governing Partners: State-Local Relations in the United States,
Russell L. Hanson